INDIA
Social Development Report 2012
Minorities at the Margins

Council for Social Development

edited by
Zoya Hasan and Mushirul Hasan

OXFORD
UNIVERSITY PRESS

OXFORD
UNIVERSITY PRESS

Oxford University Press is a department of the University of Oxford.
It furthers the University's objective of excellence in research, scholarship,
and education by publishing worldwide. Oxford is a registered trademark of
Oxford University Press in the UK and in certain other countries

Published in India by
Oxford University Press
YMCA Library Building, 1 Jai Singh Road, New Delhi 110 001, India

ISBN-13: 978-0-19-809594-1
ISBN-10: 0-19-809594-5

Typeset in 11/13 Adobe Garamond Pro
by Excellent Laser Typesetters, Pitampura, Delhi 110 034
Printed in India by Rakmo Press, New Delhi 110 020

INDIA
Social Development Report 2012

Contents

Tables, Figures, and Boxes

FIGURES

Boxes

Foreword

I have the privilege, on behalf of the Council for Social Development (CSD), to place this fourth *India: Social Development Report* (*SDR*) in the hands of the public, particularly the development planners, policymakers, functionaries responsible for executing development programmes and projects, scholars and researchers, and our compatriots in civil society organizations. The special theme of the present report is 'minority rights'. Minorities, with a size of approximately 220 million, constitute a major strength of the nation. The overall growth and prosperity of the country is linked integrally with their development and well-being. Their economic, political, and social inclusion on the basis of equality is essential for the unity and cohesion of the country. The full exercise of their rights as citizens is the litmus test of the robustness of the functioning of the Indian democracy.

This report contains a large number of studies devoted to the socio-economic conditions of the minorities, particularly the Muslims. Some of the chapters here dealing with the rights of the marginalized sections of the population include sections on minority rights. In addition, there are eight chapters, some of them based on empirical studies carried out for inclusion in this report, dealing exclusively with the socio-economic problems confronting the minorities. Special emphasis has been put on the minority's participation in education. A chapter is devoted to 'Education and Exclusion of Muslims' and another to 'Modernization of Madrasas' in the states where the Muslim constitute fairly large proportions of the total population. The report includes two chapters on progress in the implementation of the recommendations of the November 2006 Justice Rajender Sachar Committee Report, '*Social, Economic and Educational Status of the Muslim Community of India*'.

The Sachar Committee had comprehensively documented the economic backwardness and deprivations of the Muslims along most major indicators. The studies included in this *SDR* go to confirm these findings and bring out that there has been no perceptible change in their condition since the submission of that report. A large proportion of the Muslim population, as high as 30 per cent, remains steeped in poverty. Their economic engagement is dominantly in the informal sector, either as self-employed or as wage-earners, where they have very limited bargaining strength and which remains by and large stagnant. The special programmes targeted at the Muslims, which were somewhat strengthened following the Sachar Committee recommendations, remain faulty in conception and design, and inadequately planned and financed. Hardly any conscious effort has been made to ensure the participation of the beneficiaries in the formulation, evaluation, and implementation of the programmes. Finally, this community continues to face widespread discrimination, particularly in the matter of employment.

The special development programmes for the Muslims have largely benefited the non-Muslim community because of their being area-based, that is, districts with a concentration of Muslim population being taken as basic planning units. Non-Muslims have cornered the benefits because of their political influence at the district level. Moreover, these programmes have suffered from inadequate budgetary provisions. The increases in outlays that have taken place since the Sachar Committee recommendations appear impressive, but they are far short of the total requirement of resources in order to be able to make a real dent on the socio-economic conditions of the community.

In the field of education, the Muslims are getting special benefits by way of scholarships, uniforms, hostels, etc. But it is important to underline that these facilities are designed to provide better access to a very poor quality education system. For quality is a systemic problem. Unless the existing multilayer discriminatory and poorly provided system of education is replaced by a new system based on equality and uniform application of a minimum set of norms, quality of education is unlikely to improve. Further, the additional scholarships that are made available, hostels that are being built for the students of the minority community, and the assistance that is given for modernizing madrasas still remain inadequate as compared to the total requirements. These cannot make a difference unless they are universalized to cover the entire community. And it will be politically impracticable to universalize these facilities for a particular community without universalizing it for the entire population. The Muslim community have, therefore, as high a stake as the rest of the Indian population, in joining movements for restructuring the entire educational system. This will be equally applicable to other social sectors, particularly health.

The Muslim community is undoubtedly entitled to the special programmes and projects launched for their development and other measures adopted by the government in their favour. In view of their sufficiently documented socio-economic backwardness, there could be a justification for adopting affirmative action in their favour. However, all these will be of only limited value until the community continues to be subjected to systemic biases and discriminations rooted in the social structure. Removal of discrimination will be of much greater help to the community than special measures and affirmative action taken together. Discrimination can be removed only if each and every citizen of India practises secularism in the true sense of the term. The maturity and the level of excellence reached by a society lies in the manner in which it treats its minorities. And the main responsibility for it rests with the majority community. The situation prevailing in India in this regard cannot be regarded as satisfactory.

Discrimination based, among others, on religion is specifically and categorically prohibited by the Indian Constitution. Any individual or entity violating this provision should be subjected to the harshest punishment. If necessary, additional laws should be enacted to enable the authorities to do so. Moreover, every institution or entity above a particular size, should have a special unit consisting of individuals known for their impeccable commitment to secularism, to serve as a watch-dog against religion-based discriminations and to recommend and take positive measures for enhancing the representation of the minorities in the institution, including their promotion at the highest levels.

Safeguarding the sovereignty of the nation and ensuring the security for its citizens has for long been regarded as the raison d'etre of the state. Whereas this still remains the primary justification for its legitimacy, the state has also come to play a decisive role in the development of a country, particularly in building of infrastructures and designing and running education and health systems for providing universal access to quality services in these sectors. This has been particularly true of developed countries. But it has also happened in the emerging economies of Southeast, East, and North Asia. With the onset of the new phase of globalization and liberalization starting from the early 1980s, most of the states in the world have shed responsibilities in these areas in order to pave the way for the fullest possible play of the market forces. But even the votaries of this new development strategy, like the World Bank and the International Monetary Fund, have gone out of the way to explain that what they have been advocating is not the abdication of the role of the state, but its recalibration in order to strike the right balance with the market forces. Even in the changed scheme of things, the state is still primarily responsible for the development of infrastructure and the provision of social services, though there could be differences on how to go about it.

But in India, there is an accelerating trend of the withdrawal of the state from the key sectors of the economy, particularly the infrastructure, agriculture, and social sectors. Apart from adversely affecting the growth of the economy, this policy is having disastrous consequences for the incomes, livelihood, and welfare of the poor sections of the population. The withdrawal from infrastructure development started in the early 1990s when the government embraced in a full-fledged manner the policy of liberalization and privatization. The private sector has no doubt stepped in the space vacated by the state, but it has met only a small proportion of the needs in this area. Moreover, it has not shown much interest in investing for the development of rural infrastructure like rural roads, bridges, culverts, reservoirs, and rural markets to name only a few. The consequence is that whereas in other countries the infrastructure development pioneered by the state triggered development in other sectors, in India the inadequacies of infrastructure is proving the most important constraint to development.

No significant increase has taken place in public expenditure as a proportion of gross domestic product (GDP) in key social sectors, particularly health and education. Public expenditure in health as a proportion of GDP has been stagnating at the level of a little over 1 per cent, whereas in most emerging and more developed among developing counties it is close to 3 per cent. The target of devoting 6 per cent of GDP to expenditure in education, recommended by the Kothari Commission in 1966 and nationally agreed in the following decades, is yet to be realized. The actual expenditure on education has been hovering around 3.5 per cent of GDP and has never crossed 4 per cent over the past several years. The private sector has to some extent filled in the gap in these sectors, but this has happened to a very limited extent and with far-reaching adverse consequences for the poor.

The two important ways in which the state has transferred its primary responsibilities to the private sector in these areas are: (*a*) outsourcing to the private sector; and (*b*) adopting the public-private partnership mode for development or delivery of services. This process of privatization has resulted in the continuing decay and dismantling of existing public institutions without their being replaced in any significant way by new institutions built under public-private partnership. Secondly, this has severely affected the poor by putting essential services out of their reach. Thirdly, the expectation that the withdrawal of the government from the process of production and distribution and the delivery of goods and services would remove a major cause of corruption has been belied. Instead, outsourcing and award of contracts to private operators and companies has spawned corruption on a scale much larger than could have been imagined a few years ago. Finally, the Indian state has generally been both incapable and unwilling to monitor and regulate private sector operation in order to ensure that it does not militate against public interest and is not violative of the law of the land and of the basic principles and objectives of the Constitution.

Here are a few examples of the havoc wrought by the retreat of the state:

The entire infrastructure of agricultural extension services has been dismantled. This has not been replaced by any private sector initiative.

Most of the infrastructure for agricultural research and development has been closed down or allowed to decay. Private sector research in this area has its own agenda, which is primarily to propagate and sell patented seeds and plant varieties rather than undertaking basic research.

Back in 2005, the Prime Minister announced the government's intent to establish on a public-private partnership mode 6,000 model residential schools spread all over the country for imparting high-quality secondary education. This number is a very small proportion of the total number of schools required to be built for universalizing quality secondary education. For the past several years, negotiations have been going on with the private sector for building these schools on a public-private partnership mode, but there has been very little progress so far. Newspaper reports indicate that it is apparently proving difficult to meet the private sector's demand for a deal which makes the running of these schools profitable for them. In the process, universalization of secondary education has gone by default.

As a result, there is a mushrooming of English-medium high-fee charging private schools at this level of education. Their numbers are not commensurate with the needs in this area. The infrastructure and the proportion of trained teachers in these schools are poorer than in government schools. Therefore, the quality of education in these schools does not do any credit to the nation.

Parents desire to give the best possible education to their children and for this purpose sending them to private schools has driven them to bankruptcy and indebtedness, which have crippled them economically. Also, the compulsion to opt for expensive treatment by private doctors and in private hospitals has had a more wide-ranging devastating impact on the families of the poor.

The government's withdrawal from the maintenance and expansion of quality institutions for the education of teachers, doctors, and para-medicals has led to the proliferation of private medical, engineering, and teachers' education colleges charging exorbitant fees and demanding huge capitation fees for initial admission. This has deprived the poor of whatever chances there were earlier to get their children admitted in quality government institutions in this category on the basis of merit.

There are indeed scholarships available for education in most of these institutions. Also, the number of these scholarships has been increased substantially in recent years, particularly for the children of the weaker sections of the population. But the total number of scholarships now available is still a very small proportion of the total number of the children of the poor who would like to be educated in these institutions but cannot afford to pay their fees.

Sanitation, kitchen, ambulance, diagnostic, and similar other services earlier provided in government hospitals have been outsourced to private service providers. As a result, their costs have gone up, taking them beyond the reach of the poor. This has made it difficult for the poor to be treated even in government hospitals.

The public health centres and sub-centres from which the poor stand to benefit most are in a neglected state. The private sector is not interested in taking them over as they are not profitable.

The institutions created by the government in the earlier period for the treatment, prevention, and doing research for discovering new drugs or ways for eliminating diseases of mass affliction like malaria and tuberculosis have either been closed down or allowed to decay. The private sector sees no commercial benefit in entering into this field. And in the name of research, they are mainly engaged in establishing super specialty medical centres to cater to the requirement of the richer sections of the population.

Privatization has resulted in the exclusion of the poor from the process of urbanization. Obsession with big ticket investments by the private sector for the development of infrastructure and provision of amenities in the cities has accentuated the distress among the poor city dwellers and has obliged them to shift from the centre of the city to its periphery. The facilities created by private sector investments largely through commercial borrowing, which incidentally is available mainly in big cities, have been concentrated in the better-off areas of the city and availed of mainly by the better-off section of the urban population. In the process, the poor have been deprived of the basic services which they used to get when the state was the main source for supplying them. Moreover, the functioning of users' welfare associations consisting mainly of the representatives of the rich has standardized and legitimized inequality in the cities.

There has been no abetment of the public demand for claiming essential social goods and services as a right, and for this purpose, putting some of the flagship projects of the government in the social field, on a legal basis. The most important candidate among these is the Integrated Child Development Services (ICDS). Another legislation which has been struggling to cross the Parliamentary hurdle is the food security bill. There is also pressure on the government to enact a legislation to remove the curse of shelterlessness and one to make access to minimum health services as a legal right. These demands are being made in spite of the fact that the progress in implementing legislations providing access to social services as a right has not been satisfactory. The most glaring example in this regard is the Right to Education (RTE) Act.

Instead of putting the ICDS on a legal footing, the government has recently adopted a National Policy for Children. This is an updating of the similar policy which has been in existence since 1975. This policy is likely to make little difference in the present situation because it is neither justiciable nor does it provide for the resources required for implementing its key provisions within a time-bound framework.

The adoption of a right-based approach makes it mandatory for the government to provide the services specified in the legislation and to commit the financial resources needed for this purpose. If the provisions of such legislations are not implemented, then a citizen or any entity on its behalf, has a right to approach the court to get it enforced. In a sense, this procedure itself suffers from inherent limitations. The poor, who are the worst sufferers, do not have the means to go to court. Moreover, the court's verdict is at best unpredictable. For cases are decided not necessarily on the basis of their merits, but very often under the influence of the social background and the ideological predilection of the judges.

In spite of this, the fact of the justiciability of a right-based provision improves the prospects of getting it implemented. This is better than depending on the sweet will and discretion of the government. If people know that access to a quality social service is their right, they would tend to be more proactive and determined to claim it. Thus, right-based access to services makes the government accountable to the court and provides civil society organizations a more potent tool to put pressure on the government for implementing pro-poor programmes.

At the end, I would like to place on record my deep appreciation and sincere gratitude to Zoya Hasan and Mushirul Hasan, the editors of this volume, for their prolonged diligent effort in planning this edition of the report, mobilizing the resources for compiling it, editing the manuscript, and for their own excellent intellectual input. I also take this opportunity to express my thanks to all the scholars and researchers—both of the Council and from outside—who through their articles and research work provided the material and analysis on which this report is based.

New Delhi
3 May 2013

Muchkund Dubey
President
Council for Social Development

Abbreviations

ACA	Additional Central Assistance
ADRI	Asian Development Research Institute
AHS	Annual Health Survey
AICC	All-India Christian Council
AIDWA	All India Democratic Women's Association
AIS	Alternative and Innovative Education Scheme
AIUDF	All India United Democratic Front
AMA	Assessment and Monitoring Authority
APL	Above Poverty Line
ASER	Annual Status of Education Report
ASHA	Accredited Social Health Activist
AWC	Anganwadi Centre
BADP	Border Area Development Programme
BIMARU	Bihar, Madhya Pradesh, Rajasthan, and Uttar Pradesh
BJP	Bharatiya Janata Party
BPL	Below Poverty Line
BRGF	Backward Regions Grant Fund
BSP	Bahujan Samaj Party
BSUP	Basic Services for Urban Poor
CABE	Central Advisory Board of Education
CAGR	Compound Annual Growth Rate
CBCI	Catholic Bishops' Conference of India
CBR	Crude Birth Rate
CBSE	Central Board of Secondary Education
CDR	Crude Death Rate
CDS	Current Daily Status
CES	Centre of Equity Studies
CGHS	Central Government Health Scheme
CHC	Community Health Centre
CMEPSP	Commission on the Measurement of Economic Performance and Social Progress
CMR	Child Mortality Rate
CPIAL	Consumer Price Index for Agricultural Labourers
CPIIW	Consumer Price Index for Industrial Workers
CPR	Contraceptive Prevalence Rate
CSD	Council for Social Development
CSO	Central Statistical Organisation
CSR	Child Sex Ratio
CSS	Centrally Sponsored Scheme
CSSM	Child Survival and Safe Motherhood
CSWI	Committee on the Status of Women in India
CV	Coefficient of Variation
CWDS	Centre for Women's Development Studies
CWS	Current Weekly Status
DISE	District Information System for Education

DLC   District Level Committee
DLHFS   District Level Health and Facility Survey
DRDA   District Rural Development Agency
EAG   Empowered Action Group
EC   Empowered Committee
ECCE   Early Childhood Care and Education
EOC   Equal Opportunity Commission
EU   European Commission
FAO   Food and Agriculture Organization
FMR   Female–Male Ratio
FWPR   Female Work Participation Rate
GDP   Gross Domestic Product
GNI   Gross National Income
GoI   Government of India
GoM   Group of Ministers
GSDP   Gross State Domestic Product
HCR   Head Count Ratio
HDI   Human Development Index
HDR   Human Development Report
HLC   High Level Committee
IAY   Indira Awaas Yojana
ICAR   Indian Council of Agricultural Research
ICDS   Integrated Child Development Services
ICSSR   Indian Council of Social Science Research
ICT   Information and Communication Technology
IGNDPS   Indira Gandhi National Disability Pension Scheme
IGNOAPS   Indira Gandhi National Old Age Pension Scheme
IGNWPS   Indira Gandhi National Widow Pension Scheme
IHD   Institute for Human Development
IHSDP   Integrated Housing and Slum Development Programme
IIPS   International Institute of Population Sciences
ILO   International Labour Organization
IMR   Infant Mortality Rate
IPC   Indian Penal Code
ITI   Industrial Training Institute
JBY   Janshree Bima Yojana
JNNURM   Jawaharlal Nehru National Urban Renewal Mission
JSY   Janani Suraksha Yojana
KGBV   Kasturba Gandhi Balika Vidyalaya
LIC   Life Insurance Corporation
MAEF   Maulana Azad Education Foundation
MCD   Minority Concentrated District
MCH   Maternal and Child Health
MCT   Minority Concentrated Town
MDG   Millennium Development Goal
MDM   Midday Meal
MFI   Micro Finance Institution
MGNREGA   Mahatma Gandhi National Rural Employment Guarantee Act
MGNREGS   Mahatma Gandhi National Rural Employment Guarantee Scheme
MMR   Maternal Mortality Rate

MoHFW	Ministry of Health and Family Welfare
MoHRD	Ministry of Human Resource Development
MoMA	Ministry of Minority Affairs
MoRD	Ministry of Rural Development
MP	Member of Parliament
MPCE	Monthly Per Capita Expenditure
MsDP	Multi-sectoral Development Programme
NABARD	National Bank for Agriculture and Rural Development
NAC	National Advisory Council
NAS	National Accounts Statistics
NCERT	National Council of Educational Research and Training
NCEUS	National Commission for Enterprises in the Unorganized Sector
NCM	National Commission for Minorities
NCMEI	National Commission for Minority Educational Institutions
NCRB	National Crime Records Bureau
NCRLM	National Commission for Religious and Linguistic Minorities
NDB	National Data Bank
NDC	National Development Council
NFBS	National Family Benefit Scheme
NFDC	National Finance and Development Corporation
NFHS	National Family Health Survey
NFIW	National Federation of Indian Women
NGNB	Nijo-Griho Nijo-Bhumi
NGO	Non-governmental Organization
NHP	National Health Policy
NIAI	National Identification Authority of India
NIC	National Industrial Classification
NMDFC	National Minorities Development and Finance Corporation
NOAPS	National Old Age Pension Scheme
NPE	National Policy on Education
NPEGEL	National Programme for Education of Girls at Elementary Level
NPP	National Population Policy
NRDWP	National Rural Drinking Water Programme
NREGA	National Rural Employment Guarantee Act
NRHM	National Rural Health Mission
NSAP	National Social Assistance Programme
NSS	National Sample Survey
NSSO	National Sample Survey Organisation
NUEPA	National University of Educational Planning and Administration
OBC	Other Backward Class
OECD	Organisation for Economic Co-operation and Development
PCA	Principal Components Analysis
PcPNDT	Pre-conception and Pre Natal Diagnostic Techniques
PDS	Public Distribution System
PG	Poverty Gap
PHC	Primary Health Centre
PHSC	Primary Health Sub-centre
PMAGY	Prime Minister's Adarsh Gram Yojana
PMGSY	Prime Minister Gram Sadak Yojana
PMHLC	Prime Minister's High Level Committee

PO	Post Office
PPP	Purchasing Power Parity
PRI	Panchayati Raj Institution
PS	Principal Status
PSL	Priority Sector Lending
PSU	Public Sector Undertaking
RBI	Reserve Bank of India
RNTCP	Revised National Tuberculosis Control Programme
RSBY	Rashtriya Swasthya Bima Yojana
RSS	Rashtriya Swayamsevak Sangh
RSVY	Rashtriya Sam Vikas Yojana
RTE	Right to Education
SD	Standard Deviation
SC	Scheduled Caste
SCSP	Schedule Castes Sub-Plan
SDI	Social Development Index
SDP	State Domestic Product
SDR	Social Development Report
SGSY	Swarnajayanti Gram Swarojgar Yojana
SHG	Self-help Group
SJSRY	Swarna Jayanti Shahari Rozgar Yojana
SLC	State Level Committee
SMC	School Management Committee
SNP	Supplementary Nutrition Programme
SPG	Squared Poverty Gap
SPQEM	Scheme for Providing Quality Education in Madrasas
SRC	Socio-religious Community
SS	Subsidiary Status
SSA	Sarva Shiksha Abhiyan
ST	Scheduled Tribe
TFR	Total Fertility Rate
TII	Transparency International India
TNMSC	Tamil Nadu Medical Services Corporation
TPDS	Targeted Public Distribution System
TSP	Tribal Sub-Plan
U5MR	Under 5 Mortality Rate
UID	Unique Identification
UIDSSMT	Urban Infrastructure Development Scheme for Small and Medium Towns
UIG	Urban Infrastructure and Governance
UIP	Universal Immunization Programme
UNDP	United Nations Development Programme
UNESCO	United Nations Educational, Scientific and Cultural Organization
UNFPA	United Nations Population Fund
UNHRC	United Nations Human Rights Commission
UPA	United Progressive Alliance
UPAFB	Uttar Pradesh Arabi and Farsi Madrasa Board
UPR	Universal Periodic Review
URP	Uniform Reference Period
UWSSA	Unorganized Sector Workers' Social Security Act
WPI	Wholesale Price Index
WPR	Worker–Population Ratio

Introduction

ZOYA HASAN AND MUSHIRUL HASAN[†]

Originally proposed by Durgabai Deshmukh, the concept of social development has undergone substantial changes in the last two decades in India. It has expanded to include processes of national and regional planning associated with economic growth, and comprises issues related to gender, governance, poverty alleviation, caste discrimination, tribal and minority development, health, and education to name a few. It has constantly evolved to integrate social and economic policy with the idea of an equitable and sustainable pattern of development. The attempt has been to take into account all those aspects of individual and societal well-being by addressing issues of the total well-being of people. Social development is a function of economic growth, social policy, and poverty reduction measures. In India, the debate around social development has sharpened with the arrival of neoliberalism which has widened the gulf between the rich and the poor in the world. The concentration of resources and profits in the hands of the corporate sector enjoying tax breaks and other fiscal incentives to encourage higher profitability has led to widespread austerity cuts for the substantial majority of the world's population, including in Europe and the US. The global financial crisis of 2008 aggravated the problems facing millions of people being deprived of access to decent education, work, health, social security, and the right to lead a dignified existence. The need to focus on social development is therefore particularly important at this juncture.

India has consolidated a democratic system despite the absence of the preconditions often associated with democracy in the 1950s when India first became a democratic, secular republic. More and more people participate in the elections and use them to influence party/government policies. This has ensured that political actors do not come only from the traditional upper-caste social elite, although they continue to have a disproportionate presence in public institutions and influence over policymaking. Even with all its limitations, the success of Indian democracy, which allows for a variety of voices and interests to be articulated and heard, is the single biggest achievement since Independence. While the record of representative democracy has been manifestly strong, India's record in ensuring better living standards for its people has been strikingly less effective. With the result, India is yet to become a minimally equal society. The strength of participatory democracy has not been matched with egalitarian development. The progress in improvement in living standards has been very slow and social indicators are still abysmal (Drèze and Sen 2011). An unconscionably large number of people are poor even by the most modest standards of living; universal literacy is yet to be realized; a high dropout rate from schools and a very small proportion of the population go on to higher education. In fact, any composite index of health, education, and nutrition would place India very close to the bottom in a ranking of all countries outside Africa (ibid.). In short, dramatic inequalities persist despite the existence of a robust democracy in which voters create public pressure for improved outcomes. The logic of democracy and development are

[†] Special thanks are due to Divya Kannan, Research Scholar at the Jawaharlal Nehru University, New Delhi, for providing excellent research assistance for the *Social Development Report*.

certainly not asymmetric, and yet asymmetries abound in India.

The combination of a vibrant democracy, energetic civil society, multitude of social movements, and a vibrant media ought to bring about some redistributive change; however, this has not been the case (Varshney 2000). There is no barrier to combining democratic governance with social intervention, yet in India there exists an extraordinary gap between voter choices and policy outcomes. The commitment to the idea of inclusive economic development has not made a significant impact on the daily lives of the vast majority of people in the absence of institutional means to achieve them (Krishna 2013). The unresponsiveness of political parties and government has encouraged the public to mobilize through social movements and non-governmental organizations (NGOs). It has also encouraged rights-based activism (for information, for jobs on rural public works, for food and education, and for forest land rights), which at the least makes more poor people politically aware of their entitlements to the benefits of development. The real and daunting task is to convert the dynamism of democracy and civil society movements into social commitments towards broad-based policies to overcome policy and institutional inadequacy. What is needed is much greater public engagement with the demands of justice and development which has been quite limited in India (Drèze and Sen 2011). This has proved difficult to achieve because of a pervasive imbalance of political and economic power which leads to the neglect of the basic needs of the unprivileged.

Economic growth has averaged at 8 per cent in the first decade of this century, but the benefits of growth have disproportionately gone to a small proportion of the population that has been doing very well indeed, while the bulk of the people experience little or no trickle-down benefits from growth (Chandrasekhar 2000). It is clear that the overall economic growth is necessary but not sufficient to bring about a reduction in poverty. Growth rates do not capture social reality as the demands of development go well beyond economic growth. It does not tell us anything about either per capita incomes or the quality of life of the majority of people. Amartya Sen and Jean Drèze pointed out in a recent essay that '[t]here is probably no other example in the history of world development of an economy growing so fast for so long with such limited results in terms of broad-based social progress'. Yet, the Gross Domestic Product (GDP) has been elevated to being the most important criterion for judging the country's economic achievement even though India has patently failed to meet the basic needs of decent living standards for the majority of its population. Economic development cannot be disengaged from social development since such growth would neither be possible nor sustainable in the long run unless it translates into a general improvement in living standards and enhancement of people's well-being. Growth is important for achieving development, but this requires public policies that can ensure the fruits of economic growth reach everyone. Fast economic growth is essential for the generation of public revenues to invest in social services, especially public health care and public education. Growth has to go hand in hand with more active and bold social policies to substantially change the course of development. In the comparison of fiscal expenditure on social security as a percentage of the total domestic product, India measures quite unfavourably to most countries with similar parameters (HDR 2011).

The impact of growth on living standards is crucially dependent on the nature of the growth process and its sectoral composition. In India there is a basic asymmetry between a growth model powered by the service sector, which is fuelling a large proportion of the growth rate and the source of income of the majority, which is agriculture which has declined. Indeed, a glaring manifestation of this imbalance is the disregard of agriculture even though the population dependent on agriculture and allied services is substantial. Industry has grown sluggishly and only forms about one-fourth of the GDP. The service sector was growing much faster and fuelling a large proportion of the growth rate. Large-scale employment was the key to poverty alleviation but this had not happened under the service-led growth model.

This brings up the most important issue which is this—the dissonance between growth and well-being. India is the second fastest growing economy in the world, next to China. According to official data, per capita income has grown at a rate close to 5 per cent in real terms between 1990–1 and 2009–10. But after 20 years of rapid growth, it is one of the poorest countries in the world that is often lost sight of (Drèze and Sen 2011). The country had clearly not made much headway against poverty with hundreds of millions of people steeped in poverty. It has proved difficult to reduce the number of poor at a comparably rapid pace. It is clear that rapid growth has not reduced poverty sufficiently quickly. India is home to half of the world's largest number of poor and destitute, even the most optimistic estimates hold that the number was 300 million in 2004–5. The percentage of the population below the poverty line was declining but, as the Planning Commission acknowledges, 'at a pace which is no longer acceptable given the minimalist level at which the poverty line is fixed'. Poverty becomes starker when examined alongside the concept of vulnerability. The Arjun Sengupta Committee Report estimated that 77 per cent population was poor and vulnerable defined with a minimal poverty line of Rs 20 (GoI 2007). The magnitude of poverty is also indicative of who has really benefited from changes in economic policies and the glaring shortcomings in ensuring effective implementation of public welfare and development programmes targeting the poor. The socially marginalized groups such as Scheduled Castes (SCs), Scheduled Tribes (STs), and Muslims face multiple deprivations and difficult challenges posed by the everyday discrimination and exclusion, and to a considerable extent a great systemic bias in the case of all the three groups (Kannan and Raveendran 2011). The deprivation and disparities are more glaring in the poorer states, namely, Bihar, Jharkhand, Madhya Pradesh, Odisha, Rajasthan, Uttar Pradesh, Chhattisgarh, and West Bengal which account for 55 per cent of the SC and ST population and 55 per cent of the Muslim population.

Social development has been on the development agenda since Independence not only as a means to development but also as an end in itself to enhance human functioning by increasing opportunities, capabilities, and freedom. Yet, in 2011, India was outperformed by much poorer countries in terms of human development. India ranks 134th in the 2011 UN Human Development Report (HDR), its rank in the 2011 Global Hunger Index stands at 67 out of 81, which places us below Sri Lanka (rank 36), Nepal (54), and Pakistan (59). According to HDR, malnourishment in Indian children is two times higher than children in Sub-Saharan Africa. The problem is not just that India has significantly underperformed but more importantly, progress is not commensurate with growth when the revenues available to tackle this problem have increased substantially. The vastly augmented public revenues means that the government can deploy additional resources for development purposes but this has not happened because accelerated growth does not simultaneously translate into inclusive growth. Government revenues which are about four times more than in 1990 have funded schemes such as the National Rural Employment Guarantee (Drèze and Sen 2011). Yet, it is difficult to deny the persistence of huge social and economic disparities. On most of the counts from child nutrition to lowering the incidence of poverty, outcomes have been largely disappointing.

Inequality has grown faster than at any time since Independence. India has the fifth largest concentration of dollar-billionaires in the world (after the US, Russia, China, and Germany) and also the single largest concentration of the world's poor. The ratio of billionaire wealth rose from less than 1 per cent of GDP in the mid-1990s to 23 per cent in 2008, and was 14 per cent in early 2010, after a fall and recovery. Each year the Indian government subsidizes the corporate to the tune of Rs 50,000 crores, enough for universal social services like health, education, and other social security benefits. Levels of inequality not only threaten economic well-being, they threaten and undermine the existence of democracy.

But debates over India's failure in giving its people the basic minimums seem to evade the policy framework of the past 20 years that has driven such levels of inequality. The huge new inequalities are feeding into existing ones in a society where certain groups are already disadvantaged. Thus, inequality in India is not merely economic and the challenge for the state is to ensure active intervention in the enhancement of human capabilities by reducing social inequalities also. The *India: Human Development Report 2011* released by the Planning Commission highlights the skewed income and wealth distribution, and the widening gap between the rich and the poor (GoI 2001). The distribution of assets is extremely unequal with the top 5 per cent of the households possessing 38 per cent of the total assets and the bottom 60 per cent of the households owning a mere 13 per cent. The report also highlights the fact that despite affirmative action, a high incidence of poverty persists amongst the SCs and STs as well as Muslims. One-third of the Muslim population, the report states, continues to live below the poverty line. The disparities between religious communities and socially marginalized groups call for a better integration of social and economic policies alongside substantial investment in key sectors such as education and health. This is important because the traditionally upper caste/class communities have continued to gain from their advantageous position in the social hierarchy, especially in relation to education, employment, and ownership of assets.

Like its predecessors, a substantive part of *Social Development Report 2012* deals with the key issues of social development for different sectors. Many of the chapters interrogate the concept development, its meaning for those who are deprived and disadvantaged. They focus on certain key sectors such as education, poverty, food security, and health which play an important role in the betterment of the conditions of minorities. The contributions combine empirical studies and critical analyses to explain the impact of policy interventions on social development and the challenges that remain. Together the chapters address the relationship between the country's development process and social development and the social policy discourse in contemporary India.

Jayati Ghosh traces the evolution of the idea of social development within development literature. She points out that the idea emerged from the recognition that simple indicators like GDP and per capita income do not reflect the welfare and living conditions of the mass of the people. The need was perceived, therefore, to have an all-round notion of development that takes into account various capabilities that people enjoy. This, she points out, is a fundamentally political conception since it would have to be attentive to the distribution of income and assets, domestic and international political factors, public action, and so on. Social policy, as a concept, is closely tied in with this notion of social development and implies state policy directed at enhancing social development through changing social relations, social institutions, and social welfare. There is, however, a close relationship between social development and economic growth. Without social development, growth would become unviable. Social development through a change in the distribution of assets and incomes increases the purchasing power of the bulk of the population thereby increasing demand which in turn would spur growth. It implies an improvement in labour productivity through an enhancement in the living conditions of the working people. Through the inclusion of the mass of the people in decision-making, it would contain social conflicts and create grounds for the acceptability of state policies thereby generating political stability which is a prerequisite for growth.

Himanshu's chapter on poverty traces trends in poverty and inequality in the context of the ongoing debate on poverty estimates. The recent poverty estimates released by the Planning Commission provoked a major controversy with regard to the underestimation of poverty. He points out that regardless of the ongoing controversy, data points to a general decline in poverty, but it also raises important questions about the nature of growth. Despite poverty reduction in conditions of relatively high growth, socio-economic inequalities have persisted. The phenomenon of 'jobless' growth has mostly affected vulnerable social groups. Increase in wage rates have not corresponded with the condition of employment which is showing greater informalization of workers, even within the organized sector. These trends

in inequality call for a re-evaluation of poverty assessment to understand if a decline in the latter has improved the standard of living for the bulk of the population. Unless this happens, it will be difficult to register any positive step towards poverty eradication in the country.

Muchkund Dubey's chapter discusses the implications of the Right to Education (RTE) Act on the future of school education and lives of millions of children in India. It provides an overview to assess the RTE which is still suffering from major loopholes. Although the Act has been hailed across the socio-political spectrum, Dubey highlights its major problems which affects school-going children, especially those belonging to poor and vulnerable social groups. He points out that the Act leaves outside its scope children from poorer sections, child labourers, those with special disabilities, and those enrolled in madrasas. With such a significant flaw, the Act will perpetuate existing inequalities in the school education system which does not follow a state-regulated or a common school system. By not devoting 6 per cent of the GDP to education, the government has failed to live up to its responsibility and discouraged any improvement in the quality of education. While the budget earmarked for education has increased over the past five years, it is still inadequate to expand school infrastructure and implement proper welfare programmes for children. This has only been compounded by a lack of coordination among the various ministries that look into children's comprehensive welfare. There are certain positive measures in the Act that seek to make education free and compulsory, devoid of private interests. However, in the absence of adequate funding and a statutory mechanism to oversee the implementation of the Act, education will continue to remain an exclusive commodity, and not a basic right.

On the unemployment situation in India, Praveen Jha and Avanindra Nath Thakur's analysis of employment and unemployment reveals the unfavourable trends regarding the well-being of labour, which has worsened in the neoliberal era. 'Jobless growth' has adversely affected the bulk of the working classes who have not benefited from the modest growth in employment opportunities that has been supported by the expanding services sector at the cost of the manufacturing sector, which has been plagued by political and technological limitations. Although, unemployment for males and females has declined in the rural areas, the informalization of workers has continued unabated. Certain sectors such as construction and trade have recorded a higher share in employment but these sectors have served the purposes of a few surplus-earning individuals and not impacted the working population as a whole. The implementation of Mahatma Gandhi National Rural Employment Guarantee Act (MGNREGA) has not significantly improved the employment situation in the country. The semi-skilled and educated labour force has not received any desirable employment although opportunities for unskilled labour have slowly risen. Such slow changes in the generation of quality employment have unfavourably affected socially disadvantaged groups and their work participation. Unless significant attention is paid to the primary and secondary sectors, coupled with regular wages, the rate of unemployment will take a longer period to fall and the casualization of workers will increase, affecting the standard of living of the majority of the population.

India's performance in terms of provision of adequate health services is no better. This is reflected in the poor share of less than 2 per cent of the country's GDP towards it. Mohan Rao and Oommen C. Kurian's chapter titled 'India's Health: Not Shining' encapsulates the abysmal state of health services in the country and reveals the negligible expenditure in public health care services by the state. Compared to other similarly placed developing countries in South Asia, India fares poorly on many health indices. It has the world's highest proportion of undernourished children and women, one of the highest rates of maternal mortality in the world, and the highest number of preventable and communicable diseases. However, private spending on health has disproportionately increased, causing the poor and marginalized sections of the population to remain most vulnerable to disease and starvation. There is a rising trend of public money being spent for private health care which caters to the needs of the few. The National Rural Health Mission (NRHM), which came into existence in 2005, prioritized certain states but has not been able to support a universal health coverage programme that will compel the central government to increase investment in public health as well as introduce programmes to check certain unfavourable trends. On the other side, in the name of health sector reforms, international financial institutions, NGOs and private players have entered the arena and dictate the terms of what constitutes 'basic' health coverage. Unless the government treats health as a priority and introduces critical reorganization of the public health services, the welfare of large sections of the people will remain at risk. The reason for this is the low spending on health which will also continue to pull down the processes of social development and prevent poorer social groups, including the minorities, to overcome these obstacles towards progress.

Indu Agnihotri's chapter on gender and inequality posits that a sharp decline in the overall status of women in society has to be seen as deeply connected with the economic changes which have rendered women more vulnerable on a day-to-day basis. She argues that even market relations must be contextualized within extant social forms. Liberalization and globalization have implied a decrease in the work participation rates of women. This, of course, means that more and more women have to resort to unpaid and extremely insecure forms of work. Thus, the neoliberal policies, which result in a feminization of the workforce and the hope that this would produce the modern woman, has been completely belied. These unpaid forms of work, or even paid labour such as domestic labour, can only entail a continuous cycle of poverty in which the woman has to live in perpetual insecurity. Further, there has occurred a feminization of poverty as a result of the agrarian crisis. Liberalization has seen a general neglect of the agricultural sector—through the dismantling of subsidies, weakening of the provisioning of credit, steep rises in input prices, and enormous price fluctuations owing to integration with the world market. The crisis has triggered an enormous migration from villages to the towns and cities. Such migration, however, does not lead to a change in the structure of the workforce, since it is usually circular, based as it is on extremely low-paying and informal forms of work as alternatives to agricultural work. Further, since most of these migrants are men, women increasingly constitute the mainstay of the workforce in agriculture. A general decline of agriculture, therefore, means greater immiseration for women. Important policies such as the MGNREGA have not been able to ameliorate the situation on account of certain inherent limitations, faulty implementation, and the continuation of piece-rate work. Even the new emphasis on microfinance does not readily translate into any gains for women since the microfinance institutions who get the funds lend out to the Self-help Groups (SHGs) often at extremely exploitative rates of interest.

This takes us into the related issue of regional disparities. P.M. Kulkarni and Himanshu examine the regional dimensions in the distribution of inequalities in health, education, nutrition, and income across regions in India. These are mapped across social groups—SCs, STs, Other Backward Classes (OBCs) and general castes; religious groups—Hindus and Muslims; gender divisions—male and female, and place of residence—urban and rural. The authors rely on census data from 2001, the 66th Round of the National Sample Survey (NSS) (2009–10) and the third NFHS (2005–6). At the national level, there is wide inequality as far as the above social categories are concerned. The SCs and STs perform much worse than other groups on the indicators of health, nutrition, education, and employment, while STs are generally worse-off than even the SCs. The Muslims are slightly better-off than the SCs and the STs in regard to education and employment, but they lag behind the Hindus. The Muslims perform better than the Hindus on indicators of health and nutrition but the difference is not much. Women lag behind men on all the counts, while those from rural areas are worse-off than those from urban areas. In the southern-central states, the Muslims perform well if not better than the Hindus in some respects. The reason for this could be the higher level of urbanization among the Muslims in these states. Also these states have attempted to bridge these gaps through measures like the Integrated Child Development Services (ICDS), the RTE Act, and the NRHM, even as the changes brought about as a consequence have necessarily been slow. They point out, however, that there are certain encouraging signs. For instance, in all probability due to the National Rural Employment Guarantee Act (NREGA), the poverty decline amongst the Muslims, SCs, and STs has been higher than among the Hindus and non-SC/ST population.

Another major concern is hunger and food security. Tajamul Haque's chapter, 'Challenges of Food Security', points to the need to link food security with other policies for infrastructural and technological development. Malnutrition and low levels of food absorption can be rectified only with the enhanced access to health services. An assessment of the food security situation reveals that Muslims and SC/STs do not enjoy decent nutritional security and have been unequal beneficiaries of food security related schemes. Women suffer from high levels of anaemia and both Hindu and Muslim women are no exception to this trend. In times of rising food inflation, the most vulnerable social groups, comprising landless labourers, semi-agricultural and informal sector workers, tribal communities, and OBCs are suffering the most. Of all the socio-religious communities, Muslims have the highest poverty rate at 32 per cent according to the poverty data for 2004–5, especially in urban areas where they tend to be concentrated. The country is also witnessing region-wide variations in crop production as many states are food-insufficient. Food sufficiency at a macro level requires the implementation of welfare schemes to strengthen the Public Distribution System (PDS) and special policies for the elderly, sick, and those dependent on guaranteed minimum food security.

Praveen Jha, R. Ramakumar, and Nilachala Acharya's chapter on social security examines social welfare schemes and finds them to be thoroughly inadequate. They point out that while workers in the organized sector (which accounts for a very small percentage of the workforce) have access to a minimum amount of social security (such as pension), the majority of workers in the massive unorganized sector do not have any such protection. While the National Commission for Enterprises in the Unorganized Sector (NCEUS) made recommendations for a scheme that could potentially provide social security to the unorganized sector workers, its implementation in the form of the Unorganized Sector Workers' Social Security Act has been completely watered down and therefore ineffective. Further, plans like the National Social Assistance Programme (NSAP) started in 1995–6, which aims at providing coverage to workers aged 60 and above within the unorganized sector, while registering some initial progress, has not produced any substantial results. While on the one hand, the provision of funds has not been commensurate to the needs of the programme, there is a further danger due to linking of pension benefits with the Aadhar/Unique Identification (UID) scheme which may end up excluding vast sections of the intended beneficiaries. Making calculations on the basis of the official nutritional poverty line, they find that an additional Rs 111,100 crores would be required for providing a minimum social security for the unorganized sector which would be universal in scope and which would provide for at least the minimum of nutritional requirements. This amount is equal to only a quarter of the tax exemptions provided to the corporate sector in 2011–12. It is concessions and exemptions of this kind which result in a very low tax–GDP ratio in India, in comparison with other countries. An increase in direct taxes, as against indirect taxes, which are progressive in character do not burden the poor. Thus, revenue can be effectively mobilized provided there is sufficient political will. Further, the authors also point out that instead of having a number of scattered and disjointed schemes, it is preferable to have a single universal comprehensive programme. The funds should be provided by the central government rather than state governments, since the central government has far greater access to resources.

Several chapters in this volume deal with minorities, particularly the Muslims who have been at the margins of development. They highlight their vulnerability and the reality of exclusion and discrimination which is now difficult to deny. The need for inclusion of minorities is crucial to the country's human development which seeks to protect the basic rights and livelihoods of its population. Abusaleh Shariff, Khursheed Anwar Siddiqui, Amit Sharma, and Prabir Kumar Ghosh raise some pertinent issues regarding the impact of social structure on India's GDP growth rate. By comparing various religious communities, they explain how the higher performance of the Hindu general population has been the driving force behind the maintenance of steady growth rates of 8–9 per cent at the same time as there exists extensive poverty and deprivation for a majority of the population, particularly the socially excluded groups. The per capita contribution to the economy (in rupees) by Hindu General is 270, Hindu OBCs is 135, and SCs/STs is 95.2 as compared to 167.2 of Muslims. All others contribute a share of 231.6. The Muslims, despite their illiteracy, have contributed significantly to the economy. Better higher and technical education would further their skills levels and efficiency. The key challenge is to ensure that adequate support is given to retain Muslims in the educational system and provide them with better job opportunities. The Muslims are also faring better in the modern sector services compared to those in the traditional sector pointing to the need for industrial development.

Tanweer Fazal and Rajeev Kumar's chapter 'Muslims in India' provides a comprehensive but a rather bleak picture of the situation of Muslims in four major states. Using census data and reports on human development, they compare the income, poverty, education, and work participation levels of Muslims in four states—Bihar, Uttar Pradesh, Assam, and Kerala. Their conclusions point to the Muslim community as one steeped in poverty, deprivation, and lagging behind on major social indicators such as income, literacy, work participation, and gender parity. Despite certain regional variations amongst Muslims across states, there are huge gaps between them and other communities, particularly in the case of Muslim women who lag behind the general populace in terms of educational attainment. In Assam, there is a 43 per cent illiteracy rate among Muslim women, 52.7 per cent in Uttar Pradesh, and Bihar records one of the highest at 69.1 per cent. Even in states such as Kerala which has proved high literacy rates and better health indicators for Muslims, the school retention rates are low and dropout rates are 41.2 per cent. Muslims in India are generally concentrated in urban areas but their work participation remains low. The casualization of Muslim works, many of them staying dependent on agriculture-related activities and self-employment, has not helped much to attain better income levels and reduce poverty.

Alongside, the proportion of land owned by backward Muslims is meagre.

Despite internal disparities, deprivation and inequality are common to many Muslims with low work participation rates and educational attainment. Prashant K. Trivedi's chapter 'Rural Power Structure, State Initiatives, and the Muslims', investigates the relationship between the socio-economic status of the Muslims and local economy and power structures in rural areas. It is a study of four villages in Uttar Pradesh, Bihar, West Bengal, and Assam with a substantial Muslim population. It looks at variables such as landownership, education, health, housing, electricity, and occupation and attempts to assess how these vary across different social groupings—upper castes Hindus, backward castes, Dalits, *Ashrafs*, and *Ajlafs*. There is both a spatial variation in the condition of Muslims as also a certain commonality across space among them. In all the villages the condition of the Muslim groups—particularly the Ajlafs—is quite depressing on most of the indicators. Access to education, employment opportunities, access to health, education, etc., were much better for the upper caste Hindus and the backward castes than both the Muslim groups. Further, in all the villages apart from West Bengal, the dominance of the local elite in the villages pose an enormous challenge to the implementation of any welfare schemes and programmes targeted at the empowerment of the Muslims. The marginalized groups in these villages were dominated and controlled in every aspect of life by the local elite.

The chapters by Mohammad Sanjeer Alam, 'Education and Exclusion of Muslims', and Arshad Alam, 'Madrasas and Educational Conditions of Muslims', break popular stereotypes about the Muslim community's lack of inclination towards modern education. There is a widespread assumption that most Muslims prefer religious education but substantial numbers of them attend government and primary schools. But there is a serious issue in regard to their retention and completion of secondary education. By contextualizing access to education of Muslims vis-à-vis other religious communities, it reveals a trend of convergence for Muslims in urban areas regarding educational opportunities. Mohammad Sanjeer Alam asserts that the regional dimension of educational access needs to be taken into account since Muslims in relatively better developed states enjoy better access to education. The Muslims in West Bengal and Uttar Pradesh are educationally more deprived than the SC/STs.

Arshad Alam's study focuses on the agenda of modernization of madrasas in West Bengal, Bihar, and Uttar Pradesh arguing for a policy that provides equal space for the minorities and state to be stakeholders. Tracing the history of madrasa education in these major states, he explains that the reasons for the slow modernization of madrasas lie in the disinterested attitude of the state to move beyond mere appeasement. He looks at the different kinds of madrasas such as those which are state funded and follow government syllabi. The lukewarm response to modernization programmes initiated by the setting up of state madrasa boards has been due to the varying attitudes of the Muslim community and the inefficient disbursement of funds by the state governments and centre. While on the one hand, the traditional madrasas have resisted 'state intervention', those organized under state auspices have been functioning in a haphazard manner. Both these chapters stress the need for the government to invest further in education and provide adequate infrastructure and other support systems which will benefit all socially disadvantaged groups and not just Muslims. The subtext of these analyses is also to assert that only a greater participation of minorities in the country's development trajectory can make definite changes. Otherwise, most promises and policies will remain on paper.

There has been a vigorous debate on the socio-economic backwardness and political under-representation of Muslim communities since the submission of the Sachar Committee Report (SCR). This was provoked by the appointment of the Prime Minister's High Level Committee (PMHLC) to inquire into the socio-economic status of Muslims under the chairmanship of Justice Rajinder Sachar by the United Progressive Alliance (UPA) government which submitted its report in 2006. Its priority was to examine the need for enhancing the scope of state intervention in the socio-economic development of minorities and Muslims, in particular. Some of the recommendations of the committee included the formation of an Equal Opportunity Commission (EOC) for addressing the concerns of discrimination of socially excluded groups, expanding opportunities for employment of Muslims, increase in investment in education and the recognition of madrasa degrees in civil, defence, and banking examinations, and affirmative action for the most backward sections amongst Muslims. Reactions to the Report have been predictable but it's important to examine the response of the government to the implementation of these policy recommendations.

Two chapters—Zoya Hasan and Mushirul Hasan, 'Assessing UPA Government's Policy Response to Muslim Deprivation', and Jawed Alam Khan and Pooja Parvati, 'Government's Commitment towards Development of Muslims'—analyse the implementation of the recommendations of the Sachar Committee and come to the conclusion that these have been insufficiently and scantily implemented. Hasan and Hasan show that inadequate planning, continuous discrimination, and diversion of funds to non-Muslims have affected the efficacy of development programmes targeting minorities. The comparison of the area-specific development and beneficiary-oriented approaches reveal that the Planning Commission's insistence on the former has not helped minorities in general. By choosing to consider the district as the basic planning unit, funds are being utilized for purposes that benefit non-minorities and non-Muslims better, leaving behind minority Muslims in a vulnerable position. An overemphasis on the provision of basic services has ignored the specific needs of the minority population, especially women. The scholarship schemes have yielded certain positive results and this calls for its universal implementation to ensure school retention amongst poor Muslim students.

On a similar note, Khan and Parvati make a comparative study of two districts in Uttar Pradesh and Haryana to understand the impact of Sachar Committee recommendations. Despite targeted schemes, the Muslims have been disadvantaged due to a range of social and political factors. They have unduly benefited non-Muslim populations and yet the government has been apathetic towards rectifying these measures. The districts under study are some of the poorest in the country and findings reveal a mismatch between priorities and action. Budgets are negligible and with major exclusion of the Muslims from planning and implementation, these areas continue to lag behind. Changes must be brought about to integrate Muslims into the policy schemes and a larger allotment of funds under special sub-plans must be pushed for.

The *SDR 2012* explores the developmental aspects of another important minority community, the Christians. It is usually accepted that given the Christian community's favourable social indicators, their concerns are not as pressing as the rest. However, Savio Abreu and Rowena Robinson argue otherwise in their chapter on the social development of the Christian community. They suggest that the rise of Hindutva politics in the country coupled with incidents of violence has affected the condition of the heterogeneous Christian community. The Christians are also deeply divided on lines of caste and congregational affinities. The so-called upper-caste Christians such as the Syrian Christians of Kerala, Goa, and Mangalore have enjoyed higher educational and employment attainment. But the Dalit Christians continue to face conflicts within and outside the church in terms of weak access to education, work, and safety. Anti-Christian attacks have risen and the 2007 Kandhamal killings of Christian activists and locals revealed the growing communalism fanned by right-wing Hindu forces in the region. The infliction of violence and state apathy has led the Christian community to become more inward-looking than before and they have begun to make ardent appeals for special economic packages and schemes. These issues raise significant questions on the character of Indian secularism and the need to re-evaluate the state's approach to different minority communities.

The *SDR 2012* also presents the Social Development Index (SDI) prepared by Surajit Deb. The Index encompasses six major dimensions of social development that examine barriers to inclusion. This conception, based on the principal component analysis, broadens the scope of the Human Development Index (HDI) itself. Employing recent data the SDI attempts to assess the level of development amongst various groups on the lines of caste, religion, and gender. Both Kerala and Goa have shown steady progress but indicators in other states are pointing towards an inclusive growth process. This is a positive trend but one that requires effective planning, implementation, and political will, and popular participation to ensure that all groups have access to the country's development.

Certain trends can be discerned from these contributions. One important trend apparent from the SDR is that identity-based exclusion is at the root of marginalization and social conflicts. Poverty accentuates social hierarchies of caste and gender, and ethnic and religious inequalities—those lower down these hierarchies fare much worse compared to others. The SDR's analysis of the conditions of women, Muslims, SCs, and STs demonstrates that these groups have less access to health, education, employment, housing, sanitation, food security than other communities. Imbalances in access to public goods or problems with job market discrimination are leading to worse outcomes. While this is the case across the country, the levels of inequality vary across space. In the relatively backward regions of north India, the condition of the marginalized groups is particularly bleak. The STs are the worse-off almost uniformly across the country. Further, we also find that these exclusions and deprivations are closely tied in with traditional structures of domination at the micro level. The key question is whether these unequal outcomes are the result of unfair state or market exclusion. It is evident from these studies that policies of liberalization, privatization, and globalization have taken a heavy toll on the vast majority of the population. These processes have had a particularly detrimental impact on socially marginalized groups—SCs, STs, women, and religious minorities. It is apparent from most of the contributions that aggregate economic growth does not sufficiently capture the living conditions of the people, hence an understanding of the processes which impact different aspects of the lives of the people—health, education, employment, housing, sanitation, nutrition, food security, and so on—is imperative. This renders the concept of social development and a close examination of the varied socio-economic indicators of welfare particularly important.

Compared to other marginalized groups, the Muslims lag further behind in the field of education, work participation, income betterment, and ownership of productive aspects. The failure of development programmes to deliver on its promises to the minorities and the SC and STs have aggravated the deprivation of these groups. Qualitative and survey evidence seems to suggest that there is discrimination against the Muslims in the provision of government health and educational services, and employment compared to most groups. Discrimination in employment cannot be explained by factors such as education, suggesting that market discrimination is at work. In case of the Muslims, both formal and informal structures perpetuate their exclusion. Investments in education and health have yielded positive results but these are not substantial yet. Education is the key to the development of the Muslim communities in India. The expansion of the modern economic sector and the incorporation of the Muslims within it is indispensable to the process of social development. However, the urgency of the situation notwithstanding, the state's response to the implementation of the recommendations of the SCR has been too little.

References

Chandrasekhar, C.P. 2000. 'Fragile Growth', *Frontline*, 18 January.

Drèze, Jean and Amartya Sen. 2011. 'Putting Growth in Its Place', *Outlook*, 14 November.

GoI (Government of India). 2001. *India Human Development Report 2011—Towards Social Inclusion*. New Delhi: Planning Commission.

———. 2007. Report on the 'Conditions of Work and Promotion of Livelihood in the Unorganised Sector', National Commission for Enterprises in the Unorganised Sector, August.

HDR (Human Development Report). 2011. *Sustainability and Equity: A Better Future for All*. UNDP.

Kannan, K.P. and G. Raveendran. 2011. 'India's Common People: The Regional Profile', *Economic and Political Weekly*, 46(38, 17 September): 60–73.

Krishna, Sankaran. 2013. 'The Great Number Fetish', *The Hindu*, 26 January.

Varshney, Ashutosh. 2000. 'Why Have Poor Democracies Not Eliminated Poverty? A Suggestion', *Asian Survey*, 40(5, September–October): 718–36.

Part I
Social Development and the Marginalized

1

Social Development
Some Conceptual Considerations

Social development refers to the change or transformation of social relations within a society.

In the past, the use of this term reflected a more philosophical approach about the evolutionary patterns of social progress. More recently, however, it has been seen as a somewhat separate set of changes that can interact with, alter, or even inhibit patterns of development that are based on purely economic indicators. Thus, there have been more complicated, more detailed, and slightly different definitions. For example, Morris (2010: 144) defined social development as 'the bundle of technological, subsistence, organizational, and cultural accomplishments through which people feed, clothe, house, and reproduce themselves, explain the world around them, resolve disputes within their communities, extend their power at the expense of other communities, and defend themselves against others' attempts to extend power'.

The need to separate the notion of social development from that of economic progress became particularly necessary as the poverty of certain more limited and purely material conceptions of development became more marked. Despite much analytical and empirical discussion of the need to find measures of the quality of life that go beyond simplistic measures, such as national income, Gross Domestic Product (GDP) and related estimates continue to form the core of the economic database that informs both public policy and public debate in much of the world. This is why there are increasingly more normative approaches to the concept which stress that social development should really be about putting people and conditions of life at the centre of development. This goes beyond the point that development should benefit the mass of the people, and particularly the poor, however defined. It also entails the recognition of social institutions and norms, and the various forms of social interaction between individuals within society that are not only affected by the processes of economic change, but also affect it and thereby shape economic development as well.

A BRIEF HISTORY OF THE IDEA OF DEVELOPMENT

It is probably commonplace to recognize that the 'development project', as it was used to be called, is far from complete except in a tiny handful of countries in the world. But what exactly is this project, rather what exactly constitutes 'development' in the first place? There have been different phases of international perception in this regard (Ghosh 2012). Early analysts treated it simply as a process of generating greater material prosperity leading to what is now seen as a somewhat simplistic focus on expansion of per capita income. Subsequently, there was a recognition that development implies the structural transformation of the economy, making it synonymous with industrialization and building an industrial or 'post-industrial' society as characterized by the affluent countries. Around two decades ago, the concept of human development was introduced. While the Human Development Index (HDI) reduced to incorporating health and education indicators to per capita income, the basic aim was to recognize that development implies the expansion of human capabilities, the achievement of universal access to basic needs, human security and dignity for the entire population (Haq 1995), and, subsequently, more broadly 'as a process of expanding the real freedoms that people can enjoy' (Sen 1999).

The experience of several developing countries suggests that economic growth (in terms of expansion of GDP) is neither a necessary nor always a sufficient condition for development defined in a broader sense. Rather, the nature of growth is crucial—the extent to which it generates structural changes in the economy (including industrialization) that are associated with increases in the aggregate productivity of labour; the extent to which it generates productive employment for the labour force; the extent to which it ensures that asset and income distribution changes (possibly through redistributive policies) allow the benefits of growth to reach the entire population; the extent to which the process increases the access of the population to basic goods and services that affect the quality of life and human capabilities.

Obviously, such development is not and cannot be a simple technocratic or apolitical process. Rather, it is one that relies on and is characterized by changes in income and asset distribution, and, therefore, depends critically on national and international political economy configurations. These distributional issues have both international and national aspects. Therefore, an understanding of the process of development must integrate these perspectives. It is important to note that relative prices are not either determinants of or reflective of 'efficiency', rather, they along with the markets which determine them reflect differential power configurations. So markets can be quite compatible with inadequate and even socially undesirable use of capital and labour. Nor is market functioning always benign or independent of what are typically seen as 'extra-economic' variables, either within national economies or internationally. Similarly, the distribution of income into profits, rent, and interest cannot be explained simply in terms of just economic returns to factors based on their marginal products. National income distribution reflects the social and historical factors, the level and nature of institutional development, relative class, and power configurations. This in turn implies that changing processes of production and distribution inevitably involve the clash of class interests along with the interaction of social, historical, and institutional factors.

The embeddedness of both markets and governments as inherently social institutions (as noted by Karl Polanyi) means that meaningful economics must be political economy, which recognizes the interplay of political and social forces with economic institutions and processes.

This approach gives history, society, and politics much more significant roles in the processes of growth and development at local, national, regional, or international levels, and the importance of uneven development as a characteristic and intrinsic feature of capitalist expansion also becomes evident. Thus, attitudes to development strategy and specific policies must be sensitive to distributional consequences. These distributional outcomes can then also act upon the economic, social, and political processes to determine the contours of subsequent policies. This is more than simply recognizing that there can be different 'winners' and 'losers' in a development process. Rather, history matters in a more thorough and complex way, by making the process of development an evolutionary one in which there is a continuous interplay of various social, economic, and political forces which determine actual outcomes.

SOCIAL POLICY FOR DEVELOPMENT

Mkandawire (2001: 6) defines social policy as

collective interventions directly affecting transformation in social welfare, social institutions and social relations. Social welfare encompasses access to adequate and secure livelihoods and income. Social relations range from the micro to the global levels, encompassing intra-household relations of class, community, ethnicity, gender, etc. Social institutions are the humanly devised constraints that shape human interaction, or the rules of the game in a society. It is now widely recognized that these are important determinants of economic development, which, in turn, facilitates achievements in these areas.

Thus, social policy refers broadly to that set of state interventions that directly affects social welfare, social institutions, and social relations. It is not only that these policies are necessary because the benefits of economic growth do not automatically reach all. Also inadequate social policies ultimately limit growth in the medium and long term. Social policies are justified not only from a humanitarian viewpoint. They are an economic and political need for future growth and political stability, and minimally to maintain broader public and citizen support for governments that are engaged in the process of economic transformations.

Even mainstream literature now recognizes that there are many arguments for equitable development policies. Some of these include:

- Investing in people enhances the quality and productivity of the labour force, thus improving the investment climate and, hence growth.

- Raising the incomes of the poor increases domestic demand and so encourages growth. Greater consumption ratios among lower income groups contribute to expanding the domestic market.
- Highly unequal societies are generally associated with lower rates of growth.
- Among children, poverty and malnutrition damage health, reduce body weight and intelligence thereby resulting in lower productivity in adulthood, which is a high tax for a country to pay.
- Investing in girls and women has numerous positive multiplier effects for social and economic development.
- Unequal societies are not only unjust, but also cannot guarantee social and political stability in the long term, which is a barrier to economic growth.
- Gross inequities and their associated intense social tensions are more likely to result in violent conflict, ultimately destabilizing governments and regions, and may make people more susceptible to terrorist appeals and acts.

Equitable and inclusive development requires that all members of the society gain (even if not equally) from the benefits of growth. But the benefits of economic growth do not automatically accrue to all in reasonable, let alone equitable, proportions. Therefore, one major goal of social policy has been the redistribution of incomes to ensure greater equity or ensuring greater spread of the benefits of increasing incomes. More broadly, social policy is seen as necessary for:

- Redistributing the gains from growth.
- Access to food and ensuring nutrition at affordable prices.
- Enhancing the capability of individuals with less or poor endowments to participate in economic activity, be employed, and engage with markets.
- Providing security against circumstances such as ill health, accidents, and natural calamities.
- Ensuring equitable, high quality education and health.
- Protecting those who may not be able to fend or provide for themselves such as the aged and children, and persons with disabilities.

It can easily be shown that when designed appropriately and delivered efficiently, such social policies serve as instruments of development. More and better livelihood opportunities and equitable distribution of income expand markets and enhance the potential for economic growth. By guaranteeing livelihoods and more egalitarian distribution of income, social policy enhances the share of GDP going to the lower income segments of the population. These sections of the population devote a higher proportion of their income for consumption. That results in increasing demand for goods and services. The increase in demand leads to greater production and employment, which in turn further increases (multiplies) demand for a wide range of goods and services. These multiplier effects encourage new investment and hence lead to economic development and growth.

Consider some examples. Employment programmes can create crucial capital assets and build infrastructure. Unemployment assistance supports demand during the downturn and serves as an 'automatic stabilizer' (referring to those forms of public spending that vary automatically in the appropriate direction when destabilizing changes in national income occur), which in turn reduces economic fluctuations. Social policy can increase social cohesion, reduce gender discrimination, ensure the legitimacy of the political order, and contribute to political stability. This in turn is essential for any sustainable economic growth process.

SOCIAL DEVELOPMENT AND ECONOMIC GROWTH IN INDIA

India was until fairly recently experiencing an economic boom that has been relatively prolonged with a confident capitalist class increasingly taking on the world not only in exports, but also through investments abroad, euphoria in the financial markets, and growing self-confidence among the elite, professional, and middle classes. India has been increasingly regarded (along with China) as one of the 'success stories' of globalization, likely to emerge into a giant economy in the twenty-first century. This perception has been bolstered by the apparent ability of the Indian economic growth process to withstand the worst effects of the global financial crisis and to experience only a minor slowdown of output growth rather than any actual decline in national income.

Thus, from one perspective, which tends to be the dominant one among mainstream media and policymakers, the expectations generated by more than six decades of independence have been at least partially met, in terms of a vibrant democracy on the move, especially in economic terms.

However, there are many reasons why this is at best a partial, and at worst a very misleading, perception of the Indian economic reality. This is true not just because of the fact that economic growth has not been accompanied by much improvement in basic social and human development indicators. It is also because the recent economic growth experience is based on a relatively fragile pattern of external dependence that may be hard to sustain over a medium term.

The recent high economic growth in India was related to financial deregulation that sparked a retail credit boom and combined with fiscal concessions to spur consumption among the richest sections of the population. This led to rapid increases in aggregate GDP growth, even as deflationary fiscal policies, poor employment generation, and persistent agrarian crisis reduced wage shares in national income and kept the demand for mass consumption low. There was a substantial rise in profit shares in the economy and the proliferation of financial activities. As a result, finance and real estate accounted for nearly 15 per cent of GDP in 2007–8. This combined with rising asset values to enable a credit-financed consumption splurge among the rich and the middle classes, especially in urban areas. And this in turn generated higher rates of investment and output over the upswing. The earlier emphasis on public spending as the principal stimulus for growth in the Indian economy was thus substituted in the 1990s with debt-financed housing investment and private consumption of the elite and burgeoning middle classes.

The recent Indian growth story in its essentials was, therefore, not unlike the story of speculative bubble-led expansion that marked the experience of several other developed and developing countries in the same period (Ghosh and Chandrasekhar 2009). Both history and comparative experience tell us that such a trajectory is inevitably marked by instability, unevenness, and greater vulnerability to internally and externally generated financial crises.

So the recent boom was fundamentally dependent upon greater global integration, not just in trade of goods and service, but even more significantly with respect to internationally mobile finance capital that chose to make India one of its favoured destinations among emerging markets. The dependence of GDP growth upon largely debt-fuelled consumption of a relatively small segment of the population rather than mass demand means a more limited and ultimately more fragile domestic market. Export growth in software, IT-enabled services, and some manufactures remains high, but export-oriented employment is simply not large enough to counter the effects of inadequate productive employment generation in domestic sectors. High rates of investment continue to

be driven by expectations of rapid growth of the domestic market as well as very substantial fiscal sops in the form of tax incentives and implicit subsidies, but these cannot increase beyond a point. Most of all, bubbles, whether they are driven by inflows of foreign capital or by domestic credit expansion to chosen sectors, are liable to burst, and the most adverse consequences are usually felt by those (such as workers) who did not really gain much in the period of boom.

But it is not only the fact that such growth is part of a credit-driven bubble that poses as a problem. It is the other major feature of the growth process, of the lack of spread of its benefits, which is probably of greater concern. In fact, to paraphrase Charles Dickens, while these are the best of times for some, they are also the worst of times for others (which may well include the majority of Indians) because of the growing dichotomy in conditions of living. While this has been an unfortunate feature of the Indian development process since the start, it has reached newer and sharper levels in terms of inequality and material insecurity in the past decade.

Taking a long view, there are some clear achievements of the Indian economy since Independence—most crucially the emergence of a reasonably diversified economy with an industrial base. The last 25 years have also witnessed rates of aggregate GDP growth that are higher compared to the past and also when compared with several other parts of the developing world. Significantly, this higher aggregate growth has thus far been accompanied by macroeconomic stability with the absence of extreme volatility in the form of financial crises such as those that have been evident in several other emerging markets. There has also been some reduction (although not very rapid) in income poverty.

However, there are also some clear failures of this growth process even from a long-run perspective. Despite more than six decades of Independence, the development project is nowhere near completion in India. It is also clear that over time, some elements of that project seem even less likely to be achieved than in the past, despite relatively rapid economic growth. An important failure is the worrying absence of structural change, in terms of the ability to shift the labour force out of low productivity activities, especially in agriculture, to higher productivity and better remunerated activities. Agriculture continues to account for well above half of the total workforce and more than two-thirds of the rural workforce (NSSO 2010) even though its share of GDP is now less than 15 per cent (CSO 2010). In the past decade and a half, agrarian crisis across many parts of the country has impacted adversely on the livelihood of both cultivators and rural workers, such that cultivation is barely viable, especially in the rain-fed parts of the country. Yet, the generation of more productive employment outside this sector remains woefully inadequate.

Other major failures, which are directly reflective of the still poor status of human development in most parts of the country, are in many ways related to this fundamental failure of structural transformation. These include the persistence of widespread poverty; the absence of basic food security for a significant proportion of the population and indeed evidence of growing food insecurity in terms of nutritional outcomes; the inability to ensure basic needs of housing, sanitation, adequate health care to the population as a whole; the continuing inability to ensure universal education and the poor quality of much needed school education; and the sluggish enlargement of access to education and employment across different social groups and for women in particular. In addition, there are problems caused by the very pattern of economic growth, such as aggravated regional imbalances; greater inequalities in the control over assets and in access to incomes; dispossession and displacement without adequate compensation and rehabilitation.

Seen in this light, it becomes apparent that a basic feature of the process of economic development in India has been exclusion: exclusion from control over assets; exclusion from the benefits of economic growth; exclusion from the impact of physical and social infrastructure expansion; and exclusion from education and from income-generating opportunities. This exclusion has been along class or income lines by geographical location, by caste and community, and by gender. However, exclusion from these benefits has not meant that from the system as such. Rather, those who are supposedly marginalized or excluded have been affected precisely because they have been incorporated into market systems. We, therefore, have a process of exclusion through incorporation, a process that has actually been typical of capitalist accumulation across the world, especially in its more dynamic phases. In fact, this process of simultaneous incorporation and exclusion has been especially marked in the recent phase of rapid accumulation over the past two decades, when the Indian economy has been viewed globally as 'a success story'.

Thus, peasants facing a crisis of viability of cultivation have been integrated into a market system that has made them more reliant on purchased inputs in deregulated markets while becoming more dependent upon volatile output markets in which state protection is completely inadequate. The growing army of 'self-employed' workers, who now account for more than half of our workforce, have been excluded from paid employment because of the sheer difficulty of finding jobs, but are nevertheless heavily involved in commercial activity and exposed to market uncertainties in the search for livelihood. Those who have been displaced by developmental projects or other processes, and subsequently have not found adequate livelihood in other activities, are victims of the process of economic integration, though excluded from the benefits.

In terms of employment patterns, the recent economic growth process in India exhibits a problem which is increasingly common throughout the developing world—the apparent inability of even high rates of output growth to generate sufficient opportunities for 'decent work' to meet the needs of the growing labour force. This has been widely noted in the literature on the basis of both the data emerging from the 2001 census and the more comprehensive data from the National Sample Survey Organisation (NSSO). Therefore, there is no need to repeat the evidence here. Nevertheless, it is still worth noting some of the more significant features of recent employment trends. First, the deceleration and stagnation of formal employment growth despite accelerated output growth, and the lower intensity of employment in the most dynamic manufacturing and services sub-sectors (Kannan and Raveendran 2009). Second, the stagnation of real wages of almost all categories of workers, despite rapid increase in labour productivity in some sectors, as well as rapid increase in GDP growth as a whole. This has also been associated with increasing gender gaps in wages (Ghosh 2011). Third, the increase in labour force participation rates for both men and women, including those who are actively engaged in work and those who are unemployed but looking for work, which incorporates the net effect of declining rates of labour force participation among the youth (falling within the age group of 15–29 years) and a rise for the older age cohorts. Finally, shifts in the type of employment, with declines in the proportion of all forms of wage employment and corresponding increases in self-employment, often at very low rates of remuneration. This means that around half of the workforce in India currently does not work for a direct employer, not only in agriculture, but also in a wide range of non-agricultural activities.

These unfortunate features are not because of the 'failure' of the economic growth process. Rather, they are fundamental to the accumulation process itself, which actually *requires* the continuing impoverishment of certain sections for its very success. This is because it is the ability to rely on the surpluses generated by different categories of workers as well as the new potential surpluses thrown up by land acquisition and various activities of the state that has enabled Indian capitalists to invest more (both domestically and abroad), and expand production of goods and services at an increasing rate. The process of capitalist accumulation in India has utilized the agency of the state to further the project of primitive accumulation through diverse means (including land-use change as well as substantial fiscal transfers). It has also exploited specific socio-cultural features, such as caste, community, and gender differences, to enable greater labour exploitation and, therefore, higher surplus generation. This argument is particularly evident in the case of certain kinds of workers—those engaged in petty production as self-employed workers; workers operating in segmented labour markets by virtue of social discrimination and exclusion; and women workers engaged in paid and unpaid labour. Capitalism in India, especially in its most recent globally integrated variant, has used past and current modes of social discrimination and exclusion to its own benefit, to facilitate the extraction of surplus and ensure greater flexibility and bargaining to employers when dealing with workers. So social categories are not 'independent' of the accumulation process, rather they allow for more surplus extraction because they reinforce low employment generating (and, therefore, persistently low wage) tendencies of growth.

This is what makes a specific consideration of social development in India an urgent and pressing concern. It is increasingly evident that the focus on social development is essential not only for generating greater equity within the society and polity, but also because continued economic expansion without explicit recognition of these social concerns is no longer likely to be possible.

Greater recognition and understanding of the complex social realities that have been so crucial in underpinning the recent expansion of the economy can allow for much more creative responses in terms of varying demands and forms of mobilization.

REFERENCES

CSO (Central Statistical Organisation). 2010. *National Accounts Statistics*. New Delhi: GoI.

Ghosh, Jayati. 2011. 'Social Processes in the Indian Development Story', *Social Scientist*, 39(1/2): 35–46.

———. 2012. 'Development', in Bhupinder S. Chimni and Siddharth Mallavirapu (eds), *International Relations: Perspectives for the Global South*. New Delhi: Pearson Dorling-Kindersley, pp. 167–79.

Ghosh, Jayati and C.P. Chandrasekhar. 2009. 'The Costs of Coupling: The Global Crisis and the Indian Economy', *Cambridge Journal of Economics Symposium on the Financial Crisis*, 33(July): 725–39.

Haq, Mahbub ul. 1995. *Reflections on Human Development*. New York: Oxford University Press.

Kannan, K.P. and G. Raveendran. 2009. 'Growth sans Employment: A Quarter Century of Jobless Growth in Indian Manufacturing', *Economic and Political Weekly*, 44(10, 7 March): 80–91.

Mkandawire, Thandika. 2001. 'Social Policy in a Development Context', Social Policy and Development Programme Paper No 7. Geneva: United Nations Research Institute for Social Development.

Morris, Ian. 2010. *Why the West Rules—For Now: The Patterns of History, and What They Reveal About the Future*. New York: Farrar, Straus and Giroux.

NSSO (National Sample Survey Organisation). 2010. 'Report on Employment and Unemployment in India'. New Delhi: GoI.

Sen, Amartya. 1999. *Development as Freedom*. New York: Oxford University Press.

2

Recent Trends in Poverty and Inequality

Poverty estimates based on the 66th Round (2009–10) consumption expenditure surveys were much anticipated not only because these are the first estimates of poverty after the United Progressive Alliance (UPA) took over, but also because these are the first estimates available after the Planning Commission accepted the Tendulkar Committee Report (GoI 2009) on new poverty lines. These were as much a testing ground of how the new poverty lines fare compared to the existing ones based on the Lakdawala methodology as much as they were about the 'inclusiveness' of the growth strategy of the period between 2004–5 and 2009–10, perhaps the best period of growth since Independence. The fact that these poverty estimates show almost doubling of the rate of decline in poverty compared to the 1993–4 to 2004–5 period should have been a cause of celebration. The 66th Round (2009–10) poverty estimates were the first poverty estimates of the UPA and it showed that poverty head count ratio (HCR) has declined by 7.4 percentage points or 1.47 percentage points per annum between 2004–5 and 2009–10. These are almost double the rate of decline in poverty between 1993–4 and 2004–5 at 0.74 percentage points per annum. Unfortunately, not only was the government denied this opportunity of claiming the credit of the poverty reduction, the very foundation of the poverty lines itself came into question. While the debate on measurement of poverty along with what causes poverty to decline has been a long-standing debate in Indian academia (see Deaton and Drèze 2002; Deaton and Kozel 2005; Sen and Himanshu 2004), this debate never percolated down to the middle class at least not in the misinformed and misguided way that it has in the

current context. So much so that within months of the release of the poverty estimates by the Planning Commission, the government, under public pressure, was forced to abandon these. These were kept in abeyance until a new committee, set up to examine the issue of poverty estimation, has taken a view. In the process, the planning commission also abandoned the Tendulkar Committee Report which was accepted by the Planning Commission just a year back.

The credit of this middle class outrage should go to the Planning Commission—the agency assigned the task of estimating poverty in India. On a matter unrelated to the estimates of poverty, the Planning Commission impleaded itself in the Supreme Court in a bid to justify the use of poverty estimates for targeting purposes. Given the historical experiences of targeting in the country, any such move to seek legitimacy for targeting was not only bound to create strong reactions, but also question the motive for seeking such legitimacy. This essentially was the reason for the outburst of the middle class which asked a legitimate and relevant question on the very foundation of the poverty estimates if they were to be used for targeting. It is unfortunate that the collateral damage of all this was the credibility of the National Sample Survey (NSS) data and poverty estimates which enjoy widespread credibility among economists and academic not only in India but also internationally.

While there is not much merit in the criticisms levelled against the Tendulkar poverty lines, the poverty estimates have also been questioned because of the lack of comparability of the 2009–10 official poverty estimates with the earlier estimates. This issue has arisen because of the way the National Sample Survey Organisation (NSSO) has treated transfer payments in 2009–10 compared to their treatment in the earlier Rounds. Fortunately, there is a way to make the 2009–10 poverty estimates comparable to the earlier Rounds. This chapter reports the adjusted poverty estimates as well as the unadjusted poverty estimates. After adjustment, the conclusion still remains that the percentage point annual decline in poverty between 2004–5 and 2009–10 has been faster than that between 1993–4 and 2004–5. While this result in itself may not be surprising given that the growth rate for the period between 2004–5 and 2009–10 has been the fastest since Independence and almost 50 per cent higher than the one observed between 1993–4 and 2004–5, it does raise questions on whether this poverty decline is real or not.

These issues arise not only because of the fact that the 2009–10 Round was a drought year and immediately following a recession which impacted the urban sector, particularly the manufacturing and construction sector, but also because the 2004–5 and 2009–10 periods shows the strengthening of the trend of increasing inequality since 1993–4. This trend of increasing inequality is not only observed across households and household categories, but also across states. While a part of the answer lies in the fact that this period also saw an acceleration in wage rate growth which benefited the casual labour households, which are among the most vulnerable class of households, analysis of the poverty estimates by household type, social group, and religion also confirm that the vulnerable and marginalized groups may have done better after 2004–5 than in the previous period. This element of better distribution despite increasing inequality sits uncomfortably, but is an important clue to the puzzle of faster poverty reduction after 2004–5.

While the analysis of why poverty declined faster after 2004–5 is not dealt convincingly in this chapter, some pointers towards possible explanations are offered as an explanation. This chapter primarily looks at the broad pattern of poverty after the Tendulkar Committee estimates were accepted. The chapter is structured as follows. The introductory section is followed by comments on the suitability of the poverty line along with comparison with estimates based on Lakdawala estimates, followed by the section on poverty estimates. The next section presents some indicators of inequality and poverty by social groups, household types, and religion. The concluding section looks at some possible explanations of the poverty decline in the period 2004–5 and 2009–10, with some issues for further research.

POVERTY LINE

Since the matter has become controversial and questions have been raised on the robustness of the poverty estimates, it is necessary to settle the issue at the outset before proceeding to examine trends in poverty reduction. The issue of robustness of the poverty lines have already been examined by the literature that followed the publication of the Tendulkar Committee Report. Nonetheless, it is useful to compare the estimates of poverty based on the Lakdawala Committee (GoI 1993) which existed before the Tendulkar Committee poverty lines were accepted by the government.

Even though the underlying data is the same, the Lakdawala poverty estimates show a lower decline than the Tendulkar estimates. By the Lakdawala poverty lines applied on Uniform Reference Period (URP) consumption expenditure of 2009–10, the percentage of population below the poverty line is 26.1 per cent in rural areas, 24.0 per cent in urban areas, and 25.5 per cent for the country as a whole.[1] The corresponding estimates for 2004–5 for rural, urban, and total areas were 28.3 per cent, 25.7 per cent, and 27.5 per cent, respectively. That is, percentage point decline in poverty between 2004–5 and 2009–10 is only 2.2 per cent in rural areas, 1.7 per cent in urban areas, and 2.0 per cent for all areas. Further, this also implies that the annual percentage poverty decline during 2004–5 and 2009–10 at 0.43 per cent, 0.34 per cent, and 0.40 per cent for rural, urban, and all areas, respectively, is only half of the annual percentage poverty decline seen during 1993–4 to 2004–5 at 0.82 per cent, 0.61 per cent, and 0.77 per cent for rural, urban, and all areas, respectively. This is contrary to the estimates for the same periods reported on the basis of Tendulkar poverty lines. According to Tendulkar poverty lines, the annual percentage point decline in poverty accelerated to almost double at 1.60 per cent, 0.96 per cent, and 1.47 per cent respectively in rural, urban, and all areas during 2004–10 compared to 0.75 per cent, 0.55 per cent, and 0.74 per cent, respectively, during 1993–2005.

The difference in these two methods and their underlying trend is primarily due to the way inflation is treated by both measures. The Lakdawala method was based on poverty estimates anchored on 1973–4 consumption expenditure estimates and used the Consumer Price Index for Agricultural Labourers (CPIAL) and the Consumer Price Index for Industrial Workers (CPIIW) to update the poverty lines over time for rural and urban areas. This updation was based on the Laspeyre index using commodity groups weights from the 1973–4 consumption expenditure surveys applying the commodity group specific inflation indices from these two sources (GoI 1993). A large literature has already analysed the problems using the consumer price indices from the labour bureau (CPIAL and CPIIW) (Deaton 2003; Deaton and Drèze 2002). The problems were not only the use of outdated commodity weights, but also inadequate coverage of centres (for example, CPIIW) along with problems in capturing inflation for items of consumption such as health and education, and fuel in some cases. The Tendulkar Committee sought to remove some of these anomalies by shifting away from the consumer price indices from the labour bureau to unit values implicit in the consumption expenditure surveys. The second major departure was the use of the Fisher indices which were rooted in current consumption patterns. In fact, the Tendulkar Committee only made technical adjustments to correct the anomalies in use of price indices while retaining the urban poverty estimates of the Lakdawala Committee as reference. As a result of the change in methodology, the inflation implicit in Tendulkar poverty lines between 2004–5 and 2009–10 turned out to be 1.50 per cent in rural areas and 1.49 per cent in urban areas compared to 1.60 per cent and 1.57 per cent in rural and urban areas, respectively, by the Lakdawala methodology.

The difference in the two inflation factors implicit in the Tendulkar poverty lines and the Lakdawala poverty lines is primarily due to the difference in weights used in the computation of the poverty lines. A large part of this is occurring because the structure of the basket has changed over the years with commodity groups such as food having much lower weight than what is implicit in the Lakdawala method. As against the food groups representing 80 per cent of total consumption implicit in the Lakdawala method, the Tendulkar poverty lines imply a food share of less than 60 per cent. This has happened secularly over a period of time and the weights reflected in Tendulkar methodology are a better reflection of the current consumption trends. A part of this is also due to the use of the Fisher indices by the Tendulkar method as against fixed weight of the Lakdawala method.

Even though the Tendulkar Committee revised and corrected the poverty lines for spatial prices and effectively raised the rural poverty lines, it was criticized for being an underestimate. While there may not be much merit in the arguments of those who have been criticizing the poverty line for being too low on the basis of a per capita per day basis, their concerns, however, remain valid. This is again entirely due to the doublespeak of the Planning Commission, which has not shown clarity in making its stand clear on whether these poverty lines will be used for the targeting of beneficiary households or not. While it must be made clear that there is nothing wrong with the Tendulkar poverty lines as long as it is used only as a statistical benchmark to track progress over time, it must also be made clear that neither did the Tendulkar Committee recommend using the resultant poverty estimates for targeting beneficiaries nor was this ever recommended by any other committee set up earlier to estimate poverty.

At the same time, even as a statistical tool, the absolute poverty line which is used by the Planning Commission has to satisfy the generally accepted norms of a minimum standard of living. The poverty lines recommended by the Tendulkar Committee have been tested for most of these—for example, external validation checks were carried out for the poverty line to satisfy minimum nutritional, educational, and health expenditure norms along with the ability to capture dimensions of poverty such as occupational vulnerability, literacy, and so on— (Himanshu 2010). The Committee did accept the fact that the lines met most of the norms in the majority of states, but not all.

Having said this, let us also compare it with other poverty lines. The weighted average of the Tendulkar Committee rural and urban poverty lines for 2004–5 turns out to be Rs 16.25. This is only marginally lower than the Rs 20 used by the Arjun Sengupta Committee which claimed that 77 per cent of Indians live under this poverty line. The World Bank uses a poverty line of $ 1.25 per day in Purchasing Power Parity (PPP) terms. The current poverty line, as claimed by the Planning Commission in its affidavit, is Rs 26 for rural areas and Rs 32 for urban areas. The weighted average turns out to be Rs 28 in 2009–10 prices. Using the current PPP exchange rate of Rs 19 to a dollar, the Indian poverty line is higher than that of the World Bank. The question that arises is: What about other countries and their poverty lines? Most developed countries do not use an absolute poverty line, but use a relative poverty line pegged at 60 per cent of median income or expenditure. The Tendulkar poverty lines are 92 per cent of the median in rural areas and 69 per cent of the median expenditure in urban areas in 2004–5. That is, the Indian poverty line is considerably higher than poverty lines used either in international comparisons or comparable poverty lines in other countries.

COMPARABILITY

While the Tendulkar poverty lines appear robust compared to the Lakdawala poverty lines in terms of its superiority in capturing the spatial and inter-temporal price differential, issues of robustness and comparability have also arisen in the case of the official poverty lines issued by the Planning Commission on a completely different matter. This issue of treatment of in-kind transfers as well as valuation of implicit transfers from the state which have become more important since 2004–5 has already been raised with regard to the Midday Meal (MDM) expenditures (Himanshu 2012). As mentioned earlier, this issue of implicit in-kind food transfers as a result of government schemes such as the MDM schemes has in any case arisen because the 2009–10 data includes MDM expenditure, something that was not done in the past. The inclusion of MDM expenditure as part of private household expenditure in 2009–10 consumption survey had the effect of increasing the Monthly per Capita Expenditure (MPCE) and underestimation of poverty using the official poverty lines based on the Tendulkar method. It also lowers measured inequality since the majority of the households that report MDM expenditure are concentrated at the bottom half of the distribution.

A preliminary exercise using official poverty lines suggests that after the exclusion of MDM expenditure from the total consumption expenditure of households, the actual poverty estimate for 2009–10 is 35.2 per cent in rural areas, 21.5 per cent in urban areas, and 31.5 per cent for all India as against the reported Planning Commission estimate of 33.3 per cent, 20.9 per cent, and 29.9 per cent for rural, urban, and all India, respectively. That is, the real decline in poverty during 2004–5 and 2009–10 is only 6.63, 4.3, and 5.7 percentage points in rural, urban, and all India, respectively, as against the reported estimates of 8.0, 4.8, and 7.4 percentage points by the Planning Commission. The inescapable conclusion even after this correction does remain that poverty has declined faster than it was declining in the previous period even though the extent of decline may have been overestimated by the Planning Commission. It also implies that the total number of poor in the country in 2009–10 was 373 million, 18 million more than the reported estimate of 355 million for the country as a whole. That is, the number of poor people declined not by 52 million as reported by Planning Commission, but only by 34 million.

In this context, the Planning Commission's official view appears that it is necessary to include these because after all beneficiaries are getting these transfers which leads to welfare improvement. However, since this is also the case of many other transfers which lead to measured improvement, the issue of in-kind transfers need to be looked at carefully not only from the perspective of measurement of welfare and poverty, but also comparability of poverty estimates over time since previous quinquennial surveys have not included any in-kind transfer as part of private household expenditure. Moreover, the issues are not only limited to in-kind transfers such as MDM, but also Public Distribution System (PDS) consumption which has the impact of lowered measured MPCE, but higher consumer welfare as a result of transfers either because of lower prices for the commodities or expansion of the coverage and entitlement of the households of these commodities.

Poverty Estimates

Nonetheless, since the issue of inclusion of MDM expenditure has already been brought out in the public domain, any analysis of what happened to poverty should be on the basis of estimates comparable with earlier poverty estimates. Tables 2.1, 2.2, 2.3, and 2.4 give the estimates of poverty, poverty gap (PG), and squared poverty gap (SPG) for 1993–4, 2004–5, and 2009–10.[2] The comparable measure of MPCE used for poverty estimation in 2009–10 has been labelled as adjusted MPCE because of the adjustment made by deducting the MDM expenditure from the consumption expenditure estimates (see Table 2.4). For comparison purposes, the official poverty estimates based on consumption expenditure including MDM expenditure are reported in Table 2.3. These are the same as the official poverty estimates released by the Planning Commission. All measures are estimated using unit level data and with the Tendulkar poverty lines released by the Planning Commission.

At the all-India level, based on official estimates, the decline in poverty HCR was 7.4 percentage points between 2004–5 and 2009–10 (8.0 in rural and 4.8 in urban) compared to 8.1 percentage points between 1993–4 and 2004–5 (8.3 in rural and 4.0 in urban). However, on a comparable basis, the decline in poverty HCR between 2004–5 and 2009–10 is only 5.7 percentage points (6.63 in rural and 4.3 in urban). On an annual basis, this implies a poverty reduction of 1.12 percentage points per annum (1.31 in rural and 0.79 in urban) between 2004–5 and 2009–10, higher than the comparative decline between 1993–4 and 2004–5 at 0.74 percentage points per annum (0.75 in rural and 0.55 in urban).

While the evidence on the better performance of the post-2004–5 period based on a simple measure of HCR is clearly in favour of improved performance, the same is not true once we move to higher order measures of poverty such as PG and SPG. Based on PG, the per

Table 2.1 Estimates of Poverty HCR, PG, and SPG, 1993–4

State	HCR			PG			SPG		
	Rural	Urban	Total	Rural	Urban	Total	Rural	Urban	Total
Andhra Pradesh	48.1	35.2	44.6	11.3	8.3	10.5	3.9	2.8	3.6
Assam	54.9	27.7	51.8	11.3	5.0	10.7	3.3	1.4	3.1
Bihar	62.3	44.7	60.5	15.9	11.2	15.5	5.6	4.0	5.5
Chhattisgarh	55.9	28.1	50.9	12.4	5.9	11.3	3.9	1.8	3.5
Gujarat	43.1	28	37.8	10.5	6.3	9.2	3.6	2.0	3.1
Haryana	40	24.2	35.9	9.5	4.6	8.2	3.2	1.4	2.7
Himachal Pradesh	36.7	13.6	34.6	7.3	2.1	6.8	2.2	0.5	2.1
Jammu and Kashmir	32.5	6.9	26.3	5.9	1.2	4.8	1.6	0.3	1.3
Jharkhand	65.9	41.8	60.7	16.8	10.0	15.5	5.8	3.4	5.3
Karnataka	56.6	34.2	49.5	15.0	8.5	13.1	5.5	3.0	4.8
Kerala	33.9	23.9	31.3	7.8	5.5	7.3	2.7	1.9	2.5
Madhya Pradesh	49	31.8	44.6	13.0	7.1	11.5	4.9	2.3	4.2
Maharashtra	59.3	30.3	47.8	17.3	8.1	13.9	6.9	3.1	5.5
Odisha	63	34.5	59.1	16.0	8.3	15.0	5.7	2.8	5.3
Punjab	20.3	27.2	22.4	3.7	5.2	4.1	1.0	1.5	1.1
Rajasthan	40.8	29.9	38.3	8.8	6.6	8.3	2.8	2.1	2.6
Tamil Nadu	51	33.7	44.6	13.4	7.9	11.5	5.0	2.9	4.3
Uttar Pradesh	50.9	38.3	48.4	13.0	9.6	12.3	4.5	3.5	4.3
Uttaranchal	36.7	18.7	32	6.5	4.0	6.0	1.7	1.3	1.6
West Bengal	42.5	31.2	39.4	8.7	6.9	8.3	2.6	2.3	2.5
Total	50.1	31.8	45.3	12.4	7.5	11.2	4.3	2.6	3.9

Source: All estimates have been calculated by the author from unit level data based on Tendulkar Committee poverty lines.
Notes: The MPCE measure used is Mixed Recall period. All estimates are in percentages.

Table 2.2 Estimates of Poverty HCR, PG, and SPG, 2004–5

State	HCR			PG			SPG		
	Rural	Urban	Total	Rural	Urban	Total	Rural	Urban	Total
Andhra Pradesh	32.3	23.4	29.9	7.0	4.8	6.4	2.3	1.5	2.1
Assam	36.4	21.8	34.4	7.0	4.2	6.8	2.0	1.1	1.9
Bihar	55.7	43.7	54.4	12.7	11.4	12.6	3.9	3.9	3.9
Chhattisgarh	55.1	28.4	49.4	13.7	7.2	12.7	4.9	2.6	4.6
Gujarat	39.1	20.1	31.8	9.3	3.9	7.5	3.2	1.1	2.5
Haryana	24.8	22.4	24.1	4.7	4.9	4.8	1.3	1.6	1.4
Himachal Pradesh	25	4.6	22.9	4.2	1.1	3.9	1.1	0.4	1.0
Jammu and Kashmir	14.1	10.4	13.2	2.1	2.1	2.1	0.5	0.6	0.5
Jharkhand	51.6	23.8	45.3	11.1	5.8	10.3	3.4	1.9	3.1
Karnataka	37.5	25.9	33.4	6.5	6.2	6.4	1.7	2.1	1.8
Kerala	20.2	18.4	19.7	4.4	4.0	4.3	1.5	1.3	1.4
Madhya Pradesh	53.6	35.1	48.6	12.6	8.6	11.6	4.2	2.9	3.9
Maharashtra	47.9	25.6	38.1	11.9	6.5	9.7	4.3	2.3	3.5
Odisha	60.8	37.6	57.2	17.4	9.6	16.3	6.6	3.5	6.2
Punjab	22.1	18.7	20.9	3.8	3.2	3.6	1.0	0.8	0.9
Rajasthan	35.8	29.7	34.4	7.0	5.7	6.7	2.0	1.7	1.9
Tamil Nadu	37.5	19.7	28.9	7.4	4.1	6.1	2.1	1.3	1.8
Uttar Pradesh	42.7	34.1	40.9	9.2	7.8	8.9	2.8	2.5	2.7
Uttaranchal	35.1	26.2	32.7	5.8	5.1	5.6	1.4	1.4	1.4
West Bengal	38.2	24.4	34.3	7.9	5.3	7.3	2.4	1.6	2.2
Total	41.8	25.7	37.2	9.2	5.8	8.4	2.9	1.9	2.7

Source: All estimates have been calculated by the author from unit level data based on Tendulkar Committee poverty lines.

Notes: The MPCE measure used is Mixed Recall period. All estimates are in percentages.

Table 2.3 Estimates of Poverty HCR, PG, and SPG, 2009–10, Official

State	HCR			PG			SPG		
	Rural	Urban	Total	Rural	Urban	Total	Rural	Urban	Total
Andhra Pradesh	22.8	17.7	21.1	4.7	3.8	4.5	1.5	1.2	1.4
Assam	39.9	26.1	37.9	7.3	5.9	7.2	1.9	2.0	1.9
Bihar	55.3	39.4	53.5	13.4	10.3	13.1	4.5	3.7	4.5
Chhattisgarh	56.1	23.8	48.7	12.4	6.2	11.3	3.8	2.3	3.6
Gujarat	26.7	17.9	23.0	4.6	3.6	4.2	1.2	1.1	1.1
Haryana	18.6	23.0	20.1	3.7	4.6	4.0	1.1	1.2	1.1
Himachal Pradesh	9.1	12.6	9.5	1.4	2.4	1.5	0.4	0.7	0.4
Jammu and Kashmir	8.1	12.8	9.4	1.2	1.9	1.4	0.3	0.4	0.4
Jharkhand	41.6	31.1	39.1	9.1	7.9	8.8	2.8	2.8	2.8
Karnataka	26.1	19.6	23.6	4.8	4.4	4.6	1.3	1.4	1.3
Kerala	12.0	12.1	12.0	2.3	2.1	2.2	0.7	0.6	0.7
Madhya Pradesh	42.0	22.9	36.7	10.6	5.6	9.4	3.7	1.9	3.3
Maharashtra	29.5	18.3	24.5	5.7	4.0	5.0	1.6	1.3	1.4
Odisha	39.2	25.9	37.0	9.0	5.3	8.5	3.0	1.7	2.8
Punjab	14.6	18.1	15.9	1.9	3.8	2.6	0.4	1.1	0.6
Rajasthan	26.4	19.9	24.8	4.3	3.8	4.2	1.1	1.1	1.1
Tamil Nadu	21.2	12.8	17.1	3.7	2.1	3.0	1.0	0.6	0.8
Uttar Pradesh	39.4	31.7	37.7	7.6	7.3	7.5	2.1	2.4	2.2
Uttaranchal	14.9	25.2	18.0	2.0	5.1	2.8	0.6	1.5	0.8
West Bengal	28.8	22.0	26.7	5.3	4.5	5.1	1.4	1.4	1.4
Total	33.8	20.9	29.8	6.8	4.5	6.2	2.1	1.4	1.9

Source: All estimates have been calculated by the author from unit level data based on Tendulkar Committee poverty lines.

Notes: The MPCE measure used is Mixed Recall period. All estimates are in percentages. Official estimates include expenditure on MDM in MPCE, but not comparable to earlier estimates.

Table 2.4 Estimates of Poverty HCR, PG, and SPG, 2009–10, Adjusted

State	HCR			PG			SPG		
	Rural	Urban	Total	Rural	Urban	Total	Rural	Urban	Total
Andhra Pradesh	24.9	18.7	23.2	5.3	4.3	5.0	1.8	1.5	1.7
Assam	40.7	26.1	39.2	7.8	6.1	7.6	2.1	2.1	2.1
Bihar	55.8	39.6	54.2	13.9	10.5	13.5	4.7	3.8	4.6
Chhattisgarh	58.4	24.2	52.3	14.2	6.6	12.8	4.7	2.5	4.3
Gujarat	29.2	17.8	24.9	5.5	3.9	4.9	1.5	1.2	1.4
Haryana	20.2	23.2	21.1	4.0	4.6	4.2	1.2	1.3	1.2
Himachal Pradesh	11.4	14.0	11.6	2.1	2.9	2.1	0.6	0.8	0.6
Jammu and Kashmir	8.7	12.8	9.6	1.3	1.9	1.5	0.4	0.4	0.4
Jharkhand	43.7	32.1	41.4	10.3	8.4	9.9	3.3	3.1	3.3
Karnataka	29.3	20.1	26.1	5.9	4.9	5.5	1.7	1.7	1.7
Kerala	12.7	12.9	12.8	2.6	2.4	2.5	0.8	0.7	0.8
Madhya Pradesh	44.6	23.5	39.4	11.3	5.8	10.0	4.1	2.0	3.6
Maharashtra	32.4	18.9	26.8	6.7	4.3	5.7	2.0	1.4	1.8
Odisha	41.7	26.6	39.5	10.2	5.6	9.6	3.7	1.8	3.4
Punjab	15.4	18.1	16.3	2.2	3.9	2.8	0.5	1.2	0.7
Rajasthan	27.8	20.1	25.9	5.0	4.0	4.8	1.3	1.3	1.3
Tamil Nadu	23.8	14.1	19.5	4.8	2.6	3.8	1.4	0.8	1.1
Uttar Pradesh	40.6	31.9	38.8	8.2	7.5	8.1	2.4	2.5	2.4
Uttaranchal	18.2	26.3	20.3	2.7	5.6	3.4	0.8	1.7	1.0
West Bengal	31.7	22.6	29.5	6.0	4.8	5.7	1.7	1.6	1.7
Total	35.2	21.7	31.6	7.6	4.8	6.8	2.4	1.6	2.2

Source: All estimates have been calculated by the author from unit level data based on Tendulkar Committee poverty lines.

Notes: The MPCE measure used is Mixed Recall period. All estimates are in percentages. These estimates have been arrived using adjusted MPCE measure which excludes MDM expenditure. These are comparable to poverty estimates of 1993–4 and 2004–5 reported by the Tendulkar Committee.

annum decline between 2004–5 and 2009–10 is still marginally higher at 0.31 percentage points per annum (0.34 in rural and 0.19 in urban) compared to the decline between 1993–4 and 2004–5 at 0.26 percentage points per annum (0.29 in rural and 0.16 in urban). However, for the SPG measure, the period between 2004–5 and 2009–10 turns out to be performing worse than the comparable performance between 1993–4 and 2004–5. By this measure, the per annum percentage poverty decline between 2004–5 and 2009–10 was 0.10 (0.11 in rural and 0.06 in urban) compared to 0.11 percentage points per annum (0.13 in rural and 0.07 in urban) between 1993–4 and 2004–5.

The fact that the higher order measures of poverty do not show the same improvement after 2004–5 as is shown by the simple measures of HCR does lead to obvious questions of the dynamism of poverty reduction, in particular, the issue of who gained and who lost. The evidence from the analysis of state-level data again suggests a mixed bag, but definitely in favour of higher poverty decline in richer states (or states with a low incidence of poverty to begin with) compared to poorer states which house the majority of poor. Except Odisha, most of the poorer states such as Assam, Bihar, Chhattisgarh, and Uttar Pradesh show a marginal decline or an increase in poverty. While Assam and Chhattisgarh show a higher poverty incidence in 2009–10 compared to 2004–5 by the simple measure of HCR, Bihar and Jharkhand get added to the list by the higher order measures of poverty.

Richer states with lesser poverty incidence such as Tamil Nadu, Maharashtra, Gujarat, and Andhra Pradesh, which accounted for 22 per cent of rural poor and 33.6 per cent of urban poor in 2004–5, account for 17.2 per cent of rural poor and 29.9 per cent of urban poor by 2009–10. On the other hand, poorer states of Bihar, Assam, Uttar Pradesh, and Chhattisgarh, which accounted for 37.8 per cent of rural poor and 23.9 per cent of urban poor in 2004–5, accounted for 47.2 per cent of rural poor and 27.1 per cent of urban poor in 2009–10. That is, there is relative concentration of the poor in poorer states of eastern India, while the richer states of south and western India have seen relative prosperity increasing.

INEQUALITY

In fact, the evidence on rising inequality throughout the last two decades is now available from the same consumption expenditure surveys from the NSSO. These then show the following—inequality as measured by the gini coefficient increased throughout in rural areas, but much faster in urban areas (Table 2.5). However, a better measure of the inequality between the two extremes of population is available by looking at the ratio of MPCE of top 10 per cent of the population and the bottom 10 per cent of the population (Table 2.6). Figures 2.1 and 2.2 also plot the growth rate of MPCE by MPCE deciles. Figure 2.3 presents the indices of real MPCE by consumption groups.

Table 2.5   Gini Coefficients for Rural and Urban Areas

	Rural	Urban	Total
1993–4	25.8	31.9	30.1
2004–5	28.1	36.4	34.6
2009–10	28.8	38.3	36.2

Source: Consumption Expenditure Survey, NSSO.

Table 2.6   Ratio of Average Consumption Expenditure (top 10 per cent/bottom 10 per cent)

	Rural	Urban
1993–4	5.06	7.14
2004–5	5.63	9.14
2009–10	5.94	10.33

Source: Consumption Expenditure Survey, NSSO.

In both rural and urban areas, the 1980s saw a higher growth of consumption expenditure among the lower deciles compared to the richer deciles. This pattern was reversed after 1993–4 with lower consumption deciles growing slower than the richer deciles. After 2004–5, this trend has actually accentuated with the growth rate of lower two deciles in rural areas remaining below 0.5 per cent. In the case of urban areas, while there has been an increase of growth rates across the board, the gap between growth rates of lowest deciles compared to highest deciles has continued to rise. While these do suggest increasing inequality across households, particularly among the two extremes of the distribution, the consumption expenditure estimates also suggest increasing divergence in consumption expenditure of various occupational groups. In particular, there is evidence of slower improvements among the vulnerable categories of households such as agricultural labour households and other labour households (non-agricultural labour households). This is true also for casual labour households in the urban areas whose consumption expenditures have increased slower than the overall increase in consumption expenditure. One way to analyse these is to look at the ratio of consumption expenditure of these households compared

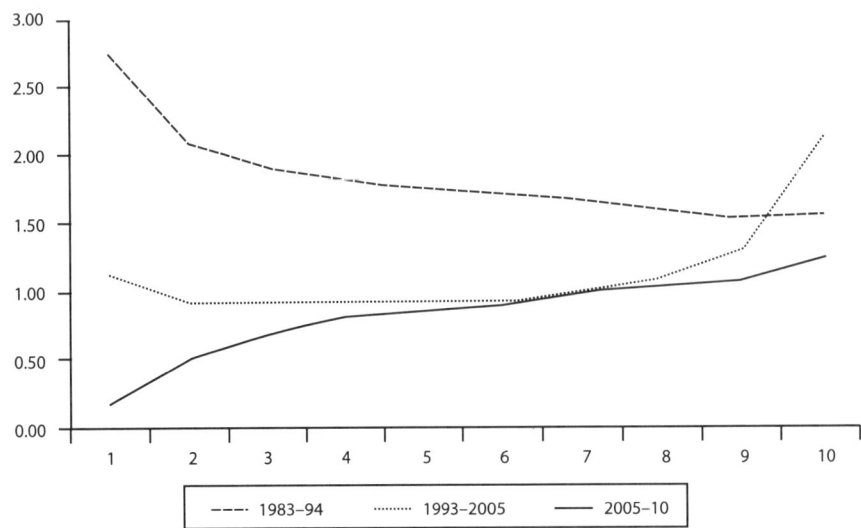

Figure 2.1 Growth Rate of Real MPCE by MPCE Deciles, Rural

Source: Author's calculation from unit level data of NSSO consumption expenditure survey.

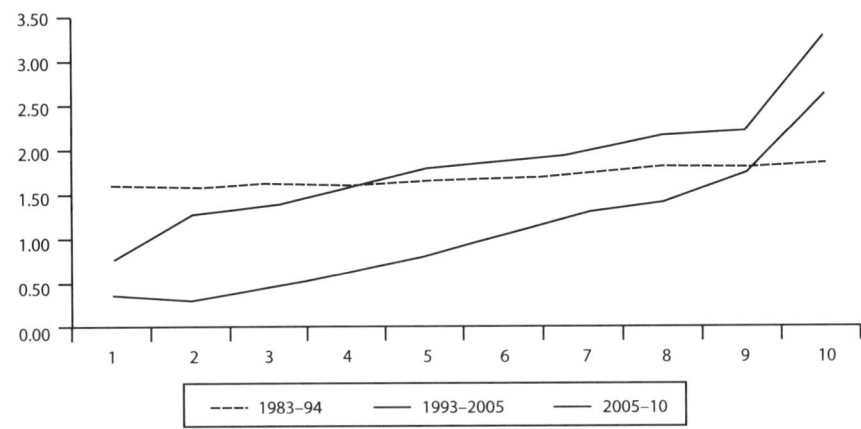

Figure 2.2 Growth Rate of Real MPCE by MPCE Deciles, Urban

Source: Author's calculation from unit level data of NSSO consumption expenditure survey.

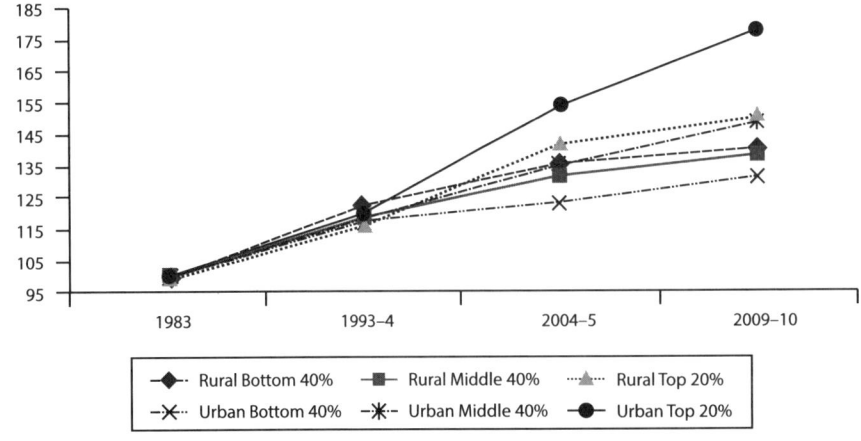

Figure 2.3 Index of MPCE by Groups (1983 = 100)

Source: Author's calculation from unit level data of NSSO consumption expenditure survey.

Table 2.7 Ratio of Average MPCE of Some Occupation Groups to Average MPCE of all Population

	Rural		Urban	
	AL/All	OL/All	CAS/All	CAS/REG
1993–4	0.78	0.95	0.61	0.54
2004–5	0.75	0.93	0.54	0.47
2009–10	0.77	0.91	0.54	0.46

Source: Author's calculation from unit level data of NSSO consumption expenditure survey.
Note: AL = Agricultural Labour; OL = Other labour; CAS = Casual Labour; REG = Regular Workers.

to overall consumption expenditure. Table 2.7 presents these ratios for 1993–4, 2004–5, and 2009–10.

Although there is some improvement after 2004–5 in the ratio of MPCE of agricultural labour households compared to all households, it has worsened for other labour households. While the average MPCE of other labour households was 95 per cent of all households' MPCE in 1993–4, this ratio was down to 91 per cent in 2009–10. Similarly, in urban areas, MPCE of casual labour households was 61 per cent of all households' MPCE, but declined to only 54 per cent by 2009–10. Also, MPCE of regular worker households has increased faster than the MPCE of casual labour households in urban areas as reflected by the ratio of MPCE of casual to regular workers' households.

Some confirmation of this trend is available from the national accounts which give the factor incomes by occupational categories. Figure 2.4 gives the break-up of factor incomes by occupational groups for 1993–4, 1999–2000, 2004–5, and 2009–10. It is clear from the figure that the highest increase has been in the share of private surplus (profits), the share of which has increased steadily from 7 per cent in 1993–4 to more than double at 16 per cent by 2009–10. On the other hand, the share of income accruing to cultivators has come down from 25 per cent in 1993–4 to 14 per cent by 2009–10. While this mirrors a decline in the share of agriculture in Gross Domestic Product (GDP), along with increasing share of non-farm incomes as seen in the case of non-farm wages and non-farm self-employed, the growth of non-farm incomes as a whole is far lower than corresponding increase in its share as seen through the national accounts. Figure 2.5 gives the corresponding break-up by employment for same years.

On the other hand, the changes in employment structure have been far slower than the corresponding changes in sectoral shares in the national accounts. An important aspect of the changing workforce structure has been the declining share of agricultural labourers and cultivators with a corresponding increase in non-farm wage workers and self-employed in non-farm activities. Also, the private share of private salaried workers has remained unchanged with a marginal decline in the share of

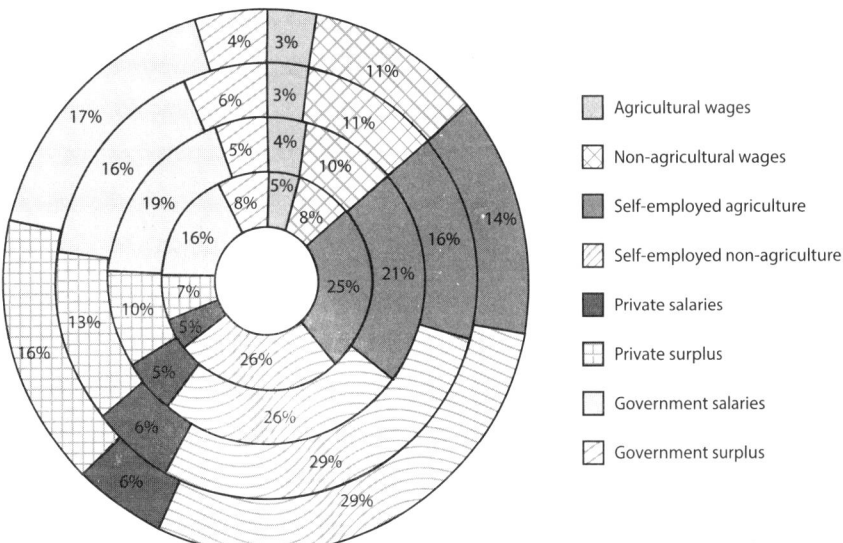

Innermost: 1993–4, Second ring: 1999–2000, Third ring: 2004–5, Outermost: 2009–10

Figure 2.4 Break-up of Factor Incomes from the National Accounts
Source: National Accounts of India, various years.

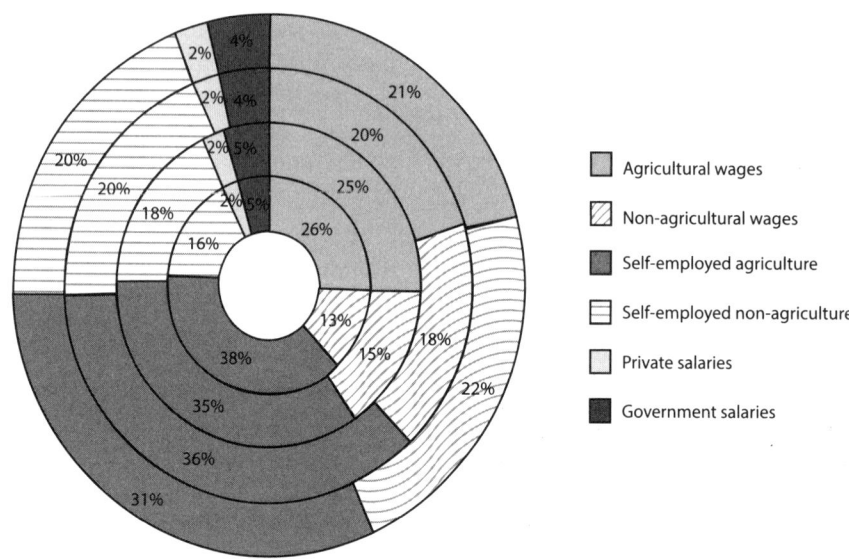

Innermost: 1993–4, Second ring: 1999–2000, Third ring: 2004–5, Outermost: 2009–10

Figure 2.5   Break-up of Employment by Various Groups from the NSS
Source: Employment and Unemployment Survey, various years.

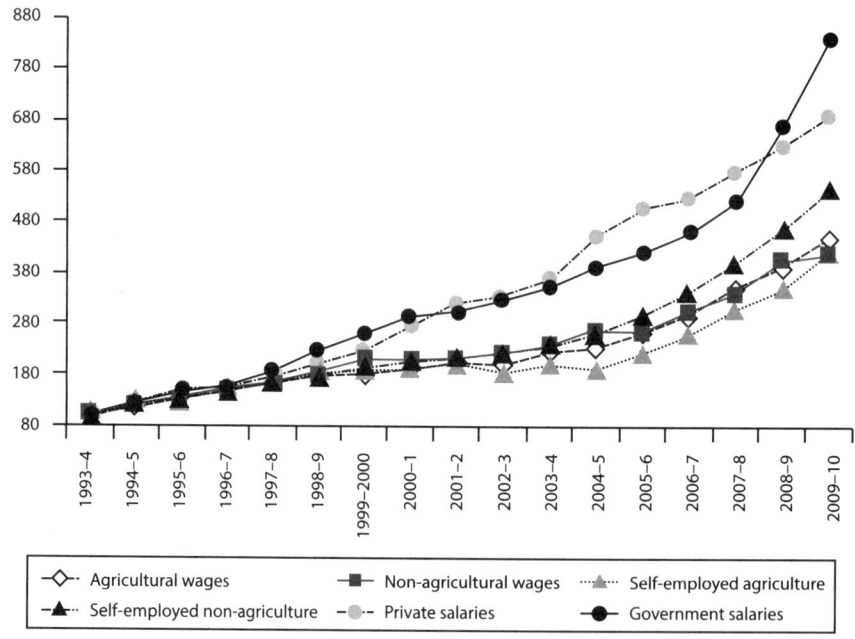

Figure 2.6   Indices of Per Worker Income of Selected Occupational Groups
Source: National Accounts and Employment and Unemployment Survey, various years.

government salaried workers. Using Figures 2.4 and 2.5, Figure 2.6 gives the indices of per worker income of the various occupational groups.

As is evident from Figure 2.6, the highest growth in per worker incomes is observed in the private salaried

workers and government salaried workers. In fact, since 1999–2000, the growth of per worker incomes of private salaried workers and government salaried workers has been almost double that of other workers.[3] On the other hand, there has been some increase and catching-up as far as workers in agriculture are concerned after 2004–5, but over a longer period, their incomes have increased by less than half of those of private and government salaried workers. The analysis carried out by Vakulabharanam (2010) also confirms the unequal gains to different classes of workers with gains to the urban elite and rural elite being much more than the rural workers and the peasantry.

SOCIAL GROUPS, RELIGION, AND HOUSEHOLD TYPES

While the evidence on inequality suggests an increasing trend, poverty estimates are not so conclusive. Analysis of poverty estimates by household types suggests higher reduction in poverty post-2004–5 among the agricultural labour households. Table 2.8 gives the poverty HCRs by household types for rural as well as urban areas. Decline in poverty among agricultural labour households was 0.65 percentage points per annum between 1993–4 and 2004–5. This increased to 2.19 percentage points per annum between 2004–5 and 2009–10. This is also true for casual labour households in urban areas. For urban casual worker households, the percentage point decline in poverty per annum increased from 0.52 percentage points per annum between 1993–4 and 2004–5 to 2.02 between 2004–5 and 2009–10. A large part of

this acceleration in poverty reduction among the casual labour households is due to the significant acceleration in the growth rate of casual wages after 2004–5.

The incidence of poverty by social groups also shows faster poverty reduction among the marginalized and vulnerable groups such as Scheduled Castes (SCs) and Scheduled Tribes (STs) compared to others. Table 2.9 gives the poverty incidence among social groups. In the rural areas, poverty reduction has been fastest among the STs followed by SCs. In fact, compared to 1993–4 to 2004–5 periods, the period after 2004–5 shows a sevenfold increase in per annum percentage point decline in poverty among STs compared to others. For SCs it increases by more than double in rural areas but only marginally in urban areas. However, the annual percentage point decline in poverty is only marginally better for the other group of households, while the trend is similar in urban areas with annual percentage point decline in poverty among STs doubling after 2004–5 compared to the decade before that, the SCs show marginal improvement in the annual percentage point decline in poverty after 2004–5 compared to the decade before 2004–5. However, for both SC and ST households in rural as well as urban areas, the annual percentage point decline is higher compared to others after 2004–5. These findings are also

Table 2.8   Poverty HCR by Household Type

Year	Rural					Urban			
	SENA	AL	OL	SEA	OTH	SE	REG	CAS	OTH
1993–4	44.0	70.3	57.0	41.8	26.5	34.2	20.6	64.5	24.1
2004–5	36.3	63.1	48.6	33.2	21.8	27.5	15.3	58.8	15.9
2009–10	28.0	49.4	39.6	26.2	14.4	21.9	11.1	47.1	12.6
2009–10 (adjusted)	29.5	52.2	41.7	27.6	16.2	22.3	11.4	48.7	13.6

Source: Author's calculation from unit level data of NSSO consumption expenditure survey.
Notes: For rural areas, SENA = Self-employed in Non-agriculture; AL = Agriculture Labour; OL = Other Labour; SEA = Self-employed in Agriculture; and OTH = Others.
For urban areas, SE = Self-employed; REG = Regular; CAS = Casual Labour Households; and OTH = Others.

Table 2.9   Poverty HCR by Social Group

Year	Rural			Urban		
	ST	SC	OTH	ST	SC	OTH
1993–4	65.8	62.2	43.9	41.0	51.6	28.2
2004–5	62.3	53.5	35.1	35.7	40.6	22.5
2009–10	47.2	42.3	28.0	30.3	34.0	18.0
2009–10 (adjusted)	50.4	44.5	29.6	31.1	34.8	18.5

Source: Author's calculation from unit level data of NSSO consumption expenditure survey.
Note: ST = Scheduled Tribe; SC = Scheduled Caste; OTH = Others. For all years, others also include Other Backward Classes.

confirmed by a similar analysis by Thorat and Dubey (2012) using the Lakdawala poverty estimates.

Incidentally, the picture is not so good as far as religious minorities such as Muslims are concerned. Table 2.10 gives the incidence of poverty by religious groups. Not only do the Muslims, the largest religious minority, do worse compared to other religions and the Hindus with a lower rate of decline on a per annum basis in the period after 2004–5, the annual percentage point decline in poverty among Muslims in rural areas also shows a lower improvement in annual decline after 2004–5 compared to the previous period between 1993–4 and 2004–5. On the other hand, they do better in urban areas not only compared to other religious groups, but also compared to their performance in the period 1993–4 and 2004–5.

* * *

The puzzle of the faster decline in poverty along with rising inequality and jobless growth does raise important questions on the dynamics of poverty reduction. This is particularly so in a period of severe drought and unprecedented inflation particularly in food. Although the period after 2004–5 did witness an acceleration of

growth rates to an average of 8.4 per cent per annum between 2004–5 and 2009–10 from less than 6 per cent per annum during the preceding five-year period, it could be argued that the drought and the global recession make it less likely to cause a significant poverty reduction as seen during 2004–5 and 2009–10. It does appear that the adverse effect of these two external shocks on rural areas was less than earlier expected despite the fact that the 2009 drought was the worst in 30 years. Although this did not lead to an absolute decline in agricultural output, it did generate inflationary pressures that could have created distress. However, some of the distress that the drought and the recession could have caused was mitigated by other measures.

Along with the poverty and inequality estimates, estimates on employment and unemployment are also available now. As is clear from Table 2.11, the high growth rate of GDP in the last five years has failed to create employment. Whereas 60 million additional jobs were created during 1999–2000 and 2004–5, only 2 million additional employments were created in the last five years for which data is available. This appears particularly worrisome considering that the previous period between

Table 2.10 Poverty HCR by Religion

Year	Rural			Urban		
	Hindu	Muslim	OTH	Hindu	Muslim	OTH
1993–4	50.3	53.4	39.7	29.6	46.4	23.8
2004–5	42.1	44.6	30.9	23.1	41.9	15.4
2009–10	33.5	36.2	22.1	18.7	33.9	14.6
2009–10 (adjusted)	35.4	38.3	23.3	19.3	34.3	14.7

Source: Author's calculation from unit level data of NSSO consumption expenditure survey.

Table 2.11 Employment Growth

Year	Rural		Urban		Total
	Male	Female	Male	Female	
	Workers in employment (in millions)				
1993–4	188	105	65	17	374
1999–2000	199	106	75	18	398
2004–5	219	124	90	25	458
2009–10	232	105	100	23	460
	Growth rates				
1993–2000	0.94	0.15	2.61	0.94	1.02
1999–2004	1.96	3.24	3.71	6.23	2.85
2004–10	1.20	−3.30	2.07	−1.42	0.10

Source: Based on employment estimates from NSSO.

1999–2000 and 2004–5 showed employment growth which was not only higher than the growth of labour force, but also the highest seen in the last four decades.

Compared to 1999–2000 to 2004–5, the period between 2004–5 and 2009–10 shows employment growth at only 0.1 per cent per annum by usual status, but somewhat higher at 1 per cent per annum by daily status. While confirming the trend of slow employment growth reported by the 2007–8 employment survey, these also confirm other trends noted earlier on changes in the status of employment and industrial distribution. The bulk of the employment generated in the last five years has been in the low productivity construction sector. Further, the data also suggest an increasing casualization of the workforce with employment swelling in the informal sector. The trend towards non-farm diversification also does not show any significant acceleration compared to the previous periods.

However, matters are complicated by the fact that the surge in employment growth after 1999 was accompanied not by higher growth in wage rates, but by their stagnation. Table 2.12 summarizes the all-India trends in wages at constant 1999–2000 prices. From this table, the trend is clearly deceleration in real wages of casual workers although it revived in the most period. That is, real wages decelerated for all workers significantly during 1999–2000 to 2004–5 and then accelerated again to the previous level. And this was true for rural and urban,

agriculture and non-agriculture, male and female, and at all levels of education.

However, although the wage rate growth of casual workers returned to a respectable rate of growth by 2009–10, the deceleration in employment growth during the same period meant that the casual workers as a category benefited less than in previous years. On the other hand, regular wages increased in rural as well as urban areas at a faster rate during 2004–5 and 2009–10 compared to the previous period when these were declining in real terms. However, analysis of regular wages by education status also confirms that except for the rural illiterates, there has been a higher rate of growth of wages for the higher educated, particularly of the graduates and above, compared to other educational categories. The ratio of the wage of regular workers with graduate and above qualifications to the wage of illiterate regular workers was around 3 in 1983 and 1993–4. This rose to 4.63 by 2009–10 (Table 2.13). The higher rate of growth of workers with higher education is consistent with the fact that a market economy with growth being driven by services and manufacturing will have higher premium to skills.

However, data also suggest that this may not entirely be a return to skills but may also to do with the distribution of productivity gains across sections of workers in the industry or the economy. Two important facts are worth noticing in this context. First, while the overall employment growth was lowest during the last five years

Table 2.12 Growth Rate of Real Wages of Casual Workers of Age 15–59 (1999–2000 prices)

| | 1993–4 to 1999–2000 | | 1999–2000 to 2004–5 | | 2004–5 to 2009–10 | |
	Agriculture	Non-farm	Agriculture	Non-farm	Agriculture	Non-farm
Male	2.8	3.67	1.38	0.67	3.33	3.00
Female	2.95	5.13	1.04	1.51	4.78	4.29
Persons	2.78	4.19	1.31	0.76	3.98	3.23

Source: Computed from NSSO employment–unemployment surveys.

Table 2.13 Growth Rate of Real Wages of Regular Workers by Education Status

| | Rural | | | Urban | | |
	1993–4 to 1999–2000	1999–2000 to 2004–5	2004–5 to 2009–10	1993–4 to 1999–2000	1999–2000 to 2004–5	2004–5 to 2009–10
Not literate	6.18	−1.67	4.11	2.63	−1	2.67
Primary	3.88	−0.57	0.84	3.42	−2.2	2.27
Secondary	4.33	−0.72	1.50	4.37	−1.74	1.73
Graduates	6.04	2	−0.70	5.27	1.91	3.51

Source: Computed from NSSO employment–unemployment surveys.

(2004–10), these were also accompanied by changes in structure of workforce characterized by increasing informalization and contractualization of the workforce. Second, the period is also characterized by a declining wage share accompanied by increasing profit share out of value added. The changing nature of workforce structure is evident for the economy as a whole where the share of informal workers in the economy gradually increased from 91.2 per cent in 1999–2000 to 92.4 per cent in 2004–5 and 93.1 per cent in 2009–10. But even more important is the fact that the percentage of informal workers also increased in the organized sector with the percentage of informal workers in the organized sector increasing from 37.8 per cent in 1999–2000 to 46.6 per cent in 2004–5 to 63.5 per cent in 2009–10. That is, two out of every three workers in the organized sector in 2009–10 were informal workers with no social security. Nonetheless, there does appear to be some case to suggest that the acceleration in growth rate of wages of casual as well as regular workers did contribute to higher incomes for the casual and regular workers and, therefore, lower poverty after 2004–5. Moreover, since recession restrained prices of manufactures, the inflation during 2004–5 and 2009–10, primarily concentrated in the primary sector itself was accompanied by a significant movement of terms of trade in favour of agriculture. This also benefited the cultivators, who are also among the largest group as far as the poor in rural areas are concerned.

However, another important defining feature of the 2004–5 to 2009–10 period has been the increase in social sector spending by the states as well as the central government. An obvious case of this is the Mahatma Gandhi National Rural Employment Guarantee Act (MGNREGA). For example, with the 66th Round showing an eight-fold increase in participation in public works over the 61st Round and a doubling even compared to 64th Round, the impact of MGNREGA is clearly visible. Recent research has confirmed the role of MGNREGA in not only influencing wage rates, but also by creating employment opportunities in non-farm sector in rural areas. While MGNREGA was largely a central-government–led programme, state governments were seen as the primary catalyst as far as food-related schemes are concerned. Most of the state governments expanded the scope of the existing programmes such as PDS and MDM by not only expanding the coverage of households eligible for benefits, but also by significantly reducing prices of essential cereals. More generally, the effects of the financial crisis were also muted because of the fiscal stimulus, which involved both a significant

step-up in construction activity in the public sector and debt relief for farmers. Taking into account that rural areas also witnessed a significant flow of resources in the run-up to the general elections in 2009, all these meant that the external shocks, although important, were not so severe as to recreate the earlier situation of sustained distress.

Seen in this backdrop, there appears to be a prima facie case of growth contributing to the poverty reduction since 2004–5. This is also consistent with the previous literature on poverty reduction where growth appears to be the primary driver of poverty reduction. While it is true that the aggregate growth rate accelerated during 2004–5 to 2009–10 compared to the period between 1993–4 and 2004–5, it is also true that the growth rate across states varied a great deal. In fact, the coefficient of variation of the State Domestic Product (SDP) across states does show an increase in the subsequent period. The notable feature of the growth rate after 2004–5 has been the emergence of the hitherto poorer states such as Bihar, Uttar Pradesh, Chhattisgarh, and Odisha emerging as states with the highest growth rates whereas the traditional drivers of growth such as the western and southern states have not seen any significant acceleration in growth rates in the latter period compared to the previous period.

However, the extent of poverty reduction does not suggest any significant positive correlation between the state's growth rates and extent of poverty reduction. Barring Odisha, which also shows a high reduction in poverty between 2004–5 and 2009–10, Bihar, Chhattisgarh, and Uttar Pradesh are among the states with negligible poverty reduction with poverty actually increasing in the case of Chhattisgarh. Most of these states also have a very high concentration of poverty, and the inability of growth to result in poverty reduction raises a question on the transmission mechanism of growth in these states. While it is difficult to argue that growth did not play a role in the significant poverty reduction in a period of rising inequality and associated factors, it is also true that the role of transfers from the state was crucial not only in insulating the poorer households from external shocks, but also in ensuring an increase in the welfare of these households.

Although a detailed analysis of the actual drivers of poverty reduction has not been attempted here, the preliminary analysis does suggest that while growth may have contributed to significant poverty reduction after 2004–5, it was also supported by increased social sector spending after 2004–5, which insulated the poorer households from the vagaries of drought, inflation, and recession and was also instrumental in ensuring better access of resources to the poor, marginalized, and vulnerable groups.

NOTES

1. The poverty estimates are based on URP monthly expenditure and do not include MDM expenditure as part of MPCE. After including the MDM expenditure, the poverty estimates stand at 24.2 per cent (rural), 23.5 per cent (urban), and 24.0 per cent (all India). However, since the original Lakdawala estimates from the Planning Commission were based on URP MPCE, which did not include MDM expenditure, all comparisons are based on comparable URP poverty estimates, excluding MDM expenditure.

2. PG and SPG are higher order measures of poverty. PG measures the depth of poverty defined as the aggregate short fall of the poor population from the poverty line. SPG measures the severity of poverty and gives higher weightage to households away from the poverty line.

3. The increase in government salaried workers after 2008–9 is primarily a result of the upward adjustment of salaries of government workers as a result of the Sixth Pay Commission.

REFERENCES

Deaton, A. 2003. 'Prices and Poverty in India: 1987–2000', *Economic and Political Weekly*, 38(4, 25–31 January): 362–8.

Deaton, A. and J. Drèze. 2002. 'Poverty and Inequality in India: A Re-examination', *Economic and Political Weekly*, 37(36, 7–14 September): 3729–48.

Deaton, A. and V. Kozel. 2005. 'Data and Dogma: The Great Indian Poverty Debate', *World Bank Research Observer*, 20(2): 177–99.

Himanshu. 2010. 'Towards New Poverty Lines for India', *Economic and Political Weekly*, 45(1, 2 January): 38–48.

———. 2012. 'India Undercounts Its Poor', *Mint*, 26 March.

GoI (Government of India). 1993. 'Report of the Expert Group on Estimation of Proportion and Number of Poor'. New Delhi: Planning Commission, Perspective Planning Division.

———. 2009. 'Report of the Expert Group to Review the Methodology for Estimation of Poverty', November. New Delhi: Planning Commission.

Sen, A. and Himanshu. 2004. 'Poverty and Inequality in India', *Economic and Political Weekly*, 39(38, 18–25 September): 4247–63.

Thorat, S. and Amaresh Dubey. 2012. 'Has Growth Been Socially Inclusive during 1993–94–2009–10', *Economic and Political Weekly*, 47(10, 10 March): 43–54.

Vakulabharanam, Vamsi. 2010. 'Does Class Matter? Class Structure and Worsening Inequality in India', *Economic and Political Weekly*, 45(29, 17 July): 67–76.

3

Free and Compulsory Elementary Education
Still a Long Distance for Indian Children

Muchkund Dubey

The Right of Children to Free and Compulsory Education Act (RTE Act), 2009, was notified and came into effect from 1 April 2010. It has been in operation for more than two and a half years now. It is well known that this new law, which was awaited with great expectation, suffers from a number of fundamental flaws. To name only a few, it leaves out of its scope children in the age group of 0–6 years, thus depriving, according to the 2011 census data, 158.7 million children of their fundamental right to education. Almost an equal number of children in the age group of 15–18 years are also beyond the pale of this legislation and, hence, deprived of their fundamental right. Second, by according legal sanctity to the multilayer hierarchical system of school education, the Act perpetuates, and will accentuate, the prevailing discrimination in the Indian school system. In the process, it also perpetuates a major factor, that is, inequality—accounting for the poor quality of school education. Third, the Act makes no commitment for the availability of resources required to universalize quality education within a specified time limit. Fourth, the norms contained in the Schedule of the Act are non-transparent, perfunctory, and mostly of a discretionary nature, which comes in the way of making them legally enforceable. They are also too few to make any real difference to the poor quality of the school education system. Fifth, the legislation does not stipulate the establishment of a statutory mechanism for overseeing its implementation, suggesting further reforms, and serving as a last court of appeal for redressing grievances. Finally, the Act does not make it mandatory to impart primary education through the medium of the mother tongue, which is a sine qua non for making school education truly inclusive.

In spite of these deficiencies, the Act was hailed in many quarters as a major victory in the century-long struggle for getting recognition for the right of Indian children to free and compulsory education and seeing this right translated into reality. This demand is vindicated in Section 3(1) of the Act which states that 'every child of the age of 6 to 14 years shall have a right to free and compulsory education in a neighbouring school till completion of elementary education'. Besides, there are several other progressive measures included in the Act, which have been on the agenda of those committed to bringing about comprehensive reforms in the school education system in India. These include:

- There will be no test for admission, either of the child or parents.
- Capitation fee for admission is prohibited.
- No child shall be detained in any class or sent back during the eight-year period of free and compulsory education.
- Annual examinations will be substituted by comprehensive and continuing evaluation.
- Admission will not be denied based on the absence of a birth certificate or other papers.
- Enrolment will take place at any time during the year.
- No child will be subjected to physical punishment or mental harassment.

- Pupil–teacher ratio will be maintained at 30:1 at the lower primary level and 35:1 at the upper primary level.
- There will be no multigrade teaching in any school.
- There will be no recruitment of para-teachers after five years.
- Teachers will not be permitted to give private tuition.
- Teachers will not be deployed for non-teaching purposes except those listed in the Act.
- Vacancies for teachers will not exceed 10 per cent of the sanctioned strength.
- Every school will have a School Management Committee, 75 per cent members of which will be parents and 50 per cent would be women.
- Private schools will be required to be registered and only registered schools will be recognized. Registration will be on the basis of their following the norms laid down in the Schedule of the Act.

The provision in the Act for the reservation of at least 25 per cent of the strength of Class I in the 'specified category' and 'unaided' schools, for providing free and compulsory education to children belonging to weaker sections and disadvantaged groups, has been regarded by many as of great significance. Some have seen in it the potentiality of bringing about a veritable social revolution. This is, however, misplaced and at best exaggerated. Instead of having any revolutionary potential, this provision is in fact a retrograde step. It will create a divide among the children of the poor—between those who will be admitted under this provision and those who will be left out. This is apart from the divide in the same school of the children of the rich who will pay for their education and those of the poor who will be provided free education. Moreover, the total number of children who will get admission in these privileged schools when this provision is fully implemented will be a small percentage falling in the age group of 6–14 years. It is estimated that there are some 20 crore students in this age group. The total capacity of the schools in these categories is about 5.4 crores. Even if the full 25 per cent of this capacity is reserved for the children of the weaker sections, the total number of children who will benefit will be only 1.36 crores, that is, 6.8 per cent of the total.

The owners of private schools are not prepared to permit even this extent of opening of their schools for the children of the poor. Soon after the Act was passed, they filed a suit in the Supreme Court to get the provision of the Act relating to 25 per cent reservation, declared ultra vires of the Constitution. The Supreme Court pronounced its verdict after a long delay in 2012, and ruled this provision to be entirely in consonance with the spirit of the Constitution.

Most of the positive measures of the Act, except that relating to the teachers' training for which the time limit is five years, are to be implemented within three years after the Act entered into force. These include:

- Making sure that there are enough schools on the ground for every child in the age group of 6–14 years to be admitted in a school in the neighbourhood.
- Appointing adequate number of teachers in order to meet the pupil–teacher ratio prescribed in the Schedule.
- Ensuring that all schools comply with the norms prescribed in the Act, relating to infrastructure facilities.
- Bringing all the out-of-school children to school.
- Ensuring that every school has a School Management Committee constituted according to the criteria laid down in the Act.

Available data, both official and unofficial, as well as the review of implementation undertaken by civil society organizations, have brought out that none of the goals with a time limit of three years are going to be realized by the end of March 2012. No systematic and comprehensive mapping has so far been done to determine the additional number of schools to be built and additional number of teachers to be recruited. Consequently, the required number of schools are not on the ground and a large proportion of the teachers required for meeting the target under the Act, are yet to be appointed. In 2010–11, not more than 5 per cent of the schools complied with all the infrastructure norms laid down in the Act.

Towards the end of 2011, 10 per cent of the schools did not have drinking water supply.[1] According to Annual Status of Education Report (ASER) survey of 2011,[2] this percentage was 16.6. Thirty-seven per cent of the schools did not have functioning lavatories.[3] Forty per cent of the schools did not have toilets separately for girls.[4] For the country as a whole, only 62 per cent of the schools visited had a playground.[5] The 2010–11 DISE data put it even lower at 47.4 per cent. The proportion of schools without libraries was 28.6 per cent.[6] More than 50 per cent of the schools had no medical facilities.[7] Only a little over 18 per cent of the schools had computers; 75 per cent of the schools had no electricity connections.[8] This percentage came down to 57 a year later.[9] Only 50.59 per cent of the schools had ramps for disabled children.[10]

The average number of teachers in an elementary school in 2011 was 4.7.[11] Thousands of schools had only a single teacher. The percentage of single teacher schools, according to the DISE data, came down from 14 in 2009 to 8.6 in 2010–11. Over half the classes visited by the ASER team were multigrade.[12] The proportion of schools compliant with the RTE norm of the pupil–teacher ratio was approximately 40 per cent both in 2010 and 2011.[13] The percentage of schools having an enrolment of 100 per cent and above and having a head master or head teacher was about 56.[14]

Enrolment is the only area where the performance of the elementary schools appear to have been up to the mark. According to the ASER 2011 data, the enrolment in these schools in rural areas was 96.7. According to the DISE 2009–10 data, the enrolment ratio in the age group of 6–13 years was 102.47. However, the attendance that year was only 70.9 per cent,[15] representing a decline over the ratio of 73.4 per cent in 2007. So far as the coverage of education is concerned, it is the attendance and not enrolment that matters. It was correctly recommended in ASER 2011 that 'it is time that attendance instead of enrolment, is used as the measure of who is in school'.

An important indicator of access to education is the retention of those enrolled. According to the Government of India (GoI 2011) data, the dropout rate was 28.86 per cent from Classes I to V, 43.9 per cent from Classes I to VIII, and 52.76 per cent from Classes I to X. These rates were much higher in some states and for Scheduled Caste (SC) and Scheduled Tribe (ST) students. In Bihar, the respective figures in the three stages were 42.45, 66.02, and 77.56. The all-India figure of the dropout rate for ST students from Classes I to X was as high as 72.1 per cent (GoI 2011).

Though there has been some progress during the review period in bringing to school the very large number of out-of-school children in India, there is no prospect of this goal being realized by the end of the target date of March 2013. According to government estimates, some 7.5 to 8 million children, constituting over 4 per cent of the total children in the age group of 6–13 years, are out of school. The latest National Sample Survey (NSS) data puts the number of such children at 2.1 crores. The figure of out-of-school children often cited by civil society organizations working in the field of school education comes to nearly 16 million children out of 220 million children in the age group of 6–13 years.[16] The Common School System Commission, Bihar in its report in 2007 had calculated that 50 per cent of the children, that is, 1.5 crores out of 3 crores, in the age group of 5–18 years were out

of school (Government of Bihar 2007). Out-of-school children fall in a variety of categories. By far the largest among them consist of those engaged in various forms of child labour. Others include street children, children of migrant workers, and those whose parents are victims of natural disasters.

During the last two and a half years, a much larger proportion of the schools at the elementary level have come to have School Management Committees (SMCs) as mandated under the RTE Act. However, a significant proportion of them still have not set up such committees. Besides, the procedure laid down in the Act, particularly with regard to the representation of parents and women in the committees, have not been followed in constituting the newly established committees nor have their functions been properly defined or adequate authority given to them to discharge their functions. Very few SMCs have prepared school development plans as mandated in the Act.

Even after the Supreme Court's verdict, very few unaided schools have provided the minimum stipulated reservation of 25 per cent at the level of Class I for the children of the weaker sections. When owners of private schools filed the case with the Supreme Court, the latter had not given any stay order. Therefore, the implementation of this clause should have commenced from 1 April 2011, taking into account the fact that one year's extension was given by the government for this provision to come into force.

In consonance with the Act, schools have started eliminating annual qualifying exams, but they have not been able to introduce in its place, a system of comprehensive and continuing evaluation. The main reason for this is that the schools do not know how to go about it as the government has not laid down the procedure for conducting such evaluations nor has any attempt been made to bring about changes in the syllabus and in the pedagogy, to conform to this requirement.

The government has not until now taken with seriousness the task of registering private schools based on their conformity with the norms and standards prescribed in the Schedule of the RTE Act. This task, like many others, was to have been completed within a period of three years after the Act came into force.

Though several states have laws to regulate private schools, these schools, by and large, remain unregulated. Among others, they continue to extract from parents exorbitant fees, including capitation fees and other charges.

It is widely recognized that the quality of elementary education in India is abysmally poor. The tests carried out by various agencies have brought out that children in elementary schools are far behind in proficiency in reading, writing, and arithmetic that they are expected to acquire in their respective class. The Supreme Court has, in its interpretation of the fundamental right to education, clarified that right to education means right to quality education. Without ensuring quality, the objectives of education cannot be realized. In the current phase of globalization, marketability has come to be recognized as the principal objective. This is a highly truncated way of looking at education.

The inculcation of values is an important aspect of quality. These values, enshrined in the Constitution of India, are those of justice, equality, non-discrimination, secularism, and respect for plurality, diversity, and fundamental freedoms. These are built into the national curriculum which is expected to be followed by all schools and reflected, with such variations as may be necessary, in the syllabus and textbooks, and pedagogy based thereon.

During the last two and a half years, very few of the measures provided in the Act designed to improve quality have been implemented. These include the building of additional schools, putting in place the required infrastructure facilities, recruiting the required number of teachers, training teachers, renovating and establishing teachers' training institutions, and ensuring truly participatory and effective school management. As teachers have the most critical role to play in ensuring quality, they should be paid salaries befitting their due status in society and their career prospects should be improved. It is also important to provide incentives to make the teaching profession attractive and satisfying. For this, teachers should be given teaching aids and awarded fellowships to improve their knowledge and career prospects. They should be given facilities to do research in order to innovate, a role in supervising schools, and a platform for regular consultation and exchange of experience among them to improve pedagogy.

In addition to the above instrumental factors, there are a number of structural factors which account for the low quality of school education in India. By far the most important among them is the inequality and discrimination characterizing the system. Quality will remain elusive so long as marginalization and exclusion remains embedded in the very structure of school education. That equality is a critical determinant of quality has been demonstrated by the experience of those countries which follow a common school system and those which have consciously adopted measures to reduce inequality and open their school education system to the children of the marginalized and the poor. In the *Development Plan for Education* issued a few years ago by the Ministry of Education of the Brazilian government, it is stated that 'the published data make it clear that the problem of quality will only be solved if the problem of inequality is also faced'.

It is problematic whether there will be any notable progress at all in enhancing the quality of school education in India so long as it is done within the framework of the existing multilayer system of education, legalized by the RTE Act. In this system, children of the poor who constitute the vast majority of the population go to government schools where the quality is very poor, whereas the elite class sends its children to specified category schools or private schools providing a better quality of education. Therefore, the elites which constitute the ruling class are not interested in the upgradation of the quality of government schools. On the other hand, in the absence of socialization in private schools, among children coming from different class backgrounds, the quality of education in these schools also leaves much to be desired. Consequently, there is an all-round degradation of quality of school education in India—both in government schools as well as in private schools.

In view of the comprehensive failure to meet the three-year deadline for achieving the major objectives of the Act, the central government is reported to be toying with the idea of extending the time limit from three to five years. In October 2012, some of the mainstream newspapers quoting government sources reported that the central government was contemplating to move an amendment to the Act to extend the time target. This provoked widespread protests from civil society organizations active in the field of school education. In the beginning of November 2012, a number of such organizations and individual activists and intellectuals addressed an appeal to the Minister of Human Resource Development of the GoI, in which they characterized the proposal for extension as 'uncalled for' and stated that this will 'harm the children's development and life chances'. They urged the government 'to respect the timeline in the Act and not seek any extension'. They warned that 'the Centre's proposed move to extend the deadline of implementation of the provisions of the RTE Act, 2009, will only strengthen the growing belief that India is not committed to the education of the children of its marginalized'.

Once the government succumbs to the political pressure for extension, this will become an unending process in which each extension will be followed by another. This will be violative of the spirit of Article 21A and the

RTE Act, which are intended to universalize free and compulsory education within a time-bound framework. This could very well justify seeking judicial intervention to prevent extension.

There are various reasons accounting for the lack of or very slow progress in the implementation of the RTE Act. First, the government did not adopt the indispensable preparatory measures for implementing the Act. The most important among them is the mapping of schools and related institutions to determine the magnitude of the task of providing free and compulsory elementary education. It was assumed that the mapping would be done during the course of the implementation of the Act. This expectation has not been realized so far.

Moreover, the government neglected the task of creating the capacity at its different levels for implementing the Act. Nor did it actively seek to achieve a convergence among different government ministries and departments capable of providing crucial inputs for implementing the Act. The ministries and departments concerned include the Ministry of Rural Development so far as its programmes on water and sanitation are concerned; the Ministry of Labour and Employment so far as child labour is concerned; the Ministry of Women and Child Development for the education of children in the age group of 0–6 years; the Ministry of Health and Family Welfare for the provision of health services and medical facilities for children; the Ministry of Science and Technology for educational aids and technology; the Department of Sports for sports facilities for children; and the Ministry of Culture so far as education in fine arts is concerned.

By far the most important constraint to implementation is the lack of adequate financial resources. The government has been non-committal on the question of providing resources needed for implementing the Act. It did not follow the usual practice of attaching a financial memorandum to the RTE Bill when it was moved in Parliament, even though it had set up a sub-committee of the Central Advisory Board of Education (CABE) Committee to calculate the additional financial resources required for providing free and compulsory education to the children in the age group of 6–14 years, and that sub-committee had made an estimate, which was included in the earlier draft of the Bill. The last minute withdrawal of the financial memorandum from the Bill raised the question as to whether the government was genuinely committed to implementing the Bill or it was rushing through the passage of the Bill only for serving political ends.

There was no doubt a substantial increase, nearing doubling, in the resources earmarked for elementary education in the Eleventh Five Year Plan as compared to that in the Tenth Plan. Against an actual expenditure of Rs 9,092 crores per annum during the Tenth Five Year Plan, the outlay in the Eleventh Plan was a little over Rs 25,000 crores per annum. Moreover, the Thirteenth Finance Commission provided to states grants-in-aid for school education amounting to Rs 25,000 crores per annum. Though these figures taken together represented a substantial increase in the resources made available for elementary education after the passage of the RTE Act, they still fell far short of the resources required, according to calculations made by expert committees appointed by the government, to universalize quality elementary education within a time-bound framework. The sub-committee of the CABE Committee had calculated in 2004 that over a period of six years from 2006–7 to 2011–14, an amount of Rs 72,347 crores per annum as additional resources would be required for realizing the objective. Thus, even the much enhanced resources provided for in the Eleventh Five Year Plan fell miserably short of the required additional resources.

The allotment for elementary education in the budget of the central government for the year 2010–11, the first year of the implementation of the Act, was Rs 25,000 crore out of which Rs 15,000 crores were for the Sarva Shiksha Abhiyan (SSA), the vehicle chosen for implementing the Act and Rs 9,300 crores for Midday Meals (MDM). This allotment was far short of the request made by the Ministry of Human Resource Development for Rs 40,000 crores and of the conservative recommendation of the Planning Commission, amounting to Rs 35,000 crores. This again put a question mark on the seriousness of the union government to implement the Act. The total allocation for the financial year 2011–12 was a little over Rs 31,000 crores and for the year 2012–13 a little over Rs 37,000 crores. Even these amounts did not come close to the required magnitude of the additional resources as calculated by the experts committees referred to above.

As far back as in 1968, the nation had set a target in the National Policy on Education (NPE) of spending 6 per cent of the Gross Domestic Product (GDP) on education. This was reiterated in the NEP of 1986 and its revised version of 1992. This target was also approved by the Indian Parliament and incorporated in successive election manifestos of major national political parties. And yet the proportion of GDP devoted to expenditure on education has never exceeded 4 per cent during the past several decades. This prolonged neglect of the target of 6 per cent is indicative of the relatively low priority which successive governments of India have accorded to education, including school education, and of its continuing unwillingness to reprioritize public expenditure in favour of education in order to meet the target of 6 per cent.

This is in contrast to the practice followed by several other developing countries which have accepted legal commitments for public funding of education. For example, in Brazil it is constitutionally mandatory for the federal government to devote 18 per cent of the federal budget and for the provincial governments to devote 25 per cent of their budgets to education. The Indonesian government has accepted a legal obligation to devote 20 per cent of its national and regional budgets combined for expenditure on education. The National Education Act of Thailand (1999) enjoins upon the state and local governments to levy educational taxes as appropriate to finance education. There is a law in Argentina obliging the state to allocate 6 per cent of GDP to education during a specified period of time.[17]

It needs to be underlined that most of the increase in resources needed for universalizing quality school education is of a once-for-all nature. At the end of the period specified for universalization, the expenditure will start tapering off and the resources needed will be only those of a recurring nature, that is, for maintaining and running facilities and institutions, and for creating additional facilities for the education of additional number of children who will enter the school-going age.

In addition to budgetary allocation, other sources from which additional resources can be mobilized are earmarking a part of the foreign exchange reserve and a part of the fund realized from the public sector disinvestment. Additional resources can also be mobilized through fiscal reforms and from the community. The *Report of the Common School System Commission, Bihar*, had, in addition, mentioned other sources such as borrowing from the National Bank for Agriculture and Rural Development (NABARD) and the social development windows of public sector banks. It is also important to bear in mind that a common school system based on the neighbourhood concept and a desired set of norms can result in substantial savings such as savings arising out of the closure of hostels; dispensing with the need for providing school transport and scholarships for students; and savings from the non-expansion of specified category and expensive profit-making private schools.

SOME RECENT ACTIONS BY THE GOVERNMENT

RECALIBRATING THE NORMS OF THE SSA

On 9 September 2010, the Cabinet Committee on Economic Affairs approved revisions in the existing norms of the SSA programme to bring them into conformity with those provided in the RTE Act. It was also decided that the SSA would be the main vehicle for the implementation of the Act. The revisions approved relate to provisions for teachers and classrooms, and support for academic supervision, research, evaluation, and monitoring. New norms, particularly those relating to the provision of free uniforms and meeting transportation costs, were also approved.

REVISION OF THE FUNDING PATTERN UNDER SSA

It was also decided to revise the funding pattern of the programme for implementing the RTE Act, between the centre and the states, to conform to the proportion of 65:35 for all states and union territories except in the case of eight states of the northeastern region where the existing sharing ratio of 90:10 will continue to apply.

AMENDMENTS TO THE RTE ACT

In April 2012, Parliament passed a legislation to amend the RTE Act mainly to provide for the following:

- Exempt madrasas, *vaidik pathshala*s, and educational institutions primarily imparting religious instructions from the application of the provisions of the Act.
- In the definition section, the words 'a child with disability' was included in the category of 'child belonging to disadvantaged group'; and it was clarified that disabled children 'shall have the right to free and compulsory education in a neighbouring school till the completion of his or her elementary education'.
- The provision in the original Act that the pupil–teacher ratio as specified in the Schedule will be ensured within six months from the date of the operationalization of the Act, was amended to provide that this goal will now be achieved within three years.

The last mentioned amendment corrects an anomaly in the original Act. When all the teachers required are to be employed within three years, how is it possible to attain the pupil–teacher ratio within six months?

The amendment relating to children with disability is basically of a cosmetic nature. This was done under the pressure of the civil society organizations working for disabled children. The amendment simply includes 'children with disability' in the category of those belonging to the disadvantaged group, which even otherwise could have been understood to be so. The amendment does not lay down additional norms such as provision of teaching aids and other facilities specific to the needs of disabled children, the appointment of teachers trained for teaching these children and the training of additional teachers for this purpose. There is also no indication in the amendment or outside it, of the additional costs involved in the education of the disabled children, let alone earmarking of actual budgetary resources for meeting such costs.

The NGOs working for disabled children have taken objection to a sub-clause in this part of the amendment which states that a child with 'severe disability' 'may also have the right to opt for home-based education'. These NGOs are apprehensive that government functionaries may take advantage of this sub-clause to isolate the disabled children from the syllabus, teaching, and environment of schools in their neighbourhood to which they are entitled to be admitted and which is the best vehicle to educate them.

The Supreme Court in a judgement in April 2012 exempted the non-aided minority schools from the application of the RTE Act. The constitutional amendment went further and excluded all minority schools—aided and unaided—from the scope of the Act. This raises the issue of reconciling Articles 29 and 30 of the Constitution with Article 21A on the fundamental right to education. The issue basically is why should the vast number of children getting education in these institutions, be deprived of their fundamental right to education. Besides, most of the madrasas come under the category of government-aided schools which are obliged under the Act, to provide free and compulsory education to a specified proportion of children admitted therein. Apart from these legal problems, there is the basic social and moral issue as to why at a time when an attempt is being made to universalize quality education through the RTE, millions of children studying in the madrasas, vaidik pathshalas, and similar educational institutions should be condemned to inferior quality education for a long, if not all time to come.

There is now also talk about the government considering another amendment to the Act which would exempt unaided schools from complying with the norm of having a playground. Thus, amendments to the Act are moved and adopted on an ad hoc basis under political pressure and as compromises with vested interests. They are not well considered, nor are they designed to deal with the basic deficiencies of the Act.

POLICY ON EARLY CHILDHOOD CARE AND EDUCATION

The government is considering the adoption of a policy on Early Childhood Care and Education (ECCE). The draft of such a policy has been prepared and circulated for eliciting the views of civil society organizations and other interested groups. The draft covers all early childhood care and education programmes and related services in public, private, and voluntary sectors that are offered to children under six years. These include anganwadi, playgroups, pre-schools, nursery schools, preparatory schools, kindergarten, and home-based care. In the preamble of the document, 'early childhood' is described as the first six years of life. It is also underlined that early childhood care and education is the indispensable foundation for lifelong learning and development and has a critical impact on success at the primary stage of education.

The First National Policy for Children was adopted in 1974 which was followed by the launching of the Integrated Child Development Services (ICDS) programme of the government in 1975. This new draft national ECCE policy thus comes 36 years after the ICDS has been in operation. The draft policy suggests extensive reforms of the ICDS, but the financial implications for carrying out these reforms have not been spelt out nor a time limit been set for completing the reform process.

ICDS is the only public-funded programme for meeting in an integrated way the needs of children below six years for their healthy growth and development. Unfortunately this public philanthropy is very poorly managed. A recent social audit of the ICDS in the district of Anantapur in Andhra Pradesh carried out by the Council for Social Development (CSD), brought out that the norms relating to the provision of services and coverage of the children are not being adhered to. Anganwadis are generally in a pitiable condition. Caste discrimination has been observed in the provision of services. The educational components of the services are hardly implemented (Venugopal 2012). In spite of this programme having been in operation for a fairly long time, malnutrition among the children in India is the widest in the world. According to some estimates, more than 60 per cent of the children in India suffer from malnutrition. Infant Mortality Rate (IMR) in India, at a little over 50, is among the highest in the developing world.

The Supreme Court of India had several years ago ordered the universalization of the coverage of ICDS.

According to the data given in the draft policy document 'out of the 158.7 million children in the below 6 years category,[18] about 75.7 million children i.e. 48 percent, are reported to be covered under the ICDS'. Thus the nation has not reached even the halfway mark on the road towards the universalization of the ICDS.

Instead of going through the charade of adopting another toothless policy document on ECCE, the right policy for the government would be to put the ICDS on a legal footing by enacting an appropriate legislation. There is every justification for taking such a step. The provision of education and other services to children in the age group of 0–6 years under the revised Article 45 of the Constitution read with Article 21 on the right to life, constitute the legal justification for making ECCE a fundamental right on the same ground as free and compulsory education for the children in the age group 6–14 years, was raised to the status of a fundamental right under Article 21A of the Constitution. The legislation, among others, should lay down the norms and standards for making the services available; should set a time target for the universalization of the services and provide for the additional financial resources required for this purpose.

LOOKING AHEAD

The tasks that lie ahead for realizing the objective of universalizing quality school education fall in two categories:

- those relating to the implementation of the provisions of the RTE Act, and
- those going beyond the RTE Act.

The measures falling in the first category should include the following:

- Speedy completion of the mapping of schools and related institutions.
- Completion of the process of the registration of private schools and of their recognition based thereon.
- Bringing to schools all out-of-school children within a specified period of time. This will require massive mobilization both by the government and the civil society organizations, and programmes for conducting bridge courses tailored to the requirement of each category of out-of-school children. This will also require the monitoring of the quality and implementation of bridge courses and ensuring that these are imparted and supervised by the neighbouring school.

- Ensuring that the elimination of annual examinations between Classes I and VIII takes place simultaneously with the institution of a system of comprehensive and continuous evaluation.
- Ensuring that each specified category and unaided school admits for providing free and compulsory education, 25 per cent of its strength in Class I, from amongst the children of economically disadvantaged communities, also ensuring that these schools do not practise any discrimination against the children so admitted.
- Ensuring that every school, except those exempted under the Act, constitutes a school management committee according to the principles prescribed and procedures laid down in the Act and that this committee is properly empowered.
- Giving the teachers the dignity, social status, and facilities they must have to be able to discharge their responsibilities. The additional number of teachers required must be recruited speedily. In this connection, the figure given by the government that only one million teachers need to be recruited seems to be an underestimation. The exact figure can be determined only by mapping and applying the norms relating to teachers. Moreover, the norms laid down in the Schedule, for infrastructure and related facilities for schools, must also be strictly applied. This alone will create an environment conducive to and provide the indispensable means for the teachers to make the contribution, expected from them, to the system. Finally, the teachers should be provided with salaries befitting the dignity of their profession and opportunities for progress in their career.

Given the constraints of a basic nature, outlined in this chapter, it is doubtful whether the above measures are at all implementable. Moreover, even if these measures are implemented, it will not necessarily bring about the universalization of quality school education in the country. For this to happen, measures going beyond the RTE Act would need to be adopted. These include:

1. The neighbourhood school concept as practised in most developed countries, having a common school system, should be introduced. This will call for delineating the neighbourhood pertaining to each school.
2. Two years of free and compulsory pre-primary education; free and compulsory education at the secondary level, that is, for children in the age group of 15–18 years, should be provided.

School education should not be seen in fragments, with one kind of treatment and provision of services at the elementary level and different kinds at the pre-primary and secondary levels. Education is the fundamental right of all the children so defined. According to the United Nations Convention on the Child Rights, to which India is a party, the definition of a child is a person up to the age of 18 years. It is, therefore, legally unjustified and ethically inadmissible to deprive children, at the latter two levels, of their fundamental right to education. Besides, the access to and the quality of education provided at one level has a critical bearing on those at the other levels. School education is, therefore, seen in almost all developed and several developing countries as a seamless process starting from a year or two of the pre-elementary level and extending up to the end of the secondary level. An Expert Consultative Group of United Nations Educational, Scientific and Cultural Organization (UNESCO) in its operational definition of basic education stated 'beyond pre-school education, the duration of which can be fixed by the State, basic education consists of at least nine years and progressively extends to 12 years'. It further stated that such education 'is free and compulsory without any discrimination or exclusion' (UNESCO 2009).

3. A far-reaching upgradation and diversification of the norms provided in the Schedule of the Act is called for. Besides, the norms should be articulated in such a manner so as to be legally enforceable.

4. A clearly delineated language policy should be introduced in the school education system. Among others, it should be made compulsory to impart education in the mother tongue of the child, at least at the pre-primary and primary levels. Adequate facilities should be provided for this purpose and teachers should be trained for imparting education through the mother tongue and teaching national and regional languages.

5. The current process of the privatization and commercialization of school education should be brought to a halt and the existing private schools should be obliged to follow the norms laid down by the government.

The experience in most developed countries and several developing countries and that in the working of the right to education till now, shows that the above measures cannot be implemented until the present mul-tilayer system of school education in India is replaced by a state-supported and state-controlled common school system based on the concept of neighbourhood schools and a comprehensive set of clearly articulated and legally enforceable norms.

Notes

1. District Information System of Education (DISE) Flash Statistics, 2009–10 and 2010–11, Elementary Education in India. Progress towards UEE, compiled by the National University of Educational Planning and Administration (NUEPA). Data coverage in the DISE for 2010 was for 35 states, 637 districts, and 1.3 million schools.

2. ASER is facilitated by a non-governmental organization (NGO) called Pratham. ASER 2011, issued in January 2012, covered 558 districts, 16,017 villages, 327,372 households, and 633,465 children. The survey team visited more than 14,000 government schools to assess progress towards compliance with the norms and standards specified in the RTE Act.

3. DISE 2009–10.

4. DISE 2010–11.

5. ASER 2011.

6. Ibid.

7. DISE 2009–10.

8. Ibid.

9. DISE 2010–11.

10. Ibid.

11. Ibid.

12. ASER 2011.

13. Ibid.

14. DISE 2010–11.

15. ASER 2011.

16. As per 2011 Census data.

17. These facts have been taken from a statement made by Kishore Singh, the United Nations Special Rapporteur on Right to Education at the meeting of the High-Level Segment on Education of the Economic and Social Council of the United Nations, 7 July 2011.

18. As per 2011 Census data.

References

GoI (Government of India). 2011. 'Status of School Education: 2009–2010'. New Delhi: Ministry of Human Resource Development (as on 30 September 2009).

Government of Bihar. 2007. 'Report of the Common School System Commission'. Patna: Government of Bihar.

Venugopal, K.R. 2012. *The Integrated Child Development Services: A Flagship Adrift.* Delhi: Konark Publishers Pvt. Ltd.

United Nations Educational, Scientific and Cultural Organization (UNESCO). 2009. 'Expert Consultation on the Operational Definition of Basic Education, 17–18 December 2007: Conclusions'. Paris: UNESCO.

4

Employment and Unemployment
Context and Prospects

PRAVEEN JHA AND AVANINDRA NATH THAKUR

Generation of opportunities for decent work and livelihood ought to be among the most important policy objectives on any meaningful agenda of economic development. On this front, the Indian experience, spanning over decades, emerges in a very poor light. One may also suggest that the prospect of any substantial shift in occupational structure, away from agriculture seems remote in India, as in most developing countries, in the near future. The 'dual economy' models and other 'modernization' paradigms that had hypothesized a relatively smooth transition in occupational structure seemed to have got it wrong in retrospect. In fact, as discussed by Jha (2003) in some detail, in most of the developing world even when the increase in the output of the non-agricultural sectors have been rapid, growth of employment in such sectors has been far from impressive. For India, the share of agriculture in total employment has reduced from 73 per cent in 1950 to about 55 per cent now, but this decline, over the same period, has been much slower than that in the share of Gross Domestic Product (GDP) (59 to 17 per cent, respectively). Also, some of the transfer of workers to non-agricultural sectors may not be due to any positive development, but on account of distress diversification (particularly in a variety of self-employed services). This may also hide the fact that sections of these people happen to be part-time agricultural workers as well. Hence, it would be reasonable to argue that in terms of labour absorption in modern manufacturing or services sector the country is not favourably placed, and a major decline in dependence on agriculture and

the transfer of labour into decent livelihood options elsewhere does not seem to be on the cards, at least not in the near foreseeable future.

Like many other developing countries, India has made inadequate progress in terms of addressing the problems of poverty, unemployment, and occupational structural transformation. Even during the first four decades after Independence, achievements on these counts were unimpressive despite the strategy of relatively autonomous development and public-sector-led industrialization which resulted in unprecedented and quite respectable growth outcomes with reference to any appropriate benchmark. The importance of radical land reforms and state-facilitated infrastructure in shaping impressive agricultural transformation and its linkage to overall rapid economic growth, poverty reduction, and the well-being of the rural masses as a whole is widely acknowledged. It has become increasingly clear that for a country like India where a large section of the population is dependent on agriculture for their livelihood, feasibility of successful agricultural transformation through any route that ignores the issue of land reforms is highly suspect. A fundamental failure of India's development throughout the dirigiste era was its inadequacy with respect to addressing the agrarian questions and the associated structural transformation. This has had profound implications for prospects of decent livelihoods for the masses in general. The inability to address the agrarian question effectively was linked to the basic contradictions inherent in the postcolonial state. Furthermore, it also implied constraints on the prospects of mobilization of resources by the state for accelerating the growth of productive forces to enhance the pace of accumulation and creation of opportunities that would have increased the participation of the poor in the growth process. Hence, it would be reasonable to argue that the failure of the dirigiste paradigm in India lay essentially not in what it attempted, but in its relative neglect of confronting the agrarian question headlong. Nonetheless, with increased government expenditure in rural areas, focus on the various direct and indirect poverty alleviation and employment-generation programmes, and many other initiatives largely confined around the upliftment of the substantial mass at the margin, have had undisputedly positive impact on the overall well-being status of the working mass in general.

Since the early 1990s, that is, during the era of neoliberal reforms, the above noted correlates of the well-being of the masses in general have come under relative pressure. As is well-known, even today vast masses of the country's population continue to eke out an existence primarily through their dependence on agriculture under extremely fragile conditions. And any prospects regarding the successful transformation of their occupational structure in the near future seems remote.

Given the contestation between various perspectives regarding employment, the following section focuses on the overall trajectory of India's development strategies and their implications for employment conditions. The next section discusses the changes in the dynamics of various indicators impacting on the well-being of workers for the period of around three decades since the early 1980s. This is followed by concluding remarks on prospects for employment and decent livelihood conditions for the labouring mass in general.

EMPLOYMENT AND INDIA'S DEVELOPMENT EXPERIENCE

THE DIRIGISTE PHASE

In the first couple of decades of the development trajectory after Independence, the promises and expectations emanating from various plan documents regarding employment generation remained largely unfulfilled. The fundamental assumption underlying official thinking, that increases in investment and national income would be accompanied by a commensurate increase in employment opportunities, was clearly off the mark.

By the early 1970s, there was a reluctant acknowledgement in official discourses that the development strategy pursued hitherto was not delivering towards the objective of creating adequate employment opportunities and the 'directly targeted programmes' of employment generation and poverty alleviation started coming into being. As it happens, both the Fifth and the Sixth Five Year Plans admitted the possibilities of real conflict between employment and growth and made a strong case for prioritizing the latter. However, even in these plans the main focus of the developmental process reverted to the traditional growth approach with the usual assumption that employment would increase with the rise in investment, irrespective of the choice of techniques. However, during these Plans there were substantial increases in government spending on target areas and for the well-being of the targeted population. Also, consequent upon the nationalization of banks and under the 'directed' lending programmes, a significant proportion of bank credits was directed to 'priority' sectors affecting a substantial section of the population. Furthermore, particularly since the early 1980s, availability of cheap credit for the middle and upper classes tended to increase noticeably. It was a combination of all these factors, inter alia, leading to a revival of GDP growth rate after almost a decade of deceleration since the mid-1970s.

Thus, during the period from the mid-1970s to late 1980s (especially between 1977 and 1991), the Indian economy underwent a phase of recovery, which was in a significant measure consumption-led and in turn gave a push to the generation of employment opportunities. However, even during this period, the organized sectors of the economy grew much faster in terms of income and output without a commensurate increase in employment. In fact, the 1980s growth of such employment was 1.5 per cent per annum, much less than the rate of population growth. Within this, the employment in the private organized sector grew at a much slower rate, averaging a growth rate of only 0.2 per cent per annum. There was a drop in labour absorption by the agricultural sector also, and agricultural employment grew at a rate substantially below the rate of population growth. Thus, the respectable rates of growth of output in agriculture and the organized private sector failed to translate into any significant acceleration of employment in these important sectors (Sen 1996).

However, though there was only small improvement in the employment scenario in 1980s, the decade was characterized by rising real wages, including real wages for unskilled workers both in rural and urban areas, and this was, in large measure, on account of the important changes that occurred in the nature of intersectoral and other linkages in the economy (ibid.). Also, as mentioned earlier, during this period the central government stepped up its revenue expenditure in rural areas by expanding employment programmes either through its own rural development schemes or by instructing banks to extend more credit for such initiatives. In fact, a major hallmark of the 1980s was a large number of 'rural development' schemes along with a plethora of special schemes for a variety of identifiable 'target' groups. Consequently, there was a noticeable growth of non-agricultural employment in rural areas. In fact, after a long period of stagnation in the share of the agricultural sector in the total workforce, a sign of decline became visible, resulting mainly from the expansion of the rural non-agricultural sector. The National Sample Survey (NSS) data show that the share of agricultural workers among all male rural workers declined steadily from 80.6 per cent in 1977–8 to 71.7 per cent in 1989–90 and for rural females this share dropped from 88.1 per cent in 1977–8 to 81.4 per cent in 1989–90 (as noted in Jha 1997). As was highlighted by several researchers, the true significance of this shift is probably better understood in incremental terms. These figures imply that non-agricultural sector absorbed about 70 per cent of the total increase in the rural workforce between 1977–8 and 1989–90. Moreover, 22.3 per cent of all casual labour days spent on non-agricultural activity in 1987–8 were on public works programmes of the government, showing a significant rise from 17.7 per cent in 1977–8 and 14.9 per cent in 1983. Nearly 60 per cent of all new government jobs created during this period went to rural areas. Thus, the agency of the state played a key role in diversifying opportunities for the rural poor.

There were some other factors which facilitated the shift of workers from the agricultural to non-agricultural sector. In certain regions, the industrial development and growth of services linked to this created employment opportunities not only in the tertiary sector, but also in small-scale industry in rural areas. In fact, the growth of rural non-agricultural employment was the main factor behind the rise in rural wages between 1977–8 and 1989–90. Possibly, a spillover of the positive developments in rural areas also led to an increase in employment in urban areas, although this was mostly of a casual nature in industrially or commercially developed regions. According to NSS data (as noted in Jha 1997), the share of casual workers among males in urban employment increased from 13 per cent in 1977–8 to 16 per cent in 1989–90. The share of casual workers among females in urban employment increased from little above 25 per cent in 1977–8 to around 28 per cent in 1983 and then declined to around 22 per cent in 1989–90. One of the probable causes of decline in the women's share in urban casual employment during the second half of the 1980s may be on account of an increase in the real wages and income of a section of such households above a threshold level. There is some evidence to suggest that such an increase at times results in withdrawal of women from paid work. In any case, the point worth emphasizing here is that given the limited geographical spread of such direct links to modern industry and commerce, in most areas the pivotal role in the expansion of rural and non-agricultural employment was played by the expansion of government expenditure.

Nevertheless, it is important not to overstate the gains of the 1980s. Although increases in employment and wages improved the condition of rural workers even at the lower rungs in the economic hierarchy, their employment diversification into non-agriculture continued to have many characteristics of a 'distress' phenomenon, given the overall tendency of labour use in agriculture. The main sectors providing this type of non-agricultural employment were secondary sectors like construction, mining, and small-scale manufacturing, and there is evidence that over time, the incidence of poverty among those employed in some of these sectors became larger than in agriculture.

The increases in government spending undoubtedly increased the industrial and overall growth rates; the latter being at well above 5 per cent per annum for the decade of the 1980s was a significant improvement over the long-run trend growth rate of around 3 per cent for the preceding three decades. Moreover, as emphasized earlier, increased government spending resulted in some positive employment as well as income effects for the masses. But as it became evident by the late 1980s, the specific strategy of pump-priming had a clear downside to it. Much of the increased expenditure was through a borrowing spree by the government—both internally and externally. Furthermore, a very substantial part of the external borrowing was from commercial sources. Not unexpectedly, a combination of these elements led to a sharp increase in the gross fiscal deficit of the government as well as in the external debt and debt-service payments.

The enormous increase in external debt, a growing portion of which consisted of short-term borrowings, exposed the economy to the caprices of international lenders and investors, and particularly to the danger of sudden capital flight due to 'confidence crises'. The foreign reserves of the country during this time were depleted to abysmally low levels and in this backdrop, the then government launched a major stabilization and structural adjustment programme by accepting the conditionalities imposed by Bretton Woods Institutions (the International Monetary Fund and the World Bank) in the name of economic reforms. As is well-documented now, launched in July 1991, these reforms represented a sharp break from the dirigiste regime of the past four decades and put the country on quite a different policy route in its economic journey (for detailed accounts of these, see Chandrasekhar and Ghosh 2002; Patnaik and Chandrasekhar 1995 among others).

THE REFORM ERA

Given this backdrop, it is of utmost importance to assess the implications of the globally ascendant neoliberal policy regimes for the employment scenario and overall well-being of labour. Persistence of high levels of unemployment in different regions of the global economy during the recent decades of neoliberal reforms lend strong support for the view that the macroeconomic policies based on such doctrines are hardly consistent with a progressive employment agenda, even in structurally more favourably placed economies, let alone in the more adverse circumstances prevailing in most developing countries. As is well-known, among the major premises of neoliberalism was the argument that in the case of developing countries the inward-looking capital-intensive import substitution policy had resulted in a bias against agriculture and other employment-intensive activities, with respect to both the domestic and external markets. Thus, labour utilization had been well below potential. It was hoped by the advocates of neoliberalism that the marketist reforms would rectify this bias and facilitate a surge of investment, both from domestic and foreign sources, in labour-intensive projects with significant export-orientation. All available evidence since the ascendancy of the neoliberal economic policy package confirm that the expectations regarding greater labour utilization in the global economy, through changes in structure as well as intensity of employment have not been realized.

In much of the developing world, there is overwhelming evidence to support the view that the employment elasticity of whatever growth that has occurred in recent years has been extremely low. Even more striking is the negative elasticities that emerge in some cases, also in a range of manufacturing sectors that are typically thought of as being labour-intensive (Chandrasekhar and Ghosh 2002). This work also reports that the employment scenario for aggregate industry, rather than just manufacturing, has been as grim during the period under consideration. The *inescapable* conclusion that emerges is

thus that the period of globalization and liberalization has been far off the mark as regards creating a conducive scenario from the point of view of employment expansion. Clearly, the hopes of the advocates of neoliberal marketist reforms have not materialized.

In fact, such a development is hardly surprising. As Patnaik has argued in several of his writings (for example, see his 2006 work), employment elasticity of growth tends to fall sharply with a shift from a dirigiste to an open economic regime due to several factors. These include, inter alia, (a) growing dominance of finance capital which militates against the growth of the real sectors; (b) changes in the nature of production processes which tend to be more capital intensive; and (c) imitation of the lifestyle of the developed country by the elite of the developing countries. The net effect of all these is a growing divergence between growth of output and that of employment.

Returning to the Indian experience, by all accounts the problem of widespread unemployment across all sectors of economy has tended to become progressively more serious after the introduction of economic reforms. The rate of employment generation during the recent years has fallen considerably and the unemployment rate, on current daily basis as per the NSS Rounds, went up to over 9 per cent in 2004–5 from around 6 per cent in 1993–4. However, during the most recent phase between 2004–5 (61st Round) and 2009–10 (66th Round), a slight improvement on the unemployment front is visible, which is mainly attributed to the enactment of the Mahatma Gandhi National Rural Employment Guarantee Act (MGNREGA), indeed, for the country as a whole any symptom of generation of quality employment in any significant manner is still nowhere near reality. Moreover, during the entire period of planned development, not unexpectedly, an increase in the incidence of unemployment has been sharper for relatively more vulnerable social and economic groups. Various major data sources such as the Economic Census of 2001, the Population Census of 2001, Employment Exchange statistics for different years, the various rounds of NSS, among others, have acknowledged the increasing gravity of the unemployment problem.

In fact, approximately within a decade of the launching of neoliberal reforms, two of the initiatives of the Planning Commission, the task force on employment opportunity headed by M.S. Ahluwalia, and the special group on Targeting Ten Million Employment Opportunities per year headed by S.P. Gupta, had examined the relevant trends in some detail and indicated that the adverse employment experience of the 1990s may get further aggravated in the subsequent years. Similar conclusions have been reached by almost every official report and other studies since then. It has been suggested by some that even with a high GDP growth rate of 8 per cent per annum, the unemployment rate may touch more than double of the current one by the end of the Twelfth Five Year Plan.

The obvious important message emerging from these numbers is that during the period of neoliberal reforms, challenges of labour absorption for Indian economy have been further aggravated. Moreover, even the traditional parking lot, namely, agriculture, is unable to perform the function of the residual sector, and the rural areas have borne the brunt of sharp deceleration in employment generation. In fact, the much talked about process of diversification of employment from the mid-1970s to the late 1980s, away from agriculture and primary activities and towards a variety of non-agricultural avenues, has tended to come under pressure and the growth of latter has also slowed down considerably. As is well-known, it was primarily on account of very significant acceleration in public expenditure in rural areas in the 1970s and the 1980s that the above noted diversification had gathered momentum. However, the 1990s witnessed a policy shift for the worse in this regard.

Apart from the quantity of employment, the issue of quality is also important as the overwhelming proportion of workers employed in the informal sector (accounting for about 93 per cent of the country's labour force) work under extremely vulnerable conditions and low wages. Thus, the country has a large count of the working poor who remain entrapped in low productive activities and persistent poverty. Furthermore, increasing casualization and marginalization are the growing features of the labouring landscape in the formal sector itself. Not unexpectedly, along with the employment trends, most indicators relating to the well-being of workers have come under substantial pressure during the era of neoliberal reforms.

The performance of the Indian economy in the neoliberal regime continues to be a subject of intense debate, especially in the context of provisions of adequate and sustainable livelihood options for a large section of the population. The essential picture that emerges is one of overall worsening in employment and conditions of work even though there has been a significant acceleration in output growth in the manufacturing and services sector. As regards the agricultural sector, its performance has tended to worsen considerably not only with respect to

employment, but also output growth. Fundamentally, there has been a change in the pattern of growth where the non-agricultural sector has shown substantial acceleration in output per worker compared to the agricultural sector, and thus the gap between the two has tended to increase substantially. Furthermore, employment content of the growth process has gone down significantly during the reform era. In particular, rural India which houses more than two-thirds of the working population of our country has been among the worst hit during the period of economic reforms.

Factors like substantial compression of rural development expenditures, increasing input prices, vulnerability to world market price fluctuations due to greater openness, inadequate or non-existent crop insurance, and substantial weakening of the provisioning for credit, along with the government's apathy to the demand for remunerative prices for farm produce are among the obvious causal correlates of the contemporary agrarian crisis in the country.

It is to be expected that in a period of agrarian distress, agricultural labourers are likely to be affected the most, through adverse impacts on wages and employment opportunities directly in agriculture and indirectly through multiplier effects in non-agriculture activities as well.

The Employment and Unemployment Scenario since the Early 1980s

LABOUR FORCE PARTICIPATION RATE

The discussion about the labour force participation rate and its direction of movement can hardly be detached from that of the employment conditions and any change in the participation of females at the margin is particularly more sensitive towards the overall working environment as well as income conditions. During the last three decades, in spite of the long-term stability, significant fluctuations in the labour force participation rate was observed in various rounds of the surveys and such fluctuations are often related to transitory features such as a good or bad agricultural year, particularly in rural areas. For instance, the increase in female participation experienced between 1999–2000 and 2004–5 may have occurred because of the need to substitute male workers, who were looking for better opportunities outside agriculture in a distressed agricultural year. Else, it could be a reflection of the need to supplement household earnings in a bad year.[1] In other words, higher participation rates as in 2004–5 are neither necessarily a reflection of improved performance on employment availability nor do they reflect any permanent change in the structure of the labour market, particularly in this case. Further, this can be substantiated by the fact that these rates have slid in 2009–10 (Table 4.1). In case of urban males and females, no significant changes have been observed during the period under consideration here, that is, from 1983 to 2009–10. However, a marginal rise in this rate for urban females was visible during the year 2004–5, which may be on account of the downturn of the economy due to long and sustained agrarian distress for most parts of rural India. Consequently, higher participation of females might be a factor, as considered by many, to overcome the inadequacies regarding their family income. In the following two surveys, in 2007–8 and 2009–10, the decline in the labour force participation rate is very clearly observed in urban areas also (Table 4.2).

WORKER–POPULATION RATIO

It is important to look at the trends of worker–population ratio (WPR) in order to get the overall condition of employment as it is a broad indicator of the availability of job opportunities.[2] On the whole, this has remained at the same level for almost three decades now. However, variation in the WPR in different Rounds of NSS was quite observable (Table 4.3), which, to a certain extent, reflects the changing employment conditions during the relevant periods. The increased government expenditure and, consequently, significantly large expansion of employment opportunities in rural areas during the decade of the 1980s had a clear impact on the overall WPR in rural areas between 1983 and 1993–4. Over this period the WPR in rural areas increased by 1 percentage point on the 'usual basis', 2 percentage points on the 'weekly basis', and more than 2 percentage points on the 'daily basis'. This rise in WPR, particularly higher on 'CDS (Current Daily Status) basis' indicates the rising work opportunities created by various self-employment and casual wage employment programmes in rural areas during the above noted period. However, the neoliberal regime was marked by a sharp reduction in the overall public expenditure and various subsidies in rural areas.

Table 4.1   Labour Force Participation Rate in Rural Areas

NSS Round	Rural Male				Rural Female			
	PS	PS + SS	CWS	CDS	PS	PS + SS	CWS	CDS
38 (1983)	54	55.5	53.1	52.1	25.2	34.2	23.7	21.8
43 (1987–8)	53.2	54.9	52.6	52.5	25.4	33.1	23	22.2
50 (1993–4)	54.9	56.1	54.8	53.4	23.7	33.1	27.5	23.3
55 (1999–2000)	53.3	54	53.1	51.5	23.5	30.2	26.3	21.9
61 (2004–5)	54.6	55.5	54.5	53	25	33.3	28.7	23.7
64 (2007–8)	55.1	55.9	54.7	53.6	22	29.2	24.5	20.4
66 (2009–10)	54.8	55.6	54.8	53.6	20.8	26.5	23.1	19.7

Source: Various Rounds of NSS survey reports.
Notes: PS = Principal Status; SS = Subsidiary Status; CWS = Current Weekly Status; CDS = Current Daily Status.

Table 4.2   Labour Force Participation Rate in Urban Areas

NSS Round	Urban Male				Urban Female			
	PS	PS + SS	CWS	CDS	PS	PS + SS	CWS	CDS
38 (1983)	53.1	54	52.7	52.1	12.9	15.9	12.8	11.9
43 (1987–8)	52.8	53.4	52.7	52.3	12.9	16.2	13.1	12.5
50 (1993–4)	54.2	54.3	53.9	53.4	13.2	16.5	15.1	13.4
55 (1999–2000)	53.9	54.2	53.9	52.9	12.6	14.7	13.8	12.3
61 (2004–5)	56.6	57.1	56.6	56.1	14.9	17.8	16.7	15
64 (2007–8)	57.3	57.6	57.2	56.8	12.6	14.6	13.8	12.5
66 (2009–10)	55.6	55.9	55.6	55	12.8	14.6	14.1	12.9

Source: Various Rounds of NSS survey reports.

Therefore, the decade of the 1990s experienced a decline in the absorption capacity in the rural economy as a whole, and consequently a fall in WPR was observed for both males and females during the same period. After a noticeable dip in this rate during 1999–2000, there was a marginal recovery in 2004–5, for both males and females in rural areas, which is of course rooted in the increased labour force participation rate particularly for females (which may well be distress-driven) in both urban and rural areas. For the next two Rounds in 2007–8 and 2009–10, while the WPR for rural male remained more or less stagnant, it declined for the rural female. This indicated an overall worsening of the employment-generation scenario in the rural areas. Now, if we exclude the employment opportunities created by MGNREGA during this period, one can infer that the ability of the entire rural economy to generate decent livelihood conditions during the neoliberal era has remained very limited.

For the entire period from 1983 to 2009–10, the above rate marginally improved for urban males (Table 4.4). However, a significant decline in the rate has been observed in both rural and urban female categories during the same period. In spite of high and sustained GDP growth for last three decades, the overall WPR for person as a whole has shown a decline during the period between 2004–5 and 2009–10, which clearly indicates a disheartening situation on the employment-generation front. For urban females though WPR has shown a decline on the 'usual basis', it showed a marginal increase on both 'weekly' and 'daily' basis over the period 1983 to 2009–10. Like males, WPR for females also showed a significant decline during 2004–5 to 2009–10. This clearly disproved the notion of a positive relationship between the growth rate of GDP and employment creation in any sizable manner under the current neoliberal reform era.

In terms of additional employment generation over the last three decades, it is clear that the rate of growth of rural employment had risen at an annual rate of 1.72 per cent between 1983 and 1993–4 before it nosedived

Table 4.3 Worker–Population Ratio in Rural Areas

NSS Round	Rural Male				Rural Female			
	PS	PS + SS	CWS	CDS	PS	PS + SS	CWS	CDS
38 (1983)	52.8	54.7	51.1	48.2	24.8	34	22.7	19.8
43 (1987–8)	51.7	53.9	50.4	50.1	24.5	32.3	22	20.7
50 (1993–4)	53.8	55.3	53.1	50.4	23.4	32.8	26.7	22
55 (1999–2000)	52.2	53.1	51	47.8	23.1	29.9	25.3	20.4
61 (2004–5)	53.5	54.6	52.4	48.8	24.2	32.7	27.5	21.6
64 (2007–8)	53.8	54.8	52.5	49	21.6	28.9	23.7	18.7
66 (2009–10)	53.7	54.7	53.1	50.1	20.2	26.1	22.3	18.2

Source: Various Rounds of NSS survey reports.

Table 4.4 Worker–Population Ratio in Urban Areas

NSS Round	Urban Male				Urban Female			
	PS	PS + SS	CWS	CDS	PS	PS + SS	CWS	CDS
38 (1983)	50	51.2	49.2	47.3	12	15.1	11.8	10.6
43 (1987–8)	49.6	50.6	49.2	47.7	11.8	15.2	11.9	11
50 (1993–4)	51.3	52.1	51.1	49.8	12.1	15.5	13.9	12
55 (1999–2000)	51.3	51.8	50.9	49	11.7	13.9	12.8	11.1
61 (2004–5)	54.1	54.9	53.7	51.9	13.5	16.6	15.2	13.3
64 (2007–8)	55	55.4	54.5	52.9	11.8	13.8	12.9	11.3
66 (2009–10)	53.9	54.3	53.6	52.2	11.9	13.8	13	11.7

Source: Various Rounds of NSS survey reports.

to 0.66 per cent between 1993–4 and 1999–2000. Subsequently, it picked up to 1.97 per cent between 1999–2000 and 2004–5 (a year of indifferent agricultural performance).[3] In urban areas, the growth rate of employment between 1983 and 1993–4 was 3.10 per cent per annum. This continued for the next decade also (that is, between 1993–4 and 2004–5) and grew at the same rate (although there was decline during the first half, but this recovered during the second half). During the next period, that is, between 2004–5 and 2009–10, though the economy witnessed a high growth rate, the total number of usual with subsidiary status workers increased only by 2.3 million. This was much in contrast to the relatively significant expansion of around 60 million during the previous period between 1999–2000 and 2004–5. During the period from 1999–2000 to 2004–5, male employment increased by 20.2 million in rural areas, while in the next period from 2004–5 to 2009–10, it rose by only 13.4 million. The corresponding figures for urban areas were 15 million and 9.8 million, respectively. Rural female employment, which rose by 18.3 million during 1999–2000 and 2004–5, registered a decline of 19.2 million between 2004–5 and 2009–10. In urban areas, female employment rose by 6.4 million in the first and declined by 1.7 million during the next period (Chandrasekhar and Ghosh 2011).

Thus, a clear mismatch between the high rate of growth of GDP and the pace of employment generation indicates a significant fall in the elasticity of employment with respect to output. In other words, the key message that gets reinforced by the latest round of NSS is that the transition to a high growth trajectory has not delivered much on the employment front. The data since the early 1990s indicate that the increase in employment seems to occur when workers, especially female workers, are pushed into the workforce by increased adversity in their economic circumstances (for example, a bad agriculture year), and there have been few positive impulses for employment. Moreover, organized manufacturing and services appear to contribute very little additional employment creation, and the expectation that these would add significantly to the generation of employment opportunities once neoliberal policies succeeded in delivering growth has hardly materialized. On the contrary, there has been a significant dip in the absolute count of workers in organized segments of the economy. These facts cumulatively suggest that in the years of high growth much of the increase in employment was in the categories of casual and self-employed workers, which had extremely adverse distributional and social welfare

implications (Chandrasekhar 2010; Chandrasekhar and Ghosh 2007; Himanshu 2011; Jha 2009).

It is generally argued that the decline in WPR during the recent period is attributed more to the fact that a significantly large proportion of persons withdrew from the labour force in order to complete their education, particularly those between the age group of 6–14 years due to the provision of compulsory primary education. Undoubtedly, the provision of compulsory primary education has had an immense effect on labour force participation rate and was in turn reflected in the decline in the WPR for the age group of 6–14 years (Table 4.5). However, a sharp decline in WPR for the age group of 15–29 years compels us not to accept the argument regarding the rise in school enrolment as the sole reason to explain the decline in WPR during the said period. Given the limited improvement in college and university enrolment, it is hard to believe that the decline in WPR in this age group is the outcome of preferring higher education over any kind of job available for them. More precisely, it becomes difficult to refute the notion that a substantial section of the population after completing their primary or secondary education is unable to find jobs. This line of argument can be further substantiated by the fact that neither formal sector employment nor any kind of regular employment has experienced adequate expansion during the recent period. It was only manual unskilled work particularly under the MGNREGA which showed some expansion during the recent years, and those who are semi-skilled or have received education of some level could barely get their desired employment. This explains the fact that there has been a continuous rise in the unemployment of the educated workers over the recent years, and those who are uneducated or merely literate are more easily capable of getting jobs than their semi-skilled and educated counterparts up to a certain level (Ghose 2008).

THE UNEMPLOYMENT SCENARIO

Contrary to what has been argued by Srinivasan (2006),[4] the unemployment rate on CDS basis is a better indicator of the level of unemployment as well as underemployment of the working population. Moreover, since in India a majority of the workers—both in rural as well as in urban areas—are casual labour and in most of the cases they are hired on a daily basis, the 'current daily basis' of measuring unemployment rate can only reflect the closer trends and pattern of unemployment for such a huge mass of the workforce both in rural and urban areas as compared to both 'usual' status and 'CWS' or Current Weekly Status. Relevant data, since the early

1980s, show a clear worsening in this respect during the reform period. In rural areas, between 1983 and 1993–4, there was a significant decline in the unemployment rate on CDS basis, both for male and female (Table 4.6).

During the next decade, between 1993–4 and 2004–5, the corresponding rates rose sharply.[5] In urban areas, however, there was a small decline in unemployment over the longer period, that is, between 1983 and 2004–5, for

Table 4.5 Worker–Population Ratio in Various Age Groups

Age Group (in years)	Year*	Rural				Urban			
		Male PS	Male SS	Female PS	Female SS	Male PS	Male SS	Female PS	Female SS
4–9	4	0.20	0.20	0.10	0.30	0.20	0.00	0.00	0.10
	3	0.20	0.10	0.10	0.20	0.20	0.00	0.10	0.20
	2	0.50	0.10	0.60	0.10	0.30	0.00	0.10	0.10
	1	0.90	1.10	1.10	0.30	0.40	1.10	0.30	0.20
	0	1.97	0.60	1.78	0.67	0.54	0.21	0.50	0.16
9–14	4	2.70	1.70	2.10	1.40	2.40	0.40	0.80	0.40
	3	5.40	1.40	4.90	1.50	4.40	0.40	2.40	0.90
	2	8.20	0.90	7.40	2.20	4.60	0.30	2.80	1.80
	1	11.20	2.60	10.40	3.70	5.90	0.70	3.50	1.00
	0	21.28	2.80	16.19	7.04	9.31	1.97	5.41	1.55
15–29	4	62.60	2.20	21.80	7.00	55.60	0.80	12.40	2.00
	3	71.20	3.00	28.80	12.20	60.50	1.80	14.30	4.10
	2	72.10	2.00	30.70	9.30	58.30	1.00	12.40	2.50
	1	74.00	3.50	31.1	13.6	60.10	1.70	13.30	4.00
	0	78.92	2.80	36.12	13.54	64.00	2.63	14.51	4.16
30–44	4	99.00	0.10	36.10	11.20	97.90	0.10	21.50	3.70
	3	98.10	0.30	45.80	15.40	97.20	0.30	25.40	5.60
	2	97.80	0.40	44.30	12.90	96.80	0.10	22.30	4.30
	1	98.40	0.20	42.50	17.30	97.40	0.10	23.00	6.50
	0	98.12	0.37	45.73	15.64	97.22	0.25	23.41	5.74
44–59	4	96.20	0.30	38.20	8.60	93.60	0.10	19.90	2.00
	3	95.80	0.40	44.40	12.50	91.70	0.60	21.70	3.50
	2	95.3	0.5	40.70	11.10	91.80	0.30	21.80	3.20
	1	96.30	0.50	40.10	14.30	93.10	0.40	23.10	5.20
	0	94.98	0.55	40.68	14.52	92.11	0.44	22.81	4.97
60 and above	4	63.60	1.00	19.00	3.60	33.50	0.60	6.10	0.90
	3	63.00	1.40	19.70	5.60	35.50	1.10	8.60	1.40
	2	62.20	1.70	17.40	4.40	38.60	1.60	8.20	1.20
	1	68.30	1.60	17.20	6.90	42.90	1.30	9.10	1.20
	0	64.08	2.69	15.52	7.09	48.50	1.72	11.60	2.20
All ages	4	53.70	1.00	20.20	5.90	53.90	0.40	11.90	1.90
	3	53.50	1.10	24.20	8.50	54.10	0.80	13.50	3.10
	2	52.20	0.90	23.10	6.80	51.30	0.50	11.70	2.20
	1	53.80	1.50	23.40	9.40	51.30	0.80	12.10	3.40
	0	61.28	2.17	28.73	10.57	58.22	1.47	13.76	3.49

Source: Various Rounds of NSS survey reports.
Notes: * 0 = 1983; 1 = 1993–4; 2 = 1999–2000; 3 = 2004–5; and 4 = 2009–10.

Table 4.6 Unemployment Rate in Rural Areas

NSS Round	Rural Male				Rural Female			
	PS	PS + SS	CWS	CDS	PS	PS + SS	CWS	CDS
38 (1983)	2.1	1.4	3.7	7.5	1.4	0.7	4.3	9
43 (1987–8)	2.8	1.8	4.2	4.6	3.5	2.4	4.4	6.7
50 (1993–4)	2	1.4	3.1	5.6	1.3	0.9	2.9	5.6
55 (1999–2000)	2.1	1.7	3.9	7.2	1.5	1	3.7	7
61 (2004–5)	2.1	1.6	3.8	8	3.1	1.8	4.2	8.7
64 (2007–8)	2.3	1.9	4.1	8.5	1.9	1.1	3.5	8.1
66 (2009–10)	1.9	1.6	3.2	6.4	2.4	1.6	3.7	8

Source: Various Rounds of NSS survey reports.

both male and female workers, but it was hardly adequate to compensate the considerable worsening in rural areas. As emphasized repeatedly in the forgoing discussion, such trends are indicative of setbacks in the generation of productive employment opportunities and deterioration in the quality of employment in the recent growth process.

However, some positive trends in the reduction in the unemployment rate are discernible during the period 2004–5 to 2009–10. In rural areas, the unemployment rate for males declined from 8 per cent in 2004–5 to 6.4 per cent in 2009–10. For rural females, the corresponding figures were 8.7 and 8.1, respectively, on a current daily basis. Similarly, in urban areas, the unemployment rate for males declined from 7.5 per cent in 2004–5 to 5.1 per cent in 2009–10, and for urban females these figures were 11.6 and 9.1, respectively. Given the trend of stagnant regular wages, increasing casualization, and persisting informality in the labour market, etc., these quantitative improvements in the unemployment rates in the recent period do not, however, indicate better quality jobs. Moreover, a decline in the

unemployment rate can be attributed more to the decline in labour force participation rate than to the creation of more jobs. Besides, in rural areas MGNREGA played a significant role. Looking at the overall capacity of the rural economy to generate additional employment, it can be inferred that whatever improvement on the employment front is visible in rural areas can be attributed to MGNREGA rather than to the rise in the systemic capacity to absorb additional labour force during the period under consideration.

STATUS OF EMPLOYMENT

Regular employment as a whole has been under tremendous pressure during the last three decades, and it is instructive to look at the relevant numbers (Tables 4.7 and 4.8). For the rural male, the proportion of regular employed, which was about 10.3 per cent in 1983, declined to 8.5 per cent in 2009–10. Also, in urban areas the share of regular employed in the male category remained more or less stagnant between 1999–2000 and 2009–10 and clearly showed a significant decline between 1983 and 2009–10. The marginal increase in regular

Table 4.7 Status of Employment in Rural Areas

NSS Round	Rural Male			Rural Female		
	Self-employed	Regular	Casual	Self-employed	Regular	Casual
38 (1983)	60.5	10.3	29.2	61.9	2.8	35.3
43 (1987–8)	58.6	10	31.4	60.8	3.7	35.5
50 (1993–4)	57.9	8.3	33.8	58.5	2.8	38.7
55 (1999–2000)	55	8.8	36.2	57.3	3.1	39.6
61 (2004–5)	58.1	9	32.9	63.7	3.7	32.6
64 (2007–8)	55.4	9.1	35.5	58.3	4.1	37.6
66 (2009–10)	53.5	8.5	38	55.7	4.4	39.9

Source: Various Rounds of NSS survey reports.

employment during the period from 1983 to 2009–10, for both rural and urban females, was not able to raise its overall share in total employment. We may also note that the annual rate of growth of regular employment was about 2 million during 1993 to 2005, which declined by around half of this rate during 2005 to 2010.

Although the data for the 61st and 66th NSS Rounds show that the rate of regular employment generation in the private organized sector has picked up recently, it is also clear that this was more than offset by stagnation or even a decline in the share of regular employment in all other categories, mainly in the unorganized sector. In fact, it is quite striking that over 80 per cent of all new jobs created in the recent years have been of a casual nature and construction alone accounting for a substantial share. In other words, in spite of the high growth rate in the economy, the process of casualization of labour has been on the rise during the last two decades. A substantial segment of workers who are unable to find even casual employment often remain 'self-employed', which, to a large extent, are either underemployed or disguisedly unemployed[6] (Table 4.9). There are overwhelming evidences that the process of casualization and contractual employment is continuously increasing in the organized sectors as well (Bhalla 2008; Dutta 2005; Mathur and Mishra 2007; Nanda and Kaur 2008; Neethi 2008; among others.)

WORKFORCE STRUCTURE

As has been mentioned at the outset, the prospects for successful transfer of a substantial mass of workers away from the low productive primary sector towards high productive secondary and tertiary sectors remained very much limited during the entire course of development both in urban as well as rural areas. Moreover, even if there is some sluggish trend showing a shift of the workforce from primary to the other two sectors, the transition from substantially large informal to formal economy has remained nearly unnoticeable. By looking at the share of the workforce in various industries of origin, it is not very difficult to arrive at such conclusions (Tables 4.10, 4.11, and 4.12). In rural areas, for the last three decades, the

Table 4.8 Status of Employment in Urban Areas

NSS Round	Urban Male			Urban Female		
	Self-employed	Regular	Casual	Self-employed	Regular	Casual
38 (1983)	40.9	43.7	15.4	45.8	25.8	28.4
43 (1987–8)	41.7	43.7	14.6	47.1	27.5	25.4
50 (1993–4)	41.7	42	16.3	45.8	28.4	25.8
55 (1999–2000)	41.5	41.7	16.8	45.3	33.3	21.4
61 (2004–5)	44.8	40.6	14.6	47.7	35.6	16.7
64 (2007–8)	42.7	42	15.4	42.3	37.9	19.9
66 (2009–10)	41.1	41.9	17	41.1	39.3	19.6

Source: Various Rounds of NSS survey reports.

Table 4.9 Unemployment Rate in Urban Areas

NSS Round	Urban Male				Urban Female			
	PS	PS + SS	CWS	CDS	PS	PS + SS	CWS	CDS
38 (1983)	5.9	5.1	6.7	9.2	6.9	4.9	7.5	11
43 (1987–8)	6.1	5.2	6.6	8.8	8.5	6.2	9.2	12
50 (1993–4)	5.4	4.1	5.2	6.7	8.3	6.1	7.9	10.4
55 (1999–2000)	4.8	4.5	5.6	7.3	7.1	5.7	7.3	9.4
61 (2004–5)	4.4	3.8	5.2	7.5	9.1	6.9	9	11.6
64 (2007–8)	4	3.8	4.7	6.9	6.6	5.2	6.5	9.5
66 (2009–10)	3	2.8	3.6	5.1	7	5.7	7.2	9.1

Source: Various Rounds of NSS survey reports.

share of the workforce in primary sectors declined only by 15 per cent points while the contribution of GDP of the primary sector has declined by more than 30 per cent points. Moreover, manufacturing and electricity, which constituted a significant proportion of the total organized workforce showed almost stagnant growth in its share in total employment. However, construction, trade and related sectors, and transport, which remained largely unorganized and relatively low paid sectors, have shown visible growth in their contribution in accommodating additional employment. So, though a significant proportion of the workforce remained 'employed', their employment in the unorganized sector prevented them from enjoying adequate livelihood support. In majority of the

Table 4.10   Structure of Employment in Rural Areas

NSS Round	Rural Male			Rural Female		
	Primary	Secondary	Tertiary	Primary	Secondary	Tertiary
38 (1983)	77.5	10	12.2	87.5	7.4	4.8
43 (1987–8)	74.5	12.1	13.4	84.7	10	5.3
50 (1993–4)	74.1	11.2	14.7	86.2	8.3	5.5
55 (1999–2000)	71.4	12.6	16	85.4	8.9	5.7
61 (2004–5)	66.5	15.5	18	83.3	10.2	6.6
64 (2007–8)	66.5	16.2	17.3	83.5	9.7	6.8
66 (2009–10)	62.8	19.3	17.8	79.3	13	7.6

Source: Various Rounds of NSS survey reports.

Table 4.11   Industry of Employment for Rural Male

Activities (Rural Male)	1983	1987–8	1993–4	1999–2000	2004–5	2007–8	2009–10
Agriculture and allied activities	77.5	74.5	74.1	71.4	66.5	66.5	62.5
Mining and quarrying	0.6	0.7	0.7	0.6	0.6	0.6	0.8
Manufacturing	7.0	7.4	7.0	7.3	7.9	7.7	7.1
Electricity	0.2	0.3	0.3	0.2	0.2	0.2	0.2
Construction	2.2	3.7	3.2	4.5	6.8	7.7	11.4
Trade, hotels, etc.	4.4	5.1	5.5	6.8	8.3	7.6	8.2
Transport, etc.	1.7	2.0	2.2	3.2	3.8	4	4.2
Other services	6.1	6.2	7.0	6.2	5.9	2.8	5.6

Source: Various Rounds of NSS survey reports.

Table 4.12   Industry of Employment for Rural Female

Activities (Rural Female)	1983	1987–8	1993–4	1999–2000	2004–5	2007–8	2009–10
Agriculture and allied activities	84.7	86.2	85.3	83.3	83.3	83.5	78.9
Mining and quarrying	0.4	0.4	0.3	0.3	0.3	0.3	0.3
Manufacturing	6.9	7.0	7.6	8.4	8.4	7.4	7.6
Utilities	0.0	0.1	0.0	0.0	0.0	0.0	0.0
Construction	2.7	0.9	1.1	1.5	1.5	2.0	4.2
Trade, hotels, etc.	2.1	2.1	2.0	2.5	2.5	2.3	3.1
Transport, etc.	0.1	0.1	0.1	0.2	0.2	0.2	0.3
Other services	3.0	3.4	3.6	4.6	4.6	4.6	5.7

Source: Various Rounds of NSS survey reports.

cases, these sectors, in the absence of any substantial rise in the absorption capacity of formal sectors, act as the last resort of employment.

Similarly, in urban areas the transition of the workforce in the above mentioned direction remained severely limited, and this limitation has been more pronounced in urban areas than that of in rural areas. In other words, it is clear (Tables 4.13, 4.14, and 4.15) that the share of the total workforce in primary sectors has declined by only around 5 percentage points during the entire period of around three decades. Further, and unfortunately enough, the share of the manufacturing sector in the total workforce has declined significantly over the entire period, that is, from 1983 to 2009–10, both for urban males and females. Only construction and trade, and related sectors witnessed some rise in the share of total employment which, however, fails to reflect any positive change in the structure of the workforce towards formalization of employment at any significant scale.

* * *

For almost three decades now, the Indian economy has witnessed remarkable and sustained progress in the overall growth. However, this high growth in GDP has been characterized by some disturbing trends with respect to both quantity and quality of employment and well-being of labour in India. For much of this period, the tertiary sector (rather than manufacturing) has been the major player in the 'economic success' story—both in terms of the value added and, on a much smaller note, with respect to employment generation. An extremely low share of high-earning individuals in certain segments of the economy (largely in the tertiary sector) obviously suggest that positive employment implications for the entire workforce in general, even on this account, have been limited. Further, persistent dualism in the manufacturing sector, which is largely a result of structural factors as well as policy bottlenecks and failures, has limited the prospects of a dynamic role for this sector in the economy. It is a combination of such factors, inter alia, which explains why the expectation that the high rate of growth

Table 4.13   Structure of Employment in Urban Areas

NSS Round	Urban Male			Urban Female		
	Primary	Secondary	Tertiary	Primary	Secondary	Tertiary
38 (1983)	10.3	34.2	55	31	30.6	37.6
43 (1987–8)	9.1	34	56.9	29.4	31.7	38.9
50 (1993–4)	9	32.9	58.1	24.7	29.1	46.2
55 (1999–2000)	6.6	32.8	60.6	17.7	29.3	52.9
61 (2004–5)	6.1	34.4	59.5	18.1	32.4	49.5
64 (2007–8)	5.8	34.3	59.7	15.3	32.3	52.4
66 (2009–0)	6	34.6	59.3	13.9	33.3	52.8

Source: Various Rounds of NSS survey reports.

Table 4.14   Industry of Employment for Urban Male

Activities (Urban Male)	1983	1987–8	1993–4	1999–2000	2004–5	2007–8	2009–10
Agriculture and allied activities	10.6	9.1	9.0	6.5	6.1	5.8	5.9
Mining and quarrying	1.2	1.3	1.3	0.9	0.9	0.6	0.7
Manufacturing	26.8	25.7	23.5	22.4	23.5	23.5	21.9
Utilities	1.1	1.2	1.2	0.8	0.8	0.7	0.7
Construction	5.1	5.8	6.9	8.7	9.2	9.5	11.5
Trade, hotels, etc.	20.4	21.5	21.9	29.4	28.0	27.8	27.0
Transport, etc.	10.4	9.7	9.7	10.4	10.7	10.9	10.5
Other services	24.7	25.2	26.4	19.0	20.8	21.0	21.8

Source: Various Rounds of NSS survey reports.

Table 4.15 Industry of Employment for Urban Female

Activities (Urban Female)	1983	1987–8	1993–4	1999–2000	2004–5	2007–8	2009–10
Agriculture and allied activities	31.5	29.4	24.7	17.6	18.1	15.3	11.8
Mining and quarrying	0.7	0.8	0.6	0.4	0.2	0.3	0.3
Manufacturing	26.7	27.1	24.1	24.0	28.2	27.5	25.8
Utilities	0.2	0.2	0.3	0.2	0.2	0.2	0.4
Construction	3.2	3.7	4.1	4.8	3.8	4.3	5.1
Trade, hotels, etc.	9.5	9.8	10.0	16.9	12.2	12.8	12.8
Transport, etc.	0.6	1.2	1.3	1.8	1.4	1.8	1.5
Other services	26.7	27.8	35.0	34.2	35.9	37.8	42.7

Source: Various Rounds of NSS survey reports.

would be accompanied with a commensurate growth in employment opportunities has been belied. For the overwhelming chunk of the working masses, several adverse processes have been unleashed during the regime of neoliberal reforms. In other words, as discussed by many scholars, the neoliberal trajectory has pushed the Indian economy increasingly towards 'jobless growth'. Thus, the benefits of growth are largely appropriated by the surplus earners (as the share of surplus in the output has been increasing disproportionately), and the overwhelming mass of workers has remained largely excluded from the current growth process. Hence, it is hardly surprising that almost all the indicators of well-being of labour in India have shown relative deteriorating trends during this period.

In contrast to the decade of the 1980s, which had witnessed some improvement in the well-being indicators of the labour, in large measure on account of the range of government policies, the period since the early 1990s emerges in a different light. The decline in government activities and downsizing of the public investment has led to the significant squeeze in overall employability of the economy as whole. The agriculture sector, which continues to be the largest employment provider, has been among the worst hit and lost its capacity to absorb labour. Moreover, acceleration in adoption of capital-intensive techniques across different economic sectors along with increasing tendencies of casualization and in-formalization of the workforce has aggravated the overall employment scenario. The unemployment rate has risen and there are clear evidences of qualitative deterioration of working conditions for the overwhelming majority of workers. The unorganized sector, largely characterized by low earnings, job insecurity, lack of social security, and poor working environment has tended to increase its share further during the reform era. The additional

employment opportunities in the tertiary sector, though very small in proportion to its share in national income, are less likely to absorb the poor, who are mostly unskilled. More precisely, most of the relevant indicators reflecting the well-being status of the workers in general clearly show a relative deteriorating trend, particularly during the last two decades. The generation of employment under the neoliberal regime has come under tremendous pressure. Moreover, employment creation in the formal sector has undergone severe limitations during the same period. The share of regular employment both in rural and urban areas has witnessed a sharp reduction over the entire period of the last three decades or more. Any evidence of successful transformation towards the formalization of the workforce is almost missing during the entire course of development and the situations remained even grimmer during the last two decades under the neoliberal reform period. Declining WPR among the younger population is also indicative of the lack of employment opportunities for the educated and semi-skilled labour force entering the job market. Till 2004–5, there was clear evidence of a sharp deceleration of the real wage rate in rural as well as urban areas along with rising trends of the unemployment rate on 'CDS basis'. However, with the initiation of MGNREGA, some of the trends regarding the deceleration in the real wage rate and upward movement of the rate of unemployment seem to be halted at least for the time being. Nonetheless, any improvement even in these indicators on a permanent basis without having fundamental change in the structure of current policy regime seems extremely remote in the near future.

NOTES

1. These possibilities are corroborated also by the fact that in good agricultural year 2007–8, while male participation rates increased marginally, that of women fell significantly.

2. As is well acknowledged, the impact of residual absorption of labour is also included in this ratio.

3. However, taking the period from 1999–2000 to 2007–8 (a good agricultural year) this rate declined significantly to 1.27 per cent.

4. Srinivasan gives more importance to CWS basis for measuring unemployment rather than to CDS basis.

5. In 2007–8, for male workers, it reached the level even higher than that of in 1983.

6. Of course exception to such a trend would be a very small proportion of self-employed skilled workers who have done extremely well as self-employed, due to the opening of the new avenues like the expansion of information and communication technology (ICT).

References

Bhalla, G.S. 2008. 'Globalization and Employment Trends in India', *The Indian Journal of Labour Economics*, 51(1): 1–23.

Chandrasekhar, C.P. 2010. 'India's New, High-Growth Trajectory: Implications for Demand, Technology and Employment', Presented at the 52nd Annual Conference of ISLE, Dharwad, 17–19 December.

Chandrasekhar, C.P. and Jayati Ghosh. 2002. *The Market That Failed: A Decade of Neoliberal Economic Reforms in India*. New Delhi: Leftword Books.

———. 2007. 'Recent Employment Trends in India and China: An Unfortunate Convergence'. Available at www.macroscan.com (accessed 5 April 2012).

———. 2011. 'The Latest Employment Trends from the NSSO'. Available at www.macroscan.com/fet/jul11/fet140711NSSO.htm (accessed 4 October 2012).

Dutta, Puja Vasudeva. 2005. 'Accounting for Wage Inequality in India', *The Indian Journal of Labour Economics*, 48(2): 273–96.

Ghose, Ajit K. 2008. 'Globalization and Employment in Developing Countries', *The Indian Journal of Labour Economics*, 51(4): 497–504.

Himanshu. 2011. 'Employment Trends in India: A Re-examination'. *Economic and Political Weekly*, 46(37, 10 September): 43–59.

Jha, Praveen. 1997. *Agricultural Labour in India*. New Delhi: Vikas Publishing House.

———. 2003. 'Issues Relating to Employment in India in the Era of Globalization', *Social Scientist*, 31(11/12, November–December): 47–65.

———. 2009. 'The Well-being of Labour in Contemporary Indian Economy: What's Active Labour Market Policy Got to Do With It?' Employment Working Paper No. 39, Employment Analysis and Research Unit, Economic and Labour Market Analysis Department, International Labour Organization, Geneva.

Mathur, Ashok and Sunil Kumar Mishra. 2007. 'Wages and Employment in the Indian Industrial Sector: Theory and Evidence', *The Indian Journal of Labour Economics*, 50(1): 83–110.

Nanda, Paramjit and Veerpal Kaur. 2008. 'Impact of Globalization on the Labour Market in India: Evidence from the Manufacturing Sector', *The Indian Journal of Labour Economics*, 51(4): 545–57.

Neethi, P. 2008. 'Contract Work in the Organized Manufacturing Sector: A Disaggregated Analysis of Trends and Their Implications', *The Indian Journal of Labour Economics*, 51(4): 559–73.

Patnaik, Prabhat. 2006. 'A Model of Growth of the Contemporary Indian Economy', *Economic and Political Weekly*, 42(22, 2–8 June): 2077–81.

Patnaik, Prabhat and C.P. Chandrasekhar. 1995. 'Indian Economy under Structural Adjustment', *Economic and Political Weekly*, 30(45, 25 November): 3001–13.

Sen, Abhijit. 1996. 'Economic Reforms, Employment and Poverty: Trends and Options', *Economic and Political Weekly*, 31(35–37, September): 2459–78.

Srinivasan, T. N. 2006. 'Employment and Unemployment since the Early Seventies', Working Paper No. 306, December, Stanford Center for International Development, Stanford.

5

India's Health
Not Shining

MOHAN RAO AND OOMMEN C. KURIAN

Commencing with Independence in 1947, India has indeed made some gains in health. The Infant Mortality Rate (IMR) was 134 per thousand live births at the time of Independence (GoI 2002a) and has declined to around 47 in 2010. The Crude Birth Rate (CBR), reflecting the huge mortality load, stood at 39.9 in 1941–51, declined to 22.1 in 2010. The Crude Death Rate (CDR) declined from 27.4 in 1941–51 to 7.2 in 2010 (GoI 2011a). As a consequence, expectation of life at birth is now in the mid-Sixties, from a figure in the early Thirties at the time of Independence. Nevertheless, as the data we survey reveals, India has worse health indices than a number of comparable developing countries in the world. Table 5.1 provides data on health indices in India, Sri Lanka, China, Brazil, and Thailand in relation to their public spending on health.

We see, then, that health achievements in India have been extremely modest indeed, compared to these other countries, and that there is a clear association with public

health spending that we shall examine later. But to make a beginning, India has one of the lowest public health expenditures in the world, with not surprisingly, a very high proportion of private spending. It is not, therefore, surprising that we have one of the highest proportions of undernourished children and women in the world, one of the highest rates of maternal mortality in the world, and the highest load of preventable and communicable diseases. Yet, the very first health policy adopted by the Government of India (GoI) in 1983 set out to provide 'universal, comprehensive primary health care services, relevant to the actual needs and priorities of the community' (GoI 1983: 3). India is also a signatory to the Alma Ata Declaration which resolutely states that

[t]he Conference strongly affirms that health, which is a state of complete physical, mental and social well-being, and not merely the absence of disease or infirmity, is a fundamental human right and that the attainment of the highest possible

Table 5.1   Health Indices in India, China, Brazil, Sri Lanka, and Thailand in Relation to Public Health Expenditures

Indicator	India	Thailand	China	Sri Lanka	Brazil
IMR	50	12	17	13	17
Under 5 mortality rate	66	13	19	16	21
Fully immunized (%)	66	98	95	99	99
Birth by skilled attendants	47	99	96	97	98
Per capita government expenditure on health (PPP $)	39	247	203	66	483

Source: *World Health Statistics*, World Health Organization (WHO), 2011.

level of health is a most important world-wide social goal whose realization requires the action of many other social and economic sectors in addition to the health sector. (WHO 1978: 2)

Realizing the profound weaknesses of the health care system, the GoI initiated the National Rural Health Mission (NRHM) in 2005 to strengthen the health infrastructure, with special reference to particularly vulnerable Empowered Action Group (EAG) states. Despite the stated NRHM objective of raising the outlays for public health from 0.9 per cent of gross domestic product (GDP) to 2–3 per cent of GDP by 2012 and expanding public health infrastructure substantially, we still see the proportion hovering above 1 per cent. According to the 2010 *Bulletin on Rural Health Statistics in India*, there is a shortage of 19,590 sub-centres, 4,252 primary health centres (PHCs), and 2,115 community health centres (CHCs) in India. Worse is a crippling shortage of human resources all down the line (Rao *et al.* 2011) An evaluation in 2011 (Husain 2011) observed that while the improvements in the status of health infrastructure and human power have fallen far short of what was originally planned, there was some positive impact on indicators, such as immunization, institutional deliveries, and antenatal care. Rao and Choudhury (2012) observed that despite the adoption of NRHM, public expenditure on health increased only marginally to 1.2 per cent of GDP in 2009–10. This resulted in poor quality of preventative care and poor health status of the population and forced the population to seek private care, resulting in very high out-of-pocket spending.

The NRHM aimed to reduce the IMR to 28/1,000 live births, the Maternal Mortality Rate (MMR) to 100/100,000 live births, and the Total Fertility Rate (TFR) to 2.1 by 2012. With IMR at 47 and MMR at 210 in 2010, it is clear that only the TFR goal is anywhere near the goal set with 21 states and union territories already achieving replacement levels of fertility. This achievement is an indication of the focused attention that fertility control has been receiving. The fact that IMR and MMR are still lagging behind may be seen as evidence that the success of family planning programmes is mostly at the cost of potential quality and access improvements in health care, in general, and Maternal and Child Health (MCH), in particular. The fact that many states responded to the increase in the centre's health allocations to NRHM by reducing their own expenditure acted as an additional impediment (Duggal 2009). The latest status report of NRHM, however, shows that the utilization of funds in the states has considerably improved over the last few years as the absorptive capacity has gone up. It concludes that the change is taking place, but it needs to happen faster. The 'neglect of the public system of care has been colossal and it will take time to set right a dysfunctional system' (GoI 2011b: 58).

Clearly, then, there is a profound mismatch between the aims we have set out for ourselves and our achievements. What could be the reasons for this? Is this the lack of political will? Is it a question of good plans improperly implemented? Is it that our achievements have been overtaken by population growth? These, indeed are some of the explanations conventionally proffered to explain our failures. Or have we, in fact, managed to create a health service system that we wanted to create? In other words, is this in fact a story of success? This chapter presents data on India's health indices, including some data on trends over time, and in a brief discussion, highlights some of the major reasons for India's failures in achieving acceptable health standards in the population.

LIFE EXPECTANCY AT BIRTH

Figure 5.1 provides us information on life expectation at birth. The fact that India commenced the twentieth century with average life expectations in the early Twenties, the life expectation in early agricultural societies is of course a result of colonial famines and epidemics. With the decline of death rate commencing in the 1920s, life expectations commenced a secular, although unremarkable, increase. One feature of singular importance is that in India, unlike other parts of the world, female life expectations over much of the twentieth century remained below that of males. This was, of course, a result of the huge gender differentials in infant and early childhood mortality. From the 1980s onwards this pattern has reversed with female life expectations being slightly more than male life expectations. The 1980s was also the period of maximum decline in infant and child mortalities. This is, of course, not to deny the continuing gender discrimination in life chances in the country, but that the data seems to indicate that overall improvements in female life chances seem to be governed by overall improvements in health in the population at large. That is to say socio-economic disadvantage undergirds gender disparities.

The life expectancy at birth for males was 62.6 years as compared to 64.2 years for females according to 2002–6 estimates. What the data also reveals is the pervasive nature of health inequalities in India. A female child born in rural Kerala (life expectancy 76.1 years) could

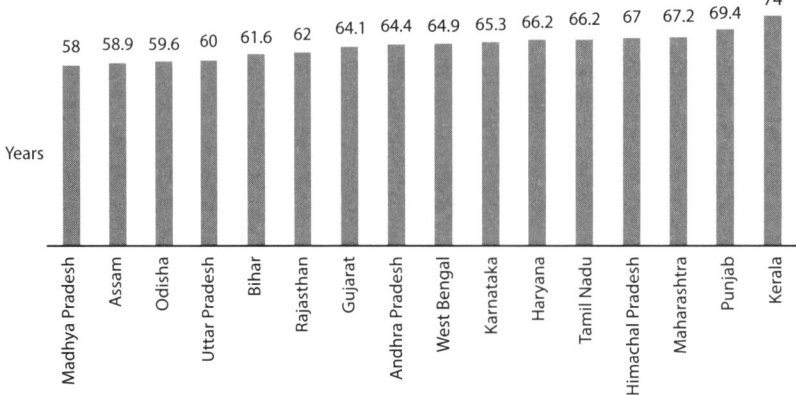

Figure 5.1   Life Expectancy at Birth
Source: GoI 2011c.

expect to live almost 20 years longer than a male child born in rural Madhya Pradesh (56.7 years). Across states, life expectancy was higher in urban areas. Surprisingly, despite all the hype about development in Gujarat, the life expectation there was lower than in Karnataka, Maharashtra, Punjab, and Haryana, not to mention, Tamil Nadu and Kerala (GoI 2011c).

INFANT MORTALITY RATE

Table 5.2 presents data on the IMR by sex and residence among the major states in the country. India, again, is unique in that it is one of the few countries with higher female IMRs than male. This is of course despite the well-attested biological superiority of the female infant, attesting to the widespread anti-female biases in India's society. What is also remarkable is the marked and persistent rural urban differences. There are marked interstate differences too—Kerala at 13 has the lowest IMR while Odisha (61), Uttar Pradesh (61), and Madhya Pradesh (62) have the highest IMRs. Together these latter states account for a substantial proportion of India's population. There is no straightforward relationship to socio-economic development. It is seen that Bihar and Haryana have the same IMR. Similarly, the richer state of Punjab has a higher IMR than the relatively poorer West Bengal. What is, however, clear is that we did not reach even our 1983 health policy goal of lowering the IMR to less than 60 in all states of India by 2000, or the 2002 health policy goal of lowering IMR further to 30 by 2010.

The gap between IMRs of boys and girls, along with the overall decline in female IMRs, suggests explicit discriminatory practices against girls. The regional variation in gender bias confirms that the states of northwest India are more anti-female than the states of the south and east.

Latest National Family Health Survey (NFHS) figures show that the IMR is 66.4 among the Scheduled Castes (SCs), 62.1 among the Scheduled Tribes (STs), 56.6 among other disadvantaged groups, and 48.9 among Others. Data from the same NFHS Round indicate that the IMR among households with a low standard of living was 70.4 compared to 29.2 among households with a high standard of living. The post-neonatal mortality rate is more than three times as high in households with a low standard of living as in households with a high standard of living and child mortality is almost seven times higher (IIPS 2007).

According to GoI (2011a), every sixth death in the country still pertains to that of an infant. Of all the states, Kerala, Tamil Nadu, and Maharashtra have already achieved the Millennium Development Goal (MDG) goal of an IMR of 28 by 2015, while Delhi and West Bengal are in close proximity to that achievement. IMR for the country declined by 30 points in the last 20 years at an annual average decline of 1.5 points, of which rural IMR fell by 31 points and urban IMR by 16 points. Still, one in every 20 children at the national level; one in every 18 children born in rural areas; and one in every 29 children born in urban areas die within one year of birth (GoI 2011a).

The rate of the decline of IMR has seen fluctuations and has been a matter of concern particularly in the context of a slowdown over the last 20 years. IMR declined at a very low rate of around 1 per cent during the decade of 1961–71, followed by a five-year period of actually negative decline, with an increase in IMR from 129 in 1971 to 140 in 1975—an increase of 8.53 per cent (Gupta and Trivedi 2008). Thereafter, there was a steady decline at an increasing rate up till 1990—the five-year

Table 5.2   Infant Mortality Rates by Sex and Residence in India and Major States, 2010

India and Major States	Total			Rural			Urban		
	Total	Male	Female	Total	Male	Female	Total	Male	Female
India	47	46	49	51	50	53	31	30	33
Andhra Pradesh	46	44	47	51	50	51	33	29	36
Assam	58	56	60	60	59	62	36	35	38
Bihar	48	46	50	49	47	51	38	36	40
Chhattisgarh	51	48	54	52	49	55	44	41	46
Delhi	30	29	31	37	32	42	29	28	29
Gujarat	44	41	47	51	48	54	30	28	33
Haryana	48	46	49	51	51	52	38	35	42
Himachal Pradesh	40	35	47	41	35	48	29	29	29
Jammu and Kashmir	43	41	45	45	43	47	32	28	37
Jharkhand	42	41	44	44	43	46	30	28	31
Karnataka	38	37	39	43	42	44	28	28	28
Kerala	13	13	14	14	14	15	10	10	11
Madhya Pradesh	62	62	63	67	66	67	42	41	42
Maharashtra	28	27	29	34	33	35	20	19	21
Odisha	61	60	61	63	62	63	43	40	46
Punjab	34	33	35	37	36	39	28	27	29
Rajasthan	55	52	57	61	58	64	31	29	34
Tamil Nadu	24	23	24	25	25	26	22	22	22
Uttar Pradesh	61	58	63	64	61	67	44	44	45
West Bengal	31	29	32	32	31	33	25	24	27

Source: GoI 2012a.

rate of decline being 11.63 per cent in 1976–80 and a high 16.67 per cent in 1986–90. However, the decade of structural adjustment policies (the 1990s) saw the IMR stagnating at very low rates of decline—a low 7.5 per cent between 1991–5 which further decelerated to 5.56 per cent between 1996 and 2000. This was even lower than the rate of decline of the 1960s. However, there was some acceleration in the rate of decline of IMR after 2000. Between 2001 and 2005, IMR declined at 12.12 per cent, a rate further accelerated to 17.54 per cent for 2006–10, comparable to that of the 1980s (GoI 2011a).

In sum, not only is the IMR still unconscionably high, with marked rural–urban differences and differences among states and regions, there are even more marked social differences between groups within the population and among the genders. Hence, the Dalits, Adivasis, and Other Backward Classes (OBCs) bear a disproportionate burden of infant deaths, as indeed do the poor in general. Thus, in addition to regional factors, class, caste, and gender interact to contour the differentials in morbidity and mortality.

UNDER 5 MORTALITY RATE

Like the IMR, the Under 5 Mortality Rate (U5MR) is also considered a sensitive index of health achievement and of socio-economic development. Table 5.3 presents the relevant data.

As is evident, Assam (83), Madhya Pradesh (82), Uttar Pradesh (79), Odisha (78), and Rajasthan (69) have extremely high levels of U5MR; Kerala (15) and Tamil Nadu (27) are among the lowest. Although not depicted in the table, Goa's U5MR is at the second lowest level after Kerala. India is also unique in the marked and persistent gender differences even up to this age. Although gender differences are present both in urban and rural areas, they are more marked in rural settings. What is important to remember, however, is that rural–urban differences are significantly greater than gender differences.

Table 5.3   Under 5 Mortality Rate by Sex and Residence in India and Major States, 2010

India and Major States	Total			Rural			Urban		
	Total	Male	Female	Total	Male	Female	Total	Male	Female
India	59	55	64	66	61	71	38	36	40
Andhra Pradesh	48	46	51	53	52	55	36	32	40
Assam	83	79	87	88	83	93	42	41	42
Bihar	64	60	68	65	61	70	47	46	47
Chhattisgarh	61	52	70	63	54	72	48	42	54
Delhi	34	33	35	42	42	42	33	31	34
Gujarat	56	52	60	65	63	67	39	33	46
Haryana	55	51	59	58	54	61	47	41	53
Himachal Pradesh	49	43	57	50	43	59	37	40	34
Jammu and Kashmir	48	46	50	51	50	52	33	28	40
Jharkhand	59	52	66	63	55	71	35	32	38
Karnataka	45	43	47	49	47	51	36	34	38
Kerala	15	14	16	16	14	18	12	12	13
Madhya Pradesh	82	79	85	88	84	92	54	55	53
Maharashtra	33	31	35	39	37	42	23	22	25
Odisha	78	76	79	81	81	82	46	41	50
Punjab	43	38	48	49	43	56	31	30	33
Rajasthan	69	60	79	76	67	86	42	35	51
Tamil Nadu	27	26	28	30	28	32	24	24	24
Uttar Pradesh	79	71	87	82	74	92	60	59	60
West Bengal	37	37	38	40	39	40	28	26	30

Source: GoI 2012a.

This emphasizes the point made earlier about socio-economic differences undergirding gender differences. Again, Gujarat does worse than Karnataka, Maharashtra, and indeed even Haryana and Punjab in U5MR. U5MR for the country declined by 54 points (rural IMR by 57 points vis-à-vis urban IMR 30 points) in the last 20 years at an annual average decline of 2.7 points (GoI 2011a).

While the urban U5MR has already achieved the MDG target and male–female differentials in mortality have narrowed over the years, stark rural–urban differentials remain a major concern. Between 1990 and 1995, U5MR declined by 17.8 per cent, but the rate declined to 12.37 per cent in 1995–2000, and further to a low of 9.41 per cent in the 2000–5 period. However, there was an acceleration in the rate of decline in the five years that followed and U5MR fell between 2005 and 2010 by an impressive 16.88 per cent. At the same time, despite consistent decline over the last 20 years at rates higher than 10 per cent per five-year periods, the rural U5MR is still at unacceptably high levels.

According to the NFHS III, in rural areas the U5MR was 82, while in urban areas it stood at 51.7 (IIPS 2007). In urban areas it was 32.8 among households with a high standard of living, while it stood at 92.1 in households with a low standard of living, highlighting, of course, the conditions of life in urban slums. In rural areas, the U5MR was an astonishing 94.7 among Dalit households, 99.8 among Adivasi households, and 78.7 among the OBCs, compared to 68.2 among others. Again, in rural areas, households with a low standard of living had levels of 100.9, more than three times higher than in better-off households in urban areas and almost three times higher than in better-off households in rural areas. Again, the data here draw attention to the interlocking of class and caste in the distribution of the mortality load. The uncertainty of childhood survival implies that women continue to bear a higher load of pregnancies and the associated morbidities and mortalities. This is particularly the case with poorer sections of the population in poor and deprived areas. All too often, of course, such women belong to the lower castes or are Adivasis.

Nutritional Status

The latest NFHS data shows that despite a bourgeoning economy, growing for the better part of last decade at around 8 per cent, the nutritional crisis has reached alarming proportions. The figures establish that malnutrition rates in many parts of the country are comparable to or worse than most Sub-Saharan African countries. Almost half of the children under 5 years of age (48 per cent) are stunted and 43 per cent are underweight. Worse, 24 per cent are severely stunted and 16 per cent are severely underweight. Wasting, signifying chronic hunger, is quite a serious problem in India as well, affecting 20 per cent of children under 5 years of age. While it is true that undernutrition is substantially higher in rural areas than in urban areas, even in urban areas, 40 per cent of children remain stunted and 33 per cent remain underweight (IIPS 2007).

NFHS III results also show that anaemia is very common and on the rise in India. As high as 70 per cent of all under-5 children are anaemic, of whom 40 per cent are moderately anaemic and 3 per cent are severely anaemic. Among women, anaemia affects 55 per cent, while among men the prevalence is 24 per cent. Anaemia is considerably higher in rural areas, among children of women with no education, among Dalits and Adivasis, and among children in households in the lower wealth quintiles. In fact, the NFHS III data shows that prevalence of anaemia among children between 6 and 35 months has increased from 74 per cent in 1998–9 to 79 per cent in 2005–6. This increase is largely due to a worsening of the situation among young children in rural areas. It is alarming that even in a state like Haryana, which is considered developed, more than 80 per cent of children in the age group of 6–35 months were anaemic. It was seen that the only states in which less than half of children are anaemic are Goa (38 per cent), Manipur (41 per cent), Mizoram (44 per cent), and Kerala (45 per cent) (ibid.).

The prevalence of anaemia for ever-married women too has increased from 52 per cent in NFHS II to 56 per cent in NFHS III. Interestingly, obesity is also rapidly becoming a substantial problem among several groups of women in India, particularly urban women, well-educated women, women from households with a high standard of living, and among Sikhs. Fifteen per cent of ever-married women are overweight or obese, up from 11 per cent in NFHS II. Obesity is particularly prevalent for both men and women in Delhi, Kerala, and Punjab (IIPS 2007)·

In short, the nutritional situation testifies to the wide inequalities in the country—a substantial population lacking adequate food while a small minority suffers from alimentary excesses.

Sex Ratio

The female–male ratio (FMR) in the world—that is, the number of females per 1,000 males—is 990. Western Europe has a figure of 1,064 females per thousand males, in Africa the figure is 1,015. Asia, as a whole, has FMRs of 953, but India shares extremely negative sex ratios with a number of her neighbours in Asia. Values of less than 950 females per 1,000 males are found in the countries of West Asia (940), Pakistan (929), India (933), Bangladesh (939), and China (941)—an arc of anti-female countries, cutting across cultures and religions.

India has seen a steady decline of the sex ratio over the twentieth century. The 1901 Census showed 972 females per 1,000 males. It declined steadily to 946 in 1951, 941 in 1961, and 930 in 1971. Indeed the historic 1974 'Report of the Committee of the Status of Women in India' brought this centre stage as an indicator of the dismal status of women in the country (GoI 1974). The 1981 Census threw up a happy figure of 934 females per 1,000 males. Some people optimistically thought that this indicated a halt in the decline in the sex ratio. The 1991 figure, however, showed otherwise: it revealed a further decline to 927. The 1981 figure, it is now accepted by demographers, was caused by a significant under-counting of females due to a decline in the quality of the 1971 Census. Demographers have agreed that the 1991 and 2001 Censuses are free from this infirmity. This is to say that the 2001 Census figures, of 933 females per 1,000 males, are real and indicative of an improvement in the overall survival of females. Have we then turned the corner?

Both the 2001 and 2011 Censuses seem to indicate so with the sex ratio increasing from 933 to 940 (Table 5.4). There are only three states where the sex ratio has declined—Bihar, Jammu and Kashmir, and Gujarat. Researchers consider Jammu and Kashmir's decline 'too large' to be plausible (Navaneetham and Dharmalingam 2011). Bihar's decline could plausibly be related to male outmigration. While the reasons for the decline of the sex ratio in these states need to be studied, the fact that it had done so in a state like Gujarat is a comment on its pattern of development. Gujarat happens to be the only major state where the sex ratio declined both in the 1990s as well as later, although the rate somewhat decelerated in the past decade when compared to the 1990s. According to Navaneetham and Dharmalingam, who based their estimates on the provisional 2011 Census figures, the regional pattern in sex ratio in 2011 follows a long trend—that of relatively less 'masculine' sex ratio in the south and east compared to the north. While an improvement in the enumeration may be a factor in the improved ratio, a greater survival rate among women contributed the most (ibid.).

Table 5.4 Sex Ratio in India and Major States, 2001 and 2011

India and Major States	Total Sex Ratio	
	2001	2011
India	933	940
Andhra Pradesh	978	992
Assam	935	954
Bihar	919	916
Chhattisgarh	989	991
Delhi	821	866
Gujarat	920	918
Haryana	861	877
Himachal Pradesh	968	974
Jammu and Kashmir	892	883
Jharkhand	941	947
Karnataka	965	968
Kerala	1,058	1,084
Madhya Pradesh	919	930
Maharashtra	922	925
Odisha	972	978
Punjab	876	893
Rajasthan	921	926
Tamil Nadu	987	995
Uttar Pradesh	898	908
West Bengal	934	947

Source: Census 2011.

CHILD SEX RATIO

The overall sex ratio could turn feminine simply because more men than women have migrated. But the Juvenile or Child Sex Ratio (CSR) is not subjected to this limitation. And it is this that is deeply worrying. Despite the slight overall improvement in the sex ratio, the CSR in India as a whole has declined significantly—from 945 in 1991 to 927 in 2001 to 914 in 2011.

This decline in the CSR has been particularly notable in Uttar Pradesh (916 to 899), Sikkim (963 to 944), Madhya Pradesh (932 to 913), Maharashtra (913 to 883), and, among the southern states, Andhra Pradesh (961 to 943). Surprisingly, Punjab and Haryana—part of the Bermuda triangle for missing females—have buckled the trend. However, in spite of an improvement between 2001 and 2011, these states still have the lowest CSRs (less than 850) in 2011 (Table 5.5).

A 2003 report simply titled 'Missing', prepared by the United Nations Population Fund (UNFPA), Ministry of Health and Family Welfare, and the Census Commissioner, which mapped the adverse CSRs in India captures the decline in the number of girls (UNFPA 2003). It reveals that 70 districts in 16 states and union territories recorded a more than 50 point decline in the CSR between 1991 and 2001. This decline had spread to regions and populations hitherto considered immune, namely, the states of the south and west of India and populations of Dalits and Adivasis. What is also interesting is that the decline was more marked in the more developed and better-off regions and in more literate and better-off social groups. What is significant, of course, is that the worsening of the sex ratio was most marked in those states which can claim to be better governed, and have a higher density of private medical care services and lower birth rates. The worsening of CSR continues with the latest Census estimates too.

The worsening of the CSR in the last 10 years point to a further widening of the gender mortality gap—continuing anti-female rates of infant and child mortality—as well as a decrease in the sex ratio at birth through sex selective abortion. The preference of a son and the low status of women are the two underlying causes for discrimination against female children in India. According to Navaneetham and Dharmalingam (2011: 16): 'A girl child is about 40 per cent more likely to die than a male child in her first year of life, and 61 per cent more likely to die between her first and fifth birthdays.' They suggest that while sex selective abortion and female neglect jointly contributed to low sex ratio in states like Punjab and Haryana, sex selective abortion may have contributed proportionately more than female neglect in states like Gujarat, Delhi, and Chandigarh.

Sex ratio at birth data from 2011 Census is not published yet. As given in Table 5.6, sex ratio at birth for most of the last decade was recently published as part of the 'Statistical Report 2010' (GoI 2011e). In India, a normal sex ratio at birth would be about 105 male births for 100 female births, or, on the average, 953 females per

Table 5.5   Child Sex Ratio in India and Major States, 2001 and 2011

India and Major States	Child Population in the Age Group 0–6		Population Aged 7 and Above	
	2001	2011	2001	2011
India	927	914	934	944
Andhra Pradesh	961	943	981	997
Assam	965	957	929	953
Bihar	942	933	914	912
Chhattisgarh	975	964	992	995
Delhi	868	866	813	866
Gujarat	883	886	927	923
Haryana	819	830	869	885
Himachal Pradesh	896	906	980	983
Jammu and Kashmir	941	859	884	887
Jharkhand	965	943	935	948
Karnataka	946	943	968	971
Kerala	960	959	1,072	1,099
Madhya Pradesh	932	912	916	933
Maharashtra	913	883	924	931
Odisha	953	934	976	985
Punjab	798	846	888	899
Rajasthan	909	883	923	935
Tamil Nadu	942	946	993	1,000
Uttar Pradesh	916	899	894	910
West Bengal	960	950	929	946

Source: Census 2011.

1,000 male children. However, sex ratio at birth estimates for 2008–10 reveal an all-India figure of 905 females per 1,000 males, despite some minor improvements across the last six years or so. This is indicative of the continuing practice of sex selective abortion. Figures below the national average of sex ratio at birth are seen in Punjab (831), Haryana (848), Uttar Pradesh (870), Jammu and Kashmir (873), Rajasthan (877), Delhi (884), Maharashtra (895), and Gujarat (903). UNFPA notes, based on the analysis of SRS data, that the number of girls missing in India on account of sex selective abortion was around six lakh per year. It was estimated that during 2001–8 for the country as a whole, on an average nearly 5 per cent of female births did not occur because of prenatal sex selection (UNFPA 2011).

CAUSES OF DEATH IN INDIA

Data presented in Registrar General of India (2008, cited in GoI 2011f and Vellakkal n.d.) revealed, as shown in the Figure 5.2, that non-communicable diseases are now the leading causes of death in the country, constituting 42 per cent of all deaths. Communicable, maternal, perinatal, and nutritional conditions constitute another 38 per cent of deaths, while injuries and ill-defined causes each constitute 10 per cent of deaths. It is suggested that the majority of ill-defined causes are for older people (aged 70 or above) and most of the ill-defined deaths are likely to be caused due to non-communicable diseases.

Rural areas report more deaths due to communicable, maternal, perinatal, and nutritional conditions (41 per cent) compared to urban areas. The proportion of deaths due to non-communicable diseases is less in rural areas (40 per cent) than in urban areas (56 per cent). The leading cause of death is cardiovascular disease (19 per cent), followed by respiratory diseases (9 per cent), diarrhoeal diseases (8 per cent), perinatal conditions (6.3 per cent), respiratory infections such as acute pneumonia (6.2 per cent), tuberculosis (6 per cent), malignant and other neoplasms (5.7 per cent), senility (5.1 per cent), unintentional injuries and other (4.9 per cent), and symptoms,

Table 5.6   Sex Ratio at Birth in India and Major States, 2004–6 to 2008–10

India and Major States	Total				
	2004–6	2005–7	2006–8	2007–9	2008–10
India	892	901	904	906	905
Andhra Pradesh	917	915	917	919	920
Assam	920	939	933	931	928
Bihar	881	909	914	917	912
Chhattisgarh	961	969	975	980	985
Delhi	847	871	877	882	884
Gujarat	865	891	898	904	903
Haryana	837	843	847	849	848
Himachal Pradesh	872	931	938	944	942
Jammu and Kashmir	838	854	862	870	873
Jharkhand	888	927	922	921	919
Karnataka	917	926	935	944	943
Kerala	922	958	964	968	966
Madhya Pradesh	913	913	919	926	921
Maharashtra	879	871	884	896	895
Odisha	934	933	937	941	938
Punjab	808	837	836	836	831
Rajasthan	855	865	870	875	877
Tamil Nadu	955	944	936	929	927
Uttar Pradesh	874	881	877	874	870
West Bengal	931	936	941	944	938

Source: GoI 2012a.

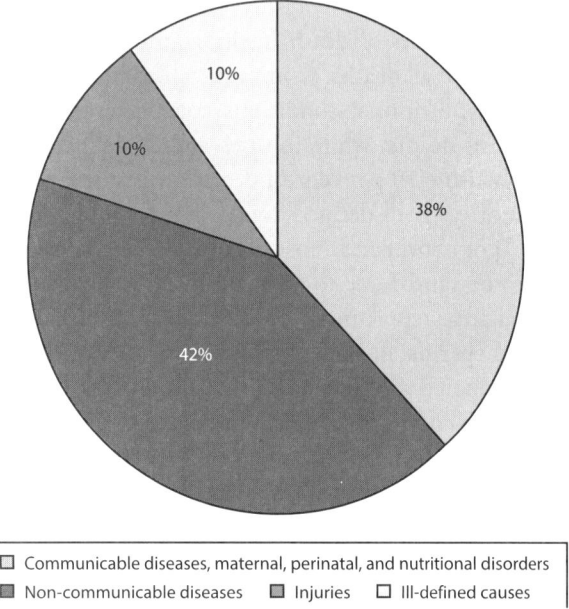

☐ Communicable diseases, maternal, perinatal, and nutritional disorders
■ Non-communicable diseases   ■ Injuries   ☐ Ill-defined causes

Figure 5.2   Causes of Death in India, 2008
Source: GoI 2011f.

signs, and ill-defined conditions (4.8 per cent). Among the age group of 25–69, cardiovascular disease caused 25 per cent of the total deaths. Furthermore, it is the leading cause of death among both males and females (GoI 2011f). It is also reported that there is a marked regional variation in India in the distribution of leading cause of deaths.

What the data indicates is that we have what has been described as a double burden of diseases—communicable diseases continue to be important causes of death, although increasingly non-communicable diseases are dominating. What is also extremely interesting is that non-communicable diseases such as hypertension and diabetes are increasingly prevalent among populations suffering from chronic undernutrition, and are not, therefore, classically susceptible to these. WHO (2006) notes that undernutrition is a double burden for poor people, as the poorest groups in the society have high rates of both undernutrition and obesity. In Asian countries, between 3 and 15 per cent of households have both an overweight and underweight person, usually an underweight child and an overweight adult. These households are most often seen among the urban poor. Mohan *et al.* (2011) observe that a recent survey in Kerala reported one of the highest diabetes prevalence rates (14.6 per cent) so far in a rural setting. Even among the urban poor in north India, high rates of obesity (14 per cent), dyslipidaemia (27 per cent), and diabetes (10.3 per cent) have been reported (ibid.). Such non-communicable diseases also lead to distress financing and very high levels of health expenditures. For instance, catastrophic expenditure among poor people who suffered acute coronary syndrome in Kerala was as high as 92 per cent (ibid.). In short, the conventional thinking here of 'life style' causes begs to be re-thought.

MATERNAL HEALTH

Although reliable national estimates of maternal mortality are not available for many countries, South Asia is believed to have among the highest MMRs in the world. Within the South-Asian region too, India has higher MMRs than her neighbours, Sri Lanka and Pakistan. Despite the fact that maternal health and mortality were issues of serious concern that partly motivated the launch of the family planning programme in India, MMR continues to be extraordinarily high. That is to say, gender disadvantage becomes particularly marked during the reproductive years. The latest maternal mortality estimates by UNFPA published in a report titled 'Trends in Maternal Mortality: 1990 to 2010' shows that globally, the total number of maternal deaths decreased from 543,000 in 1990 to 287,000 in 2010. Likewise, the global MMR declined from 400 maternal deaths per 100,000 live births in 1990 to 210 in 2010, representing an average annual decline of 3.1 per cent. At the country level, India and Nigeria accounted for a third of global maternal deaths, with India at 19 per cent (56,000) and Nigeria at 14 per cent (40,000). Between 1990 and 2010, India managed a reduction of 66 per cent in MMR. While this may seem significant, one has to add that in the same period, Maldives (93 per cent), Bhutan (82 per cent), Iran (81 per cent), Nepal (78 per cent), and Bangladesh (70 per cent) did much better on this front (UNFPA 2012).

One of the MDGs is the reduction of maternal mortality. For India, this means that by 2015 the MMR should be reduced by 75 per cent from the all-India 2000 figure of about 425 maternal deaths per 100,000 live births.[1] The data below indicate that we are way off the mark and unlikely to achieve anything even close. Table 5.7 presents the data on the MMRs among the major states in the country.

Table 5.7 Maternal Mortality Ratio in India and Major States, 2007–9

India	212
Andhra Pradesh	134
Assam	390
Bihar	261
Chhattisgarh	269
Gujarat	148
Haryana	153
Jharkhand	261
Karnataka	178
Kerala	81
Madhya Pradesh	269
Maharashtra	104
Odisha	258
Punjab	172
Rajasthan	318
Tamil Nadu	97
Uttar Pradesh	359
West Bengal	145

Source: GoI 2011c.

The states of Assam (390), Uttar Pradesh (359), Rajasthan (318), Madhya Pradesh (269), and Odisha (258) have amongst the highest MMRs in the world, higher even than Sub-Saharan Africa, indicating that it is not merely a function of birth rates. While it is indeed the case that the MMR is extremely high in India, it is also the case that this is primarily due to the poor health status of women in general. In all age groups, causes related to pregnancy account for 12 per cent of all deaths. In other words, causes other than pregnancy and childbirth account for the larger proportion of deaths, so that solutions to the problem focusing on maternal deaths alone would be to miss the woods for the trees (Qadeer 1998). For instance, more women who are not pregnant die due to causes associated with anaemia than pregnant women. Similarly, deaths due to communicable diseases far outweigh that due to maternal mortality.

The trend of major causes of maternal death in rural India over a period of time shows no significant changes. Haemorrhage and sepsis top the direct cause list, and anaemia the indirect. Abortion-related deaths show a downward trend, while toxaemia and malposition of the foetus remain almost at the same level. In short, they attest not only to the poor health status of women in general, but to the lack of adequate health facilities during pregnancy and childbirth, in particular the lack of emergency obstetric care. It is, however, imperative to bear in mind that it is not just any woman who dies during pregnancy and childbirth. It is likely to be a woman, still young, above all poor, probably from the Dalit, Adivasi, or other backward communities, with little access to health care. The health worker does not bother about her health unless she is a target for family planning. She avoids the public health system for a variety of reasons—inconvenient timings, unavailability of doctors and medicines, and the fact that she is harshly treated. She prefers a private doctor, often a quack, who treats her with an injection and perhaps a long list of drugs in a prescription she cannot afford to fill. This happens repeatedly over a period of time when she is always kicked around between a collapsing public health system and an exploitative private health care system. The family would have gone through extraordinary efforts to collect funds for her, selling whatever assets they possess. Desperately ill, she finally dies at the government hospital in the nearest town. She is, in all probability, a landless agricultural labourer with extraordinarily low wages. She would have been born poor, undernourished, and politically powerless. Managing somehow to survive, she is married early, underfed, and anaemic, and working herself to the bone to maintain her family. She would also have suffered infant and child deaths, in addition to repeated pregnancies.

It is a commonplace assumption that maternal deaths among such populations is either due to ignorance or the fact that medical care is delayed. This assumption is seriously flawed because it ignores the extraordinary efforts families make, as several studies have shown, to save the lives of women (Basu 2006). This is not surprising given the salient role women play in both production for the family and its reproduction. The assumption, above all, ignores the enormous structural constraints to health care access and the fact that not enough efforts have been made to ease them, especially for marginalized populations. Indeed, this assumption is a convenient form of victim blaming. See Box 5.1.

REPRODUCTIVE HEALTH

India commenced MCH and family planning services in the First Five Year Plan. Indeed, India was one of the first countries in the world to initiate an official policy and programme for family planning. During the initial years, the focus was on antenatal care and training of traditional birth attendants to provide safe deliveries, along with family planning, which has always stood at the heart of the programme, its raison d'etre. Subsequently, under the Child Survival and Safe Motherhood (CSSM) programme launched in 1992, the focus was on encouraging institutional deliveries, along with the Universal Immunization Programme (UIP). These programmes have been integrated into the Reproductive and Child Health Programme launched in 1996.

Despite these initiatives, however, as the data we surveyed earlier revealed, they have failed to have the expected impact in reducing the MMR or indeed the IMR and Child Mortality Rate (CMR). The NFHS III

Box 5.1 The Grass Widows of Bihar

In Rasiabharna village in Darbhanga district, for example, none of the 15 grass widows interviewed had ever received any pre natal or post natal assistance from the health centre in the village. Nor were they aware of such facilities. Only two were immunized against tetanus during their last pregnancy and that too by quacks. The absence of tetanus vaccination is especially significant in view of the fact that a majority of the deliveries here are carried out at home, mostly by family members or untrained *dais* or traditional birth attendants, locally also known as *chamains*. It is not as though government services are completely absent from the rural areas of Bihar. The government, in fact, makes its presence felt in a big way for family planning and for pulse polio vaccination—which only puzzles the villagers. 'Everyone asks me to protect my child from polio, but I say polio will pose a threat only if my child survives diarrhoea,' complains Bachia Devi of Kiratpur village.

Bachia, an illiterate grass widow, works as an agricultural labourer, while her husband is an agricultural labourer in Punjab, who returns to the village occasionally. They belong to the musahir sub-caste of Dalits, those who eat mice to survive. Bachia supports her in-laws and her children on her appalling wages, which is much less than the stipulated agricultural wage. She is hardly able to feed herself and is grossly anaemic. Her husband's wages, when he sends them, go to pay off the middleman who recruited him to work in Punjab. She has lost four babies due to diarrhoea. The fourth baby died six days after receiving pulse polio drops. Bachia now refuses to get her fifth child—1-year-old Banaiya—vaccinated. An unknown fear grips Bachia whenever polio vaccinators visit her hut. For her, polio is not a life-taking disease but diarrhoea is.

Source: Jha 2004.

provides data indicating that MCH performance and coverage has been extremely unsatisfactory. Despite some improvements, they fall far short of targets.

There are also significant disparities between states. Goa, Kerala, and Tamil Nadu consistently rank in the top five while Uttar Pradesh, Bihar, and Rajasthan show a consistently poor performance. Women not receiving antenatal checkups are spread disproportionately from among the Dalits, Adivasis, and OBCs. The likelihood of having received antenatal care at all, as well as antenatal care from a doctor, increases sharply with the household's wealth index. Among mothers in households with the lowest wealth quintile, 59 per cent received antenatal care and only 23 per cent received antenatal care from a doctor. By contrast, among mothers in households in the highest wealth quintile, 97 per cent received antenatal care and 86 per cent received antenatal care from doctors. Only 12 per cent of births to women in the lowest wealth quintile households were assisted by a doctor, compared with 78 per cent of births to women in households in the highest wealth quintile. In addition, just 17 per cent of births to women who belong to STs were assisted by a doctor, compared with 47 per cent of births to women who belong to the general category (IIPS 2007).

Similarly, according to the NFHS III, vaccination coverage under the UIP left a lot to be desired. In urban areas, just 57 per cent of children had received all immunizations by 12 months of age, while in rural areas only 38.6 per cent had. There is very little improvement in full immunization coverage between NFHS II in 1998–9 (42 per cent) and NFHS III in 2005–6 (44 per cent). Also, NFHS III found that only 24 per cent of children from households in the lowest wealth quintile were fully vaccinated, compared with 71 per cent of children from households in the highest wealth quintile. It also found that a smaller proportion of Muslim children (36 per cent) were fully vaccinated than children of any other religion, who range in coverage from 44 to 67 per cent. Also, a much smaller percentage of ST children (31 per cent) were fully vaccinated than those belonging to any other status.

Boys (45.3 per cent) were more likely to have received immunization than girls (41.5 per cent). Only 26.1 per cent of children of illiterate mothers were fully immunized, as compared with 75.2 per cent of children of mothers who had completed high school. Dalit children (39.7 per cent), Adivasi children (31.3 per cent), and OBC children (40.7 per cent) are less likely to be immunized than others (53.8 per cent). Only 24.4 per cent of children from households with a low standard of living were fully immunized as compared with 71 per cent of children from households with a high standard of living. Immunization coverage ranges from 21 per cent in Uttar Pradesh to 80.9 per cent in Tamil Nadu among the major states. In short, not only are there marked differences in health status, the health system mirrors these with differential outreach and performance.

Critics have argued that one reason for the failure of MCH programmes, indeed for a host of other programmes, has been the focus on vertical programmes in general and the family planning programmes in particular (Rao 2004). However, the TFR has declined over the years along with a decrease in mortality. Here again, interstate differentials are striking—India's TFR, according to SRS 2010 figures, is 2.5. While 21 states and union territories—Andaman and Nicobar Islands, Goa, Puducherry, Manipur, Tamil Nadu, Kerala, Tripura, Chandigarh, Andhra Pradesh, Himachal Pradesh, Jammu and Kashmir, West Bengal, Punjab, Delhi, Maharashtra, Daman and Diu, Karnataka, Mizoram, Nagaland, Sikkim, and Lakshadweep—have already achieved the replacement level, 8 states have TFR between 2.1 and 3.0. Only six states/union territories—Bihar, Uttar Pradesh, Rajasthan, Madhya Pradesh, Meghalaya, and Dadra and Nagar Haveli—have TFR more than 3.0 (GoI 2011f). The TFR has declined from 5.2 to 4.5 during 1971 to 1981 and from 3.6 to 2.5 during 1991 to 2010. The TFR in rural areas has declined from 5.4 to 2.8 from 1971 to 2010 whereas the corresponding decline in urban areas has been from 4.1 to 1.9 during the same period (GoI 2012a). At present, a rural woman (with a TFR of 2.8) at the national level would have about one child more than an urban woman (with a TFR of 1.9), on average. In other words, as could be expected, states which are lagging behind in the epidemiological transition and have a weak health care delivery system, are also the states lagging behind significantly in the demographic transition. It is nevertheless significant that the fertility for the whole country has declined significantly. The TFR for the country declined by 1.3 points (down by more than a child); the rural TFR by 1.3 points and urban TFR by 0.9 point over the last two decades. Thus, current policy initiatives, especially those initiated by several states, focusing on a two-child norm to be encouraged through punitive disincentives and targets and are not only in contravention of the National Population Policy (NPP), but also seriously misplaced (Rao 2010). Interestingly, the latest NFHS figures reveal that the fertility rate that is currently sought, 2.13, is lower by just 0.47 child (that is by just about 20 per cent) than the current TFR of 2.6. This is to say, if unwanted births could be reduced, the TFR would drop to the replacement level of fertility. Indeed, this is acknowledged in the NPP, which therefore marks as its priority, meeting the unmet need for health and family planning.

A study carried out in five states (Andhra Pradesh, Haryana, Odisha, Rajasthan, and Madhya Pradesh) indicated that the fall out of the imposition of the two-child norm on Panchayati Raj Institutions (PRIs) had been exactly as anticipated. The largest number of cases of disqualification from contesting elections was with reference to this law. Women formed 41 per cent of those disqualified. Dalits, Adivasis, and OBCs formed an overwhelming 80 per cent of those disqualified. The study also found no evidence to support the contention that the law induced adoption of the small family norm, nor indeed that members of the PRIs were seen as role models. What it did find was evidence of desertion of wives, denial of paternity, neglect of female infants, non-registration of births and non-immunization of daughters to avoid registration. Equally significantly, there was evidence of forced abortions and pre-birth elimination of females (Mahila Chetna Manch 2004). In short, the framers of this law utterly ignored how patriarchy and class intersect in India, to deny women and the marginalized communities a place in the sun. Indeed, that the law itself serves to further victimize them.

What is also important to acknowledge is that given the age structure of the population, population growth will continue despite the fall in the birth rate due to what demographers call momentum, that is, the effect of a young age structure caused by high population growth rates in the recent past. With a large proportion of the population—almost 60 per cent—below the age of 30, further growth of population is inevitable, unless of course mortality increases, which cannot be the aim of policy. Population momentum continues to contribute as much as two-thirds of current population growth.

Health Finances

The Indian health system is plagued with serious problems such as sharp inequalities in health, insufficient coverage, unequal access, poor quality, and costly health care services. These serious deficiencies are not fortuitous. They have been primarily caused by the patterns of financing of health in India. It has been shown that per capita public health spending is an extremely significant variable affecting life expectancy at birth across Indian states. According to calculations by Choudhury and Kumar (2011), the association between per capita gross

state domestic product (GSDP) and life expectancy at birth disappears with the inclusion of per capita public health spending. It was added that factors such as the priority assigned to health, equitable provisioning and reach of health services, quality of health care, the institutional milieu in which service delivery takes place, and complementary investments in sectors other than health, such as basic education, nutrition, sanitation, and water, are equally important (ibid.).

One extremely important cause for the high morbidity and mortality rates in the country, along with, of course, widespread hunger and poverty, is the shockingly low public investment in health. As the National Health Policy (NHP) itself acknowledged, 'public health investment over the years has been comparatively low, and as a percentage of GDP, has declined from 1.3 per cent in 1990 to 0.9 per cent in 1999' (GoI 2002b: 7). As Table 5.8 reveals, health expenditure has declined as a proportion of the total plan from 3.3 per cent in the First Plan to 1.9 per cent in the Eleventh Plan. In GDP terms, according to Deolikar et al. (2008), public spending on health in India peaked at about 1.6 per cent of GDP and 4 per cent of the government budget in the mid-1980s. During the 1990s, government health spending failed to keep up with the expanding economy, and by 2001 it constituted 0.9 per cent of GDP and 2.7 per cent of the government budget. These numbers fell to 0.8 per cent and 2.4 per cent, respectively, by 2005. However, from the 2006–7 budget this trend got somewhat reversed with increased allocations to social sectors. Compared to health expenditures, family planning expenditures have shown a relative increase. What is also striking is the decline in the allocation to control of communicable diseases.

This proportion of health expenditure is below the average of low-income countries and even Sub-Saharan Africa. The average health expenditure, as a proportion of GDP for low-income countries, is 1 per cent, while the average in countries of Sub-Saharan Africa is 1.7 per cent (World Bank 2000). More significantly perhaps, India has one of the highest levels of private financing of health care expenses, with out-of-pocket expenditure estimated to account for 78 per cent of total expenditures. Indeed, only a handful of very poor countries show a higher proportion of private funding (GoI 2009). Interestingly, it was found that most of (74 per cent) the out-of-pocket expenditure was incurred for outpatient treatment. Drugs accounted for 72 per cent of the total private out-of-pocket expenditure (Kumar et al. 2011).

The high proportion of regressive funding for health care implies that the poor, who often have greatest need

Table 5.8   Expenditure on Health and Family Welfare

Period	Plan Outlay on Health and Family Welfare in Different Plan Periods					
	Health	Family welfare	Sub-total	Total plan	% of health to total	% of family welfare to total
First Plan (1951–6)	65.2	0.1	65.3	1,960	3.33	0.01
Second Plan (1956–61)	140.8	5	145.8	4,672	3.01	0.11
Third Plan (1961–6)	225.9	24.9	250.8	8,576.50	2.6	0.3
Annual Plan (1966–9)	140.2	70.4	210.6	6,625.4	2.1	1.1
Fourth Plan (1969–74)	335.5	278.0	613.5	15,778.8	2.1	1.8
Fifth Plan (1974–9)	760.8	491.8	1,252.6	39,426.2	1.9	1.2
Annual Plan (1979–80)	223.1	118.5	341.6	12,176.5	1.8	1.0
Sixth Plan (1980–5)	1,821.0	1,010.0	2,831.0	97,500.0	1.9	1.0
Seventh Plan (1985–90)	3,392.9	3,256.3	6,649.2	1,80,000.0	1.9	1.8
Annual Plans						
1990–1	960.9	784.9	1,745.8	61,518.1	1.6	1.3
1991–2	1,042.3	856.6	1,898.9	65,855.8	1.6	1.3
Eighth Plan (1992–7)	7,575.9	6,500.0	14,075.9	434,100.0	1.7	1.5
Ninth Plan (1997–2002)	12, 073.0	14,170.0	26,243	859,200.0	1.4	1.6
Tenth Plan (2002–7)	31,020.0	27,125.0	58,920.0	1,484,131.0	2.1	1.8
Eleventh Plan (2007–12)	41,092.92	90,558.00	136,147.00	2,156,571.00	1.9	4.2

Source: GoI 2011c and 2012b.

for health services, and the least ability to pay for them, bear the highest proportion of health care costs. Selvaraj and Karan using the norm of one dollar poverty line, calculate that during 1999–2000, approximately 32 million people in India were pushed below the poverty line due to high out-of-pocket payments for health care (Selvaraj and Karan 2012).

Total health expenditure from all the sources was Rs 1,337,763 million during 2004–5, constituting 4.25 per cent of the GDP. Of the total health expenditure, the share of the private sector was at the maximum with 78.05 per cent, the public sector at 19.67, while external flows contributed 2.28 per cent (GoI 2009). In India, the states typically account for about 75 per cent of total public spending on health, with the rest being borne by the centre. The proportion of health expenditure in the major states, which was in the range of 6–7 per cent during the 1980s, came down to about 5 per cent during the 1990s, the decade of the reforms. Even in the post-NRHM era, when the centre has started putting in more funds for health, it was observed that there would be state fund fungibility in that state governments tend to substitute their health sector funding with that of central funding (Duggal 2009).

Table 5.9 provides data on per capita public spending on health among the major states. As is evident, Bihar has the least spending followed by Uttar Pradesh, Madhya Pradesh, Assam, and Odisha. A substantial proportion, close to 80 per cent of these state expenditures are, however, geared towards payment of salaries alone, especially in the BIMARU (Bihar, Madhya Pradesh, Rajasthan, and Uttar Pradesh) states. This, of course, is indicative of not high salaries to personnel, but the remarkably low spending on health. Clearly, low public spending is not only related to poor health system performance and outreach, it is also a primary reason for high private sector reliance and regressive and high out-of-pocket expenditures.

Here then, it seems, lies the singular explanation for poor performance in the health sector—poor public sector spending. These are of course a result of political decisions made over this period, which was accompanied by a squeeze on finances. This is a consequence of reforms of the health sector, when issues of governance came to the fore. As in many other countries, then, reforms were slated to increase health inequalities and were not fortuitous outcomes of the policy process. Again, these decisions were in line with policy prescriptions emerging out of the World Bank and institutions owing allegiance

Table 5.9   Per Capita Public and Private Expenditure in Health by States and Union Territories, 2004–5

	Expenditure (in Rs '000)			Expenditure (in Rs)		In %	
	Public expenditure	Private expenditure	Total expenditure	Per capita public	Per capita private	Public expenditure as share of GSDP	Public expenditure as share of state expenditure
Major states							
Andhra Pradesh	15,166,809	69,133,745	84,300,554	191	870	0.72	3.22
Assam	4,546,276	17,217,791	21,764,067	162	612	0.86	3.08
Bihar	8,264,168	37,256,449	45,520,617	93	420	1.12	4.12
Gujarat	10,673,668	40,606,301	51,279,969	198	755	0.57	3.06
Haryana	4,609,237	19,866,486	24,475,723	203	875	0.49	3.19
Himachal Pradesh	4,003,601	5,598,467	9,602,068	630	881	1.74	4.98
Karnataka	12,901,254	33,041,496	45,942,750	233	557	0.87	3.77
Kerala	9,431,012	87,545,011	96,976,023	287	2663	0.88	4.65
Madhya Pradesh	9,375,858	41,694,492	51,070,350	145	644	0.87	3.19
Maharashtra	20,900,906	103,402,991	124,303,897	204	1008	0.55	2.88
Odisha	7,010,724	27,553,390	34,564,114	183	719	0.98	4.41
Punjab	6,322,375	28,456,190	34,778,565	247	1112	0.65	3.01
Rajasthan	11,283,333	34,868,833	46,152,166	186	575	0.98	3.90
Tamil Nadu	14,334,228	66,562,101	80,896,329	223	1033	0.71	3.43
Uttar Pradesh	22,805,122	151,006,063	173,811,185	128	846	0.92	3.86
West Bengal	14,485,984	91,102,485	105,588,469	173	1086	0.69	4.32

Source: GoI 2009.

to it. The squeeze on resources for primary health care is the single most important factor for the dismal state of primary health care services in the country. This is not to deny that tertiary health care needed substantial strengthening. However, to draw attention to the fact this has occurred at the cost of lower levels of health care.

It is often argued that one reason why the government has introduced expenditure cuts is that there is a squeeze on government finances. Over the 1990s, the government was either less willing or unwilling to collect taxes even at levels that existed before the onset of reforms. Thus the tax GDP ratio had declined from more than 13 per cent in 1990–1 to 9 per cent in 2000–1. Lately, tax/GDP ratio has improved substantially, supported by a robust economic growth rate of 8–9 per cent in GDP. However, there has not been a corresponding increase in health investments. India also has a huge amount of uncollected revenues in terms of corporate tax exemptions that amounts to many times the entire expenditure on public health, medicine, and family welfare by the central and state governments combined.

It is a fact that investments in health have started receiving a higher priority primarily because of the perceived role that good health of the working population in accelerating and sustaining economic growth, and also to a lesser extent because of the growing recognition of health as a human right (Choudhury and Shiva Kumar 2011). The GoI announced in 2005 that public spending on health will be stepped up from the current level of 1 per cent of GDP to 3 per cent over the next five to seven years. The Working Group on Health Care Financing, including Health Insurance for the Eleventh Five Year Plan in 2006, the Approach Paper to the Eleventh Five Year Plan in 2006, the Eleventh Five Year Plan document (2007–12), the High Level Expert Group of the Planning Commission on Universal Care in its report in 2011, as well as the Steering Committee on Health for the Twelfth Five Year Plan—all of these endorse the target of 3 per cent of GDP to health. In all probability the Twelfth Five Year Plan document too will have it. However, to achieve that these projections, calculations reveal that the nominal per capita health expenditures will have to go up from Rs 267 in 2005–6 to Rs 2,430 by the target year—which is 2015 by the current consensus (ibid.). At the current rate, it is, however, clear that such eventuality is highly unlikely.

PRIVATE SECTOR IN HEALTH CARE

Any generalization about the private sector in the country would be hazardous, if not foolish, since it comprises a large and heterogeneous group of actors and institutions. On the one hand are state-of-the-art super-speciality corporate hospitals in urban areas that even the middle classes find difficult to access, and which are the hub of the health tourism industry that the government promotes. On the other hand are the vast numbers of ill-qualified individual practitioners who provide the bulk of curative care in the country, primary level care in particular. Between the two, is a range of not-for profit non-governmental organizations (NGOs), trusts, charitable and religious institutions providing medical and health care. A growing concern is that some of these have recently changed character and ought to be classified as for-profit institutions. At the same time, a number of high-tech, for-profit hospitals are registered as trusts and research centres to avail of tax concessions.

As the Tenth Plan document notes, there is no uniform nation-wide system of registering either practitioners or institutions in the private sector. Nor is there any system for obtaining and analysing information about this large sector (GoI 2002b). After 2002, the government stopped compiling and disseminating data on the private health sector. Studies on the private sector in India are thus plagued by unavailability of data, with the sector unwilling, by and large, to share data with even academic investigators.

Based on admittedly unreliable available data, one study estimates that 93 per cent of hospitals and 64 per cent of hospital beds in India are in the private sector (Nandraj 2000). Available government data on the growth and share of private and public sector hospitals and beds in the country clearly reveal that the share of private hospitals has increased remarkably between 1974 and 2002, while that of beds has shown an increase, although not as significant as in the number of institutions.[2] While there are exceptions, the majority of these are small institutions, with 85 per cent of them with less than 25 beds. Most such institutions offer maternity and general services, and are managed by doctor entrepreneurs. Tertiary speciality and super-speciality private institutions comprise only 1 to 2 per cent of the private sector institutions (GoI 2002b). The distribution of private sector facilities and doctors between states and regions is even more inequitable than the public health facilities, reflecting the tendency to concentrate in better-off states and in better-off regions (Dantas 2011). In the case of public services, the rural–urban divide is shown in Figure 5.3. It is clear that while beds are concentrated in urban areas, hospitals are not. Similar national-level data is not available for private hospitals. However, what is to

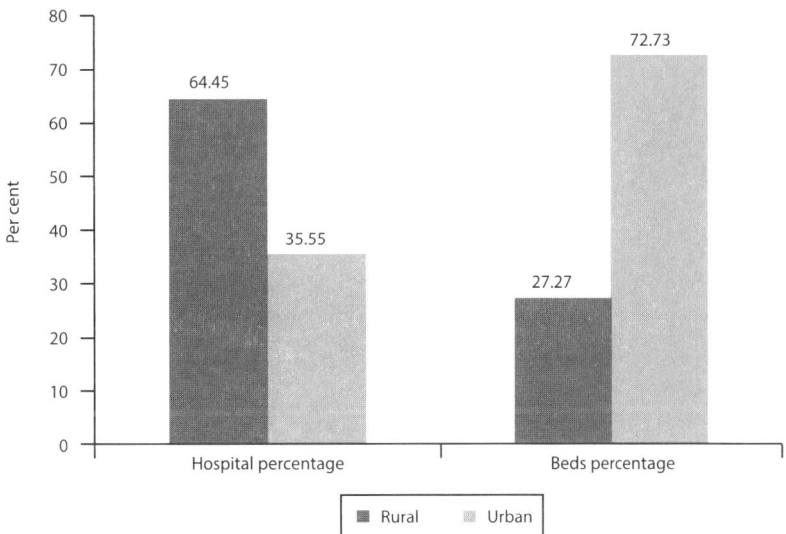

Figure 5.3   Distribution of Hospitals/Hospital Beds, Public, 2010
Source: GoI 2011d.

be remembered is that given the varied nature of private health care as a category, the bulk of medical care in rural areas, and a not-insignificant amount in urban areas, is provided by unqualified medical practitioners, estimated to be about one million. While the quality of medical care is said to be dubious, this is not a characterization that sticks to the unqualified medical practitioners alone. Figure 5.4 shows that in the year 2002—the last year where such figures are available—74 per cent hospitals as well as 38 per cent of beds were in the private sector. This figure suggests that across states the average size of a private hospital may be much less than the average size of a government hospital.

The private sector today dominates the public in both inpatient care and in outpatient care. The reasons for this are many, and include the fact that medicines are not available in the public sector and indeed there are significant shortfalls of human power. It is also due to the preoccupation of public health services with the vertical programmes in general and the family planning programme in particular. Data from the National Sample Survey's (NSS) 60th Round show that reasons for preference to the private sector for treatment as compared to the government varies across rural and urban areas. The main reason, 'Not satisfied with medical treatment by govt doctor/facilities', contributes nearly 41 per cent and 45 per cent in rural and urban areas, respectively. Twenty-one per cent in rural and 14 per cent in urban settings have reported 'distance' as the reason for not availing gov-

ernment services in 2004. 'Long waiting' was the reason in 8 per cent of rural and 16 per cent in urban settings. Other reasons, including non-availability of facilities and specific services, contribute 30 per cent and 26 per cent in rural and urban areas, respectively (GoI 2007).

The private sector accounts for around 80 per cent of all outpatient care at the all-India level and more than 60 per cent of all inpatient care. However, immunizations and ante-natal care are overwhelmingly provided by public sector facilities. There are also significant interstate variations. The better-off states with a well-developed private sector such as Maharashtra, Kerala, Haryana, and Punjab show more utilization of private facilities. On the other hand, poorer states with poorly spread private facilities continue to show the predominance of the public sector. Across the country, an interesting finding which perhaps explains the increasing neglect of public health is that the middle classes have now forsaken the public sector (Baru 1998). It is this class, which is increasingly 'seceding' from the nation, that provides the social base for the health sector reforms of increasing privatization under way.

With substantial sections of the population utilizing private health care facilities, the costs of such care assumes great importance, especially as the NHP notes that households typically reduce their spending on essential needs, including nutritional ones, in order to access medical care. Indeed, as we already noted, medical care costs have emerged as a leading cause of indebtedness in

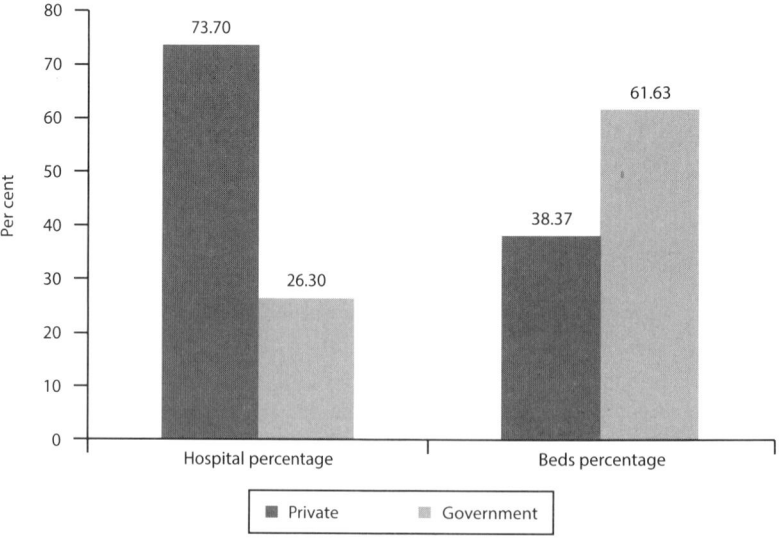

Figure 5.4   Distribution of Hospitals/Hospital Beds, Public and Private Sectors, 2002
Source: GoI 2003.

the population. The difference in costs between the private and public sector varies significantly across states, with a sharp rise in medical costs across the board. Over the last two decades, the proportion of untreated ailments due to financial reasons has been going up continuously. The largest proportions untreated due to this reason are from Maharashtra, Rajasthan, West Bengal, and Karnataka (GoI 2007).

The situation is bad even for outpatient treatment. As GoI (ibid.) indicates, in urban India, 9 per cent of the non-hospitalized treatments are met by borrowing, sale of assets, etc. This was as high as 25 per cent for the lowest group of the class with Monthly Per Capita Expenditure (MPCE) less than Rs 300. Fifteen per cent of the SC and OBC depended on borrowing/sale of assets in urban areas for meeting the expenses of non-hospitalized treatment. Clearly, this cannot be allowed to continue on grounds of equity, if not for epidemiological considerations.

There is a general assumption that private medical care is of a vastly superior quality than that provided in the public sector. There is, however, little empirical data to substantiate this claim. A study of private hospitals in Chennai revealed that this sector has grown without any state policy to regulate its growth and development. As a result, the sector had grown without any regard to norms for infrastructure. There has also developed a complex network of private hospitals and physicians with diagnostic centres involved in policies of 'scalping'. It also shows a strong tendency to over-provide care, depending on the patient's ability to pay (Muraleedharan 1999). Another study of the private sector in rural Maharashtra revealed that only 55 per cent had registration, only 38 per cent maintained records of any kind, and that a remarkably high proportion lacked basic facilities. It also showed that close to 30 per cent were being run by doctors not trained in the allopathic system of medicine; they were being run without adequate facilities and human power, with only 2 per cent employing trained nurses. Of the hospitals, 39 per cent operated without a full-time doctor. Only 10 per cent of hospitals had an ECG monitor, 65 per cent a sterilizer, and 56 per cent an oxygen cylinder (Nandraj and Duggal 1997). Yet another study found that caesarean sections were performed three times more in private hospitals than public ones (Homan and Thankappan 1999). A study in Mumbai reported widespread malpractices, with cutbacks for referrals—the scalping referred to—of the order of 40 per cent of the fees charged by laboratories and specialists. It also found widespread false billing and irrational treatment practices (Yesudian n.d.).

A study of prescription practices in Satara district found a high proportion of irrational prescriptions among doctors in both the public and private sectors. Although doctors with postgraduate degrees tended to use a higher proportion of rational drugs, they also tend to prescribe more drugs than necessary. Public sector prescriptions were more rational than private sector prescriptions. Indeed, irrational prescriptions in the private sector were more than double that in the public (Phadke et al. 1995). Another study by CEHAT in 2011 of 261 nursing homes (less than 30 beds) from 11 districts of Maharashtra found that found that most hospitals did not fulfil the minimum requirements as laid down in the law. The study found that 56 per cent of the hospitals under study did not have a single qualified nurse, more than 50 per cent hospitals did not have a resident doctor, and only 14 of 114 maternity homes had a midwife (Bhate-Deosthali and Khatri 2011).

One undoubted contribution of the private sector, especially during the period of reforms, has been the sharp masculinization of the sex ratio at birth as we saw earlier. This is of course a gift to the upwardly mobile classes—eliminating daughters before birth. For example, in 2001 Delhi's CSR stood at 868 girls per 1,000 boys; in 2011, the number of girls has fallen to 866. The ratio is also alarmingly lower than the national average of 914 girls per 1,000 boys. The CSR was lowest in the southwest district—which includes relatively affluent areas such as Vasant Vihar, Vasant Kunj, Delhi Cantonment, R.K. Puram, Moti Bagh, and others—in 2001. In 2011, not only has it continued to be the lowest, but also fell further by 10 points (Express News Service 2011). This well-off and educated population was thus achieving population stabilization, at the cost of population balance.

Perhaps the most telling comment on the private sector was during the plague epidemic in Surat of 1994. The epidemic itself is partly attributed to the decay of the public health system, including the slashing of budgets for the control of communicable diseases (Qadeer et al. 1994). But once the epidemic commenced, it was observed that the majority of private practitioners fled the city, while the government doctors tried, with hands tied with lack of medicines and funds, to fight the epidemic (Shah 1997).

Thus, issues of quality of care that plague the public sector are not unique to it. Indeed the private sector provides the lead and sets norms for a culture of medicalization that the public sector is often forced to emulate. Yet, without taking many of the systemic factors that ail the public sector into account, efforts at reforms in the health sector all too often are facile and simplistic, and involve increasing public subsidies to the private sector. While the private sector has thus grown its quality, outcomes and cost have not been issues coming under a strong regulatory mechanism.

HEALTH SECTOR REFORMS

Citing inefficiencies of the public system and financial stringency, India commenced health sector reforms. What was not clearly articulated was that these moves were initiated at the behest of international financial institutions to which we were indebted. The mantra was of course that of better efficiency. This section briefly surveys the experience from the last two decades.

The data reviewed on the health scenario and of the health system in India unfortunately project a none-too-happy picture. A small study, widely quoted, for example, reveals the dismal state of public health services, even as it indicates that people spend substantially on health care largely provided by unqualified persons in the private sector where services were even worse (Banerjee *et al.* 2004). Yet, over the 1990s as India embarked upon the structural adjustment programme, as we saw earlier, state spending on health declined. The decline in public investments was matched with growing subsidies to the private sector in health care in a variety of ways. What is interesting is that while wide-ranging reforms in the health sector were initiated, the NHP itself makes no reference to this important policy change.

In essence, the reforms intend to reduce the role of the state in provisioning of health care, while confining its role to that of regulation and that of a financier of care provided by the private sector. The efforts underway in India could thus be seen as part of much larger processes shaping the health sector globally; in developing countries at the instance of international financial institutions. Given the fact, however, of the desperate poverty of large sections of the population, of the widespread prevalence of hunger, of the huge morbidity and mortality loads, and the abysmal role of the state in health sector provisions in the country, the direction of such reforms as carried out in other countries further curtail health care access to the poor.

Health sector reforms in India have taken a variety of forms aimed at improving efficiency and effectiveness, and the quality of care provided by public health services. Some of these include contracting, various public–private partnerships of dubious credibility involved directly in health care provision, user fees in public health facilities, and privatization of public facilities. In a sense, govern-ment was investing its efforts in creating push factors in the public sector, and, at the same time, pull factors in the private sector, through various engagements involving direct and indirect subsidies.

Contracting has emerged as an important new mechanism for improving the efficiency of services in the public health sector. Some or all aspects of health facilities and functions could be contracted out to private parties, including clinical, para-clinical, and non-clinical functions. The rationale for contracting was that it reduced costs, introduced greater flexibility in the use of labour, or could be utilized to provide services in areas that were under-served. In India contracting has been initiated under the blindness programme, the AIDS control programme, and franchising arrangements have been set up with private providers under the Revised National Tuberculosis Control Programme (RNTCP) (Nandraj *et al.* 2001). Many non-clinical support services in public hospitals have also been contracted out. The PHCs have been contracted to NGOs; indeed this was the suggestion of an influential World Bank (1995) document.

There is not enough documentation on the transfer of public health facilities to private providers on a contract basis. One recent case involves the transfer of ownership of a public tertiary care hospital in Mumbai as part of a state health system project funded by the World Bank (Nandraj *et al.* 2001). The municipal corporation of Mumbai has taken a policy decision to hand over many of its peripheral hospitals to the private sector. In a controversial move, a peripheral hospital was also handed over to a private medical college that did not have the necessary clinical facilities; the Medical Council of India had not recognized the concerned medical college. Other cities, such as Ahmedabad, have handed over facilities to NGOs.

The nature of the contract between government and the private sector has always been asymmetric and skewed towards the latter (Datta 2009). There have been many instances where services had been contracted without any accountability in the form of clear deliverables. Most of these arrangements were so arbitrary that the contracts had no clauses for exit or even penalty. It was noticed that there are no standard treatment protocols nor were there any provisions for grievance redressal. It was also found that there was no transparency in these processes, as no criteria had been set out at all. In a recent review which covered 30 public–private partnerships in reproductive health services in India, Sundari Ravindran observed that barring a handful, there exist very few assessments of the contribution of such partnerships. This is especially true of partnerships that do not involve the GoI or state governments. Being completely private initiatives, it is not clear who the projects are accountable to. A comprehensive assessment of these initiatives is a crying need (Ravindran 2011).

It is still too early to assess the benefits and pitfalls of these experiments but they need to be examined for the benefits, if any, they bring to the poor. It could be argued that this transfer of public resources to private sources represents further strengthening of a private health care system that has shown itself to be exploitative and not sensitive to wider social concerns. This does not then represent moves to improve the administrative and managerial efficiency of the public health system as a whole, but instead a simplistic response to a complex problem.

Another scheme has been the provision of a range of incentives to the private health sector through provision of land at throw-away prices, grant of customs duty exemptions for import of sophisticated medical technology, and loans from financial institutions at low interest rates. These incentives have been provided for both private for-profit and not-for-profit institutions. A study indicated that these had been utilized primarily by urban-based institutions that had not always provided free services to the poor as they were expected to as per the terms of the contractural agreement (Bhat 1998). Further, there were no mechanisms to monitor the project, with the government's limited institutional ability to do so.

Any effort to improve public health in the country must not only emphasize the important determinants of health but also the salient role of public spending. The reforms, however, singularly lack a health system perspective and instead comprise an agglomeration of projects with an implicit belief that the market will cure the problems that ail the health system.

Current Efforts to Achieve Universal Health Coverage

Universal access to health care has been in focus lately, and recently, three documents that are very significant for the future of public health in the country were released. The first being the Approach Paper to the Twelfth Five Year Plan; the second, a report that was submitted by the Planning Commission's High Level Expert Group; and the third being the report of the Steering Committee on Health for the Twelfth Plan. The general recommendations favour a 'national health package' to be implemented by public and private providers. The most likely scenario towards any expansion of health care towards universalization seems to be one through a mechanism similar to

Rashtriya Swasthya Bima Yojana (RSBY), which has been in operation for almost four years now.

While it is commendable that the Twelfth Plan Approach Paper rightly identifies many problems that plague India's health system, and even gives some suggestions in the right direction like the linking of new medical and nursing colleges to district hospitals in under-served districts and the recommendation of the Tamil Nadu Medical Services Corporation (TNMSC) as a tested model for procurement and distribution of drugs, the general course it takes is worrying indeed. There are indications that health policy is taking a direction where the focus is going to be on the private sector strengthening rather than the expansion of the public sector. The section of the approach paper, on health care financing starts with the line, 'public financing of health care does not necessarily mean provision of the service by public providers' and goes on to recommend private sector participation through a government funded health insurance plan for every citizen along the lines of the RSBY, which will provide some 'basic' universal health care.

However, this separation of provisioning and financing is bound to have a long-term impact on the health system particularly when it is accompanied with 'patient choice', 'competition', and the profit motive that is implicit in the approaches that are being promoted. In a policy atmosphere where a consensus is being reached regarding a model of care where privately provided health care is publicly financed largely through tax revenues, astonishingly, despite all evidence, a 'benign' private sector is also emerging in health policy documents—with the ability and willingness to serve the interests of the poor. Donor pressure to channelize subsidies through the private sector rather than focus on public provisioning and the mounting evidence against user charges in public facilities—another innovation that was recommended by donors, primarily the World Bank, in the 1980s to cure the ills of the Third World's health systems—have contributed to the newfound focus on insurance-based solutions.

The Steering Committee on Health for the Twelfth Five Year Plan specifically recommended leveraging 'strengths of private sector', although subject to strict checks and balances. It is very clear that the private sector is going to be the focus and the major partner in any effort to expand health coverage. It reflects the global trend where the state is increasingly shifting from being the major provider of services to financier for a minority of the poor for a selected and very limited set of needs. After RSBY was already recommended by the Planning Commission as the model on which universal care in India should be based, a pilot project is being announced in Odisha with the support of ICICI Bank where 10 outpatient visits for a family of five will be included per year in the package. It is not clear how serious issues such as supplier-induced demand, price discrimination (charging the insured more), and cost escalation that affect RSBY in many states are going to be addressed while it is scaled up.

* * *

Our survey of the health scenario in the country presents a rather bleak picture. It is, therefore, not at all surprising that the latest Human Development Report puts India at the 134th position out of a total of 187 countries (UNDP 2011). Among the 47 countries in the 'Medium Human Development' group, India is the eighth from the bottom. All this reflects well the low priority that health gets from policy planners. It points towards the crying need for substantially higher government health expenditure, which should result in a credible and accessible public health system, rather than quick fix solutions depending on the private sector.

Our health performance does not sit well with the fact that we have an elite that thinks of the country in terms of an economic powerhouse or as an emerging superpower. The task ahead is long and arduous—fulfilling the expectations of building a public health system, universal, free and comprehensive as envisaged before Independence in the Bhore Committee report.

Notes

1. The NRHM sets a target of an MMR of 100 by 2012.
2. Central Bureau of Health Intelligence reports of various years up to 2003.

References

Banerjee, A., A. Deaton, and E. Duflo. 2004. 'Health Care Delivery in Rural Rajasthan', *Economic and Political Weekly*, 39(9): 944–9.

Baru, R.V. 1998. *Private Health Care in India: Social Characteristics and Trends*. New Delhi: Sage Publications.

Basu, Alaka. 2006. 'Methodological and Cultural Assumptions Underlying Small-Scale Research on Safe Motherhood Initiatives', Paper presented at the conference 'Safe Motherhood Initiatives: Contributions from Small-Scale Studies', in Roger Jeffery, Patricia Jeffery, and Mohan Rao, 'Safe Motherhood Initiatives: Contributions from Small-Scale Studies', *Indian Journal of Gender Studies*, 14(2, May–August 2007): 285–94.

Bhat, R. 1998. 'Private Health Care Sector in India: Issues Arising out of Its Growth and the Role of the State in Strengthening Public-Private Interaction', Unpublished paper. Ahmedabad: Indian Institute of Management.

Bhate-Deosthali, Padma and Ritu Khatri. 2011. *Health Care in the Private Sector: A Study of Private Hospitals in Maharashtra*. Mumbai: Center for Enquiry into Health and Allied Themes.

Choudhury, Mita and A.K. Shiva Kumar. 2011. 'Improving India's Health: The Significance of Public Financing', in Praveen Jha (ed.), *Progressive Fiscal Policy in India*. New Delhi: Sage Publications, pp. 406–21.

Dantas, Anandi. 2011. *Mapping of Urban Health Facilities in Maharashtra*. Mumbai: Center for Enquiry into Health and Allied Themes.

Datta, A. 2009. 'Public-Private Partnerships in India: A Case for Reform?' *Economic and Political Weekly*, 44(33, August): 73–8.

Deolikar, Anil B., Dean T. Jamison, Prabhat Jha, and Ramanan Laxminarayan. 2008. 'Financing Health Improvements in India', *Health Affairs*, 27(4): 978–90.

Duggal, Ravi. 2009. 'Sinking Flagships and Health Budgets in India', *Economic and Political Weekly*, 44(33): 14–17.

Express News Service. 2011. 'Child Sex Ratio Dips Further, Southwest District Worst Hit', *Indian Express*, New Delhi.

GoI (Government of India). 1974. 'Towards Equality: The Report of the Committee on the Status of Women in India'. New Delhi: Ministry of Education and Social Welfare.

———. 1983. *National Health Policy*. New Delhi: Ministry of Health and Family Welfare.

———. 2002a. *Health Information of India 1999*. New Delhi: Ministry of Health and Family Welfare.

———. 2002b. *National Health Policy*. New Delhi: Ministry of Health and Family Welfare.

———. 2003. *The Health Information of India 2003*. New Delhi: Central Bureau of Health Intelligence.

———. 2007. *Select Health Parameters*. New Delhi: Ministry of Health and Family Welfare and World Health Organization.

———. 2009. *National Health Accounts 2004–05*. New Delhi: Ministry of Health and Family Welfare.

———. 2011a. *Sample Registration System Bulletin 2011*. New Delhi: Office of the Registrar General.

———. 2011b. *Meeting People's Health Needs in Partnership with States—The Journey So Far 2005–2010*. New Delhi: NRHM.

———. 2011c. *Family Welfare Statistics in India*. New Delhi: Ministry of Health and Family Welfare.

———. 2011d. *National Health Profile 2010*. New Delhi: Central Bureau of Health Intelligence.

———. 2011e. 'SRS Statistical Report 2010'. New Delhi: Office of the Registrar General.

———. 2011f. 'Annual Report to the People on Health'. New Delhi: Ministry of Health and Family Welfare.

GoI (Government of India). 2012a. 'Sample Registration System Statistical Report 2010'. New Delhi: Office of the Registrar General.

———. 2012b. *National Health Profile 2011*. New Delhi: Central Bureau of Health Intelligence.

Gupta, Indrani and Mayur Trivedi. 2008. 'The Slow Decline in the Infant Mortality Rate in India: Can Governance Be an Explanation?' *Journal of Health and Development*, 4(1): 87–102.

Homan, R.K. and K.R. Thankappan. 1999. *An Examination of Public and Private Sector Sources of In-patient Care in Trivandrum District, Kerala*. Thiruvananthapuram: Achuta Menon Centre for Health Services.

Husain, Zakir. 2011. 'Health of the National Rural Health Mission', *Economic and Political Weekly*, 46(4): 53–60.

IIPS (International Institute of Population Sciences). 2007. *National Family Health Survey (NFHS 3) 2005–06*. Mumbai: International Institute of Population Sciences.

Jha, Dhirendra K. 2004. 'The Grass Widows of Bihar', in Mohan Rao (ed.), *An Unheard Scream: Reproductive Health and Women's Lives in India*. New Delhi: Zubaan, pp. 67–86.

Kumar, Shiva A.K., Lincoln C. Chen, Mita Choudhury, Shiban Ganju, Vijay Mahajan, Amarjeet Sinha, and Abhijit Sen. 2011. 'Financing Health Care for All: Challenges and Opportunities', *Lancet*, 377(9766, February): 668–79.

Mohan, Sailesh, K. Srinath Reddy, and D. Prabhakaran. 2011. *Chronic Non-communicable Diseases in India: Reversing the Tide*. New Delhi: Public Health Foundation of India.

Mahila Chetna Manch. 2004. 'Two Child Policy and Its Implications for Women', Unpublished report for the Ministry of Health and Family Welfare. Bhopal.

Muraleedharan, V.R. 1999. 'Characteristics and Structure of Private Hospital Structure in Urban India: A Study of Madras City', Small Applied Area Research Paper 5, Bethesda, Washington, DC.

Nandraj, Sunil. 2000. *The Private Health Sector: Concerns, Challenges and Options*. Mumbai: Center for Enquiry into Health and Allied Themes.

Nandraj, S. and R. Duggal. 1997. *Physical Standards in the Private Health Sector—A Case Study of Rural Maharashtra*. Mumbai: Center for Enquiry into Health and Allied Themes.

Nandraj, S., V.R. Muraleedharan, R.V. Baru, I. Qadeer, and R. Priya. 2001. *Private Health Sector in India: Review and Annotated Bibliography*. Mumbai: Center for Enquiry into Health and Allied Themes.

Navaneetham, K. and A. Dharmalingam. 2011. 'Demography and Development: Preliminary Interpretations of the 2011 Census', *Economic and Political Weekly*, 46(16): 13–17.

Phadke, Anant, Audrey Fernandez, L. Sharda, Pratibha Mane, and Amar Jesani. 1995. *A Study of Supply and Use of Pharmaceuticals in Satara District*. Pune: The Foundation for Research in Community Health.

Qadeer, Imrana. 1998. 'Reproductive Health: A Public Health Perspective', *Economic and Political Weekly*, 33(41): 2675–84.

Qadeer, Imrana, K.R. Nayar, and R.V. Baru. 1994. 'Contextualising Plague: A Reconstruction and an Analysis', *Economic and Political Weekly*, 29(47): 2981–9.

Rao, M. Govinda and Mita Choudhury. 2012. 'Health Care Financing Reforms in India', Working Paper 2012-100. New Delhi: National Institute of Public Finance Policy.

Rao, Mohan. 2004. *From Population Control to Reproductive Health: Malthusian Arithmetic*. New Delhi: Sage Publications.

———. 2010. 'Why Penalize People', in A.K. Shiva Kumar, Pradeep Panda, and Rajani Ved (eds), *Oxford Handbook of Population and Development*. New Delhi: Oxford University Press, pp. 41–9.

Rao, Mohan, Krishna D. Rao, A.K. Shiva Kumar, Mirai Chatterjee, and T. Sundararaman. 2011. 'Human Resources for Health in India', *Lancet*, 377(9765): 587–98.

Ravindran, T.K. Sundari. 2011. *Public–Private Interactions in Reproductive Health Services in India: A Mapping*. Mumbai: Center for Enquiry into Health and Allied Themes.

Registrar General of India. 2008. *Summary Statistics of Causes of Death India*. New Delhi: Registrar General of India.

Shah, Ghanshyam. 1997. *Public Health and Urban Development: The Plague in Surat*. New Delhi: Sage Publications.

Selvaraj, Saktivel and Anup K. Karan. 2009. 'Deepening Health Insecurity in India: Evidence from National Sample Surveys since 1980s', *Economic and Political Weekly*, 44(40): 55–60.

UNDP (United Nations Development Programme). 2011. 'Sustainability and Equity: A Better Future for All', Explanatory note on 2011 HDR composite indices. Available at http://hdrstats.undp.org/images/explanations/IND.pdf (accessed on 5 June 2012).

UNFPA (United Nations Population Fund). 2003. *Missing: Mapping the Adverse Child Sex Ratio in India*. New Delhi: UNFPA.

———. 2011. *Trends in Sex Ratio at Birth and Estimates of Girls Missing at Birth in India (2001–2008)*. New Delhi: UNFPA.

———. 2012. *Trends in Maternal Mortality: 1990–2010*. Geneva: UNFPA, World Health Organization, World Bank, and United Nations Children's Fund.

Vellakkal, Sukumar. n.d. *Economic Implications of Chronic Diseases in India*. New Delhi: South Asia Network for Chronic Disease.

World Bank. 1995. 'India: Policy and Finance Strategies for Strengthening Primary Health Care Services', Report No. 13042-IN. Washington, DC: Population and Human Resource Division.

World Bank. 2000. *World Development Report 1999–2000: Entering the 21st Century*. New Delhi: Oxford University Press.

World Health Organization. 1978. *Health for All through Primary Health Care: Report of the International Conference on Primary Health Care*. Geneva: World Health Organization.

———. 2006. *Noncommunicable Disease and Poverty*. Geneva: World Health Organization.

Yesudian, C.A.K. n.d. *Behaviour of the Private Sector in the Health Services Market of Mumbai*. Mumbai: Tata Institute of Social Sciences.

6

Gendering Social Analysis, Contextualizing Gender
Women in Neoliberal India*

Indu Agnihotri

In times when words and their meanings are regularly being turned around, it may be useful to examine the axiomatic phrase based on centuries of philosophical thought—that the position of women in a society is an indicator of the level of social progress as per Fourier and other Utopian Socialists. To make the centuries of wisdom handed down in different societies in similar but different words relevant today, it may be worthwhile to arrive at a more contemporary rendering of this axiom, which may perhaps then read as follows: the depth and level of social crisis in a given society, at specific conjunctures, such as the present, may be measured by the extent to which the women of that society are seen to be unequal and denied any measure of justice.

If violence is a manifestation and reflection of an escalation of social conflict, then the sharp increase in figures related to crimes against women should send shock waves down those entrusted with the responsibility of governance and ensuring that law and order prevails. Even as the women's movement has continuously drawn attention to the violence faced by women in 'normal' times, the present scenario is disturbing, to say the least. Further, while the extent and measure of violence may not be a sufficient tool to analyse social trends, nor even of women's status for that matter, the unprecedented scale on which violence is today being perpetrated against women, and its social acceptance, cannot be ignored.

Turning a critical eye to this phenomenon, based on analytical tools that the social sciences provide, may help us to identify the depth of social crisis, what lies at the root of pervasive social turmoil, gripping both urban and rural India, and how this affects different sections with uneven ferocity. While macro developments in India should be sufficient to set alarm bells ringing for social scientists, there is a strong case today for turning a gendered lens to lend a critical edge to understanding the depth of the crisis in our society today.

Available indicators, in general, point to a visible deterioration and obstacles in achieving the goals of social progress despite high levels of growth. While it would be nobody's case that women are alone in the discrimination they face, data with regard to sex ratio and women's employment gives an insight into how highly gendered and exclusionary current social development processes are. In globalized times, as inequality rises and justice is denied, the axe clearly appears to fall more heavily on women and, as a quick glance through official statistics shows, the buck ultimately stops at the women. Across classes, castes, regions, and religions they face denial, discrimination, and, increasingly, reprisals for non-adherence to 'norms' imposed by self-styled gatekeepers of social morality. The fact that deep-seated inequalities based on gender persist is a comment on the quality of governance and the commitment of our ruling elites to

---

* This chapter was written much before the events of December 2012 in Delhi when the issue of violence, particularly sexual violence, against women acquired unprecedented visibility in the public domain. Hence, it may not address issues raised in the course of the last few months.

the constitutional goals and is not merely the result of patriarchal mindsets.

The visible decline in social indicators provides a disturbing picture, in sharp contrast with official pronouncements on development and growth and a verbal commitment to social justice and inclusive growth. At the same time it is essential to examine some emerging trends, which are not always clearly visible when only annual or latest data is referred to. Just as the roots of patriarchy constantly need to be traced back to social structures, it is important to recognize that the making of a social crisis transcends calendar years. It stems from a deeper social malaise which is often linked to macro structures and the policy orientation of successive governments in power. Together with historically inherited inequalities and prejudices, these provide the context in which exclusions and discriminations shape emerging sites of social conflict and determine how specific groups become more vulnerable. The declining status of women, their heightened social vulnerability, including their propensity to persistently emerge as prime targets in this, deserves deeper academic analysis than this short piece can provide. Nevertheless, an attempt is made here to cull out features from the unfolding social development scenario to point to the linkages that exist between women's specifically gendered experience of discrimination and oppression, even as they are members of larger social groups, which are differentially and adversely affected by macro processes. Often aspects of these are presented by the media as human interest stories, attracting attention, either as stories of success or of victimhood. While these serve their own purpose, they sometimes detract from a more sustained analysis of social trends.

The Context

The most significant area of concern is the picture on the economic front. Given the crisis in the advanced economies, and increasing realization of its depth at the global level, there is a visible 'dark mood', if not virtual panic in the Eurozone, even as the US claims to have overcome the shock tremors triggered by the crisis in 2007. In India, from time to time, satisfaction is expressed both at how India withstood the global financial crisis and the fact that the economy has shown buoyancy, even if there has been a slowdown in comparison with earlier years when there was double digit growth. We are, apparently, still in a 'high growth' phase.

For 2012–13, the Economic Advisory Council of the Prime Minister 'expects to see a fall in food grain output especially in the kharif season and also possible decline in some commercial crops, particularly cotton and sugarcane'. While there may be output losses it is of the view that overall farm sector Gross Domestic Product (GDP) would register a positive growth of around 0.5 per cent. The increase in GDP arising in manufacturing is estimated at 4.5 per cent, and growth in the mining and quarrying sector is projected at 4.4 per cent overall, for the economy. The Council assumes that an average growth of 6.7 per cent in 2012–13 can be realistically expected. While the agriculture growth rate will be lower than the last year, there can be a distinct improvement in the performance of the mining sector and a moderate improvement in the manufacturing sector.[1]

The picture on the ground, however, is not so bright. Even as the economy has had a slow rate of growth, inflation in mid-2012, stood at 7.3 per cent and was likely to persist. Most alarming is the steep increase in prices of primary food, including vegetables, milk, fruit, and meat apart from pulses, over the last several years. It is officially acknowledged that the 'present level of inflation has to come down, in order to allow for stable conditions for healthy investment climate and equitable economic growth'.

While the discussion on economic aspects is generally conducted in the context of macro issues and policies in a global context, the need to understand and analyse how these impinge on the daily lives of women is greater. The ongoing changes have added considerable volatility in society and this impacts the relationship between gender, citizenship, and entitlements in a very fundamental way. It is important to draw the connections between these social trends and ongoing development processes in order to develop analytical frameworks which allow us to identify and understand the linkages and how these need to be addressed.

Surprisingly, of late, academic scholarship appears to be inclined to shy away from such intersecting analysis and exploration of the ground reality, even as the need to do so is greater. It is almost as if the fragmentation that afflicts society is also reflected in the scholarship emerging in the contemporary context. While a fair amount of effort is being spent on theoretical discussions, the concepts and frameworks of analysis being deployed do not appear to be sufficiently sensitive to the factors that shape consciousness or spur action. In fact dependence on conceptual categories which have emerged from vastly different socio-historical contextual frames appears to be getting reinforced. There is an urgent need to bridge the widening gap between critical social enquiry and the challenge of confronting the processes of social change on the ground. As at the time of the anti-imperialist struggle, this task needs to be undertaken with equanimity and a resoluteness that does not compromise the pursuit of social enquiry nor does it tailor itself to contingent political demands or funding agendas which, more than anything else, today shape research agendas through a negotiation of social movements. In recent decades, there has been a tendency to deny the links between social classes and the reflection of their interests in ideological formations which have surfaced on the political firmament. Such trends blur the material basis of social oppression and blunt the social transformatory edge of contemporary movements. This poses serious challenges to those committed to advancing the goal of equality for women and identifying the issues as well as connections between these macro processes and the social crisis facing us all. The success of the women's movement shall lie in how soon and seriously it understands and accepts this challenge. In the absence of a critical framework to understand the roots and varied manifestations of the social crisis, it may continue to focus on 'issues' while missing out on underlying processes which fundamentally determine social change.

DEVALUATION OF WOMEN'S STATUS

If this was not so evident earlier, it is now amply clear that there has been an all-pervasive devaluation of women's status, even as some individual women may have made it to the top. There is a widespread acceptance of a public perception of women as an economic and social burden. This lies at the bottom of the systematic elimination of girl children in contemporary India. As noted after the release of the 2011 Census data, 'the consistent decline in the sex-ratio throughout this century sums up the fate of women in India. It is even more alarming to see that the decline has now set in so deeply that the 0–6 age group shows a sharp difference between the survival rate for the male and female child'. Clearly, the long-term implications of such a demographic transition and a trend towards reversal of the age pyramid, which is amply clear with regard to women, are yet to be realized. There is both a rapid 'greying' of the population in India, and a visible trend towards increase in the population of females as compared to males in the age group of 60 and above, though this is spread unevenly across states (GoI 2011: 6).

Meanwhile, the 2011 Census made it clear that the all-India child sex ratio (CSR) had fallen from 927 to 914 girls per 1,000 boys over the last decade. The steepest and unparalleled decline, of the magnitude of 82 points, in

recent decades, in Jammu and Kashmir may need more specific examination. Leaving aside the fact that this may reflect issues with regard to data collection, it may also indicate how conflict situations render women vulnerable in more ways than one recognizes. More critical is the fact that

major states such as UP, MP, Rajasthan & Maharashtra have shown sharp declines. Orissa, Uttaranchal, Delhi and Andhra have also reported lower levels. The data from Manipur and Assam are unfavourable to girls. Thus in 2011, for the first time in recorded Indian history, we see declines against girls in all regions, South, North, East, West and North East at the State level.[2]

In comparison, though the 2001 Census had also registered declining patterns, these were largely 'confined to North Western India, South Gujarat and the prosperous districts of Maharashtra'. It should be noted that 'the exceptions to the declines over the 2001–11 intercensal decade have been Punjab which has shown a modest rise while Haryana, Himachal and Gujarat have shown marginal improvement'; it still has to be recognized that 'Haryana and Punjab still have the lowest child sex ratio in 2011' and that in Gujarat and Haryana there are indeed several districts which have worsened in 2011. Haryana has the worst child sex ratio and six of the ten worst districts of the country are in this state (George 2011: 7) (see Table 6.1).

Table 6.1   Sex Ratio over Time

Total Population	1971	1981	1991	2001	2011
	931	935	927	933	940
Population aged 0–6 years	964	962	945	927	914

Source: Census of India 2011, GoI, New Delhi.

In Madhya Pradesh, Uttar Pradesh, Rajasthan, Andhra Pradesh, at the district level there is a 'near universal decline', indicating that

intensification of the practice of foetal sex determination in districts which had already witnessed masculine levels in 2011 and further spread to districts which were not affected in 2001 is the highlight of this Census. For instance in MP, the only exception has been Bhind which has remained at around 820, while two Districts in Nagaland have reported a fall of 80 points! An examination of the worst ten districts—where ratios have suddenly come down to 800—showed that two of these, Beed and Pithorgarh are in Maharashtra and Uttarakhand, respectively. Compared to this, in the past Census all the worst Districts were in Punjab and Haryana. ... (George 2011: 5; see also Table 6.2)

Table 6.2   Sex Ratio of Total Population and Child Population in the Age Groups 0–6 and 7+ years in States, 2001 and 2011

India	2001	2011	2001	2011	2001	2011
	933	940	927	914	934	944
Jammu and Kashmir	892	883	941	859	884	887
Himachal Pradesh	968	974	896	906	980	983
Punjab	876	893	798	846	888	899
Chandigarh*	777	818	845	867	767	812
Uttarakhand	962	963	908	886	973	975
Haryana	861	877	819	830	869	885
NCT of Delhi*	821	866	868	866	813	866
Rajasthan	921	926	909	883	923	935
Uttar Pradesh	898	908	916	899	894	910
Bihar	919	916	942	933	914	912
Sikkim	875	889	963	944	861	883
Arunachal Pradesh	893	920	964	960	878	913
Nagaland	900	931	964	944	890	929
Manipur	974	987	957	934	977	995
Mizoram	935	975	964	971	930	976
Tripura	948	961	966	953	945	962
Meghalaya	972	986	973	970	971	989
Assam	935	954	965	957	929	953
West Bengal	934	947	960	950	929	946
Jharkhand	941	947	965	943	935	948
Odisha	972	978	953	934	976	985
Chhattisgarh	989	991	975	964	992	995
Madhya Pradesh	919	930	932	912	916	933
Gujarat	920	918	883	886	927	923
Daman and Diu*	710	618	926	909	682	589
Dadra and Nagar Haveli*	812	775	979	924	779	752
Maharashtra	922	925	913	883	924	931
Andhra Pradesh	978	992	961	943	981	97
Karnataka	965	968	946	943	968	971
Goa	961	968	938	920	964	973
Lakshadweep*	948	946	959	908	946	951
Kerala	1,058	1,084	960	959	1,072	1,099
Tamil Nadu	987	995	942	946	993	1,000
Puducherry*	1,001	1,038	967	965	1,006	1,047
Andaman and Nicobar Island*	846	878	957	966	831	868

Source: Census of India 2011, GoI, New Delhi.
Note: * Based on Statement 13 Census of India 2011, sex ratio of total population and child population in the age group 0–6 and 7+ years: 2001 and 2011.

Beed, which has in recent months reported some of the worst cases of sex selective abortions, reports 'the cheapest place for sex determination in the state … for a mere 500 Rs foetal sexing is available!' (George 2011).

While sex determination tests and pre-birth elimination of girls is linked to social/cultural practices, it cannot be denied that there is active collusion of the state and society in this, including that of members drawn from the medical profession. There is continued failure to implement the Pre-conception and Pre Natal Diagnostic Techniques (PcPNDT) Act. This includes allowing misuse of ultrasound machinery, little or no monitoring of the clinics, and violation of the mandatory guidelines with regard to maintenance and submission of records. Cases registered under the Act are few and far, and conviction rates would perhaps be the lowest for any crime committed! There are serious lapses in notification of guidelines and even blatant violation of these while constituting Monitoring Committees and Supervisory Authority, as is obvious from the fact that many of those caught in sting operations by the media in several states were found to be sitting on these committees. The media itself has been found guilty of carrying advertisements or reports which display a son preference and a blatant anti-girl child bias. Several cases are pending on this count before media regulatory bodies. The medical profession has largely been in denial mode on this unethical practice, with most crying foul every time a crime is registered against one of their fraternity, even as the blame is pushed on to unregistered/unqualified medical practitioners/quacks.

A critical issue pertains to official policy and its overriding concern with 'population growth', overlooking visible links between strategies of reducing the rate of population growth and sex determination. The years 2001–11 have seen the sharpest decline in population growth rate since Independence and a far greater visible spread of preference for a son across states and districts. But the clear link with the continued focus on curbing the growth rate in population is consistently overlooked. Worse still is the enforcing of the two-child norm with most 'scheme' based benefits provided by states today being linked to the two child family norm as a 'condition of eligibility'. Women's organizations have repeatedly pointed to the need for withdrawal of these conditions/conditionalities forthwith, if any reversal of trends with regard to child sex ratio is to be achieved.

Pointing to the social acceptability of pre-birth elimination of girl children, scholars have emphasized that

understanding the economic and social factors that lead to a skewed child sex ratio requires moving from the immediacy of reproductive decisions. It is necessary to grasp the nature of change and not assume a straightforward continuity with tradition … the more thorough elimination of daughters can only be explained if we accept that what was the obverse of son-preference—daughter undesirability—has now become daughter-aversion. Daughter-aversion as an emotion and practice has become the common sense with a life of its own, quite apart from son-preference.... [T]he fact that some people do also want and care for a daughter does not take away from the social force of daughter-aversion.(John *et al.* 2009: 18)

There is also enough evidence to establish a clear relation between affluence, the advance and spread of new reproductive technologies, and violence against the girl child, with ratio being more adverse for regions and states marked by high per capita income, overlapping with the more affluent, urban sections. Western India, more developed than the east, shows lower sex ratio and urban patterns also show faster disappearance of the girl child than in rural areas. Punjab and Haryana have the largest number of districts with the lowest sex ratio, while Kerala, which has had better ratios in the past, has begun to show a decline in the juvenile sex ratio. A clear link can also be established with the proliferation of ultrasound clinics performing sex-determination tests leading to sex-selective abortions. The plea that 'what is required are state policies that actually seek to create the conditions for meaningful life chances, beginning with those of girls and women', clearly takes on a specific meaning in this context (John 2011: 12).

Furthermore, the emerging scenario with regard to new and assisted reproductive technologies is particularly grim. In a study of surrogates with field work undertaken in Anand, Gujarat, it was found that all the 42 women in the sample were mothers. Only 1 came from a family with a monthly income of Rs 10,000; 10 were drawn from families with a monthly income of Rs 1,500 and below; and 6 others came from families earning between Rs 5,000 and Rs 8,000 per month. The increase in surrogacy serves as a crude reminder of what is increasingly being made available to women as 'work', as per the definitions coined by some women's studies scholars (Pande 2009). Others have pointed out that reproduction has become a thriving global business that is inadequately regulated, with evidence to show that inequalities of first world/third world countries are reinforced through such commercial surrogacy. The women's movement in turn faces the challenge of pushing for 'regulation' of a fast expanding fertility tourism business, even as it focuses on the ethical issue of 'commercial surrogacy' and urges the government to stop the commodification of women's bodies, and a re-colonizing of women in the developing world through marketization of their reproductive capacities.

These apparently modern technologies pose several other questions as they, like markets, function in correlation with existing social structures. They cannot be seen to be 'good' or 'efficient' in the abstract and their impact should be examined with regard to the hierarchies prevalent. The marketization of assisted reproduction offers glaring examples of how 'traditional' social prejudices, stereotypes of motherhood, and son preference co-exist. Questions have been raised about the absolute 'faith of the middle class in technology to deliver the goals of economic, social and environmental justice' (Qadeer 2010: 9). Similar ethical, social, and developmental concerns have been expressed by scholars about how these technologies reconfigure ideologies of motherhood and relationships between the north and south even as they reinforce global/regional inequalities (Gupta 2012; Sarojini *et al.* 2011).

While sex ratio, population policies, and assisted reproductive technologies require specific attention in view of their direct consequences in the lives of women, equally serious is the increasing morbidity and declining health of women along with children and the general population.

The problem of the highest number of underweight children in India, this being double those of Sub-Saharan Africa, is now being highlighted. In Maharashtra, Odisha, Bihar, Madhya Pradesh, Uttar Pradesh, and Rajasthan one in two children continue to be underweight. Apart from the problem of high poverty levels these also have a close link with the nature of health facilities, institutional delivery schemes as well as entitlements to maternity protection schemes. The Maternal Mortality Rate (MMR) in India continues to be high, at 212 per lakh live births with a mother dying every 10 minutes. As per a recent study, of an estimated 315 million women in the age group of 15–49, constituting 54.6 per cent of the female population, 138 million or 44 per cent are workers. These women would be eligible for maternity benefit cover in accordance with their constitutional entitlement. However, of this, '132 million or 95.6% are informal workers—that is, workers who are not eligible for any form of social security' (provident fund, gratuity, pension, health care, maternity benefit) (GoI and ILO 2012: 201). National Sample Survey Organisation (NSSO) data showed that in 2004–5 only 0.4 million women or

0.3 per cent of the workforce were eligible for health care and maternity benefits. It is further seen that the Janani Suraksha Yojana (JSY), 'the only maternity-linked assistance available to women not linked to their worker status', covers women below poverty line (BPL). Further, the clause of the minimum age of 19 to be eligible for this support

ignores the existence of fertility below 19 years as a result of marriage before the legal age and early motherhood. The limit up to two children ignores the high fertility among vulnerable groups such as ST/SC and the poor. Further, the scheme shares many limitations of any targeted scheme. Although JSY has been shown to have a significant effect on increasing antenatal care and in-facility births, it has also been shown to have left the poorest and least educated women out of its reach…. (Ibid.: 204)

It is observed that since the country registered economic growth with no commensurate growth in employment, particularly in the organized sector 'data on rising inequality and poverty in absolute numbers point to the need to protect women's employment and interventions to guarantee a minimum level of wages and income' (see ibid.: 201–5).

UNDERSTANDING DEVALUATION OF WOMEN: EXPLORING LINKAGES

A fundamental issue that needs to be addressed is what has contributed to such a marked devaluation of women? While it would be difficult to argue that economic factors have a direct or mechanical impact on women's lives, there is an urgent need to examine the impact of ongoing macro processes, how these influence the daily lives of women and understand their linkages with emerging trends.

Over the past decade and more, much has been written about women's work with regard to home-based work and self-employment, where women are mostly located. The National Commission for Enterprises in the Unorganized Sector (NCEUS) assessed that over 92 per cent of the total workforce in our country—nearly 32.3 per cent of which were women—was located in the unorganized sector. It has been further observed that 'the rosy image of new productive opportunities emerging from self-employment because of a vibrant fast—growing economy is unfortunately far from the truth for most such workers, even in the urban areas which are currently seen as more economically dynamic' (Ghosh 2009: 117).

Scholars have drawn attention to the fact that contrary to the 'assumption that globalization leads to feminization of labour', NSSO's Employment and Unemployment data for India 2009–10 shows a steep fall in female work participation rates and that 'gender dimensions of employment trends in India need to be centre staged in the general discussions on employment and jobless growth under liberalization'. Further, of the three employment/ activity status categories of workers recorded in official data collection—self-employed, regular salaried, and casual labour—a higher proportion of the female workforce is always found to be concentrated in the 'self-employed'. Attention has been drawn to the fact that 'an aspect of the data that is missed relates to how much of women's work participation is in the form of unpaid labour', for 'concealed within the aggregate figures for the self-employed is a large unpaid segment, which contributes to the production economy, but without receiving any independent payment/income for their labour'.

Unpaid work here in fact refers not to domestic work such as cooking, cleaning and child care, but to economic activities—defined as all the market activities in production of goods and services for exchange, as well as non-market activities which result in production of primary goods for own consumption or relate to the own-account production (such as construction of houses, roads, wells, manufacture of machinery, tools, and also construction of any private or community facilities free of charge) or in the capacity of either a labourer or a supervisor. In 2009–10, more than two-thirds of them were in community and personal services (which includes domestic workers, teachers, launderers, beauticians, etc.), a little less than one fourth were in manufacturing (primarily home-based piece-rated work).[3]

In the past the tendency has been to see unpaid work by women as being solely a feature of 'traditional' production systems/sectors that are outside the contemporary monetized value exchange economy associated with 'modern' capitalist social relations, but this is no longer acceptable. A notable fact is that in urban India, the share of unpaid labour increased when the Female Work Participation Rate (FWPR) rose and declined when FWPR fell, pointing to the need to look at unpaid work, 'when assessing the implications of any increases in work participation trends for urban women', as well as to the link between these trends and the devaluation of women. These trends pose the need for women's studies analysts to undertake closer scrutiny and monitoring of the definitional aspects of data collection both with regard to NSSO and the Census.[4]

There is also a need to assess whether recent economic developments have succeeded in breaking down societal bias and discrimination as seen in projected roles and the sexual division of labour? Does globalization confront patriarchal bias at the ideological and structural level, which, when seen in conjunction with class, caste, region, and religion form the basis of denial of equality and dignity to women in India? Are the state and its policies more favourable to the promotion of equality? It is important to address these questions since one of the justifications for recent changes has been the glamour surrounding the image of this 'new woman'.

In fact it has been seen that the features of the labour market in India 'indicate the lack of positive dynamism in job opportunities for the bulk of women'. Between 1999–2000 and 2004–5 real wage trends in India showed a decline 'for both regular and casual women workers, and have hardly increased much even compared to more than a decade earlier'. Further,

real wages of regular women workers declined for every category of education level and in both rural and urban areas! Over the 11 year period between 1993–94 and 2004–05, real wages grew noticeably only for female graduate workers in both rural and urban areas. For rural women with secondary and higher secondary education, average real wages for regular work actually declined slightly. And there was a real sharp fall in average real wages for regular work of illiterate urban women workers. This probably reflects the changing composition of the regular female workforce in urban areas and the growing share of those engaged in domestic service, which is among the lowest paid of urban activities. (Ghosh 2009: 79–80)

Similarly, a survey conducted amongst home-based women workers in Delhi, during 2009, pointed to the dismal condition of these women: after working on an average of nearly seven hours a day along with other family members, the home-based workers in Delhi manage to earn only Rs 32.54 per day, whereas the daily minimum wage for unskilled workers in Delhi is Rs 140. They got work only for an average of 16 days a month. During the early months of 2009, a large number complained of 'shrinking work availability and further decrease in piece rates' (All India Democratic Women's Association 2009).

The Rural Context: Where the Majority of Women Live

India has seen over a quarter of a million farmers' suicides between 1995 and 2010. The National Crime Records Bureau's (NCRB) report on 'Accidental Deaths & Suicides in India' for 2010 placed the number at 15,964. The cumulative 16-year total from 1995—when the NCRB started recording farm suicide data—appears to be 2,56,913, prompting this to labelled as the 'the worst-ever recorded wave of suicides of this kind in human history' (Sainath 2011). In 2009 alone 17,368 farm suicides were reported (Sainath 2010). Even going by the official data, 'on average nearly 16,000 farmers committed suicide every year over the last decade or so' and that 'every seventh suicide in the country was a farm suicide'. It is at the same time argued that the number of suicides also may be an underestimation of the actual numbers, given the fact that the police often adopt

a rather strict and stringent definition of a farmer in identifying a farm suicide. The title to land was taken as the criterion for identifying the farmer and this often left out a genuine farmer from the count. For example, a tenant farmer who leased in land and hence did not have a title to the land could be denied the status of a farmer; so also a farmer if the title was in his father's name.

Further, since the 'criterion generally adopted in these records for identifying a farmer is title to land and since the title is generally in the name of male head of the household it is very likely that a female farmer who commits suicide will not be recorded as a farmer in these records', apart from the fact 'the high concentration of farm suicides among males in fact represents an objective reality' (Nagaraj 2008: 6–7).

Attention has been drawn to the adverse impact of the 'distinct slowdown in agricultural growth since the mid-1990s' on the livelihood base of rural people, since 'the slowdown has occurred in all the sub-sectors of agriculture, including livestock and horticulture which were the main drivers of agricultural growth in the immediate past'. It is believed that 'a large number of proximate and structural factors have contributed to the decline of agriculture. The foremost among them is the reduced developmental role of state in investment in irrigation, flood control, research, extension, and institution building in the context of liberalizing agriculture' (Reddy and Mishra 2009: xiv). Economic reforms initiated in 1991 have set the Indian economy on a 'high growth path, making it one of the leading emerging market economies of the world. The institutional shift from planned but slow growth process to market-driven rapid growth has, however, been accompanied by rising income and regional disparities, deceleration in the reduction of poverty, and rural distress embedded in agrarian crisis' (ibid.: 3). A direct result of this has been a continuous decline in the share of agriculture in the total GDP but very slow diversification of the workforce away from agriculture. Slow growth of employment in the formal

sector and in agriculture, results in 'structural rigidity' inhibiting the shift of the labour force from agriculture to non-agriculture. The relative productivity of workers in agriculture has declined from 28.7 per cent of non-agricultural productivity in 1972–3 to 19.9 per cent in 2004–5. Concentration of the workforce in agriculture combines with more insecure casual work, self-employment, and the declining share of rural employment.

Undoubtedly the agrarian crisis is one of the foremost questions before the nation albeit from different perspectives. Despite the importance of agriculture in our economy, Gross Capital Formation in agriculture and allied sectors as a proportion of overall GDP has remained stagnant at around 2.5–3 per cent between 2004–5 and 2009–10. Growth in agriculture and allied activities decelerated even as economic growth touched striking rates. GDP growth rates for agricultural and allied activities for the year 2008–9 were -0.1 per cent even though the year 2008–9 witnessed a 'record harvest'. This implies that prices for agricultural commodities were low and resulted in poor returns for cultivators.[5]

Since in India the majority of women live in rural areas and their income and livelihood continue to be linked to agriculture and the rural job environment in a significant way, stagnation in agricultural growth has been a major concern. The significance of the agrarian crisis, from the perspective of women, is greater.

One phenomenon which attracted official attention in this context was growing rural indebtedness. It was recognized that

in the present liberalised trade and market regime, farmers are exposed to price volatility because of fluctuations in domestic production and wide fluctuations in international prices. Currently, no adequate and effective risk mitigating measures exist to counter the adverse impact of such fluctuations. Further, rapid changes in information and space technology which hold immense potential have hardly been used to provide timely weather signals to the farmers and thereby mitigating the weather induced risks. (GoI 2007: 1)

Since the mid-1990s, large sections of the farm households have been facing a great deal of distress as a consequence of decline in agricultural income, erosion of their repayment capacity, and increased debt burdens. Reversal of this trend would require not only adequate institutional credit to farmers but also undertaking steps to revive agriculture which would help increase credit absorptive capacity of farmers (ibid.). Ironically, the Report did not pay any attention to the specific impact rural debt has on women's lives and gender relations. Meanwhile, the Farmers' Commission, while urging the government to take significant and immediate steps to attend to the goal of 'Making Hunger History…, drew attention to the "the feminisation of agriculture"', which 'due to male out-migration, needs specific attention with reference to gender-sensitive farm and credit policies. All research, development and extension programmes in agriculture, and all services must be engendered' (GoI 2006: para 1.5.5 xi, p. 23).

The National Policy for Women in Agriculture, adopted by the National Commission for Women, also drew attention to the pivotal role played by women in agriculture and the distress faced by those working in the sector. It noted that

any statement of policy has to take into account this recent sharp decline in the growth of the agricultural sector in our country. The National Policy on Farmers has talked of measures to counteract this, but the impact of this decline on women has additional dimensions. The increased feminization of agricultural work and labour means concentration of women in a sector which is already experiencing severe decline. Because of this the destitution of the agrarian population due to the crisis has also meant a feminization of poverty.

It observed that

rising agrarian distress has also led to increase of *violence against women*. It must be remembered that apart from the problems of livelihood and employment, women anyway have to endure the inequities of a patriarchal system both in the family and in the world outside. When livelihood and employment have been threatened, the discrimination and violence perpetrated on women as women also tend to increase. (See National Commission for Women 2009; emphasis added)

Insufficient attention paid by the state to agriculture since Independence and, specifically over the last two decades remains a significant issue. It has been shown that 'public investment and expenditure on agriculture in India have grown only slowly and have not decisively increased even after more than 60 years of independence'. While public capital formation and expenditure do show a moderate rise in the 2000s,

a revival of India's agricultural growth requires a far greater thrust to public spending. Major and medium irrigation projects require special attention, as irrigation is instrumental not just in raising yields, but also the number of days of employment for labourers. Increasing public investment in agricultural research and extension is central to bridging the yield gap that persists. Formal credit flows to agriculture have

to specifically target small and marginal farmers, and emphasis should move away from generating agricultural growth by channeling credit to agri-business firms and corporate players in agriculture. If India's second green revolution has to contribute to an accelerated reduction of poverty, hunger and malnourishment, it undoubtedly has to be a state-led project. (Ramakumar 2012: 7)

Decline in public investment in agriculture in India was visible since the 1980s. This 'accelerated further in the 1990s. By the end of 1990s public investment in agriculture and allied activities was only about 1.6% of agriculture GDP and about 6.6% of total gross capital formation in the public sector' (Ramachandran and Rawal 2009: 58). Over the years, the results of such policies have become more clearly visible, with the Economic Survey for 2008–9 noting that growth in agriculture and allied activities decelerated from 4.9 per cent in 2007–8 to 1.6 per cent in 2008–9. It was noted that 'agricultural growth also turned negative, adding a further dampener', that is, in addition to the slowdown effect in the economy which was very visible in the manufacturing sector (GoI 2008–9). The figures of actual year-on-year growth rates in the agriculture/allied sector were 5.1 per cent and 4.2 per cent for 2005–6 and 2006–7, respectively. There are several related issues which need to be understood with regard to the agrarian crisis—of availability of land and resources; state investment in agriculture or the lack of it; agricultural credit, the poor performance of credit cooperatives and regional rural banks, the inability of commercial banks to meet their targets for agricultural lending, and the high cost of rural banking. Studies have pointed to shrinking opportunities for rural credit and the consequences of this (Ramachandran and Swaminathan 2006).

It is hidden from no one that with the decline in state investment in the rural sector, micro-credit and Self-help Groups (SGHs) were peddled as a strategy in which women were seen to play a pivotal role. Till very recently, uncritically, the Bangladesh experience was seen as a success story in this regard, though subsequently the fault lines within this began to show up in a glaring manner. While the non-governmental organization (NGO) sector's response to this has been in the form of evaluations of the success of the micro-credit initiative(s), this issue has been discussed at great length in the women's movement for several years now and the limitations as well as problems with this growth path have been raised at different levels by the women's movement. Even as media began to report on harassment and suicides linked to some of the unethical practices and 'strategies' adopted by the banking sector under the micro finance institution (MFI) came to be known, the years 2010–11 saw mass protests, including by the National Federation of Indian Women (NFIW) in Andhra Pradesh for example and also from the All India Democratic Women's Association (AIDWA). These drew attention to the problem of lack of institutional credit and the policing and 'extortionist' methods adopted by agencies on the count of recovery. In an effort to address women's needs at the policy level, AIDWA, the largest organization of women in India, urged the Reserve Bank of India (RBI) to make women a separate category for Priority Sector Lending (PSL). In a memorandum addressed to the Chairperson of the Committee to Re-examine the Existing Classification and Suggest Revised Guidelines with regard to PSL Classification and Related Issues, RBI, the AIDWA raised the issue of current eligibility criteria for classification as PSL for the categories of the priority sector. These include direct and indirect finance to agriculture, micro and small enterprises, micro credit, educational loans, and housing loans. The AIDWA urged that women should be a separate sub-category under PSL. It argued that although women form a large part of these priority sectors, they are invisibilized due to widely prevalent gender discriminatory attitudes and practices, and as a result, so are their credit needs. The demand was that at least 30 per cent of the credit allocations for different sections in the PSL should flow to women within that specific category; at least 30 per cent loans in the micro and small enterprises category of collateral free loans up to 10 lakh should be reserved for women; and that the definition should include women in vending, informal sector, and home-based workers, and that a monitoring mechanism be set up under the PSL to check the amount of funds being accessed by women. Along with this the demand was raised for the taking out of MFI from PSL, since the MFIs use credit under PSL to give loans to women's SHGs at much higher rates of interest due to which women have to pay more than they would if they had direct access to bank loans although one of the arguments put forward to justify support to MFIs is the poor banking network. Decrying the coercive and criminal practices of the MFIs, organizations pointed to the bitter experience of women SHGs with MFIs which was symbolized by the tragic suicides of women in Andhra Pradesh. The AIDWA urged government agencies to strengthen rural banking through other avenues and models, along with Grameen Banks, so as to extend credit facilities to uncovered areas. The AIDWA memorandum pointed out that while the quantum of bank loans disbursed to MFIs

during 2009–10 more than doubled to Rs 8,062 crores while the increase in bank loans to SHGs had, comparatively, slowed down and that banks are choosing to lend more to MFIs rather than to SHGs. Welcoming the attention paid to issues such as the interest cap, margin cap, and income limit of borrowers, it was noted that these measures have been largely undermined by setting an exorbitantly high cap of 26 per cent per annum rate of interest, given the fact that studies have shown that a margin of 2 per cent is more than adequate for these institutions to cover their costs. The AIDWA drew attention to the fact that many women become indebted to moneylenders due to household emergencies. Hence it would be useful to formulate a scheme to assist them to prepay this amount. Further, it urged that a comprehensive data base be maintained for all loans and advances made to women in the different segments of PSL, in an effort to ensure that the interests of the large section of women from the marginalized and deprived sections would be better served by the banking sector.[6]

However, in sharp contrast to these pressures from the movement, what are the issues that the government has identified at the top? If the current line of thinking and recent policy measures announced are an indication these are—legalizing tenancy since it is argued that restrictions on leasing in and leasing out of land should be removed since this closes the option of augmenting holding, and income for the small farmers, and occupational diversification, especially, though not exclusively, for the large farmers; reforms in agricultural marketing, which are effectively aimed at helping at best big farmers; reducing input subsidies by dismantling the present subsidy regime in agriculture since 'the system has become addicted to subsidies', and action aimed at a 'retreat without disarray'.[7] It would be unwise to prolong this discussion here given the limitations of space and the significant attention given to *The Land Question and the Marginalized*, in Part II of Social Development Report 2010, and the incisive chapter on Land Reforms (Saxena 2011), in the same. However, it is important to emphasize that links need to be continuously drawn between gender aspects, women's lives, and the agrarian question.

POVERTY, CRISIS, AND MIGRATION

How do women and men respond to the growing pressure of poverty and the need for survival? Migration clearly emerges as one strategy and scholars have drawn attention to widespread rural distress which has led to large-scale migration, often of the circular type. However, this process itself is gendered and has a tremendous impact on the family unit and on women, children, and on those left behind. The long absences from home, or of near ones from home, add to the material and psychological insecurity of women, causing pressures and requiring negotiations with the extended family members. Given patriarchal traditions, women end up coping with several problems which are further exacerbated by the uncertainty of the timing and size of remittances on which the precarious household economy ultimately depends. This, in turn, pushes women and children from poor labouring households to participate in the labour market under adverse conditions. The impact of migration on women is complex; however, it is seen that patriarchy continues to restrict and influence women's entry into the labour market and also the scope of their autonomy, leave alone the emotional stress and heightened vulnerability that the new environment poses for all migrant workers, but more specially for women.[8]

Developments in other sectors of the economy, over the years, have been no more encouraging, more so in the wake of the global recession and financial crisis. Job cuts and retrenchment have further added to apprehensions of imminent loss of employment and erosion of incomes and standards of living. Women and workers were affected adversely due to the closure and curtailment of activities. Along with agriculture, the prolonged crisis in the tea industry, which employs women in large numbers, also severely impacted women and their families, as did the price collapses in coffee and rubber, at different points of time over the last many years.

The NCEUS, in its observations on the global recession and financial crisis, noted that 'the impact of the crisis is not restricted to the larger, organised segments of industry and is indeed of a much more serious nature among those engaged in the informal economy'. These people gained little when the economy grew rapidly. As we have shown on the basis of consumption estimates, during the period of growth (1993–4/2004/2005), consumption expanded rapidly in roughly the top two deciles, fuelling the growth, but the benefits of this growth principally bypassed the vast majority of the population (77 per cent) who remained poor or vulnerable with an average per capita daily consumption below Rs 20 (less than 50 cents). However, during the current slowdown, it is precisely these people, the poor and vulnerable, engaged in informal sector enterprises or informally employed by the formal sector, who will be affected the most adversely.[9]

Meanwhile, the Planning Commission in 2011 gave an affidavit to the Supreme Court stating that a person is to be considered 'poor' only if his or her monthly spending is below Rs 781 (Rs 26 per day) in rural and Rs 965 (Rs 32 per day) in urban areas, exposing how unrealistic 'poverty lines' are. While these sums could not meet the minimal nutrition needs at current prices, it was being argued that they would take care of all needs of the average citizens. What remains a concern is the fact that nearly 450 million people in India actually subsist below these levels. The results are there for all to see—malnutrition is rampant and many, especially children are underweight, stunted, sickness-prone, and have no access to any kind of health care. Of these, the majority belong to the Scheduled Castes (SCs) and Scheduled Tribes (STs). As remarked by a well-known scholar who raised questions about the credibility of these laughable figures in what is now being called The Republic of Hunger, 'the official poverty lines do not measure poverty anymore; they measure destitution' (Patnaik 2011). As pointed out by Patnaik, the Planning Commission had made a huge mistake in changing the definition of poverty line which was originally defined on the basis of an expert committee recommendation in 1979. (Patnaik 2004). Historically it is known that food insecurities and growing inflation are a matter of great concern for women who are often drawn into struggles against these.[10]

The need to explore links between economic processes and increasing violence was similarly highlighted by another study undertaken of workers in small-scale informal sectors in the wake of the global financial crisis. The research looked into agriculture, auto parts, engineering industry, *chikan* craft, home-based garments, and gems and jewellery industries. The study highlighted the increase in tensions, conflict, and violence, including domestic violence. This was also accompanied by reduction in food consumption, reduced expenditures in essentials such as education and health. This has to be understood along with the debate on food security, reduction of state investment, and expenditure in primary health care and social sector spending (UNDP 2009).

More recently, a study focusing on gender with reference to internal migration in India, across over 20 states has pointed to the severe consequences of the agrarian crisis and shrinking of job opportunities for women (CWDS 2012). It identifies increase in short-term circular migration by both men and women in the face of a rapidly declining share of agriculture in the country's GDP, accelerated growth primarily in services, and to a lesser extent also industry which has not generated commensurate demand in terms of employment, for which women have paid the main price of reduced employment.

Despite the push towards distress migration induced by the agrarian crisis, a pullback also appears to be operating given the predominantly temporary nature of the developing employment regime, and the widespread inability of migrants at lower ends of the economy to sustain social reproduction without a periodic retreat to the village economy, even as the village economy is not providing sufficient employment. It observed that there were structural limitations to the migration enterprise under the current growth/development path in effecting (*a*) durable or structural sectoral/occupational shifts away from agriculture for women workers, (*b*) escape from or transformation of degrading semi-feudal social relations based on caste hierarchies and patriarchy, and (*c*) escape from the massive employment crisis that women face in India. Despite a degree of social assertion, the persistence of structural constraints reinforced entrenched patriarchies in the macro-process and in the highly gendered labour market, which were equally visible in processes of migration. Further, in circular migration based brick-making (across the country) and sugarcane cutting (in western and southern India), women's wage work itself was found to be subsumed in labouring units comprising male/female pairs or family units, despite serving segments of capital accumulation-oriented modern industries, such as sugar mills. Combined with piece rates, this leaves no scope for independent income, even as legal quantification of individual women's work value becomes difficult. This is compounded by a cycle of advance and debt-based tying of such labouring units, generally through contractors. Further, there was limited evidence of diversification of women's employment through migration, with greater concentration of women in a relatively narrow band of occupations, with differentiation moving along the fault lines of entrenched caste and community hierarchies. More medium- and long-term migration among women from upper caste communities correlated with relatively greater levels of diversification into various types of services while migrant women workers from the SCs and STs were concentrated in hard manual labour-based short-term and particularly circular migration linked occupations, with little scope for social advance. This was accompanied by a distinctive movement towards a major concentration of women in paid domestic work, mainly through urban-wards migration. This was found to cut across all castes/tribes/community lines. The study concluded that the macro- and meso-level findings challenge some assumptions that have become commonplace in approaches to women's work and work-based migration. The low shares of women in labour migration for

industry and diversified services run counter to the assumption that liberalization and globalization lead to feminization of labour and related migration. In fact, the escalated devaluation of women's traditional work appears to be confronted with employment constriction and a narrow range of options, rather than compensation for loss of earlier employment through adequate expansion/diversification in paid employment opportunities for women.[11]

The availability or absence of work, along with the conditions under which work is performed by women, remains crucial, especially if the circumstances of their life and condition are to be critically evaluated. Central to any study on aspects of work, and labour, particularly in rural India, is the existence and extent of free/unfree labour. The extent and nature of coercion, bondage, and tied labour are common reference points in analysis and descriptions of rural India. These inevitably centre around stories of impoverishment, distress, survival, and the viability of agriculture. While some of these are issues which have dogged the study of rural India since the period of the colonial economy, the story of the ravaging of the rural economy in the present context appears to be scripted with not much different—much of the labour and immigration is on the basis of advance and 'tied' conditions with regard to wages, terms of payments, and the sectors in which women are mobilized continue to be plagued by contractor-driven mobilization of labour.[12]

Field surveys conducted as part of the Centre for Women's Development Studies' (CWDS) multi-state, multi-sector study on gender and migration amply demonstrated that the crisis stalking the length and breadth of the rural economy resulted from a failure to address critical issues of social change in the context of growth while the differential impact of the crisis was a result of both structural aspects as well as production patterns and regimes, and differentiation within the rural classes, which together determine the dynamics in rural India. The lack of homogeneity of social groups, a marked feature of rural India, despite the broad pattern of an urban–rural divide also affected the women across social groups and communities differently and differentially. Nevertheless, gender-based discrimination persisted and women from castes and communities pitched at lower levels were seen to be affected more severely by prejudices and the differential impact of growth processes. During fieldwork the impact of sectoral crisis faced by different industries, such as the handloom crisis and the implications for women from artisanal families stood out very sharply. This often also impinged directly on the lives of women from the minority community. Similarly, the decline of other occupational groups, including forest dwellers and those based on common property resources was marked. These mainly included tribals—those designated as 'denotified tribes', potters, and artisanal groups who increasingly complained of a lack of availability of resources. This was often also accompanied by a loss of skills and status, including specifically for women. Despite not being seen as 'workers' in common social perceptions, women played a key role in operations within the domestic units of artisanal production and with the loss of work in the 'traditional' occupational sectors women's status within these caste/occupational groups also appears to be undergoing a change (Agnihotri *et al.* 2012).

While in women's studies by now the subject of the invisibility of women's work in artisanal and subsistence-level household-based activity of women is well known, less recognized is the even more glaring subsumption of women's labour under the 'family' unit within sectors where production and accumulation are directly for surplus and profit. Both these forms of non-recognition and invisibility need to be understood and addressed at the level of public policy, though the approach requires that a distinction be made between the two, given the nature, role, and purpose they perform in capitalist production regimes. However, both underscore the fact that there is a need to explore the links between changing gender relations and links with prevailing economic processes. This is necessary if devaluation of women's status is to be understood and addressed, both within the individual family as well as at a social level. Further, studies point to the need to interrogate these aspects from women's own differential social location. This is necessary also if caste- or community-based patterns of gender discrimination and oppression are to be specifically and meaningfully addressed, going beyond slogans of caste identity and pride. Given the scale and high level of uneven development in India, another feature that has to be constantly factored in is that of regional disparities. It is interesting to see that while the community, family, and the household repeatedly figure in discussions on rural India, social scientists are yet to focus on how these are changing, beleaguered, and may even be felt in a dispersed form under economic pressure, despite an ever widening discourse on gender.

Understanding Violence against Women

In recent years women have increasingly been at the receiving end of unprecedented violence. These crimes against women in India have to be seen in the larger context and the dislocations and disruptions that are a marked feature of the social life in India today. The anger this has fuelled is reminiscent of the sharp turn that social conflict took in the pre- and post-emergency days, marked by the crisis of the 1970s in the history of this country. While activists grapple with the impact and search for ways to address these intensified attacks in their multiple geographical and social locations, the fact is that since the increased violence has its roots in growing inequalities and heightened social conflict, resolution of these is not possible at the level of the women's movement alone.

While violence is an issue the women's movement has had to face from the 1970s, the scale and proportion that violence against women and children has assumed today has not been adequately fathomed by social analysts. More disturbing is the high level of social acceptability of and acquiescence to this violence. What accounts for this increase and how is it to be understood at a social level? It cannot be understood or seen merely as the perverse behaviour of individuals who perpetrate it even though these perpetrators must be brought to book. While the media usually highlights specific incidents when these happen, it is imperative that we understand the context in which this violence is inflicted, made socially acceptable. Perpetuation of it on a continued basis is made possible within a context determined by the broader social matrix. The parameters of defining this context need to define women going beyond a narrow gender discourse to locating the vulnerability of women in their specific locations in society.

Data on crimes, specifically the increasing instance of domestic violence brings out the sharp increase. It has been observed that while the 'silent crime' of domestic violence is rampant in Indian homes, the fact is that 'the violence is so abusive that it forms the largest category of crimes against women, as officially recorded by the NCRB over the years 1995–7. It was also found that while on other counts there often appears a north–south divide, there was none to be seen when it came to crimes against women. There has been continual increase in the rate of crimes against women since 1996. It is observed that the crimes against women reported an increase of 1.7 per cent over 2000 and 24.2 per cent over 1996 respectively (GoI 2009). Crimes against women have continued to increase even when the rate—defined as the 'number of crimes' per 100,000 population—of cognizable crimes in the country showed a decreasing trend. In an overview of crime in India, the NCRB provided data in 2009, to show that kidnapping and abduction had registered an increase of 475.2 per cent between 1953 and 2008, while murder had seen an increase of 234.3 per cent in the same period.

The Bureau started recording rape separately only in 1971 and this had shown an increase of 791.5 per cent by 2010.[13] Crimes against women, it may be noted, started appearing as a separate head in the Crimes in India report only since 1995. The NCRB data shows that between 1999 and 2009 the incidence and rate of crimes against women registered a percentage share increase of 50.1 per cent. Between 1996 and 2006 the incidence and rate of crime against women registered a percentage share increase of 42.4 per cent, with 43.9 per cent of the incidents in 2009 being incidents of cruelty by the husband and relatives reflecting a broad pattern over the years with some variations in annual figures. Similarly, incidents of dowry deaths have shown a steady increase through these years. In 2009 and 2010, the number of incidents of dowry deaths registered under Section 302/304 Indian Penal Code (IPC) in India was 8,383 and 8,391, respectively, while cases registered under Section 498-A were 89,546 and 94,041, respectively.[14] There has been an almost consistent increase in crimes against women, with only a slight temporary dip being registered in the year 2003.[15]

While the household emerges as an important site as social conflict intensifies, what has been more intriguing and shocking is growing violence against women in public spaces. This is obvious from the issues focused on by the movement through the last several decades. The major heads of crime continue to be dowry and dowry-related deaths, rape—within which incest and child abuse feature prominently—cruelty by the husband, and kidnapping and abduction. To ignore this brutal exploitation and oppression of women conveys a sense of the paralysis that has hit both politics and society. Meanwhile at the official level there is a visible shift from an earlier attitude of prevarication by the state and judiciary, in the name of a supposed 'gender balancing'. Instead of exerting pressure to strictly enforce the existing laws, the thrust of the official machinery, and sections of the judiciary and executive has been in the direction of reversing some of the gains made in the wake of widespread support for the sustained struggle in the 1980s. Even as the crime data in India with reference to women is alarming, discussions in official circles, including at the level of parliamentary debate, have in fact been oriented to dilution of laws brought in to check crimes against women. These issues were raised by women's organizations in course of discussion with the Rajya Sabha, in December 2010.[16]

While violence in general has increased, the situation with reference to conflict zones continues to be a grim reminder of the seriousness of the situation. The areas affected by armed conflict being a case in point. Violations by instruments and agencies of the state, assigned the charge of protecting and upholding the law, have perhaps the worst record. Developments in the states of Jammu and Kashmir, Manipur, and much of the other violence-affected areas conveys a sense of the weaknesses and vulnerabilities of our democracy and above all the need for effective monitoring of human rights violations by official agencies.

In countries such as India even as the incidence of crimes has gone up, what is more alarming is the fact that everyday forms of violence have increasingly become more acceptable socially and it is only specific 'incidents' of violence that attract attention. The discussion and societal reflection on violence more so in the media is effectively focused on the response to it. This comes out sharply in cases such as the horrendous crime committed on the streets of Guwahati, some months ago. Equally alarming has been the issuing of diktats and aggressive assertion by forces broadly representing the 'moral brigade'. While till some years ago such assertions were confined to protests by the saffron brigade and its various front organizations on specific occasions such as Valentine's Day and others, the frequency with which fundamentalist statements or diktats are issued and sought to be imposed is on the rise, be it in the name of village/khap panchayats, or other such bodies. More disconcerting is the impunity with which these are allowed to impose their will on free citizens, especially the women of India. A similar impunity is witnessed in the case of crimes committed in the name of 'honour' as seen in the state of Haryana, where the movement first took up such incidents to make such unconstitutional assertions visible. While these crimes were first being associated with rural India, clearly urban modern India is in no way free from this malaise. If official response is an indicator, the seriousness of the situation is yet to be fathomed. Though in Haryana itself some couple protection homes have been set up and other such measures have been implemented under pressure from the movement (All India Democratic Women's Association 2010). The aggressive projection of fundamentalist identities and ideologies, and their espousal by major political formations in the Indian scenario, further constricts the space within which the debate on women's rights is carried out and narrows the scope for advance of democratic rights for all.

What prompts such violence and what allows society to become immune to such flagrant violation of the rights and dignity of women?

While there is no doubt that the violence inflicted on women is also part of a wider trend towards criminalization, there is no doubt that the vulnerability of women, being part of the most oppressed sections exposes them to a specific gender-based attack which adds an element of commonality to their lives despite the obvious fact that they are not a homogenous group. Modern-day consumerism has much to do with this phenomenon which sees women as an object of consumption. Ironically, in recent months, attempts to show this violence as provoked (by the women) or to put the blame on trends representing embracing of values that are un-Indian have also increased. There has been a highly charged and prejudiced public debate with members of the National Commission for Women, ministers at the state level in Karnataka particularly and police officers, including from Uttar Pradesh, and more recently, Haryana, openly coming out with statements which ascribe the reason for such violence to women themselves while women activists have taken strong objection to this. These seek to pass the blame on to the victims of violence and attacks, even as they absolve both society and those guilty of crimes.

GENDER BALANCING BY THE STATE: IN SEARCH OF POSITIVE INTERVENTIONS

NATIONAL RURAL EMPLOYMENT GUARANTEE ACT

Enacted by the UPA government in 2005, the National Rural Employment Guarantee Act (NREGA) was initially implemented in 200 poverty-ridden districts was later extended to provide 100 days' work on a household basis in all districts, based on the principle of self-targeting and declaration of the need and intent to undertake work as per the schemes being implemented in different districts. While women were not specifically targeted/or even mentioned in the first instance, interventions by women's organizations provided for one-third reservation for women under the Act. However, while in the first few years wages remained a major issue, non-issuing of cards in the name of women emerged as a major constraint on women getting work under the schemes launched. Women's organizations also drew attention to productivity norms and rates of payments given the nature of tasks assigned, which did not allow for equal wages to women, apart from non-implementation of clauses such as that for provision of child care/crèches on work sites (CWDS-FORCES 2010–11).

As per reports and reviews of NREGA it is assessed that 47 per cent of the person-days of work generated have been by women, and that women have received a total of Rs 53,000 crores as wages under the Act between 2006–7 and 2011–12 financial year. However, there are reports of significant inter-state variations, with Kerala showing the highest participation by women and Uttar Pradesh and Jammu and Kashmir showing low levels. Southern states appear to perform better as is the case with regard several other state sponsored programmes and indicators. It is claimed that the Mahatma Gandhi National Rural Employment Guarantee Act (MGNREGA) has 'reduced traditional gender wage discrimination, particularly in the public works sector' (GoI 2012: 21).

The NREGA is seen as a major strategy to deal with poverty and unemployment and is now being cited as adding restrictions on labour migration. There has been criticism from agencies such as the World Bank that this has checked labour mobility and acted as a constraint on economic growth (GoI 2012). The World Bank's observations have drawn wide critical response even as NREGA continues to be cited as a major factor behind labour shortages in urban India.

It is observed that 'the agriculture labour shortage is not caused entirely by MGNREGA and that the impact of MGNREGA' has several dimensions which include rural participation rates by drawing into the workforce many who were not active workers, and making work accessible on wages and employment conditions that are better than what prevailed earlier (ibid.). Attention has also been drawn to the issue is that of wage rates. While NREGA generally envisages a daily wage rate, its manner of implementation represents a combination of time-rate and piece-rate and the need to focus on the nature of work undertaken and its links with broader issues of rural economy.

The grimness of the unfolding scenario is visible at various levels and in various sectors. For example, in the post-liberalization period the picture in the handloom sector, for instance, has changed from one of moderate to slow growth to decline in the 1990s. Handloom production is characterized by region-specific diversity. It cannot be reduced to or understood merely in terms of abstract demand and supply principles of the market. Highlighting the importance of linkages with the local economy, reports have pointed out that the recent 'emphasis on export-orientation as a strategy of survival is not only against the very nature of handloom production but is likely to be suicidal for the handloom weavers'.

EDUCATION

In this larger scenario, one aspect that has held out hope in the last decade has been the development on the education front though that still remains disappointing in terms of expectations, achievements, and aspiration. Enrolment rates for girls have been steadily going up though gaps in rural urban terms persist. Equally serious is the lack if not total absence of facilities in the remote and interior parts of the country, more specifically in tribal areas. The Muslim minority has often been cited in discussions on India lagging behind with reference to goals on the education front.

More recently, studies conducted by the National University of Educational Planning and Administration (NEUPA) show that the enrolment of Muslim students in primary schools is registering an increase, at a time when overall enrolment is either stagnating or even declining in some states. Between 2007–8 and 2010–11, Muslim enrolment in Classes I to V (primary) shot up by 25 per cent and for Classes VI to VIII (upper primary) by 50 per cent across the country, according to data collected from the country's 1.36 million elementary schools for Classes I to VIII as a whole, this marked a rise of 31 per cent. In the same period, total enrolment in Classes I to V inched up by just 1 per cent and for Classes VI to VIII by 12 per cent. For Classes 1 to VIII, this marked a rise of 4 per cent. The enrolment of girls has blazed ahead even faster than boys in the Muslim community. For primary sections, the enrolment for Muslim girls increased by 26 per cent compared to just 1 per cent increase in the enrolment of all girls. For upper primary sections, the enrolment for Muslim girls increased 54 per cent while for all girls it rose 15 per cent. For Classes I to VIII, the enrolment was up 33 per cent for Muslim girls against an overall average of 5 per cent (Varma 2012).

THE PREVENTION OF SEXUAL HARASSMENT AT THE WORKPLACE

While the Women's Reservation Bill is still to be adopted, nearly one and a half decades after the landmark Vishakha Guidelines from the Supreme Court, the Lok Sabha has finally adopted the Sexual Harassment of Women at Workplace (Prevention, Prohibition and Redressal) Bill, 2010. As laid down in the Supreme Court guidelines, the definition of sexual harassment includes any unwelcome act or behaviour, demand for sexual favours, making sexually coloured remarks, or showing pornography, and any other physical, verbal, or non-verbal conduct of a sexual nature. The Bill comprehensive in its definition

of sexual harassment and in the areas/sectors it seeks to cover, makes it mandatory for all offices, hospitals, institutions, and other workplaces to have an internal complaints redress mechanism, with non-compliance being punishable. While an attempt has been made to address some of the concerns earlier expressed by women's organizations in that it includes domestic workers in its ambit, nevertheless serious lacunae remain, primarily with regard to women in the informal sector. It leaves out women agricultural workers, who, as discussed above, continue to form a large segment of the unorganized labour force, including under the MGNREGA. At the same time women working in fisheries, forests, or in construction work sites, roads, stations, trains, etc., have not been brought under its purview. Women employees in the armed forces are also not covered by this law. The restriction in the number of workers to less than 10 in the unorganized sector has no justification.

While many of these issues, discussed over the last few years with reference to the draft in circulation persist, the most unacceptable part is the inclusion of a penalty clause which allows for penal action against the complainant, if retained, will defeat the very purpose of this legislation. Women's organizations had specifically asked for the removal of the 'complaint with malicious intent' clause. This goes against the very spirit of the Vishakha guidelines, which had explicitly stated that the complainant should in no way be victimized. Retention of this clause shall go against bringing justice to those who are victims of sexual harassment and, in fact, shall act in a manner to restrain them for filing complaints of sexual harassment, a fact that had been noted by the Parliamentary Standing Committee. The context in which women seek and perform work continues to be insecure and the assumption that cases which are/ may not be proven arise from falsehood and malicious intent cannot be upheld, merely because the charge could not be proven.

There is a need to address some of these issues even as an emphasis needs to be placed on the enquiry in a time-bound manner and to be conducted and recommendations followed up with appropriate action in a more time-bound manner.

DEVELOPING FRAMEWORKS TO ANALYSE WOMEN'S DECLINING STATUS

The focus on violence in this piece is not to suggest that the status of women can be understood only in terms of growing violence against women. Nor is it being argued that women's status should be fathomed by focusing on gender aspects in isolation from overall paradigms of development. This was a point emphasized by the Committee on the Status of Women in India (CSWI's) report *Towards Equality* several decades ago (GoI 1975). Rather it is being argued that the extent to which increased economic pressures wreak havoc in the social milieu and specifically mount pressure on family life is yet to be realized and that the violence inflicted on women is not isolated from these trends. What is surprising is that while the crisis of the economy is located in and is a direct fall-out of the macro policies that have shaped the economy over the last two decades, the solutions sought to the violence that these processes unleash are often in the domain of human rights and abstraction from macro-policies. In somewhat similar fashion, the adverse impact of development policies is sought to be countered by refurbishing the foundations of the family. Within women's studies too there has been a trend to pursue the cultural studies framework to explore the roots of denial, discrimination, and oppression in cultural formations. While as historical explorations these undoubtedly serve a long-term purpose by developing an understanding. However, if analysis remains confined to these, the urgency of addressing women's status, denial of dignity, and increasing devaluation shall be lost on both state and society. The need of the hour is to accompany interpretation of cultural representations with exploring the material basis of these concrete suggestions so as to also provide for addressing the continuing decline in social indicators on virtually all counts through policy interventions.

A central paradox of the unfolding scenario and its implication for women there is a growing burden of work, accompanied by a pervasive pressure to struggle to find work in order to survive in the face of loss of livelihood, with resources increasingly going out of the hands of people and corporate power, and increasing control over these. Women are under severe pressure to find alternate means of livelihood at a time when high growth is accompanied by shrinking opportunities for the mass of people, including women. This is accompanied by fast changing consumerist lifestyles and modernist aspirations. Under siege are both, production as well distribution/consumption patterns based on age-old social hierarchies and patterns of exclusions even as the parameters for reconfigured hierarchies, discriminations, and denials demand attention from more egalitarian perspectives. However, the neoliberal policy framework is oriented to building a system which is complacent and complicit with both the age-old hierarchies and ever emerging new forms of denials and discriminations. Official agencies—national and international—have incorporated a focus on gender

relations as the location for addressing women's rights. This serves a purpose and follows a method. But we would do well to remember and continuously remind ourselves that women's social identity, even as it is based on their belonging to the female sex, is in fact shaped by the complexity of their being embedded in wider social relations and formations. A crisis in the latter affects women and their links with society in its entirety. Fragmentation of strategies for redressal too will serve only a partial purpose.

The family, which is seen as a primary location for the woman, is not and never has been only a unit of residence or mere physical habitation. It has served the purpose of socialization and provided moorings, even as these have stemmed from known privileges to some and known/unknown prejudices against others, including patriarchal moorings to social institutions. As an institution it is, perforce, also under pressure in view of the changes it is exposed to, particularly in order to perform its role of intra-household resource allocation in view of emerging constraints and obligations. Further, since these are to be reworked within the given socio-cultural context, prevailing norms of gender relations assume importance. Whereas often this is seen and interpreted in terms of the specificity of households, the fact is that gender relations and social norms are shaped in the context of a socio-political dynamic within the regional, national, and even an international context. This may be mediated by individual families through caste- or community-based identities. While social activists have been open to exploring the links that the South Asian context provides for the reworking of patriarchy, especially in the context of fundamentalism, a similar scrutiny of links between the fundamentalist order, neoliberalism, and currently prevalent models of governance has been lagging behind in the academic domain. It has been significantly concluded that the fundamentalisms prevalent in the South Asian region are all firmly entrenched in patriarchy and retrogressive ideologies. The fact that imperialist impulse driving the modern-day capitalism and the pace of modernization is comfortable with such compromises and even steps in to exploit these so-called 'cultural' legacies and identities has not yet been sufficiently explored.

It is these links which have in fact significantly shaped the discourse on women's rights in India and other parts of South Asia, while also bringing the women's movement in direct conflict with both the cultural and politico-ideological formations. The fact remains that the current scenario of insecurity, vulnerability, and denial of equality as well as dignity to women and men, stands in direct contrast with the urges and aspirations which emerge from the ground. Social movements and the women's movement, have interpreted emerging modernity as offering hope and new opportunities to uphold the dignity of a woman—dignity as measured by her sense of self-worth, her power to choose freely what she will be, and the means by which she believes she will achieve her ends. These, in course of time, have come to be seen as determined by the individual's ability to assert rights through an enabling environment. However, the material conditions as well as current ideological formations in the political domain are in fact running counter and do not allow for realization of these goals. The fact that globalization enhances women's vulnerability in their multiple roles as citizens, as members of exploited and marginalized groups as well as specifically on a gender-based identity today makes it representative of the hegemonic paradigm within which both inequality and patriarchy prosper. This must be recognized by all those who wish to interrogate the phenomenon of growing inequality and violence that women are subjected to and interlinkages between these phenomenon and the macro processes need to be drawn at all points. Historically, capitalism has been seen as the harbinger of a civil society premised on liberty and equality. There is sufficient evidence to show that the results of growth strategies currently being pursued in India are contrary to these claims. For a historian, these times reflect possibilities which can take different and opposite historical directions depending on the political thrust and orientation. For this reason women have a stake in ongoing debates as well as in the interrogation and contestation of prevailing development paradigms.

Notes

1. *Economic Outlook 2012/13*, Economic Advisory Council of the Prime Minister, pp. 4–6.

2. Census of India 2011, GoI, New Delhi.

3. This section draws upon trends analysed and data presented in Mazumdar and Neetha (2011). Also see Mazumdar (2012).

4. Ibid.

5. Economic Advisory Council to the Prime Minister, New Delhi, February 2011, p. 2.

6. See AIDWA Memo dt. 24 November 2011, submitted to M.V. Nair, Chairperson, Committee to Re-examine the Existing Classification and Suggest Revised Guidelines with regard to PSL Classification and Related Issues RBI, New Delhi.

7. *Economic Outlook 2012/13*, Economic Advisory Council, pp. 59–61.

8. Ravi S. Srivastava's acceptance speech for the V.V. Giri National Labour Award, 2009, titled 'Internal Labour Migration and Elements of Migration Policy for India'.

9. NCEUS Note submitted to GoI on 'The Global Economic Crisis and the Informal Economy in India: Need for Urgent Measures and Fiscal Stimulus to Protect Incomes in the Informal Economy', on 26 November 2008.

10. See movement documents from AIDWA, India, and also Thompson (1991).

11. Based on Mazumdar and Agnihotri (forthcoming in 2013).

12. For more discussion on forms of labour, see Misra (2011).

13. *Crime in India 2010*, Compendium, NCRB, MHA, and GoI, New Delhi, p. 12.

14. *Crime in India 2009*, Compendium, NCRG, MHA, and GoI, New Delhi, Table 5(A), p. 81.

15. NCRB reports for relevant years.

16. Also see Resolution on 498-A, National Consultation on 'Marital Violence and 498 –A', organized by AIDWA and ISWSD, 12 November, 2011, New Delhi.

References

Agnihotri, I., I. Mazumdar, and N. Neetha. 2012. *Gender and Migration Negotiating Rights: A Women's Movement Perspective, Key Findings.* New Delhi: Centre for Women's Development Studies.

All India Democratic Women's Association. 2009. *Report on the Conditions of Work of Home-based Women Workers in Delhi.* Delhi: All India Democratic Women's Association.

———. 2010. *In the Name of Honour: Let Us Love and Live.* New Delhi: All India Democratic Women's Association.

CWDS (Centre for Women's Development Studies). 2012. 'Gender and Migration: Negotiating Rights: A Women's Movement Perspective (Key Findings)', supported by IDRC and CRDI, March. New Delhi: CWDS. Available at http://www.cwds.ac.in/researchPapers/GenderMigrationNegotiatingRights.pdf.

CWDS-FORCES. 2010–11. 'Assessment of Child Care Component under NREGA: A Study of Rajasthan, Uttar Pradesh, and Jharkhand', FORCES, 2010–11, unpublished.

George, Sabu. 2011. 'Child Sex Ratio Patterns from Census 2011: Preliminary Observations', *Women's Watch*, (April–June): 5–8.

Ghosh, Jayati. 2009. *Never Done and Poorly Paid Women's Work in Globalizing India.* New Delhi: Women Unlimited.

GoI (Government of India). 1975. *Towards Equality.* New Delhi: GoI.

———. 2006. *National Commission on Farmers, Final Report.* New Delhi: National Commission on Farmers, Ministry of Agriculture.

GoI (Government of India). 2007. *Report of the Expert Group on Indebtedness, Banking Division*. New Delhi: Department of Economic Affairs, Finance Ministry.

———. 2008–9. Economic Survey 2008–9, Chapter 2. New Delhi: GoI.

———. 2009. *Crime in India*, no. 49. New Delhi: National Crime Records Bureau, Ministry of Home Affairs.

———. 2011. *Situation Analysis of the Elderly in India*. New Delhi: Ministry of Statistics and Programme Implementation.

———. 2012. *MGNREGA Sameeksha: An Anthology of Research Studies on the Mahatma Gandhi National Rural Employment Guarantee Act, 2005, 2006–12*. Delhi: Orient BlackSwan.

GoI and ILO (International Labour Organization). 2012. *Maternity Protection in India: A National Assessment*, August. New Delhi: Ministry of Labour and Employment, GoI and ILO.

Gupta, J.A. 2012. 'Reproductive Biocrossings: Indian Egg Donors and Surrogates in the Globalized Fertility Market', *The International Journal of Feminist Approaches to Bioethics*, 5(1, Spring): 25–51.

John, M., R. Kaur, and R. Palriwala. 2009. 'Dispensing with Daughters: Technology, Society, Economy in North India', *Economic and Political Weekly*, 44(15, 11 April): 16–19.

John, Mary E. 2011. 'Census 2011: Governing Populations and the Girl Child', *Economic and Political Weekly*, 46(16, 16 April): 10–12.

Mazumdar, Indrani. 2012. 'A Volatile World: Women's Employment Situation in Liberalization Led Growth in India', Unpublished, CWDS.

Mazumdar, Indrani and Indu Agnihotri. Forthcoming in 2013. 'Traversing Myriad Trails: Gender and Migration across India', in Thanh-Dam Truong, Des Gasper, J. Handmaker, and S.I. Bergh (eds) *Migration, Gender and Social Justice: Perspectives on Human Insecurity*, vol. 9, *Hexagon Series on Human and Environmental Security and Peace*. Heidelberg, New York, Dordrecht, and London: Springer.

Mazumdar, Indrani and N. Neetha. 2011. 'Gender Dimensions: Employment Trends in India 1993–94 to 2009–10', *Economic and Political Weekly*, 46(43, 22 October): 118–26.

Misra, Lakshmidhar. 2011. *Human Bondage Tracing its Roots in India*. New Delhi: Sage Publications.

Nagaraj, K. 2008. 'Farmers' Suicides in India: Magnitudes, Trends and Spatial Patterns', March. Madras: Madras Institute of Development Studies.

National Commission for Women. 2009. *National Policy for Women in Agriculture*. Delhi: National Commission for Women.

Pande, Amrita. 2009. 'Not an "Angel", Not a "Whore": Surrogates as "Dirty" Workers in India', *Indian Journal of Gender Studies*, 16(2): 141–173

Patnaik, Utsa. 2004. *The Republic of Hunger and Other Essays*. New Delhi: Three Essays Collective.

———. 2011. 'How Little Can a Person Live on?' *The Hindu*, 30 September.

Qadeer, Imrana. 2010. *New Reproductive Technologies and Health Care in Neo Liberal India: Essays*. New Delhi: Centre for Women's Development Studies.

Ramachandran, V.K. and Madhura Swaminathan. 2006. *Financial Liberalization and Rural Credit*. New Delhi: Tulika Books.

Ramachandran, V.K. and Vikas Rawal. 2009. 'The Impact of Liberalization and Globalization on India's Agrarian Economy', *Global Labour Journal*, 1(1, 12 March): 56–91.

Ramakumar, R. 2012. 'Large-scale Investments in Agriculture in India', *IDS Bulletin*, Special Issue: *Standing on the Threshold: Food Justice in India*, 43(Issue Supplements, 1 July): iii–ix, 1–129.

Reddy, D.N. and Srijit Mishra. 2009. *Agrarian Crisis in India*. New Delhi: Oxford University Press.

Sainath, P. 2010. '17,368 Farm Suicides in 2009', *The Hindu*, 27 December.

———. 2011. 'In 16 Years, Farm Suicides Cross a Quarter Million', *The Hindu*, 29 October, Mumbai.

Saxena, K.B. 2011. 'Land Reforms: Unfinished Agenda or Reversal of Policy', *India: Social Development Report 2010: The Land Question and the Marginalized*. New Delhi: Oxford University Press and Council for Social Development, pp. 173–93.

Sarojini, N., V. Marwah, and A. Shenoi. 2011. 'Globalisation of Birth Markets: A Case Study of Assisted Reproductive Technologies in India', *Global Health*, 7(1, 12 August): 27.

Thompson, E.P. 1991. *Customs in Common: Studies in Traditional Popular Culture*. London: Merlin Press.

UNDP (United Nations Development Programme). 2009. *Global Economic Crisis Impact on the Poor: A Synthesis of Sector Studies*. New Delhi: UNDP India.

Varma, Subodh. 2012. 'Muslim Girls' Enrolment in Primary Schools Up 33% against Average of 5%', TNN, *The Times of India*, 20 August.

7

Regional Dimensions of Inequalities

P.M. Kulkarni and Himanshu

Since Independence, there have been perceptible improvements in the socio-economic conditions of India's population. Literacy has increased over the years and now a vast majority of men are literate as are a majority of women. Mortality has declined at all ages with the result that an Indian now expects to live for over 65 years. Real incomes have increased, and the growth in per capita income has been impressive during the last two decades in spite of an enormous growth in population. Agricultural production has shown good progress and per capita food availability has risen though there are some year-to-year fluctuations. Industrial production is substantially greater than in the past. Many channels of communication are available now and these have become easily accessible to most sections of the society. But the development has not been uniform across space. Some regions, especially some states, have done much better than others in education, health, incomes, and poverty reduction. This is well-recognized in India, and government policies pay special attention to the regions lagging in the process of development, special programmes are introduced for these, and additional financial assistance is provided.

But there are inequalities within states as well. In a stratified society like India, social and economic conditions are known to vary substantially across castes and religions. Socio-economic conditions also differ between rural and urban areas, and between males and females. Since the overall level of socio-economic development is not yet high in the country, inequalities imply that some sections are much more deprived of basic needs than others. Many communities in India have traditionally been excluded from education and denied access to assets and public services. Caste has been a major stratifying factor in India and differentials by caste in various aspects of living have long been noted. In particular, those belonging to the Scheduled Castes (SCs) have for long faced severe discrimination in various spheres, including education and have generally been prevented from ownership of agricultural land. Those belonging to the Scheduled Tribes (STs) were deprived of many opportunities in the past on account of isolation, and some amount of isolation persists even now. It has also been recognized that certain other sections of society also remained socially and educationally backward compared to others. These are broadly called the Other Backward Classes (OBC). Issues of disparities by caste, the pathways and implications, have been discussed extensively in literature on social and economic development in India (Thorat 2006).

Precepts and injunctions of religions may have a bearing on certain aspects of development. Besides, religious affiliation by itself brings in isolation and exclusion, depriving many from accessing public services. Religious minorities often do not get adequate share in power in a democratic system of governance, and it has been noted that the representation of some minorities in economic and social institutions in India is well below their share in population. The Report of the Prime Minister's High Level Committee (PMHLC) on Socio-Economic Conditions of Muslims in India (Sachar Committee) has systematically presented the evidence on the nature and extent of religious disparity (PMHLC 2006).

Rural populations have poor access to infrastructure and to various social and economic services as compared to the urban. Educational institutions, especially those of higher education, are generally located in urban areas. This is also true of health facilities. In spite of the network of primary health centres (PHCs), many villages do not have any health delivery facility. Employment opportunities in the secondary and tertiary sectors are also primarily in urban areas. Poor transport means that rural populations cannot easily enjoy the benefits located in urban areas.

Women have traditionally been kept out of many spheres of economy and education. While this had been the case in most societies around the world, Indian women too suffered from social exclusion though such exclusion is no longer as widespread as in the past. There has been an improvement in the schooling of girls and female literacy has risen impressively in the recent years. Yet, the level is short of that of male literacy and the gender gap is wide in higher education. In many sectors of employment, female participation is still quite meagre. Besides, political power continues to be male-dominated. There is neglect of women in health care with the result that early childhood mortality for girls in India is higher than that for boys in contrast to the world pattern. Moreover, in the recent decades, sex selection achieved with the use of modern technology has severely affected the child sex ratio (CSR) aggravating the population sex imbalance.

Efforts have undoubtedly been made, by governments and other organizations, to eliminate or at least minimize inequalities in development by introducing affirmative action and other special schemes for weaker sections of the society. This includes reservations in the central and state legislatures for SCs and STs, and additionally for women in municipal and village panchayats. There are reservations in government-controlled or aided educational institutions and in public sector employment for SCs, STs, and OBCs. Other forms of affirmative action, such as financial support, have also been introduced. But given that some of the inequalities, especially those by caste and gender, are deep rooted, large differences remain. A number of reports, including the series of Social Development Reports prepared by the Council of Social Development (CSD) and the Human Development Reports (HDRs) commissioned by the Planning Commission and various state governments and research organizations have documented regional and social differentials in various aspects of social and economic development (CSD 2006, 2011; Desai *et al.* 2010; Institute of Applied Manpower Research 2011; especially the papers by Bose 2006; Dubey 2011; Jodhka 2011; Raju 2006; Sujaya 2011; Thorat 2006; and Tilak 2006 from these reports). Besides, individual researchers have analysed the differentials and tried to establish linkages of these with historical developments and recent state actions.

Furthermore, given India's heterogeneity, the nature and pattern of inequalities is not expected to be uniform across space. While caste has been a major factor in social structure and SCs have faced exclusion throughout India, the nature of caste discrimination and inter-caste relationships has not been uniform. Similarly, though male domination has been widely prevalent through most of the country, gender relations in the south have been different from those in the north (Karve 1968). In particular, women in the southern, eastern, and tribal regions have faced much less exclusion than others. Moreover, social movements for elimination of caste and gender-based discrimination arose in some parts earlier than in others. The movements in Maharashtra and Tamil Nadu are prominently noted in literature, but there have been other movements as well, at different times, and of different nature (for a review, see Shah 2002). It is likely that social disparities have narrowed in regions that had active social revolutionary or reform movements. Besides, many policies on eliminating discrimination and on affirmative action fall within the ambit of state governments and some have been ahead of others in this. For instance, reservations for backward classes were introduced in parts of southern India long before such policies were brought in nationally and in other regions. There is reason to believe, therefore, that the nature and severity of inequalities could conceivably differ across regions. Thus, not only does the level of development vary regionally, the inequalities also possibly do. The focus of this chapter is on this issue.

INDICATORS AND DATA

The three important facets of human development are education, health, and income. These are used in the construction of the Human Development Index (HDI) used by the United Nations and we look at differentials in these. However, the indicators used here are not identical to those used in the HDI for reasons mentioned ahead. First, for education, instead of literacy, we prefer to use the percentage of population in the age range of 20–34 years that completed high school as the indicator. Literacy has risen in India, but since the level of literacy for middle and older ages hardly changes, the level for the entire adult population reflects to a large degree the effects of past educational development. Instead, literacy for young age groups correctly indicates recent educational development. But since most children have been entering school in the recent past, the level of literacy of young population is not likely to show much differential. On the other hand, many children drop out early and do not complete high school. High school completion is the minimum requirement for most of the employment in the modern sector. Therefore, the percentage of those completing high school gives a good indicator of education. Given that high school involves 10 years of schooling, only those above 16 years should be covered assuming children enter school at the age of 6. But since many begin school at a later age—this is especially true in rural areas—and some repeat a grade in school, only those above 20 years are included. Further, we restrict the age range to 20–34 years so that recent educational development is captured. Data on educational achievement for social groups and by gender are available from India's decennial Censuses. The latest Census is of 2011; however, as data on educational level are yet to be released, we fall back on the 2001 Census. The Census provides cross-tabulations of persons by age and educational achievement (highest level completed) by sex, place of residence (rural or urban), and by religion as well for SCs and STs. This allows us to compute the percentage of persons of ages 20–34 that have completed high school for each sex, rural and urban areas, each major religion, and SCs and STs. However, in a few states like Punjab, Haryana, and Delhi, there is no ST population and naturally no indicator could be computed for them. At this stage of India's development, the level of tertiary education is quite low overall and hence no effort is made to examine differentials in college education here.

The most commonly recognized outcome of health is mortality, or, to put it in a positive way, survival. Life expectancy (expectation of life at birth) comprehensively captures mortality at all ages. But computation of life expectancy involves construction of a life table which, in turn, requires data on age-specific death rates. Since the coverage of the civil registration in India is far from complete, data from this system cannot be used. The Sample Registration System has been providing age-specific death rates for large states by sex and place of residence, but not by social groups. Therefore, life expectancy as such cannot be computed for social groups. However, the National Family Health Survey (NFHS), a large nationwide survey that has been carried out three times so far in India—in 1992–3, 1998–9, and 2005–6—gives estimates of infant and early childhood mortality for socio-economic classes including for major religions, and SCs and STs (IIPS and Macro International 2007). The under 5 mortality rate (U5MR), which is the proportion of births dying before completing five years of age, expressed in terms of deaths

per 1,000 births, captures mortality up to the age of 5, that is, infant as well as child mortality, and is used as an indicator of health. One must note that this is a negative indicator: the higher the value, lower the survival. The data from the latest survey, NFHS III are used here.

Undernutrition is a major factor responsible for the high morbidity and high mortality among Indian children. This is assessed using anthropometric measures based on weight and height. For children, height can be compared to the standard height for that age, and weight can be compared to standards for the height as well as the age. International standards have been established by the World Health Organization (WHO) for each sex for *weight at a specified age (in months), for height at a specified age, and for weight at a specified height*. An individual child's nutritional status is reckoned on the basis of the z-score on the international reference for the child's age and sex. Low height relative to age, called *stunting*, indicates chronic undernutrition resulting from long deprivation in nutrition or long persistence of some disease, causing growth retardation. Low weight at a given height, called *wasting*, indicates acute undernutrition. Weight for age is a composite measure and takes into account chronic as well as acute undernutrition resulting from the lack of food or continuous persistence of diarrhoea or other diseases in the period just before the measurement. Children with weight less than two standard deviations below the reference median for that age (weight < Reference Median—2 standard deviations for the age) are considered to be *undernourished* and those with weight less than three standard deviations below the median as *severely undernourished*. Since wasting is less common in India than stunting, and there is a strong association between stunting and undernourishment, we focus on the weight for age measure of undernutrition. The NFHS has collected data on weight and height of children under 5 years of age and tabulated by the degree of undernourishment (IIPS and Macro International 2007). Specifically, we use the percentage of children with weight below the international reference median for the age minus two standard deviations, as assessed in the latest round of the NFHS III (carried out during 2005–6), as the indicator of undernutrition.

The NFHS being a household sample survey, the estimates are subject to sampling errors. Estimates based on very small samples have unacceptably large sampling errors and hence are not provided by survey reports. The overall sample sizes in small states were less than 3,000 households; thus, for some social groups within these, the samples were quite small. Therefore, differentials in child mortality by social groups are not available for small states. Besides, even in large states, samples for some religions are small and estimates for these are not given by survey reports. Though these estimates can be computed from data files, given the small sample sizes, sampling errors are very high. Estimates are available, by and large, for Hindus and Muslims in most states (though not all) but for Sikhs and Christians in only a few states. As mentioned earlier, in some states—Punjab, Haryana, and Delhi—there is no ST population, while in some states populations of OBCs are quite small, and in some the share of the 'other' group is very small. Thus, comparisons across all social groups or religions are not possible in many states, but wherever estimates were available, comparisons are made.

Per capita income is a well-accepted indicator of income. However, household surveys find it extremely difficult to collect information on income and instead concentrate on consumer expenditure. The National Sample Surveys (NSS) obtain data on household consumption expenditure in periodic rounds, collected meticulously using a schedule that has a detailed list of various items of expenditure, and provide tabulations by monthly per capita consumer expenditure (NSSO 2011). Moreover, the survey data files allow computation of expenditure distributions for various social groups. But instead of mean (or median) monthly per capita consumer expenditure, we prefer to use the level of poverty as an indicator here. The percentage of population living below a certain level of income or consumption (the 'poverty line'), the head count ratio (HCR), gives an idea of deprivation, and this measure is well-accepted in debates on development in India. Generally, poverty lines are arrived at for individual states separately for rural and urban areas on the basis of some objective criteria and the lines are updated to account for changes in prices. The issue of what should be accepted as the poverty line has been contentious—both with regard to the criteria and the methodology—but the lines provided by the Planning Commission are used by the government and considered as 'official' estimates. Recently, the Tendulkar Committee proposed a new methodology for setting the poverty line. Estimates for states have been worked out according to this approach (Tendulkar Committee 2009). Applying the same lines, it is possible to estimate the poverty level for various social groups from the unit-level data of the NSS. Accordingly, HCRs of poverty have been obtained for social groups within states based on the expenditure data from the 66th Round of the NSS that was carried out during 2009–10.

Like the NFHS, estimates from the NSS, being a sample survey, are subject to sampling errors and sample sizes for social groups can indeed be quite low. Therefore, it is not possible to study differentials in small states. Again, even in large states, sample sizes for some social groups are too small to permit an assessment of differences.

For assessing disparities, the level for a category is compared to that for a reference category. In case of social groups, the indicator for SC, ST, or OBC is compared to that for the 'Others' (that is, communities other than SCs, STs, and OBCs) which is treated as a reference group. The indicators for females are compared to those for males, for rural population to those for urban, and for Muslims to those for Hindus. No comparison is made for other religions since Sikh, Christian, Buddhist, and Jain populations are not large in most states and as a result indicators are not available for these communities, thereby preventing an assessment of regional pattern.

The disparity can be measured as simple gap, that is, gap between a social group and the reference group, or as a ratio. The Sopher's Index, computed as a log of the odds ratio is suited to indicators that are in the form of proportions (or percentages). However, for the sake of simplicity, only the gap measure of disparity, that is, the gap between the level of one group and the reference group is used here.

We first examine the inequalities at an all-India level and then proceed to view these at the level of the state and see how inequalities vary regionally and specifically whether there is some regional pattern.

INEQUALITIES AT THE NATIONAL LEVEL

The selected indicators at the all-India level are shown in Table 7.1 for various groups: male and female; SC, ST, OBC, Others (those other than the SC, ST, and OBC); the two large religions, Hindus and Muslims; and for rural and urban areas. Women do not do as well as men in high school education. Note, however, that a majority of men in the age range of 20–34 years have also not completed high school. Among the SCs and particularly the STs, the level is much lower than others (non-availability of a separate category as the OBCs in the Census prevents an assessment of the level of OBCs and thus the reference here is to all non-SC/ST population that includes the OBCs as well). The educational level of 'others', that is, those other than the SCs, STs, and OBCs is expected to be higher than of the OBCs (note that education is a criterion in the identification of the OBCs) and the gaps between the 'others' and the SCs and STs would be even wider. Muslims have lower levels of high school completion than Hindus (by about 10 percentage points), but are marginally better-off than the SCs. Among the rural population, the level of high school education is much lower than the urban (23 per cent in contrast to 49 per cent), but this is partly an artefact of rural to urban migration being selective with regard to education; educated persons from villages move to urban places for employment in large numbers, thereby raising the level of education in urban areas. Therefore, we have not explored rural–urban differences in school education further.

The overall world pattern is that infant and early childhood mortality is higher among boys than girls. However, in India, girls face greater risk than boys. This is especially so for those aged between 1 and 5, as seen from the data from the Sample Registration System (Registrar General 2010). Relative neglect of girls in health care, including treatment in case of illness, is cited as a factor behind this. U5MR is the highest among the STs (96 per 1,000), followed by the SCs, OBCs, and 'Others' (59 per 1,000) in this order. Muslims do marginally better than Hindus in child survival. U5MR among Sikhs and Christians is lower than both Hindu and Muslim levels (IIPS and Macro International 2007). As expected, child mortality is much higher in rural areas than urban.

In terms of nutritional status, the pattern of differentials is fairly similar to that of U5MR. The STs fare worse than the SCs, and both groups worse than

the OBCs and in turn, the 'others'. Urban children are much less undernourished than rural; the gap is quite wide. However, levels of undernourishment among Muslims and Hindus are nearly equal as are those for boys and girls.

The level of poverty among the STs is much higher (by 20 percentage points) and among the SCs notably higher (by 15 points) than the non-SC/ST population. Poverty among Muslims is higher than among Hindus by about five points. Since poverty is reckoned at the household level, the issue of the male–female gap does not arise.

Overall as a group, the STs are relatively the most deprived followed by the SCs. Muslims fare poorly in education and have higher level of poverty than Hindus. But in health matters, Muslims have a small advantage over Hindus. Women lag behind men in education and girls face a greater risk of mortality than boys do. As expected, the urban population scores over the rural in all the aspects considered.

REGIONAL VARIATIONS IN INEQUALITIES

Is the nature and extent of inequality similar in nature across regions of the country? To address this question, indicators are obtained at the state level and inequalities are examined. As noted earlier, many of the indicators are available only for large states and hence most of the discussion is based on these. We first look at the indicator of education, namely, the percentage of persons of

Table 7.1   Differentials in Some Indicators of Education, Health, and Poverty in India

Category	% Persons Ages 20–34 Who Completed High School, 2001 Census	U5MR, 2005–6 NFHS III	% Children under Five Years Underweight, 2005–6 NFHS III	% Below Poverty Line, 2009–10
All	30.7	74.3	42.5	29.8
Male	38.4	69.7	41.9	NA
Female	22.7	79.2	43.1	NA
SC	18.7	88.1	47.9	40.6
ST	13.9	95.7	54.5	45.4
OBC	NA	72.8	43.2	NA
Others	34.8*	59.2	33.7	24.9*
Hindu	31.3	76.0	43.2	29.7
Muslim	20.2	70.0	41.8	35.4
Rural	22.5	82.0	45.6	33.8
Urban	48.9	51.7	32.7	20.9

Sources: High school completion: Computed from 2001 Census data CDs of Social and Cultural Tables, Registrar General, India; Under-five mortality rates and nutritional status: IIPS and Macro International 2007; Poverty ratios: Computed by Himanshu from NSS 66th Round data files, using the Tendulkar Committee methodology.
Note: * These figures relate to all the population except SC and ST, that is 'Others' and OBCs.

ages 20–34 that have completed high school. These are presented in Table 7.2 for states and for various groups (for some earlier work, see Kulkarni 2007). It is seen that the high school completion rate is generally higher among men than women, with Kerala as an exception. But the gender gap varies as seen from the table and the map in Figure 7.1. Female disadvantage is very high (over 20 percentage points) in Bihar and Jharkhand, and fairly wide (15–20 points) in many states. On the other hand, Punjab, Delhi, Goa, Sikkim, Nagaland, and Mizoram

show mild gaps of less than 10 points. No regional pattern is discernible though. In particular, contrary to expectation, we do not see any north–south pattern in gender disparity.

Muslims are at a huge disadvantage in high school education, of over 20 points, in Haryana, Uttarakhand, Delhi, Manipur, and Himachal Pradesh, and in most of the northern and eastern states the gaps are moderate to high. On the other hand, the gaps are generally narrow and sometimes negative in the southern states (except

Table 7.2   Percentage of Persons Aged 20–34 Who Completed High School in India, Various Groups

State	All	Male	Female	SC	ST	Non-SC/ST	Hindu	Muslim
India	30.7	38.4	22.7	18.7	13.9	34.8	31.3	20.2
Jammu and Kashmir	33.0	41.5	23.1	20.3	13.4	36.5	42.9	26.3
Himachal Pradesh	46.8	54.3	39.2	32.2	32.2	52.4	47.3	22.0
Punjab	44.0	47.5	40.1	24.8		51.1	49.2	
Uttarakhand	39.6	48.1	31.5	20.4	23.0	44.4	42.9	13.8
Haryana	36.7	45.7	26.6	18.2		40.9	38.1	10.0
Delhi	53.4	56.8	49.1	30.0		57.8	55.1	27.2
Rajasthan	21.1	30.4	11.3	12.1	10.3	25.0	20.9	12.4
Uttar Pradesh	25.6	35.0	16.0	13.9		28.7	27.8	14.6
Bihar	23.2	33.9	12.7	10.2		25.8	24.8	14.1
Sikkim	27.7	31.5	23.2	16.8	26.4	28.7	28.7	
Arunachal Pradesh	25.4	32.6	17.6		21.3	31.1	32.7	
Nagaland	34.0	38.5	29.1		33.2	39.0	40.7	
Manipur	46.5	52.8	40.2	50.3	34.4	52.6	56.3	30.4
Mizoram	26.4	27.9	24.9		26.4	27.0	32.7	
Tripura	19.3	24.4	14.2	14.6	10.5	25.3	20.4	8.8
Meghalaya	23.4	26.2	20.7		20.2	39.7	36.8	18.3
Assam	30.0	35.5	24.6	23.5	28.6	30.7	36.0	16.6
West Bengal	22.4	27.5	17.2	11.8	6.4	27.0	26.3	10.0
Jharkhand	25.9	36.0	15.9	13.0	15.2	32.6	28.0	19.8
Odisha	27.9	35.9	20.1	16.6	9.1	36.9	28.1	26.8
Chhattisgarh	23.8	33.5	14.4	21.4	11.5	30.7	22.7	37.8
Madhya Pradesh	23.4	31.1	15.3	15.2	6.9	29.9	22.5	23.4
Gujarat	32.9	39.1	26.3	30.7	17.3	35.9	33.1	23.5
Maharashtra	41.1	49.7	31.6	34.4	16.9	44.2	41.3	30.7
Andhra Pradesh	30.9	40.8	21.2	22.3	10.3	34.3	30.2	34.6
Karnataka	36.8	44.8	28.6	24.3	18.3	40.6	36.9	28.9
Goa	53.5	56.1	50.7			53.9	51.0	34.5
Kerala	48.1	46.7	49.4	32.6		50.4	50.2	31.2
Tamil Nadu	31.5	37.6	25.7	22.4		33.9	30.7	29.1

Source: Computed from 2001 Census data CDs of Social and Cultural Tables, Registrar General, India.
Note: Percentages are not shown where the population of the group in the state is below 2 per cent.

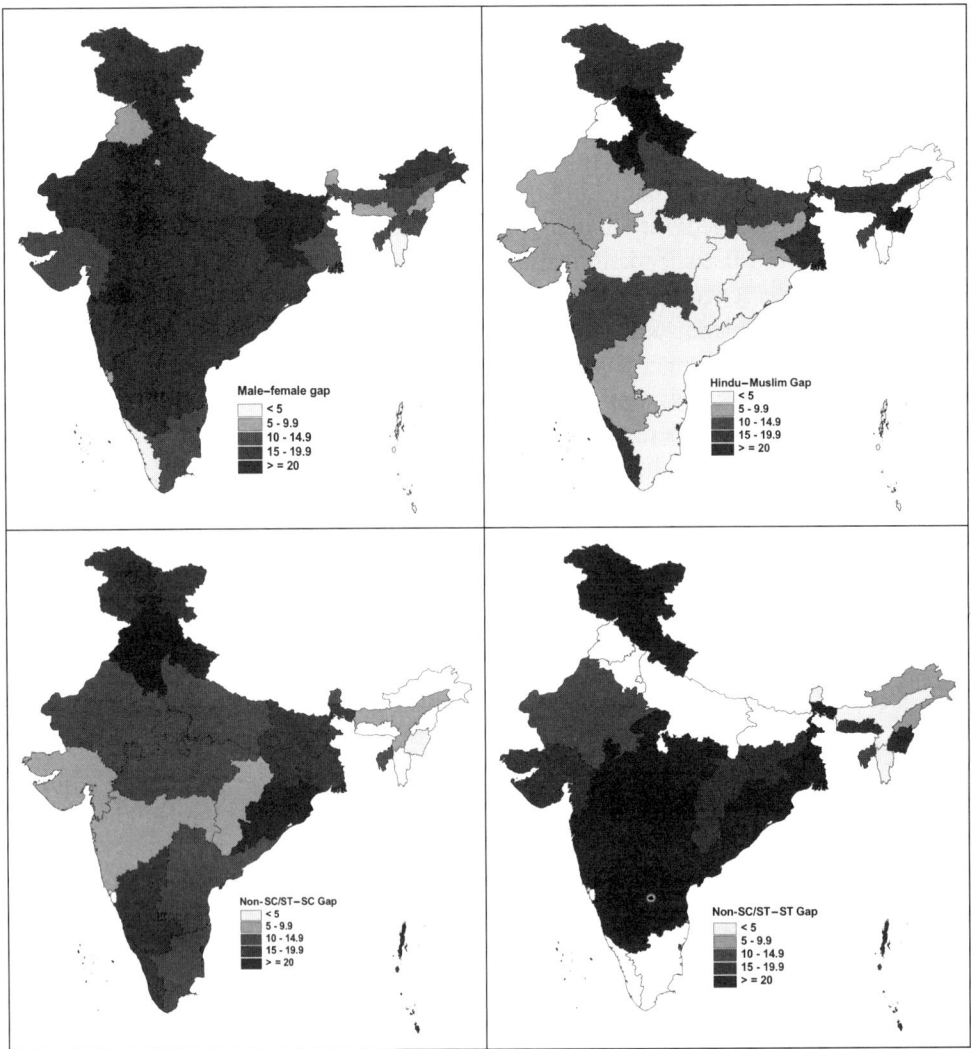

Figure 7.1   Intra-state Differentials in Percentage of Persons Aged 20–34 Who Completed High School

Source: Census 2001.

Note: Blank indicates that the indicator for one of the comparison groups was not obtained due to small population share (less than 2 per cent) of the group in the state.

Kerala) and in central India. We do see some regional pattern here—wide gaps in northern and eastern states and narrow in southern and central (see the map in Figure 7.1). It must be noted that a majority of Muslims in the southern and central states reside in urban areas and this factor has kept the Hindu–Muslim gap low.

The SCs fare poorly compared to the others (non-SC/ST) in all the states. But the gap is narrow in the north-eastern region and Gujarat. On the other hand, in Delhi, Punjab, Haryana, and Uttarakhand, the SCs are most disadvantaged. The STs in the central tribal belt running from Maharashtra to West Bengal face high deprivation in acquiring high school education. This is also the case

in Karnataka (Figure 7.1). In the northeastern regions, on the other hand, the picture is mixed. While Meghalaya, Manipur, and Tripura show moderate gaps, in Assam, Mizoram, and Sikkim, the differences are quite small. In fact, with the exception of Tripura, the STs in the north-eastern states and Himachal Pradesh perform better than the STs in other states in high school completion.

Overall, when it comes to education, some regional patterns are seen. Muslims are relatively deprived in the northern-eastern states, but not in the southern-central states. Similarly, the STs in the central tribal belt are highly deprived. The disadvantage of SCs is widespread but is severe in the Delhi–Punjab region.

Girls do face greater risk of early childhood mortality than boys overall. However, in some states—West Bengal, Odisha, Himachal Pradesh, Andhra Pradesh, and Karnataka—boys have a higher U5MR than girls; this is in conformity with the world pattern. In some other states, the gaps are quite narrow in either direction, and, thus, no inequality as such is seen. But girls in Uttar Pradesh and Bihar are at a much greater risk of mortality than boys in these states, the U5MR for girls being higher by over 20 points than for boys; Rajasthan, Gujarat, and Assam also show moderate female disadvantage.

At the all-India level, Muslim children are at a slight advantage than Hindu children, the U5MR for Muslims being lower than among Hindus. In most of the south-ern and central states, child mortality among Muslims is much lower than among Hindus, greater urbanization of Muslims makes a difference. In a few states the gap is narrow either way. But Muslim children are at a relative disadvantage in Assam, Haryana, West Bengal, and Bihar (see maps in Figure 7.2).

Early childhood mortality among the SCs is higher than other population in almost all the states (for some earlier work, see Baraik and Kulkarni 2006; Sujaya 2011; see also Table 7.3). The SC disadvantage is extremely high, over 40 points, in Rajasthan, Uttar Pradesh, and Uttarkhand, and very high, over 30 points, in many other states. With the exception of Punjab and Delhi, health conditions of the SCs in the northern region are very

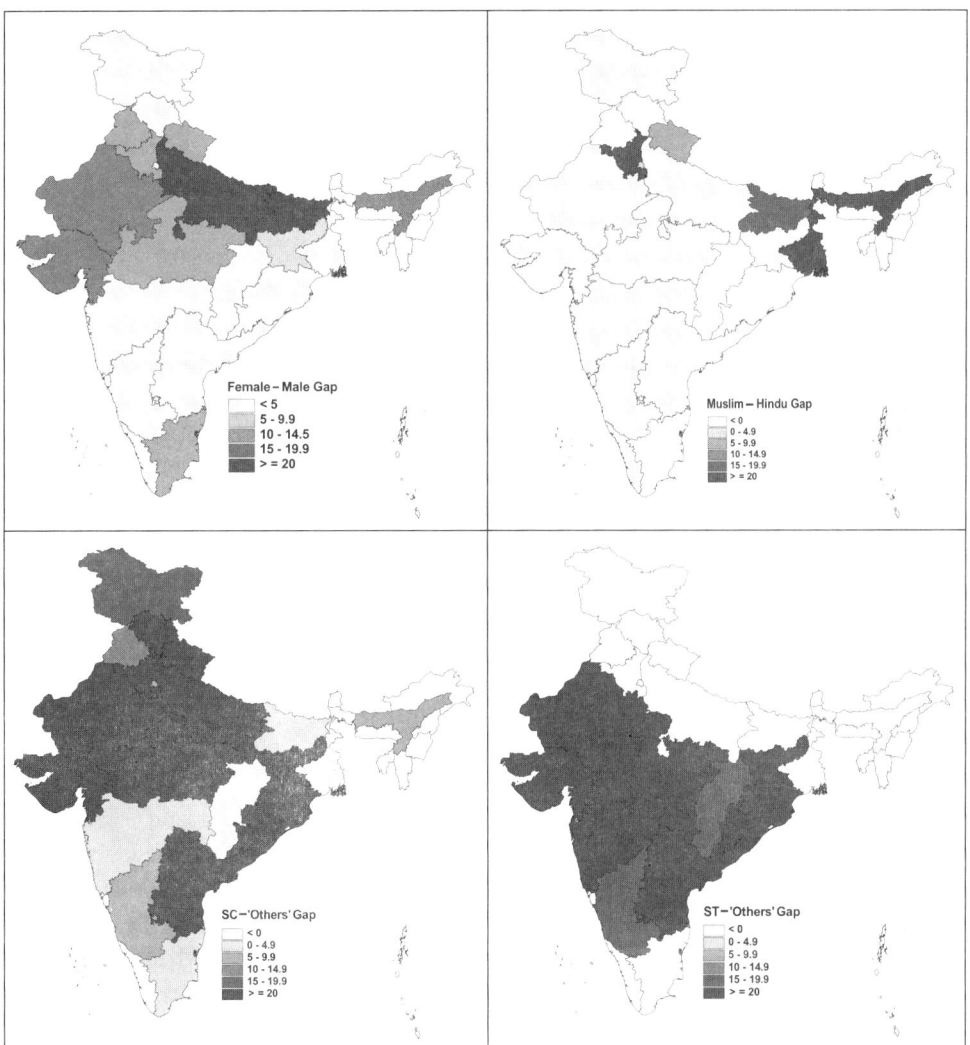

Figure 7.2   Intra-state Differentials in Under 5 Mortality Rates, 2005–6

Source: NFHS III, 2005–6.

Note: Blank indicates that the estimate for one of the comparison groups was not available due to small sample size in the state.

Table 7.3   Under 5 Mortality Rate, in India and Large States, Various Groups

State	All	Male	Female	SC	ST	OBC	Others	Hindu	Muslim	Rural	Urban
India	74.3	69.7	79.2	88.1	95.7	72.8	59.2	76.0	70.0	82.0	51.7
Jammu and Kashmir	53.8	53.9	53.7	72.2		55.1	53.3	55.2	53.9	53.9	53.3
Himachal Pradesh	42.7	49.3	35.8	63.4		36.9	33.1	41.8		44.1	29.6
Punjab	54.6	51.3	58.9	61.5			50.5	56.3		56.2	51.4
Uttarakhand	70.1	67.6	72.9	97.3		83.9	52.2	72.4	80.9	75.3	53.6
Haryana	58.8	55.2	63.0	73.9		62.3	49.7	55.9	86.3	64.4	41.4
Delhi	46.4	47.2	45.5	51.3		47.5	43.2	46.4	48.0	72.8	48.5
Rajasthan	93.3	87.7	99.4	123.1	113.8	80.8	69.9	95.8	77.5	97.6	76.4
Uttar Pradesh	112.3	100.9	124.7	135.1		111.0	87.7	115.8	101.1	116.9	94.8
Bihar	95.0	82.7	108.3	113.1		84.7	108.9	91.5	108.9	96.2	87.2
Assam	95.2	90.3	100.3	110.7	83.2	76.4	100.9	83.3	114.7	98.9	67.4
West Bengal	65.4	74.8	55.7	46.6			70.4	57.6	80.0	68.8	52.9
Jharkhand	112.4	111.1	113.7	121.3	138.5	100.8	92.7	105.0	91.4	123.6	63.7
Odisha	94.7	103.7	84.4	91.8	136.3	83.5	64.2			100.7	59.3
Chhattisgarh	105.5	107.7	103.3	78.1	128.5	98.3	109.3	105.0		116.1	55.7
Madhya Pradesh	108.2	103.6	112.7	110.1	140.7	97.6	79.9	110.5	89.3	114.1	86.6
Gujarat	77.0	72.2	82.5	86.6	115.8	78.1	55.7	80.7	48.0	90.5	54.0
Maharashtra	53.4	55.8	50.7	50.2	69.8	57.8	47.4	57.8	28.6	67.2	36.9
Andhra Pradesh	78.7	85.6	71.1	96.1	112.0	73.1	63.2	82.0	60.0	89.3	55.3
Karnataka	66.2	71.4	60.6	65.4	77.9	63.8	60.4	68.8	57.2	77.4	45.9
Kerala	19.5	22.3	16.6			12.9	20.7	19.1	18.6	22.2	13.8
Tamil Nadu	45.0	42.3	47.9	48.3		44.6		48.3		52.9	34.7

Source: IIPS and Macro International 2007.

Note: Due to small sample sizes, rates for small states and for certain categories in some states are not given.

unfavourable. But conditions of the STs are even worse and the U5MR for the STs is much higher than other population in almost the entire central tribal belt. We, however, do not have differentials in U5MR in the small northeastern states (on account of small sample sizes); the STs in Assam are not poorly placed compared to others, but mortality is high for all sections in the state.

Children in rural areas are at a disadvantage in matters of health and this is reflected in high U5MR. The rural gaps are generally wide throughout the country but there are exceptions: Jammu and Kashmir, Punjab, Bihar, and Kerala show narrow gaps. But no regional pattern as such is seen here.

In nutritional status, girls fare worse than boys in many states, but the order reverses in quite a few (Table 7.4). Overall, the male–female differences are quite narrow. It is in order to note here that the international reference trajectories of weight for age are obtained separately for boys and girls and the comparisons are made with the

values for the respective sex; thus, the deprivation seen here is relative. Undernourishment is higher among SC children than others in all the states. The disparity is high, over 20 percentage points, in Jammu and Kashmir and Bihar, and moderate, 10–20 points, in many states. At the other end, Delhi, Rajasthan, Assam, West Bengal show relatively low gaps (see maps in Figure 7.3). The STs are at a great disadvantage in most of the central tribal belt but not in Assam and Himachal Pradesh (again, small samples prevent an assessment of differentials in the small northeastern states). There are hardly any Hindu–Muslim differences, with most states showing small gaps in either direction. But Muslim children in Haryana and Assam have poorer nutritional status compared to Hindu children in the respective states.

Thus, in matters of child health conditions, though at the national level girls are poorly placed compared to boys, the pattern is not uniform across states. No Hindu–Muslim disparity is seen in the southern-central region

Table 7.4 Percentage of Children Under 5 Years Who Are Underweight, in India and Large States, Various Groups

State	All	Male	Female	SC	ST	OBC	Others	Hindu	Muslim	Rural	Urban
India	42.5	41.9	43.1	47.9	54.5	43.2	33.7	43.2	41.8	45.6	32.7
Jammu and Kashmir	25.6	24.0	27.4	47.7	35.7	28.1	18.8	31.8	23.0	27.9	15.8
Himachal Pradesh	36.5	37.3	35.7	42.9	25.0	57.0	29.0	36.8		37.8	23.6
Punjab	24.9	23.9	26.3	33.9		23.3	17.8	28.8		26.8	21.4
Uttarakhand	38.0	37.8	38.3	44.5	50.4	46.8	32.3	37.7	42.7	42.1	24.3
Haryana	39.6	40.3	38.7	49.4		46.0	32.4	38.4	51.2	41.3	34.6
Delhi	26.1	27.0	25.1	30.0		27.7	23.7	26.2	31.1	22.5	26.5
Rajasthan	39.9	40.3	39.5	44.5	46.8	36.7	37.1	39.8	41.5	42.5	30.1
Uttar Pradesh	42.4	41.2	43.7	48.0	.	43.7	32.3	42.7	41.4	44.1	34.8
Bihar	55.9	54.3	57.8	69.6		55.0	46.1	55.0	59.8	57.0	47.8
Assam	36.4	34.4	38.4	43.0	18.2	29.1	38.2	31.6	43.6	37.7	26.1
West Bengal	38.7	37.4	40.0	40.0	59.7	22.7	37.0	37.7	40.3	42.2	24.7
Jharkhand	56.5	57.7	55.3	56.0	64.3	55.7	42.7	55.3	51.4	60.7	38.8
Odisha	40.7	39.4	41.9	44.4	54.4	38.1	26.0	40.5		42.3	29.7
Chhattisgarh	47.1	46.9	47.2	46.4	52.8	46.5	27.2	48.0	26.4	50.2	31.3
Madhya Pradesh	60.0	59.5	60.6	62.6	71.4	57.8	45.3	60.3	59.8	62.7	51.3
Gujarat	44.6	46.6	42.4	45.9	64.5	46.4	35.3	44.8	43.2	47.9	39.2
Maharashtra	37.0	36.7	37.3	41.7	53.2	33.0	32.6	38.5	29.1	41.6	30.7
Andhra Pradesh	32.5	31.7	33.4	38.5	41.5	32.6	24.2	33.3	25.4	34.8	28.0
Karnataka	37.6	38.7	36.3	41.7	41.9	37.9	32.6	38.2	36.8	41.1	30.7
Kerala	22.9	24.0	21.8	32.6		21.5	20.6	25.4	22.6	26.4	15.4
Tamil Nadu	29.8	31.5	28.0	40.2		26.3	15.9	31.8	15.0	32.1	27.1

Source: IIPS and Macro International 2007.
Note: Due to small sample sizes, rates for small states and for certain categories in some states are not given.

where Muslims are highly urbanized. However, gaps are wide in some states—Assam, West Bengal, and Bihar—which have large Muslim populations. Children belonging to the SCs have generally poor health condition and this condition prevails throughout the country and the STs in the central tribal belt are at a huge disadvantage compared to the non-tribal population.

As seen from Table 7.5, poverty among the STs is much higher (by over 20 percentage points) than other populations in most states (the assessment was possible only in states with large enough ST populations). The exceptions are Assam, Jammu and Kashmir, and Karnataka where the gap is small or in either direction. But in the case of Assam, poverty is high in all sections and though the STs seem to be better placed than others, conditions are not good. In almost the entire central tribal belt, STs are much poorer than others (maps in Figure 7.4). By and large, poverty among the SCs is also higher than among others. Again, Assam is an exception because of high poverty for

all and Jammu and Kashmir and Gujarat show narrow gaps. In some states, notably, Assam, Gujarat, Haryana, West Bengal, Jharkhand, and Uttarakhand, Muslims are much poorer than Hindus, with the deficit exceeding 10 points. On the other hand, in most of the southern states and in Madhya Pradesh, where Muslims are highly urbanized, the gaps are narrow, on either side. Bihar and Jammu and Kashmir also show narrow gaps. By and large poverty ratio for urban populations are less than for rural. But since the poverty lines for rural and urban areas are not the same, no inferences are drawn on rural–urban disparities in this case.

Do we see any regional pattern in inequalities? Clearly, though there are regional variations in the degree of inequality and sometimes even in the direction, no common pattern is discernible. But for some categories, a broad pattern is seen. First, the STs are highly deprived in all respects—education, child health, and income—compared to others throughout the central tribal belt,

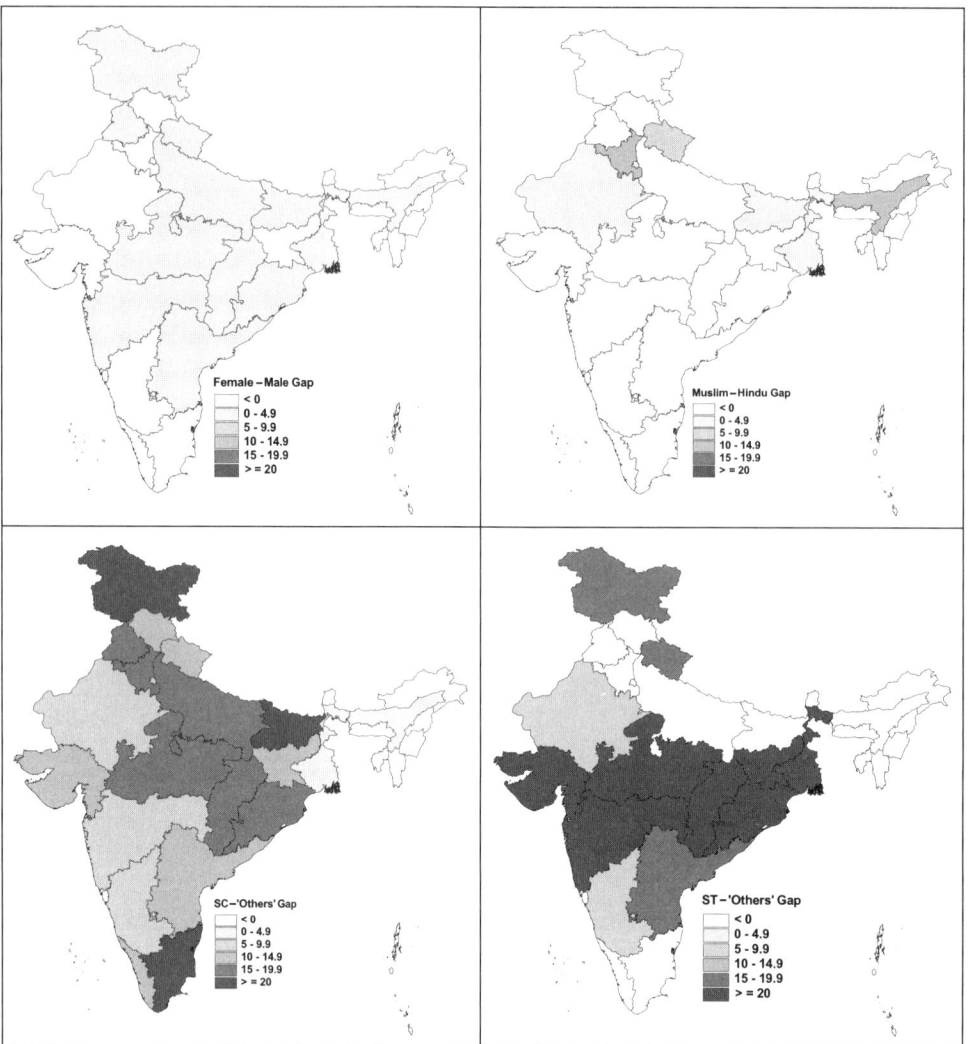

Figure 7.3   Intra-state Differentials in Percentage of Children below 5 Who Are Underweight, 2005–6

Source: NFHS III, 2005–6.

Note: Blank indicates that the estimate for one of the comparison groups was not available due to small sample size in the state.

from Maharashtra to West Bengal, whereas in Assam all sections do poorly (the STs are not relatively more deprived, but all groups are highly deprived). The ST population does fairly well in the predominantly tribal northeastern states in educational achievement and, in fact, better than the STs in the central belt.

The SCs also fare poorly compared to the non-SC/ST population in all respects and, with a few exceptions, in all the states. The degree varies; the SC level of poverty is much higher than others in Punjab and Haryana, and of child mortality in Uttar Pradesh and Bihar. Overall, though the SCs are undoubtedly a deprived section of population, the degree seems to be high in north-

central India, in the regions stretching from Punjab to Bihar.

In most of the large northern and eastern states, Muslims are relatively worse-off than Hindus in all respects. On the other hand, in the southern states and adjoining regions, Muslims do as well as or even better than Hindus in some respects. Muslims are much more urbanized than Hindus and this benefits them in matters of education and health.

It is pertinent to mention here that the differentials discussed above are 'gross' differences. In many analyses, net differences, that is, differences after statistically controlling for other background factors are computed.

Table 7.5   Percentage of People Below the Poverty Line in India and Large States, Various Groups, 2009–10

State	All	SC	ST	Others	Hindu	Muslim	Rural	Urban
India	29.8	40.6	45.4	24.9	29.7	35.4	33.8	20.9
Jammu and Kashmir	9.4	10.7	3.9	9.2	6.6	11.4	8.1	12.8
Himachal Pradesh	9.5	14.9	22.0	6.0	9.3	28.8	9.1	12.6
Punjab	15.9	29.2		7.3	18.1		14.6	18.1
Uttaranchal	18.0	21.5	18.6	15.3	15.3	28.0	14.9	25.2
Haryana	20.1	37.8		12.1	19.4	33.8	18.6	23.0
Rajasthan	24.8	37.1	35.4	18.7	24.7	31.7	26.4	19.9
Uttar Pradesh	37.7	52.3		32.9	36.3	46.2	39.4	31.7
Bihar	53.5	67.7		49.2	54.0	52.2	55.3	39.4
Assam	37.9	36.6	31.9	40.1	30.9	53.6	39.9	26.1
West Bengal	26.7	32.7	31.6	24.5	24.0	34.4	28.8	22.0
Jharkhand	39.1	43.5	51.3	31.5	38.0	49.0	41.6	31.1
Odisha	37.0	47.1	62.7	24.0	36.8	38.0	39.2	25.9
Chhattisgarh	48.7	60.1	65.0	39.6	51.3	15.7	56.1	23.8
Madhya Pradesh	36.7	41.7	60.9	27.9	38.2	27.6	42.0	22.9
Gujarat	23.0	21.8	47.6	17.7	21.9	37.6	26.7	17.9
Maharashtra	24.5	34.7	48.5	19.8	23.7	28.5	29.5	18.3
Andhra Pradesh	21.1	24.5	37.6	19.4	21.2	22.6	22.8	17.7
Karnataka	23.6	34.4	24.2	21.1	24.6	20.7	26.1	19.6
Kerala	12.0	27.4		10.4	12.1	15.2	12.0	12.1
Tamil Nadu	17.1	28.8		14.7	17.8	12.7	21.2	12.8

Source: Computed by Himanshu from NSS 66th Round data files, using the Tendulkar Committee methodology.
Note: Due to small sample sizes, rates for small states and for certain categories in some states are not given.

When the background factors are associated it is necessary to control for other relevant factors before inferences about cause–effect relationships are drawn. But in the present discussion, the issue is of existing disparities and for this one needs to look at gross differences as has been done here.

WILL SOME RECENT INITIATIVES MATTER?

As the existence of inequalities by social group, religion, sex, and place of residence has been well-recognized for some time, government policies and programmes have sought to minimize these. Many of the continuing programmes address issues of health, hunger, education, poverty, and have some element of affirmative action built in. These include the Integrated Child Development Services (ICDS) scheme, various education programmes, poverty alleviation programmes, as well as other initiatives as part of the planning process and normal developmental activities. In certain aspects, the goal of a policy is to attain universalization which would naturally ensure equality.

Besides, there is some affirmative action in favour of women and those from socially disadvantaged sections of the society. This is in the form of reservation in education, employment, additional facilities in services, additional allowances, and incentives. Finally, certain schemes are specifically introduced for socially disadvantaged groups. The last decade has seen some fresh major efforts.

In the case of education, in particular for elementary education, universalization is the goal. This has been sought to be achieved in successive programmes for long, and some progress has clearly been made. In 2002, the 68th Amendment to the Constitution made elementary education a fundamental right. The Sarva Shiksha Abhiyan (SSA) was introduced to achieve universalization of elementary education. The Right to Education Act (The Right of Children to Free and Compulsory Education Act of 2009), commonly labelled as the RTE, provided the legal framework to achieve it. As the Act has been introduced very recently, we need to wait to see how well it has been implemented and what has been

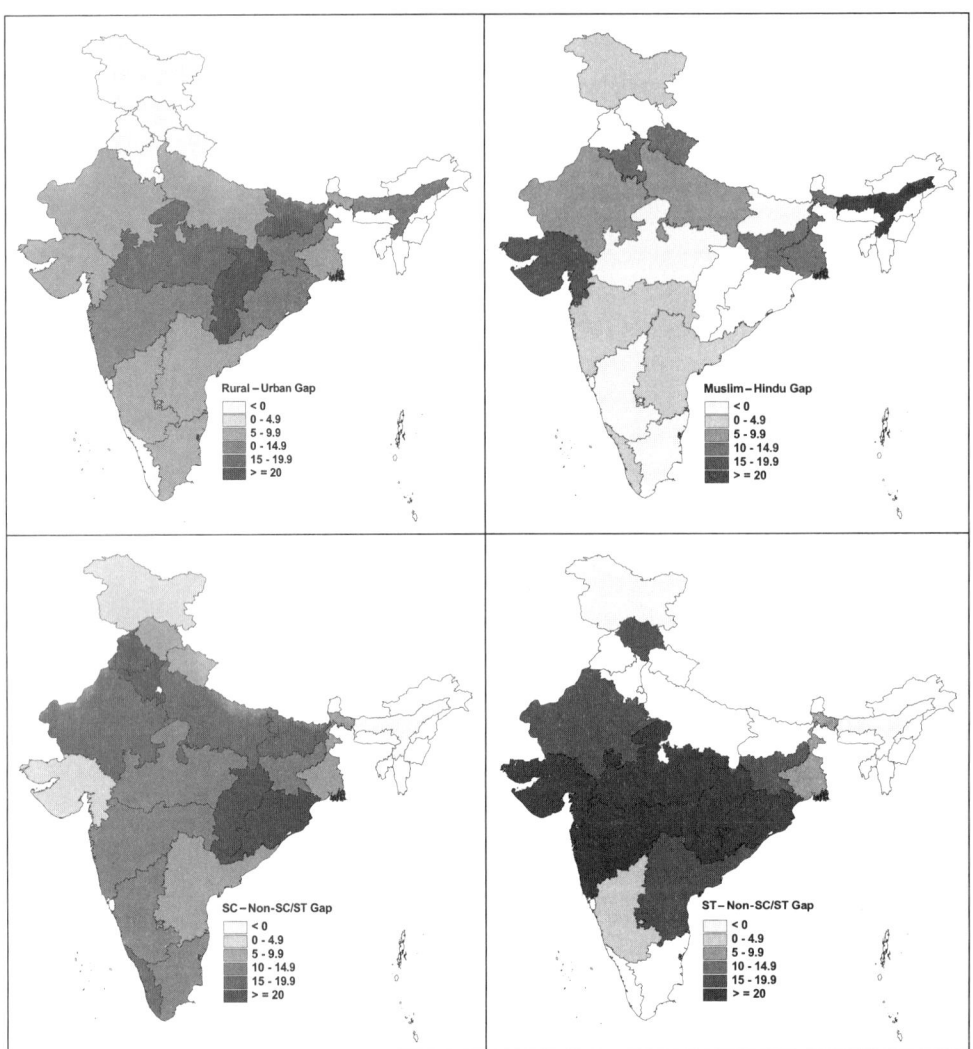

Figure 7.4   Intra-state Differentials in Percentage of Population Below the Poverty Line

Source: Based on NSS 66th Round, 2009–10, Tendulkar Committee Methodology.
Note: Blank indicates that the estimate for one of the comparison groups was not available due to small sample size in the state.

the impact. Once the 2011 Census data on education are available, one would be able to see if there is substantial improvement in the level of education. However, the RTE relates to ages up to 14, which cover elementary education, but high school education is not under the purview of the RTE per se. Dubey (2011) has suggested that the act should have covered ages 15–18 as well so as to achieve universalization of high school education. But in school education there are heavy dropouts at an early stage during elementary education, and if these could be checked by the various provisions made for implementation of the RTE, the level of continuation of students will improve, thereby raising high school completion in turn. However, this is a long process and even assuming that continuation of children in schools is raised, it will take some time for it to translate into high school completion. Besides, it has generally been the experience that during the process of development some sections move ahead of others opening up gaps and later the others catch up narrowing and ultimately closing the gap. The high school completion levels in India, as seen from the 2001 Census, were quite low or moderate for all sections, and certainly nowhere near universal. Thus, India is at an early stage of development in this matter, and the gaps might actually widen for some time, as some sections move towards universality, and will narrow only later as others follow with some lag. Therefore, we actually expect widening of the differentials in high school education though for literacy as such the gaps are likely to narrow. It is pertinent to note here that two new research scholarships, the Rajiv Gandhi Fellowship for SC and ST students, and the Maulana Azad Fellowship for religious minorities, have been introduced recently. These will directly impact doctoral studies but also indirectly encourage higher education among the SCs, STs, and minorities. Thus, the schemes have the potential to reduce disparities in higher education. But it is too early to see if an impact has been made.

Public health programmes in India address both preventive and curative care. Health services are primarily the responsibility of state governments, but the central government has introduced various schemes and provided funds for maternal and child health services and for control of certain diseases. The programmes have been recast and strengthened over time and there has been notable reduction in mortality including during early childhood. The National Rural Health Mission (NRHM) was a major initiative introduced in 2005 (MoHFW 2005). While the NRHM covered a host of issues, two key innovations were the Janani Suraksha Yojana (JSY) and Accredited Social Health Activist (ASHA). The JSY was designed to promote safe deliveries by providing financial support to women who opt for institutional delivery or for delivery by skilled health professionals. The ASHA scheme called for identification of a social worker from the village, the ASHA, who would promote maternal and child health care, sanitation, and nutrition. The NRHM has focus on states that have had poor health indicators, essentially those in the central-eastern region. Thus, the NRHM is expected to reduce regional variations between rural and urban areas and between states which have good indicators (southern and some western and eastern states) and the high focus states. Besides, in the reports to be provided by the service-providers of the NRHM, information on services provided to weaker sections is mandatory. This would keep some pressure on the workers to ensure that no section is ignored because of its social status. Furthermore, in some incentives and compensation, the poor are given additional benefits. Thus, the NRHM, by focusing on less developed areas and disadvantaged sections, is expected to reduce inequalities.

The NRHM has been functioning for some time now. The mission was announced in 2005 and the implementation framework prepared in 2006. We now have some evidence of the functioning of the NRHM from the Annual Health Survey (AHS) that was carried out in 2010–11 in nine states that had poor health conditions. Table 7.6 shows some indicators from the NFHS III (conducted during 2005–6, before the NRHM was implemented) and the AHS conducted in 2010–11 reveals distinct improvement in many. In particular, the levels of institutional delivery and delivery attended by health professionals have increased very sharply since the NRHM was introduced. The level has now crossed 70 per cent in Odisha, Rajasthan, Madhya Pradesh, and Assam. Translating these improvements into declines in maternal and child mortality will take some time (the surveys cover mortality for a period of three years prior to the survey date or year). We do not as yet have detailed information on coverage by social groups and hence are not in a position to see if differentials have narrowed. But given that a vast majority of women in some of the large states now get professional health assistance level at

Table 7.6   Recent Changes in Maternal and Child Health Coverage for Nine States

State	% of Deliveries Conducted in Institutions		% of Deliveries Assisted by Health Professionals		% of Children 12–23 Months Fully Immunized	
	NFHS III 2005–6	AHS 2010–11	NFHS III 2005–6	AHS 2010–11	NFHS III 2005–6	AHS 2010–11
Assam	22.4	57.7	31.0	70.1	31.4	59.0
Bihar	19.9	47.7	29.3	53.5	32.8	64.5
Chhattisgarh	14.3	34.9	41.6	49.5	48.7	74.1
Jharkhand	18.3	37.6	27.8	47.1	34.2	63.7
Madhya Pradesh	26.2	76.1	32.7	82.0	40.3	54.9
Odisha	35.6	71.3	44.0	75.2	51.8	55.0
Rajasthan	29.6	70.2	41.0	76.2	26.5	70.8
Uttar Pradesh	20.6	45.6	27.2	51.3	23.0	45.3
Uttarakhand	32.6	50.5	38.5	56.9	60.0	75.4

Sources: For NFHS III, see IIPS and Macro International 2007; and for AHS, see Registrar General 2012.

delivery, all sections must have benefited. Yet there is a long way to go for Uttar Pradesh and Bihar.

The Mahatma Gandhi National Rural Employment Guarantee Act (MGNREGA) that was introduced in 2006 assures employment in rural areas for up to 100 days in a year for those in need. As seasonal unemployment is common among the rural population, supplementary employment is expected to help poverty alleviation. Reports on employment generation for the past six years show that about half of the employment (assessed from the number of person-days) under this scheme is provided to the SCs and the STs (Table 7.7). While this means that the weaker sections have benefited, the quantum of benefit seems to have been small. The total employment under this scheme has not crossed 3000 million person-days in a year and given that the size of India's rural labour force exceeds 300 million, the incremental employment is not large. However, there is evidence of a reduction in poverty gaps over time, especially since 1993–4 (Thorat and Dubey 2012). In particular, poverty decline among the Muslims, SCs, and STs was greater than among the Hindus and non-SC/ST population. There is a move towards equality whether due to MGNREGA or otherwise.

Table 7.7 Number of Person-days (in lakh) of Employment Provided under MGNREGA, India, 2006–7 to 2011–12

Year	Total	SC	ST	Women
2006–7	9,050	2,295	3,299	3,679
2007–8	14,368	3,942	4,206	6,109
2008–9	21,633	6,336	5,502	10,357
2009–10	28,360	8,645	5,874	13,641
2010–11	25,715	7,876	5,362	12,274
2011–12	21,142	4,661	3,838	10,187
Total	120,268	33,755	28,081	56,247

Source: Department of Rural Development, Ministry of Rural Development, Government of India (GoI), Mahatma Gandhi National Rural Employment Guarantee Act Implementation Status Report for various financial years. Available at http://nrega.nic.in (accessed 10 August 2012).

✳ ✳ ✳

The existence of regional variations in inequalities mean that programmes of affirmative action would have to be designed on a regional basis. In regions that are relatively developed, the prevalence of large disparities shows failure to adequately respond to the needs of weaker sections. Why should the conditions of the STs in relatively developed states such as Maharashtra and Gujarat be so poor in spite of special programmes in place? Similarly, the condition of the SCs in prosperous Punjab and Haryana is a matter of concern. On the other hand, in regions that have a low level of development, disparities mean high deprivation for large sections of population. This is the case with Muslims in the northern and eastern states.

But there are certain common issues as well. As school enrolments become universal, near universal literacy will also follow in course of time. But secondary education is far from becoming universal. In 2001, in only two states, Delhi and Goa, a majority of young adults had completed secondary education. By now a few states would have joined this group but most would take some time to do so. Naturally, a vast majority of the SCs, STs, and Muslims as well as women in most of the country would be far from achieving a high level of secondary school completion. This means that they would have very low opportunity to find the much sought after white-collar employment in the organized sector. Similarly, health conditions in India, though better than in the past, are nowhere near those in developed countries and are short of conditions in many developing countries. As a result, for the more deprived sections, health conditions are miserable. With a few exceptions, poverty in most states is fairly high in spite of the declines in the poverty ratio that have occurred. Again, this implies that poverty in some sections of population is quite high.

There is, undoubtedly, recognition of the disparities and steps are being taken to reduce these. Overall development accompanied by affirmative action has probably helped narrow down the gaps between the socially backward classes and others but gaps do remain and the objective of eliminating inequalities is far from being achieved. Clearly, affirmative action has not been adequate or its implementation has been faulty. This calls for closely monitoring the performance of the ongoing schemes, augmenting the allocation of resources, and bringing in innovations.

REFERENCES

Baraik, Vijay and P.M. Kulkarni. 2006. 'Health Status and Access to Health Care Services: Disparities among Social Groups in India', Working Paper Series, 1(4). New Delhi: Indian Institute of Dalit Studies.

Bose, A.B. 2006. 'Child Development in India', in *India: Social Development Report*. New Delhi: Oxford University Press, pp. 151–79.

CSD (Council for Social Development). 2006. *India: Social Development Report*. New Delhi: Oxford University Press.

CSD (Council for Social Development). 2011. *India: Social Development Report 2010—The Land Question and the Marginalized*. New Delhi: Oxford University Press.

Desai, Sonalde B., Amaresh Dubey, B.L. Joshi, M. Sen, Abusaleh Shariff, and Reeve Vanneman. 2010. *Human Development in India: Challenges for a Society in Transition*. New Delhi: Oxford University Press.

Dubey, Muchkund. 2011. 'Universalizing School Education—A Missed Opportunity' *India: Social Development Report 2010—The Land Question and the Marginalized*. New Delhi: Oxford University Press, pp. 80–7.

Institute of Applied Manpower Research. 2011. *India Human Development Report 2011—Towards Social Inclusion*. New Delhi: Oxford University Press.

IIPS and Macro International. 2007. *National Family Health Survey (NFHS-3), India, 2005–06*. Mumbai: IIPS.

Jodhka, Surinder S. 2011. 'Dalits and Development', *India: Social Development Report 2010—The Land Question and the Marginalized*. New Delhi: Oxford University Press, pp. 51–61.

Karve, Irawati. 1968. *Kinship Organization in India*. Bombay: Asia Publishing House.

Kulkarni, P.M. 2007. 'Human Development Differentials among Social Groups', *State, Markets and Inequalities—Human Development in Rural India*. New Delhi: Orient Longman, pp. 621–62,

MoHFW (Ministry of Health and Family Welfare). 2005. *National Rural Health Mission (2005–12), Mission Document*. New Delhi: Ministry of Health and Family Welfare, GoI.

NSSO (National Sample Survey Office). 2011. *Key Indicators of Household Consumer Expenditure in India, 2009–10, NSS 66th Round*. New Delhi: Ministry of Statistics and Programme Implementation, GoI.

PMHLC (Prime Minister's High Level Committee). 2006. *Social, Economic and Educational Status of the Muslim Community of India*. New Delhi: Cabinet Secretariat, GoI.

Raju, Saraswati. 2006. 'Locating Women in Social Development', *India: Social Development Report*. New Delhi: Oxford University Press, pp. 77–95.

Registrar General. 2010. *Compendium of India's Fertility and Mortality Indicators 1971–2007: Based on the Sample Registration System (SRS)*. New Delhi: Office of the Registrar General, Ministry of Home Affairs, GoI.

———. 2012. *Annual Health Survey 2010–11, District Level Factsheets*. New Delhi: Office of the Registrar General, Ministry of Home Affairs, GoI.

Shah, Ghanshyam. 2002. *Social Movements in India: A Review of Literature*. New Delhi: Sage Publications.

Sujaya, C.P. 2011. 'Women, Disparities and Development', *India: Social Development Report 2010—The Land Question and the Marginalized*. New Delhi: Oxford University Press, pp. 32–50.

Tendulkar Committee. 2009. *Report of the Expert Group to Review the Methodology for Estimation of Poverty*. New Delhi: Planning Commission, GoI.

Thorat, S.K. 2006. 'Empowering Marginalized Groups: Policies and Change', *India Social Development Report*. New Delhi: Oxford University Press, pp. 64–78.

Thorat, Sukhadeo and Amaresh Dubey. 2012. 'Has Growth Been Socially Inclusive during 1993–4—2009–10?' *Economic and Political Weekly*, 47(10): 43–53.

Tilak, Jandhyala B.G. 2006. 'Education—A Saga of Spectacular Achievements and Conspicuous Failures', *India: Social Development Report*. New Delhi: Oxford University Press, pp. 33–49.

8

Challenges of Food Security

TAJAMUL HAQUE

Food security is generally defined as a situation 'when all people, at all times, have physical, social and economic access to sufficient, safe, and nutritious food to meet their dietary needs and food preferences for an active and healthy life' (FAO 1996). A close look at this definition would reveal that there are seven essential elements of food security. First, there should be adequate food available for all people through either local production or imports. Second, people should have adequate income or purchasing power to buy food, if they do not produce any or enough food for self-consumption. Third, available food should be safe to eat for a healthy life. Fourth, the available food should have proper nutritional value so that nobody suffers from malnutrition or undernutrition. Fifth, adequate quantities of different varieties of food should be available according to food preferences of people of any social group or geographical region. Sixth, people should have proper food absorption or utilization capacity which is conditioned by their access to safe drinking water, sanitation, health care, and even nutrition education. Seventh, adequate, safe, and nutritious food should be accessible by all.

This chapter analyses the challenges of food security in India primarily from the angles of the above mentioned seven elements of food security. The secondary data were collected from various published government and non-government sources and analysed to arrive at the conclusions.

KEY QUESTIONS

The key questions concerning food security in India could be listed as follows:

1. Does India produce enough, albeit diverse food items in a sustainable manner in response to rising demand, resulting from population and income growth?
2. Do people of different socio-economic strata in the country possess adequate purchasing power to buy enough food according to their dietary needs and preferences especially in view of rising food prices in recent times?
3. Do people of all social groups in the country have access to sufficient nutritious food?
4. Does India have an appropriate policy, infrastructure, and institutions for effective food delivery and distribution at the village and household levels?
5. Do all people in the country have access to safe drinking water, sanitation, health care, and education for food absorption and utilization?
6. What are the major technological, infrastructural, institutional, and policy constraints to sustainable food security?

The answers to these questions would throw adequate light on the problems and prospects of sustainable agriculture and food security in India.

DEMAND–SUPPLY SITUATIONS OF MAJOR FOOD ITEMS

India is self-sufficient in the production of all important food items, excepting pulses, oilseeds, and meat. In 2011–12, it produced about 257.4 million tons of foodgrains against an estimated demand of 234.3 million tons (Table 8.1). The production of rice was estimated at

104.3 million tons against the demand of 98.8 million tons, and the production of wheat was an all-time high at 93.9 million tons against the demand of 77.4 million tons. However, the production of pulses was only 17.2 million tons against the demand of 19.9 million tons, while oilseeds production was only 33.6 million tons against a demand of 53.4 million tons. The production of sugar was 25.0 million tons against the annual demand of 23 million tons. Similarly, the production of vegetables, fruits, and milk far exceeded the demand, while the production of fish marginally exceeded its demand. The production and demand of eggs was in balance, but production of meat fell short of demand by about 1.7 million tons. It would be further seen from Table 8.1 that the present level of foodgrains production is higher than what has been projected as the demand in 2020.

TRENDS IN FOOD PRODUCTION

During the past one decade, the production growth rate has been quite uneven among various crops (Table 8.2). The production of rice which is a major staple food for most Indians has been growing only at the rate of about 1.8 per cent per year, slightly higher than the growth rate of population. However, production growth rates of wheat (2.6 per cent), bajra (3.4 per cent), maize (5.8 per

cent), pulses (3.5 per cent), oilseeds (5.0 per cent), fruits (5.7 per cent), vegetables (4.8 per cent), milk (4.3 per cent), fish (3.6 per cent), and meat (3.1 per cent) were higher than the population growth rates. The production growth rates of jowar and ragi, which were once important sources of food and nutrition in southwest India, were negative. Another important factor that needs to be kept in mind in this respect is that although the production of high value food items such as fish, milk, meat, fruits, and vegetables were quite high, the demands for them are rising fast and consequently their prices tend to be persistently high. Further, there were wide regional variations in the production growth rates of almost all food articles.

It would be seen from Table 8.3 that during 2000–1 to 2010–11, the Compound Annual Growth Rates (CAGRs) of per capita cereal production were negative in Bihar (–4.9 per cent), Jharkhand (–4.1 per cent), Kerala (–4.0 per cent), Meghalaya (–1.5 per cent), Mizoram (–8.5 per cent), Punjab (–0.40 per cent), Sikkim (–1.1 per cent), Tamil Nadu (–2.7 per cent), Uttar Pradesh (–0.8 per cent), Uttarakhand (–1.4 per cent), West Bengal (–0.8 per cent), Andaman and Nicobar Islands (–3.4 per cent), Daman and Diu (–2.8 per cent), Dadra and Nagar Haveli (–4.3 per cent), and Puducherry (now Puducherry)

Table 8.1   Estimated Production Demand Gaps in Selected Food Items

Commodity	Estimated Production in 2011–12 (million tons)[1]	Estimated Demand 2011–12 (million tons)[2]	Projected Demand in 2020 (million tons)[1]
Rice	104.3	98.8	117.0
Wheat	93.9	77.4	98.0
Coarse cereals	42.0	38.2	38.0
Pulses	17.2	19.9	25.0
Foodgrains	257.4	234.3	277.0
Oilseeds	33.6	53.4	71.0
Edible oils			
Sugarcane	357.7	322.5	NA
Sugar	25.0	23.0	NA
Vegetables	146.6	83.1*	189.0
Fruits	74.9	53.7*	124.0
Milk	121.8	89.1*	173.0
Meat	4.8	6.5*	9.3
Eggs	2.1	2.2*	NA
Fish	8.3	7.7*	14.0

Sources: [1] GoI 2013: vol. II and [2] Ministry of Agriculture, GoI.
Note: * These demand figures have been estimated by the author.

Table 8.2 CAGR and Variability in the Production of Major Food Items, 2000–1 to 2011–12

Items	Annual Growth Rate (%)	CV (%)	Items	Annual Growth Rate (%)	CV (%)
Rice	1.8	9.30	Total oilseeds	5.0	20.36
Wheat	2.6	10.89	Sugarcane	2.1	14.04
Jowar	–1.0	7.17	Vegetables	4.8	13.57
Bajra	3.4	24.87	Fruits	5.7	13.79
Maize	5.8	22.13	Milk	4.3	14.18
Ragi	–0.8	19.29	Fish	3.6	12.22
Small millets	0.9	20.56	Meat	3.1	30.31
Barley	1.3	12.30			
Coarse cereals	2.7	12.85			
Cereals	2.3	10.13			
Total pulses	3.5	14.73			
Total foodgrains	2.4	10.33			

Source: Estimated based on the data collected from the Ministry of Agriculture, GoI.

(–4.5 per cent). The highest annual per capita production growth rate of cereals was in Gujarat (10.5 per cent) followed by Goa (10.0 per cent), Chhattisgarh (7.3 per cent), and Nagaland (5.9 per cent). In the case of pulses, states such as Gujarat (12.3 per cent), Jharkhand (10.9 per cent), Manipur (20.8 per cent), Rajasthan (13.9 per cent), Uttarakhand (7.2 per cent), Sikkim (7.3 per cent), Odisha (5.8 per cent), Chhattisgarh (5.1 per cent), and Himachal Pradesh (6.5 per cent) had a relatively higher per capita annual growth. But several states had negative growth rates of pulse production, which included Assam (–0.4 per cent), Bihar (–3.6 per cent), Goa (–2.6 per cent), Kerala (–12.2 per cent), Meghalaya (–1.8 per cent), Punjab (–9.2 per cent), Tamil Nadu (–3.8 per cent), Tripura (–2.6 per cent), Uttar Pradesh (–2.4 per cent), West Bengal (–3.4 per cent), Daman and Diu (–5.8 per cent), Dadra and Nagar Haveli (–2.4 per cent), and Puducherry (–11.7 per cent). The states like Bihar, Jharkhand, Kerala, Daman and Diu, Andaman and Nicobar Islands, and Mizoram with already low levels of per capita production of cereals and pulses must have locally faced more shortages of these food commodities due to negative growth in recent years. Similarly, states such as Bihar, Assam, Goa, Kerala, Punjab, Tamil Nadu, Tripura, West Bengal, and Puducherry have very low levels of per capita production of pulses and negative annual growth which should be a cause for concern.

In the case of high-value items such as milk, fish, eggs, meat, fruits, and vegetables too there were regional variations in the per capita production growth rates (see

Table 8.3). Bihar had highest annual growth rate of per capita milk production (6.9 per cent), followed by Andhra Pradesh (5.6 per cent), Odisha (4.6 per cent), and Jharkhand (3.1 per cent). But Arunachal Pradesh (–6.2 per cent), Jammu and Kashmir (–0.5 per cent), Karnataka (–0.8 per cent), Kerala (–0.7 per cent), Meghalaya (–0.7 per cent), Mizoram (–4.3 per cent), Chandigarh (–1.1 per cent), Dadra and Nagar Haveli (–1.2 per cent), Daman and Diu (–4.2 per cent), Lakshadweep (–0.6 per cent), and Puducherry (–0.1 per cent) had negative growth of per capita milk production. The levels of per capita milk production in the northeastern states of Assam, Arunachal Pradesh, Meghalaya, and Mizoram are already very low and, therefore, negative growth rates in recent years would have caused further hardship. The annual growth rate of meat production was highest in Haryana (37.0 per cent) followed by Punjab (34.7 per cent), Tamil Nadu (26.1 per cent), Chhattisgarh (21.1 per cent), Tripura (19.8 per cent), Goa (14.9 per cent), Uttar Pradesh (9.4 per cent), Puducherry (8.1 per cent), and Andhra Pradesh (7.6 per cent).

The states which witnessed negative growth in per capita production of meat included Arunachal Pradesh (0.6 per cent), Jammu and Kashmir (–1.6 per cent), Kerala (–2.7 per cent), Meghalaya (–1.7 per cent), West Bengal (–3.5 per cent), Andaman and Nicobar Islands (–2.6 per cent), Delhi (–0.6 per cent), Lakshadweep (–0.4 per cent), and Jharkhand (–0.2 per cent). In the case of fish production, the best performing states included Chandigarh, Haryana, Chhattisgarh, Andhra Pradesh, Karnataka, Punjab, Rajasthan, Uttar Pradesh, and

Table 8.3 CAGR of Per Capita Production of Major Food Items in India, 2000–1 to 2010–11

State/Union Territory	Rice	Wheat	Jowar	Ragi	Cereals	Total Pulses	Total Oilseeds	Food-grains	Milk	Eggs	Meat	Fish	Vegetables	Fruits
Andhra Pradesh	0.35	3.81	-7.78	-9.41	1.21	2.02	-3.35	1.26	5.59	3.93	7.62	5.97	15.14	3.18
Arunachal Pradesh	3.36	-2.82	NA	NA	2.08	0.52	-1.08	2.03	-6.22	13.44	-0.58	-0.82	-9.66	-3.76
Assam	0.12	-6.21	NA	NA	0.01	-0.39	-1.96	0.00	-0.10	-2.34	4.76	1.86	-1.59	1.22
Bihar	-7.57	-3.00	10.17	-13.57	-4.88	-3.62	-1.85	-4.81	6.92	2.04	2.20	-0.04	3.83	0.82
Chhattisgarh	7.79	2.65	0.03	-2.81	7.26	5.05	7.17	7.07	0.53	1.58	21.10	6.85	9.82	20.19
Goa	-2.89	NA	NA	-15.55	9.98	-2.62	9.11	9.49	2.09	-20.01	14.89	2.09	-3.49	1.14
Gujarat	10.25	17.90	1.74	-1.75	10.52	12.25	9.46	10.66	2.91	11.95	2.31	-0.77	9.14	9.97
Haryana	0.69	0.00	2.67	NA	0.37	2.86	3.45	0.39	0.46	11.41	37.02	8.75	6.03	2.34
Himachal Pradesh	-0.89	6.78	NA	-7.82	1.13	6.47	-3.86	1.25	2.60	0.83	0.33	-0.98	7.42	13.25
Jammu and Kashmir	-0.18	9.19	0.00	NA	0.92	0.40	4.23	0.92	-0.52	0.82	-1.56	-1.74	5.55	5.94
Jharkhand	-5.79	2.24	-27.63	-17.16	-4.08	10.86	12.73	-2.68	3.05	-5.26	-0.16	-5.29	6.81	7.08
Karnataka	-0.63	-0.14	-1.99	-3.15	0.57	3.51	-3.34	0.86	-0.83	2.34	0.80	5.23	6.47	2.99
Kerala	-4.02	NA	18.02	-19.16	-4.04	-12.17	-5.43	-4.11	-0.74	-2.64	-2.71	-0.33	2.44	3.04
Madhya Pradesh	4.14	2.68	1.08	-19.19	1.98	2.16	5.02	2.02	1.70	-1.75	5.54	-0.11	5.40	9.39
Maharashtra	1.87	7.65	-2.90	-2.41	2.24	5.01	7.53	2.74	1.29	0.71	8.35	-0.78	2.34	-0.76
Manipur	1.84	0.00	NA	NA	2.43	20.84	33.53	2.77	0.07	3.52	0.05	0.75	12.12	6.49
Meghalaya	-1.05	-22.38	NA	NA	-1.48	-1.82	-1.37	-1.49	-0.71	-1.17	-1.74	-3.32	0.42	0.07
Mizoram	-9.42	NA	NA	NA	-8.46	2.41	-5.39	-7.88	-4.34	0.83	0.67	-2.81	7.91	10.54
Nagaland	5.23	-6.04	-21.85	0.00	5.88	5.65	3.74	5.87	2.96	4.24	13.47	2.43	-11.99	-6.64
Odisha	2.62	-11.86	-5.13	-1.24	2.81	5.79	2.93	2.95	4.64	10.77	11.30	1.73	-0.88	2.78
Punjab	0.37	-0.74	-100.00	NA	-0.35	-9.20	-3.27	-0.36	0.41	-0.29	34.72	3.91	3.28	8.52
Rajasthan	3.45	0.68	12.03	NA	3.25	13.88	10.34	4.44	3.45	-0.34	3.99	3.18	5.35	11.04
Sikkim	-1.37	-13.35	NA	-4.76	-1.12	7.34	0.18	-0.50	0.33	1.34	0.00	1.35	6.01	8.34
Tamil Nadu	-3.83	0.00	-3.57	-5.50	-2.68	-3.82	-5.67	-2.72	1.66	9.04	26.10	0.58	2.73	7.05
Tripura	1.75	-12.87	NA	NA	1.74	-2.64	-4.53	1.70	0.04	1.76	19.79	3.81	2.74	2.16
Uttar Pradesh	-1.56	-0.08	-6.28	-100.00	-0.75	-2.40	-3.95	-0.83	1.79	0.83	9.40	4.42	-0.23	6.94
Uttarakhand	-2.94	0.29	NA	-2.98	-1.42	7.20	4.74	-1.25	0.84	9.06	1.36	-6.73	1.60	4.83
West Bengal	-0.81	-3.16	-33.25	-2.24	-0.80	-3.43	0.79	-0.83	1.11	0.53	-3.54	2.58	2.65	2.71

(Contd.)

Table 8.3 (Contd.)

State/Union Territory	Rice	Wheat	Jowar	Ragi	Cereals	Total Pulses	Total Oilseeds	Food-grains	Milk	Eggs	Meat	Fish	Vegetables	Fruits
Andaman and Nicobar Islands	-3.55	NA	NA	NA	-3.41	10.47	NA	-3.08	0.19	0.85	-2.64	1.62	7.43	4.89
Chandigarh	NA	NA	NA	NA	NA	NA	NA	NA	-1.11	2.09	1.45	17.85	-1.56	-1.56
Dadra and Nagar Haveli	-3.93	-13.55	-0.45	-5.50	-4.30	-2.41	-9.09	-3.94	-1.22	3.62	0.00	-6.05	-12.54	NA
Daman and Diu	-3.91	NA	NA	NA	-2.81	-5.79	NA	-3.59	-4.21	-8.48	0.00	-6.45	-19.22	NA
Delhi	17.09	-0.69	-3.20	NA	1.47	4.66	-7.37	1.49	2.99	-46.33	-0.59	-14.42	-5.86	-1.93
Lakshadweep	NA	NA	NA	NA	NA	NA	NA	NA	-0.61	5.09	-0.36	-1.58	NA	0.26
Puducherry	-4.36	NA	0.00	-18.27	-4.45	-11.74	0.29	-4.73	-0.06	-0.61	8.07	-3.00	-18.64	-7.81
All India	-0.61	0.57	-2.34	-3.76	0.35	3.40	4.10	0.54	2.05	3.32	6.30	1.69	5.83	3.98

Source: Calculated by the author based on data collected from the Ministry of Agriculture, GoI.

Tripura, while the worst performing states with negative growth were Arunachal Pradesh, Jammu and Kashmir, Himachal Pradesh, Kerala, Madhya Pradesh, Maharashtra, Meghalaya, Mizoram, Dadra and Nagar Haveli, Daman and Diu, Delhi, Lakshadweep, Puducherry, Uttarakhand, and Jharkhand (Table 8.3). Per capita vegetable production per year increased with higher rates in Andhra Pradesh (15.1 per cent), Manipur (12.2 per cent), Chhattisgarh (9.8 per cent), Gujarat (9.1 per cent), Himachal Pradesh (7.4 per cent), and Sikkim (6.0 per cent). But states such as Arunachal Pradesh, Assam, Goa, Nagaland, Odisha, Uttar Pradesh, Chandigarh, Dadra and Nagar Haveli, Daman and Diu, Delhi, Puducherry had negative growth rates of vegetable production per capita. Of these, Arunachal Pradesh, Goa, Nagaland, Chandigarh, Dadra and Nagar Haveli, Daman and Diu, Delhi, and Puducherry have at present very low levels of vegetable production per capita. The annual growth rate of per capita fruit production was highest in Chhattisgarh (20.2 per cent) followed by Himachal Pradesh (13.2 per cent), Madhya Pradesh (9.4 per cent), Sikkim (8.3 per cent), Tamil Nadu (7.1 per cent), and Uttar Pradesh (6.9 per cent). But Arunachal Pradesh (–3.8 per cent), Maharashtra (–0.8 per cent), Nagaland (–6.6 per cent), Delhi (–1.9 per cent), and Puducherry (–7.8 per cent) had negative growth rates of per capita fruit production.

The per capita net availability of cereals and pulses—including imports and opening stock and excluding exports—dropped in the recent years, while that of edible oils and sugar improved due to increased production as well as imports (Table 8.4). During 2011–12, about 9 million tons of edible oils were imported. In the case of pulses, import of about 2 to 3 million tons per year did not significantly improve the per capita availability. The decline in per capita availability of cereals is largely accounted for by exports of rice and decline in the production of coarse cereals like jowar and ragi in the recent years.

STABILITY AND SUSTAINABILITY OF FOOD PRODUCTION/SUPPLY

Indian food supply system has been more or less stable in the recent years. Even during the major drought years in 2002 and 2009, the shortfall in production could be easily made up by huge stock in the central pool. In the case of pulses and edible oils, the domestic production system could not meet the demand; therefore, these had to be imported in huge quantities. It would be seen from Table 8.5 that the coefficients of variation were relatively high in the production of pulses, oilseeds, milk, eggs, and meat while the coefficient of variation (CV) was comparatively very low in the case of rice, wheat, and jowar. Of course, dependence on imports poses a challenge in terms of their adequate availability in international market and also affordability of prices. But sustainability of domestic production of several food commodities poses many

Table 8.4 Per Capita Net Availability of Food Items and CAGR

Year	Per Capita Net Availability				
	Cereals (gm/day)	Pulses (gm/day)	Foodgrains (gm/day)	Edible oils (kg/yr)	Sugar (kg/yr)
	Per capita net availability				
1961–2 to 1963–4 (TE)*	394.20	63.60	457.80	3.20	5.00
1971–2 to 1973–4 (TE)	395.73	46.43	452.17	2.93	6.37
1981–2 to 1983–4 (TE)	410.23	38.73	448.97	5.13	9.23
1991–2 to 1993–4 (TE)	443.63	37.37	481.00	5.77	13.13
2001–2 to 2003–4 (TE)	417.80	31.50	449.30	8.63	16.13
2008–9 to 2010–11 (TE)	402.73	36.80	439.53	13.20	17.90
	CAGR				
1961–2 to 1973–4 (TE)	0.039	–3.097	–0.124	–0.866	2.446
1971–2 to 1983–4 (TE)	0.361	–1.797	–0.071	5.756	3.787
1981–2 to 1993–4 (TE)	0.786	–0.359	0.692	1.170	3.586
1991–2 to 2003–4 (TE)	–0.598	–1.693	–0.679	4.118	2.079
2001–2 to 2010–11 (TE)	–0.523	2.246	–0.313	6.253	1.496

Source: Economic Survey, various years, GoI; CAGR or Compound Annual Growth Rate calculated by the author.
Note: * TE stands for triennium ending.

Table 8.5 Coefficients of Variation in Production of Major Food Items in India by States, 2000–1 to 2011–12 (in %)

State/Union Territory	Rice	Wheat	Jowar	Ragi	Cereals	Total Pulses	Total Oilseeds	Food-grains	Milk	Eggs	Meat	Fish	Vegetables	Fruits
Andhra Pradesh	19.32	33.10	23.92	29.77	19.47	16.37	31.16	18.88	23.16	14.38	22.96	25.84	42.02	18.23
Arunachal Pradesh	20.64	17.18			14.65	12.08	9.29	14.50	24.77	83.33	31.84	5.54	40.06	1.81
Assam	13.00	17.17			12.65	6.60	9.28	12.52	4.50	4.84	18.24	11.71	29.41	13.49
Bihar	24.57	11.74	37.85	40.88	14.32	11.41	9.84	13.87	33.08	18.07	10.28	10.38	3.47	11.38
Chhattisgarh	25.75	14.99	22.77	12.65	24.60	20.07	30.13	23.98	8.86	11.46	96.68	36.32	31.72	46.53
Goa	14.13	49.38	24.04	42.16	51.78	24.51	35.58	48.37	11.56	95.61	81.37	167.95	55.06	38.05
Gujarat	29.84			28.68	29.76	32.25	36.92	29.94	17.90	52.17	24.07	7.24	19.54	20.35
Haryana	12.85	8.77	24.89	27.43	9.88	23.21	16.13	9.87	7.99	58.77	142.20	42.90	17.69	17.30
Himachal Pradesh	11.45	25.89			14.90	44.31	32.46	14.72	13.45	10.31	12.84	5.75	18.67	34.95
Jammu and Kashmir	11.61	26.42	69.47		11.62	8.45	63.77	11.55	6.84	9.09	2.02	4.34	20.06	22.34
Jharkhand	38.97	22.14	110.99	61.27	34.76	47.13	84.97	33.84	20.34	20.15	5.81	41.09	8.00	32.25
Karnataka	24.14	25.71	19.13	26.95	23.11	29.22	21.44	23.17	9.32	16.86	7.79	23.30	25.73	15.53
Kerala	11.61		56.81	71.14	11.64	38.12	32.04	11.70	10.69	21.54	42.91	8.88	13.38	4.77
Madhya Pradesh	20.03	17.14	19.54	110.25	13.19	19.13	26.28	14.01	14.61	16.48	45.18	15.39	15.26	49.67
Maharashtra	15.48	35.65	8.80	16.73	13.70	23.79	30.65	15.19	10.21	6.16	45.91	4.72	23.12	4.85
Manipur	13.42	0.00	105.48	0.00	15.26	98.32	256.00	16.27	6.29	17.37	4.12	7.04	48.61	18.94
Meghalaya	8.30	93.67			7.13	7.47	4.08	7.02	7.11	4.35	5.45	15.50	13.94	14.16
Mizoram	50.38	86.69			46.50	30.10	37.21	44.33	14.09	13.79	16.28	11.25	58.25	59.14
Nagaland	18.32	38.16	13.17	8.98	17.67	21.75	16.78	17.26	17.41	16.57	46.19	8.74	15.84	80.24
Odisha	19.82				19.74	25.01	19.89	19.73	24.40	53.09	49.64	12.48	13.40	17.89
Punjab	8.39	4.68	68.31	12.73	5.11	29.53	11.91	5.08	7.09	10.04	107.41	23.68	14.85	27.86
Rajasthan	31.75	13.70	55.24		22.45	55.13	35.68	25.21	21.90	6.23	17.51	26.40	16.69	30.89
Sikkim	4.45	30.35			4.12	36.53	9.30	6.14	10.24	16.40	0.00	10.97	23.26	29.54
Tamil Nadu	22.97	0.00	12.48	26.39	20.90	24.26	17.45	20.71	16.18	39.39	93.65	9.82	16.05	25.90
Tripura	9.72	53.81			9.54	9.24	20.04	9.42	9.23	21.51	60.77	29.95	28.86	10.12
Uttar Pradesh	10.71	8.50	22.91	52.03	7.71	11.74	11.63	7.19	13.57	10.91	59.99	22.00	41.20	24.79
Uttarakhand	6.69	8.43		7.03	4.53	31.47	26.85	4.72	9.50	33.85	19.91	52.87	5.54	4.01

West Bengal	5.98	10.43	45.32	4.00	5.31	15.70	13.35	5.15	8.43	6.37	19.39	14.51	15.87	11.57
A and N Islands	14.26				13.27	69.60	53.28	11.58	7.47	9.17	45.72	20.99	29.06	14.72
D and N Haveli	17.12	29.08	17.03	15.16	15.67	9.04		14.08	29.63	28.45	0.00	8.94	55.18	70.38
Delhi	41.72	15.09	49.84		11.13	34.68	63.97	11.19	23.25	63.27	10.77	75.59	19.06	68.31
Daman and Diu	8.09				29.12	6.71		22.72	0.00	37.43	15.78	25.57	20.35	44.07
Chandigarh									3.71	18.19	14.49	56.30	0.00	0.00
Lakshadweep									22.25	20.06	47.65	14.05	85.16	5.27
Puducherry	10.55		88.89	44.95	10.87	82.58	47.54	11.30	9.53	12.34	39.42	17.31	71.62	46.64
All India	8.04	8.66	5.40	20.21	8.88	14.07	20.70	9.11	14.18	16.99	30.31	12.22	13.57	13.79

Source: Calculated by the author based on data collected from the Ministry of Agriculture, GoI.

challenges as well as opportunities. The sustainability of the rice–wheat system in major producing regions such as Punjab and Haryana faces a problem of deterioration in soil health and depletion of groundwater. In the case of cereals, pulses, oilseeds, fruits, vegetables, livestock, and fisheries there are huge technological or yield gaps, bridging of which can improve their production and productivity. But utilization of any such yield potentials would require extensive extension credit and marketing support (ICAR 2008). Besides, adequate technological and institutional preparedness to meet the challenges of climate change would be required as there are indications that climate change may adversely impact the food security situation in different parts of the country.

TRENDS IN PER CAPITA CONSUMPTION OF MAJOR FOOD ITEMS

Table 8.6 shows the trends in per capita consumption of major food items in rural and urban India, during 1993–4 to 2009–10. It would be seen from the table that per capita consumption of rice, wheat, coarse cereals, and pulses declined over time in both rural and urban areas, but that of edible oils, vegetables, milk, eggs, and chicken increased. The per capita consumption of meat, however, not only fluctuated, but showed a declining trend and that of fish improved marginally. In terms of per capita consumption of calories and proteins, there were declining trends overtime in both rural and urban areas, although the use of fats increased substantially (Table 8.7). The decline in calorie intake was observed across all economic classes. But the falling per capita calorie consumption in the bottom quartile from 1,659 kc in 1993–4 to 1,624 kc in 2004–5 and of bottom deciles from 1,490 kc in 1993–4 to 1,485 in 2004–5 was a cause for concern (Deaton and Drèze 2009).

INCIDENCE OF POVERTY AND MALNUTRITION BY REGION AND SOCIAL GROUP

Despite the fact that India is self-sufficient in the production of major food items, economic access to food by people is limited due to poverty and inequality. Based on Tendulkar Methodology, about 33.8 per cent rural population and 20.9 per cent urban population in India continued to live below the poverty line in 2009–10 (Table 8.8). The total number of poor persons was estimated at 354.7 million, comprising 278.2 million in rural areas and 76.5 million in urban areas. Further, the incidence of rural poverty was as high as 56.1 per cent in Chhattisgarh, 55.3 per cent in Bihar, 55.9 per cent in Dadra and Nagar Haveli, 47.4 per cent in Manipur,

42.0 per cent in Madhya Pradesh, and 41.6 per cent in Jharkhand. In urban areas also, the incidence of poverty was quite high in Bihar (39.4 per cent), Jharkhand (31.1 per cent), Manipur (46.4 per cent), Daman and Diu (33.0 per cent), and Uttar Pradesh (31.7 per cent). The poor people lack not only adequate purchasing power to access sufficient, safe, and nutritious food, but also many of them live in hunger.

The incidence of poverty in rural areas was comparatively higher among Scheduled Tribes (STs) (47.7 per cent) and Scheduled Castes (SCs) (42.3 per cent) against 33.8 for all social groups. In urban areas however, it was highest among SCs (34.1 per cent), followed by STs (30.4 per cent) as against the average poverty rate of 20.9 per cent. The religious community-wise incidence of poverty data for 2009–10 was not available. However, based on the earlier estimates for 2004–5, the incidence of poverty was highest among Muslims (32 per cent) followed by Hindus (29 per cent), Christians (15 per cent), and Sikhs (6 per cent). It would be seen from Table 8.9 that in rural areas, incidence of poverty was disproportionately higher among Hindus, Muslims, Buddhists, and lower among Sikhs but in urban areas it was disproportionately very high among Muslims.

Even though the incidence of poverty dropped by 8 per cent in rural areas and 4.8 per cent in urban areas, during 2004–5 to 2009–10, the income inequality (Lorenz ratio) increased from 0.28 in 1993–4 to 0.30 in 2009–10 in rural areas and from 0.34 in 1993–4 to 0.37 in 2004–5 and 0.38 in 2009–10 in urban areas. The poverty gap (PG) increased from 38.4 per cent in 1993–4 to 39.7 per cent in 2009–10 in rural areas, and from 42.8 per cent in 1993–4 to 46.8 per cent in 2009–10 in urban areas. Also the incidence of poverty among agricultural labourers was as high as 46.1 per cent in 2004–5.

In estimating the food poverty line, the minimum required calorie intake per capita was 2,100 kc for urban areas and 2,400 kc for rural areas. By these norms, about 50 per cent of India's population remained calorie poor. In fact, there were declining trends in average calorie intake during 1993–4 to 2004–5 in rural areas of all the states, excepting Assam and Kerala, and also the intake of protein declined in all states excepting Assam, Kerala, and Maharashtra (Table 8.10). In urban areas the average calorie intake declined in most places, excepting Assam, Kerala, Punjab, Tamil Nadu, Bihar, and Uttar Pradesh. The intake of protein declined in Haryana, Karnataka, Madhya Pradesh, Maharashtra, Odisha, Rajasthan, and West Bengal. The prevalence of calorie undernourishment was as high as 29.1 per cent in Tamil Nadu,

Table 8.6 Per Capita Consumption of Different Commodities in India

Year	Rice (kg)	Wheat (kg)	Coarse Cereals (kg)	All Cereals (kg)	All Pulses and Pulse Products (kg)	Vegetables (kg)	All Edible Oil (kg)	Milk (l)	Eggs (no.)	Fish (kg)	Goat Meat/ Mutton (kg)	Chicken (kg)
Rural (per annum)												
1993–4	82.61	52.56	27.86	163.03	9.25	32.97	4.5	47.94	7.79	2.19	0.73	0.24
1999–2000	80.18	54.14	20.44	154.76	10.22	40.15	6.08	46.11	13.26	2.56	0.85	0.49
2004–5	77.62	50.98	18.86	147.46	8.64	35.53	5.84	47.09	12.29	2.45	0.57	0.61
2009–10	74.7	53.03	10.34	138.08	7.92	49.14	7.74	50.09	21.08	3.27	0.57	1.5
Urban (per annum)												
1993–4	62.42	54.02	12.53	128.97	10.46	35.41	6.81	59.5	18.01	2.43	1.34	0.37
1999–2000	62.05	54.14	10.59	126.78	12.17	42.46	8.76	62.05	25.06	2.68	1.22	0.73
2004–5	57.31	53.05	10.59	120.94	9.98	38.57	8.03	62.17	20.93	2.51	0.85	1.03
2009–10	56.64	52.82	4.6	114.05	9.6	50.11	9.95	65.19	32.53	2.9	1.11	2.19

Source: National Sample Survey Organization (NSSO), 50th, 51st, 61st, and 66th Rounds, quoted in GoI 2011b.

Table 8.7 Average Per Capita Consumption of Calories, Protein, and Fats (per day)

Year	Calories (kc)		Protein (gm)		Fats (gm)	
	Rural	Urban	Rural	Urban	Rural	Urban
1983	2,240	2,070	63.5	58.1	27.1	37.1
1987–8	2,233	2,095	63.2	58.6	28.3	39.3
1993–4	2,153	2,073	60.3	57.7	31.1	41.9
1990–2000	2,148	2,155	59.1	58.4	36.0	49.6
2004–5	2,047	2,021	55.8	55.4	35.4	47.4

Source: Deaton and Drèze 2009.

Table 8.8 Number and Percentage of Population Below Poverty Line by States, 2009–10

States	Rural		Urban		Total	
	% of persons	No. of persons (in lakh)	% of persons	No. of persons (in lakh)	% of persons	No. of persons (in lakh)
Andhra Pradesh	22.8	127.9	17.7	48.7	21.1	176.6
Arunachal Pradesh	26.2	2.7	24.9	0.8	25.9	3.5
Assam	39.9	105.3	26.1	11.2	37.9	116.4
Bihar	55.3	498.7	39.4	44.8	53.5	543.5
Chhattisgarh	56.1	108.3	23.8	13.6	48.7	121.9
Delhi	7.7	0.3	14.4	22.9	14.2	23.3
Goa	11.5	0.6	6.9	0.6	8.7	1.3
Gujarat	26.7	91.6	17.9	44.6	23.0	136.2
Haryana	18.6	30.4	23.0	19.6	20.1	50.0
Himachal Pradesh	9.1	5.6	12.6	0.9	9.5	6.4
Jammu and Kashmir	8.1	7.3	12.8	4.2	9.4	11.5
Jharkhand	41.6	102.2	31.1	24.0	39.1	126.2
Karnataka	26.1	97.4	19.6	44.9	23.6	142.3
Kerala	12.0	21.6	12.1	18.0	12.0	39.6
Madhya Pradesh	42.0	216.9	22.9	44.9	36.7	261.8
Maharashtra	29.5	179.8	18.3	90.9	24.5	270.8
Manipur	47.4	8.8	46.4	3.7	47.1	12.5
Meghalaya	15.3	3.5	24.1	1.4	17.1	4.9
Mizoram	31.1	1.6	11.5	0.6	21.1	2.3
Nagaland	19.3	2.8	25.0	1.4	20.9	4.1
Odisha	39.2	135.5	25.9	17.7	37.0	153.2
Puducherry	0.2	0.0	1.6	0.1	1.2	0.1
Punjab	14.6	25.1	18.1	18.4	15.9	43.5
Rajasthan	26.4	133.8	19.9	33.2	24.8	167.0
Sikkim	15.5	0.7	5.0	0.1	13.1	0.8
Tamil Nadu	21.2	78.3	12.8	43.5	17.1	121.8
Tripura	19.8	5.4	10.0	0.9	17.4	6.3
Uttar Pradesh	39.4	600.6	31.7	137.3	37.7	737.9
Uttarakhand	14.9	10.3	25.2	7.5	18.0	17.9
West Bengal	28.8	177.8	22.0	62.5	26.7	240.3
Andaman and Nicobar Islands	0.4	0.01	0.3	0.004	0.4	0.01
Chandigarh	10.3	0.03	9.2	0.92	9.2	0.95
Dadra and Nagar	55.9	1.02	17.7	0.25	39.1	1.27
Daman and Diu	34.2	0.22	33.0	0.54	33.3	0.75
Lakshadweep	22.2	0.03	1.7	0.01	6.8	0.04
All India	33.8	2782.1	20.9	764.7	29.8	3546.8

Sources: GoI 2012.
Note: Based on Tendulkar Methodology.

Table 8.9 Distribution of Population and Incidence of Poverty by Religious Community, as of 2004–5

Religious Group	Rural		Urban	
	Share of population	Share of poor	Share of population	Share of poor
Hindus	82.3	84.1	75.6	68.9
Muslims	12.0	12.4	17.3	27.9
Christians	2.1	1.2	2.9	1.4
Sikhs	1.9	0.3	1.8	0.4
Buddhists	0.7	0.9	1.1	1.2
Jains	0.1	–	1.1	0.1
Other religious groups	0.8	1.0	0.2	0.2
All religious groups	100.0	100.0	100.0	100.0

Source: GoI 2011a.

Table 8.10 Per cent Change in Macronutrient Intake, Rural and Urban India, 1993–4 to 2004–5

States	Rural			Urban		
	Calorie	Protein	Fat	Calorie	Protein	Fat
Andhra Pradesh	−2.78	−1.97	23.16	0.40	2.62	23.78
Assam	4.24	6.46	27.14	1.66	4.49	19.48
Bihar	−3.12	−3.99	23.48	0.09	1.30	23.55
Gujarat	−3.56	−4.14	7.38	−1.78	4.37	9.67
Haryana	−10.64	−11.22	3.36	−5.00	−4.87	10.12
Karnataka	−11.00	−11.43	18.53	−4.05	−1.69	15.16
Kerala	2.49	9.06	24.77	1.53	8.21	21.35
Madhya Pradesh	−10.86	−6.67	24.03	−6.15	−2.68	7.69
Maharashtra	−0.31	1.64	23.88	−7.14	−6.13	4.59
Odisha	−8.00	−8.35	20.27	−5.40	−3.50	0.71
Punjab	−7.36	−10.71	−1.84	2.92	2.59	13.59
Rajasthan	−11.74	−12.34	−3.60	−3.11	−3.76	9.30
Tamil Nadu	−2.23	−4.06	19.84	0.68	1.03	21.24
Uttar Pradesh	−4.64	−6.39	5.63	0.47	3.01	11.89
West Bengal	−6.38	−5.11	23.83	−5.63	−2.65	14.33
All India	−4.92	−5.32	13.06	−2.46	−0.35	13.10

Source: NSSO reports on nutritional intakes in India, various rounds.

28.6 per cent in Kerala, 28.1 per cent in Karnataka, and 27.0 per cent in Maharashtra. The proportion of underweight children of less than 5 years age was about 42.5 per cent in the country. It was as high as 59.8 per cent in Madhya Pradesh, 57.1 per cent in Jharkhand, 50.1 per cent in Bihar, and 47.6 per cent in Chhattisgarh (GoI 2011a).

It would be further seen from Table 8.11 that about 36.4 per cent Hindu women and 35.2 per cent Muslim women, 23.3 per cent Christian women, and 17.7 per cent Sikh women suffer from acute energy deficiency. In several states including Assam (45.7 per cent), Bihar (49.7 per cent), Haryana (47.7 per cent), Odisha (64.1 per cent), West Bengal (42.8 per cent), Meghalaya (40.9 per cent), and Tripura (48.2 per cent) the percentage of Muslim women with body mass index less than 18.5 was very high, that is, more than 40 per cent. In the case of Hindu women this was relatively very high in Bihar

(44 per cent), Chhattisgarh (44 per cent), Jharkhand (41.8 per cent), Madhya Pradesh (42.3 per cent), and Odisha (41.2 per cent). In the case of Christian community, the chronic energy deficiency was high in Odisha (42.3 per cent) and Uttar Pradesh (44.8 per cent).

Besides, about 72 per cent urban children and 81 per cent rural children were anaemic in 2005–6. Also about 55.9 per cent Hindu women, 54.7 per cent Muslim women, 50.4 per cent Christian women, and 39.2 per cent Sikh women were anaemic. Among various social

Table 8.11 Percentage of Women with BMI less than 18.5 by Major Religious Communities, as of 2005–6

States	Hindus	Muslims	Christians	Sikhs
Andhra Pradesh	34.5	27.6	31	33.3
Assam	33.3	45.7	37.8	
Bihar	44	49.7		
Chhattisgarh	44	29.4	32.2	40
Delhi	14.9	18.6	9.2	8.8
Goa	29.8	25.7	23.5	
Gujarat	36.4	37.3	57	24.8
Haryana	31.5	47.7		17.1
Jharkhand	41.8	47	43	20.8
Karnataka	36.7	26.8	24.3	
Kerala	20	15.6	14.3	
Madhya Pradesh	42.3	37.2	15.4	14.3
Maharashtra	37.8	23.7	11.3	18.8
Odisha	41.2	64.1	42.3	14.3
Punjab	21.3	22.1	9.6	17.2
Rajasthan	37.1	36.1	19.3	41.5
Tamil Nadu	29.3	20.7	21.9	
Uttar Pradesh	36	36.6	44.8	19.4
West Bengal	38.1	42.8	34.3	13.9
Arunachal Pradesh	22.2	30.8	15.8	
Himachal Pradesh	30.4	21.1		37.6
Jammu and Kashmir	32.1	21		8.9
Manipur	15	22.6	12.7	
Meghalaya	23.3	40.9	11.2	
Mizoram	9.5	39	14.6	
Nagaland	21.3	32.5	16.2	
Sikkim	12.2	25.3	11.5	
Tripura	36.8	48.2		
Uttarakhand	30.1	30.1	32	29.4
Andaman and Nicobar Islands				
Chandigarh				
Dadra and Nagar Haveli				
Daman and Diu				
Lakshadweep				
Puducherry				
All India	36.9	35.2	23.3	17.7

Source: National Family Health Survey (NFHS) III, quoted from GoI 2011a.

groups, this was highest among STs (68.5 per cent), followed by SCs (58.3 per cent), Other Backward Classes (OBC) (54.4 per cent), and others (51.2 per cent). Among Hindu women, the incidence of anaemia was highest in Assam (71.6 per cent), followed by Jharkhand (68.2 per cent), Tripura (66.4 per cent), West Bengal (63.8 per cent), and Jammu and Kashmir (60.5 per cent). Among Muslim women, this was highest in Bihar (68.1 per cent), Uttarakhand (64.6 per cent), Haryana (63.4 per cent), Jharkhand (61.8 per cent), and West Bengal (61.3 per cent). Among Christian women, about 89.7 per cent women in Assam, 75.8 per cent in West Bengal, and 70.9 per cent in Tripura were anaemic (GoI 2011a). Besides, iodine deficiency and vitamin A deficiency were common across all social groups.

UNEMPLOYMENT AND WAGE RATES

According to the 64th Round of National Sample Survey (NSS; as per current daily status), for the year 2007–8, about 8.3 per cent Hindus, 8.8 per cent Muslims, 9.8 per cent Christians, and 6.9 per cent Sikhs were unemployed. The incidence of unemployed among Muslim youth was high in Goa (18.6 per cent), Kerala (18.0 per cent), Tamil Nadu (16.6 per cent), Tripura (15.0 per cent), and Karnataka (12.9 per cent). Among Hindu youth, it was high in Jharkhand (11.5 per cent), Kerala (21.6 per cent), Tamil Nadu (17.2 per cent), and Tripura (19.0 per cent). Besides, as of 2007–8, the average wage earnings of casual labourers in the country were only

Rs 79 per day for male and Rs 51 for female workers. In the agricultural sector, it was as low as Rs 48 for female and Rs 67 for male workers. Even for regular employees in agriculture, it was only Rs 65 for female and Rs 96 for male workers which can hardly ensure food security for them, especially in view of rising food price inflation. The rate of annual growth of wages has also been lower than that of food price inflation. Considering the country as a whole, the hunger index was 20 per cent (GoI 2011a).

IMPACT OF FOOD PRICE INFLATION

Inflation robs poor people of their already low purchasing power and makes them more vulnerable in terms of food insecurity. The poor people adjust with inflation by either skipping one meal or reducing the quantity and quality of food. It would be seen from Table 8.12 and Figure 8.1 that during 2004–5 to 2011–12, the wholesale price index (WPI) of most food items abnormally increased. The WPI either doubled or more than doubled in the case of pulses, mutton, and fish while that of foodgrains increased by 80.7 percentage points, milk by 94.0 percentage points, and fruits and vegetables by 83.1 percentage points. The retail and consumer price indices for these commodities would have increased even more due to rising price spread.

FACTORS INFLUENCING FOOD ABSORPTION

Inadequate supply of safe drinking water, safe quality food, sanitation arrangements, and access to public

Table 8.12   Yearly WPI of Selected Commodities (base: 2004–5 = 100)

Commodities	2005–6	2006–7	2007–8	2008–9	2009–10	2010–11	2011–12
Foodgrains	107.26	122.41	130.88	145.30	166.36	174.43	180.72
Cereals	105.99	116.74	127.86	143.09	161.18	169.67	176.23
Pulses	113.34	149.18	144.93	155.84	190.76	196.86	201.82
Vegetables	113.71	114.28	137.07	141.89	161.80	182.83	179.26
Fruits	103.27	109.68	114.38	129.08	136.17	163.17	186.37
Fruits and vegetables	108.00	111.78	124.63	134.86	147.76	172.05	183.15
Milk	101.01	108.98	114.58	123.24	146.41	175.88	194.01
Mutton	105.05	117.81	124.79	139.50	175.06	187.17	200.10
Fish (inland)	118.14	108.52	101.38	101.37	152.63	193.43	250.82
Fish (marine)	103.20	120.97	125.65	146.23	160.53	222.84	246.72
Egg	102.12	104.83	119.89	126.47	143.58	165.44	181.79
Eggs, meat, and fish	106.29	112.77	116.37	125.38	151.48	190.13	214.33
Sugar	109.67	109.57	93.40	108.54	166.79	165.02	173.44
Edible oils	94.08	102.45	116.02	121.55	114.38	120.58	135.72

Source: Office of the Economic Adviser to the GoI, Ministry of Commerce and Industry.

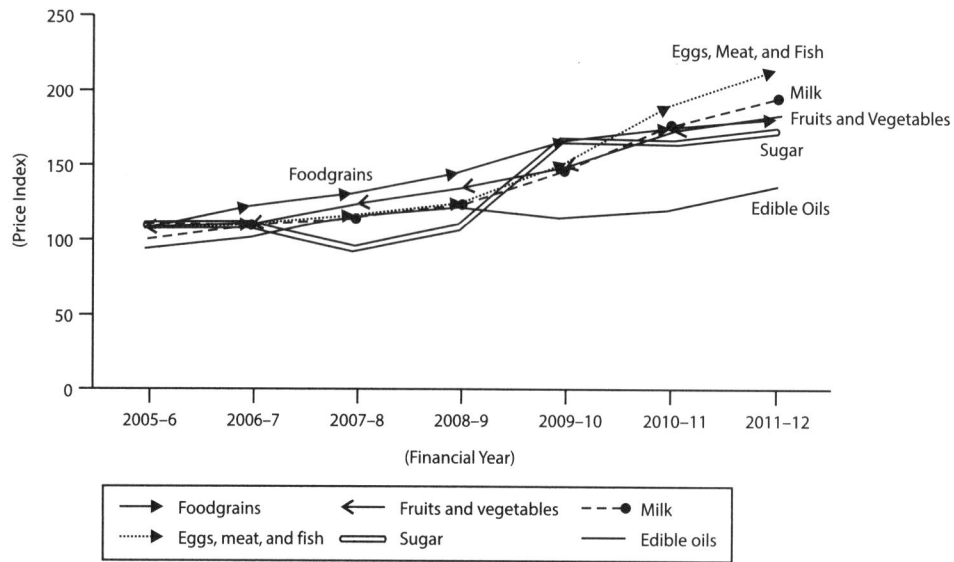

Figure 8.1 Yearly WPI of Selected Agricultural Commodities (base: 2004–5 = 100)
Source: Based on Table 8.12 in this chapter.

health services are some major food security challenges in India in relation to food absorption. According to the 65th Round of NSS for the year 2008–9, about 90.4 per cent households in rural areas and 93.9 per cent in urban areas had access to improved sources of drinking water. But in several states, the percentage of households with improved sources of drinking water was relatively much lower. These states include Assam (83.3 per cent), Jharkhand (67.4 per cent), Rajasthan (84.0 per cent), Manipur (49.1 per cent), Mizoram (44.4 per cent), Nagaland (64.4 per cent), Sikkim (72.0 per cent), Tripura (80.2 per cent), and Lakshadweep (33.5 per cent). In the rural areas of Jharkhand (63.4 per cent), Manipur (38.9 per cent), Mizoram (20.4 per cent), and Lakshadweep (28.3 per cent) an even lower proportion of total households had access to improved sources of drinking water. Considering the country as a whole, only about 30.1 per cent rural households and 74.3 per cent urban households used tap water. The proportion of rural households using tap water was less than 10 per cent in several states including Assam (6.3 per cent), Bihar (1.1 per cent), Chhattisgarh (7.6 per cent), Jharkhand (3.5 per cent), Madhya Pradesh (9.1 per cent), Odisha (5.8 per cent), and West Bengal (7.8 per cent). Taking into consideration both rural and urban households in India only about 35.8 per cent of Muslim households, 43.6 per cent Hindu households, 48.0 per cent Christian households, and 49.3 per cent Sikh households

had access to tap water (GoI 2009). However, access to tap water was much less than these national average figures for all religious communities in the states of Assam, Bihar, and Jharkhand. For all religious communities, open well was the main source of drinking water in Kerala and Nagaland (Table 8.13).

Besides, nearly 49.2 per cent households in India, 65.2 per cent households in rural areas, and 11.3 per cent in urban areas had no latrines. Only 28.5 per cent households in the country, 11.7 per cent in rural areas, and 70.7 per cent in urban areas had septic tanks or flush toilet facilities (Table 8.14). Considering both rural and urban areas, the states with a higher percentage of households not having latrines include Bihar (74.1 per cent), Chhattisgarh (72.9 per cent), Jharkhand (74.7 per cent), Karnataka (51.5 per cent), Madhya Pradesh (70.2 per cent), Odisha (78.7 per cent), and Rajasthan (63.6 per cent) (GoI 2010). It would be further seen from Table 8.15 that about 52.5 per cent Hindu households, 35.8 per cent Muslim households, 22.1 per cent Christian households, and 24.7 per cent Sikh households in the country did not have any toilet or latrine. Only 10.3 per cent of Hindu households, 35.4 per cent Muslim households, 46.9 per cent Christian households, and 45.9 per cent Sikh households had septic tanks or flush toilets. Majority of the Hindu households in Andhra Pradesh, Bihar, Chhattisgarh, Gujarat, Jharkhand, Karnataka, Madhya Pradesh, Odisha, Rajasthan, Uttar Pradesh, and

Table 8.13 Distribution of Households by Source of Drinking Water by Major Religious Communities, 2008–9

States	Hindus			Muslims			Christians			Sikhs		
	Tap	Tube well	Well	Tap	Tube well	Well	Tap	Tube well	Well	Tap	Tube well	Well
Andhra Pradesh	64.9	22.8	7.6	75.6	14.3	2.6	68.0	25.8	3.0			
Assam	10.8	60.3	20.9	7.7	72.0	11.4	6.9	30.0	26.5	12.2	87.8	
Bihar	7.2	88.4	3.4	9.1	87.7	2.5	13.5	86.5		1.5	98.2	
Chhattisgarh	17.0	74.1	7.7	59.3	33.0		13.7	39.0	47.3			
Delhi	83.8	11.2	0.0	89.2	10.0					96.4	0.7	
Goa	83.4	0.3	10.3	88.5		11.5	91.8		8.2			
Gujarat	56.8	33.7	5.5	78.8	18.0	2.0	59.7	35.1	0.1	52.8	25.3	
Haryana	67.6	29.6	1.6	34.3	47.8	7.6				70.1	28.1	
Jharkhand	9.3	66.0	22.9	9.7	59.6	30.1	10.1	38.8	50.9	61.9	38.1	
Karnataka	77.6	12.7	6.5	81.2	11.5	4.1	74.4	4.1	15.1			
Kerala	23.0	3.2	70.8	13.1	3.3	82.9	31.8	2.1	59.3			
Madhya Pradesh	21.4	59.5	16.6	49.8	42.5	4.3	65.1	34.9		71.8	15.4	12.8
Maharashtra	73.8	12.9	8.4	79.4	8.3	4.8	82.7	0.5	10.4	93.4		
Odisha	14.9	65.1	17.1	32.5	59.7	7.9	6.1	70.0	13.3			
Punjab	68.7	30.3	0.0	64.2	34.3	0.0	28.5	71.5	0.0	44.1	54.9	
Rajasthan	42.1	39.3	8.3	64.4	19.3	5.3	36.7	54.2	7.4	67.9	9.6	1.9
Tamil Nadu	84.6	7.2	2.1	88.6	5.9	1.8	79.5	8.6	3.2			
Uttar Pradesh	11.2	83.4	4.9	12.5	85.3	1.4	39.8	60.2	0.0	47.2	52.8	
West Bengal	32.8	60.3	4.7	15.9	81.6	1.8	31.2	43.1	21.3	86.7	13.3	
Arunachal Pradesh	73.7	20.3	3.2	76.0	14.7	0.7	81.8	7.2	3.3			
Himachal Pradesh	79.1	7.4	3.8	72.9	12.7	2.0				98.5	0.7	
Jammu and Kashmir	61.9	22.3	1.0	79.0	7.4	0.9	83.9	16.1	0.0	35.9	60.8	
Manipur	42.4	10.3	0.8	16.7	26.6	1.9	25.6	5.2	7.2			
Meghalaya	51.9	18.1	14.1	16.8	57.2	26.1	61.3	4.5	8.5			
Mizoram	37.8	0.0	0.0	58.1			43.0	3.0	0.2			
Nagaland	30.8	4.9	44.3	2.1	3.3	87.4	28.0	4.4	36.7			
Sikkim	69.6	0.0	0.0	77.7			70.4	0.0	0.0			
Tripura	33.4	41.9	19.9	30.8	45.6	17.5	36.4	46.2	15.9			
Uttarakhand	64.9	21.2	0.0	56.2	43.5	0.0	56.8	43.2	0.0	49.3	50.7	
Andaman and Nicobar Islands	84.0	0.8	9.8				99.6		0.1			
Chandigarh	97.5	2.2										
Dadra and Nagar Haveli	39.5	45.2	12.7	91.7	8.3		98.3	1.7				
Daman and Diu	67.1	31.5	0.9	99.9	0.1		84.8					
Lakshadweep	94.1	0.5	5.3	3.8	7.1	84.2						
Puducherry	96.6	0.5	0.5	69.8	0.0	28.5	97.7	0.0	0.0			
All India	43.7	43.6	8.9	35.8	51.8	9.2	48.0	15.2	25.3	49.3	48.5	0.2

Source: GoI 2009.

Table 8.14 Distribution of Households by Type of Toilet Facility, 2008–9

States	Rural		Urban	
	Septic tank/flush	No latrine	Septic tank/flush	No latrine
Andhra Pradesh	29.9	64.3	85.3	11.2
Assam	18.2	13.5	84.8	0.9
Bihar	11.8	79.8	61.9	27.7
Chhattisgarh	11.3	82.3	64.3	31.5
Delhi	84.5	7.5	92.8	1.2
Goa	40.6	36.2	87.6	9.6
Gujarat	26	67.3	79.5	7.3
Haryana	29.6	45.3	73.5	8.4
Jharkhand	7.3	84.1	70.6	24.5
Karnataka	7.4	75.2	72.8	11.3
Kerala	21.7	5.3	50.6	1.5
Madhya Pradesh	10.5	85.3	66.2	24.3
Maharashtra	31.6	60.7	89.4	5.9
Odisha	7.3	88.2	56.2	29.1
Punjab	32.1	36.2	84.1	5
Rajasthan	8.2	82.1	70.3	12.6
Tamil Nadu	23.7	73.5	79.1	16
Uttar Pradesh	23.2	53.5		
West Bengal	14.8	41.7	73.4	5.6
Arunachal Pradesh	23.9	16.2	61.5	0.1
Himachal Pradesh	47.8	46.5	87.5	8.8
Jammu and Kashmir	17.2	34.9	71.3	11.8
Manipur	21.8	1.1	51.6	0
Meghalaya	14.8	11.4	79.1	0.2
Mizoram	32.1	1.2	82.3	0
Nagaland	32.6	3.1	70.1	1.3
Sikkim	68.9	2.5	98.9	0
Tripura	5.2	3.4	48.6	0.9
Uttarakhand	12.6	79.2	72.8	14.2
Andaman and Nicobar Islands	47.5	39.9	93.9	6.1
Chandigarh	90	9.6	99.4	0.6
Dadra and Nagar Haveli	32.2	53.2	87.1	7.1
Daman and Diu	8.4	31.9	986.7	6.4
Lakshadweep	21.7	0	62	1
Puducherry	34.6	65.4	84.8	9.1
All India	17.9	65.2	77.3	11.3

Source: GoI 2009.

Table 8.15 Distribution of Households by Type of Toilet Facility by Major Religious Communities, as in 2008–9

States	Hindus		Muslims		Christians	
	Septic tank/flush	No latrine	Septic tank/flush	No latrine	Septic tank/flush	No latrine
Andhra Pradesh	44.6	50.2	65.5	28.4	46.8	50.9
Assam	32.0	8.6	11.8	19.7	16.1	26.0
Bihar	20.2	71.0	23.1	57.8	38.9	60.2
Chhattisgarh	20.4	73.8	78.6	14.4	24.5	64.1
Delhi	92.3	1.7	88.8	1.9	100.0	0.0
Goa	60.3	24.8	55.3	39.0	74.7	13.7
Gujarat	41.2	50.6	48.9	34.5	46.0	51.3
Haryana	43.3	32.9	30.9	63.4	100.0	0.0
Jharkhand	17.6	60.8	12.8	63.9	33.2	60.4
Karnataka	29.9	54.3	40.1	35.4	59.1	10.0
Kerala	28.1	5.3	20.5	1.4	42.6	3.1
Madhya Pradesh	22.5	72.6	53.6	39.3	50.7	28.3
Maharashtra	59.6	34.1	74.4	18.1	89.4	0.8
Odisha	15.0	78.8	36.4	56.0	5.6	93.3
Punjab	63.1	19.9	54.2	31.3	47.2	52.4
Rajasthan	23.5	65.8	36.9	45.7	43.5	56.2
Tamil Nadu	47.2	49.3	75.7	19.7	69.5	23.3
Uttar Pradesh	22.6	71.4	35.7	46.8	90.9	9.1
West Bengal	38.5	25.1	18.2	41.0	32.7	36.6
Arunachal Pradesh	40.3	9.2	33.4	10.9	25.7	8.2
Himachal Pradesh	51.9	42.9	50.8	47.0	90.0	10.0
Jammu and Kashmir	32.5	63.1	27.7	7.8	16.1	0.0
Manipur	32.6	0.7	12.7	0.8	25.2	0.7
Meghalaya	40.0	0.0	13.6	0.0	26.5	10.3
Mizoram	44.4	0.0	85.9	0.0	59.0	0.0
Nagaland	61.1	4.0	4.2	10.2	42.7	2.4
Sikkim	72.7	2.5	98.6	0.0	80.8	0.2
Tripura	14.0	2.8	6.2	3.5	10.4	0.0
Uttarakhand	34.5	44.6	27.7	21.4	18.5	79.1
Andaman and Nicobar Islands	55.1	34.7	97.0	1.0	77.9	17.4
Chandigarh	98.3	1.7	92.9	7.1	100.0	0.0
Dadra and Nagar Haveli	46.4	43.6	38.4	0.0	0.0	21.9
Daman and Diu	32.5	24.0	85.7	4.8	68.2	16.0
Lakshadweep	89.0	0.0	29.9	0.5	0.0	0.0
Puducherry	68.7	27.3	81.9	9.4	80.0	14.6
All India	34.7	52.5	35.4	35.8	46.9	22.1

Source: GoI 2009.

Jammu and Kashmir did not have any toilet or latrine. Similarly, majority of Muslim households in Bihar, Haryana, Jharkhand, and Odisha, and that of Christian households in Andhra Pradesh, Bihar, Gujarat, Jharkhand, Odisha, Punjab, Rajasthan, and Uttarakhand had no toilet facility. In fact, the proportion of households without toilets was much higher for SCs and STs and OBCs. About 69 per cent ST households, 65 per cent SC households, and 54 per cent OBC households in the country were without toilets (GoI 2009).

Public Health Care

The data sourced from NFHS III for the year 2005–6 show that only about 34.4 per cent households had access to public health care, while 64.8 per cent was dependent on private health care facility (Table 8.16). The access to public health care facility was very low in several states including Bihar (6.7 per cent), Punjab (19.3 per cent), and Uttar Pradesh (15.3 per cent).

Incidence of HIV/AIDS, Tuberculosis, and Malaria

India has the third largest number of people living with HIV/AIDS. The estimated number of people living with HIV/AIDS was 2.27 million in 2008. According to the World Health Organization (WHO) Global Report, tuberculosis is a major health problem in India. The tuberculosis mortality rate was as high as 0.33 million every year. Malaria is another acute parasitic illness which resulted in 1,055 deaths in 2008. While undernourishment is one of the reasons for tuberculosis, malaria spreads due to stagnant water storage. Even though the incidence of HIV/AIDS, tuberculosis, and malaria have shown declining trends in recent years, in many areas, people continue to suffer.

The Vulnerable Groups

Judged by the three crucial factors of food security, namely, physical availability, economic access, and food absorption, the most vulnerable groups in the country are landless labourers, marginal farmers, and other unorganized sector workers in the villages and slum dwellers in urban areas. The condition of women among these categories of people is even worse. They suffer from food insecurity and malnutrition on account of landlessness or semi-landlessness, low level of unemployment, low wages, high food price inflation, shelterlessness, lack of access to safe drinking water, poor sanitation, etc. Also in the absence of education and skills there is hardly any scope for their upward mobility.

Table 8.16 Source of Health Care: Percentage Distribution of Households by Public and Non-public Health Care Provision, 2005–6

States	Public Medical Sector		
	Urban	Rural	All
Andhra Pradesh	26.2	25.5	25.8
Assam	49.8	69.1	65.2
Bihar	10.5	6.0	6.7
Chhattisgarh	26.8	38.9	36.3
Delhi	28.6	37.9	29.3
Goa	28.1	31.5	29.6
Gujarat	16.8	35.2	27.5
Haryana	27.3	27.9	27.7
Jharkhand	27.1	20.7	22.3
Karnataka	23.3	44.6	36.0
Kerala	45.8	52.1	50.0
Madhya Pradesh	38.2	37.1	37.4
Maharashtra	22.0	36.8	29.7
Odisha	62.2	79.0	76.2
Punjab	17.8	20.2	19.3
Rajasthan	59.2	74.7	70.2
Tamil Nadu	47.5	57.6	53.0
Uttar Pradesh	16.2	15.0	15.3
West Bengal	22.7	31.7	28.8
Arunachal Pradesh	69.0	87.7	82.6
Himachal Pradesh	78.5	83.3	82.7
Jammu and Kashmir	41.4	72.6	62.9
Manipur	71.7	82.4	79.0
Meghalaya	48.7	70.5	64.9
Mizoram	88.1	93.6	90.6
Nagaland	36.9	57.8	52.1
Sikkim	83.4	94.0	91.8
Tripura	58.8	84.5	80.0
Uttarakhand	47.1	43.4	44.5
All India	29.6	36.8	34.4

Source: NFHS III, quoted from GoI (2011a).

According to official estimates, about 10 per cent households do not own any land and the percentage of those who do not own any land other than homestead is as high as 41.6 per cent. The proportion of pure landless households that do not own even homestead land was as high as 31 per cent in Sikkim, 22 per cent in Arunachal Pradesh, 18 per cent in Maharashtra, 17 per cent in Tamil Nadu, and 14 per cent in Andhra Pradesh (GoI 2006).

Landless and houseless people are most vulnerable because they have neither land to produce food for self-consumption nor have income to purchase adequate, safe, and nutritious food. Besides, shelterlessness or slums do not provide hygienic condition for food absorption, even if they have access to some food. They are the poorest of the poor in the villages and citizenless without food cards or any identity card in the cities. Women remain more vulnerable because they do not own any land and have relatively low levels of employment and wages. Besides, in a situation of shortage, they are tradition-bound to feed the husband and children first and eat only the residues. Besides, there are about 90 million elderly people in India, 75 per cent of whom live in rural areas of which 48 per cent are women and 55 per cent are widows. The majority of elderly women has no income security and 'therefore' suffer from acute food insecurity and deprivation. The relative deprivation of women is more across all castes and communities in India (GoI 2011a).

Government Policies and Programmes

In order to ensure food and nutritional security of all people, the Government of India (GoI) has initiated a number of schemes in the past. These are:

1. Targeted Public Distribution System (TPDS) of food, which aims at subsidized food supply to poor and semi-poor households.
2. Annapurna Scheme for free supply of 10 kg of foodgrains to senior citizens belonging to the category of destitute.
3. Midday Meal (MDM) scheme for school children. During 2011–12, about 2.7 million tons of foodgrains were allocated under the MDM scheme.
4. Integrated Child Development Services (ICDS) for children up to six years of age including health checkups, immunization, supplementary feeding, advice on health and nutrition, etc.

   There are also other schemes such as the Mahatma Gandhi National Rural Employment Guarantee Scheme (MGNREGS), the Social Assistance Programme, etc., which aims at improving the poor people's economic access to food.
5. The MGNREGS provides a legal guarantee for 100 days of employment in a financial year to adult members of any rural household who are willing to do public work-related unskilled manual work at a statutorily fixed minimum wage.
6. Social assistance or social protection programmes, provides old age pension, maternity benefit, insurance, etc. The poor people have no doubt received some benefit from all such schemes. But due to governance deficit or implementation gaps, the overall impact is far from satisfactory.

Targeted Public Distribution

India has a large system of public food distribution, currently called TPDS. There are about five lakh fair price shops through which rice and wheat are distributed at highly subsidized rates to both poor and semi-poor households. The Food Corporation of India and other state agencies procure food from farmers at the minimum support prices fixed by the government and maintain stocks and distribute to the poor through fair price shops at subsidized rates. As on 1 July 2012, about 30.7 million tons of rice and 49.8 million tons of wheat were in the central pool stock as against the buffer norms of 11.8 million tons rice and 20.1 million tons wheat (Table 8.17). The people below the poverty line are provided 35 kg of foodgrains per month at highly subsidized rates. About 65.2 million below poverty line (BPL) families are covered by TPDS. Besides, families above poverty line also are supplied with food at subsidized rates, depending upon their availability in the central pool. During 2011–12, about 59 million tons of foodgrains were distributed through the fair price shops.

However, the TPDS suffers from several weaknesses, including (*a*) high exclusion and inclusion errors, (*b*) non-viability of many fair price shops, (*c*) failure in fulfilling the price stabilization objective, and (*d*) leakages (GoI 2008: vol. II). In rural India, the Public Distribution System (PDS) shared hardly 13.2 per cent of total household consumption of rice and 7.3 per cent of household consumption of wheat. In the relatively poorer states such as Bihar, Odisha, and Uttar Pradesh the contribution of PDS to household consumption of rice and wheat was less than 1 per cent to 3 per cent (GoI 2007). First of all, the PDS off-take was low in these states and second, there was a huge gap between PDS off-take and PDS consumption. Besides, only 36 per cent of the poor had either BPL or Antyodaya cards in the country. Only 22.7 per cent fair price shops were viable (GoI 2008). Moreover, the cost of administering TPDS is quite high. The rising food subsidy bill poses a problem of sustainability of any such inefficient and ineffective food distribution system. Currently, the government is considering to introduce food stamps, multi-application

Table 8.17 Actual Stock Position and Buffer Norms
of Rice and Wheat during July 2000–
July 2012 (in million tons)

Date	Rice		Wheat	
	Actual stock	Buffer norm	Actual stock	Buffer norm
July 2000	14.5	10.0	27.8	14.3
January 2001	20.7	8.4	25.0	8.4
July 2001	22.8	10.0	38.9	14.3
January 2002	25.6	8.4	32.4	8.4
July 2002	21.9	9.8	41.1	14.3
January 2003	19.4	11.8	28.8	8.4
July 2003	11.0	9.8	24.2	14.3
January 2004	11.7	11.8	12.7	8.0
July 2004	10.8	9.8	19.2	14.3
January 2005	12.8	11.8	8.9	8.4
July 2005	10.1	9.8	14.5	17.1
January 2006	12.6	11.8	6.2	8.2
July 2006	11.1	9.8	8.2	17.1
January 2007	12.0	11.8	5.7	8.2
July 2007	11.0	9.8	12.9	17.1
January 2008	11.5	11.8	7.7	8.2
July 2008	11.2	9.8	24.9	20.1
January 2009	17.6	11.8	18.2	11.2
July 2009	19.6	11.8	32.9	20.1
January 2010	24.4	13.8	23.1	11.2
July 2010	24.3	11.8	33.6	20.1
January 2011	25.6	13.8	21.5	11.2
July 2011	26.9	11.8	37.1	20.1
January 2012	29.7	13.8	25.7	11.2
July 2012	30.7	11.8	49.8	20.1

Source: Monthly Food Bulletins, various issues, Department of Food and Consumer Affairs, GoI.

smart cards, and web-enabled systems to remove the above mentioned deficiencies. But they have their own limitations in the Indian context. The major problems with the food stamps system are that any counterfeiting of stamps may derail the whole system and there would be an erosion in the value of coupons, unless linked with inflation which would erode the gain and confidence of the people. Some state governments introduced a scheme of providing rice to poor people at subsidized rates say Rs 2 per kg of rice which worked well in some parts of Tamil Nadu and Andhra Pradesh. Recently the states of Chhattisgarh and Gujarat have introduced IT in the management of PDS which seems to have improved the food distribution system, through reduction of leakages. Besides, in Chhattisgarh, cooperatives play an important role in food distribution, at the local level which is generally viewed as a good model.

NATIONAL FOOD SECURITY BILL 2011

In order to ensure right to food to all its citizens, GoI tabled the National Food Security Bill on December 2011 which is yet to be passed as an Act. The stated objective of the Bill is 'to provide for food and nutritional security in human life cycle approach, by ensuring access to adequate quantity of quality food at affordable prices to people to live a life with dignity and for matters connected there with or incidental thereto'. The Bill in its present form provides statutory entitlements for subsidized ration for 75 per cent of population in rural areas (with 46 per cent people in priority category) and 50 per cent of urban population (with 28 per cent in priority category). The Bill proposes to provide 7 kg of foodgrains per person per month for priority households not exceeding Rs 3/2/1 per kg of rice/wheat/coarse cereals and not less than 3 kg of foodgrains per person per month for general households at prices not exceeding 50 per cent of the minimum support prices.

While this may be well intentioned, the proposed Bill has been criticized by many concerned people for several reasons such as (*a*) not simultaneously addressing the sustainability of required production, decentralized procurement, storage, and distribution; (*b*) no adequate mention of nutrition; (*c*) still targeted and not universal; (*d*) ineffective grievance redressal mechanism; (*e*) no role for local-level institutions; (*f*) inadequate provision dealing with transparency and accountability; (*g*) omissions of provisions for malnourished children, out of school children, community kitchens, prevention of starvation, etc., as suggested by the National Advisory Council; and (*h*) provision to replace food entitlements with cash transfers by the central government on its own terms, etc.

It is expected that these concerns will be addressed in the Act when it is passed.

KEY CHALLENGES

Despite the fact that India has achieved macro-level food self-sufficiency in a broader sense, the food security system in the country remains weak in several respects. First, the country is still deficient in the production of pulses, edible oilseeds, and coarse cereals. Second, the yield levels of some cereal and pulse crops have started plateauing in several regions mainly due to technology fatigue and soil health deterioration which poses a threat to stability and sustainability of the food security system. Third, the incentives to produce more fruits and vegetables for the farmers are missing as the benefits of high retail prices go mainly to the traders and not to the farmers. Fourth, although the production growth rates of meat, fish, and milk are reasonably high the demand for these commodities is rising at faster rates and, therefore, there should be special efforts to increase their production and marketing arrangements for price stability. Fifth, there is a lack of purchasing power on the part of a substantial number of households to access adequate, safe, and nutritious food according to their dietary needs and preferences, as reflected by the high incidence of poverty and malnutrition. Sixth, the food safety concerns have not been adequately addressed by the government as quality of food articles, especially vegetables, is often questioned due to high chemical content. Seventh, the existing food delivery system at the village and household level has several deficiencies due to lack of transparency, accountability, and non-viability of fair price shops. Eighth, still a significant number of poor households especially in rural areas do not have access to safe drinking water, sanitation, and health care which fail them to convert even smaller quantities of food into nutrition. Ninth, the landless poor in the villages and slum dwellers in urban areas, especially women, are more vulnerable than others in terms of food and nutrition insecurity. This is truer about elderly women who do not have any regular source of income. Besides, there are various technological, infrastructural, institutional, and policy constraints to sustainable agriculture and food security, including availability of quality seeds and other inputs, credit, markets and appropriate technology, and price policies for sustained agricultural growth and food security.

The Way Forward

The right to food is a basic human right. Therefore, all human beings should be entitled to access adequate, safe, and nutritious food in a stable manner. However, it is also true that the existing food policy in India is non-sustainable in the long run for a variety of reasons which cannot be elaborated here for lack of space. First, there should be ICT-led more transparency and efficiency in the public food distribution system and beneficiaries of TPDS should be organized into cooperatives and self-help groups (SHGs) and manage the fair price shops themselves at the local level for checking corruption and food diversion. Second, all farm households should be enabled through appropriate technological and institutional support and incentives to produce adequate basic

food materials for themselves, and also produce surplus for feeding others and generate income to purchase other required food and non-food items that cannot be produced by them with available land and other resources in their possession. Third, every landless family in rural areas should be allocated homestead plot of at least 10 cents in size in the name of either the woman or jointly in the name of the woman and man which will enable a beneficiary to construct a house if she/he does not have one and use the additional space for taking up some economic activities such as cultivation of vegetables, fruits, goat rearing, poultry, etc., thereby enhancing her/his food and nutritional security. The states of West Bengal and Odisha have already initiated such a scheme in the past few years, which are yielding positive impacts in terms of improved food security of the beneficiary households. In West Bengal, a total of 62,167 families received land through the Nijo-Griho Nijo-Bhumi (NGNB) scheme till March 2013 (see Box 8.1).

Fourth, there should be effective implementation of the Hindu Succession Act and also enactment of similar Acts for other communities, for providing equal land rights to women aside from redistribution of available government land, *bhoodan* land, and ceiling surplus land to them. Fifth, all slum-dwelling households should be given food card to access subsidized food, as a matter of right or entitlement. Sixth, every adult person in both rural and urban areas should be entitled to adequate quality education and skills for accessing high paid jobs or taking up entrepreneurship that will enable them to purchase food from the market, if needed, according to their dietary needs and preferences leading to a decent life. Currently, there are huge untapped yield potentials in crops, horticulture, and livestock which should be utilized through appropriate technological, infrastructural, institutional, and policy interventions. Seventh, food price inflation must be maintained at a low level as the persistently high food price inflation risks the poor people not only with low availability of food and nutrition but also of hunger and starvation death. Eighth, every household should be provided with safe drinking water, sanitation, and basic health care facilities for prevention and control of diseases and conversion of food into nutrition. Last but not the least, production and productivity of not only food crops, but also fruits, vegetables, meat, fish, egg, and chicken should be substantially enhanced to meet the growing demand for these food items as people's incomes rise. In the past few years, the impact of food price inflation has been felt more in respect of fruits, vegetables, milk, meat, fish, and eggs.

Box 8.1   The Story of an Erstwhile Landless Woman in Kalna District, Burdwan, West Bengal

Shubhankari Nag lived in a small rented shelter without any security, till recently. She received a five decimal plot of land under the NGNB scheme of the Government of West Bengal on 27 March 2012. Now she says as follows:

I worked hard in the hope of enhancing my family's income, but options were few. Now after getting land and house from the government, things are changing. I have nurtured a small kitchen garden; fresh vegetables from my garden supplement our diet. I can even sell a portion to earn a little. I am also rearing cows. I now generate about Rs 200 per month which goes into supporting my children's education. I have never felt so happy before.

Figure 8.2   Shubhankari Nag
Source: Wings, Department of Land and Land Reforms, Government of West Bengal, 2012.

REFERENCES

Deaton, A. and Jean Drèze. 2009. 'Food and Nutrition in India: Facts and Interpretations', *Economic and Political Weekly*, 44(7): 42–65.

FAO (Food and Agriculture Organization). 1996. *Report on Food for All*. Rome, Italy: World Food Summit.

GoI (Government of India). 2006. *Household Ownership Holdings in India*, NSSO, 59th Round. New Delhi: GoI.

———. 2007. *Report on 'Public Distribution System and Other Sources of Household Consumption'*, 2004–5, NSS, 61st Round, Report no. 510. New Delhi: Ministry of Statistics and Programme Implementation.

———. 2008. *Eleventh Five Year Plan*. New Delhi: Planning Commission, GoI.

———. 2009. *Report on Housing Conditions and Amenities in India*, NSSO, 65th Round, Report no. 535. New Delhi: GoI.

———. 2011a. *India Human Development Report*. New Delhi: Institute of Applied Manpower and Research and Oxford University Press.

———. 2011b. *Agricultural Statistics at a Glance*. New Delhi: Ministry of Agriculture.

———. 2012. *Press Note on Poverty Estimates*, 2009–10, March. New Delhi: GoI.

———. 2013. *Twelfth Five Year Plan*. New Delhi: Planning Commission, GoI.

ICAR (Indian Council of Agricultural Research). 2008. *State Specific Technological Interventions for Higher Agricultural Growth*. New Delhi: Indian Council of Agricultural Research.

9

Social Security in India

PRAVEEN JHA, R. RAMAKUMAR, AND NILACHALA ACHARYA

The notion of social security in academic discourses has conceptually been a complex and open-ended one as is clearly evident from the history of its evolution. At the most basic level, social security is organically connected with the competing visions of development, associated deprivations, and the policy wherewithal to address the same. The conception put forth by the International Labour Organization (ILO) is a good operational benchmark for assessing policies towards social security. The ILO's Social Security (Minimum Standards) Convention, 1952 (No. 102) establishes worldwide-agreed minimum standards for all nine branches of social security. These branches are: medical care; sickness benefit; unemployment benefit; old-age benefit; employment injury benefit; family benefit; maternity benefit; invalidity benefit; and survivor's benefit. Further, the ILO has extended its social security definition by adding *general protection against poverty and social exclusion* into the existing nine branches of social security.

Apart from that of the ILO, there are other international classifications of the scope of social security, such as by the European Commission, Organisation for Economic Co-operation and Development (OECD), and the United Nations. However, all the branches of social security defined by these international organizations, which constitute social protection or security, have been covered by the ILO's extended social security definition. For the ILO, social security is a term that denotes *protection* against economic and social distress caused by a fall in income resulting from death, old age, sickness and employment injury, maternity, and temporary unemployment. However, there is also substantial litera-

ture that makes a strong case for adding the provisions of *promotional* support to the provisions of *protective* coverage in a vision of social security.[1] It may be useful to recall here the argument proposed by Drèze and Sen that makes a distinction between these different aspects of social security, namely, *protection* and *promotion*: 'the former is concerned with the task of preventing a decline in living standards and the later refers to the enhancement of general living standards and to the expansion of basic human capabilities of the population, and will primarily have to be seen as a long term challenge' (Drèze and Sen 1989: 16). Further, they regard social security as an *objective* to be pursued through *public means* rather than a narrowly defined set of particular strategies. The basic idea of social security is to use social means to prevent deprivation, and vulnerability to deprivation (Drèze and Sen 1991). In a similar vein, we may recall the conception advanced by Abram de Swaan (1988) that social security arrangements are collective remedies against adversity and deficiency.

Based on such conceptions, there have been several policy dialogues, globally and regionally, to chart a broad roadmap and to highlight elements that need to be prioritized towards the goal of broad-based social security provisioning. The well-known World Summit for Social Development in Copenhagen in 1995, which was reaffirmed through the 2000 UN Millennium Declaration for Reduction of Poverty, was one such exercise. At the 2010 UN Summit on the Millennium Development Goals (MDGs), the idea of a universal 'social floor' was introduced based on recognition of the fact that it is possible to eradicate poverty and provide social security for all.

In many countries, both in developing and developed worlds, social security has come to mean a wide variety of schemes and programmes, usually taken up by the state for the benefit of the public at large or the poorer sections whose basic entitlements are yet to be fulfilled. As noted earlier, in contemporary discourses, social security takes into account both *protective* and *promotional* aspects, and thus the constitutive elements entering the canvas of social security is very large. Hence, for policy priorities one needs to state clearly the norms, needs, and requirements in a particular context and at a specific socio-economic conjecture.

ROLE OF THE STATE (INDIA) IN THE PROVISIONING OF SOCIAL SECURITY

Social security is seen as one of the fundamental human rights. This has been recognized in a number of international legal instruments, in particular the Declaration of Philadelphia (1944) and the Universal Declaration of Human Rights (1948) adopted by the General Assembly of the UN. Further, the Constitution of India, in the Directive Principles of State Policy, enjoins the state to direct its policy towards securing, inter alia, that the citizens, men and women equally, have the right to an adequate means of livelihood [(Article 39(a); Bakshi 2009]. The state shall also, within the limits or its economic capacity and development, make effective provision for securing the right to work, to education, and to public assistance in cases of unemployment, old age, sickness, disablement, and in other cases of undeserved want (Article 41; Bakshi 2009).

However, on the whole, during the period since Independence, India's policymakers have not been able to achieve even a fraction of the promises enshrined in the country's Constitution. As is commonly agreed, our social security system is quite inadequate when compared even to several countries in the Third World with similar income levels, although the story across states is not entirely the same. For instance, a couple of states, notably Kerala and Tamil Nadu, have put in place schemes which try to address some of the core concerns much better than most of the states in the country. But on the whole, for the country at large, the scenario has remained quite bleak.

CASE FOR A NEAR-UNIVERSAL SOCIAL SECURITY

Though the importance of universal social security is being increasingly recognized as an integral part of progressive public policy, in the most developing countries, only a fraction of the population has been covered under the safety net of social security. It is quite clear that people without social security coverage in developing countries usually work in the informal sector of the economy. The case is similar with regard to India where about 93 per cent of its labour force is in the informal sector. As mentioned, social security is a human right and only a fraction of the total world's population actually enjoys that right, while the majority lacks comprehensive and adequate coverage. As is noted, 'more than half of world's population lack any type of protection at all. In sub-Saharan Africa and South Asia, the number of people with access to even the most rudimentary protection is estimated to be less than 10 percent' (ILO 2010: 7).

As mentioned earlier, some level of partial protection by social security measures exists in nearly all countries, though only a minority of countries provide protection in all branches. In many countries social security coverage is limited to a few branches and only a minority of the population has both legally and effectively access to existing social security schemes (ibid.). Further, the same report mentioned that 'only one-third of countries globally (inhabited by 28 per cent of the global population) have comprehensive social protection systems covering all branches of social security and between 20 per cent to 60 percent of the global population enjoys only basic social protection' (ibid.: 33).

Given the fact that there still remain many countries in the world where social security coverage is low, the Global Campaign on Social Security and Coverage for All, as mandated by the ILO Conference, 2001, it was expected that the countries need to put in place a set of basic social security guarantees for all residents as soon as possible, while planning to move towards higher levels of provisioning.

As it happens, in the case of India, none of these nine branches mentioned in the standard definition of social security by the ILO have been institutionalized for the entire population in the country as part of official policy. In fact, according to a press release of the Government of India (GoI), 'it is of the view that each country should decide the level of its own Social Protection Floor and there should not be prescription of a Uniform Social Protection Floor for all countries. Social protection should be implemented depending on the national social and economic circumstances in member states'.[2]

Nevertheless, India's search for an 'indigenous' social security system appears to be continuing eternally. Further, contrary to the original conception, social security is increasingly seen as a 'dole' or giving everybody something for nothing. What is required today is a return to the original conception of social security as a 'fundamental right' of every citizen, which ought to be guaranteed by the law of the land.

We may also emphasize here that a framework of social security should be visualized in the context of development and well-being indicators in any society. In this context it may be worth recalling that with respect to even the most basic well-being indicators, the scale, intensity, and persistence of deprivations in India is extremely disturbing. In the following section, we illustrate this with reference to a couple of core development indicators.

DEVELOPMENT DEPRIVATIONS IN INDIA: SOME ILLUSTRATIONS

As is well known, income or consumption poverty is often used as shorthand to capture the economic well-being of people. However, there is almost a consensus among social scientists by now that such a view of poverty is too narrow and it is absolutely necessary to go beyond hunger and malnutrition and include several other features in conceptualizing poverty, such as deprivation (or poor access) in terms of clothing, shelter; basic social services, including primary health care, sanitation, education, and others; political powerlessness, socio-cultural marginalization and exclusion, among others (Sen 1992). By any reckoning, development deficits in India are huge. Let us look at a few such deficits with respect to some of the most commonly used indicators in contemporary discussions, including those constituting the so-called MDGs. As per the available information, South Asia, after Sub-Saharan Africa is the worst performer in terms of approaching the 2015 MDGs targets. Among the indicators not related to environmental concerns, progress relating to only one, namely, the percentage incidence of poverty, is approximately on track; none has yet been met; progress towards half the targets is too slow and will not lead to the expected 2015 MDGs scenario, and the rest show little progress or even retrogressions. As already mentioned, only proportional poverty reduction seems to be on track; however, it may not mean a substantial change in the absolute number of the poor (even by official definitions of poverty).[3]

For instance, according to an estimate by Patnaik (2004),[4] 'the proportion of rural population unable to access 2,400 calories daily climbed from 75 per cent in 1993–4 to a record high of 87 per cent by 2004–5. The corresponding percentages for urban India, where the nutrition norm is lower at 2,100 calories, are 57

and 64.5'. As the National Sample Survey Organisation (NSSO) data show, per capita availability of foodgrains has been falling since the early 1990s and the current level is among the lowest recorded for the last half century. Since the early 1990s, it has declined from 177 kg per person per year to 155 kg and this figure is quite close to those recorded around the infamous Bengal famine of the 1940s. Unfortunately, the dominant discourses within the government as well as within the academia dismiss the need to urgently address this issue by justifying the fall in foodgrain consumption as a matter of voluntary choice, instead of recognizing the devastating effects of such developments.

Similarly, with regard to the incidence of poverty, in terms of the percentage of population with less than $ 2 a day Purchasing Power Parity (PPP), India is close to 80 per cent. Further, as per the recent survey (NSSO 68th Round, 2011–12), 50 per cent of the rural population belong to households having average daily per capita consumption expenditure equivalent to Rs 25.22, and for the urban areas 50 per cent of population belong to households having average daily per capita consumption expenditure equivalent to Rs 39.32 (see Table 9.1). Recent evidence suggests that poverty is increasingly concentrated in a few geographical locations and among specific social groups, particularly the Scheduled Castes (SCs) and Scheduled Tribes (STs) (Radhakrishna and Rao 2006).

As per the MDGs, 27 and 32 per 1,000 live births respectively are target numbers for Infant Mortality Rate (IMR) and Under 5 Mortality Rate (U5MR) by 2015 (for details, see UN Millennium Project 2005: 4). Current trends, if continued, will fall far short of the targets and in fact IMR is not expected to be less than 46 (in 2015). As per the most recent data (2010, as reported by the World Bank) IMR is 46 and U5MR is 63. Furthermore, as expected, there are huge disparities between rural and urban areas. As regards the coverage of children, in the age group of 12–23 months, as per recommended norms for vaccinations, the relevant figures for 1991–2, 1998–9, and 2005–6 were 36, 42, and 44 per cent, respectively. Apart from the fact that the coverage happens to be disturbingly low, the progress in the recent years appears to have been almost stalled.

Similarly, child malnutrition is extraordinarily high in India, with close to 43 per cent of children under five years suffering from it. Data for 2005–6 (National Family Health Survey or NFHS III) show that 46 per cent of children under three years in India are underweight, showing a decline of merely 1 per cent in relation to the previous 1998–9 survey. The progress, if one can call

Table 9.1 Extent of Development Deprivations in India

Indicators	Values
Population below $2 a day (%)*	80.6
Rural population belonging to household having an average monthly per capita consumption expenditure equivalent to Rs 757, that is, Rs 25.22 per person per day (NSS, 68th Round, 2011–12, GoI) (%)	50
Urban population belonging to household having average monthly per capita consumption expenditure equivalent to Rs 1,180, that is, Rs 39.32 per person per day (NSS, 68th Round, 2011–12, GoI) (%)	50
Literacy rate (overall) (%)	74.04
Female literacy rate (%)	65.46
Ratio of female to male secondary enrolment (%)	92
Ratio of female to male tertiary enrolment (%)	73
Employment to population ratio, aged 15+, total (%)	54
Employment to population ratio, aged 15–24, total (%)	34
Share of women employed in the non-agricultural sector (% of total non-agricultural employment)	18.1
Proportion of seats held by women in national parliaments (%)	11
Immunization, measles (% of children aged 12–23 months)	74
IMR (per 1,000 live births), 2010	48
U5MR (per 1,000 live births), 2010	63
Adolescent fertility rate (births per 1,000 women aged 15–19), 2010	79
Incidence of tuberculosis (per 100,000 people)	185
Tuberculosis case detection rate (all forms) (%)	59
Improved sanitation facilities (% of population with access)	34
Immunization, measles (% of children aged 12–23 months)	74
Births attended by skilled health staff (% of total)	47

Source: World Development Indicators. Available at http://ddp-ext.worldbank.org/ext/ddpreports/ViewSharedReport?&CF=&REPORT_ID=1336&REQUEST_TYPE=VIEWADVANCED (accessed 3 August 2012).
Note: * Taken from Radhakrishna 2008.

it that at all, is substantially lower than the 5 per cent decline experienced between 1991–2 and 1998–9. Poor nutrition can also be seen in the widespread prevalence of anaemia among children in the age group of 6–35 months, which affected almost four out of five children in 2005–6, and it shows a worsening of the situation compared to 1998–9 when three in four children in the relevant age group were anaemic.

In almost more than six decades since Independence, one of the most disappointing aspects of India's development has been its notable failure to rise up to the challenge of universalizing primary education. It currently houses the largest number of illiterates compared to any other country and has the dubious distinction that every third illiterate in the world is an Indian. Despite the rhetoric of according highest priority to universalize elementary education soon after Independence, India's record of progress has been a dismal one. As per the most recent decennial Census, conducted in 2011, the average rate of literacy at the national level is only 74 per cent

and the scenario for female literacy is still at a lower count (65.46 per cent) (see Table 9.1).

It is worth stressing that the divide between urban and rural India, in terms of most indicators of well-being, is huge. As reported by the GoI, with regard to indicators of access to safe water, *pucca* houses, literacy, formal education, and life expectancy, the gap is truly alarming. For instance, as per most recent data, slightly less than half of all births (47 per cent) are assisted by professional personnel nationwide. Similarly, only 34 per cent of the total population have improved sanitation facilities. Furthermore, not only is deprivation concentrated in certain regions, but it is also disproportionately high among historically marginalized groups such as the SCs, STs, and others. For instance, data on landlessness shows that in 1999–2000, around 40.9 per cent of all rural households were landless, but this figure was substantially higher at 55.5 per cent for SC households and at 64.5 per cent for SC agricultural labour households (Jha 2006, based on NSSO 1999–2000 data). The extreme poverty of such groups renders them most vulnerable for exploitation and violation of their human rights, with 80 per cent to 90 per cent of all bonded labourers in India belonging to the SCs and STs.

In sum, the extent of development deprivation in India, as is noted in the foregoing, seems quite disturbing. It is more than evident, for those who care to see, that the promise of a wonderland by the magic of the market will continue to elude very large segments of India's population. Hence, there is an urgent need for a comprehensive social security provisioning which would take care of at least a couple of well-being indicators for the masses.

CURRENT STATUS RELATING TO PUBLIC EXPENDITURE TOWARDS SOCIAL SECURITY

Globally, through various international conventions and declarations,[5] the principles concerning the financial guarantees of social security systems have been put forth and discussed at length. It has also been pointed out that adequate resources for the financing of social policies in general and social security policies in particular would not be possible unless sound economic and financial policies are in place. Obviously, one could argue what constitutes 'sound economic and financial policies'. Nonetheless, better economic and financial policies could enable the state to finance a comprehensive social security measure, which in turn would facilitate substantial poverty reduction. For instance, according to the ILO, social security transfers reduce poverty by at least 50 per cent in almost all OECD countries and reduce income inequality by about 50 per cent in many European countries (Cichon 2008). The same study also found that less than 2 per cent of global gross domestic product (GDP) is needed to provide a basic set of social protection benefits for people in poverty. Hence, to have a comprehensive social security in place, it requires significant investments of public resources.

Let us look at the global scenario on investments in social security vis-à-vis the position of India in this regard. The ILO report mentioned that, 'on average, 17.2 percent of global GDP is allocated to social security' (2010: 3). Similarly, alternative measurements[6] reveal that, on average, countries in the world allocate 10.9 per cent of their respective GDP to social security. While considering the size of population in different countries as a weight to compute mean percentages of GDP, the result shows that for the average resident, only 8.4 per cent of the GDP of the country is allocated as social security benefits in the form of cash and in-kind transfers. As per the same measure (weighted population measure), countries in Asia

and the Pacific spend 5.3 per cent of its GDP (average), whereas countries in Western Europe, and Central and Eastern Europe have been spending 25.1 and 18.9 per cent, respectively, of their respective GDP towards social security measures. On the same count, India was spending 1.68 per cent of its GDP during 2000 and 2010–11 (the latest available year), this has increased to 4.05 per cent of GDP.[7]

Provisioning social security through budgets is crucial for a country such as India. It is crucial in the sense that as many as half of its population are under the so-called official 'poverty line'. State provisioning for both the dimensions, for example, promotional and protective measures of social security can reduce poverty and vulnerability to a great extent. Before discussing the adequacy of such public resources for a *modest social security measure*, let us have a look at the existing budgetary provisions on social security in the country during the last couple of years.

As mentioned, there is no such unanimous view in the existing literature regarding what comprises social security measures, hence, in this chapter we have tried to look at the quantum of public expenditure towards social security not from the point of view of simply both the dimensions (protective and promotional) of social security measures, rather what is there in the budgets of union and state governments of India on various social security programmes and schemes (as per the functional classification of budgets in India). As per such classifications, there are two such broad categories available for both organized and unorganized sector workers and/or their family members.

PUBLIC PROVISIONING TOWARDS PENSION AND OTHER RETIREMENT BENEFITS FOR ORGANIZED SECTOR WORKERS/FAMILY

As per the functional classification of budgets in India, budgetary provisions under 'pension and other retirement benefits' is exclusively meant for the organized sector workers and/or their family members, whose share in the country's present employment scenario is less than 7–8 per cent. Budget expenditure on pension and other retirement benefits includes expenditure on superannuation and retirement allowance, commuted value of pensions, compassionate allowance, gratuities, family pensions, pensioner charges in respect of high court judges, contribution to pensions and gratuities, contributions to provident fund, pensions to employees of state-aided educational institutions, pensions of employees of local bodies, pensions to legislatures, pensions and other retirement benefits of the president of India, leave encashment benefits, ex-gratia payments arising out of special volunteer retirement scheme to central government employees declared as surplus, government contribution for the defined contribution pension scheme, medical treatment for Central Government Health Scheme (CGHS) pensioners, pension expenditure for defence personnel, and others.

Data presented in Table 9.2 show that the union government (including the union territory of Puducherry) was spending Rs 22,208 crores during the fiscal year 2006–7, which increased to Rs 57,659 crores in 2010–11. The increase of expenditure during this period has been 159.6 per cent. This stiff rise of such expenditure noticed during the later period, that is, during 2009–10 and 2010–11, is primarily owing to the implementation of the recommendations of the Sixth Central Pay Commission. Similarly, Rs 44,759 crores has been spent by all states during 2006–7, which increased to Rs 108,511 crores during 2010–11. However, the growth of increase of such expenditure by all states during this period was reported at 132 per cent. For the country as a whole, pension and other retirement benefits amounted to Rs 68,972 crores in 2006–7, which further increased to Rs 166, 170 crores in 2010–11 at current prices. Thus, the overall growth of expenditure is 141 per cent under the relevant budgetary heads. A phenomenal percentage growth of expenditure on these heads has been noticed by the states such as Sikkim (225) followed by Mizoram (223), Jharkhand (206), Chhattisgarh (190), Arunachal Pradesh (182), and Uttar Pradesh (160) during the period of analysis (see Table 9.2). Again the growth performance of such expenditures by states largely accounted for the implementation of the recommendations of the Sixth Central Pay Commission at their respective states.

Though there has been a very significant growth of total nominal expenditure towards pension and other retirement benefits during the period of analysis, when we deflate the same (by using GDP deflator, 2004–5 prices), in real terms the growth of such expenditure is substantially lower (79.7 per cent).

As is evident from the relevant data, the union and state governments of India together have been spending 7 per cent of its total budget annually (on an average during the period 2006–7 to 2010–11), towards pension and other retirement benefits. The share of such expenditure out of the total budgetary expenditure of both the union and state governments was 6.35 per cent during 2006–7 and reached 8.42 per cent during 2010–11. Similarly, the share of same in the country's GDP was 1.61 per cent in 2006–7, which has increased to 2.11 per cent during 2010–11. The trend shows an increase one during the period of analysis (see Table 9.3). The important point worth mentioning here is that these budgetary provisions only ensure the retirement benefits of such organized sector workers/family members, including defence personnel.

BUDGETARY PROVISIONS ON SOCIAL SECURITY MEASURES FOR PUBLIC AT LARGE

There are provisions in the budgets of the union and state governments towards social security programmes for those who are not being covered under the provisions of statutory pension and other retirement benefits.

Again, here we have attempted to trace only those budget expenditures, which are falling under the *protection* measures of social security in India. Essentially, these heads of budgetary expenditures are expenditure under social security and welfare, nutrition, labour and employment, etc.[8] A cursory look into the trend of such expenditures in India (expenditure carried out by both the union and states) though it exhibits an increasing one is quite inadequate to take care of the need of what constitutes a *modest* social security measure. Data presented in Table 9.4 show trends of such budgetary expenditures for a period of 2006–7 to 2009–10, across states.

As is evident from the relevant data presented in Table 9.4, the union and state governments together were spending Rs 24,689 crores towards social security and welfare, nutrition, and labour and employment in 2006–7 which increased to Rs 68,901 crores during 2009–10. The union government was spending Rs 3,832 crores towards these heads in 2006–7 and there was almost a four-fold increase in it within one year (Rs 13,343 crores in 2007–8). Further, by 2009–10, the relevant figure had reached Rs 19,688.8 crores. However, the real growth of such expenditures over the period (when we deflate the same by using 2004–5 prices, GDP deflator), has been seen quite inadequate. For instance, the real expenditure under these heads was Rs 22,270 crore during 2006–7 which increased to Rs 51,219 crores in 2009–10 with a growth of only 130 per cent.

Growth of expenditures under these heads by a couple of states, during the period 2006–7 and 2009–10, have been very impressive. States like Chhattisgarh (450) that top the list followed by West Bengal (349), Assam (249), and Andhra Pradesh (158) have been provisioning higher budgetary allocations towards provisioning social security compared to other states of India.

The important point to note is that budgetary provisioning towards pension and other retirement benefits

Table 9.2   Expenditure on Pension and Other Retirement Benefits by the Union, Union Territory, and State Governments of India during 2006–7 to 2010–11 (in Rs cr and current prices)

Year/Units	2006–7	2007–8	2008–9	2009–10	2010–11	% Increase in 2010–11 over 2006–7
A *Union and Union Territory governments*						
Union government $	22,103.8	24,261.0	32,940.6	56,148.6	57,405.4	159.7
Union territory government, Puducherry	104.2	120.0	165.7	289.0	253.6	143.5
Total A	22,207.9	24,381.0	33,106.2	56,437.7	57,659.1	159.6
B *State governments*						
Andhra Pradesh	4,150.5	5,092.1	5,518.5	6,339.0	9,609.4	131.5
Arunachal Pradesh	78.8	108.8	113.6	182.9	222.2	181.9
Assam	1,177.9	1,340.7	1,437.4	1,769.3	2,384.5	102.4
Bihar	2,497.1	2,788.9	3,479.0	4,318.7	6,143.9	146.0
Chhattisgarh	624.7	684.5	930.8	1,233.8	1,810.3	189.8
Goa	147.5	140.1	213.9	344.0	373.8	153.5
Gujarat	2,396.0	2,979.4	2,962.8	4,513.0	5,779.4	141.2
Haryana	1,173.3	1,297.5	1,614.2	2,390.4	3,094.3	163.7
Himachal Pradesh	911.8	949.3	1,153.9	1,348.5	2,105.4	130.9
Jammu and Kashmir	1,020.9	1,193.0	1,269.4	1,567.6	2,241.8	119.6
Jharkhand	679.0	818.3	988.4	1,680.8	2,081.1	206.5
Karnataka	2,495.9	3,240.6	4,112.6	3,408.3	4,069.9	63.1
Kerala	3,294.6	4,924.5	4,686.4	4,705.5	5,767.5	75.1
Madhya Pradesh	1,751.7	1,964.3	2,433.0	3,077.2	3,766.5	115.0
Maharashtra	3,542.5	4,191.3	5,153.0	6,132.5	8,884.0	150.8
Manipur	238.9	205.8	267.1	292.8	400.1	67.5
Meghalaya	117.5	134.7	171.8	207.9	299.6	155.0
Mizoram	77.3	97.1	126.0	164.3	249.5	222.8
Nagaland	201.7	259.7	229.0	279.1	336.0	66.5
Odisha	1,484.6	1,801.4	2,075.0	3,283.4	4,011.0	170.2
Punjab	1,905.4	2,432.6	2,829.8	3,357.4	5,309.3	178.6
Rajasthan	2.116.2	2,564.2	3,322.1	4,886.8	5,150.7	143.4
Sikkim	49.2	50.2	59.5	125.7	160.1	225.2
Tamil Nadu	5,429.6	6,017.0	7,734.5	8,384.9	11,768.1	116.7
Tripura	267.4	315.3	356.4	559.9	654.8	144.9
Uttar Pradesh	4,849.6	6,136.2	6,926.3	11,074.4	12,617.8	160.2
Uttarakhand	527.0	622.9	828.3	1,047.3	1,141.7	116.6
West Bengal	3,552.7	3,995.4	4,432.8	6,510.6	8,078.0	127.4
Total B (all states)	46,759.2	56,345.7	65,425.4	83,185.8	108,510.8	132.1
Grand total (A + B)	68,967.2	80,726.7	98,531.6	139,623.4	166,169.8	140.9
Total expenditure (at 2004–5 prices)*	62,209.7	68,856.0	78,770.0	103,792.7	111,786.5	79.7

Source: Compiled by the authors from the base data given in the Combined Finance and Revenue Accounts of the union and state governments in India, Comptroller and Auditor General, various years.

(Contd.)

Table 9.2   (*Contd.*)

Notes: @ Expenditure on pensions and other retirement benefits includes: (*a*) superannuation and retirement allowance, (*b*) commuted value of pensions, (*c*) compassionate allowance, (*d*) gratuities, (*e*) family pensions, (*f*) pensioner charges in respect of high court judges, (*g*) contribution to pensions and gratuities, (*h*) contributions to provident fund, (*i*) pensions to employees of state-aided educational institutions, (*j*) pensions of employees of local bodies, (*k*) pensions to legislatures, (*l*) pensions and other retirement benefits of the president of India, (*m*) leave encashment benefits, (*n*) ex-gratia payments arising out of special versus to central government employees declared as surplus, (*o*) government contribution for defined contribution pension scheme, (*p*) medical treatment for CGHS pensioners, (*q*) other pensions, (*r*) pension expenditure on navy, (*s*) pension expenditure on army, and (*t*) pension expenditure on air force.

$-Expenditure on pension payments pertaining to Delhi is debited to the Union Government Accounts as the GoI has not transferred the Pension Scheme to NCT Delhi.

* Constant prices (2004–5 prices) have been computed using GDP deflator.

Table 9.3   Share of Expenditure on Pension and Other Retirement Benefits in Total Budgetary Spending and GDP of the Country

Items/Year	2006–7	2007–8	2008–9	2009–10	2010–11
Total expenditure under pension and other retirement benefits (in Rs cr and current prices)	68,967.2	80,726.7	98,531.6	1,39,623.4	166,169.8
Total budgetary spending (by both the union and states)@ (in Rs cr and current prices)	1,086,592	1,243,597	1,519,081	1,833,730	1,973,762
Total GDP of the country# (in Rs cr and current market prices)	42,93,672	4,986,426	5,582,623	6,550,271	78,77,947
Share of expenditure on pension and other retirement benefits to total expenditure (in %)	6.35	6.49	6.49	7.61	8.42
Share of expenditure on pension and other retirement benefits to GDP (in %)	1.61	1.62	1.76	2.13	2.11

Source: Computed by authors from the basic data given in the Combined Finance and Revenue Accounts of the union and state governments, Comptroller and Auditor General, various years, and *Indian Public Finance Statistics, 2010–11*, Ministry of Finance, GoI.

Notes: @ Includes non-development expenditure, development expenditure, and loans and advances.

Data for 2009–10 and 2010–11 are revised and budget expenditure, respectively.

GDP at market prices and are based on CSO's National Accounts 2004–5 series.

(those especially meant for the organized sector workers/family members) accounted for 139,623 crores (comprising 7.61 per cent and 2.13 per cent of total budgetary expenditure and country's GDP, respectively) in 2009–10, whereas the expenditure towards provisioning of social security for *others* (more than 90 per cent of the country's population) amounted to only Rs 68,900.7 crores (see Table 9.4). Lest there be any misunderstanding, we are not suggesting any whittling down of the provisions for the organized sector employees; rather the issue is how to upscale protections for those constituting the base of the pyramid.

EXISTING SOCIAL SECURITY SCHEMES IN INDIA: A SKETCH

At present, in India, the nature of social security schemes that benefit people after they cross the age of 60 years are different for the organized and unorganized sectors. As mentioned, in the organized sector, there is (*a*) the civil service pension system for government employees, where a pension is received after retirement; (*b*) gratuity, where a one-time lump sum retirement payment is received; (*c*) provident fund, which is a contributory scheme of employers and employees and where the employee receives his contribution as well as a matching grant of the employer at retirement and so on.

However, for the unorganized sector, social security schemes are almost non-existent in India as a whole. This is particularly so for the aged, who are/were workers in the unorganized sector. Only a handful of states have social security schemes for the aged worth the name. Among all states, Kerala has the most wide-ranging set of social security schemes for the benefit of the aged in the unorganized sector and within other vulnerable

Table 9.4 Expenditures by Union, Union Territory, and State Governments towards Social Security and Welfare and Nutrition during 2006–7 to 2009–10 (in Rs cr)

	Year/Units	2006–7	2007–8	2008–9	2009–10	% increase/decrease in 2009–10 over 2006–7
A	*Union and Union Territory governments*					
	Union government	3,666.7	13,154.3	19,300.0	19,459.5	431
	Union territory government, Puducherry	165.3	189.1	211.6	229.3	39
	Total A	3,832.0	13,343.4	19,511.6	19,688.8	414
B	*State governments*					
	Andhra Pradesh	2,172.7	2,839.8	5,472.0	5,609.5	158
	Arunachal Pradesh	51.9	68.2	72.8	89.6	72
	Assam	257.9	353.1	523.5	900.2	249
	Bihar	958.1	1,126.2	1,584.1	2,469.1	158
	Chhattisgarh	390.0	602.7	1,704.6	2,144.0	450
	Delhi	360.6	384.1	685.4	842.2	134
	Goa	114.6	193.9	177.0	204.3	78
	Gujarat	856.2	1,009.6	1,241.7	1,911.9	123
	Haryana	942.4	1,089.0	1,231.3	2,151.1	128
	Himachal Pradesh	172.1	211.2	314.5	370.2	115
	Jammu and Kashmir	278.5	271.6	364.3	591.5	112
	Jharkhand	490.9	730.0	900.0	1,019.3	108
	Karnataka	1,170.8	1,825.6	2,449.1	3,366.1	187
	Kerala	618.2	833.9	913.0	1,173.3	90
	Madhya Pradesh	883.1	1,091.7	1,438.1	2,266.0	157
	Maharashtra	1,811.1	2,141.9	2,720.8	3,447.7	90
	Manipur	126.2	111.5	110.6	123.8	-2
	Meghalaya	60.4	54.9	65.4	107.8	78
	Mizoram	63.1	58.5	60.5	65.3	4
	Nagaland	93.1	84.4	87.6	86.5	-7
	Odisha	838.2	926.1	1,142.5	1,364.4	63
	Punjab	493.3	257.7	775.7	935.3	90
	Rajasthan	727.1	893.9	1,098.7	1,271.0	75
	Sikkim	21.8	32.2	36.6	46.0	111
	Tamil Nadu	2,619.5	3,648.9	4,284.8	4,801.4	83
	Tripura	120.5	169.3	219.1	246.7	105
	Uttar Pradesh	2,853.3	3,757.4	5,056.8	6,388.8	124
	Uttarakhand	223.0	265.8	287.6	336.5	51
	West Bengal	1,088.6	1,774.3	2,755.0	4,882.6	349
	Total B (all states)	20,857.4	26,807.3	37,773.0	49,212.0	136
	Grand total (A + B)	24,689.4	40,150.7	57,284.6	68,900.7	179
	Total expenditure (at 2004–5 prices)*	22,270.3	34,246.6	45,795.5	51,219.2	130

Source: Computed by authors from the basic data given in the Combined Finance and Revenue Accounts of the union and state governments, Comptroller and Auditor General (various years), GoI.

Notes: @ Expenditure on social security includes:

Expenditure on rehabilitation, social welfare, National Social Assistance Programme (NSAP), and debt relief for farmers and other social security programmes as listed in the combined finance and revenue accounts of union and state governments of India. Expenditure on distribution of nutritious food and beverages includes expenditure on special nutrition programmes and Midday Meals (MDM) and expenditure on labour, employment and trainings related expenditures are covered under labour and employment head.

* Constant prices (2004–5 prices) have been computed using GDP deflator.

groups. Kerala has social security schemes for the aged for agricultural labourers, construction workers, disabled persons, widows, handloom workers, fishermen, traditional artists, and so on. Of all the welfare schemes in Kerala, a major share of the beneficiaries belongs to three schemes: (*a*) the agricultural workers' pension scheme; (*b*) destitute and widows' pension scheme; and (*c*) the special pension for the physically handicapped.

Similarly, the distribution of pensions to rural unorganized workers in Kerala is undertaken through different welfare funds constituted by the government (Duvvury and George 1997). In Kerala, there are more than 20 welfare funds for unorganized workers. Estimates show that welfare funds cover about 50 per cent of all the unorganized workers in Kerala. In general, the funds for these institutions are generated through contributions over a period of time from workers, employers, and the government. The benefits from welfare funds to workers can be divided into three types. First, some funds provide provident fund benefits to members upon superannuation, a monthly pension, and a gratuity payment. Presently, monthly pensions were provided by 8 of the 19 funds. Secondly, some funds provide social insurance benefits to members, such as a payment for medical treatment or physical disability. Thirdly, some funds provide different types of welfare assistance to members, such as assistance for children's education, marriage of daughters, and construction of houses.

Apart from Kerala, most states have some form of old-age pension schemes in place. A few states have pensions for agricultural labourers, a few have pensions for widows, and a few have allowances for the physically handicapped. This apart, a few other states also provide employment injury benefits for the unorganized sector workers. However, there are wide variations in the coverage, nature of benefits, and eligibility conditions in these schemes, not to speak of efficiency in implementation across states. States like Kerala and Tamil Nadu have an excellent record in both coverage and implementation of many schemes. Even the Unorganised Sector Workers' Social Security Act, which came into force in 2009, is merely an enabling legislation; it does not seek to put on the statute books any specific comprehensive scheme of social security.

SOCIAL SECURITY SCHEMES SUGGESTED BY THE NATIONAL COMMISSION FOR ENTERPRISES IN THE UNORGANIZED SECTOR REPORT

A major development happened in 2005, as the GoI appointed the National Commission for Enterprises in the Unorganized Sector (NCEUS) to examine the various issues concerning workers in the unorganized sector, which included the question of social security also. In 2006 itself, the NCEUS gave a detailed report to the government that contained the draft outline of a social security scheme.[9] As on 2005, there were about 423 million informal workers in India. The scheme submitted by the NCEUS was to cover this section completely within five years. The cover was called National Minimum Social Security and it was based on an insurance-cum-state assistance model. The scheme included different aspects of social security, such as health (hospitalization for self and family) and maternity, life and disability, and old age security in the form of state pension for those belonging to poor households and a provident fund for others. The minimum social security benefits suggested by the NCEUS were the following:

1. Hospitalization cover up to Rs 15,000 and sickness cover for the registered worker during hospitalization at Rs 50 per day for a maximum period of 15 days;
2. maternity benefit of Rs 1,000 (maximum) per delivery;
3. personal accident cover in the event of death of earning head of family to the tune of Rs 25,000;
4. two options for old age security: (*a*) monthly old age pension of Rs 200 per month to all poor (below poverty line or BPL) old-aged (60+) workers; and (*b*) provident fund to all other workers (who are required to contribute to the national social security scheme).

The NCEUS also suggested the formation of a National Social Security Board, which would execute the scheme. This Board would handle a National Social Security Fund and would help formulating policies, provide technical assistance, and allocate funds to the states. There were to be similar boards at the state level too with its administrative network spread down to the local level through workers' facilitation centres. Workers registering for the scheme were to be given social security cards.

Typically workers, employers, and the government were to contribute to the fund in the ratio of 1:1:1. Where the employer could be identified, the employer was to pay Re 1 per day per worker. However, given the difficulties in identifying employers in the informal sector, the NCEUS suggested that the contributions of such workers be paid by the government. Thus, when the employer was not identified, the contribution was to be shared by the central and state governments in the ratio of 3:1 (Rs 0.75 per day per worker by the centre and Rs 0.25 per day per worker by the states). The government was also to pay the contributions of the poorer households (23 per cent of workers) also given their inability to contribute on a regular basis. Thus, it was recommended that the central government pay Re 1 per day for BPL workers.

Within the recommended insurance-cum-state assistance model, the state-assistance model was limited to the payment of old age security and the rest was based on the insurance model. The NCEUS recommended a cashless model for hospitalization expenses; here, beneficiaries could access hospital services from designated health care institutions. For this purpose, it recommended public health care institutions, cooperatives, and charitable institutions as well as private hospitals that meet the minimum requirement of infrastructure. The question of life insurance was recommended to be handled by either public sector insurance companies, such as the Life Insurance Corporation of India (LIC) or post offices. The NCEUS was enthusiastic about the post office network across the country and its use in handling social security contributions. They were to act as book-keepers of the social security system by keeping accounts as well as making payments to the service providers.

For above poverty line (APL) workers, a provident fund model managed by a mutual fund was recommended. It recommended a guaranteed annual return of 10 per cent from the fund, so that the savings of the workers are not subjected to the vagaries of the capital market. The financing of the scheme was to be managed by the central government by imposing cess on trades or commodities or through a social security tax or a combination of these or any other means. The NCEUS estimated that the cost of financing the scheme would be equivalent to about 0.5 per cent of the GDP, when all the 300 million workers are covered in the fifth year.

The Unorganized Sector Workers' Social Security Act, 2008

Based on the recommendations of the NCEUS, the GoI enacted the Unorganized Sector Workers' Social Security Act (UWSSA), 2008. This Act provides for the constitution of a National Social Security Board, which shall recommend social security schemes, namely, life and disability cover, health and maternity benefits, old-age protection, and any other benefit as may be determined by the government for the unorganized workers.

The rules under the Act have been framed and the Act came into force vide notification dated 14 May 2009.

The National Social Security Board was constituted on 18 August 2009 and held its meetings to consider extension of existing schemes to other unorganized workers and formulation of other social security schemes for these workers. The Board recommended that Rashtriya Swasthya Bima Yojana (RSBY) providing health and maternity benefits, Janshree Bima Yojana (JBY) providing death and disability cover, and the Indira Gandhi National Old Age Pension Scheme (IGNOAPS) be extended to certain categories of unorganized workers.

Problems with the UWSSA, 2008

The UWSSA Bill tabled in Parliament in 2007 was a watered down version of the recommendation given by the NCEUS. The Bill was referred to the Standing Committee of the Parliament, which substantially rewrote the Bill, and restored many features originally present in the NCEUS recommendations. However, these recommendations of the Standing Committee were ignored by the government and a version similar to the tabled version was put up for approval of the Parliament in 2008. The Bill was passed and thus the UWSSA, 2008 came into force. The UWSSA, 2008 has been severely criticized for its inadequacy by the former members of the NCEUS themselves. Below we provide a long quote from a critique by K.P. Kannan:[10]

(a) The Act is more in the nature of an enabling legislation because it states that "The Central Government shall formulate, from time to time, suitable welfare schemes for unorganized workers …" [Section 3(1)].
(b) It has not accepted the proposal of the NCEUS and the Parliamentary Standing Committee for creating a national fund but states that schemes notified by the government may be fully or partly funded.
(c) By providing for notification of schemes as and when the government deems necessary, the Act provides for specification such implementation mechanisms in the concerned schemes as may be necessary thus providing for no common implementation system.
(d) In the light of the above, the Act does not provide for an empowered implementing body but provides for constitution of national and state level social security boards that are basically advisory in character.
(e) While the Act states that 'State governments may formulate and notify, from time to time, suitable welfare schemes', it is indeed a superfluous one because the state governments do have the power to legislate on social security for workers, including the unorganised workers, since the subject of Labour is in the Concurrent List of the Constitution….

While this national legislation is an important first step, it has indeed made further progress towards universalisation (i.e. coverage of all unorganised workers with limited economic means) not only a difficult but complicated task. The neoliberal lobby within the government was opposed to such a legislation right from the beginning but when it realised that total opposition would be politically unacceptable, it did not spare any effort to water down, indeed puncture, a right-based social security entitlement at every stage.

In order not to appear that the Act is indeed is more of a promise and hence an empty one in terms of immediate impact, the Government decided to provide a Schedule to the Act specifying a number of schemes as proof of its commitment to formulate schemes. As it turned out, eight of the ten schemes included in the Schedule 1 were ongoing, mostly small schemes for specified segments of workers; two were relatively new schemes that were announced a few months before the enactment in December 2008. The last two schemes have the potential to cover a much larger segment of unorganized workers than the earlier schemes but currently they are restricted to only those 'below the poverty line' and rural landless households respectively.…

The eight existing schemes included in the Schedule I of the Act are: (i) Indira Gandhi National Old Age Pension Scheme, (ii) National Family Benefit Scheme, (iii) Janani Suraksha Yojana, (iv) Handloom Weavers' Comprehensive Welfare Scheme, (v) Handicraft Artisans' Comprehensive Welfare Scheme, (vi) Pension to Mastercraft persons, (vii) National Scheme for Welfare of Fishermen and Training and Extension, (viii) Janshree Bhima Yojana, (ix) Aam Aadmi Bhima Yojana (Life Insurance Scheme for Common People), and (x) Rashtriya Swastha Bhima Yojana (National Health Insurance Scheme).

THE NATIONAL SOCIAL ASSISTANCE PROGRAMME

Within the overall umbrella of social security, one important element is the social security of the aged. With most developing countries passing through different stages of demographic transition, the size and share of population in the age group of 60+ years is growing. In India, in absolute terms, the population aged 60+ years numbered 12.1 million at the 1901 Census and 77 million at the 2001 Census. According to some projections the number of people aged 60+ years is likely to rise further to about 140 million by 2021. The share of population, aged 60+ years was 7.4 per cent in 2001; the share was higher for women at 7.8 per cent and lower for men at 7.1 per cent. Within India, states in the advanced stages of demographic transition, such as Kerala, had more than 10.5 per cent of their population aged 60+ years in 2001.

Alongside, the old-age dependency ratio (that is the number of people aged 60+ as a share of the labour force in the age group of 15–59 years), which was 10.9 per cent in 1961, rose to 13.1 per cent in 2001. In 2001, old-age dependency ratio was higher in the rural areas at about

14 per cent compared to the urban areas at about 10 per cent. Data from the NSSO show that the share of 60+ population that was not fully economically independent for their day-to-day maintenance was about 65 per cent in India in 2004–5; the corresponding share for women was about 85 per cent.

Let us examine NSAP which was started in the year 1995–6 as a centrally sponsored scheme (CSS). However, in the subsequent period, this NSAP has been modified into a state plan (Central Assistance to States and Union Territory Plans) scheme and is in operation since 2002–3. Currently, NSAP comprises of five schemes, namely, (a) IGNOAPS, (b) Indira Gandhi National Widow Pension Scheme (IGNWPS), (c) Indira Gandhi National Disability Pension Scheme (IGNDPS), (d) National Family Benefit Scheme (NFBS), and (e) Annapurna (nutrition).

For getting benefits under NSAP, the applicant must belong to a BPL family according to the criteria prescribed by the GoI. As per the revised eligibility criteria, new beneficiaries will be identified from BPL list prepared by the states/union territories as per guidelines issued by the Ministry of Rural Development (MoRD) for the BPL Census 2002. The central contribution of pension under the IGNOAPS is Rs 200 per month per beneficiary up to 79 years and Rs 500 per month per beneficiary from 80 years onwards and the state governments may contribute over and above this amount. At present, old-age beneficiaries are getting anywhere between Rs 200 to Rs 1,000 depending on the state contribution.

The NSAP is implemented in most states/union territories by the respective social welfare departments. It is implemented by the Rural Development Department in the states of Andhra Pradesh, Assam, Goa, Meghalaya, and West Bengal; by the Department of Women and Child Development in Odisha and Puducherry; by the Revenue Department in Karnataka and Tamil Nadu; and by the Department of Labour Employment and Training in Jharkhand. In terms of geographical coverage, the NSAP extends to both the rural as well as urban areas.

Under NSAP, 100 per cent central assistance has been extended to the states/UTs to provide the benefits in accordance with the norms, guidelines, and conditions laid down by the central government. In the National Development Council (NDC) meeting held in 1997, several chief ministers of the states suggested transferring the CSS to states. As a result of the review of the CSS by the Planning Commission in consultation with the MoRD, GoI, it was decided to transfer NSAP including

Annapurna to the state plan from the year 2002–3. At present, funds for these schemes are released as additional central assistance to state plans. The funds are allocated by the Planning Commission and allocated among the states by the MoRD and released by the Ministry of Finance on the recommendation of the MoRD.

Status of budgetary allocation and expenditure under NSAP since 2002–3

As mentioned, the money allocated under NSAP has been routed through an additional central assistance to the states and union territories since 2002–3. Looking at the year-wise budget allocated under NSAP since 2002–3 reflects that during the initial years of its inception, a meagre amount has been allocated, especially during the Eleventh Five Year Plan period. However, a quantum jump has been noticed, particularly since 2008–9. For instance, the amount allocated was to the tune of Rs 680 crores in 2002–3 reached Rs 4,500 crores in 2008–9 and further it has increased to Rs 8,382 crores in current year's budget estimate (that is, the 2012–13 budget estimate). With regard to the release of allocated money under NSAP, hardly any deviations can be noticed. But, the rate of actual expenditures seem lagging far behind expect for a couple of years since its implementation. The information given in Table 9.5 exhibits the trend of money allocated, released, and expenditures made under NSAP since 2002–3.

What is clear from the information above is that the coverage of NSAP is limited to a very small proportion of the potential beneficiaries. In this regard, it is important to note the findings put forwarded by the mid-term review of the Eleventh Five Year Plan by the Planning Commission, which has made a few suggestions on the way forward in NSAP. Some of the suggestions are quoted verbatim below:

1. Pensions need to be indexed to inflation. States need to make their share of payment under IGNOAPS.
2. NFBS must cover deaths of any adult member of the family in a BPL household, without limiting it to the breadwinner.
3. National schemes for maintenance of orphans, street children, and other most vulnerable sections also need to be started.
4. With the transfer of programme implementation to states from 2002–3 [and hence change from a Centrally Sponsored Schemes (CSS) to Additional Central Assistance (ACA) in budgetary terms], reporting and monitoring by the GoI has weakened. These systems need to be strengthened.
5. The previous fund flow model of pension transfers directly to DRDAs (District Rural Development Agencies) may be preferable to routing through state treasuries. The latter encourages diversion of National Old Age Pension Scheme (NOAPS) for other purposes (Gujarat, Jharkhand and Odisha made no NOAPS payments in some of the early years of this decade). In Bihar, Jharkhand, West Bengal, and Manipur there are reports of delays of

Table 9.5   Budget Allocation and Expenditure on NSAP (including Nutrition) during 2002–3 to 2011–12

Year 1	Allocation (in Rs cr) 2	Releases (in Rs cr) 3	Total Expenditure Reported (in Rs cr) 4	Total Expenditure as % of Total Allocation 5 = (4 / 2) × 100
2002–3	680.0	657.1	594.1	87.4
2003–4	679.9	602.3	656.0	96.5
2004–5	1,189.9	1032.0	863.4	72.6
2005–6	1,190.0	1189.7	1033.9	86.9
2006–7	2,489.6	2489.6	1968.3	79.1
2007–8	2,891.5	2889.7	3123.1	108.0
2008–9	4,500.0	4500.0	3961.5	88.0
2009–10	5,200.0	5155.5	4914.9	94.5
2010–11	5,162.0	5162.0	5346.1	103.6
2011–12 RE	6,607.6	NA	NA	NA
2012–13 BE	8,382.0	NA	NA	NA

Source: Annual Report 2011–12, Ministry of Rural Development, GoI.
Notes: NA = Not Available; BE = Budget Estimate; and RE = Revised Estimate.

many months thanks to the state treasury route being adopted.

6. Documentary requirements for proving eligibility and identity have proved extremely onerous to beneficiaries who are among the most vulnerable. It is to be hoped that the use of the Unique Identification (UID) (once available) will ease some of these pressures.

7. Many states have devised somewhat arbitrary and harsh exclusion criteria which have been applied in a mechanical manner that discriminates against some of the most vulnerable. Even having a living adult son meant exclusion in some cases. Such practices must be stopped.

8. Shifting to payment through post offices or banks is a significant step in ensuring transparency. But as under Mahatma Gandhi National Rural Employment Guarantee Act (MGNREGA), where density of banks/Post Offices (POs) is low or because of lack of adequate staff, people have had to suffer great hardships in the transition period. Aged and disabled people may not be able to reach the PO or banks at all. The banking correspondent model with UID biometrics could be a way out by providing payments at the doorstep in a transparent manner.

There many problematic elements in this set of recommendations. For instance, the use of Aadhaar/UID scheme to provide pensions and other benefits is fraught with dangers of massive exclusion. It is well proven that fingerprints and iris scans of people above the age to 60 are difficult to record, de-duplicate, and authenticate. For these reasons and more, the standing committee on finance of the Parliament had recently rejected the National Identification Authority of India (NIAI) Bill 2010. The report of the Committee noted that 'the [Aadhaar] scheme is full of uncertainty in technology' and is built upon 'untested, unreliable technology'. It criticized the UIDAI for disregarding (*a*) the warnings of its Biometrics Standards Committee about high error rates in fingerprint collection; (*b*) the inability of Proof of Concept studies to promise low error rates when 1.2 billion persons are enrolled; and (*c*) the reservations within the government on 'the necessity of collection of IRIS image'. The report concluded that, given the limitations of biometrics, 'it is unlikely that the proposed objectives of the UID scheme could be achieved'. The Proof of Concept reports of the UIDAI have shown that those above 60 years of age had the 'highest rejection rates' at authentication tests.

Yet, the Planning Commission recommended the use of Aadhaar in old-age pension schemes.

PROPOSAL FOR A MODEST SOCIAL SECURITY: HOW MUCH DOES IT COST?

As mentioned at the outset, in this chapter we are demanding a near-universal social security provision with a modest amount of assistance from the state. As is well known, any proposal to expand the scope of social protection meets familiar criticisms, which include the issues of financial affordability, viability, problems relating to the delivery mechanism, and others. Without neglecting the merits of such criticism (which we do not wish to engage with in a detailed manner here), the simple point we would like to make here is the following.

Proposals such as the one advanced by the NECUS, 2006 (draft proposal of the Unorganized Sector Workers' Social Security Act) for the unorganized sector or variations thereof are eminently feasible without hurting the exchequer in any crippling fashion. Let's first recall the estimates for the above noted NCEUS, 2006 proposal. The NCEUS, in its proposed scheme suggested that when all the informal workers are covered, the union government contribution will be Rs 20,583 crores (including pension to BPL workers and administrative expenses), and the contribution of state governments will be Rs 4,819 crores by the end of financial year 2010–11. In total, as per the projection of 8 per cent GDP growth, this worked out to 0.48 per cent of GDP for the year 2010–11. The scheme was supposed to cover 30 crores unorganized workers and the scheme is to be completed within a period of five years (that is, by the end of 2010–11) covering one-fifth of the eligible informal workers every year. The proposed scheme also covers health insurance for self and family with a cover of hospitalization up to Rs 15,000; maternity up to Rs 1,000 per delivery; disability allowance up to 15 days at Rs 50 per day; accidental death cover for workers of Rs 25,000, and life insurance of Rs 15,000. The old age security for all workers above 60 years belonging to BPL households is supposed to get pension at Rs 200 per month and other workers will have a provident fund. With regard to contributions, the scheme suggested that Re 1 per day or Rs 365 per year by worker, employer, and government. In view of the difficulties in identifying employers, the government is to pay employers' contribution also, that is, Rs 730 per year in the ration of 3:1 by the union and state governments. Further, the contribution of workers belonging to BPL households need to be paid by the union government.

In the proposed social security scheme for the unorganized sector by the NCEUS, 2006, there is no denying the fact that the scheme, if implemented, in its full terms and sprit, would have addressed most of the concerns, if not all, that many scholars raising today. Of course, there are several limitations with regard to the proposed legislation by the NECUS. Here we are attempting a similar kind of social security scheme which could be implemented with a slight variation.

To consider what constitutes adequate means of livelihood, Patnaik (2012) advocates two such categories.

The first, used in much international discussion, is to define 'adequate' in the sense of avoidance of poverty, which in India is defined officially as access to 2,100 calories per person per day in urban areas and 2,400 calories (later reduced to 2,200 calories) per person per day in rural areas. The daily per capita expenditure level at which this was achieved in 2009–10 was Rs 36 in rural (for 2,200 calories) and Rs 65 in urban areas, whose weighted average is Rs 46. At current prices this would be equivalent to around Rs 60; in which case the monthly pension amount on this criterion should come to Rs 1,800. The other approach, the one adopted by the Pension Parishad, sees pensioners as 'workers' and hence entitled to a proportion of the wage income as pension. Based on this, the Parishad has demanded half the monthly minimum wage rate, or a flat amount of Rs 2,000 at the current price, whichever is higher.[11]

It may be noted that Prabhat Patnaik's suggestion is reminiscent of the ILO's advocacy that *general protection against poverty and social exclusion* should be an important concern in any vision of social security. As is well-known, there is a huge debate and controversy with regard to official poverty measurements, which we do not wish to engage with here. In our judgement, there is substantial merit in pegging the conception of poverty to calorie requirement in a context of widespread food insecurity and malnutrition.

As mentioned in the foregoing, Prabhat Patnaik's estimates suggests that a wage which was just about equivalent to keep a person above the calorie-based poverty line

(2,200 kcal per person per day) comes to Rs 1,800 per month (at current prices). Taking the count of workers in the unorganized sector close to 47 crore,[12] and with average size of household as close to five members, the total number of households in the unorganized sector works out to be approximately 10 crore.

Further, assuming that the wage equivalent of the above noted calorie-based poverty line (Rs 1,800) may be appropriate to take care of the key contingency expenditures of a typical household in the unorganized sector with respect to a basket of social security provision, the calculation in Table 9.6 gives us a possible benchmark. Sure enough, the suggested benchmark is arbitrary but in our judgement it may be reasonable approximation.[13]

If these 10 crores households be provided at Rs 1,800 per month, as social security assistance, the total amount to be required annually comes Rs 216,000 crores. Further, if we deduct the present provision of Rs 68,900 crores (latest year available is 2009–10) towards social security and labour, and employment-related expenditures in the budgets, the rest of the amount needed to be provisioned comes to Rs 147,000 crore, which is roughly 2 per cent of country's GDP (see Table 9.1).

ISSUES RELATING TO ADEQUACY OF RESOURCES: IS SOCIAL SECURITY REALLY UNAFFORDABLE?

The frequently asked question is: where would the government get these additional resources to finance such a proposal of social security provisioning? Of course, there is no one simple and agreed answer to this question, but our claim is that it is certainly not beyond the means of the union government. One can get into a detailed discussion of possible means to augment resources (for instance, through wealth tax, expansion of the coverage of services for taxation, better tax compliance mechanisms, and others); however, even if one ignores such possibilities of resource mobilization, it is quite clear that a degree of rationalization in the total quantum of revenue foregone through exemptions made by the union government can help a great deal in putting a social security provision in place.

Table 9.6 Costing Provisioning of Social Security in India

Units	Amount per Month	Amount per Year (in Rs cr)
10 crore households	Rs 1,800 per month per household (Rs 12 per day per person)	216,000
Present provision of social security and labour welfare (during 2009–10, by the union and all state governments)		68,900
Amount to be required		147,100

Source: Computed by authors.

Information given in Table 9.7 show that the union government during the fiscal year 2011–12 had foregone tax to the extent of Rs 529,432 crore, due to exemptions/deductions/incentives in the union government tax system, which is almost equivalent to 6 per cent of country's GDP. It is worth noting here that even the previous and present finance ministers have voiced their concern on the issue of exemptions and revenue foregone on several occasions. We are not making a blanket argument for and against exemptions and revenues foregone; however, the point we are stressing here is that when it comes to ensure the social security, one needs take a call on provisioning for the same vis-à-vis a whole range of exemptions provided to the corporate sector as also the other economic actors. Even if half of the tax revenue forgone presently because of the plethora of exemptions in the central government tax system get collected, it would generate additional tax revenue worth 3 per cent of GDP which would be more than enough to have a comprehensive social security legislation.

Of course, there are several arguments and justifications put forward with regard to the tax exemptions made in the union government tax system to the corporate sector, claiming that tax exemptions would enhance the capacity of the economy, particularly through contributions from the industry sector. Tax exemptions need to be minimized, carefully designed and justified with sound social and economic reasons.

Further, the overall magnitude of public resources available to the government in India has been grossly inadequate in comparison to several other countries, mainly owing to the low magnitude of tax revenue collected in our country. The total tax revenue collected by the centre and states (combined) has fallen from (the already low level of) 17.4 per cent of GDP in 2007–8 to 14.7 per cent of GDP in 2010–11 budget estimate (GoI 2011). India's tax–GDP ratio compares poorly against those of several other countries. Hence, it is necessary

for the government to take strong measures for stepping up the country's tax–GDP ratio which would enable our government to provide more resources for budgetary spending on crucial entitlements for people.

There is a possibility to increase tax base, particularly, the direct taxes, which is of more progressive in nature to finance developmental needs of the state. It is clear from the fact that India's tax system, which collects almost two-thirds of the revenue from indirect taxes and only one-third from direct taxes, is regressive as compared to the tax system of many other countries (that collect a much higher proportion of tax revenue from direct taxes). If India is to move towards a more progressive tax system, the government should rely more on direct taxes (such as, corporation tax, personal income tax, and wealth tax).[14]

In a similar fashion, several other proposals have been made on how to finance additional resource requirements for provisioning comprehensive social security measures in India. For instance, the proposal put forward by the NCEUS, which had suggested a set of cesses to finance a far more modest social security scheme.

* * *

Social security measures in India, on the whole woefully inadequate, are scattered over dozens of schemes and programmes, and there is an urgent need to think of a comprehensive framework. Even if we add up all the existing schemes relating to social security, they touch only the fringe of the problem. First, they are an assortment of specific schemes rather than an expression of a rights-based comprehensive social security scheme. Second, they do not provide universal coverage. Leaving aside the pension schemes of the organized sector, the others, as they are, target specific groups of unorganized sector workers. Even when not tied to specific occupational categories, such as the IGNOAPS, they cover only the BPL population, whose size is arbitrarily fixed by the Planning Commission at a ludicrously low level. Third, a large number of

Table 9.7 Amount of Revenue Foregone in Central Government Budgets (in Rs cr)

Items	2007–8	2008–9	2009–10	2010–11	2011–12
Corporate income tax	62,199	66,901	72,881	88,263	51,292
Personal income tax	38,057	37,570	45,142	50,658	42,320
Excise duty	87,468	128,293	169,121	198,291	212,167
Customs duty	153,593	225,752	195,288*	174,418*	223,653*
Gross total (1+2+3+4)	341,317	458,516	482,432	511,630	529,432

Source: Compiled from the Union Budget, *Statement of Revenue Forgone*, various years.
Note: * custom duty foregone less export credit.

them insist on some contribution from the beneficiaries, which is again a problematic issue.

As is well known, in India social security is on the concurrent list as per its Constitution, but in our judgement the union government should take primary responsibility for putting in place a comprehensive social security framework. The reason for such a view is that given the nature of fiscal federalism in place, the union government has been enjoying much wider authority/space in terms of augmenting resources compared to the states of the Indian Union. Hence, it is high time to go for a comprehensive social security scheme (or combination of schemes/programmes) in place with appropriate institutional mechanism. Of course, when we are talking about the appropriate institutional mechanism in place, the obvious responsibility should be shouldered by the union government as it has enormous fiscal power to devise and put things in place (Jha 2011).

As is evident from our discussion in the foregoing sections, the experience of India since Independence has, on the whole, been disappointing with reference to addressing the social security of the masses in general. There have been hesitant and limited sporadic efforts, instead of a coherent policy approach of any significance. Further, one often comes across a whole range of arguments in official circles regarding the inadequacy of resources with respect to public provisioning for social security. This must be debunked. It is well known that countries with per capita incomes currently comparable to several developing countries, including India, were able to put in place significant social security provisions towards the late nineteenth and early twentieth centuries. Even if we want to have a comprehensive social security measure in place, we need only one-fourth of the amount of revenue forgone, etc., to various actors in the central tax system. But, what is lacking is a strong political will.

Notes

1. However, the relative merits and demerits of either approach is a controversial one as there is no conclusive evidence to show that the former always result in a trade-off between growth and equity and the latter always involves an equitable growth (Kannan 1999).

2. See http://www.labour.nic.in/pib/PressRelease/RS-ComprehensiveLabour.pdf.

3. For details, see UN Millennium Project (2005).

4. For further details, see Utsa Patnaik (2006).

5. For further details, refer to ILO's Income Security Recommendation, 1944 (No. 67), the Medical Care Recommendations, 1944 (No. 69), and the Social Security (Minimum Standards) conventions, 1952 (No. 102).

6. For further details on these measurements, refer to ILO (2010).

7. For details, see ILO (2010: Annex Table 25, p. 259).

8. For details, please see notes to Table 9.4 in this chapter.

9. See http://www.ilo.org/wcmsp5/groups/public/@ed_emp/@emp_policy/documents/meetingdocument/wcms_125979.pdf.

10. See http://www.hivos.net/Hivos-Knowledge-Programme/Publications/Pubs/The-challenge-of-universal-coverage-for-the-working-poor-in-India, pp. 18–19.

11. For further details, one may look at 'For a Universal Old Age Pension Plan', *The Hindu*, 10 May 2012. Available at http://www.thehindu.com/opinion/lead/article3401455.ece (accessed 16 July 2012).

12. As is evident from the Committee Report (GoI 2012), estimation of the total number of unorganized sector workers is quite difficult, still we quote 471 million workers in the unorganized sector, and size of the household is 4.9 [as per 2011 Census (provisional)] with the projected dependency ratio 55.6 per cent for the year 2010 (ILO 2010).

13. It is worth noting here that there have been several government committees and commissions since Independence with the mandate of examining issues such as: 'minimum wage', 'floor wage', and others. However, there is little agreement on how things should be arrived at and a whole range of views have been expressed on this subject. To give an example, the 15th Labour Ministers' Conference, which had recommended that for agricultural labourers, minimum wage rates should be worked out by taking into account the cost of 2,700 calories, 18 yards of cloth per person, and 20 per cent of the value of these requirements to cover the other miscellaneous basic costs of living (Jha 1997).

14. For further details on this, refer to, 'Public Provisioning for Social Security Schemes in India', a note prepared by the Centre for Budget and Governance Accountability, mimeo, New Delhi, submitted to the Pension Parishad on May 2012.

References

Bakshi, P.M. 2009. *The Constitution of India*. New Delhi: Universal Law Publishing Co. Pvt. Ltd.

Cichon, M. 2008. *Building the Case for a Global Social Floor*. Geneva: ILO.

Swaan, Abram de. 1988. *In Care of the State*. Oxford: Polity Press.

Drèze, J. and A.K. Sen. 1989. *Hunger and Public Action*. Oxford: Clarendon Press.

———. 1991. 'Public Action for Social Security', in E. Ahmad, J. Drèze, J. Hills, and A. Sen (eds), *Social Security in Developing Countries*. Oxford: Oxford University Press, pp. 1–40.

Duvvury Nata, and Sabu M. George. 1997. 'Social Security in the Informal Sector—A Study of Labour Welfare Funds in Kerala', mimeo. Trivandrum: Centre for Development of Imaging Technology.

GoI (Government of India). 2011. *Indian Public Finance Statistics 2010–11*. New Delhi: Ministry of Finance.

————. 2012. *Report of the Committee on Unorganised Sector Statistics*, National Statistical Commission, February. Available at http://mospi.nic.in/mospi_new/upload/nsc_report_un_sec_14mar12.pdf?status=1&menu_id=199 (accessed 30 July 2012).

ILO (International Labour Organization). 2010. *World Social Security Report—Providing Coverage in Times of Crisis and Beyond.* Geneva: ILO.

Jha, Praveen. 1997. *Agricultural Labour in India*. New Delhi: Vikas Publishing House Pvt. Ltd.

————. 2006. 'Land and Poverty', mimeo. New Delhi: Centre for Economic Studies and Planning, Jawaharlal Nehru University.

————. (ed.). 2011. *Progressive Fiscal Policy in India*. New Delhi: Sage Publications.

Kannan, K.P. 1999. 'State-assisted Social Security for Poverty Alleviation and Human Development: Kerala's Record and its Lessons', mimeo. New Delhi: Institute of Human Development and Indian Society of Labour and Economics.

Patnaik, Utsa. 2004. 'Neoliberal Roots', *Frontline*, 25(6, 15–18 March), Chennai. Available at http://www.hindu.com/fline/fl2506/stories/20080328250601700.htm (accessed 15 October 2012).

————. 2006. 'Poverty and Neo-liberalism in India', mimeo. New Delhi: Centre for Economic Studies and Planning, Jawaharlal Nehru University.

Patnaik, Prabhat. 2012. 'For a Universal Old Age Pension Plan', *The Hindu*, 10 May. Available at http://www.thehindu.com/opinion/lead/article3401455.ece (accessed 16 July 2012.)

Radhakrishna, R. (ed.). 2008. *India Development Report*. New Delhi: Oxford University Press.

Radhakrishna, R. and K. Hanumantha Rao. 2006. 'Poverty, Unemployment and Public Intervention in India', *Social Development Report*. New Delhi: Oxford University Press, pp. 1–17.

Sen, Amartya. 1992. *Inequality Re-examined*. Oxford: Clarendon.

UN Millennium Project. 2005. *Investing in Development: A Practical Plan to Achieve the Millennium Development Goals*. New York: UN Millennium Project.

Part II
Minorities

10

How Social Structure Impacts the Gross Domestic Product

Role of Education and Diversity in India[*]

Abusaleh Shariff, Khursheed Anwar Siddiqui, Amit Sharma, and Prabir Kumar Ghosh[†]

The poor in fact face multidimensional disadvantages in employment, educational attainment, skills, nutrition, health, and other economic opportunities (Shariff 1999; Shariff et al. 2004; Unni 2007). While the poor are ready and willing, they often do not find paid work due to low educational attainment and poor work skills. Such deprivations enhance the economic wedge and inequality between the poor and the rich, as the latter are the recipients of the higher income during the post-reform period in India (Desai et al. 2010; Shariff 1999). Such inequality is intense and widespread as the disadvantaged constitute a high share in India's total population. One of the most enduring relationships, which express higher income levels, is with the levels of education. This chapter, therefore, explores the relationship between *levels of education* and *the share of Gross Domestic Product (GDP)*, and then whether this relationship is consistent amongst various socio-religious categories of people across India. It provides dominant leads into policy initiatives needed to improve provisioning of higher levels of education to the youth across India, and identifies communities who require a special policy focus.

Generally, the disadvantaged are prone to many types of distresses and vulnerabilities during the whole of their life cycle. Educational deprivation and lack of employment opportunities are the two greatest disabilities which enhances deprivation. The relationship that people have with their local environment, such as the social forces, institutions, and cultural values that sustain and contest them, determine the opportunities through which people contribute to the national GDP. Overall, the extent to which the newly evolving economic (reforms) changes could harm a subsistence system as opposed to benefiting it, in other words, the extent to which communities can be adversely affected by the impact of economic and social change, are to be studied and understood as well.

The poor are trapped in the disadvantages, distresses, and vulnerabilities cyclically—today they are disadvantaged and do not have education, good health, or skills required to get remunerated proportionately to their hard work, and as a result of which they are highly prone to severer distresses and vulnerabilities during the subsequent periods. Thus, one finds a vicious cycle in which the poor are trapped, intensifying distresses and

---

[*] This is a substantially revised version of the chapter available at http://www.usindiapolicy.org/documents/publications/USIPI-Publication-03-Social-Web.pdf.

[†] The authors acknowledge Ramesh Kolli, Senior Adviser, NCAER-CMCR, and former ADG, CSO, and Poonam Munjal, Senior Research Fellow, NCAER-CMCR, for their conceptualizing the methodological innovations used in this chapter.

vulnerabilities which transcend generations with limited opportunities to escape the poverty trap.

Often the responsibility of a government is to achieve and sustain high growth in economic and other developmental spheres; yet, it has to aim to ascertain a socially secure and value-based human life to its citizens. In the contemporary phase of relatively higher growth trajectory in India, it is essential that development is inclusive and broad-based so that clearly identifiable disadvantaged groups get an equal opportunity to crash out of the vicious cycle of poverty. Identifying the disadvantaged groups, providing them with appropriate policy advantages, and enabling groups to reap the demographic dividends are worthwhile policy directions.

India is a highly diverse society in terms of caste, religion, region, place of residence such as rural and urban areas, language, and so on. Most of the deprivations such as poverty, illiteracy, and low productivity register high correlations to the above cited attributes. It is but natural that any study of diversity and development must identify the economic disadvantageous associated with such attributes and also assess the role the education system plays in contributing to India's inclusive economic growth (GoI 2006).

ESTIMATING THE ECONOMIC CONTRIBUTION IN NATION BUILDING

The analysis and discussion in this chapter intends to empirically evaluate the contribution of different socio-religious communities (SRCs)[1] to Indian 'GDP'. It also estimates the value added made by the SRCs at different levels of education. Such an analysis is built upon the estimates of the workforce participation according to the SRCs and levels of education. This analysis, therefore, has made it possible to highlight the relative productivity differential according to the SRCs and hence identify the disadvantaged groups or communities. It is obvious that the lower the productivity level or value added, the higher the level of disadvantage; and such evidence should compel the governments to devise more pro-poor and just polices so as to ensure a durable and balanced social structure and harmonious living.

METHODS AND MATERIALS

The estimates of the GDP shares according to specified socio-religious groups were possible by linking data from the 66th Round of National Sample Survey Organisation (NSSO) for the year 2009–10 and sectoral GDP estimates given by the National Accounts Statistics (NAS) (CSO 2011). This is a rare feat of sorts, as such an

exercise of this nature has never been undertaken in India or abroad; although a few have identified the need to undertake such an analysis for the sake of resolving a number of puzzles in the Indian growth and equity story (see World Bank 2011a, 2011b). In the following analysis, the intersectoral labour shares extracted from the NSSO are reconciled with the sectoral GDP estimates so as to approximate the relative share of the SRCs to the GDP. The analysis further extends to understand the relationship between the value added so derived and the level of education of the labour force. The depth of analysis extends to a unique and rare segregation of the service sector into the 'traditional services' and 'modern services'. The analytical and empirical process leads to an estimation of the SRC-specific GDP productivity quotients for easy understanding and interpretation.

DECOMPOSING GDP: WAGE AND NON-WAGE INCOME

The GDP measures monetary value of all goods and services produced in the economy within a given period, normally during a year. All goods and services produced by various economic activities like agriculture, forestry, fishing, mining, manufacturing, government services, private services, community and personal services, etc., are included in the calculation of the GDP. The GDP thus measures the total value of final goods and services produced by domestic institutions during the reference period.

The Indian economy is subdivided into 9 broad groups, which are further divided in 13 sectors, and a number of sub-sectors at 2, 3, and 4 digit levels. The NAS provides estimates of the GDP originating in broad groups and sectors at different levels. Statement number 76.1 of NAS-2011 provides distribution of GDP into wage (compensation to employees) and non-wage (operating surplus/mixed income) income for these groups of the Indian economy. Wage and non-wage decomposition of the GDP for all broad sectors can be done using wage (compensation to employees) data. Consumption of fixed capital and operating surplus/mixed income is treated as non-wage income.

At the first step, the NAS information on GDP broad and main sectors is decomposed into wage and non-wage incomes. In case of 50 sub-sectors for which the wage component is not available from the NAS, the wage distributions from the NSSO 66th Round are used. The NSSO provides information on workers' weekly wages in various sectors/industries of the economy at the at 5 digit NIC-2004 classification. The sub-sectoral wage incomes are decomposed by using the share of weekly wage of each sub-sector and subsequently aggregated into broader sectors of the economy. Further, by subtracting these sub-sectoral wage incomes from the sub-sectoral GDP, non-wage income is also estimated. That is,

GDP (sub-sector)—Wage payments (sub-sector) = Non-wage income (sub-sector)

In the second stage, the non-wage income is decomposed into public and private categories, as the operating surplus of the public sector does not directly accrue to households' income. Data on the operating surplus of the public sector is taken from the NAS for all the broad 9 groups and 13 main sectors. The structure of the total GDP thus derived is used to disaggregate the sectoral operating surplus within the sub-sectors. This sub-sectoral operating surplus of the public sector (which is not accruable to households' income) is subtracted from the sub-sectoral non-wage income so as to derive the private non-wage income, which accrues as the households' income. The estimates thus derived encompass just about 96.6 per cent of all national GDP and is distributed and allocated across the SRCs engaged in different sectors and sub-sectors of the Indian economy. In this analysis, the wage component of the GDP has been worked out to be Rs 1,887,092 crores, which is 32 per cent of the GDP, and the non-wage income as Rs 4,035,357 crores, 68 per cent of GDP for the year 2009–10.

SECTORAL/SUB-SECTORAL SHARES OF GDP FOR LEVELS OF EDUCATION AND THE SRCs

The 66th Round NSSO survey on Employment and Unemployment provides information on individual wage and salary earnings and monthly household consumption expenditure in different sectors of the economy as per the National Industrial Classification (NIC-2004) codes. These data are amenable for decomposition according to levels of education and the SRCs. In all, as per the NIC classification, the GDP flowing from the whole economy is collapsed into 943 sub-sectors and further aggregated into 61 sectors. The percentage share of the GDP from each of the levels of education and each SRC in wage income (wages and salaries) and the household monthly consumption expenditure of self-employed individuals in the sub-sectors are estimated. Applying these shares at successive levels of education and for the SRCs categories in the wage income for a particular sub-sector, the wage component of the GDP is estimated. The non-wage component of sub-sectoral GDP is distributed across educational levels and SRCs

using the share of consumption expenditure of respective categories reporting themselves as self-employed in that particular sub-sector.[2]

> Wage payments accruing to a 'educational category'/SRC = % shares in wages and salaries of that community (estimated from the NSSO survey) × total wage payments in sub-sector estimated in Step 1.
> Non-wage income accruing to a 'educational category'/SRC = % share in monthly household consumption expenditure of individuals reporting self-employed of that community (estimated from the NSSO survey) × total Non-wage income in sub-sector.

> Where non-wage income in that sub-sector = GDP of sub-sector – total wage payments in that sub-sector minus operating surplus of public sector in that sub-sector.

EMPIRICAL ANALYSIS

The first section here presents the growth and structure of the Indian GDP during the last six decades. The second section discusses the results of the exercise that investigates the relative shares of different 'levels of education' and various SRCs in different sectors of the economy and the labour force.

GROWTH AND STRUCTURE OF THE INDIAN GDP

All the sectors of the Indian economy—agriculture, industry, and services—have shown growth over the last six decades. During the past over three decades, the highest growth in the economy as well as contribution to the GDP is credited to the services sector followed by industry and the agriculture sectors. In the following section, the growth in the Indian economy as well as the sectoral GDP and structure (share of different sectors to the GDP) in the last six decades are examined.

Decadal growth of Indian GDP during 1950s–2013

India, for many years has been an eye-catcher for the global investors and services providers because of a large pool of educated and easily trainable youth, as a result of which, India is now a hub for outsourcing. India's services sector, therefore, is following an outstanding growth trajectory, especially in the last two decades. The Indian GDP growth faced a dip in the 1970s, but revamped in the 1980s. The 1990s saw sustained growth of around 6 per cent and further more than 7 per cent in the last decade (Figure 10.1). The decline in the 1970s is attributed to the two sharp declines in the growth of the agriculture sector—first in 1975–6 (from 12.9 per cent in 1974–5 to –5.8 per cent in 1975–6) and second in 1978–9 (from

2.3 per cent in 1977–8 to –12.8 per cent in 1978–9). The steep fall in the agriculture sector's growth in the two years affected the whole economy as well as the growth in other sectors since the Indian economy was primarily dependent on agriculture contributing the highest share in the economy followed by the services sector, and industry being at the bottom until the 1970s.

Structure of Indian GDP during 1950s–2013

As stated above, till the late 1970s, the highest share to the Indian GDP was accrued from the agriculture sector followed by the services sector and then the industry sector. The 1970s was the time when the transformations in the structure of the Indian GDP started. During 1978–9, the agriculture sector was superseded by the services sector and during the second half of the 1990s (beginning 1995–6) the industry sector also superseded the agriculture sector relegating it to be less significant in terms of the sectoral composition of the national GDP (Figure 10.2).

The decadal sectoral compositional structure of India's GDP at factor cost at 2004–5 prices shows that

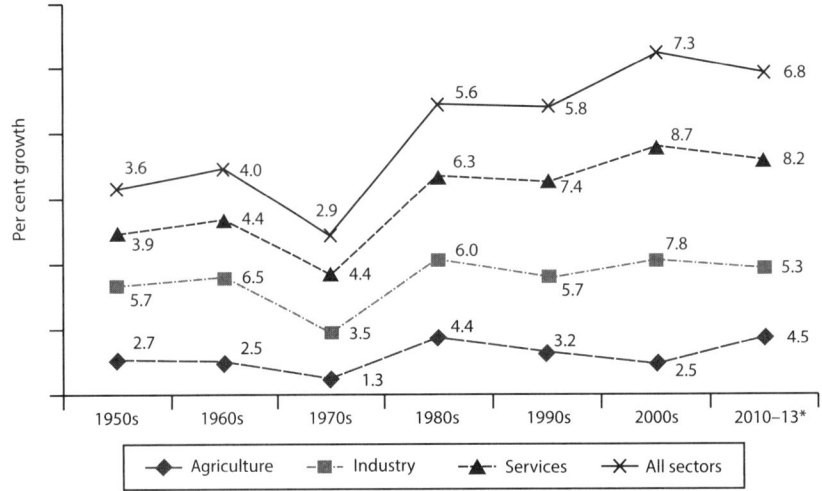

Figure 10.1   Sectoral and Overall Growth in the Indian Economy

Source: Based on authors' calculations.
Note: * Advanced estimated of GDP published by the Central Statistical Organization (CSO) are used for the year 2012–13.

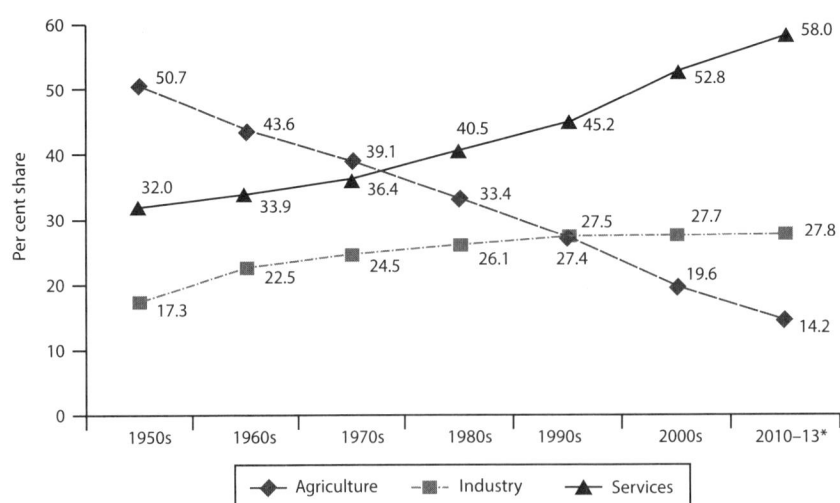

Figure 10.2   Sectoral Shares in GDP during the Last Six Decades

Source: Based on authors' calculations.
Note: * Advanced estimated of GDP published by the CSO are used for the year 2012–13.

in the last decade, the share of services to the GDP was about 53 per cent, while agriculture and industry sectors contributed 19.6 and 27.7 per cent, respectively. The sectoral composition of the GDP has changed significantly since the last six decades. The share of agriculture (and allied activities) sector declined by 31.1 per cent points from a high of 50.7 per cent in the 1950s to as low as 19.6 per cent in the 2000s. The share of the industry sector has shown an increase of 10.4 per cent points from the 1950s through the last decade. However, the services sector's contribution to the GDP has increased by a massive 21 per cent points from 32 per cent in 1950s to 52.8 per cent during the 2000s.

Year-over-year growth and structure of the Indian GDP in the last decade

From a review of growth and structure of the GDP in the last 13 years, it is clear that the Indian GDP growth reached a historical high at more than 9.5 per cent in 2006–7. It is clearly demonstrated in Figure 10.3 that both the growth in the share of services sector to the GDP has picked up momentum even at a faster pace after 2005–6. Stagnation in the share of industries sector, continuous momentum in growth in the share of services sector, and continuous decline in the share of agriculture to the GDP can even be seen in the year-wise GDP structure of the last decade (Figure 10.4).

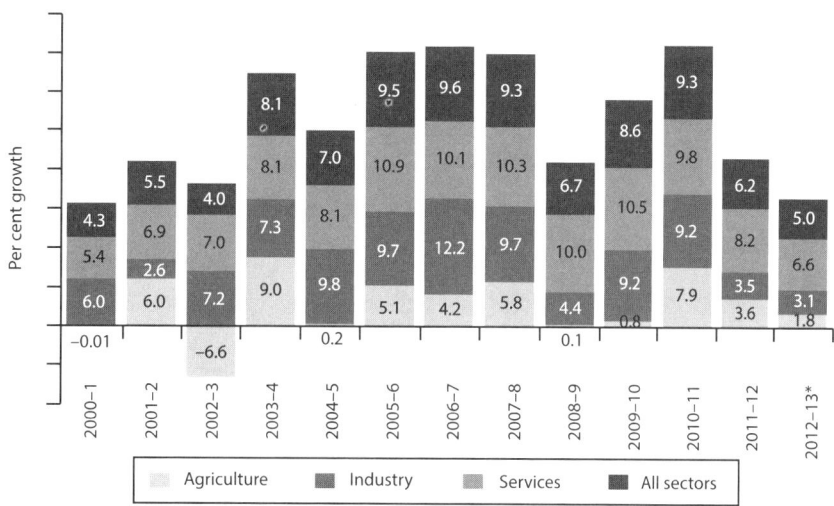

Figure 10.3   Sectoral Growth in GDP during the Last Decade

Source: Based on authors' calculations.

Note: * Advanced estimates of GDP published by the CSO are used for the year 2012–13.

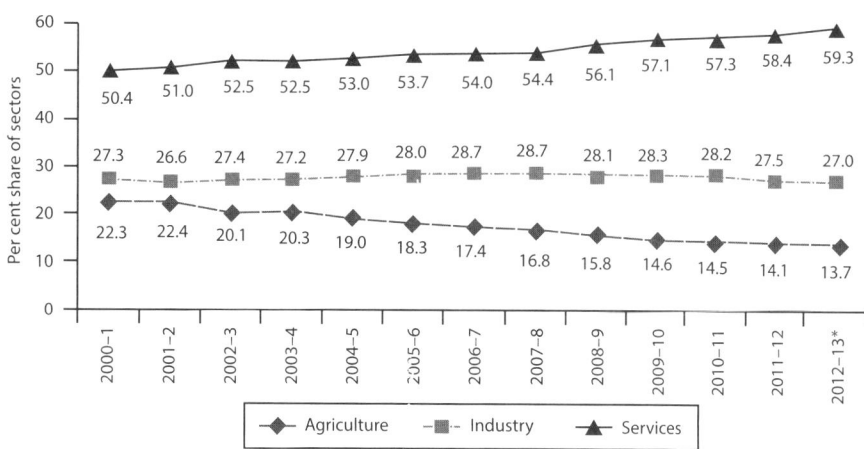

Figure 10.4   Structural Shares of GDP during the Last Decade

Source: Based on authors' calculations.

Note: * Advanced estimates of GDP published by the CSO are used for the year 2012–13.

The Social Dimensions of GDP

The most recent GDP structure by levels of education and SRCs, and associated sectoral workforce as well contributions and relative productivity levels for the year 2009–10 are presented ahead.

Estimates of the GDP according to the 'Levels of Education' and SRCs

The overall structure of the workforce employed in different sectors and associated contribution to the GDP suggests a harsh reality; that more than half of the workforce is employed in the agriculture sector which generates only about 18 per cent of the GDP thereby being

the least efficient sector in the India economy (see Figure 10.5). On the other hand, the services sector is most rewarding, which by employing just about 28 per cent of the workers contribute more than 55 per cent to the GDP. The industries sector employs about 21 per cent of the workforce and contributes to about 27 per cent of the GDP.

GSP shares according to the 'Levels of Education'

Figure 10.6 highlights the shares of different levels of education in the workforce and GDP in the Indian economy.

It is a well-established fact that through decades of research across the world, education is the foremost driving force for any kind of development. The economic

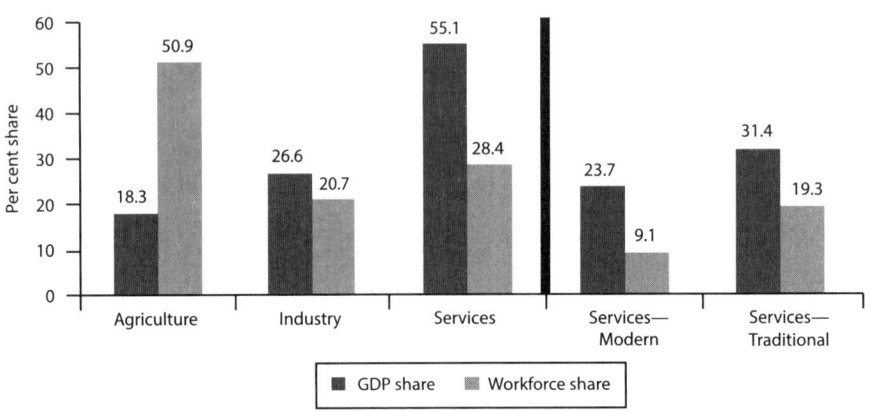

Figure 10.5   Sectoral GDP and Workforce Share, 2009–10
Source: Based on authors' calculations.

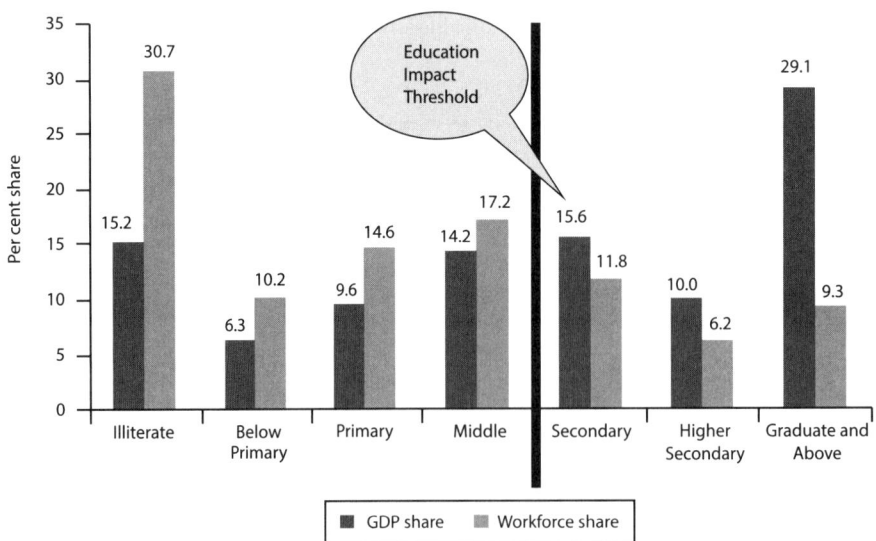

Figure 10.6   Shares in GDP and Workforce by Level of Education
Source: Based on authors' calculations.

development of an individual and even a nation is highly correlated with education, which is also an outcome of the analysis in this chapter. The estimates (in Figure 10.6) show that illiterates' share in the workforce (30.7 per cent) is twice their share in the GDP (15.2 per cent); on the other hand, only about 9 per cent of highly educated (graduates and above) contribute over 29 per cent of the GDP. Note also that up to middle-class-level education, the share in workforce is higher than the respective share in the GDP; once this threshold level of education is crossed, the per cent share in GDP supersedes the per cent share in the workforce, and this difference increases sharply with an increase in the level of education. If the efficiency quotients—that is, the ratio of share in the GDP and the share in workforce—are observed (more

on this ahead and in Table 10.1), one finds that the impact of education on the GDP is prominent and they are highly correlated.

ESTIMATES OF THE CONTRIBUTION TO THE GDP BY VARIOUS SRCS

All sectors together

The following section is a discussion about the relative contributions to the GDP by various SRCs—categories exclusively created for the purpose of this chapter. It is not surprising that the upper-caste Hindus generate most of the GDP (see Figure 10.7). They constitute about 20 per cent of the workforce and generate 34 per cent of the total GDP, which is highest in terms of volume for

Table 10.1 Efficiency Quotients (EQ*)

		Agriculture	Industries	Modern Services	Traditional Services	All Services	All Sectors
Illiterate		0.8	0.7	0.4	0.6	0.6	0.5
Below primary		0.9	0.9	0.8	0.6	0.6	0.6
Primary		0.9	0.8	0.5	0.7	0.6	0.7
Middle		1.1	0.9	0.6	0.8	0.7	0.8
Secondary		1.2	1.1	1.0	1.1	1.1	1.3
Higher secondary		1.3	1.3	0.9	1.4	1.2	1.6
Graduate and above		2.0	2.5	1.2	2.6	1.7	3.1
Hindu General		1.3	1.8	1.2	1.5	1.4	1.7
Hindu OBCs		1.0	0.9	0.9	0.9	0.9	0.8
Hindu SCs/STs		0.7	0.7	0.8	0.6	0.7	0.6
Muslims		1.1	0.8	1.1	0.9	0.8	1.0
All others		1.7	1.5	1.1	1.1	1.2	1.4
Hindu General	Illiterate	1.0	0.9	0.4	0.7	0.6	0.6
	Up to middle	1.3	1.0	0.7	1.0	0.8	0.9
	Above middle	1.7	2.5	1.3	1.6	1.7	2.5
Hindu OBCs	Illiterate	0.9	0.6	0.3	0.7	0.5	0.5
	Up to middle	1.0	0.8	0.5	0.8	0.6	0.7
	Above middle	1.2	1.4	1.0	1.2	1.2	1.6
Hindu SCs/STs	Illiterate	0.8	0.5	0.3	0.5	0.4	0.4
	Up to middle	0.7	0.7	0.5	0.6	0.5	0.5
	Above middle	0.8	1.0	1.2	0.8	1.2	1.3
Muslims	Illiterate	0.9	0.7	0.3	0.7	0.5	0.7
	Up to middle	1.1	0.7	0.7	0.8	0.6	0.8
	Above middle	1.4	1.6	1.3	1.6	1.5	2.2
All others	Illiterate	1.1	0.7	0.5	0.6	0.5	0.6
	Up to middle	1.9	0.9	0.8	0.7	0.6	0.9
	Above middle	2.1	2.8	1.3	1.2	1.5	2.5

Source: Based on authors' calculations.
Note: * Share of GDP divided by share of labour.

any set forming a community. This is followed by Hindu-Other Backward Classes (OBCs), who in the economy share 36.6 per cent of the labour force and 31 per cent of the total national GDP. The Hindu-Scheduled Castes/Scheduled Tribes (SCs/STs) constitute about 27.6 per cent of the labour force and contribute 16.5 per cent of the national GDP. The Muslims, the largest of the minorities, constitute slightly less than 11 per cent in the workforce and contribute just a bit more than this same percentage to the GDP. The other minorities, mostly the Christians, Sikhs, etc., who constitute about 5 per cent in the workforce, contribute 7.3 per cent to the GDP. On the whole, it is clear that the minorities, including the Muslims, do contribute substantially, approximately equal (a bit more, but not less) to their share in population to the GDP.

Sectoral Structure of Workforce and GDP according to the SRCs

In the following section, the shares of the SRCs, both in the workforce and respective sectoral GDP for agriculture, industry, and services, are discussed.

AGRICULTURE

The agriculture sector was the main driving force for the Indian economy from time immemorial till the late 1970s when the services and industry sectors took over as the major contributors to GDP. Currently, a major proportion of the agriculture labour force is constituted of the Hindu OBCs (39.5 per cent) and Hindu SCs/STs (32 per cent). Only about 16.6 per cent of the labour force in this sector is represented by the upper-caste Hindus followed by Muslims (7.3 per cent) and other

minorities (4.5 per cent). More than 38 per cent of the GDP generated in this sector is credited to the OBC Hindus, 24 per cent to Hindu SCs/STs and the rest about 37 per cent to the upper-caste Hindus and other minorities including the Muslims (Figure 10.8). The Muslim community's contribution to the GDP is just above their share in the labour force, suggesting a positive contribution.

INDUSTRY

Major contribution of 32 per cent to the industry sector's GDP comes from the Hindu OBCs who constitute more than 35 per cent in the workforce. This is followed by the Hindu-SCs/STs who have about 30 per cent share in labour contribution and about 19 per cent to the GDP. The upper-caste Hindus are relatively less in the industrial labour force with 16.4 per cent share but generate about 29 per cent of the sector's GDP suggesting their superior productivity. However, the Muslims constitute 13.5 per cent of the industrial workforce and contribute only 11 per cent of the GDP, suggesting that they are trapped in low-productive informal technical occupations (Figure 10.9).

SERVICES SECTOR

As mentioned earlier, the services sector is disaggregated into 'modern' and 'traditional' services. Modern services generally require education and skills. They include the technology-aided services such as information technology, computer-related services, communication, air transport, communication, banking, finance, insurance, legal services, accounting, research and development, media, public administration and defence, education, medical

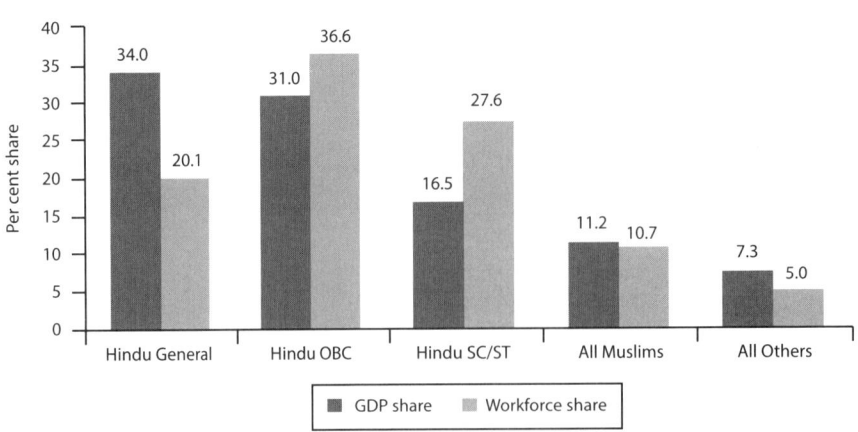

Figure 10.7   SRCs' Shares in GDP and Workforce
Source: Based on authors' calculations.

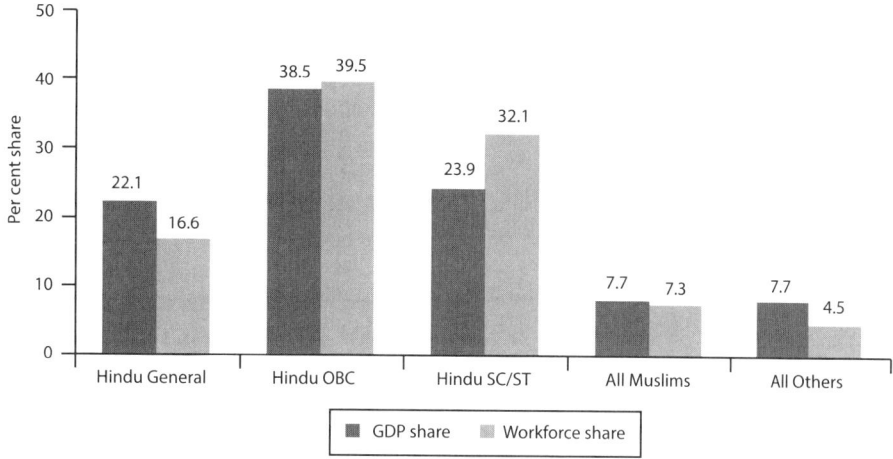

Figure 10.8   Agriculture: SRCs' Shares in GDP and Workforce
Source: Based on authors' calculations.

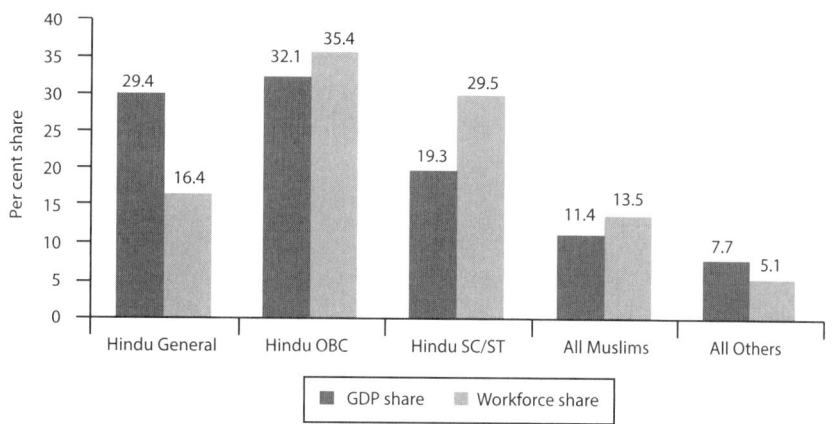

Figure 10.9   Industries: SRCs' Shares in GDP and Workforce
Source: Based on authors' calculations.

and health, and radio and TV related services, etc. The traditional services include services which generally do not require specialized educational skill and technological support such as trade, hotel and restaurants, storage, rail-road-water transport, real estate, artisanship, personal services (washing, hairdressing, and sanitary services, etc.), and so on. The following analysis presents estimates according to the services sub-sectors separately, thereby giving additional perspectives in the overall services sector.

One of the dominant distinctions between the sub-sectors is that 'traditional sector' workers are mostly illiterate, only 35 per cent reporting secondary and above level of education; on the other hand all employed in the 'modern sector' are all well-educated (75 per cent educated up to secondary or above level) and urban-oriented and

a substantial number are the upper-caste Hindus. Figure 10.10 represents the services sector's as well as the two sub-sectors' GDP and workforce composition by levels of education.

The traditional services sector has a share of 57 in GDP generated by the services sector and it employs 68 of total workers engaged in services sector. The modern services sector has a share of 43 per cent in GDP and 32 per cent in the workforce within the services sector (see Figure 10.11). The per capita GDP generated through employment in the two sub-sectors also vary significantly. Per capita GDP generated through the modern services sector (Rs 418,118 per annum) is 61 per cent higher than that generated through traditional services sector which was Rs 259,437 per annum.

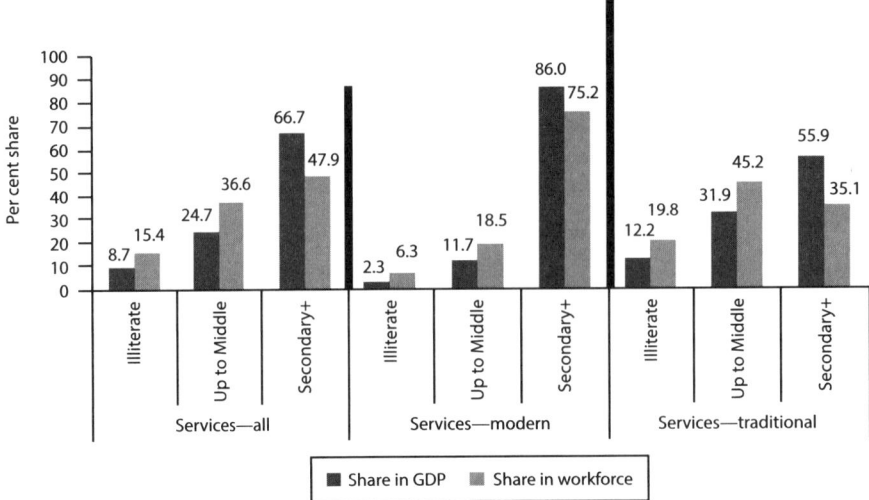

Figure 10.10   Services Sector

Source: Based on authors' calculations.

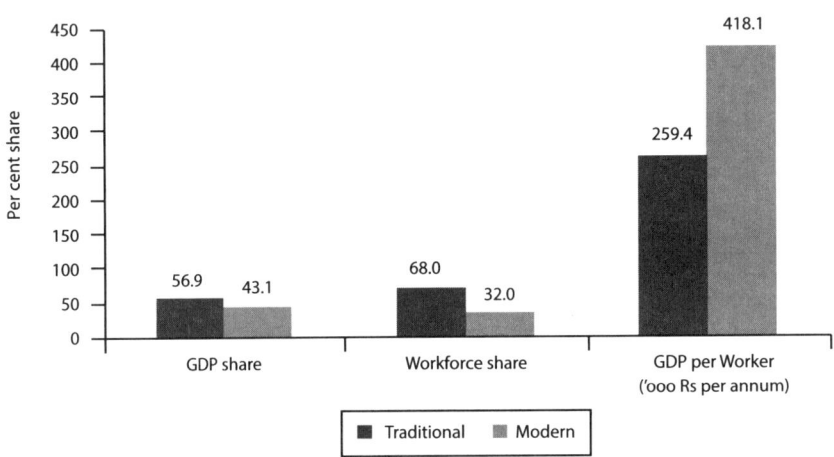

Figure 10.11   Per Worker GDP and Shares of Modern and Traditional Services in Services Sector's Total GDP
and Workforce

Source: Based on authors' calculations.

Modern services

Modern services sector is the most efficient sector in India. Note that it employs just over 9 per cent of all labour force and produces just less than one quarter of all GDP in India. Modern services sub-sector is dominated by the upper-caste Hindus with about 38.6 per cent in the labour force contributing about 45 per cent in the sectoral GDP. This is followed by large shares of the Hindu OBCs and Hindu SCs/STs having about 28 per cent and 18 per cent shares in the workforce, respectively, while for both the communities the contributions to the GDP are relatively less by almost 4 per cent than their

respective contributions to the workforce. About 7 per cent of the Muslim community labour force contributed 8 per cent to the GDP. Since educational achievements are major determinants of employment in this sector, those lower educated who worked in this sub-sector have contributed much less to the GDP.

In the modern services sector, the upper-caste Hindus, other minorities, and Muslims are the only communities which contribute to the nation's GDP higher than their shares in the sector's workforce; however, the difference between the share in GDP and the share in the workforce is not much for the minorities including Muslims but it is quite high (about 6 percentage points) for the upper-caste Hindus, the making the Hindu higher caste population most efficient workers employed in the modern services sector (see Figure 10.12).

In the following (see Figure 10.13) the SRC-wise share of the workforce employed in modern services as per cent of the SRCs' total workforce as well as the total workforce of the SRCs employed in the services sector are discussed. Note that only 9 per cent of the total labour force is employed in modern services, which contribute to 23.7 per cent to the GDP (see Figure 10.5).

It is useful to know the shares of SRCs in modern services as a percentage to respective SRCs' total workforce and also as a percentage of the entire workforce employed

in the modern services (see Figure 10.13). Interestingly, more than 17 per cent of all the upper-caste Hindu workforce is employed in the modern services alones which is the highest share from among all the SRCs considered in this analysis. This is followed, interestingly again, by the other minorities (Christians, Sikhs, etc., excluding Muslims) whose about 16 per cent of the workforce is employed in the modern services sector, which is the second highest share. Not a very large proportion of the workforce is associated with the modern services sector as percentage of the respective total workforce of the Hindu OBCs (7 per cent) and the Hindu-SCs/STs and the Muslims which is about 6 per cent each, as compared to the upper-caste Hindus and other minorities. This share of workers

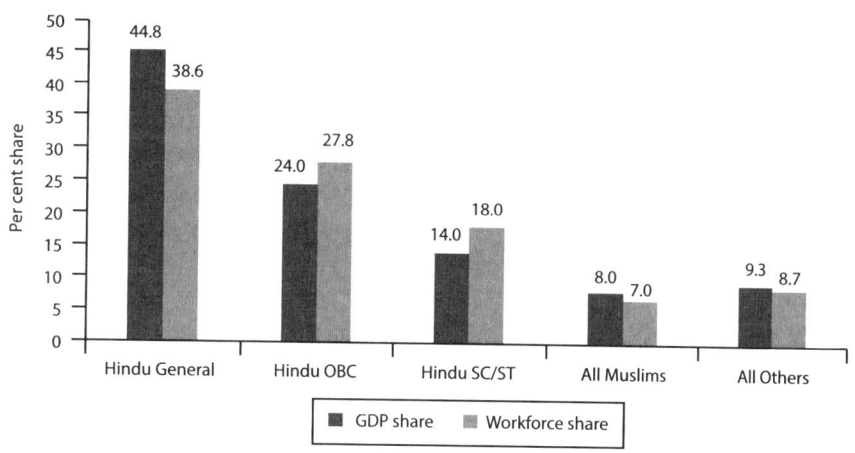

Figure 10.12   Shares in GDP and Workforce in Modern Services according to SRCs
Source: Based on authors' calculations.

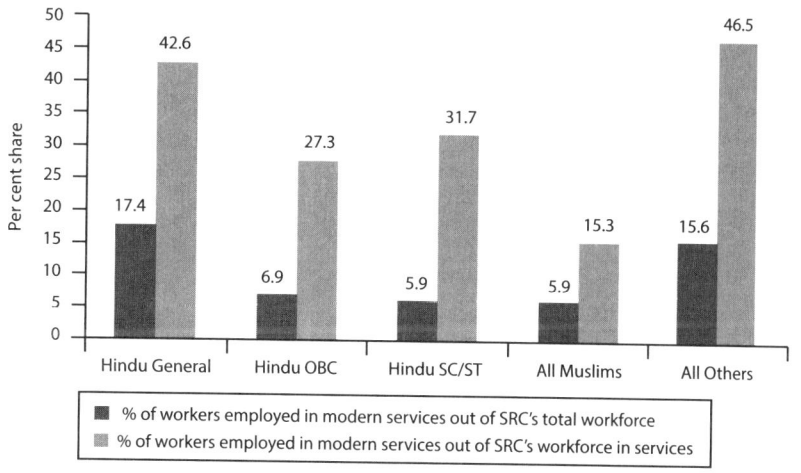

Figure 10.13   Modern Services: Share of Workers in Total Workforce and Total Workforce of Services Sector
Source: Based on authors' calculations.

in the modern services in case of the other minorities and upper-caste Hindus constitute, respectively, about 46 per cent and 42 per cent of all workers in the overall services thus suggesting that the Other Minorities (other than the Muslims) and upper-caste Hindus do not normally participate in the traditional services sector as much as the Muslims and non-upper-caste Hindu workers do.

At a second level are the Hindu SCs/STs and Hindu OBCs who have relatively better shares working in the modern services of 32 per cent and 27 per cent, respectively, from out of their total services sector employment. Interestingly again, it is the Muslims who seems to have less opportunities to get employed in the modern services sector employment, as is evident that only about 15 per cent share of labour from out of the total services sector are employed in the modern services sub-sector. These estimates and analysis highlight the existence of a considerable amount of 'discriminatory practices' in the choice and recruitment of the workforce in the modern services sector which encompass both public and private sector employment.

Traditional services

About 19 per cent of the total labour force is employed in traditional services, which contributes to more than 31 per cent of the GDP (see Figure 10.5). The traditional services sector contributes more than one and a half times in the GDP than its own share to the labour force. In many ways this is more efficient than the agricultural sector, yet it is the inefficient sector within the services sector. Note that the modern services sector contributes to the GDP

about 2.6 times than its share in labour. The traditional services sector's labour force consists of 37 per cent of the upper-caste Hindus, about 31 per cent of Hindu OBCs, 18 per cent of each of the Muslims and SCs/STs (Figure 10.14).

The share of workers by the SRCs as a percentage of SRCs' total workforce and workforce in the services sector is presented in Figure 10.15. Contrary to the common belief, only about 13 per cent of Hindu-SCs/STs workers are employed in the traditional services (as defined by the NSSO). On the other hand, about 33 per cent of all Muslim workforce is employed in the traditional sector, which is the highest of all communities compared in this chapter. Also about 85 per cent all Muslims working in the services sector are working in traditional services, which is the highest compared to any other community; for example, this proportion is about 73 per cent for Hindu OBCs and 68 per cent for Hindu SCs/STs. Thus, the Muslims are the largest segment of the traditional (mostly low-skill-based artisanal) sector workforce in India and they are trapped in low productivity occupations. The Muslims are more efficient in modern services than in traditional services when compared with other SRCs except for the upper-caste Hindus. It is in this sector, therefore, that the government must think to initiate programmes backed with technological upgradation while ensuring a slow transformation of the workforce from the traditional to modern services. Programmes promoting private initiatives for skill formation and modernized production system must to be undertaken by state governments. Further financial incentives and

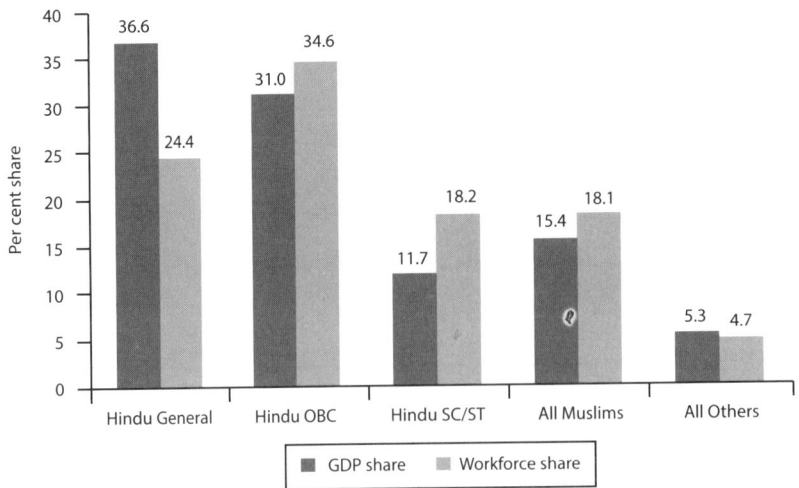

Figure 10.14   SRCs' Shares in GDP and Workforce within the Traditional Services Sector

Source: Based on authors' calculations.

access to credit from the Indian public and private banking networks have to be put in place.

Educational interaction with SRCs

Since the structure of GDP is highly varying across the two major variables, namely, socio-religious groups and education, it is also, to a certain level, of utmost importance to understand the variations in one variable (that is education) across the another (social) variable (that is, socio-religious groups) in the present context.

Information on levels of highest educational attainment for different socio-religious groups are presented in Figure 10.16. It is established through decades of research that low educational attainment is a major hurdle faced by India (and also by most of the world's developing and underdeveloped nations) in the process of sustainable development. But the situation is ever severer for the disadvantaged groups like Hindu SCs/STs/OBCs, and Muslims. Hardly 11 per cent of the Hindu STs are above the middle-class pass, followed by Hindu SCs (12.3 per cent), Muslims (13.3 per cent), and Hindu OBCs (19.2 per cent). However, comparatively, Hindu Generals have the highest level of education—over 37 per cent at levels above middle class followed by the Other Minorities

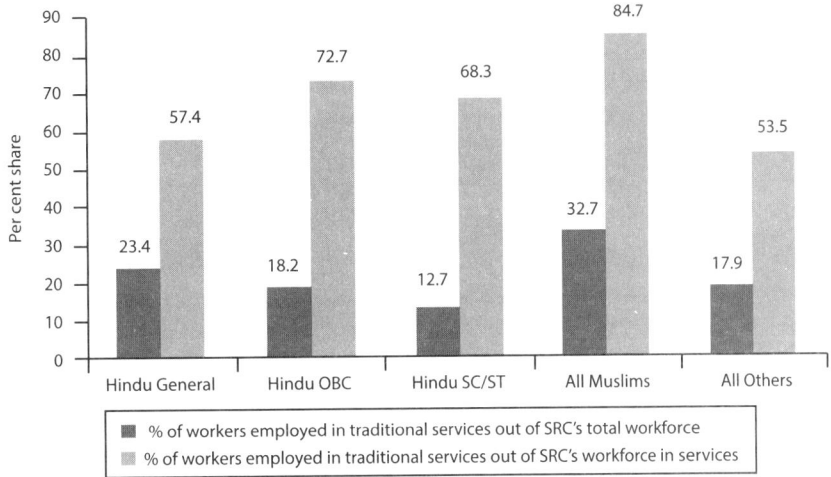

Figure 10.15   Traditional Services: Share of Workers in Total Workforce and Total Workforce of Services Sector
Source: Based on authors' calculations.

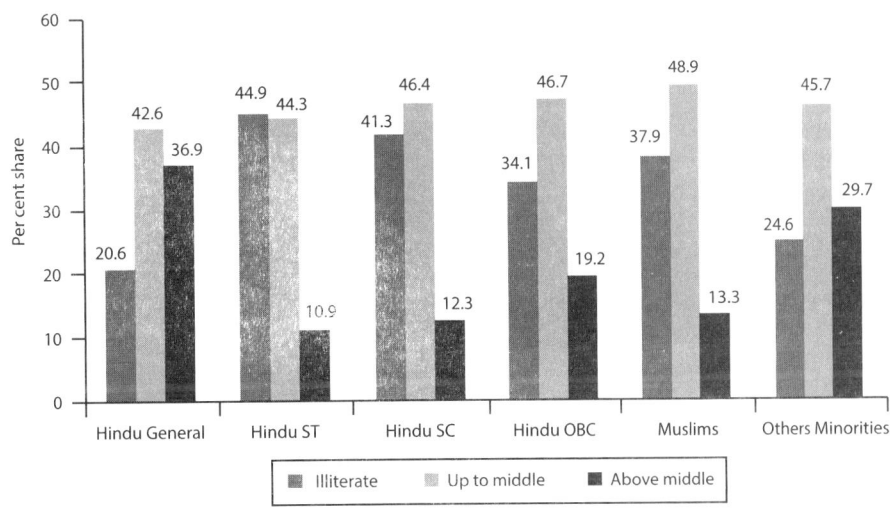

Figure 10.16   SRC-wise Distribution of Populations by Levels of Education
Source: Based on authors' calculations.

(about 30 per cent). An in-depth analysis is in order and research should be carried out for understanding the inequality and inclusiveness in the growth process of India. A brief analysis on this is presented ahead.

In this context, this analysis suggests that even after attaining a certain level of education, the disadvantaged communities show a lower level of efficiency and hence a lower level of development. The efficiency quotients estimated for different communities at different levels of education suggests high variation. For example, the Other Minorities and Hindu General sections of the population are at the top of the list at each level of education. Efficiency of the two top communities is followed by the Muslims, Hindu OBCs, and Hindu SCs/STs at each level of education. This in a way opens doors to further research to answering why educational attainment

also does not aid equally in the development of each community equally, and why the Hindu Generals and other minorities show higher level of efficiency leading to higher levels of economic and social development (Figure 10.17) compared with the same level of educated from the other deprived communities. The detailed efficiency quotients and per worker rupee value (GDP) are given in Tables 10.1 and 10.2 at different levels of education and for different SRCs.

However, a unique feature of the Muslim community which is consistent across different periods has been the fact, even at the lower levels of education and even if they are illiterate their relative contribution is comparable or even better than all the other communities in India. There is a strong suggestion to the fact that access to higher education and skills for the Muslims in

Table 10.2   Per Capita GDP (rupee value per annum in '000)

		Agriculture	Industries	Modern Services	Traditional Services	All Services	All Sectors
Illiterate		48.5	125.3	152.3	156.2	155.7	79.1
Below primary		52.9	150.1	314.0	157.8	178.8	98.7
Primary		53.8	153.9	224.0	164.1	172.2	104.3
Middle		63.7	174.1	270.1	203.4	216.1	132.2
Secondary		69.7	254.0	438.2	300.5	341.2	211.3
Higher secondary		72.6	361.7	385.6	355.1	367.4	256.5
Graduate and above		114.2	550.4	514.7	674.6	563.3	498.2
Hindu General		76.2	368.0	485.7	390.0	430.8	270.6
Hindu OBCs		55.8	185.8	361.4	232.3	267.6	135.0
Hindu SCs/STs		42.6	134.0	323.8	166.6	216.4	95.2
Muslims		60.3	173.2	477.4	221.0	260.3	167.2
All others		97.7	309.9	447.8	291.6	364.3	231.6
Hindu General	Illiterate	54.9	178.8	197.6	169.2	174.0	92.0
	Up to middle	72.3	202.8	325.8	235.2	253.9	147.4
	Above middle	97.6	524.5	516.9	517.5	517.2	408.1
Hindu OBCs	Illiterate	49.8	129.6	137.7	170.8	167.2	79.2
	Up to middle	55.7	166.7	249.8	174.7	184.3	109.4
	Above middle	70.0	288.5	407.9	352.3	378.0	247.8
Hindu SCs/STs	Illiterate	43.6	105.2	126.7	135.7	134.2	66.7
	Up to middle	40.8	139.1	199.8	142.6	155.2	85.5
	Above middle	44.4	203.9	434.5	271.1	363.4	207.4
Muslims	Illiterate	53.1	145.1	177.2	156.2	157.6	106.9
	Up to middle	62.2	144.8	376.0	176.6	190.4	134.1
	Above middle	80.4	324.5	553.9	413.3	465.4	357.6
All others	Illiterate	64.3	142.0	217.7	144.8	164.8	95.7
	Up to middle	106.7	187.0	241.1	193.6	209.1	148.6
	Above middle	121.8	576.5	520.1	400.9	467.8	401.0

Source: Based on authors' calculations.

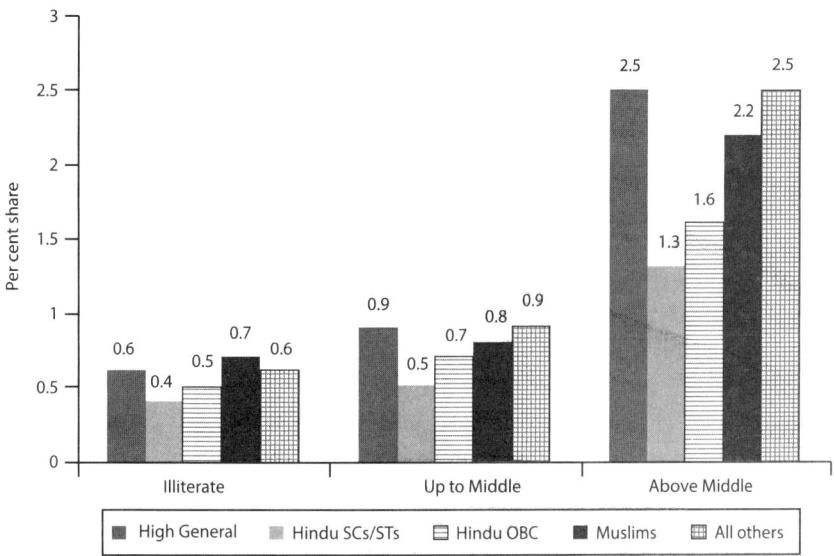

Figure 10.17   Efficiency Coefficients of SRCs by Levels of Education
Source: Based on authors' calculations.

fact consistently contributes to GDP with greatest levels of efficiency. They are the most productive, although at very high levels of education they sustain high levels next only to the Hindu General and the Other Minority categories.

DISCUSSION

The above analysis highlights the following: the Hindu-General population is the driving force of the economic growth thus far and their efficiency quotient has been high in terms of the total economy. While the Hindu Generals are the frontrunners in efficiency quotient in the modern services sector, the differentials in other sectors are much lower. This provides us with strong signals as to how India's GDP can be sustained, say at 7–8 per cent or increased to 10–12 per cent per annum. The Hindu OBCs, Hindu SCs/STs, and Muslims would contribute at higher levels of efficiency if provided technical education and opportunities to participate in modern services and industrial activities. The levels of higher education amongst the Dalits, Muslims, and Hindu OBCs must be immediately raised through multiple policies and public action.

How should the share of SCs/STs, Muslims, and Hindu OBCs be increased in various sectors of the Indian economy. Firstly, all these communities must be encouraged to improve their education at the elementary, matriculate, and graduation levels. This can be done through a combination of affirmative actions favouring these communities. Regular schools and colleges must be provided near the community living spaces, the teacher profile must be altered, especially at lower levels of education, and incentives should be offered to girls and the poorest of the poor. At the higher and technical levels of education, the current system of reservations can be extended to make entry into the educational system easier without compromising standards that are required for higher education. No country in the world has developed using only first- and second-rank achievers! What is needed is an improvement in the efficiency quotient and there is strong evidence that this need not be restricted to the upper castes in India. The question of reservations or quotas has to be understood differently in the case of higher and technical education and specialized employment. In the case of education, reservation only assists entry into the educational institution, but the final assessment benchmarks are fixed. Thus, while one can expect a lower success rate amongst those admitted on quotas, the system does not lower the standards of the educational system as a whole. Reservations can be based on an increased number of seats supported by enhanced hard and software and infrastructure. So far as employment is concerned, reservations favouring Hindu SCs/STs, Muslims, and Hindu OBCs will help to find an adequate number of teachers, professors, doctors, engineers, and scientists who would stay put in the country and might even be willing to spread out across the vast Indian hinterland. The efficiency coefficients and per capita per annum contribution to the GDP of different SRCs are given in Tables 10.1 and 10.2).

Appendix

Limitations of the Study

Due to the non-availability of data on the rate of return to capital, the consumption expenditure of self-employed reported individuals has been used to distribute the capital income. Here, consumption expenditure is assumed to be the proxy for their incomes and savings, and the capital part of the GDP is distributed accordingly. Methodology provided in this chapter needs improvement; however, it provides insight to the contribution made by various SRCs to the economy and calls for affirmative action to be taken for equitable growth.

Technical Note: Selection of Sectors

In this exercise, 61 sectors of the Indian economy are identified for which data on the aggregate GDP from NAS, employment, weekly wage earnings, and monthly consumption expenditure by SRCs from the NSSO are available. As per the objective of the study, GDP data with its break-up into wage and non-wage incomes is required. The CSO provides GDP data for 61 sectors of the Indian economy, but the GDP break-ups into wage and non-wage income are only for the broad and main sectors. The sectors for which data on GDP and its break-up into wage and non-wage as provided in the NAS are as follows:

Statement I: Broad and Main Sectors of the Indian Economy

1. Agriculture, forestry, and fishing
   (i) Agriculture
   (ii) Forestry and logging
   (iii) Fishing
2. Mining and quarrying
3. Manufacturing
4. Electricity, gas, and water supply
5. Construction
6. Trade, hotels, and restaurants
   (i) Trade
   (ii) Hotels and restaurants
7. Transport, storage, and communication
   (i) Railways
   (ii) Transport by other means
   (iii) Storage
   (iv) Communication
8. Financing, insurance, real estate, and business services
   (i) Banking and insurance
   (ii) Real estate, ownership of dwellings, and business services
9. Community, social, and personal services
   (i) Public administration and defence
   (ii) Other services

The GDP data along with its wage and non-wage components for all the above sectors is available in the Statement number 76.1 of NAS-2011. The first step is to decompose the GDP data into wage and non-wage incomes for the following sub-sectors for which only GDP data is available.

Statement II: Sub-sectors of the Indian Economy for which Break-up of GDP into Wage and Non-wage is not Available

1. Manufacturing
   (i) Production, processing, and preservation of meat, fish, fruits, vegetables, and oils
   (ii) Manufacturing of dairy products
   (iii) Manufacturing of grain mill products
   (iv) Manufacturing of other food products
   (v) Manufacturing of beverages
   (vi) Manufacturing of tobacco products
   (vii) Spinning, weaving, finishing of textiles, etc.
   (viii) Wearing apparel
   (ix) Leather and fur products
   (x) Wood and wood products
   (xi) Furniture
   (xii) Paper and printing, etc.
   (xiii) Rubber, petroleum products, etc.
   (xiv) Chemical and chemical products
   (xv) Non-metallic products
   (xvi) Basic metals
   (xvii) Recycling
   (xviii) Metal products and machinery
   (xix) Electrical machinery
   (xx) Other manufacturing
   (xxi) Transport equipment
2. Electricity, gas, and water supply
   (i) Electricity
   (ii) Gas
   (iii) Water supply
3. Trade, hotel, and restaurants
   (i) Maintenance and repair of motor vehicles
   (ii) Sale of motor vehicles
   (iii) Repair of personal and household goods
   (iv) Wholesale and retail trade
4. Transport, storage, and communication
   (i) Road transport
   (ii) Water transport
   (iii) Air transport
   (iv) Services incidental to transport

5. Banking and insurance
    (i)   Banking
    (ii)   Insurance
6. Financing, insurance, real estate, and business services
    (i)   Dwelling
    (ii)   Real estate
    (iii) Renting of machinery and equipment
    (iv)   Computer and related activities
    (v)   Legal services
    (vi)   Accounting and bookkeeping
    (vii) Research and development
7. Community, social, and personal services
    (i)   Education
    (ii)   Coaching centre
    (iii) Medical and health
    (iv)   Membership organizations
    (v)   Private households with employed persons
    (vi)   Washing and cleaning of textiles
    (vii) Hairdressing and other beauty treatment
    (viii) Custom tailoring
    (ix)   Funeral and related activities

DECOMPOSITION OF GDP INTO WAGE AND NON-WAGE INCOME

In the first step, the contribution of each of these sub-sectors to GDP is broken down into wage and non-wage incomes using data from the NAS.

For all the 9 broad sectors and for 13 major sectors as listed in Statement 1, the NAS provides estimates of both GDP originating in the broad sector/main sector and wage payments made in that sector. Using the basic national income identity that the sum of all factor payments is identical to the value added, it is an easy task to derive the non-wage (capital) income in each sub-sector. That is,

GDP in sub-sector – Wage payments in sub-sector = Non-wage income in sub-sector

For the decomposition of GDP of all the sub-sectors (51) for which the wage component is not available in the NAS, the wage distribution is extracted from NSSO 66th Round data. The NSSO provides information on weekly wages paid to workers in the different sectors/industries of the economy. Applying this structure to the controlled sectoral wages of the respective group/sectors as given in the NAS will give the wages for all the sub-sectors. (Step 1.)

Based on national income identities, the wage payments in each sub-sector are then subtracted from the GDP originating in that sector to get the non-wage (or capital) income.

After decomposing the GDP into wage and capital incomes, the next step was to decompose the capital income into public and private. This has been done because the operating surplus of the public sector does not accrue to households. For all the broad 9 groups and 13 main sectors, data on the operating surplus of the public sector is taken from the NAS. The structure of the total GDP has been used to disaggregate the sectoral operating surplus within the major sectors. This sub-sectoral operating surplus of the public sector is subtracted from the sub-sectoral total non-wage income to get the private non-wage income.

Operating surplus of public sector	210,781
Total GDP	6,133,230
GDP distributed among SRC	5,922,449
Wage	1,887,092
Non-wage	4,035,357

The total GDP distributed across different SRCs is Rs 5,922,449 crores, 96.6 per cent of the total GDP. Wage component of GDP is Rs 1,887,092 crores, which is 32 per cent of GDP and the non-wage income is Rs 4,035,357 crores, 68 per cent of GDP.

SHARE OF SRCS IN GDP OF EACH SECTOR AND SUB-SECTOR

The percentage share of each SRC in the income (wages and salaries) and household monthly consumption expenditure of individuals who reported themselves as self-employed in the sub-sectors identified earlier can be estimated as explained under the section titled 'Methods and Materials' earlier in this chapter.

Non-wage income is the major component of GDP (68 per cent) and there is no data available on the rate of return to different individuals in different sectors. The NSSO provides information on household monthly consumption expenditure and the occupation (wage-earners, salary-earners, and self-employed) of all individuals engaged in different sectors of the economy. It is assumed that the higher the consumption expenditure the higher will be the share in capital income.

Combining these percentages (of wage and salary earnings and household monthly consumption expenditure) and the wage and non-wage income estimated earlier, the share of each SRC in the wage and non-wage income of the respective sector is obtained in absolute terms.

Wage payments accruing to SRC = % share in wages and salaries of that community estimated from NSSO survey × Total wage payments in sub-sector estimated in Step 1

Non-wage income of that SRC is obtained as follows:

Non-wage income accruing to SRC = % share in monthly consumption expenditure of self-employed reported individuals of that community estimated from NSSO survey × Total non-wage income in sub-sector

where

non-wage Income in that sub-sector = GDP of sub-sector – Total wage payments in that sub-sector minus operating surplus of public sector in that sub-sector

Notes

1. The SRC in the Indian context was first conceived by the popularly known Sachar Committee Report (SCR). Given the size and distribution of various social, religious, and caste groups, the categories identified are (*a*) the SCs and STs together, (*b*) the Hindu OBC (self-reported), (*c*) all other Hindus as a general Hindu category, (*d*) the Muslims, the largest of the minorities, and (*e*) all other minorities all together form a sizable 5–6 per cent of the total population.

2. The NSSO provides information on household monthly consumption expenditure and the occupation (wage-earners, salary-earners, and self-employed) of all individuals engaged in different sectors of the economy. The share in monthly con-

sumption expenditure of those individuals who have reported themselves as self-employed is used to decompose the capital part of the GDP across SRCs in different sectors of the economy as there is no such direct data available on capital earnings of the individuals. It has been assumed that the expenditure of an individual is the proxy for his income and savings.

References

Desai, S., A. Dubey, B.L. Joshi, M. Sen, A. Shariff, and R. Vanneman. 2010. *Human Development in India*. New Delhi: Oxford University Press.

GoI (Government of India). 2006. *Social, Economic and Educational Status of the Muslim Community of India: A Report* (Sachar Committee Report). New Delhi: Prime Minister's High Level Committee, GoI.

CSO (Central Statistical Office). 2011. *National Account Statistics*. New Delhi: CSO, GoI.

Shariff, A. 1999. *India Human Development Report*. New Delhi: Oxford University Press.

Shariff, A., P.K. Ghosh, and A. Sharma. 2004. 'Food and Nutritional Status of the Poor in India: A State Level Analysis', in M.S. Swaminathan and Pedro Medrano (eds), *Towards Hunger Free India*. Chennai: East West Books (Madras) Pvt. Ltd, pp. 21–56.

Unni, J. 2007. 'Earnings and Education among Social Groups', in Abusaleh Shariff and Maithreyi Krishnaraj (eds), *State, Markets and Inequalities*. Delhi: Orient Longman, pp. 663–701.

World Bank. 2011a. *Perspectives on Poverty in India: Stylized Facts from Survey Data*. Washington, DC: World Bank.

———. 2011b. *Poverty and Social Exclusion in India*. Washington, DC: World Bank.

11

Muslims in India

A Study of Socio-economic and Educational Levels in Four Focus States[*]

Tanweer Fazal and Rajeev Kumar

At Odds with the Stereotypes: An Overview of the Muslim Situation in India

Muslims constitute 13.4 per cent of the Indian population,[1] making them the largest religious minority in the country. Though spread out in almost the entire country, major concentration of Muslims can be found in certain states. In terms of absolute numbers, four of the larger states of India, namely, Uttar Pradesh, West Bengal, Bihar, and Maharashtra have more than 10 million Muslims residing within their boundaries. Curiously, the Muslim population tends to be concentrated in certain districts. In 2001, India had 593 districts, but more than half of the Indian Muslims were found to be concentrated in just 76 of them. However, in only 20 districts did Muslims constitute a majority. In 38 districts, Muslims comprised between 25 and 50 per cent, and in a large number of districts (182), their population ranged between 10 and 25 per cent. In terms of place of residence, Indian Muslims have been inclined towards settling in towns and cities. As a result, the urban proportion of the Muslim population (16.9 per cent) is higher than their presence in rural areas (12 per cent). In total, 36 per cent of the Muslims live in urban areas as compared to the national average of 28 per cent.

An appallingly low level of literacy and inadequate work participation emerge as two major indicators of Muslim deprivation. In 2001, literacy among Muslims was 59.1 per cent, which was much below the national average of 65.1 per cent. If rural–urban disaggregation were to be taken into account, Muslim literacy fell nearly 11 percentage points below the national average in the urban areas. However, the picture does not appear so grim if state-wise analysis is considered. In nearly 10 states of India, literacy levels of Muslim populations are higher than the average. Invariably, all these states have a higher literacy among Muslim women as well. Despite a somewhat promising return in literacy figures in these states, Muslims continue to exhibit a very low work participation ratio. Therefore, the argument that a narrow Worker–Population Ratio (WPR) amongst Muslims is a fall-out of their low literacy levels fails to hold ground (Table 11.1). However, going by the Census statistics, the low WPR of Muslims is primarily because of the marginal participation of Muslim women in 'economic activity' so defined. At the all-India level, the WPR of Muslim women is only 25 per cent, while the national average remains at 44 per cent.[2]

Income, Expenditure, and Poverty Levels

In 2006, the Sachar Committee findings indicated a high rate of unemployment among Muslims—lower than Scheduled Castes (SCs)/Scheduled Tribes (STs), but

* This chapter is based partially on the study, 'Muslims in India: Specific Vulnerabilities and Needs', commissioned by Oxfam India.

Table 11.1   Muslim Literacy and Work Participation, All India

State	Literacy			Work Participation Rate		
	Muslim	Muslim women	State	Muslim	Muslim women	State
Odisha	71.3	62.3	63.1	26.9	6.8	38.8
Gujarat	73.5	63.5	69.1	32.7	13.0	41.9
Madhya Pradesh	70.3	60.1	63.7	32.8	16.9	42.7
Chhattisgarh	82.5	74.0	64.7	32.3	15.0	46.5
Maharashtra	78.1	72.9	76.9	32.4	12.7	42.5
Andhra Pradesh	68.0	59.1	60.5	33.8	16.8	45.8
Karnataka	70.1	63.0	66.6	36.4	19.9	44.5
Arunachal Pradesh	57.7	44.9	54.4	45.0	18.4	44.0
Jharkhand	55.6	42.7	53.6	31.6	18.8	37.5
Tamil Nadu	82.9	76.2	73.5	31.8	11.9	44.7

Source: Census 2001, Registrar General and Census Commissioner, GoI.

higher than all other categories such as Other Backward Classes (OBCs) and Hindu high castes. The Muslim propensity was more towards self-employment than the relatively secure salaried jobs. This was found to be particularly true in the urban areas of the country. The NSSO (National Sample Survey Organisation) Survey (2009–10) further validates the abovementioned trend in Muslim employment and earnings. The tendency towards self-employment was noticeably higher among OBC Muslims with nearly half of their households involved in self-employment (49.6 per cent) (Table 11.2).

In the villages, nearly a quarter of Muslims, both OBCs (25.8 per cent) and upper castes (24.6 per cent), are self-employed in non-agricultural activities. Compared to the Muslim OBCs, however, a good section of the Muslim upper castes are also self-employed in agriculture (24 per

cent). Yet, their proportion is much lesser than high caste non-Muslims (44.4 per cent), non-Muslim OBCs (35.9 per cent), and even the STs (37.2 per cent) (Table 11.3). This indicates that in the landownership pattern, Muslim upper castes as well as Muslim OBCs fall behind other Socio-religious Communities (SRCs), the deprivation of the latter is greater than the former in this regard.

Nearly half of the landowning Muslim households (46.9 per cent) could be termed as marginal with the size of land not exceeding 0.025 hectares. Compared to the Muslim upper castes (36.4 per cent), Muslim OBCs are more marginalized in this context with more than one-third (36.4 per cent) of them owning tiny patches of land (less than 0.01 hectares) (Table 11.4). Over all, the Muslim household condition is at par with SCs (44.8 per cent less than 0.025 hectares) and worse than all other

Table 11.2   Household Main Source of Income, Urban, All India

SRC	Self-employed	Regular Wage-/Salary-earning	Casual Labour	Others
ST	23.1	38.7	21.3	17.0
SC	26.2	39.3	25.2	9.3
OBC	34.7	37.1	16.9	11.3
Other non-Muslims	34.9	45.8	4.5	14.8
Muslim OBC	49.6	22.8	18.1	9.5
Muslim upper caste	42.8	35.7	13.5	8.0
All Muslims	45.5	30.4	15.5	8.6
All non-Muslims	33.0	41.2	13.1	12.7
Total	34.7	39.8	13.5	12.1

Source: NSSO 2009–10.

Table 11.3 Household Main Source of Income, Rural, All India

SRC	Self-employed in Non-agriculture	Agricultural Labour	Other Labour	Self-employed in Agriculture	Others
ST	6.8	33.5	13.1	37.2	9.4
SC	13.6	36.8	22.1	17.1	10.3
OBC	16.2	23.5	13.4	35.9	10.9
Non-Muslim high caste	16.0	13.3	8.1	44.4	18.2
Muslim OBC	25.8	21.5	18.5	17.8	16.3
Muslim upper caste	24.6	23.9	17.1	24.0	10.5
All Muslims	24.9	23.2	17.5	21.4	13.0
All non-Muslims	14.4	25.9	14.4	33.2	12.1
Total	15.5	25.6	14.8	31.9	12.2

Source: NSSO 2009–10.

Table 11.4 Household Landholding, All India (in hectares)

SRC	0 to 0.01	0.011 to 0.025	0.026 to 0.2	0.201 to 0.999	1 to 1.999	2 to Max
ST	26.7	5.9	10.7	29.6	14.5	12.6
SC	39.3	15.5	15.1	21.2	5.1	3.8
OBC	26.0	11.0	12.2	26.7	12.2	11.9
Non-Muslim high caste	18.3	9.6	13.2	25.9	14.2	18.8
Muslim OBC	36.4	12.5	24.5	16.7	4.6	5.2
Muslim upper caste	27.6	18.1	18.5	25.3	6.9	3.6
All Muslims	31.1	15.8	20.8	22.0	6.1	4.2
All non-Muslims	27.8	11.2	12.9	25.5	11.1	11.4
Total	28.1	11.7	13.8	25.1	10.6	10.7

Source: NSSO 2009–10.

SRCs. Consequently, a high proportion of Muslims in rural areas (25.9 per cent) is either involved in agricultural labour or are self-employed in non-agricultural activities (24.9 per cent).

A high degree of unemployment, coupled with low incomes and insecure employment, contributes to a high level of poverty among Muslims of India. The Sachar Committee recorded Muslim poverty (31 per cent) as second only to the SCs (35 per cent) at the all-India level, while in urban areas, Muslims were the poorest (38.4 per cent) followed by the SC/STs (36.4 per cent) (PMHLC 2006: 157). According to the latest Planning Commission estimates, Muslim urban poverty ratio, at 33.9 per cent, was the highest among all SRCs.

Poverty estimates in terms of Monthly Per Capita Expenditure (MPCE) also confirm Muslims as the poorest in the urban areas. In the MPCE quintiles for the urban areas, a majority of Indian Muslims (67.7 per cent) fall in the poorest two quintiles followed by the SCs (65.7 per cent) (Table 11.5). Compared to the rest of the population, poverty among Muslims is more pervasive and rampant. The Muslim backwards were found to be the worst lot with nearly three-fourths of them (71.7 per cent) falling in the poorest two quintile of urban MPCE. The Muslim condition is slightly better in the rural areas, where only half of their population (52.5 per cent) populated the poorest quintiles.

EDUCATIONAL ATTAINMENT

Muslims, both males and females, are second only to the SCs/STs amongst the illiterates of the country. Muslim women constitute the most educationally deprived social category, their status comparable only with SC/ST women. Interestingly, the gender gap amongst Muslims is highest at the level of illiterates, but narrows down at higher levels of education. This suggests a higher rate of

Table 11.5   Distribution of Persons by MPCE Quintiles, All India

SRC	1		2		3		4		5	
	Rural	Urban	Rural	Urban	Rural	Urban	Rural	Urban	Rural	Urban
ST	41.3	36.6	20.8	20.9	16.9	19.9	14.2	12.7	6.8	9.9
SC	30.7	40.5	24.9	25.2	19.8	16.4	14.4	10.9	10.2	7.1
OBC	23.0	28.7	21.9	25.6	20.9	20.6	19.5	16.0	14.8	9.0
Hindu high caste	10.6	12.3	16.5	16.2	20.3	22.2	22.9	23.9	29.7	25.4
Muslim OBC	25.6	46.4	26.0	25.3	19.3	16.0	16.3	7.4	12.8	4.9
Muslim upper caste	26.4	35.6	26.4	28.5	19.9	17.4	17.1	12.5	10.2	6.2
All Muslims	26.2	40.7	26.3	27.0	19.5	16.7	16.8	10.1	11.2	5.5
All non-Muslims	24.6	24.2	21.4	21.5	20.0	20.5	18.3	18.3	15.8	15.5
Total	24.8	26.8	22.0	22.4	20.0	19.9	18.1	17.0	15.2	14.0

Source: NSSO 2009–10.

dropouts among Muslim men compared to their women. Further, the difference between male and female enrolment in primary or above levels was also found to be low among Muslims (see Table 11.6).

The NSSO (2007–8) data on current attendance reveals that among all SRCs, Muslims (both boys and girls) have the highest figures for having never attended school (which is higher than SCs and STs). They also have the least entry for those enrolled in primary or above levels (Table 11.7).

However, having entered an educational institution once, the probability of dropping out was higher among Muslim boys. Both in rural as well as urban areas, the dropout rate was a significant 4–5 per cent points lower for Muslim girls. This highlights the yearning among Muslim girls to take to education provided they are able to get enrolled.

MUSLIM SITUATION IN FOUR FOCUS STATES: BIHAR, UTTAR PRADESH, ASSAM, AND KERALA

MUSLIM SITUATION IN BIHAR

In Bihar, Muslims constitute 16.5 per cent[3] of the population which amounts to nearly 10 per cent of the country's total Muslim population. The 38 districts of the state could be categorized into districts of high (above state average of 16.5 per cent), medium (between 10 to 16.5 per cent), and low intensity (below 10 per cent) of the Muslim population. Large conglomerations of Muslims are found in the northern part of the state. Central Bihar and southern Bihar districts, barring Bhagalpur and Gopalganj, report a medium to low concentration of Muslim population (Table 11.8).

Traditionally, Bihar's economy is dominated by the agricultural sector. Around 90 per cent of the population

Table 11.6   Distribution by Educational Level, All India

Educational Level	ST/SC		OBC		Hindu High Castes		Muslim OBC		Muslim Upper Castes		All Muslims		Total	
	Male	Female	Male	Female	Male	Female	Male	Female	Male	Female	Male	Female	Male	Female
Not literate	35.6	53.2	26.9	45.1	15.9	26.9	37.6	51.7	32.2	43.5	34.7	47.3	27.9	43.7
Below primary	21.6	18.4	20.0	17.7	15.1	14.7	22.5	19.5	23.6	20.5	23.1	20.0	19.8	17.5
Primary	18.0	14.1	17.5	15.2	15.0	16.4	16.7	12.1	19.1	18.1	18.0	15.4	17.1	15.2
Upper primary/ middle	12.8	7.9	15.7	10.7	15.6	13.7	11.6	8.8	11.3	8.7	11.4	8.7	14.3	10.3
Secondary/higher secondary	9.3	5.4	15.3	9.0	24.1	18.8	9.4	6.6	10.6	7.5	10.0	7.1	14.9	9.9
Above higher secondary	2.7	1.0	4.6	2.3	14.3	9.6	2.2	1.2	3.2	1.7	2.8	1.5	6.0	3.4

Source: NSSO 2007–8.

Table 11.7 Distribution by Current Attendance Status, Ages 5 to 29, All India

SRC	Never Attended				Dropped Out				Attending Pre-primary or Informal				Currently Enrolled in Primary or Above			
	Rural		Urban		Rural		Urban		Rural		Urban		Rural		Urban	
	Male	Female	Male	Female	Male	Female	Male	Female	Male	Female	Male	Female	Male	Female	Male	Female
ST	15.1	29.3	7.7	14.3	33.2	27.9	34.7	33.2	0.9	0.8	1.3	1.1	50.8	42.1	56.3	51.4
SC	13.8	24.7	9.4	14.2	33.4	30.4	41.5	37.4	0.8	0.8	1.0	1.2	51.9	44.2	43.1	47.3
OBC	9.2	19.9	4.8	8.3	33.6	31.4	39.6	39.6	0.9	0.7	1.0	0.9	56.3	48.1	54.6	51.2
Other non-Muslims	4.2	8.0	2.6	4.1	35.1	39.5	37.7	38.5	1.0	0.8	1.5	1.1	59.7	51.8	58.2	56.3
Muslim OBC	22.1	35.8	16.2	20.6	27.4	23.2	39.2	35.3	1.4	1.2	1.6	1.7	49.2	39.8	43.0	42.5
Muslim upper caste	15.3	22.0	9.3	14.5	33.3	33.4	44.6	40.6	0.9	0.7	1.4	2.2	50.5	43.8	44.8	42.7
All Muslims	18.6	28.3	12.7	17.5	30.4	28.8	42.2	38.2	1.1	0.9	1.4	2.0	49.9	42.0	43.7	42.4
All non-Muslims	10.1	20.0	4.9	8.0	33.8	32.2	39.0	38.5	0.9	0.8	1.2	1.0	55.2	47.1	54.8	52.5
Total	11.2	21.1	6.4	9.8	33.4	31.8	39.6	38.4	0.9	0.8	1.3	1.2	54.5	46.4	52.8	50.5

Source: NSSO 2007–8.

Table 11.8 Distribution of Districts by Concentration of Muslim Population

Concentration of Muslim Population	District (Muslim Population in %)
High	Bhagalpur (18%), Siwan (18%), East Champaran (19%), West Champaran (21%), Muzaffarpur (15%), Sitamarhi (21%), Darbhanga (23%), Madhubani (18%), Purnia (37%), Araria (41%), Kishanganj (78%), Katihar (43%), Supaul (17%), Gopalganj (17%)
Medium	Rohtas (10%), Gaya (12%), Nawada (11%), Banka (12%), Jamui (12%), Begusarai (13%), Saran (10%), Sheohar (16%), Vaishali (10%), Samastipur (10%), Saharsa (14%), Madhepura (11%), Khagaria (10%), Kaimur (10%), Aurangabad (10%)
Low	Bhojpur (7%), Buxar (6%), Jehanabad (8%), Munger (8%), Nalanda (7%), Lakhisarai (4%), Shekhpura (6%), Patna (8%)

Source: Census 2001, Registrar General and Census Commissioner, GoI.

still lives in rural areas where agriculture, along with animal husbandry, has been the mainstay of their livelihood. Majority of the Muslims of Bihar too live in the rural areas (87.6 per cent). In Bihar, as elsewhere, the average size of Muslim households is larger than the others (6.8 in rural and 6.9 in urban areas compared to 6.1 and 6, respectively, for the general population). While fertility is a shade higher than the others, the other contributing factor to bigger household sizes is the higher sex ratio among the Muslims of Bihar.

A 2006 survey sanctioned by the state's Minority Commission found the community steeped in poverty, with very low income levels, endowed with less amount of land, land-related and non-land-related resources, engaged in low-paid jobs in the unorganized sector or in self-employment activities (ADRI 2004: iii). The community's literacy rate (42 per cent) is 5 per cent below the state's average (47 per cent), and the gender gap in literacy is an astounding 20 per cent with female literacy reporting as low as 31.5 per cent. Although in work participation Muslims are able to catch up with the others,

their employment in low-paying and insecure sectors makes their condition distressing. Thus, among cultivators, the Muslim share is only 19.8 per cent, while the corresponding figure for the state is 29.3 per cent. Conversely, their share in agricultural labour (51.5 per cent) is higher than any religious community in Bihar (with 48 per cent as state average). Again, Muslim employment in the insecure household industry (5.8 per cent) was also reported to be higher than all (3.9 per cent).[4]

Income, employment, and poverty level

Nearly 45 per cent of urban Muslims and 38 per cent of rural Muslims count amongst the poorest. Over the years, the poverty level amongst Muslims has only worsened as the poverty estimates of NSSO 2009–10 shows nearly 80 per cent of Bihar Muslims populating the poorest two quintiles of MPCE in rural areas and close to 90 per cent in urban spaces. In both urban as well as rural Bihar, Muslims are equivalent to the SCs and worse-off than the OBCs of the state (see Table 11.9). Among Muslims however, there is little variation among upper

Table 11.9 Distribution of Persons by MPCE Quintiles, Bihar

Social Group	1		2		3		4		5	
	Rural	Urban	Rural	Urban	Rural	Urban	Rural	Urban	Rural	Urban
ST/SC	54.2	74.1	27.7	12.2	9.1	2.0	6.8	4.4	2.2	7.3
OBC	46.1	56.9	24.9	24.9	16.2	12.9	9.1	3.7	3.8	1.7
Hindu high caste	23.2	25.2	25.2	24.0	18.5	30.7	19.8	10.4	13.3	9.8
Muslim OBC	46.1	67.3	34.2	26.9	11.6	3.3	6.5	2.6	1.6	0.0
Muslim upper caste	54.6	56.5	27.7	21.5	14.1	16.8	2.0	4.4	1.6	0.8
All Muslims	48.8	64.1	32.1	24.3	11.8	8.1	5.6	3.2	1.6	0.3
Total	45.8	53.0	26.6	23.3	14.2	14.7	9.2	5.1	4.2	3.8

Source: NSSO 2009–10.

and low caste Muslims in so far as poverty indices are concerned.

A majority of Muslims in the villages are either agricultural labour (39 per cent) or are self-employed in non-agricultural activities (21.5 per cent). In fact, after the SC/STs (46.1 per cent), the proportion of agricultural workers among Muslims is the highest. Within Bihar Muslims, a much higher proportion of Muslim OBCs constitute agricultural labour (45.4 per cent) when equated with Muslim upper castes (25.5 per cent) (Table 11.10).

The NSSO 2009–10 data testifies to the low level of landholdings among Muslims of Bihar. More than three-fourths of the Muslim households in rural Bihar (76.5 per cent) had land of sizes less than 0.2 hectare or half-an-acre. The corresponding figure for the SCs, OBCs, and Hindu high castes was 83 per cent, 63 per cent, and 30 per cent, respectively (Table 11.11). Among Muslims, however, Muslim upper castes had a larger share of the land holdings as compared to the Muslim backwards. Thus, for the Muslims of rural areas, particularly for those from the OBCs, cultivation is barely a source of subsistence.

In urban areas too, Muslim households are more dependent on self-employment (58.4 per cent) than the regular salaried positions (13.4 per cent). Here again, casual labour among Muslims (13.6 per cent) is second only to the SC/STs (18.3 per cent). Surprisingly, casual labour among Muslim upper castes in urban areas is higher than that among Muslim OBCs. This is plausibly because Muslim OBCs, coming from occupational castes, are more inclined towards self-employment (59.8 per cent) (Table 11.12).

As wage employment is limited, many Muslims in the urban areas are self-employed. The Bihar Minorities Commission Survey (see ADRI 2004) found that artisan-based activity was one area were Muslim self-employment was found to be present (4.4 per cent). On the other hand, only a handful of Muslims were engaged in manufacturing. In rural areas, nearly 23 per cent of them were engaged in such low-paying self-employment activities as bidi-making, tailoring, rickshaw-pulling, petty shopkeeping, and others. In the urban areas, 42.5 per cent of Muslim households were engaged in such economic activities (ADRI 2004).

Table 11.10   Household Main Source of Income, Rural, Bihar

Social Group	Self-employed in Non-agriculture	Agricultural Labour	Other Labour	Self-employed in Agriculture	Others
ST/SC	17.8	46.1	13.2	14.1	8.7
OBC	23.5	28.0	9.0	28.9	10.7
Hindu high caste	22.2	13.5	3.8	49.0	11.5
Muslim OBC	20.1	45.4	6.9	14.8	12.8
Muslim upper caste	28.0	25.5	11.8	29.4	5.3
All Muslims	21.5	39.0	8.8	20.1	10.5
Total	21.7	32.5	9.4	26.2	10.2

Source: NSSO 2009–10.

Table 11.11   Household Landholding, Bihar (in hectares)

Social Group	0 to 0.01	0.011 to 0.025	0.026 to 0.2	0.201 to 0.999	1 to 1.999	2 to Max
ST/SC	47.3	21.2	13.7	13.8	3.4	0.7
OBC	21.3	16.0	26.2	24.5	7.0	5.0
Hindu high caste	11.1	7.2	12.5	30.1	24.3	14.8
Muslim OBC	33.2	16.9	34.9	10.9	2.2	2.0
Muslim upper caste	17.2	10.9	33.7	30.1	7.0	1.1
All Muslims	27.7	14.9	33.9	18.5	3.5	1.6
Total	28.0	16.2	22.3	21.3	7.6	4.5

Source: NSSO 2009–10.

Table 11.12   Household Main Source of Income, Urban, Bihar

Social Group	Self-employed	Regular Wage-/Salary-earning	Casual Labour	Others
ST/SC	33.7	16.4	18.3	31.6
OBC	57.5	11.5	11.6	19.5
Hindu high caste	37.1	30.3	1.0	31.6
Muslim OBC	59.8	13.7	12.1	14.4
Muslim upper caste	54.4	13.5	16.3	15.8
All Muslims	58.4	13.4	13.6	14.6
Total	49.9	16.7	10.3	23.1

Source: NSSO 2009–10.

Educational attainment

The 2001 Census reports Bihar's literacy rate (48 per cent) as India's lowest. Indicators for Muslims are considerably worse than the state average. In rural areas, Muslim literacy at 39 per cent was only better than the SC/ST (27 per cent), while a huge gender gap (21 per cent) between Muslim males (49 per cent) and females (28 per cent) was noticed. The gap between male (71 per cent) and female (57 per cent) literacy was, however, reduced to some extent amongst the urban Muslims. Over all, Muslim literacy remained far behind the state's average of 72 per cent in urban areas and 44 per cent in the rural areas.[5] The NSSO 2007–8 further confirms their educational deprivation. Overall, Muslims perform slightly better than the SCs and remain far behind all other SRCs (Table 11.13).

A large proportion of them, both men (51.7 per cent) and women (69.1 per cent), are simply illiterate, while another substantial section (26.7 per cent males and 19.6 per cent females) are just literates without even reaching the primary level. Noticeably, the educational profile of the Muslim community contained a very small portion of the population that had reached secondary or higher secondary levels, and in this, their performance was at par with the SCs of Bihar.

On the subject of children out of school, the Muslim situation was found to be worse (Table 11.14). In this regard, the educational deprivation of Muslim children was similar to the SCs in the state. Compared to the Muslim boys, a higher proportion of Muslim girls (38 per cent) in rural areas was out of school, however, in the urban areas, this was inverted with Muslim girls (28.8 per cent) showing greater propensity towards enrolment than the boys (34.7 per cent).

MUSLIM SITUATION IN UTTAR PRADESH

One-sixth of India's population lives in Uttar Pradesh. The most populous state also has the largest concentration of the Muslim population. Though Muslims constitute 18.5 per cent of the state's population, in absolute numbers, they far outscore the community's population in any other state. Muslims are spread all across the 72

Table 11.13   Distribution by Educational Level, Bihar

Educational Level	ST/SC		OBC		Hindu High Castes		Muslim OBC		Muslim Upper Castes		All Muslims		Total	
	Male	Female	Male	Female	Male	Female	Male	Female	Male	Female	Male	Female	Male	Female
Not literate	56.5	75.4	36.4	59.9	16.9	30.9	55.2	73.8	44.9	59.5	51.7	69.1	40.8	61.4
Below primary	22.4	15.5	25.1	19.8	18.6	19.8	25.5	17.1	29.8	25.7	26.7	19.6	23.9	18.8
Primary	9.7	5.7	13.9	9.7	11.6	15.1	10.3	4.7	13.4	7.7	11.2	6.0	12.3	8.8
Upper primary/ middle	5.6	1.9	11.2	5.4	13.6	13.2	4.6	2.4	3.9	2.9	4.7	2.5	9.3	5.1
Secondary/higher secondary	4.8	1.4	11.1	4.7	25.7	16.8	3.2	1.6	5.0	3.7	3.9	2.4	10.4	5.0
More than higher secondary	1.1	0.1	2.3	0.5	13.6	4.3	1.1	0.4	2.9	0.6	1.7	0.4	3.3	0.9

Source: NSSO 2007–8.

Table 11.14   Percentage of Children between 6 and 14 Years Not Attending School, Bihar

SRC	Rural		Urban	
	Male	Female	Male	Female
SC	30.6	41.1	33.8	34.2
OBC	17.4	27.5	15.7	12.1
Hindu high caste	9.3	7.9	10.5	7.9
Muslim	32.0	38.0	34.7	28.8
All	21.9	30.6	20.2	17.8

Source: NSSO 2007–8.

districts of the state; however, their concentration varies considerably. The Muslim population of the state could be distributed into high concentration (population share above 33 per cent), medium concentration (between 19 to 33 per cent), and low concentration (below 19 per cent). Of the four geographical regions of the state, a major portion of the Muslim population (46.9 per cent) inhabits the western region, followed by the eastern (36.3 per cent) and the central region (14.9 per cent). Districts forming part of the Bundelkhand cultural region such as Jhansi, Hamirpur, Chitrakoot, and others have a minuscule presence of Muslims (see Table 11.15).

Acute differences in the level of human development prevail among the different social and religious groups in the state. Muslims fare worse insofar as their socio-economic situation is concerned. Their literacy rate, in 2001, at 47.8 per cent was sizably lower than state's average of 56.3 per cent. The gap was even more marked if male literacy alone was to be taken into account—just 57.3 per cent compared to 68.8 per cent for all communities. On the other hand, Muslims in Uttar Pradesh demonstrate an increased pace of urbanization (36 per cent) compared to the state's average of 21 per cent. Much of this is owing to the fact that Muslims in Uttar Pradesh do not count much amongst the landowners and cultivators.[6] Neither

do they populate the rank of agricultural workers. Big cities and towns, towards which they look for opportunities and better life too fail to provide succour. According to the State Human Development Report (2007), a sizable section of the Uttar Pradesh Muslims comprise the urban poor.

Although falling behind all other religious groups in terms of developmental indices, Muslims in Uttar Pradesh return a better sex ratio (918) than the state's average (898). This has not necessarily enhanced the position of Muslim women in other spheres. In keeping with the national trend, work participation among Muslim women remained marginal at 12.4 per cent, while literacy among them was nearly 5 points below the state's average female literacy.

Income, employment, and poverty levels

In Uttar Pradesh, inequalities are sharp between various social groups. In general, the social hierarchy of caste and religion is replicated in the economic sphere as well with Muslims, OBCs, and SC/STs lagging far behind. This gets reflected in their work participation, too, where Muslims (29.1 per cent) lagged behind the state average of 32.5 per cent. Only 25.7 per cent of the Muslim work populace is constituted of cultivators, whereas the state's average is 41.1 per cent. On the other, a disproportionately large proportion of Muslim workers populate the undefined 'other' works category, which could suggest a high degree of casualization. Though less represented among agricultural workers, Muslim employment in the household industry emerges as much greater than the other communities (11.9 compared to the average of 5.6).[7] The 2009–10 Round of the NSSO also shows Muslim households being largely dependent on low-paying and less secure economic activities. In the rural areas, the proportion of Muslim households comprising agricultural labour (15.8 per cent) is equivalent to that of the SC/STs of the state (17.4 per cent). However, it is

Table 11.15   Region-wise Percentage Distribution of Population by SRC, Uttar Pradesh

Region	Total Population	Hindus	Muslims	Christians	Sikhs	Buddhists	Jains	Others
Bundelkhand	5	5.7	1.9	5.3	1.5	2.5	14.1	2.8
Central region	18.4	19.2	14.9	19.6	25.8	23	9.1	24.8
Eastern region	43.1	44.9	36.3	29.6	10.5	39.8	6.6	44.4
Western region	33.5	30.2	46.9	45.5	62.2	34.7	70.3	27.9
All	100	80.61	18.5	0.13	0.41	0.18	0.12	0.05

Source: Estimated by Abusaleh Shariff using the percentage distribution of 2001 Census and total population of the districts from Census of India 2011, cited in Shariff 2011.

in self-employment in the non-agricultural sector in the rural areas that Muslims (27.2 per cent) far outscore all other social groups. Remarkably, little variation in employment is observable between households of Muslim OBCs and Muslim upper castes (Table 11.16).

More than half of the Muslim population (55.1 per cent) in urban areas is dependent on self-employment while they are sparsely represented (less than ST/SCs and OBCs) in regular wage-earning employment. The existence of casual labour among Muslims was also found to be higher than the average (12.7 per cent), although it was significantly less than the ST/SCs (24.9 per cent) (Table 11.17). Again, little variations could be observed between Muslim OBCs and Muslim upper castes insofar as the employment pattern was concerned.

A sizable (44.4 per cent) of the Muslim population, according to Planning Commission estimates of 2009–10, falls below poverty line thus making the state second only to Assam (53.6 per cent) in Muslim poverty. This is further confirmed by the 2009–10 Round of NSSO whereby MPCE figures reveal that Muslim poverty peaks in the urban area compared to the rural ones (Table 11.18). In urban areas, nearly 90 per cent of the Muslims

appear in the poorest two expenditure brackets. Nevertheless, both in the towns and the villages, Muslims fill the rank of the poorest among all SRCs.

Ownership of landholdings too seems to be meagre among Muslims. Table 11.19 shows that among Muslims possessing land, a majority of them (38 per cent) are marginal owners with their farm size not exceeding 0.01 hectares. A quarter of the Muslims could be termed as middle farmers with their landholdings between 0.2 and 1 hectare. In the category of owners of the largest farm sizes that is above 2 hectares, Muslims are rarely to be found. In this they were worse off than the SCs. The disparity is stark when compared with Hindu high castes that have the largest presence among big land-owners with ownership of more than 2 hectares.

Educational attainment

In general, Uttar Pradesh performs poorly in educational attainment. This is established by the disparity that exists between the literacy rate of the state (56.26 per cent) and the national average (64.8 per cent). The state also retains a huge gender gap in literacy of 30 per cent points, which compares unfavourably with the gap at the national

Table 11.16   Household Main Source of Income, Rural, Uttar Pradesh

Social Group	Self-employed in Non-agriculture	Agricultural Labour	Other Labour	Self-employed in Agriculture	Others
ST/SC	14.1	17.4	32.8	26.6	9.1
OBC	15.8	9.0	12.7	55.1	7.4
Hindu high caste	10.8	3.3	5.6	65.6	14.7
Muslim OBC	29.8	15.9	15.8	24.4	14.1
Muslim upper caste	21.6	12.6	22.8	31.3	11.7
All Muslims	27.2	15.8	17.7	26.2	13.2
Total	16.0	11.3	18.1	44.7	9.8

Source: NSSO 2009–10.

Table 11.17   Household Main Source of Income, Urban, Uttar Pradesh

Social Group	Self-employed	Regular Wage-/Salary-earning	Casual Labour	Others
ST/SC	34.3	30.1	24.9	10.8
OBC	47.3	27.7	17.5	7.6
Hindu high caste	36.4	40.3	1.5	21.9
Muslim OBC	59.5	15.0	18.7	6.8
Muslim upper caste	50.0	22.7	11.9	15.4
All Muslims	55.1	18.6	16.1	10.2
Total	43.5	30.2	12.7	13.6

Source: NSSO 2009–10.

Table 11.18   Distribution of Persons by MPCE Quintiles, Uttar Pradesh

SRC	1		2		3		4		5	
	Rural	Urban	Rural	Urban	Rural	Urban	Rural	Urban	Rural	Urban
ST/SC	34.9	55.2	30.0	24.7	19.2	7.3	10.0	7.2	5.9	5.5
OBC	26.4	56.4	27.2	17.5	21.9	14.8	16.5	8.4	8.0	3.0
Hindu high caste	10.3	15.5	19.4	18.1	28.9	25.5	21.7	19.0	19.8	21.9
Muslim OBC	29.3	73.9	31.2	19.2	22.1	4.3	10.7	2.3	6.7	0.4
Muslim upper caste	28.4	50.3	27.0	31.9	21.8	11.3	14.7	3.6	8.1	3.0
All Muslims	28.9	65.0	30.2	24.0	21.7	6.9	12.1	2.8	7.1	1.4
Total	26.6	46.3	27.1	20.4	22.2	14.9	14.9	9.9	9.1	8.5

Source: NSSO 2009–10.

Table 11.19   Landholdings by SRC, Uttar Pradesh (in hectares)

Social Group	0 to 0.01	0.011 to 0.025	0.026 to 0.2	0.201 to 0.999	1 to 1.999	2 to Max
ST/SC	28.3	9.8	23.9	32.0	4.5	1.6
OBC	16.7	6.5	14.2	41.5	14.5	6.6
Hindu high caste	10.1	6.5	6.9	37.2	20.2	19.1
Muslim OBC	41.2	9.4	19.6	24.6	4.0	1.2
Muslim upper caste	32.0	14.5	16.9	26.0	4.9	5.7
All Muslims	38.2	10.8	18.9	25.3	4.2	2.6
Total	21.8	8.0	16.4	36.0	11.2	6.6

Source: NSSO 2009–10.

level (21 per cent points). The literacy figures show a further climb down when it comes to Muslims. Of all the religious communities in the state, Muslim literacy at 47.8 per cent is at the bottom. A gender gap of nearly 20 per cent points between males (57.3 per cent) and females (37.4 per cent) further compounds the problem (Table 11.20).

Table 11.20   Literacy Rate by Gender and Religion, Uttar Pradesh

Religion	Total	Male	Female	Gender Gap
Uttar Pradesh	56.3	68.8	42.2	26.6
Hindus	57.9	71.2	43.1	28.2
Muslims	47.8	57.3	37.4	19.9
Christians	72.9	78.1	67.4	10.8
Sikhs	71.9	72.2	52.6	19.6
Buddhists	56.2	70.3	40.3	30.1
Jains	93.2	95.9	90.3	5.6

Source: Census 2001, Registrar General and Census Commissioner, GoI.

In the 2007–8 NSSO survey, illiteracy among Muslim men was found to be excessively high (43.1 per cent), higher than all other SRCs such as the SCs/STs (39.1 per cent) and OBCs (30.46 per cent). The survey revealed that in Uttar Pradesh, very few Muslim men had attained education till higher secondary (7.3 per cent) and beyond (2.2 per cent). At the same level, all other SRCs had scored over Muslims. The scenario was worse when it came to women, a large majority of whom were reportedly illiterate (58.6 per cent). Like their male counterparts, their proportion of illiteracy was highest amongst all SRCs be it SCs/STs (59.3 per cent), OBCs (52.2 per cent), or Hindu high castes (29.9 per cent) (Table 11.21).

The gravity of the situation is also to be understood by the fact that a very large number of Muslim children in the school-going age (6–14 years) were found to be out of school. Here again, the pattern appeared universal across residence and gender. Curiously, the percentage of out of school children—both male and female—was higher in urban areas (31.5 per cent for males and 38.8 per cent for females) than in rural areas (23.6 per cent for males and

Table 11.21   Distribution by Educational Level, Uttar Pradesh

Educational Level	ST/SC		OBC		Hindu High Castes		Muslim OBC		Muslim Upper Castes		All Muslims		Total	
	Male	Female	Male	Female	Male	Female	Male	Female	Male	Female	Male	Female	Male	Female
Not literate	39.1	59.3	30.4	52.2	16.6	29.9	43.8	61.1	39.9	52.7	43.1	58.6	32.5	51.6
Below primary	22.9	17.9	22.4	19.0	18.1	15.1	23.5	19.6	26.5	20.5	24.2	19.8	22.2	18.3
Primary	14.9	11.3	14.5	12.3	12.9	14.6	15.5	8.4	12.8	11.0	14.5	9.3	14.4	11.9
Upper primary/ middle	12.5	6.7	15.6	8.2	15.9	13.5	8.9	5.4	8.6	5.9	8.8	5.5	13.7	8.2
Secondary/higher secondary	8.4	4.1	13.5	7.0	22.6	17.3	6.8	4.8	8.6	7.2	7.3	5.5	12.6	7.6
More than higher secondary	2.1	0.7	3.6	1.4	13.9	9.6	1.6	0.7	3.6	2.7	2.2	1.3	4.7	2.5

Source: NSSO 2007–8.

34.2 per cent for females) (Table 11.22). This could be owing to abject conditions of poverty in which a majority of the urban Muslims in Uttar Pradesh live.

Table 11.22   Percentage of Children between 6 and 14 Years Not Attending School, Uttar Pradesh

SRC	Rural Male	Rural Female	Urban Male	Urban Female
ST	15.3	8.0	0.0	21.7
SC	15.3	19.3	24.6	27.1
OBC	10.9	11.7	11.2	16.3
Non-Muslim high caste	5.5	7.4	4.5	4.0
All Muslims	23.6	34.2	31.5	38.8
Total	13.4	17.0	18.8	24.0

Source: NSSO 2007–8.

MUSLIMS IN ASSAM

In Assam, Muslims constitute nearly one-third or 31 per cent of the total population of the state. Most of Assam's population resides in the valleys between the two major river systems—the Barak and the Brahmaputra. The former on the southern part of the state along the border with Bangladesh has three districts while the bulk of the population lives in the 24 districts lying in the latter. Less densely populated are the two hill districts of Karbi-Anglong and North Cachar Hills, set in the low-lying hills that separate the two valleys. The Muslim population varies considerably between an extreme high concentration (above state average of 31 per cent) to an extremely low turnout (below 10 per cent). The remaining could be categorized as medium concentration, with the Muslim population ranging roughly between 10

and 30 per cent. Ten districts of the state report a very high concentration of Muslims of which six are Muslim-majority.

Both the Barak and Brahmaputra valleys hold substantial population of Muslims; however, significant cultural difference exists among Muslims of Assam. The Muslims of the Brahmaputra valley are socially divided into two groups—indigenous Muslims and immigrant Muslims with the former having a privileged position among the Assamese. They are mostly engaged in trade or other non-cultivating professions. In contrast, the immigrant Muslims are primarily an agricultural group, are bereft of modern education, and are relegated to a low status in Assamese society (Dev and Lahiri 1985: 1). Immigrant Muslims, too, have adopted the Assamese language and culture and are referred to as '*na assamese*' (new Assamese).

Unlike other parts of the country, an overwhelming percentage of the Muslim population (93 per cent) stays in the villages and is dependent on agriculture for living. In the villages, however, apart from being cultivators, a fairly large proportion of Muslims constitute agriculture labour (21.3 per cent) in which they far outnumber the state's average (13.2 per cent). Their literacy rate, in 2001 (48.4 per cent), was a good 15 per cent points below the state's average (63.3 per cent). This reflected in their low work participation (29.1 per cent) as well. Most appalling was the condition of Muslim women in Assam of whom only 9.7 per cent in the working age had been able to join the workforce. In the sex ratio, however, Muslims presented better results—938 compared to the average of 935—which showed signs of further improvement in the 0–6 age group (971 for Muslims compared to the average of 965 for all).[8]

Income, employment, and poverty level

According to the Planning Commission estimates of 2009–10, 53.6 per cent of Muslims in rural Assam live under conditions of acute poverty. Thus, in the state's 39.9 per cent poor population, the Muslims have a major slice. More than 50 per cent of the Muslims in the rural areas fall in the poorest two quintiles (54.9 per cent) of MPCE. The condition of urban Muslims is equally pitiable with 49.3 per cent counting among the poorest. Among social groups, Muslims are the worse off in rural areas and are listed next only to the SCs in urban areas (see Table 11.23).

Landownership among Muslims remains limited. Most of the Muslim cultivators are middle farmers with farm holdings ranging between 0.2 to 2 hectares of agricultural land (50.2 per cent). Muslims have the largest share (12.3 per cent) of marginal farmers (0 to 0.025 hectares). In relation to the size of land that they hold, except for SCs, all other social groups including the OBCs, STs, and Hindu high castes have an edge over them (Table 11.24).

Educational level

The literacy rate, as mentioned above, falls far behind the average. Moreover, the huge gender gap (gap of 16 per cent points) calls for appropriate and urgent intervention. The Muslim lag in education is further analysed by comprehending the comparative level of education that different communities have been able to attain. Educational levels among Muslims, across gender, tends to fall sharply beyond the primary level. In the NSSO figures for levels of education, a drop of nearly 10 per cent points is seen after the primary level. Such a sharp decline beyond the primary level is not witnessed in case of any other SRC be it the SCs, STs, OBCs, or Hindu high castes (Table 11.25).

A high level of illiteracy prevails among Muslims females (43 per cent), which is much above the state average (32.2 per cent). Moreover, Muslims seem to have kept away from higher education. The proportion of their population having achieved higher secondary level or beyond was found to be poorer than that among the SC/STs and OBCs of the state. Poor economic status as well as lesser probability of securing employment could be the possible reasons dissuading Muslims from taking to higher education. Educational deprivation of Muslims of Assam was noted in the Sachar Committee Report (SCR) as well. Among all SRCs, Muslims (7–16 years) reported the least years of schooling. Muslim backwardness in education has continued over the years. More

Table 11.23   Distribution of Persons by MPCE Quintiles, Assam

SRC	1		2		3		4		5	
	Rural	Urban	Rural	Urban	Rural	Urban	Rural	Urban	Rural	Urban
ST	21.6	16.5	24.4	26.9	15.5	17.0	24.9	11.4	13.6	28.2
SC	24.6	42.5	22.7	23.3	21.7	18.3	18.3	14.3	12.7	1.6
OBC	16.5	28.6	19.2	21.0	23.4	19.7	25.0	21.2	15.8	9.5
Hindu high caste	14.8	22.0	20.5	18.8	28.2	32.0	20.8	16.8	15.6	10.5
Muslims	25.8	42.0	29.1	7.3	19.7	18.9	17.4	11.6	8.0	20.2
Assam	21.1	28.8	23.9	18.6	21.5	24.6	21.2	15.7	12.5	12.3

Source: NSSO 2009–10.

Table 11.24   Landholdings by Size of Land and SRCs, Assam

SRC	0 to 0.01	0.011 to 0.025	0.026 to 0.2	0.201 to 0.999	1 to 1.999	2 to Max
ST	0.7	4.1	16.8	30.8	23.2	24.5
SC	4.1	6.5	29.9	36.3	13.1	10.1
OBC	5.5	4.0	19.6	29.6	27.2	14.0
Hindu high caste	2.4	2.1	27.8	44.8	12.1	10.8
Muslims	6.4	5.9	17.0	38.3	21.9	10.6
Assam	4.6	4.7	20.6	35.4	21.4	13.4

Source: NSSO 2009–10.

Table 11.25 Distribution by Educational Level, Assam

Educational Level	ST/SC		OBC		Hindu High Castes		All Muslims		Total	
	Male	Female	Male	Female	Male	Female	Male	Female	Male	Female
Not literate	21.1	35.2	16.2	25.8	14.0	21.0	32.0	43.0	21.8	32.2
Below primary	26.4	22.9	18.9	16.7	18.7	20.9	29.9	24.9	24.0	21.4
Primary	20.0	20.2	20.8	25.9	17.3	19.7	17.8	18.1	19.0	21.0
Upper primary/middle	17.0	12.4	21.0	17.5	18.0	15.2	11.3	8.1	16.5	13.1
Secondary/higher secondary	14.1	8.4	19.9	13.0	23.7	20.2	8.1	5.5	15.7	11.1
More than higher secondary	1.4	0.9	3.2	1.2	8.3	3.1	1.0	0.4	3.1	1.3

Source: NSSO 2007–8.

recently, a survey of out-of-school children (2010) found Muslims returning the highest percentage of children in the age group of 6–13 (6.19 per cent) who had either never attended school or were not enrolled at the time of the survey (PMHLC 2006: Appendix Table 4.2).

MUSLIMS IN KERALA

Muslims in Kerala constitute one-fourth of the state's population (24.7 per cent by Census 2001). Of the three broad geographical regions—Malabar, Kochi, and Travancore—Muslims are largely concentrated in the Malabar belt, the region along the northern coast of Kerala. Six of the 14 administrative districts of Kerala, fall in the Malabar region, and in each of these districts the Muslim share crosses the state average. However, Muslims constitute a majority only in Malappuram (68.53 per cent). Christians who constitute 19 per cent of the state's population are more concentrated in the Kochi and Travancore areas, while Hindus of Kerala are more evenly distributed across the state.

Contrary to the demographic trend in most parts of the country, the extent of urbanization among the Muslims of Kerala is weak. However, it is much in keeping with the general inclination of the state's population. Thus, while 25.4 per cent of the Kerala Muslims inhabit the urban areas, it is consistent with the average urbanization of the state (26 per cent). Unlike popular belief, lower urbanization does not affect the social development of Kerala's populations. This also holds true for the Muslims of the state. Their literacy rate at 89.45 per cent is only a shade behind the state's average of 90.9 per cent. But when compared with the national average (64.8 per cent) and average literacy of India's Muslims (59.1 per cent), the Kerala Muslims are far ahead. Their female literacy at 85.5 per cent too suggests that the social development of Kerala Muslims do not display much gender bias. This

is reflected in the sex ratio (1,082) too, which despite lagging behind the state's average (1058) is far ahead of the national average (941). Although the decadal (1991–2001) growth rate of the population among Muslims is higher (15.8 per cent) when compared with the state's average growth rate (9.4 per cent), the rate of growth of Muslims is fast declining.

Despite high male and female literacy, Muslims of Kerala perform poorly in work participation (23.2 per cent) when compared to the state average of 32.3 per cent. A pull-down factor is extreme low participation of Muslim women (5.9 per cent), although the male participation falls behind considerably (42 per cent) compared to the average WPR of 50.2 per cent. The 2001 Census found a section of the Muslim workforce employed as agricultural labour (11.8 per cent). Majority of them were neither cultivators nor household industrial workers, rather they filled the category of other works (79.5 per cent), which could suggest a high degree of self-employment.[9]

Income, employment, and poverty levels

Table 11.26 shows a disproportionately high level of self-employment among Muslims in general (46.9 per cent). This high propensity of self-employment is suggestive of the fact that other sectors with secured earnings remain out of reach for them. Therefore, among regular salaried employees, the proportion of Muslims is found to be less than even the SCs/STs. While nearly 28 per cent of the non-Muslim OBC workers find employment in salaried jobs, only 17 per cent of the Muslim OBCs have been able to enter the same. Notably, there is also a very high degree of casualization among Muslim workers.

Interestingly, for the Muslims of Kerala, insecure employment has not necessarily manifested in lower earnings. In terms of household MPCE, Muslim situation is

Table 11.26 Employment Status by Category of Workers, Kerala

SRC	Self-employed			Regular Workers			Casual Workers		
	All	Male	Female	All	Male	Female	All	Male	Female
ST/SC	16.1	14.9	18.6	19.4	16.0	25.9	64.5	69.1	55.5
OBC	36.6	36.1	37.8	22.9	18.5	33.0	40.5	45.4	29.3
Upper caste non-Muslims	47.6	45.3	52.3	28.5	27.9	29.9	23.9	26.8	17.8
Muslim OBC	46.7	46.8	46.1	17.4	17.2	19.0	35.9	36.1	34.9
Muslim upper caste	68.9	84.2	52.8	13.9	12.8	15.1	17.2	3.0	32.1
All Muslims	46.9	46.9	46.5	17.4	17.1	19.0	35.7	36.0	34.5
Total	38.4	37.7	39.9	23.2	20.5	29.6	38.5	41.8	30.5

Source: NSSO 2009–10.

similar to many other SRCs. Compared to urban areas, Muslim households appear to be more prosperous in the rural areas where most of the Kerala Muslims live. Nearly 11 per cent of the state's rural households fall in the poorest two quintiles and the corresponding figure for Muslims is almost the same. In the urban areas of Kerala, of course, Muslim are more impoverished with nearly 38 per cent of their households populating the poorest two quintiles (Table 11.27).

Nearly 58 per cent of the landed Muslims fall in the category of middle peasantry. Within Muslims, Muslim OBCs appear to be more endowed with land than the Muslim upper castes. Muslim presence among large land-holders remains minimal (Table 11.28).

In accordance with their poor landownership, a very high percentage of Muslim workers are self-employed in non-agricultural activities. Among Muslims, it is the OBCs who are more inclined towards self-employment

Table 11.27 Distribution of Households by MPCE Quintiles, Kerala

SRC	1		2		3		4		5	
	Rural	Urban	Rural	Urban	Rural	Urban	Rural	Urban	Rural	Urban
ST/SC	10.7	34.2	16.5	14.0	23.5	19.6	18.8	20.6	30.6	11.6
OBC	4.5	15.5	7.1	21.1	12.2	27.5	20.2	18.4	55.9	17.6
Non-Muslim high caste	1.4	5.0	2.6	10.6	6.2	20.4	16.6	22.2	73.2	41.8
Muslim OBC	3.4	17.0	8.0	21.5	13.3	22.3	24.3	18.6	51.0	20.6
Muslim upper caste	0.0	0.0	3.6	12.9	1.2	0.0	49.3	74.3	45.9	12.8
All Muslims	3.4	16.9	8.0	21.4	13.1	22.0	24.6	19.1	50.9	20.5
Total	4.1	14.2	7.2	17.4	12.1	23.7	19.9	19.9	56.8	24.9

Source: NSSO 2009–10.

Table 11.28 Rural Landholding, Kerala (in hectares)

SRC	0 to 0.01	0.011 to 0.025	0.026 to 0.2	0.201 to 0.999	1 to 1.999	2 to Max
ST/SC	15.1	35.6	37.0	7.4	2.3	2.7
OBC	6.5	19.4	56.3	14.7	2.3	0.8
Non-Muslim upper caste	3.9	8.6	48.5	28.4	8.1	2.6
Muslim OBC	13.4	16.5	58.5	10.4	0.4	0.8
Muslim upper caste	37.7	0.0	39.0	21.5	1.8	0.0
All Muslims	13.9	16.5	58.0	10.5	0.4	0.7
Total	8.4	17.5	51.8	17.1	3.7	1.6

Source: NSSO 2009–10.

than Muslim upper castes. The inequities are evident as upper-caste non-Muslims count among the biggest land-owners as well as among those who are self-employed in agriculture (owner-cultivators). Comparatively, the Muslim situation is better than the SC/STs and worse than the non-Muslim OBCs of the state (Table 11.29).

Educational attainment

Muslims of Kerala are evenly placed with all other religious communities in consistently maintaining a high literacy figure (89.4 per cent). However, when it comes to educational attainments, Muslims figure poorly. The NSSO survey found educational level among Muslims peaking at upper primary level. Muslims display little interest in higher levels of education such as secondary and higher secondary. A very small proportion of the surveyed population had attained education beyond higher secondary level such as graduation or postgraduation. In fact Muslims fared worse than SC/STs in seeking higher education (Table 11.30).

High literacy, therefore, has not ensured a high retention rate. The data for the current educational status of the surveyed population shows a high degree of dropouts. The dropout rate is highest among the SCs/STs (46 per cent), followed by OBCs and Muslims. Among Muslims, the dropout rate is much higher for OBCs (41.5 per cent) than the Muslim upper castes (32 per cent).

Among those who dropped out (in the age group of 6–14 years), only a minuscule percentage of Kerala Muslims (1.5 per cent) had never attended school. Most of them had attained education at least till primary level. Therefore, Muslims, along with other communities, do have an equal access to schooling and are able to attain at least primary level of education. The reasons for dropping out, therefore, needs to be further probed (Table 11.31).

* * *

Despite the inherent diversity, Muslims of India, as per our study, do reflect commonality in terms of certain

Table 11.29   Rural Household Type, Kerala

SRC	Self-employed in Non-agriculture	Agricultural Labour	Other Labour	Self-employed in Agriculture	Others
ST/SC	9.9	34.8	37.5	1.3	16.6
OBC	18.8	12.4	36.3	12.6	20.0
Non-Muslim high castes	15.7	11.6	18.3	25.5	28.9
Muslim OBC	25.6	7.3	27.6	8.7	30.8
Muslim upper castes	12.7	0.0	28.6	10.6	48.2
All Muslims	25.3	7.2	27.6	8.7	31.2
Total	18.0	14.1	29.2	14.2	24.6

Source: NSSO 2009–10.

Table 11.30   Distribution by Educational Level, Kerala

Educational Level	ST/SC		OBC		Other Non-Muslims		Muslim OBC		Other Muslims		All Muslims		Total	
	Male	Female	Male	Female	Male	Female	Male	Female	Male	Female	Male	Female	Male	Female
Not literate	15.1	22.8	11.5	14.3	9.2	10.2	15.3	16.7	15.9	14.3	15.3	16.6	12.2	14.8
Below primary	15.3	15.7	14.8	15.4	12.6	13.2	18.5	17.4	22.6	12.3	18.5	17.2	15.2	15.3
Primary	20.5	15.1	19.7	17.8	15.6	16.2	22.5	18.2	33.1	46.9	22.6	18.8	19.4	17.3
Upper primary/ middle	30.0	22.8	25.8	23.0	21.4	20.8	23.3	26.7	9.1	10.0	23.2	26.4	24.5	23.2
Secondary/higher secondary	13.9	18.8	18.3	19.4	25.8	24.0	16.4	16.8	8.5	7.6	16.3	16.6	19.3	19.9
Above higher secondary	5.3	4.8	9.9	10.1	15.5	15.6	4.0	4.2	10.9	9.0	4.1	4.4	9.5	9.6

Source: NSSO 2007–8.

Table 11.31 Percentage of Children between 6 and 14 Years Not Attending School, Kerala

SRC	Never Attended	Dropped Out	Currently Attending Non-formal (including pre-primary)	Primary and Above
ST/SC	1.6	46.0	1.0	51.4
OBC	1.4	41.5	2.1	55.0
Non-Muslim high caste	1.0	32.0	1.7	65.3
Muslim OBC	1.5	41.5	1.8	55.1
Muslim upper caste	0.0	32.0	0.0	68.0
All Muslims	1.5	41.2	1.8	55.6
Total	1.4	39.8	1.8	57.1

Source: NSSO 2007–8.

socio-economic indicators. Thus, across India, and in almost all the four focus states, Muslims lag behind most other SRCs in terms of educational attainment. Even in states such as Kerala where Muslim literacy is comparatively high, their school retention rate remains low. Again, in almost all the states under study, Muslims have low work participation, the pull-down factor being very low participation of Muslim women in the workforce. This also manifests in their income and expenditure as Muslims, with Kerala being the exception, count amongst the poorest in the other three states. Predominantly, the all-India pattern that emerges is of a community steeped in poverty, having low educational attainment, bereft of land and other immoveable assets, and largely dependent on self-employment in low-income activities.

NOTES

1. As per Census 2001, Registrar General and Census Commissioner, GoI.
2. Ibid.
3. As per Census 2001, Registrar General and Census Commissioner, GoI.
4. 'The First Report on Religion Data', Census 2001, Registrar General and Census Commissioner, GoI, p. 1.
5. As per Census 2001, Registrar General and Census Commissioner, GoI.
6. Ibid.
7. 'The First Report on Religion Data', Census 2001, Registrar General and Census Commissioner, GoI, p. xlix.
8. Ibid.
9. Ibid.

REFERENCES

ADRI (Asian Development Research Institute). 2004. *Socio-economic and Educational Status of Muslims in Bihar*. Patna: ADRI and Bihar State Minority Commission.

Dev, Bimal J. and Dilip Lahiri. 1985. *Assam Muslims: Politics and Cohesion*. New Delhi: Mittal Publications.

PMHLC (Prime Minister's High Level Committee). 2006. 'Prime Minister's High Level Committee on Social, Educational and Economic Status of the Muslim Community of India: A Report', PMHLC (Sachar Committee). New Delhi: Cabinet Secretariat, GoI.

Shariff, Abusaleh. 2011. 'Post-Sachar Education and Employment: Uttar Pradesh, Is There a Reason to Cheer?' Paper presented at the Institute of Objective Studies, New Delhi, 1 October.

12

Education and Exclusion of Muslims

MOHAMMAD SANJEER ALAM

Education has long been seen as a creator of life chances. It has also been recognized as a great equalizer or leveller. There is wider consensus in both theoretical and empirical literature that widespread education in society leads to removal of iniquities in asset ownership, capabilities, and opportunities, a condition that not only enables individuals to acquire their rightful place in society but also promotes social cohesion and sustainability.[1] Thus, given the fact that the benefits of education accrue to both individuals and the wider society they are part of, social equity in education has significant bearings on social development.

During the past few decades, India has made rapid strides in expanding educational opportunities, leading to remarkable democratization of the education system. For instance, the number of primary schools during the period between 1951–2 and 2004–5 has increased by 3.7 times. The number of upper primary and secondary/higher secondary schools has increased by more than 20 times, each during the same period. The number of colleges for general and professional education has increased manifold, 28 and 15 times, respectively. Similarly, during the period between 1950–1 and 2004–5, overall enrolment at primary and upper primary stages has seen a 7 and 17 time increase, respectively. The growth in enrolment has been more spectacular at secondary and senior secondary levels (about 25 times since 1951–2). Overall, enrolment in higher education has increased from 1.7 million in 1950–1 to 10.48 million in 2004–5 at an average annual growth rate of 10.04 per cent.[2] To be brief, the current cohort of school-age children today—irrespective of social origin, economic circumstances, and geographic locations—enjoys far greater chances of accessing the

education system, attending schools or colleges and completing a given stage of education than their grandparents and parents did.

However, the overall rosy picture quite often tends to conceal more than what it reveals, especially in a country which is geographically as vast and socially and culturally as diverse as India. It is because social disparities in education may increase rather than decrease even during the period of rapid expansion of educational opportunities, for it is the advantaged/privileged section that first appropriates the benefits of enhanced educational opportunities. In other words, educational disparities in the given level of education continue to persist until almost all children of the privileged/dominant sections of society are accommodated in that level of education. This has led to the hypothesis of 'maximally maintained inequality' (Raftery and Hout 1993). In India, as a matter of fact, access to educational opportunities even at lower stages continues to remain unequal along several axes of regional and social stratifications despite the remarkable expansion of educational opportunities. It is now well documented that religion is one of the most pervasive axes of educational disparities, and that the Muslim community of India, the largest religious minority group, has fallen way behind other socio-religious communities (SRCs) (Alam 2012; Hasan and Menon 2004; Hussain 2005; SCR 2006; Shariff and Razzack 2006).

This chapter seeks to assess how Muslims are positioned in the education system vis-à-vis others and if and how far they have been benefiting from rapidly expanding educational opportunities in the country. The chapter is structured as follows. The first section spells out, although briefly, various processes that seem to have shaped and reshaped the overall socio-economic status of Muslims. The next section presents an overview of literacy and educational development among Muslims using recent data sources at the national level. The third section attempts to contextualize educational access and attainment among Muslims. This is followed by an analytical discussion of the factors that underlie educational disadvantages among Muslims vis-à-vis others. The last section concludes the discussion.

The Wider Context

India is a multi-religious country and, in fact, is home to almost all major religions of the world, though in varying proportions. The followers of Islam, that is, Muslims, have constituted an important element of the Indian social fabric for over a millennium. Islam, a non-Indic religion, entered India through different routes and at various points in time. However, in course of time, a large number of indigenous people, mostly belonging to lower castes and classes, also embraced Islam (Ahmad 1978; Ahmad 1999; Ahmad and Chakravarti 1981). As a result of conversion, on the one hand, and getting influenced by acculturation processes in the given socio-spatial context due to deeper interaction with the wider society, on the other, Muslims developed their cultural traits expressed in terms of language, customs, dresses, dietary habits, caste-like or occupation-based groupings, and so on under a distinct regional mould (Ahmad 1999). In brief, the 'Muslim social' is even more complex and complicated than other communities.

In undivided India, Muslims as a collective accounted for slightly less than a quarter of the total population.[3] A slightly higher proportion of them compared to the general population lived in urban centres, although there were pronounced regional variations. For example, about 1.9 and 3.5 per cent of Muslims in Assam and Bengal, respectively, lived in urban areas as opposed to 42 and 27 per cent in Central Province and Berar and United Province, respectively.[4] In general, Muslims had the same source of livelihood as the general population. An overwhelming majority of them was engaged in agriculture, though a good number of them were also artisans. At the time of Partition in 1947, the Muslim community, as various colonial official reports indicate, was by and large represented in the sphere of education and in public employment in proportion to its share in total population. The Partition of the country, however, seriously altered the social and economic structures of the Muslim community as it denuded the base of social strata comprising middle and upper classes (Hasan 1997; Imam 1975).

In 2001, Muslims with a population of 138 million accounted for about 13.4 per cent of the total population in the country.[5] Unlike other minority communities, Muslims are unevenly distributed across the length and breadth of the country. At the national level, the proportion of Muslims varies from 66.9 per cent in Jammu and Kashmir and 30.9 per cent in Assam to 5.5 per cent in Tamil Nadu. Of the total Muslim population in the country, over half (53 per cent) lives in just four states, namely, Assam, Bihar, Uttar Pradesh, and West Bengal. The four southern states—Andhra Pradesh, Karnataka, Kerala, and Tamil Nadu—together account for one-sixth of the total Muslim population in the country. At the sub-national level, while there is hardly a district that does not have Muslim population, there are 20 districts (out of 594 districts in 2001) across states where the Muslims form the majority community. There are another 38 districts that have substantial Muslim population, accounting for over a quarter of total population but below 50 per cent. About 35.7 per cent of the Muslims, as against 27.8 per cent of the overall population, lives in towns and cities of different sizes, though there are considerable variations across states. For example, while fewer Muslims live in urban areas in Assam (6.4 per cent), they are predominantly urban in Tamil Nadu (72.8 per cent), Maharashtra (70.0 per cent), and Madhya Pradesh (63.5 per cent).

As the Muslim community consists of groups drawn from different social origin and occupational practices, they are represented in almost all kinds of occupations and economic situations with pronounced regional variations. As far as the current situation is concerned, the Muslim community as a whole stands economically disadvantaged relative to other communities—predominantly Hindus (SCR 2006; also see Table 12.1). Overall, the prevalence of poverty among Muslims is considerably high as compared to the general population. Labour force participation rates among them are much lower than the national average. While the proportion of main workers among Muslims is lower and that of non-workers is higher, indicating a higher unemployment rate among them, further questions may need to be asked about the extent of the informal economic sector in relation to the Muslims. Statistics indicate that the vast majority of workers among the Muslims are concentrated in the lower rungs of economic opportunities, although they are represented across occupations. Disproportionately large proportions among them are self-employed and/ or engaged in home-based enterprises, including small trades, petty business, and street vending. As employees, much larger proportions of Muslims than others are casual workers, indicating their relatively lower access to and participation in well-paying or regular salaried jobs (Table 12.1).[6] What is, however, disturbing is the fact that while there has been substantial progress in the sum total of the socio-economic conditions of people in the country in recent decades, the socio-economic conditions of Muslims have worsened (Shariff and Razzack 2006).

EDUCATIONAL ATTAINMENT: AN OVERVIEW

This section provides an overview of the educational status of Muslims vis-à-vis other SRCs using the most recent available data sources.[7] As Muslims like any other communities are internally differentiated and reflect diversity in accessing socio-economic and educational opportunities, an attempt is made here to analyse their educational status vis-à-vis the referent group with references to such internal differentiations. Keeping this in view, five social categories are identified for the analysis:

1. Muslim OBC (Muslims reported to be as Other Backward Classes)
2. Muslim Other (Muslims other than those reported as OBCs

3. Hindu SC (Hindu Scheduled Castes)
4. Hindu OBC (Hindus reported to be as Other Backward Classes)
5. Hindu Other (Hindus other than Scheduled Castes/ Scheduled Tribes and Other Backward Classes)

LITERACY

Although defined as one's ability to read, write, and understand a simple statement in any language, literacy is seen as a crucial indicator of educational development for it is highly correlated with other indicators of education. Generally, higher the literacy rate of a group, greater is its participation in the educational opportunities.

Of the four major religious groups—Hindus, Muslims, Christians, and Sikhs—Christians with a literacy rate of 80.3 per cent is the most literate community, followed by Sikhs (69.4 per cent) and Hindus (65.1 per cent). The overall literacy rate of Muslims (59.1 per cent) is not only lower than the national average, but is the lowest of all religious groups. It is true of both males and females. However, the relative gap between Muslim and Hindu males is much higher than between females of the two religious groups (Table 12.2).

What has been the trend over time? Is the trend one of convergence? Or are Muslims falling further behind

Table 12.1   Economic and Employment Status of Muslims

Parameters	Year	All	Hindu	Muslim	Muslim–Hindu Ratio
% of workers	2001*				
Main workers		48.1	49.1	42.2	.86
Marginal workers		13.0	13.5	10.4	.77
Non-workers		38.9	37.5	47.5	1.27
% of regular salaried	2004–5**				
Government sector		34.2	35.3	23.7	.67
Public/private Ltd.		13.1	13.9	6.5	.47
Enterprise types	2004–5***				
Informal sector (rural)		88.5	87.7	94.2	1.07
Informal sector (urban)		79.1	76.9	92.1	1.19
Formal sector (rural)		11.5	12.3	5.8	.47
Formal sector (urban)		20.9	23.1	7.9	.34
MPCE[1] (current prices)	2004–5**				
MPCE (urban)		1105	1139	804	.70
MPCE (rural)		579	568	553	.97
Incidence of poverty	2004–5**				
Poverty ratio (urban)		29	27	44	1.63
Poverty ratio (rural)		28	28	33	1.78

Sources: * Census of India 2001, Religion Table.
    ** SCR 2006.
    *** *National Sample Survey 2004–5.*
Note: [1]MPCE refers to monthly per capita expenditure.

Table 12.2   Literacy Rates by Religious Groups, 2001

Gender	All Religions	Hindus	Muslims	Christians	Sikhs	Hindu–Muslim Disparity Index*
All	64.8	65.8	59.1	80.3	69.4	0.05
Male	75.3	76.2	67.6	84.4	75.2	0.06
Female	53.7	53.2	50.1	76.2	63.1	0.03

Source: Census of India 2001.

Notes: Literacy rate calculated for population aged 7 years and above.

  * Disparity index measures the extent of disparity between two mutually exclusive groups or subsets of population. Here, disparity between groups is computed using the disparity index developed by Kundu and Rao (1985). The index is expressed as follows: DS = log (X_2/X_1) + log $(200-X_1)/ (200-X_2)$; where X_1 and X_2 represent literacy rates of the relatively disadvantaged and advantaged groups, respectively. Larger the value, greater the disparity. In the present case, the referent group is Hindus, that is, the advantaged group relative to Muslims.

the rest with rising literacy rates in the country? Table 12.3 presents literacy rates by age cohorts for different SRCs. Clearly, literacy rates for younger age cohorts are much higher than the older ones, consistent with the rising awareness of education and participation in schooling in recent decades. In overall terms, the current generation (7–14 years) is twice as likely to be literate as their parents and grandparents were. This observation holds true across SRCs. The Hindu–Muslim disparity seems to have slightly decreased in recent decades as indicated by lower disparity values for younger age cohorts.

However, a closer scrutiny suggests that much of the observed reduced Hindu–Muslim disparity in literacy rates in younger cohorts is not because of the recent upsurge in literacy rates among Muslims but owing to the slower rate of increase in the literacy rates of the Hindu Other, consequently slowing down the pace of progress for Hindus as a whole. And, the slower rate of increase in the literacy rates of the younger cohorts of Hindu Other can be explained by the fact that their literacy level has already reached a stage where there is not much scope

for any significant increase. If we leave aside the Hindu Other category, the growth of literacy among Muslims has been taking place at a much slower rate than the Hindu OBCs and SCs. As Figure 12.1 reveals, the literacy rates of Hindu OBC and Muslim Other were almost at the same level in 1940s/1950s (age cohort 50+), but the former seems to have overtaken the latter in 1960s/1970s. The gap thereafter further widened. What is even more important to note is that while in the past (the generation born in 1940s of age cohort 50+), literacy rate among the SCs was the lowest of all, the generation born in 1980s surpassed Muslim OBC, and those born in 1990s seem to have left behind even the Muslim Other (Figure 12.1). It thus implies that if current trends continue, the Muslims as a community will be the last in the queue to attain universal literacy.

ENROLMENT AND PARTICIPATION

The proportion of children on roll or actually attending educational institutions is a good measure of current participation in and utilization of educational opportunities.

Table 12.3   Literacy Rates among SRCs by Age Cohorts

Age Cohort	All SRC	Muslims			Hindus				Disparity Index	
		OBCs	Others	All Muslims	SCs	OBCs	Others	All Hindus	Hindu–Muslim	Muslim Others–Muslim OBC
7–14	86.0	74.3	80.1	79.1	84.3	87.6	94.6	87.1	0.05	0.04
15–24	80.8	71.7	76.6	75.3	75.5	80.8	93.1	81.3	0.07	0.03
25–49	62.3	50.6	56.4	54.0	50.5	60.5	82.4	62.8	0.07	0.05
50+	42.7	31.6	38.6	35.3	28.7	38.2	64.4	42.8	0.09	0.09
7+	68.1	59.2	65.1	63.1	60.5	66.8	83.0	68.3	0.04	0.05

Source: *National Family Health Survey* (Raw Data Set), 2005–6, IIPS, Mumbai.

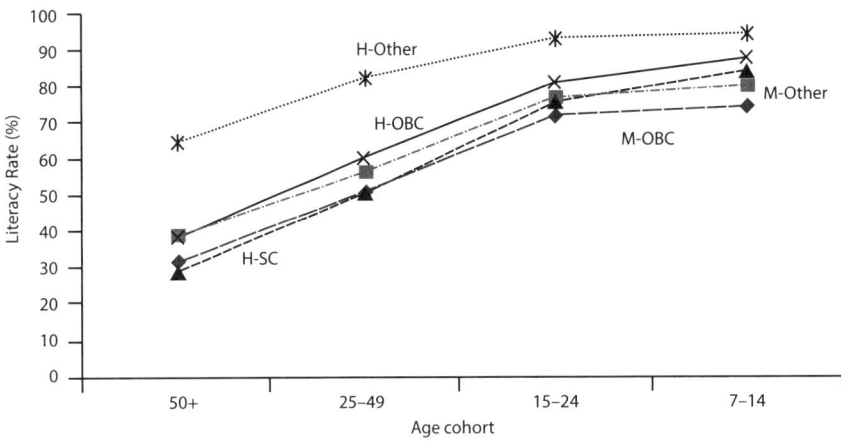

Figure 12.1   Progress in Literacy Rates across SRCs
Source: *National Family Health Survey* (Raw Data Set), 2005–6, IIPS, Mumbai.

Since enrolment is a flow variable and can be improved within a relatively short period of time (Shariff and Razzack 2006), the enrolment level of a group reflects its propensity to acquire education.

As the DISE 2009–10 statistics show, Muslim children accounted for about 13.5 per cent and 11.9 per cent of all the children enrolled at primary stage and upper primary stage, respectively, and thus consistent with the share of Muslims in total population (DISE 2011). According to NSSO (2007–8), about 46.2 per cent of Muslim children aged 5–29 were enrolled as against 52.7 and 58.3 per cent of children belonging to Hindus and Christians, respectively. Table 12.4 presents a little more detailed account of levels of participation in educational opportunities. Overall, seven out of 10 children in the age group of 6–18 attended schools during the school year 2005–6. As expected, the level of participation in schooling was higher at lower ages than at upper ages. For instance, while eight out 10 children attended schools in the age group of 6–14, the corresponding ratio for ages

15–18 was roughly 5:10. This implied a higher incidence of discontinuation or dropping out from school at the elementary level.

Remarkable disparities exist across SRCs. At one extreme are the children of Hindu–Other, of whom nine out of 10 in the age group of 6–14 attended schools, indicating that they are on the verge of attaining universal elementary education. On the other extreme stand the children of Muslim OBC who are least likely to attend school in the relevant age group, although even the children of Muslim Other are not better-off as compared to the SCs, leave alone the Hindu OBC or Hindu Other. And this holds true across age groups. What is, however, interesting to note is that while the children of Muslim OBC in general are less likely to attend school as against those of Muslim Other, the gap between them tends to close with advancing age/stage of education. In fact, the disparity between the two becomes too small at the upper age/stage to warrant attention (Table 12.4).[8]

Table 12.4   Proportion of Children Attending School/College, 2005–6

Age Cohort	All SRC	Muslims			Hindus				Disparity Index	
		OBC	Other	All	SC	OBC	Other	All	Hindu–Muslim	Muslim Others–Muslim OBC
6–10	76.5	61.6	66.6	66.1	75.4	78.2	87.1	78.4	0.08	0.04
11–14	80.0	64.6	67.9	67.2	77.0	83.3	91.5	82.3	0.09	0.03
15–18	47.4	33.4	34.1	34.1	41.4	49.6	64.3	49.6	0.17	0.01
6–18	69.8	55.2	58.4	58.0	66.6	72.2	81.9	71.8	0.10	0.03

Source: *National Family Health Survey* (Raw Data Set), 2005–6, IIPS, Mumbai.

Withholding internal differentiation, the gap between Hindus and Muslims not only persists across age groups, it gets widened with advancing age. However, the disparity between the two rises abruptly after the age of 14, as indicated by doubling of disparity value in the age group of 15–18. It suggests that while for most households the elementary level is the critical point where the calculation of potential gains, risks, and opportunity costs sets in, leading to discontinuations, nonetheless this calculus grips Muslim households far more than others. As a result they are likely to spur their children to abandon studies in favour of jobs. This calculus, however, takes a heavy toll among Muslims as compared to others.

EDUCATIONAL LEVELS

Completed educational level is one of the most crucial indicators of educational attainment. It provides information about the population which is not just literate but has actually experienced some years of formal schooling or has completed an exact grade/stage of education, no more or no less. In India though overall completed levels of education remain quite low as compared to many developing countries, the Muslims appear to be particularly disadvantaged (Table 12.5). Compared to the Hindus, while both Muslim males and females are equally likely to complete the primary/middle level, they nonetheless fall far behind their counterparts among the Hindus after the elementary stage. Hereafter, the disparity between the Hindus and Muslims rises abruptly. The lower rate of completion of upper levels of education can be explained by lower level of participation of the Muslims in the post-elementary stage, as seen earlier. It thus suggests that the obstacles to educational advancement among the Muslims lie at the school level.

However, a look at the current situation, that is, the proportion that finished college and above in the age group of 18–25, reveals an even more disappointing picture (Figure 12.2). The Muslims in general not only appear to lag way behind the Hindus as a whole, they are pushed even below the SCs, leave aside the Hindu OBC and the Hindu Other. Overall, the proportion of those who finished college among Hindus was almost double that of Muslims. Even the Muslim Other is not better-off. They are only marginally ahead of the SCs and finish far behind the rest. For instance, the Hindu OBC and Hindu Other were three and 1.5 times, respectively, as likely to finish college as Muslim Other.

WHERE DO MUSLIM CHILDREN STUDY?

One of the characteristic features of the school system in India is diversity in school types. There exists a variety of schools offering differential learning opportunities and educational outcomes. While most students still attend government schools, the proportion of school-going children attending private schools in both rural and urban areas has increased considerably in recent years (Juneja 2011; Kingdon 1996). This has been largely because of the failure of the public education system to meet the demands for schooling and the deteriorating standard of learning and teaching in the existing government schools (De et al. 2000).

As popular perceptions have it, Muslim children largely attend madrasas to acquire religious education rather than schools, the sites of modern education. However, recent empirical evidence debunks this popular perception. It is reported that about 30 and 66 per cent of all enrolled Muslim children aged 7–16 years attend private and government schools, respectively, as against 29 and 71 per cent, respectively, for others. Thus, only 4 per cent of Muslim children enrolled in the relevant age group attended madrasas (SCR 2006), and this is despite the fact that madrasas are of different kinds. First, there is a distinction between *maktab* and madrasa and many children attending the former also attend schools. Secondly, there

Table 12.5 Educational Levels by Religion, 2001

Educational Level	Muslims			Hindus			Other Religions			Hindu–Muslim Disparity Index		
	Total	Male	Female	Total	Male	Female	Total	Male	Female	Total	Male	Female
Primary/middle	27.6	32.0	22.9	27.2	31.7	22.4	29.1	31.6	26.6	0.00	0.00	0.00
Secondary/senior secondary	12.6	16.2	8.9	17.6	22.8	12.2	24.5	27.9	21.1	0.15	0.15	0.14
Graduate and above	3.6	5.0	2.0	6.9	9.3	4.4	9.4	10.7	8.0	0.29	0.27	0.34

Source: Computed from Census of India 2001, Table C9.
Note: The relevant populations for calculating educational levels are as follows: Primary/middle = population aged 14+; secondary/senior secondary = population aged 17+; graduation and above = population aged 20+.

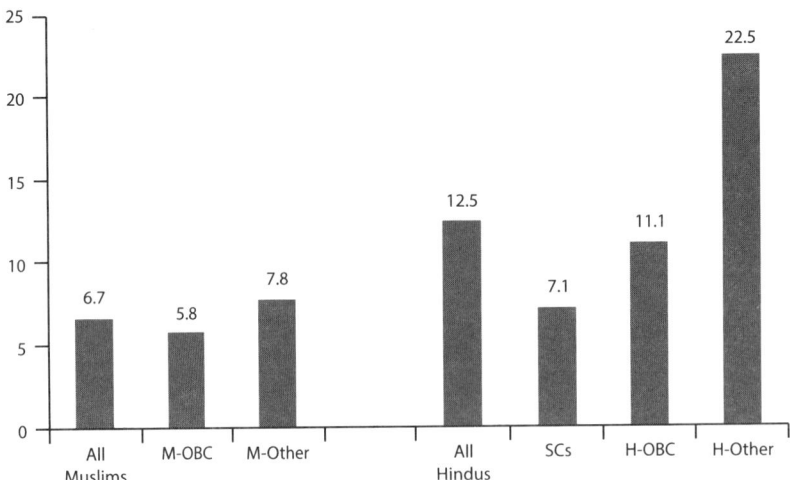

Figure 12.2   Proportion of Population (aged 18–25) Who Completed College and Above, 2005–6
Source: Computed from *National Family Health Survey*, 2005–6.

are many madrasas with public funding which do follow the general system of education. They thus bear close affinity to schools. There is yet another kind of madrasa which is unaided and private, irrespective of whether recognized or not, but do follow the general system of education. In all, four out of six madrasas (excluding maktab) follow the general system of education (NCERT 2005). Thirdly, in many situations, even non-Muslim children attend madrasas. For example, the madrasas in West Bengal have a fairly large number of non-Muslim children on rolls (SCR 2006). Given this, it may be safely concluded that the choice of schooling among Muslims is not significantly different from the wider society.

To sum up this section, Muslims in the overall context lag way behind other religious communities on any indicator of education. Rapid expansion in educational opportunities in recent decades has actually worked to the disadvantage of the Muslims as educational disparities between them and other SRCs have widened, rather than narrowed down. While this generalized picture is quite useful in taking into account the extent of religious differentials in the sphere of education, it is not very educative as accessing educational opportunities for individuals even within the given social group/community varies a great deal across types of residence, economic positioning, and indeed across developmental/regional contexts in which they live. It also implies that inter-community differences in educational attainment may vary along these lines. The following section attempts to look at access of Muslims to educational opportunities vis-à-vis other SRCs at disaggregated levels.

CONTEXTUALIZING ACCESS TO EDUCATION

In India, educational development has taken place differentially across regions and also in terms of *rural* and *urban*. Access to education is also determined a great deal by where one resides. How do Muslims fare vis-à-vis other communities, predominantly the Hindus in diverse locations? Indeed, overall access of the Muslims improves in cities and towns in the company of others, and the trend is one of convergence as we move from rural to urban areas. And yet they lag even behind the SCs/STs irrespective of age cohorts, not to speak of non-SC/ST Hindus. It is also important to note that while disparities get reduced in the age group of 6–14 as we move from rural to urban areas, this trend is reversed in the upper age group of 15–18 years. In other words, the Muslims in towns and cities are more likely to be lagging behind other SRCs than in rural areas.

Historically, availability of and access to educational opportunities has varied a great deal across geographical regions, and in fact, the spatially embedded pattern of educational development has remained unchanged for decades (Nuna 1993; Raju 1991; Raza *et al.* 1992; Sopher 1980). Thus, *regional locations* are seen to be associated with educational advantage or disadvantage. As it is evident from Table 12.6, the Muslims living in the relatively developed states/regions[9] have much better access to educational opportunities than those in backward states. Unlike the Muslims in backward states, the Muslims in relatively developed states are ahead of the SCs/STs and closer to, if not at par with, non-SC/ST Hindus as far as participation in education is concerned.

Table 12.6   Participation in Education of SRCs by Residence, Economic Class, and Region

Background Characteristics	6–14 Years			15–18 Years			Hindu (non- SC/ST)– Muslim Disparity Index	
	Muslims	Hindus		Muslims	Hindus		6–14	15–18
Residence		SC/ST	All other		SC/ST	All other		
City	73.1	80.7	88.7	39.8	49.6	67.0	0.08	0.22
Town	73.1	79.2	87.0	39.1	48.5	67.0	0.08	0.24
Rural	64.0	72.1	81.5	30.9	35.5	49.5	0.11	0.21
Economic Class								
Rich	82.2	89.0	91.8	50.1	63.5	73.2	0.06	0.17
Middle	69.0	83.5	85.4	28.1	41.7	47.5	0.10	0.23
Poor	54.9	67.1	73.9	18.7	27.9	34.5	0.13	0.27
Region								
Forward	81.7	80.7	87.9	44.8	43.8	55.5	0.04	0.10
Backward	61.0	69.6	79.9	27.7	35.5	53.4	0.12	0.29

Source: *National Family Health Survey* (Raw Data Set) 2005–6.

It thus seems to suggest that greater the availability of educational opportunities, as in the advanced region, the lower the level of disparity between groups.

Economic or class location of a child is not only expected to determine whether or not he/she may enter school, but also how long he/she, if enters school, will stay the course. Generally speaking, higher the economic class children belong to, greater is their chance of being in school and for a longer duration. This is because education is an activity that involves investment of certain amount of time, energy, and money. Obviously, different classes, measured in terms of wealth, would be able to invest in children's education differentially. Besides, they would also significantly differ in terms of aspirations for and value attached to education. In brief, even if perceived value of education is widespread and education for a few years may be available for free, all sections of society would not go in for education of their children in equal terms. Only those families/households would choose to educate their children that could afford the cost of education and see accruing tangible benefits in education. As can be seen in Table 12.6, participation in and duration of schooling varies considerably across economic classes and this is true of both Hindus and Muslims. Although the Muslims lag behind Hindus as a whole as well as SCs/STs in the corresponding economic classes, the disparity between Hindus and Muslims narrows down considerably as we move up the economic ladder. It suggests that improvement in economic conditions has a more positive impact on schooling among Muslims than Hindus.

To sum up the discussion so far, while the Muslims lag way behind the rest of population including the SC/STs, hitherto the most excluded social group, their educational disadvantages are, however, not uniform across socio-economic and spatial contexts. While this gives insights into what may underlie access differentials in educational opportunities, it remains simplistic and, in turn, is less educative. Also, it does not enable us to understand the mechanism through which different factors either independently or in combination work out intergroup disparity because the factors constraining participation in education are often interrelated and mutually reinforcing and therefore not always easily distinguishable. In this context, it is essential to systematically disentangle the impact of underlying factors influencing educational chances of individuals and the groups they are member of. Only then it would be possible to understand the mechanism through which intergroup inequality is worked out. Thus, what follows is an analytical discussion of the factors that are supposedly responsible for relative educational disadvantage among the Muslims.

WHAT AILS EDUCATION AMONG MUSLIMS? A DISCUSSION

Before we proceed to understand the complex mechanism that works out intergroup educational inequality, it may not be out of place to look through, though cursorily, the conventional explanations accounting for relative educational disadvantages facing the Muslim community. While a number of explanations have been proffered to account for relative educational deficits among the Muslims, the following are the most salient ones.

RELIGIO-CULTURAL ETHOS

A popular view explains the relative educational lag among the Muslims by referring to Islamic theology and the cultural ethos of the Muslims. It has been argued that Islamic prescription of education hinders the Muslims from acquiring modern education imparted in schools because Islam places a high premium on religious education. Muslims, therefore, prefer to send their children to madrasas to study Islamic theology and thereby fulfil their religious requirements and maintain their socio-cultural ethos (Baig 1974; Borooah and Iyer 2005; Sharma 1978; Vajpeyi 1989). It is also argued that Muslim societies in general accord a low status to women by not allowing them to go outside home either for education or for work. In other words, one of the reasons for lower educational attainment among Muslims is their treatment of women and that unless girls are treated as well as boys, the Muslim community will continue to suffer educationally. In brief, to those who view Islamic theology and cultural ethos of the Muslims as potentially the most powerful factor preventing them from taking advantage of educational opportunities, the reasons for disparate levels of education among Muslims are rooted in factors internal to the community itself.

MINORITY GROUP COMPLEX AND SYSTEMIC DISCRIMINATION

A second view accounts for educational deficits among the Muslims by referring to the policy of deliberate neglect of the community by the state. It has been contended that Muslims are denied access to educational opportunities in many and subtle ways. In the first place, educational institutions managed by the Muslim community are discriminated against in financial, legal, and recognition matters. Secondly, a rather surreptitious way of keeping Muslim children out of school is the utter neglect of Urdu, especially in north India where it happens to be the mother tongue of a large number of Muslims. Slowly but gradually, Urdu has been driven out as a medium of instruction even at the primary level in many states of north India (Farouqui 2002). Thirdly, school curriculum is heavily culturally biased with disproportionate exposition to Hindu traditions and mythologies that stand in direct conflict with religious values of the Muslims. Thus, the lack of Urdu-medium schools combined with an unfavourable school curriculum have made Muslim parents reluctant to send their children to government schools, particularly Hindi-medium schools, which lack sensitivity to the socio-cultural ethos of the Muslim community (Ansari 1992; Vasfi 1989). Simply put, Muslim parents are in a way forced to send their children to madrasas—the only site available to the community that preserves its religious and cultural values and meets its educational and intellectual needs. It is, therefore, not surprising if participation of the community in modern education largely provided by the state is much lower than the Hindus. Thus, from this perspective, the factors underlying educational disadvantages among Muslims are external to the community.

HISTORICAL TRAJECTORIES UNFAVOURABLE TO MUSLIMS

A third explanation traces the root of educational and developmental lag among the Muslims in historical processes underlying development of modern education in India and debunks the theory built around essentialist constructs of the socio-cultural ethos of the Muslim community. It has been argued that the educational lag among Muslims is, in fact, rooted in the history of uneven educational development in India. During the British period, educational development was concentrated in favoured locations, that is, the port cities of the presidencies. Educational opportunities spread beyond these enclaves of development at slower pace. A vast majority of the Muslims was living outside the boundaries of an evolving metropolitan culture in these favoured locations vis-à-vis the colonial economy. British capitalism and the system of education thus entered the Muslim-concentrated areas much later, and as a consequence they failed to make a mark in the new system of education (Seal 1968; Smith 1946). It took them a long time to catch up with other communities, but this process of 'catching up' suffered a severe blow in the wake of Partition of the country and the formation of Pakistan in 1947. It is argued that a large chunk of educated middle, professional, and upper classes of the community, especially from north India, migrated to Pakistan and those who stayed behind were poor artisans, agricultural labourers, petty shopkeepers, and small peasants who constituted the bulk of illiterates. Thus, the partition of the country not only denuded the base of the educated strata of the Muslim community substantially, but also left the community bereft of leaders and role models who could have acted as a catalyst to aspirations for education and white-collar jobs (Imam 1975). Put another way, educational disadvantages among the Muslims could be attributed, though partly, to historical trajectories that placed them in disadvantaged positions, socially and economically, rather than their aversion to modern education.

OVERALL POOR SOCIO-ECONOMIC CONDITIONS OF MUSLIMS AND ATTENDANT LOWER DEMAND FOR EDUCATION

A fourth explanation attributes educational backwardness among the Muslims to the social and economic situations they are placed in and demand for education in those situations in general. Implicitly though, this line of argument suggests that relative educational deficits among the Muslims are neither due to their unwillingness to acquire modern education nor because of discriminatory practices against them. Rather, this could be explained by the prevailing socio-economic conditions experienced by them and the perceived cost and benefit of education in such conditions (Ahmad 1981). Generally speaking, it is the upper and middle strata that are not only capable of investing in education, but also aspire for white-collar professions. As a rule, it is likely that middle/upper classes Muslims would take to education as others. But the number of people within this strata has been quite less compared to other communities[10] and has not expanded to a significant extent during the past few decades (Shariff and Razzack 2006), leading to an overall lower demand for education among them. In other words, when the Muslims are compared to others as an undifferentiated category, they appear to be lagging behind.

However, these explanations/formulations have too many problems to be acceptable.[11] Not only does the following multivariate analysis and underlying discussion help scrutinize the above explanations, it also problematizes relative educational deficits among the Muslims. The ensuing analysis uses logistic regression[12] as an analytical statistical tool to probe the net effects of the predictable variables such as age, gender, residence, region, religion, and economic class on the participation of children (aged 6–18) in schooling. The results of binary logistic regression are presented in four Models (Ms). In M_1 estimates of the net effects of independent variables for all are presented. M_2 estimates the net effects for age cohorts 6–14 and 15–18 separately. M_3 and M_4 compare the net effects of independent variables for religious groups (Hindus and Muslims) and regions separately.

Table 12.7 presents the net effects of predictor variables on the probability of participation in schooling. It can be observed that *age* and *gender* of the children are strong predictors of participation in schooling. In general, as seen in the preceding section, higher the age of the child the lower is he/she likely to be studying. Control-

ling for all other variables, the children aged 15–18 are three times less likely (1.0/.267 = 3.74) to be studying as against those aged 6–14 (M_1 and M_2). With minor changes, this observation holds true irrespective of gender, developmental context, and other socio-economic characteristics of household. There is a large body of literature that has highlighted the reasons why children with increasing age, particularly beyond the age of 14, tend to show lower probability of continuing study. One of the main reasons is the increasing cost of schooling with advancing grades/stages. This becomes a matter of particular concern for poor or low income households, for whom opportunity cost, leave aside the direct cost, of schooling turns out to be very high as the children grow up (Kanbargi and Kulkarni 1991; Lieten 2000). However, while opportunity cost has a more significant role to play in the case of boys than girls, the negative association between schooling and age in case of girls can largely be attributed to distance to schools and marriage as the universal construct.

Overall, gendered location seems to have a profound impact on access to schooling. It can be observed that girls have lower probability of getting enrolled compared to boys even after controlling for household characteristics and developmental context (M_1 and M_4). In the Indian socio-cultural framework, sons are privileged over girls in many respects and for diverse reasons. Son preference in education primarily stems from two intertwined and reinforcing reasons, that is, gender division of labour and perceived differential returns on investment in education for sons and daughters (Caldwell 1985; Unni 1995). Gender division of labour has implications not only for socialization of children (that is, to prepare them for their adult roles appropriate to sex, man and women), but also for the economic value of education. Not only are girls not expected to work outside the home, the perceived return to investment in education of girls is seen far less tangible than for boys.[13] The reason being while sons remain at home when they marry, daughters move away after getting married. To put it differently, the economic benefit that might accrue from a daughter's education would be enjoyed by her affinal relatives rather than her natal family. On the contrary, girls' education is seen inconsistent with their perceived role in the private domain, that is, domestic work, caregiving, and the task of reproduction.

Economic well-being of households is found to be the most crucial determinant of schooling (Banerjee 2000; Jabbi and Rajyalakshami 2001). Overall, the children of poor households are much less likely to participate in

Table 12.7   Odds Ratio for Attending Educational Institutions

Predictor Variables	Model 1 (All)	Model 2 (Age)		Model 3 (Religion)		Model 4 (Region)	
		6–14	15–18	Hindu	Muslim	Forward	Backward
Age							
6–14 (rc)	1.000			1.000	1.000	1.000	1.000
15–18	0.627*			.615*	0.587*	.557*	0.645*
Gender							
Boys (rc)	1.000	1.000	1.000	1.000	1.000	1.000	1.000
Girls	.852*	0.898*	0.756*	0.827*	0.941*	0.897*	0.825*
Residence							
Urban (rc)	1.000	1.000	1.000	1.000	1.000	1.000	1.000
Rural	0.995**	1.056	0.943*	0.993*	1.068**	0.949**	1.029
Economic class							
Poor (rc)	1.000	1.000	1.000	1.000	1.000	1.000	1.000
Others	1. 630*	1.551*	1.842*	1.650*	1.516*	1.566*	1.638*
Region							
Forward (rc)	1.000	1.000	1.000	1.000	1.000		
Backward	0.894*	0.784*	.913*	0.834*	0.686*		
Religion							
Hindu (rc)	1.000	1.000	1.000			1.000	1.000
Muslim	0.648*	0.705*	0.540*			0.678*	0.621*
Other	1.260*	1.129*	1.596*			1.335*	1.302*

Source: Computed from NFHS household data set of 2005–6, IIPS, Mumbai.

Notes: (rc) refers to reference category.

   * denotes significance at 1 per cent level.

   ** denotes significance at 5 per cent level.

schooling as compared to the rest. The negative association between being poor and schooling stands out across age cohort, religion, and developmental contexts (M_1, M_3, and M_4). This is neither unexpected nor surprising for two reasons—cost of schooling and home environment (lack of motivational resources). Even if there might be a higher level of aspiration for education in poor households, the perceived or real cost of schooling in such households would be too high to afford. Therefore, they may choose not to put their children in school. Even as they choose to do this, they are likely to withdraw their children early because it would become difficult to bear the cost of education as they grow up. Moreover, the home environment in the poor households is often not conducive to schooling. The lack of parental involvement and motivation for doing well in school leads to disinterestedness among children, which eventually results in discontinuation from study even at the early stage. On the contrary, relatively economically affluent households have both material and motivational resources to invest in their children's education for longer years.

In overall terms, those living in relatively advanced regions, regardless of other factors such as age, religion,

economic well-being, and so on, are more likely to participate in education than those in relatively backward states/regions (see M_1). It is because in a milieu of widespread educational opportunities as well as socio-economic development, even the poorer or less advantaged segments of the population envision the possibilities of educating their children. On the other hand, in the context of restrictive opportunities as in the backward states, the privileged segment of the population, as the theory of *social closure* suggests (Murphy 1988), tends to monopolize scarce, resources including, education by closing off opportunities for the less advantaged segments in various ways.

Let us now turn to what happens to educational disparities between religious groups under study when the influence of all other factors is accounted for. Controlling for all other variables, religion indeed emerges as a significant contributing parameter in creating disparities. Compared to Hindus, the odds are heavily weighted against the Muslim children. Overall, the probability of Muslim children not being in school is 1.5 times that of Hindus in the age group of 6–14 (M_2). The gap further increases with advancing age and the probability of

Muslim children not being in school in the age group of 15–18 becomes 1.8 times that of Hindus (odds ratios of Hindus to those of Muslims = 1.0/0.540 = 1.85; M_2). This indicates higher dropouts among Muslims with advancing age. This is further confirmed by the results in M_3. As suggested earlier, the elementary stage serves as a terminal stage more for the Muslims than the Hindus. Interestingly, while both Hindu and Muslim girls are less likely to be in school than boys, the gender disparity among Muslims is less than among Hindus, negating the popular perception about discrimination against the schooling of girls among Muslims (M_3).

It can be seen that controlling for all other variables, the impact of being rich and poor on attending schools/colleges is as strong for the Muslims as for others (M_3), that is, Muslim and Hindu households experiencing similar economic conditions are equally likely to access educational opportunities. It thus rejects the essential construct of the Muslims, which tends to treat them as homogeneous in regard to their response to modern education as in other matters.

Developmental context/regions also does intercept the observed disparity between the Muslims and Hindus, although some gaps remain. For example, in the forward states/regions the probability of Muslim children not being in school is 1.4 times that of Hindus compared to 1.6 times in the backward states (M_4). In other words, withholding educational deficits among Muslims relative to Hindus, the Muslims living in relatively developed states are much better placed than in the backward ones as far as participation in education is concerned. This could be explained by two factors other than economic ones. First, compared to Muslims in the relatively backward states, much larger proportions of Muslims in the relatively advanced/developed states live in urban areas (about 55 per cent as against 35.8 per cent for the region as a whole). Given the fact that urban areas stand out in sharp contrast to the countryside in terms of educational opportunities, it can be proposed that a very high level of urbanization among Muslims may have weakened, if not completely offset, the impact of certain constraining factors specific to Muslims. Second, while many states of the region such as Kerala, Tamil Nadu, and Karnataka have witnessed concerted efforts at the community level for educational advancement, such initiatives have been lacking in other parts of the country.[14]

In the light of the above discussion, relative educational deficits among Muslims can be placed and understood in a complex rather than a simplistic framework. This is no denying the fact that Muslims as a whole fall far behind the rest of the population in terms of educational access and attainment, although considerable variations occur according to socio-economic characteristics of household and regional locations. Given the fact that endowment differences combined with location of residence in general explain a large part of intergroup educational difference; and that only a minuscule proportion of Muslim children attend madrasas, the thesis that *religious* and *cultural ethos* of Muslims is the culprit for their lower educational attainment is untenable.

The explanation along the lines of *minority complex* and *systemic discrimination* also poses too many problems to prove its application. For one thing, even though perceived or actual discrimination may be assumed to have impacted participation of Muslims in educational opportunities, yet how much effect it has cannot be quantified and statistically tested. Secondly, Muslims live in different situations (majority/minority). In many situations, they form the majority group and they may be expected to influence the developmental processes or allocation of publicly provided goods and services in their favour in those situations. By implication, discriminatory perception stemming from their minority status cannot be framed as universally impacting Muslims' access to education. Also, we have already seen that developmental contexts intercept the educational attainment of individuals (both Hindus and Muslims) quite significantly. Muslims in relatively advanced states are as much likely to access educational opportunities as others, predominantly non-SC/ST Hindus. Seen in this context, the claim that the Muslims in general are prone to discriminatory treatment by the state and its agencies, and this largely prevents them from acquiring modern education, would be unsustainable. However, the potential of this perspective to explain part of educational deficits among Muslims cannot be entirely dismissed. It has some relevance, though in specific contexts, for in certain contexts (largely in the northern and eastern states) there exists as inverse relationship between the relative size of the Muslim population and availability of basic amenities including schools (Alam 2009; SCR 2006). Given that aspiration for and access to education is not independent of availability of educational opportunities, lack of educational opportunities in predominantly Muslim habitations has serious implications for equalizing access of Muslims to education.

Socio-economic characteristics of households and the associated demand for education appear to be a powerful analytical formulation as it explains the greater part of educational deficits among Muslims relative to others.

Educational decisions are after all made in the households and the economic well-being of the household exerts a profound influence on whether and how long a child will be put in school. In other words, larger the base of a group or sub-group with people having resources to invest in education or are engaged in white-collar occupations, higher would be its participation in educational opportunities. Historically, the spread of education among both Hindus and Muslims has always shown such a class character (Alam 2012). Currently, as seen at the outset of this chapter, Muslims in overall terms cut a sorry figure in the sphere of economy and employment, and that disproportionately a large proportion among them relative to other communities is likely to be poor and likely to engage in such occupations where aspiration as well as demand for education is generally low. As a result, when we compare the educational status of Muslims as a whole vis-à-vis other communities the whole community appears to be lagging behind. However, 'attribute disadvantages' do not, at least at the macro-level, fully account for differential access to education. It is here the supply side factor come into the picture and assumes significance. As discussed earlier, predominantly Muslim habitations in certain parts of the country are particularly marked by lack of schools and other basic facilities. Needless to say, the presence of educational opportunities in the localities inhabited by vulnerable groups such as Muslims serves as the extra push required by them in the context of unequal power relations (Alam and Raju 2007).

THE UPSHOT

Undoubtedly, education is a powerful instrument of dismantling several forms of social inequalities. It enables individuals to acquire the rightful place in society and structures of opportunities. Social equity in education, therefore, constitutes an important element of social and human development. While there has been rapid expansion of educational opportunities, access to and participation in education remains far from equal, and religion emerges as the most pervasive axes of inequality. Whichever educational indicators one takes into account, the Muslims as a whole lag way behind other communities. In fact, in certain contexts, they tend to have fallen even behind the SCs/STs, hitherto the most marginalized communities in the country. In other words, educationally, the Muslim community constitutes the most excluded segment of society.

The reasons for lower levels of access of the Muslims to educational opportunities are diverse and intertwined in complex ways. At the macro-level, while the correlates of educational access/attainment influence access of the Muslims to educational opportunities much the same way as they do others and the impact is as strong for them as for others, some gaps still remain. Put another way, endowment differences between the Muslims and Hindus alone fall short of fully explaining educational differentials between the two groups. The residual gap between these two communities may exist because of structural/institutional barriers, such as the relative lack of availability of basic amenities, including educational opportunities in the Muslim-concentrated areas, although the state is under constitutional obligation to ensure that no child is denied education just because of lack or absence of educational opportunities.

There are various approaches to address intergroup inequalities in education in multiethnic, multicultural, and multireligious countries. In the Indian context, two schools of thought stand out. One approach suggests that inequities in education are rooted in the design of the education system itself. Not only is it marked by the overall lower level of educational attainment, but also by unequal distribution of opportunities across regions (rural/urban and developed/underdeveloped) and sectors of education. In other words, social disparities in education will diminish with the rise in educational attainment and further democratization of the education system. The other approach advocates conscious efforts to eliminate disparities by way of affirmative action in favour of disadvantaged groups. It thus implies that educational expansion alone will not reduce disparities across social groups. As it turns out, even rapid expansion of educational opportunities does not lead to reduction of disparities. Disparities tend to reduce significantly only when the participation of the privileged segment in a particular level or grade reaches the saturation point. Hence, this means that the 'expansionist approach' will take a long time to equalize access to educational opportunities for the disadvantaged segments such as the Muslims. Viewed thus, affirmative action in education for the Muslims is the best way to enable them to catch up with others in a relatively short period of time.

NOTES

1. For a useful review of literature on the benefits accrued from education, see Kingston *et al.* (2003).

2. See *Selected Educational Statistics 2004–5*, Ministry of Human Resource Development, Government of India (GoI).

3. As per the 1941 Census, Muslims accounted for about 24.2 per cent of the total population of India, whereas Hindus, 69.5 per cent. Also see Davis (1949).

4. See Census of India 1921, Superintendent were Government Printing, Calcutta.

5. See Census of India, 2001, Office of Registrar General, GoI.

6. Also see SCR (2006).

7. One of the problems of stocktaking of socio-economic conditions of religious groups in India has been a lack of dependable statistics cross-classified by religion. In post-Independent India and until recently, there has been a complete blackout about how different religious communities have benefited from the developmental processes. It was in 1987–8 when the National Sample Survey Organization for the first time divulged statistics on different parameters of socio-economic development cross-classified by religion. After Independence, the Census of India also chose not to tabulate and publish educational and economic data for religious groups until the 2001 Census, although it duly published figures relating to demographic attributes/characteristics of different religious groups. While different sources of data are used for the analysis, the National Family Health Survey (NFHS) data set that includes a number of indicators of education is used for detailed investigation. The NFHS is a large-scale survey covering all India and arguably India's one of the most rigorous and scientific and nationally representative surveys.

8. Part of it could be attributed to benefits of affirmative action policy that the Muslim OBCs receive in the company of OBCs as a whole. This, however, needs further investigation.

9. The classification of states into forward and backward regions is applied to 16 major states of India, which account for about 96 per cent of total population of the country. Forward region includes the following states: Punjab, Haryana, Maharashtra, Gujarat, Andhra Pradesh, Karnataka, Kerala, and Tamil Nadu. Backward region comprises the following states: Assam, Bihar, Jharkhand, West Bengal, Odisha, Uttar Pradesh, Madhya Pradesh, and Rajasthan. Geographically, relatively developed states are situated in the southern and western parts of the country and are contiguous, except for Punjab and Haryana which are separated by Rajasthan from all other states in this group. Backward states, on the other hand, are in the northern and eastern parts of the country and are geographically contiguous. The two geographically distinctive regions differ not only in terms of geographical attributes and resource base but also in terms of socio-economic and educational development. Also and broadly speaking, the relatively advanced or forward states have a clear edge over the backward states in terms of administrative efficiency and delivery mechanisms.

10. As mentioned earlier, for a large part of the colonial period, the Muslim community lacked an indigenous capitalist class developing into a modern one. The formation of the middle class among the Muslims took place at a much later date compared to the Hindus. Broadly, the class structure among the Muslims before Independence was characterized by a very broad base comprising poor Muslims with a thin layer of middle and slightly thick upper strata. Thus, there were either very rich (mostly from the feudal class) or poor Muslims. Also see Ashraf (1975) and Misra (1961).

11. See Alam (2012) for a critical appraisal of these explanations.

12. Logistic regression, in brief, estimates the probability of an event to occur. It is a generalized linear model used for binomial regression, making use of several predictor variables, which may be either numerical or categorical. For example, the probability that a child will be in school might be predicted from knowing his/her socio-economic background. Logistic regression predicts the log odds of the dependent variable, which could be written in the following form: $z = b_0 + b_1X_1 + b_2X_2 + ... + b_kX_k$;

In the equation z is the log odds of dependent variable; b_0 is the constant and there are 'k' independent (X) variables, in the present instance giving the characteristics of ith child. If X_1 is a binary (0, 1) variable, as is the present case, then $z = X_0$ (that is, the constant) for the '0' group on X_1 and equals the constant plus the b coefficient for the '1' group. To illustrate, the dependent variable in the present analysis is dichotomous and coded 1, if a child attended school or educational institution in the calendar year 2004–5, and 0 otherwise. In Table 12.7, exp (β) is the odds ratio—the ratio of the probability an event (for example, attending school) occurs divided by the probability of the corresponding non-event (not attending). In Table 12.7, the odds ratio for the referent group is 1.0. If the odds ratio of the group which is being compared with the referent group is greater than 1.0, it indicates that the independent variable increases the likelihood of a child's being in school as against the referent group. In case the odds ratio is below 1.0, it means that the independent variable decreases the likelihood of a child's being in school as against the referent group.

13. For a useful review of literature on this, see Bhatty (1998).

14. In the southern states there exists for a long time now a well-established network of Muslim educational societies. On this, see Mohammad (2007).

References

Ahmad, S. Shamim and A.K. Chakravarti. 1981. 'Some Regional Characteristics of Muslim Caste Systems in India', *Geo Journal*, 5(1): 55–60.

Ahmad, A. 1999. *Social Geography*. Jaipur: Rawat Publications.

Ahmad, Imtiaz (ed.). 1978. *Caste and Social Stratification among Muslims*. New Delhi: Manohar.

———. 1981. 'Muslim Educational Backwardness: An Inferential Analysis', *Economic and Political Weekly*, 16(36): 1457–65.

Alam, M. Sanjeer. 2009. 'Is Relative Size of Minority Population Linked to Underdevelopment?' *Economic and Political Weekly*, 44(47): 17–21.

———. 2012. *Religion, Community, and Education: The Case of Rural Bihar*. New Delhi: Oxford University Press.

Alam, M. Sanjeer and Saraswati Raju. 2007. 'Contextualizing Inter and Intra- Religious and Gendered Literacy and Educational Disparities in Rural Bihar', *Economic and Political Weekly*, 42(8): 1613–22.

Ansari, A. 1992. 'Educational Backwardness of Muslims', *Economic and Political Weekly*, 27(42): 2289–91.

Ashraf, K.M. 1975. 'Political History of Indian Muslims', in Zafar Imam (ed.), *Muslims in India*. New Delhi: Orient Longman, pp. 50–1.

Baig, M.R.A. 1974. *Muslim Dilemma in India*. Delhi: Vikas Publishing House.

Banerjee, Rukmani. 2000. 'Poverty and Primary Schools', *Economic and Political Weekly*, 35(10): 799–802.

Bhatty, Kiran. 1998. 'Educational Deprivation in India: A Survey of Field Investigation', *Economic and Political Weekly*, 33(27and 28): 1731–40 and 1858–69.

Borooah, Vani K. and Sriya Iyer. 2005. 'Vidya, Veda and Verna: The Influence of Religion and Caste on Education in Rural India', *Journal of Development Studies*, 41(8): 1369–404.

Caldwell, J. 1985. 'Educational Transition in Rural South India', *Population and Development Review*, 11(1): 185–205.

Davis, Kingsley. 1949. 'India and Pakistan: The Demography of Partition', *Pacific Affairs*, 22(3): 254–64.

De, Anuradha, Manabi Majumdar, Meera Samson, and Claire Noronha. 2000. *Role of Private Schools in Basic Education*. New Delhi: Ministry of Human Resource Development and National Institute of Educational Planning and Administration.

DISE (District Information System for Education). 2011. *Elementary Education in India, State Report Cards 2008–9*. New Delhi: National University Educational Planning and Administration.

Farouqui, Ather. 2002. 'Urdu Language and Education', *Economic and Political Weekly*, 37(25): 2406–7.

GoI (Government of India). 2001. *Census of India*. New Delhi: Office of the Registrar General of India.

Hasan, Mushirul. 1997. *The Legacy of a Divided Nation*. New Delhi: Oxford University Press.

Hasan, Zoya and Ritu Menon. 2004. *Unequal Citizens: A Study of Muslim Women in India*. New Delhi: Oxford University Press.

Hussain, Zakir. 2005. 'Analysing Demand for Primary Education: Muslim Slum Dwellers of Kolkata', *Economic and Political Weekly*, 40(2): 137–47.

Imam, Zafar (ed.) 1975. 'Some Aspects of the Social Structure', *Muslims in India*. New Delhi: Orient Longman, pp. 70–110.

Jabbi, M.K. and C. Rajyalakshami. 2001. 'Access to Education of Marginalized Social Groups in Bihar', in A. Vidyanathan and P.G.R. Nair (eds), *Elementary Education in Rural India—A Grass Roots View: Strategies in Human Development*. New Delhi: Sage Publications, pp. 395–458.

Juneja, Nalini. 2011. 'Access to What? Diversity and Participation', in R. Govinda (ed.), *Who Goes to School: Exploring Exclusion in Indian Education*. New Delhi: Oxford University Press, pp. 205–47.

Kanbargi, R. and P.M. Kulkarni. 1991. 'Child Work, Schooling and Fertility in Rural Karnataka', in R. Kanbargi (ed.), *Child Labour in the Indian Subcontinent: Dimensions and Implications*. New Delhi: Sage Publications.

Kingdon, Geeta G. 1996. 'Private Schooling in India: Size, Nature and Equity Effects', *Economic and Political Weekly*, 31(51): 3306–14.

Kingston, P.W., R. Hubbard, B. Lapp, P. Schroeder, and J. Wilson. 2003. 'Why Education Matters?' *Sociology of Education*, 76(1): 53–70.

Kundu, A. and J.M. Rao. 1985. 'Inequity in Educational Development in India: Issues in Measurement, Changing Structure and Its Socio-Economic Correlates with Special Reference to India', in Moonis Raza (ed.), *Educational Planning—A Long Term Perspective*. New Delhi: NIEPA.

Lieten, G.K. 2000. 'Children, Work and Education', *Economic and Political Weekly*, 35(2): 2171–8

Misra, B.B. 1961. *The Indian Middle Class*. London: Oxford University Press.

Mohammad, U. 2007. *Educational Empowerment of Kerala Muslims: A Socio-historical Perspective*. Calicut: Other Books.

Murphy, R. 1988. *Social Closure: The Theory of Monopolization and Exclusion*. Oxford: Clarendon Press.

NCERT (National Council of Educational Research and Training). 2005. *Seventh All India Education Survey*. New Delhi: NCERT.

Nuna, S.C. (ed.). 1993. *Regional Disparities in Educational Development*. New Delhi: South Asian Press.

Raftery, Adrian E. and Michael Hout. 1993. 'Maximally Maintained Inequality: Expansion, Reform, and Opportunity in Irish Education, 1921–75', *Sociology of Education*, 66(1): 41–62.

Raju, Saraswati. 1991. 'Gender and Deprivation: A Theme Revisited with a Geographical Perspective', *Economic and Political Weekly*, 26(49): 2827–39.

Raza, Moonis, A. Ahmad, and S.C. Nuna. 1992. *School Education in India*. New Delhi: National Institute of Educational Planning and Administration.

SCR (Sachar Committee Report). 2006. New Delhi: Cabinet Secretariat, GoI.

Seal, Anil. 1968. *The Emergence of Indian Nationalism*. Cambridge: Cambridge University Press.

Shariff, Abusaleh and Azra Razzack. 2006. 'Communal Relations and Social Integration', *India: Social Development Report*. New Delhi: Oxford University Press, pp. 96–110.

Sharma, K.D. 1978. *Education of a National Minority: A Case of Indian Muslims*. New Delhi: Kalamkar Prakashan.

Smith, W.C. 1946. *Modern Islam in India: A Sociological Analysis*. New Delhi: Usha Publication. Reprint 1979.

Sopher, D.E. (ed.). 1980. 'Sex Disparity in Indian Literacy', in *An Exploration of India: Geographical Perspective on Society and Culture.* New York: Cornell University Press, pp. 130–90.

Unni, Jeemol. 1995. 'Returns to Education by Gender among Wage Employees in Urban India', Working Paper No. 63. Ahmedabad: Gujarat Institute of Development Studies.

Vajpeyi, Dhirendra. 1989. 'Muslim Fundamentalism in India: A Crisis of Identity in a Secular State', in D. Vajpeyi and Yogendra K. Mallick (eds), *Religious and Ethnic Minorities in South Asia.* New Delhi: Manohar, pp. 50–70.

Vasfi, Ausaf Saied. 1989. 'The Ramayana and Mahabharata in Schools', *Radiance*, (April): 23–9.

13

Madrasas and Educational Conditions of Muslims

Arshad Alam

Starting from the Gopal Singh Commission (1980), the National Policy of Education (1986) and the more recent Sachar Committee Report or SCR (2006), Muslims have been generally acknowledged as an educationally backward minority. The role and position of madrasas within the Indian Muslim society and its contribution to Muslim education has been debated since the last two decades. While some have pointed out that due to its outmoded curriculum, madrasa education has become irrelevant to the needs of modern Muslim society, others have suggested its role in increasing Muslim literacy and suggested ways in which the structure of madrasa education can be improved. This chapter is thus an attempt to chart out the expanse, nature, and character of madrasa education in India. While doing so, the chapter first interrogates the idea of permanence associated with madrasas. It is argued that madrasas also do have a history and that they have been fundamentally altered during the process of colonialism. The second part of the chapter tells us how the system has evolved during the post-Independence period and about the variety of madrasas in India. In doing so, this part will also chart out the growth of madrasas and how the state has worked with its agenda of modernization. Analysing the three specific states of Uttar Pradesh, West Bengal, and Bihar to see how the modernization agenda has affected madrasas in each of these states forms the third part of the chapter. The fourth and final part seeks to uncover the linkages between madrasas and Muslim education, and argues for a transformative policy on madrasas in which both

the state as well as the Muslim community must become the stakeholders.

MADRASAS AND COLONIALISM: FROM *DUNIYA* TO *DEEN*

Writing about Egypt, the anthropologist Gregory Starrett argues that madrasas serve the aims of 'functionalization' by which he means a process whereby 'elements of Islamic tradition like the madrasa come to serve the strategic or utilitarian ends of another discourse' (1998: 9). Building on this perspective, one can say that madrasas in India are 'functional' for a whole lot of actors: for the state, whose reformist agenda serves its modernizing aims; for the Muslim Ulama (religious clerics) whose resistance to the idea of madrasa reform positions them as the custodians of Islam; for the Hindu Right whose vilification of madrasas serves to highlight the inherent malaise of Islam; and for the 'liberal' Muslims and others in whose reformist discourse madrasa reform becomes pivotal. What gets missed out in this functional usage of madrasas is the understanding of a madrasa—its relationship with the wider Muslim society, the content, method, and aims of this education, and more importantly, the history of this form of pedagogy.

It is often assumed that madrasa education has had an almost continuous existence since its inception during the medieval times. Its 'unchanging' character has at times meant that this institution has come to be regarded as an artefact of the Islamic culture. This, however, is not the case and as all other institutions of society, madrasas too, have evolved over a period of time. It is important to not understand madrasas as traditional and unchanging, but to see them as any other institution which is prone to social changes. This section will show that there was a distinct shift in the ways in which madrasas were organized and understood during the medieval and modern colonial period. This shift had to do with a redefinition of the aims and objectives of madrasa education which was largely dictated by the changing political context.

Starting from Sind and Multan (Arshad 2005), madrasas gradually moved to the northern part of the country during the twelfth to sixteenth centuries. Most madrasas were either established by the rulers or the nobles of the state, but were also at times the result of collective endeavours of the community. Endowments were made to institutions run by the state. Also, the state sometimes gave *Madad-e-Mash* grants[1] to scholars to relieve them of their financial worries. Thus, the pre-colonial madrasas were unorganized, and even in terms of curriculum there was hardly any standardization (Nizami 1996; Sufi 1941). The inclusion of books depended on a number of factors, such as the personal predilection of a teacher, availability of books, and the adherence of a traditional approach or utility in some specific context. There were teachers who were known for their special insights in certain classical works and students came to them to receive education in that particular book and obtained a certificate (*sanad*), which enabled them to teach that particular book to others. Instructions up to a certain level was in Persian, but higher education was always in Arabic (Nizami 1996). Since education was book-based, madrasas of this period did not confine themselves only to the teaching of religious subjects. Sciences of the day were also taught by the same madrasas and those desirous of a career in government or in the revenue and administration departments often studied in one of the state-funded madrasas.

The first attempt at the standardization of syllabus was made by the Mughal state in the form of *Dars-e-Nizami* (Malik 2008). This syllabus stressed the importance of rational studies such as logic, jurisprudence, philosophy, and mathematics. The Quran and the Hadith had a marginal presence in this syllabus. The Quran was studied through only two commentaries, while the Hadith through only one abridgment. Clearly, this kind of curriculum was designed to produce bureaucrats for the courts. Many who studied this curriculum served in the Mughal and later in the Awadh courts. With the decline of these courts due to colonialism, madrasas teaching this syllabus rapidly declined (Robinson 2000).

Initially, the British made use of the Muslim Qazis to understand Muslim law and culture to the extent that they established the Calcutta Madrasa in 1781 for the 'study of Muhammedan law and such other sciences that were taught in Muhhamedan schools' (Khan *et al.* 2003). However, after the establishment of English as the court language, coupled with the encouragement given to missionaries to set-up English-medium schools, the relative importance of madrasa education started to decline. Moreover, the relative wealth of the Muslim feudal and aristocratic classes had already started to decline, which translated into less donations for the establishment and upkeep of madrasas.

It was in this context that the Deoband madrasa was established in 1861. This was a new kind of madrasa in the sense that it did not rely on rich patrons for donations rather it, for the first time, successfully experimented with the idea of subscription. The second important change that Deoband inaugurated was its curriculum. Although it kept calling its syllabus *Dars-e-Nizami*, the Deoband version of the curriculum had nothing of the original *Dars-e-Nizami*. Instead of an emphasis on the rational sciences, Deoband's curriculum consisted only of religious or revealed subjects based on the Quran and the Hadith (Metcalf 2002). According to the founders of the Deoband madrasa, the Muslims in India had lost power because they were true to their *deen* (faith). All that was needed to regain the lost glory of Muslims was to teach them 'true Islam', which became the primary objective of the Deoband madrasa and other such institutions which were modelled after it. Thus, Deoband for the first time inaugurated the separation of *deeni taleem* (religious education) from *duniyawi taleem* (secular education).

This dichotomous understanding of knowledge still exists and most non-state-funded madrasas oppose modern education because for them madrasas are only meant to provide religious education. While scholars have pointed out that such an understanding impeded the growth of Muslim education, it is interesting to note that this understanding itself was a product of colonial logic. The British view of education was governed by their understanding of religion as an aspect of life to be relegated to the private sphere (Asad 1993). Madrasas were quick to position themselves as belonging to the 'private sphere' of the Muslim community, which made them somewhat immune to the influences of the modern colonial state. Even today, in debates about madrasa reform, the Ulama oppose any state intervention in the name of defending the private sphere. It is strange indeed that this colonial logic is paraded by the Ulama to block reforms of madrasas. What is even stranger is the fact that many scholars take it to be the authentic expression of Islam in India.

This brief historical understanding of madrasas tells us that it has also undergone changes in its aims, contents, and purpose of education. Three important changes took place during the interaction of madrasas with colonialism and which are present even today. The first had to do with the changing organization of financial resources—many madrasas shunned state patronage for the fear of intervention. Secondly, the curriculum became almost exclusively religious in character which meant that a section of Muslims were losing out on contemporary forms of learning. A combined effect of these two was the change in the very social composition of Muslims which accessed madrasa education. There was a time when madrasa education was accessed by the elite and upper-caste Muslim families as it provided them jobs in the government (Ahmad 1999). The stress on the religious character of madrasa education meant that upper-class upper-caste Muslim families realized that their needs were better served by institutions such as the Aligarh Muslim University which taught modern education through the English language. The madrasas, on the other hand, started catering to the lower-class lower-caste *Ajlaf* Muslims for whom madrasas provided an important means of any worthwhile learning at all. It will not be an exaggeration to say that madrasas in India today are predominantly a lower-caste Muslim phenomenon.

Madrasas in Post-Independence India: An Overview

A substantial number of madrasas continued to have suspicion of the state even in the post-Independence period and shunned any support whatsoever. Their curriculum and pedagogical methods remained unchanged since the colonial period and they came to be known as *azad* (independent) madrasas or simply as deeni madrasas (religious seminaries). Moreover, the deeni madrasas are themselves not homogenous and there are deep ideological and doctrinal differences within them. Each claims to represent and defend 'true' Islam. Thus, the *Barelwi*s, *Deobandi*s, *Jamat-e-Islami Hind*, and the *Ahle Hadees*, all have their own separate madrasa to educate their students on how their interpretation of Islam is the correct one and how other sects are deviants from the path of true Islam (Alam 2011). There is no uniformity in their curriculum, but most often they are likely to follow some variation of the Deoband syllabus (Sikand 2005). Unlike Pakistan, most madrasas belonging to different schools of thought have

no centralized structure or organization. Instead, madrasas are either associated informally with larger madrasas or with one school of thought or mostly they function independently. There are only few madrasas which are organized under an organization, such as the Rabta-e-Madaris of Deoband, the Dini Talimi Council in Uttar Pradesh, and various sectarian federations of madrasas in Kerala. To reiterate, the large majority of madrasas exist outside any such organization while these organizations themselves operate independently of the state.

However, they are not the only madrasas that make the landscape of madrasa education in India. Apart from the azad madrasas mentioned above there are those which were either established or are funded by the state in some way. In order to streamline their functioning, madrasa boards have been set in many states with a substantial Muslim population. Thus, Bihar, Uttar Pradesh, Madhya Pradesh, Rajasthan, and Assam have constituted madrasa boards to streamline the functioning of madrasas in these states. In Bihar, the madrasa board was set up in 1982 with powers of supervision and control of madrasas. In Uttar Pradesh, the Arabi and Farsi boards had been functioning like an education board for many years. The West Bengal Board has had a long existence since 1973, but has only been active after it was structured in the last few years. Since education is a state subject, these boards have devised their curriculum keeping in mind the educational curriculum of state schools. Madrasas controlled by these boards are very different as compared to azad madrasas. The curriculum of these board madrasas is not very different from state schools. Students in these madrasas learn what other students would learn at schools. The only difference is that along with the regular school curriculum, board madrasa students also read certain additional texts on Islamic religion and history. Graduates from board madrasas are entitled to seek admission in any higher secondary school or college as their certificates are recognized at par with other education boards such as the Central Board of Secondary Education (CBSE) or the Bihar or the Uttar Pradesh boards.

Growth of Madrasas

There is no reliable data to ascertain how many madrasas exist in the country. While figures for the registered or aided madrasas might be available, it is extremely difficult to get an accurate figure of the unrecognized madrasas or what are generally called azad madrasas. Ostensibly, these are established by Muslims for religious purposes, but like any other institution in society, religious madrasas also serve a whole lot of other functions, which are not always driven by faith. It is better to understand the growth of these madrasas through the concept of 'religious market' where madrasas become suppliers of commodities in demand. There is a lot of religious entrepreneurship involved in setting up of these madrasas and apart from the service of religion, these madrasas also serve the financial and other interests of individuals who establish these. Since there is no financial accountability of these madrasas as compared to the state-funded madrasas, the founder of the madrasa often runs the establishment as his personal fiefdom.[2]

Another reason for the growth of these madrasas has been the religious competition between different *maslak*s (sects) within the Muslim community. Almost all of these azad madrasas serve the function of ideological dissemination of their own maslak's interpretation of Islam. Thus, the Barelwis, Deobandis, and other maslaks have their own network of madrasas spread over the entire country. It is interesting to note that the Deobandis were the first to establish their networks, but of late the Barelwis have also started organizing themselves through their network of madrasas. What fuels this competitive religiosity and the search for 'converting' Muslims to their own interpretation of Islam is not just pure faith. Rather it is also linked with the political economy of madrasa-education in India. While most of these madrasas run on private-local donations of cash and kind, there is also the greater *zakat*[3] market in India and abroad, which is currently stimulating this competitive religiosity among the Muslims. Azad madrasas are the outgrowth of this competitive religiosity. A statement made by the Union Home Ministry in 2001 indicated that 40,000 million rupees were being channelled annually into religious institutions, including madrasas, through foreign donations.[4]

In the absence of a comprehensive survey of madrasas, conflicting figures are provided by different sources for a number of these in India. The problem is further complicated by the fact that different sources use different definitions of what a madrasa is, some confining themselves to higher levels of Islamic learning, while others include *maktab*s (elementary-level Islamic schools) as well. Thus, according to the Centre for Promotion of Science at the Aligarh Muslim University, in 1985 there were 2,890 madrasas in the country. A decade later, the Human Resource Development Ministry put the figure at 12,000 (Siddiqui 1998). In 2002, the Union Minister for Home claimed that there were around 32,000 madrasas in the country (Sikand 2005). According to this figure, most of the madrasas are located in Uttar Pradesh (10,000)

followed by Kerala (9,975), Madhya Pradesh (6,000), and Bihar (3,500). Although the figure claims that both azad and state-funded madrasas are listed here, in all probability, the number of azad madrasas is going to be higher for the simple reason that the government has no record of these institutions in various states.

STATE AGENDA OF MODERNIZATION

In order to modernize the madrasa system of education, the state has attempted to intervene through various policies from time to time. The centrally sponsored Area Intensive and Madrasa Modernization Programme (now called the Scheme for Providing Quality Education in Madrasas or SPQEM) was the first intervention in this regard. Starting in 1993, the programme gives grants to madrasas in lieu of their introducing modern subjects in the syllabus. The programme also gives financial aid for recruiting teachers who could teach those subjects. The programme has now been brought under the purview of the Sarva Shiksha Abhiyan (SSA). It is a voluntary scheme and madrasas are expected to apply for assistance. However, only registered madrasas, which have been in existence for three years, are eligible to apply for this assistance. Clearly, the programme is specifically designed for azad madrasas who teach nothing else apart from religion. Till 2006, 4,694 madrasas were provided assistance under the scheme.[5] The SSA also gives incentives under its Alternative and Innovative Education Scheme to state governments to provide free textbooks and other facilities to unrecognized madrasas. Madrasas in 99 districts in 16 states have been identified for focused attention with Bihar, Uttar Pradesh, Assam, and West Bengal being the major beneficiaries of this scheme. In the year 2005–6, about 3,500 unrecognized madrasas received support under this programme (Nair 2009).

The madrasas modernization programme did not meet with much enthusiasm from within the Muslim community. Since this was meant mostly for those madrasas teaching only Islamic education, fears of intervention and undue interference in their 'private' affairs became the standard defence of those who were opposed to any kind of modernization at all. Leaders like Syed Shahabuddin argued that the madrasas modernizing programme of the state was the proof of distrust the state harboured against the Muslim community. He was ably supported by the now deceased Principal of Deoband, Marghoobur Rahman, who said that madrasas were in no need of reform whatsoever (Sikand 2004). The bigger problem, however, was perhaps the very half-hearted attempt of the state itself. How else does one understand the reason behind the very low budget which was allocated to this programme? In the Ninth Five Year Plan, the total budget for the modernization of madrasas programmes was a meagre 91.65 crores. However, the amount actually provided was only 48 crores. And to top it all, the total amount released did not exceed 16 crores (Hamdard Education Society 2003). While the total allocation in the Tenth Plan went up to 1,060 million, nearly 75 per cent of all disbursements went towards infrastructural development. Such low allocation reflects a lack of serious intent on the part of the state and is also a pointer to the fact that there is hardly any pressure from within the Muslim community to make the state more accountable to improving the educational conditions of the Muslims.

While the low disbursement coupled with lack of enthusiasm has been one part of the problem, the other has been the haphazard manner in which the programme itself has been implemented. In Uttar Pradesh, while additional subjects had been introduced, the timetable itself was not rationalized to accommodate these subjects. There was absolute lack of competence of the existing teachers to handle these additional subjects, which reflects the lack of basic training which the programme ignored. Besides, salaries to teachers were not only inadequate but also irregular (ibid.). The report of the Hamdard Education Society also highlighted the need for setting up of a central madrasa board through which efforts at modernization of madrasas could be streamlined. This idea was taken up towards the end of 2006, when the Ministry of Human Resource Development, under the recommendation of the National Commission for Minority Educational Institutions (NCMEI) proposed the setting up of a Central Madrasa Education Board. This board was to coordinate and standardize the madrasa system while mainstreaming into the regular system. The Commission recommended that remedial initiatives should be taken by the states on an urgent basis with the most critical task being modernizing and upgrading madrasa education. The NCMEI report categorically states that 'these madrasas form a parallel education system which completely blocks the road of economic growth and prosperity for Muslims who opt for it'. Aware of the backlash that it might have to face, the report points out that 'some of the clerics want madrasas to flourish on account of their own vested interests'. It also states that 'madrasas have had the lamentable effect of keeping the downtrodden segment of the Muslim community ignorant and exploited by the privileged' (NCMEI 2009: 5).

Subsequently, the NCMEI also drafted a Central Madrasas Board Bill in 2009 which so far has not become an Act. The Bill provides for a Central Madrasa Education Board which will have representatives from almost all Muslim sects and experts on education. Apart from the powers of affiliating madrasas, the Board will have the mandate to standardize all non-theological contents of the madrasa curriculum. Moreover, this Board will also be the chief financial regulatory authority for madrasas all over India and will have the powers to review the proper functioning of any madrasa which seeks to affiliate itself to the Board through timely inspection and supervision (NCMEI 2009). It is important to note that the NCMEI had recommended that affiliation to the Board will be optional. This means that only those madrasas will come in the suzerainty of the Board which have voluntarily agreed to do so. While the reason behind this is the suspicion that many madrasas harbour against the agenda of the state, this clause may become the reason for many madrasas to opt out of the Board. Although it is too early to say what impact this might have once the Bill becomes an Act, one can say that not too many azad madrasas would be interested in getting themselves enlisted with the Board. As argued above, azad madrasas are primarily theological seminaries with a mandate to disseminate a particular interpretation of Islam. The dissemination of their Islamic world view is most important to them and it does not matter if they are deemed to be traditional. Secondly, as the NCMEI report itself notes, the founders of these madrasas have developed a vested interest in perpetuating the system as they operate without any financial accountability, either to the community or to the state. In such a state of affairs, it does not make sense to surrender their autonomy to the state and become part of the envisioned madrasa board. A clear picture of how the state has implemented its policy of modernization might emerge after understanding how it has worked at the state level since the state is the implementing agency. To get a sense of this, we have selected three states with substantial Muslim population—Uttar Pradesh, West Bengal, and Bihar.

MADRASAS AND STATE POLICY: UTTAR PRADESH, WEST BENGAL, AND BIHAR

UTTAR PRADESH

Approximately 30 million Muslims live in Uttar Pradesh, making it the state with the largest number of Muslims in India. The Muslim population in the state is around 18 per cent.[6] The literacy rate of the state is 56.3 per cent, which is lower than the national average of 64.8 per cent. While the mean years of schooling for the state as a whole is 3.43, for the Muslims it is 2.6 only. Less than 50 per cent of Muslim children are able to complete primary level of schooling in the state (GoI 2006). As many as 25 per cent Muslim children in the age group of 6–14 years have never attended school or have dropped out. The dropout rates for the Muslims in the state is the highest in the state after the Scheduled Cates (SCs) or Scheduled Tribes (STs). Against this pitiable backdrop, it is heartening to note that of late the enrolment levels of Muslims have picked up in the state. In fact, after the SCs/STs, the Muslims have recorded the highest jump in enrolment rates (ibid.). Over 15,000 maktabs and 10,000 madrasas are running in the state with an enrolment of about 0.3 million students (Nair 2009).

Madrasa education in Uttar Pradesh has been monitored by the Minorities Welfare and Wakf Department. In 1997, a separate unit called the Uttar Pradesh Arabi and Farsi Madrasa Board (UPAFB) was created for dedicated monitoring and better implementation of policies. However, almost the entire budget of the UPAFB is spent on the salaries of teachers and support staff of aided madrasas (ibid.). In 2007, the Uttar Pradesh Madrasa Education Board was set up to oversee the madrasa education in the state. According to the data available with the Board, there are 2,160 *tahtania* (primary), *fouqania* (upper primary), and *alia* (senior secondary or intermediate) recognized madrasas in Uttar Pradesh out of which 461 madrasas receive 100 per cent grants from the government.[7] However, according to a communication received through the Ministry of Human Resource Development, around 6,500 madrasas and maktabs are receiving government aid in some form from the state. Many of the children studying here are also simultaneously enrolled in state-run secular schools to avail of the provision of Midday Meals (MDMs) or other such benefits. In Uttar Pradesh, the degrees of madrasas (Maulvi, Alim, Fazil, Kamil) are recognized by the state government as equivalent to other mainstream school or college degrees which enables a madrasa student to join a regular college or university after graduating from a madrasa. This was further extended in 2010 when even the central government started recognizing these degrees.

WEST BENGAL

Almost 25.2 per cent of West Bengal's population is Muslim. The publication of the SCR and the figures for West Bengal showed the pitiable condition of its 20 million Muslims. While the overall literacy rate of the state stood at 68.7 per cent, the rate for Muslims was 57.5 per cent. Furthermore, the mean years of schooling

at 2.84 for Muslim children was also lower than the state average of 3.58. According to the SCR, only a little over 0.13 million students are enrolled in madrasas in West Bengal with more number of girls than boys. However, this figure cannot be relied upon as these data are only for those madrasas that are under the state madrasa board. Like in Uttar Pradesh, West Bengal has its share of azad madrasas called the *kharzi* madrasas, but their numbers and those of students studying therein cannot be ascertained as there are no reliable surveys of these madrasas. The state-controlled madrasas in West Bengal are divided into three different types—the junior high madrasa (Classes 1–5); high madrasa (Classes 6–10); and the senior madrasa. There are 168 junior high madrasas, 238 high madrasas, and 203 senior madrasas in the state (Gupta 2009). It is interesting to note that high madrasas have grown closer to the schools under the general system in curriculum, recruitment of teachers' admission of students, and funding patterns. This mainstreaming of content and administration might be one of the reasons why the numbers of non-Muslim students in these madrasas has risen over the years.[8] As the differences between secondary schools and high madrasas have narrowed, the options for students have become more mainstreamed. The recognition of the high madrasa examination conducted at the level of the 10th class as equivalent to the school final or *madhyamik pariksha* of the West Bengal Board of Secondary Education has played an important role in this process. Moreover, in 2001, the CBSE also granted recognition to the degrees of high madrasas which implied that students from this system can go on for higher education in the general system anywhere in the country and are considered eligible for recruitment examinations.

While the high madrasas converge increasingly into regular schools, the issue of senior madrasas remains contentious in the state of West Bengal. It is to be mentioned here that these senior madrasas are primarily theological seminaries, some with many years of history behind them. At present, the senior madrasas offer courses which roughly correspond to traditional degrees in Islamic pedagogical structures: Alim, Fazil, and Mumtazul Muhaddisin. Over the years, this theological system has been tampered with (Gupta 2009). The growing demand for useful education saw some secular subjects added to the curriculum of these madrasas. The result has been that these madrasas have deteriorated both in terms of the theological content and the secular content. In fact, less and less students are opting to secure their degrees from a senior madrasa (Gupta 2009). If they are interested in secular instruction, they would rather opt for one of the high madrasas run by the state; on the other hand, if they want a purely theological training, they would turn towards the many azad (kharzi) madrasas. In both these choices the senior madrasas lose out.

Like in the rest of India, there are no reliable figures for the kharzi madrasas in West Bengal. But it is generally believed that their numbers are far more than the state-funded madrasas. According to the Rabita-e-Madaris, an association of kharzi madrasas in West Bengal, there are about 550 madrasas of this kind in the state (Nair 2009). This is clearly an underestimation as there are no official surveys of these madrasas. More importantly, these madrasas are mostly controlled by sectarian organizations like the Jamat-e-Islami, Barelwis, and Deobandis. Since the Rabita-e-Madaris, West Bengal, is primarily a Deobandi body, others sects are reluctant to affiliate with this organization. Some of these madrasas are registered under the West Bengal Societies Registration Act, 1961. This often creates an air of official sanction, but in reality it has nothing to do with educational sanction or affiliation of any kind. These madrasas mostly subsist on community donations through the institution of zakat, and others. While the overwhelming numbers of these madrasas are concerned only with the teaching of Islamic theology, some of them teach modern subjects along with theology. In her study of 77 kharzi madrasas located in districts of Muslim concentration in West Bengal, Gupta (2009) found that madrasas that also taught modern subjects attracted the most number of students. This would mean that within the Muslims of West Bengal, there is a marked preference for modern education, and a pure theological training for their children is only a second option.

BIHAR

According to the Census of 2001, 16.5 per cent of Bihar's 110 million population are Muslims. The overall literacy rate of the state in 2001 was 47 per cent, but for the Muslims, it was considerably lower at 42 per cent (GoI 2006). Showing a substantial increase, the literacy rate in 2011 has jumped to 63.8 per cent and there are indications that the Muslims have been one of the important beneficiaries of this impressive decadal growth. Thus, Kishanganj, which has the highest concentration of Muslims in Bihar, has recorded an impressive 26 per cent growth in literacy rate from 2001 to 2011 (Government of Bihar 2012). The mean years of the schooling for Muslim children in Bihar was 2.07, which was lower than

the state average of 2.69 (GoI 2006). Muslim children are also considerably less enrolled in schools as compared to the state average.

Since 1981, there has existed a Bihar State Madrasa Education Board which earlier also oversaw the activities of madrasas in Odisha and West Bengal. Now since Odisha and West Bengal have their own madrasa boards and Jharkhand being formed into another state, the Bihar Madrasa Board controls two kinds of madrasas—aided and unaided. The aided madrasas are those that receive all funds for their functioning from the state. The unaided ones only have the status of being registered by the state, but without any financial support. However, registering with the Board makes them eligible to apply for grants from other sources such as the SPQEM and SSA programmes in madrasas. According to the Bihar Madrasa Board, there are 1,118 aided and 2,459 unaided madrasas in the state (Alam 2011). In 2010, all unaided madrasas were brought under the ambit of the state and were recognized as aided madrasas. As with states like Uttar Pradesh, it is worth mentioning that the highest concentration of these madrasas are at the primary level or what is called the *wastaniya* level, roughly corresponding to Classes 1–5. Together these madrasas cater to about 0.2 million Muslim children out of which 65 per cent is concentrated at the primary level (GoI 2006). However, this figure is an underestimation as it does not take into account the children studying in unregistered madrasas whose numbers are said to be considerable.

According to the figures available, more than 1,000 madrasas have been supported by the SSA till 2008. Also under the Alternative and Innovative Education Scheme (AIS) of the Government of India (GoI), more than 370 centres are being run by various non-governmental organizations (NGOs) in the state. However, studies suggest that implementation of government schemes has been lacking in the state. Thus, during 1999–2002, under the AIS, the central government released grants to the tune of 118.5 million rupees, but till 2002 the money was lying unspent (Nuna 2010). It has also been observed that other minority communities such as the Jains have been at the forefront of utilizing this particular grant, but there is reluctance on the part of the state government when madrasas apply for this grant. This has also been reiterated recently by a study of an NGO which argues that Muslims' share in the flagship programme for minorities has been less than satisfactory. The report also suggests that the government should expressly assert that certain programmes are exclusively meant for the Muslim minority or should have a dedicated budget component for the Muslims within all minority programmes.[9]

Madrasas between State and Community

In the wake of a polarized political situation after the emergence of Hindutva politics, the location of madrasas within the Indian Muslim society became contentious. The Hindutva tirade sought to position these madrasas as anti-Hindu and by extension anti-national, while the defenders of the institution acted as if nothing was wrong with them. The effect of this polarizing debate was that madrasas became closely linked to the question of Muslim identity. Any criticism of madrasas is deemed to be an attack on the already threatened Muslim minority. In the long run, this can become detrimental to the educational prospects of the Muslim community.

There are certain commonalities when we study the educational situation of Muslims in Uttar Pradesh, West Bengal, and Bihar, and some of the predicaments that the community faces might have to do with madrasas. In all these three states, Muslims are educationally backward as compared to the average state-level indices. In fact, the educational deprivation of Muslims in West Bengal and Uttar Pradesh is even worse than the SC/STs (GoI 2006). Hence, there are more numbers of SC/ST students who are able to complete primary and middle schooling as compared to Muslim students. As has been pointed out, the dropout levels among Muslims from primary to middle school remain very high (ibid.) and is one of the important reason why there are not enough Muslims in higher education and consequently, in terms of representation in government services. Thus, for the state of Bihar, while 40.7 per cent Muslim children complete primary education, only about 23.7 per cent of them make up to middle school, which falls to 16 per cent when they reach matriculation. For Uttar Pradesh, while 48.2 per cent complete primary schooling, only about 29 per cent reach till middle school, which further falls to 17.4 per cent at the level of matriculation. Similarly, in West Bengal around 50 per cent of Muslim children complete primary schooling, which then falls to 26 per cent at the middle school level and further to 12 per cent at the matriculation level. It is thus clear that Muslim families are unable to retain their children at schools for a longer duration of time. While poverty has been cited as a factor for high dropout rates among marginal minorities, it does not answer the question as to why some of the other marginal sections such as the SCs have been able to improve their retention in schools over the years.

Although the SCs were far behind to start with the Muslims in all these three states, they have been able to improve their educational access substantially and even rise above them in the two states of Uttar Pradesh and West Bengal in the last 60 years. Clearly then, something other than poverty has to be factored in for this pitiable educational condition of the Muslims.

Another commonality between the three states is that in terms of madrasas, they are mostly concentrated at what is called the primary level of madrasa system. Thus, in Bihar 64.4 per cent of all madrasa students is concentrated in the primary section, while in Uttar Pradesh, an overwhelming 90.4 per cent is concentrated at the primary level. Only in West Bengal Muslim children at the primary level of madrasa education constitute about 31.27 per cent, but when combined with middle level, they account for over 75 per cent of all madrasa students. It has been mentioned earlier that in many state-funded madrasas there is an inordinate burden on the Muslim child to study both streams of education. Thus, apart from their regular state syllabus, they are required to study and pass in theological subjects. This puts too much pressure on children studying in these madrasas. It has also been found out that in most of these madrasas, teachers do not have the requisite training to teach modern subjects (Hamdard Education Society 2003), meaning that they lack the ability to engage students in any meaningful way. A weak foundation at the primary stage of education might be an important reason for the persistent high dropout rates among Muslims. It should also be mentioned here that purely theological seminaries or azad madrasas are a parallel system of education as compared with government schools. This implies that Muslim children studying in these madrasas can never hope to study in a government school and that compounds the educational predicaments of Muslims in India.

It is, therefore, of utmost importance that in order to improve Muslim access and retention in education, madrasa reforms must be undertaken at a comprehensive level. The state madrasas should be made much more accountable in terms of standards and the azad madrasa or those who teach only theological subjects in the name of providing education have to be reformed. After the publication of the SCR, it became commonplace to argue that since only 4 per cent Muslim children access madrasa education, the government should forget about madrasa reform and concentrate instead on establishing more schools in Muslim-concentrated areas. There can be no argument against opening of more schools in Muslim localities. Studies have pointed out the lack of schooling facilities, especially for girls, and that should be one of the priorities of the state. However, to say that madrasas do not need reform as due to their small numbers they are incidental to the educational fate of the community is misleading because the 4 per cent figure cited by the SCR is incorrect and an underestimation.

The data on madrasas provided by the Sachar Committee came from various state madrasa boards and more importantly from the seventh all-India school survey conducted by the National Council of Educational Research and Training (NCERT). If one looks at this data, it mentions two kinds of madrasas—those that follow the system of general education (basically madrasas controlled by various state boards) and those that do not follow the system of general education (madrasas that have own curriculum and system of funding). The SCR had counted only one kind of madrasas to arrive at their erroneous figure of 4 per cent: it did not count those madrasas—and the students therein—that are not controlled by various madrasa boards. According to the NCERT figures, their numbers are much more than the state-controlled ones. Thus, the total number of madrasas that do not follow the system of general education is 11,523. The number of students studying in these madrasas is about 1.37 million. On the other hand, those who follow the system of general education number 20,435 with a combined student strength of around 0.8 million. If we total this figure then according to the NCERT data (2006), there are more than 2 million students studying in these madrasas which is almost double the figure of nearly 1 million students provided in the SCR. It also gives the enrolment figures at maktabs at around 0.76 million, which does not figure in the SCR at all.

Let us recall once again the students spread across these madrasas. The total enrolment in madrasas and maktabs combined, according to the NCERT data, is nearly 2.76 million. Almost 70 per cent of this student population is concentrated at the primary level, and within this an overwhelming majority of students are not studying the government-approved curriculum. This directly impacts the performance of Muslim students in schools, which remains poor and shows startling dropout rates. It is imperative to recognize, therefore, that madrasas could play a crucial role in alleviating the precarious educational condition of Muslims. The state response has been piecemeal and half-hearted. While the outlay has been low, modern subjects have been added haphazardly with little consideration of whether the students would be able to cope up with the additional information or not. What is required is a comprehensive reform of the madrasa education system with an aim to make it relevant to the needs of contemporary Muslim society. Sections within the Muslims have been advocating the need for such a kind of reform for a long time. It is the responsibility of the state to heed these voices. Unfortunately, the government still thinks that it is the Ulama who are the sole custodians of Muslims in India. The government need only to have attended to the report of one of its own institutions (the NCMEI) which has brilliantly articulated the need for a comprehensive madrasa reform and recommended the constitution of an all-India madrasa board. Pre-empting the reaction that this suggestion would invoke among the religious clerics, the report cautioned the state against the vested interests within the community. Despite this, the state consigned it to oblivion at the merest hint of murmurs from the Muslim clerics. A similar capitulation can also be seen in the state exempting minority institutions, including the madrasas from being brought under the purview of the Right to Education (RTE) Act. The Muslim religious campaign against this Act was and is still being articulated as an attack on Muslim identity in India. Caught between such an intransigent attitude of Muslim orthodoxy and a weak state, it seems that millions of Muslim children will have no respite from an education which does not equip them for contemporary times.

NOTES

1. The Madad-e-Mash grant was given to scholars or institutions for the services rendered to the community in general. It was also a tool for controlling the Ulama as it could be withdrawn any time if it went against the interests of the emperor.

2. This is not to suggest that all azad madrasas are run for a profit motive. There are many such madrasas that survive in penury, but are committed to the service of spreading Islamic education. However, it would not be an overstatement to say that they are few and far in between. Moreover, the Muslims themselves complain about the malpractices within these madrasas.

3. Zakat is a mandatory alms-tax on accrued wealth which the Muslims have to earmark annually.

4. See *The Hindu*, 19 May 2002.

5. Although in an official communication, the Ministry of Human Resource Development states that around 12,000 madrasas have been given grants under the scheme till mid-2012.

6. As per Census of India 2001.

7. See http://minoritywelfare.up.nic.in/schemespercent20atpercent20apercent20glancepercent202010-11.pdf (accessed 3 May 2010).

8. Citing an *Outlook* story, the SCR says that out of the total madrasa students in West Bengal, around 12 per cent are Hindus. However, a closer examination would reveal that these 12 per cent are overwhelmingly from the SC, ST, and OBC background.

9. This report by the Center for Equity Studies was widely covered in the newspapers. See *The Times of India*, 18 May 2012.

References

Ahmad, Aziz. 1999. *Studies in Islamic Culture in Indian Environment*. New Delhi: Oxford University Press.

Alam. Arshad. 2011. *Inside a Madrasa: Knowledge, Power and Islamic Identity in India*. New Delhi and London: Routledge.

Arshad, Mohd. 2005. 'Tradition of Madrasa Education', in A. Wasey (ed), *Madrasas in India: Trying to be Relevant*. New Delhi: Global Media Publications, pp. 21–36.

Asad, Talal. 1993. *Genealogies of Religion: Discipline and Reasons of Power in Christianity and Islam*. Baltimore: The Johns Hopkins University Press.

Government of Bihar. 2012. *Economic Survey 2011–2012*. Bihar: Finance Department, Government of Bihar. Available at http://finance.bih.nic.in/Budget/Economic-Survey-2012-En.pdf (accessed 3 July 2012).

GoI (Government of India). 2006. *Social, Economic and Educational Status of the Muslim Community of India: A Report* (Sachar Committee Report). New Delhi: Prime Minister's High Level Committee, GoI.

Gupta, Nilanjana. 2009. *Reading with Allah: Madrasas in West Bengal*. New Delhi and London: Routledge.

Hamdard Education Society. 2003. *Evaluation Report on Modernization of Madrasa Scheme (UP)*. New Delhi: Hamdard Education Society.

Khan, A.U., Mohammad Saqib, and Zafar H. Anjum. 2003. 'Madrasa System in India: Past, Present and Future'. Available at www.indiachinacentre.org/bazarchintan/pdfs/madrasas.pdf (accessed 9 December 2010).

Malik, Jamal. 2008. *Islam in South Asia: A Short History*. Leiden: Brill.

Metcalf, Barbara Daly. 2002. *Islamic Revival in British India: Deoband, 1860–1900*. New Delhi: Oxford University Press.

Nair, P. 2009. 'The State and Madrasas in India', Working Paper 15, Department for International Development (DFID). Available at http://www.dfid.gov.uk/r4d/PDF/Outputs/ReligionDev_RPC/WP15.pdf (accessed 14 June 2012).

NCERT (National Council of Educational Research and Training). 2006. 'Seventh All India School Education Survey: Pre Primary and Alternative Education'. New Delhi: NCERT. Available at http://www.ncert.nic.in/programmes/education_survey/pdfs/pre-primary_education.pdf (accessed 15 July 2012).

NCMEI (National Council for Minority Educational Institutions). 2009. *The Central Madrasa Board Bill 2009*. New Delhi: NCMEI. Available at http://ncmei.gov.in/writereaddata/filelinks/4ab9bf26_Output1.pdf (accessed 15 July 2012).

Nizami, K.A. 1996. 'Development of Muslim Educational System in Medieval India', *Islamic Culture*, 70(4, October): 27–54.

Nuna, Anita. 2010. 'Programs and Schemes for Education of Minorities: Evaluation of Area Intensive Scheme', in Abdul Waheed (ed.), *Minority Education in India: Issues of Access, Equity and Inclusion*. New Delhi: Serials Publications, pp. 70–87.

Robinson, Francis. 2000. *Islam and Muslim History in South Asia*. New Delhi: Oxford University Press.

Siddiqui, M. Akhtar. 1998. 'Developments and Trends in Madrasa Education', in A.W.B. Qadri, Riaz Shakir Khan, and Mohammad Akhtar Siddiqui (eds), *Education and Muslims in India Since Independence*. New Delhi: Institute of Objective Studies, pp. 72–85.

Sikand, Yoginder. 2004. 'Reforming the Indian Madrasas: Contemporary Muslim Voices', in S.P. Limaye, R. Wirsing, and M. Malik (eds), *Religious Radicalism and Security in South Asia*. Honululu: Asia Pacific Centre for Security Studies, pp. 117–46.

———. 2005. *Bastions of the Believers: Madrasas and Islamic Education in India*. New Delhi: Penguin.

Starrett, Gregory. 1998. *Putting Islam to Work: Education, Politics and Religious Transformations in Egypt*. Berkeley: University of California Press.

Sufi, G.M.D. 1941. *al Minhaj: Being the Evolution of Curriculum in the Muslim Educational Institutions of India*. Delhi: Idarah-i Adabiyat-i Delli.

14

Rural Power Structure, State Initiatives, and the Muslims

Divergent Experiences in Four States

Prashant K. Trivedi[†]

In recent years, social science research on Muslims has mainly focused on identity issues. It has often reinforced prevailing stereotypes about the Muslims in Indian society. Critical enquiry into economic, political, as well as developmental aspects of the Muslim society has been neglected owing to this lopsided perspective. For instance, most of the articles on the Muslims appearing in social science journals in the early 2000s discussed madrasa education (Alam 2003; Aleaz 2005; Ara 2006; Bandyopadhay 2002; Engineer 2001; Godbole 2001; Hartung and Reifeld 2006; Jhingran 2005; Sikand 2003). Indeed, the preoccupation of the government and media with terrorism and counterterrorism has contributed to the distortion of this debate.

Accordingly, much of the academic attention has been focused on ethnic and sectarian issues. Right-wing Hindutva forces have constantly raised the question of fertility behaviour among Muslims (Bhagat and Praharaj 2005; Dharmalingam *et al.* 2005; Engineer 2004; James and Nair 2005; Kulkarni and Alagrajan 2005; Premi 2004; Rajan 2005; Reddy 2003; Zavier and Bhat 2005). The impact of such distortions can be seen in some earlier studies even on communal riots (Brass 2004; Gupta 2004). There is no denying the fact that all these aspects have been of considerable relevance to the lives of the Muslims and society at large. However, the point of

concern is why deliberations on this community should be focused on identity issues alone. This cognitive blackout of social science research denies them their identity as a labourer, peasant, entrepreneur, member of India's burgeoning middle class, and so on.

In this context, an attempt is made here to take the discourse on the Muslims beyond these oft-repeated sectarian issues in order to recover and analyse multiple facets of the life and work of Indian Muslims.

The Sachar Committee Report (SCR) had made a similar attempt to introduce development issues to the debate on Muslims, encouraging a number of studies (Alam and Raju 2007; Alam 2009; Krishnan 2010) that discussed their experiences of participation in economy, politics, and developmental programmes. But both the SCR and the articles that followed it, which are no doubt valuable, do not throw light on the more minute power processes that operate at the local level, impinging upon the progress of the community. In this context, this chapter tries to make a departure from this academic preoccupation by taking a comprehensive look at the socio-economic and cultural conditions of Indian Muslims at the grassroot level. It is also an attempt to investigate power structures at the local level to examine the dynamics that continue to keep the Muslims marginalized despite the state's initiatives to

[†] I am thankful to Manoranjan Mohanty for his extensive comments on an earlier draft of this chapter. Thanks are also due to T. Haque for giving this opportunity to work on such an important subject. Editorial help from Sonali Mukherjee and Poornima Joshi is acknowledged with thanks.

ameliorate their condition, though limited in their nature and scope.

However, the focus on micro processes does not mean that these are seen in isolation from macro processes, such as unfolding of a neoliberal development strategy, welfare initiatives of the state, and political change. Village studies are considered useful in documenting concrete ways in which macro processes shape the lives of the people.

A number of points that are made here are widely known, but they are substantiated with newer empirical evidences and insights. Firstly, although a majority of the Muslims seem to face a kind of communal bias in public life, their development experiences may still vary not just vertically but also spatially. Needless to say, the myth of the monolithic Muslim community has already been shattered by the SCR giving way to a class-divided, caste-ridden, and culturally diverse image of the community. They suffer from multiple deprivations, from disadvantages not just of religious identity, but also of class/caste, nationality, regional backwardness, or a combination of these with varying axes of this power process in different contexts.

Though their development indicators are comparable to other marginalized groups, their subtle political assertions, both at macro and micro levels, drastically weaken their bargaining power with the state, leaving them in a more disadvantageous position than other marginalized groups. Altogether, this exploration shows that the bias against the Muslims reflects not just in the development process, but economic transactions as well. This leaves a marked impression that both the state and the market have betrayed the community.

The Study

To get an idea of spatial variations in terms of development indicators and also to represent the maximum possible Muslim population, this study was conducted in four states of India with a relatively high proportion of Muslims—Uttar Pradesh, West Bengal, Assam, and Bihar. In all the four states, one district was chosen for the study from the list of Minority Concentrated Districts (MCDs) Category A. These districts are identified by the Government of India (GoI) for development intervention on a priority basis as they were found to have below national average infrastructure facilities. Barabanki from Uttar Pradesh, Murshidabad from West Bengal, Nagaon from Assam, and Katihar from Bihar were chosen for the survey. Following the same criterion, in each district one block was selected from the list of blocks identified by the government with more than 25 per cent minority

population. In each block, one village was chosen for a household survey. While selecting the village, the diversity of demographic composition in terms of social and religious groups was taken into account to select a study area of a mixed population with a representation of different social groups. To get a comparative picture of different social groups, all households of the sample villages were surveyed using a structured schedule. The selected village in Assam was too large, so randomly selected households of the village were surveyed.

The four selected villages differ from each other in patterns of landownership, caste composition of the Muslim population, and the nature of intercommunity relations. In Ghaghsi (Barabanki, Uttar Pradesh), a larger part of the land is owned by Kurmis, whereas in Boyar (Murshidabad, West Bengal), it is dominated by upper-caste absentee owners. The same group of caste Hindus hold land in Digaliati (Nagaon, Assam). The fourth village, Salehpur (Katihar, Bihar), differs from the other villages as a Muslim zamindar possesses large tracts of land. The Muslim population in Ghaghsi and Boyar is mainly composed of Azlafs or backward Muslims, whereas the remaining two villages are inhabited by Ashrafs or upper-caste Muslims. If Ghaghsi and Digaliati could be termed as communally polarized villages, these sectarian issues appear insignificant in Boyar. Salehpur also does not exhibit communal fissures.

Macro processes, such as neoliberal development strategy, welfare initiatives of the state, and political change take different forms in varied contexts. For instance, neoliberal economic praxis appears to have reoriented the cropping pattern in Ghaghsi, where peppermint was introduced around 15 years back. As part of the government's policy to focus on external markets, cash crops have been particularly encouraged during this period. Studies on this area have shown that very little gains made out of high-yield cash crops have percolated down to labourers and other marginalized groups (Trivedi 2010).

Scholars argue that the same development paradigm has benefited a section of the urban rich and upper middle class at the cost of the rural poor. Relative neglect of rural areas in general and agriculture in particular have rendered villages devoid of any livelihood opportunities. At the same time, increased purchasing power of the urban rich reflects in the booming construction industry in metropolises where most of the Boyar workers are occupied. Rising urban–rural inequalities and absence of employment opportunities at home seem to have converted the entire Muslim working class of the village into a 'floating population'. They keep moving from one city to another for work and return home when no work is available.

Infrastructure development for faster movement of raw material, goods, and workers is another emphasis of this development strategy. The highway, along which Digaliati is located, has been converted into an eight-lane expressway. As part of its 'Look East Policy', the government has an ambitious plan to extend this road further to East Asian countries to realize the full potential of business opportunities with this region. This road has already acquired the reputation of being the fastest approach to reach several places in northeast India. Increased volume of traffic on this road has created a demand for drivers, mechanics, and vendors. Land transactions and business prospects such as dhabas and hotels have cropped up. In this case too, implications of this development vary for different segments of people.

The case of Salehpur is not very different from that of Ghaghsi. In this village also, benefits of cash crops remain confined to the hands of a few. The Bihar government plans to present the state as an attractive destination for investment and industry. Towards this end, they have done a remarkable job of connecting most of the villages in the state with all-weather roads. Salehpur is close to a newly constructed road between the towns of Falka and Katihar. The road connecting the village with this main road is under construction. This 'investor-friendly' strategy is based on the premise that provision of infrastructure and others to attract investment would address livelihood issues too. The case of Salehpur negates such an assumption as its workers have not experienced any progress in their employment pattern, although access to markets for banana cultivators has been bettered.

The nature of political change also varies in these villages; a phenomenon discussed in detail in the next section. The field study in all the villages shows that prolonged repression has not prevented people from negotiating power structures. These villages do not present a status quo in power relations as they are constantly being altered. The only exception is Digaliati where the underclass has not yet been able to make a dent in the power structure. In spite of these differences, the experience of benefiting from state initiatives does not vary too much in the three villages with the exception of Boyar. In most of the cases, dominant sections have undermined these schemes to halt economic empowerment of the marginalized. But in Boyar, in spite of the absence of the dominant landowning class, the people have not benefited much from these initiatives, an event that reflects the inadequacies of the schemes.

STUDIED VILLAGES

Ghaghsi in Fatehpur block of Barabanki is a Kurmi-dominated village in terms of landownership, sizeable population, and consequent hold over local power structure. With their numbers comprising nearly one-third of the population, this community, along with the Yadavs, controls almost half of the good quality cultivable land. This hold is also quite evident in their long-standing control of the village panchayat which ended with the defeat of a Kurmi candidate by a person from the Faqir community, a backward Muslim caste, in the last elections held in 2011. Even with this significant change, one cannot conclude that the dominant caste has lost its grip over the power structure as the landed classes, having a close interface with local bureaucracy, continue to interfere in village affairs. With over 60 per cent population, Azlaf is the largest group among Muslims, which is mainly composed of Sabzi Farosh, also known as Kabadia, the most disadvantaged community, most of whose members still earn their livelihood from the traditional occupation of selling vegetables in local markets. Price fluctuations and vegetables being a perishable item, they often incur losses that push them deep into debt trap. Some of them grow vegetables on small pieces of land they own. They are forced to grow vegetables because of limited access to capital and small size of landholdings. Unlike the rich peasantry that has enough liquidity flow to see them through the longer maturity period of profitable crops such as peppermint, the severely impoverished state of the Kabadias restricts them to cultivating only vegetables, which have relatively short maturity periods.

These agrarian issues reflect on other aspects of social development as well. Most of the Muslim children, who used to attend government schools earlier, have shifted to the local madrasa in 2009–11. The dynamics of this change, that will be discussed ahead in this chapter, also divulge reasons for not only the present state of Muslim education, but also indicate why several welfare schemes have failed to reach the poor Muslims. However, the upward mobility shown by the Faqir community is proof that not all hope is lost. The Faqirs have moved on from begging and agricultural labour with some acquiring tractors that are leased out for ploughing and transport. The current president of the village panchayat, as mentioned earlier, also hails from the Faqir community. Unlike Ghaghsi, in Boyar of Murshidabad, a larger part of the agricultural land is owned by non-resident upper-caste Hindus, mainly Brahmins. Muslims and Dalits own very little land. Despite the implementation of land ceiling laws, the landed class could still save enough land to remain the biggest landowners in the village. Though the quantum of land owned by the landed class went down after redistribution of ceiling surplus land among landless households, wide inequality still persists between the two classes. Of the two communities of Muslims and Dalits, the latter could still derive few benefits from the land reform processes in terms of allotment of ceiling surplus land and registration of their names as 'Bargadars' (registered tenants). But the Muslims were by and large bypassed in this as well. Presently, only 10 Muslims are Bargadars in a village where their population is over 60 per cent. Altogether there are 42 Bargadars in the village. Besides Bargadars, there are other informal tenants who cultivate land owned by absentee landlords, but tenancy (Bhag-chaas) terms for these people remain unsecured. In fact, in most of the cases, erstwhile wage labourers working on a particular piece of land have been asked to lease-in the same land in order to meet challenges posed by rising wages and also to transfer a part of risk to the krishak.

Staying at Bolpur, Kolkata, and other towns, these landowners control their estates through their managers who monitor agricultural operations. With rising labour wages, the landowning class had already started leasing out more and more land, but after the ouster of the Left-front government, the practice of informal tenancy has intensified. In recent times, rising input costs and falling output prices due to dismal procurement arrangements (as in the paddy season of 2011) has further complicated the picture. However, unlike in Ghaghsi where the land-owning class is politically dominant as well, absentee landlords can only be economically exploitative in Boyar.

Underdeveloped agrarian economy and insufficient employment opportunities push most of the Muslim youth of this area to metropolitan cities to work in the construction industry while women and children get engaged in bidi-making. Again, on this account, the case of Boyar differs from that of Ghaghsi where peppermint cultivation has led to a demand for labour during the peak season which has minimized outmigration from the village. In the education sector as well there is a marked difference between both the villages. In Boyar, a majority of children, irrespective of communities, attend the same government school. There is a madrasa a few kilometres away, but in the absence of modern instruction, Muslim parents do not send their children there. The government-recognized madrasa that offers both types of education is situated too far.

While in Ghaghsi and Boyar intersectionality of class, caste, and religious identity shape social discourse, the emerging question of nationality has further complicated the picture in Digaliati. Though several Bengali Muslim families have settled here for the last three to four generations, they face oppression at multiple levels on the lines of economy, religion, linguistic identity, and nationality. Every sphere of their life is dominated by caste Hindus who are not just the biggest landowners, but are also politically assertive and have close connections with larger political formations and bureaucracy. Their eagerness to display documents that establish their credentials as Indian citizens, such as voter identity cards, was reflective of their sense of insecurity.

They also tend to avoid talking about their Bengali identity and emphasize on their religious identity so as to identify themselves with the Assamese Muslims. This sense of insecurity and alienation from the state machinery is often exploited by the landed classes in tenancy relations and payment of wages. The sizeable presence of a third socio-cultural group—the Assamese Muslims—sharing religious commonality with Bengali Muslims and common linguistic identity with caste Hindus makes equations in the village even more interesting. The study tried to identify issues on which the Assamese Muslims make common cause with their Bengali counterparts and issues on which they go along with the Assamese Hindus. The quest here was naturally to decipher which identity prevails over the other in different situations.

Being located on a national highway and railway line connecting Guwahati and Dibrugarh, this village of Nagaon district in Assam provides employment opportunities to drivers, mechanics, vendors, and others, and business opportunities in terms of eating joints, petrol pumps, and real estate transactions for the landed classes. Needless to say, the villages alongside the road have comparatively better access to government schemes and infrastructure because senior officials find it easier to inspect these villages. Roha block officials admit that Digaliati has been visited several times by high-level inspection panels, including a Planning Commission team.

Moving to the fourth village, Salehpur, another story unfolds. There is a perception that abolition of zamindari was the second biggest misfortune that caused immense loss to the Indian Muslims—the first, of course, being the partition of India that divided the Muslim population in three different nations. This view is based on an assessment of the different class composition of Muslim and Hindu communities. Among the Muslims, the proportion of landlords was comparatively high and another large proportion was artisans and service castes in the absence of a sizeable peasant class. Given this scenario, when zamindari was abolished in states such as Uttar Pradesh and Bihar and tenants were given ownership rights and ceiling surplus land was distributed among the landless, land was transferred from Muslim zamindars to Hindu peasants.

The question thus arises about whether continuation of possession of land by Muslim zamindars would have been helpful for other Muslims. And what went wrong with the land reforms policy, which resulted in landlessness in sections of Muslims despite the strong urge for land? One looks forward to explore these questions in Salehpur of Katihar which is still dominated by a Muslim zamindar. Salehpur gives us the opportunity to explore class relations within a Muslim community of sheikhs. Large tracts of land are possessed by an ex-zamindar compared to smaller pieces of land by others. Only one visit to the village is enough to remind us of landlordism of the colonial period where most of the land in several villages is controlled by one family that lives in a big haveli and the zamindar keeps his own squad of *sipahi*s to run everyday affairs of the estate. The only change that has come about is that now the zamindar prefers to lease out his land on a cash rent basis for banana cultivation. This village could also be an interesting case study for land reforms experts to identify ways and means used by big landowners to evade ceiling laws including *benami* transactions, dividing the land among family members and servants, bogus sale, etc. In the context of the abysmal state of land records, an exact estimate of land possessed by the sheikh zamindar was difficult to access, but excluding small patches of land that belong to some other families, rest of the good quality land, which is less prone to frequent floods, remains under the control of the zamindar. A sizeable part of this land has been leased out to businessmen of nearby markets who grow bananas which earns them handsome profits. It remains unaffordable for most of the peasants of this village as it is capital intensive and requires advance payment of the rent.

Residents of Salehpur have a strong perception that their backwardness has a lot to do with the existence of the adjoining bigger and comparatively prosperous village Maheshpur, which is also sheikh-dominated. Historically, Maheshpur has been the seat of zamindari and Salehpur used to be the village of their labourers, tenants, and other service-providers. A similar pattern still prevails with the zamindar staying in Maheshpur and owning large tracts of land in Salehpur. Hence, the settlement pattern of Maheshpur and Salehpur reflects a demarcation along class lines within the same community. Both these villages together form the Salehpur–Maheshpur panchayat. Maheshpur, housing more voters, the village panchayat president is always elected from there, leaving residents of the other village marginalized in terms of development initiatives of the governments. In Salehpur, most of the Muslim children attend both the government school as well as the madrasa at different times of the day.

In the last panchayat polls, this particular zamindar lost the election for the post of the president. In the election previous to that, his wife had won, but he was functioning on her behalf as the president. People were not satisfied with his performance, which led to his fall in the last elections. This incident reflects a certain dynamism in the excluded strata of this village. They exercised the only opportunity they got to oppose the coercive force of the big zamindar.

MAIN FINDINGS OF THE HOUSEHOLD SURVEY

The population of sample villages has been categorized in five social groups, namely Dalits, backward Hindus, upper-caste Hindus, Ashrafs (upper-caste Muslims), and Azlafs (backward Muslims). In each village, some or the other social group had a negligible presence. In this situation, although data regarding all social groups have been presented, for comparison, those groups such as upper-caste Hindus and Ashrafs in Ghaghsi have been left out whose presence in the sample is not statistically significant. Initially, an attempt was made to study a third category among Muslims, that is, Arzal, which is somewhat equivalent to the Dalits, separately from Azlaf. But barring Uttar Pradesh, their presence was not significant enough to warrant this investigation. People were also not aware of this kind of a nomenclature. In fact, in states such as West Bengal, caste background in a Muslim household is difficult to probe. In this situation, all non-Ashraf Muslim communities have been clubbed into the all-encompassing category of Azlafs. Here, nomenclatures such as upper caste, Azlaf, and others have been used just to capture data without any attempt to legitimize them.

Since the focus is on inequality between different social groups, indices are not being compared on absolute terms. Disparities between social groups in a village have been compared with disparities between social groups of the other village. In other words, factors leading to the inequity between social groups in one village have been compared with the other village.

AGRARIAN ISSUES

The pattern of landlessness among different social groups is enough to reveal that Azlafs are the worst placed in the landownership structure, scoring higher on absolute landlessness even than Dalits, except in Boyar (West Bengal) (see Table 14.1). In this discussion, absolute landlessness is defined as not having any piece of agricultural land. In Ghaghsi (Uttar Pradesh), the proportion of individuals with absolute landlessness among Azlafs is twice the proportion of landless backward Hindus. But Boyar and Digaliati (Assam) represent slightly different situations. On the one hand, because most of the land in Boyar is owned by absentee landowners, landlessness is quite high in all social groups, but the proportion of landless households among Azlafs and Ashrafs is lower than backward Hindus and Dalits. On the other hand, for lower population pressure on land, landlessness is comparatively lower in Digaliati. But a clearer picture emerges when sources of income are factored-in. A large proportion of the households of this village reported to have no income from agriculture, giving us an impression that most of them own very small barren pieces of land which are unfit for agriculture. And only a handful of upper-caste Hindu households control large tracts of

Table 14.1   Landownership Pattern (in acres)

Village	Social Groups	Landownership in Acres								Total
		0	.01–09	.10–.50	.51–99	1.00–1.99	2.00–2.99	3.00–5.00	5.00 and above	
Ghaghsi	Dalits	26.7	0.0	36.7	26.7	6.7	0.0	3.3	0.0	100.0
(Uttar Pradesh)	Backward Hindus	20.8	0.0	23.4	9.1	16.9	13.0	13.0	3.9	100.0
	Upper-caste Hindus	0.0	0.0	0.0	0.0	0.0	100.0	0.0	0.0	100.0
	Ashrafs	0.0	0.0	100.0	0.0	0.0	0.0	0.0	0.0	100.0
	Azlafs	38.9	1.5	30.5	5.3	16.8	3.8	3.1	0	100.0
	Total	31.3	0.8	29.2	9.2	15.4	6.7	6.3	1.3	100.0
Boyar	Dalits	75.9	0.0	13.8	5.2	3.4	0.0	0.0	1.7	100.0
(West Bengal)	Backward Hindus	70.8	0.0	8.3	12.5	8.3	0.0	0.0	0.0	100.0
	Upper-caste Hindus	23.5	0.0	47.1	17.6	0.0	5.9	5.9	0.0	100.0
	Ashrafs	53.5	0.0	20.9	9.3	11.6	2.3	2.3	0.0	100.0
	Azlafs	54.3	0.0	16.4	14.7	10.3	0.0	1.7	2.6	100.0
	Total	58.5	0.0	17.8	11.6	8.1	0.8	1.6	1.6	100.0
Salehpur	Dalits	40.6	0.0	0.0	0.0	21.9	21.9	15.6	0.0	100.0
(Bihar)	Backward Hindus	100.0	0.0	0.0	0.0	0.0	0.0	0.0	0.0	100.0
	Ashrafs	60.8	2.1	0.0	0.0	10.6	19.0	6.3	1.1	100.0
	Azlafs	100.0	0.0	0.0	0.0	0.0	0.0	0.0	0.0	100.0
	Others	100.0	0.0	0.0	0.0	0.0	0.0	0.0	0.0	100.0
	Total	61.1	1.7	0.0	0.0	11.3	18.0	7.1	0.8	100.0
Digaliati	Dalits	0.0	0.0	50.0	0.0	0.0	50.0	0.0	0.0	100.0
(Assam)	Backward Hindus	13.0	8.7	30.4	4.3	30.4	4.3	4.3	4.3	100.0
	Upper-caste Hindus	11.1	.0	3.7	.0	40.7	18.5	14.8	11.1	100.0
	Ashrafs	15.6	13.7	21.8	10.0	22.7	7.6	6.6	1.9	100.0
	Azlafs	20.0	0.0	20.0	20.0	40.0	0.0	0.0	0.0	100.0
	Others	0.0	33.3	0.0	33.3	0.0	0.0	0.0	33.3	100.0
	Total	14.8	11.8	20.7	8.9	25.1	8.5	7.0	3.3	100.0

Source: 'Socio-Economic Household Survey of Different Social and Religious Groups in Four States', Council for Social Development (CSD), 2012.

Note: Because of rounding off of two decimal numbers into one decimal number, figures in all rows may not add up to exactly 100. This case applies to all tables in this chapter.

cultivable land. In Salehpur (Bihar), all Azlaf households are landless and landlessness among Ashrafs is higher than Dalits.

Beyond landlessness, if we closely look at the ownership patterns, a tendency of clustering is witnessed, which means most of the households of a particular social group cluster in a narrow range of ownership. For instance, two-third households of Ghaghsi Dalits cluster in a range between 0.1 and 1 acre as compared to a majority of the Azlaf households clustering in a range of 0.1 acre to 2.0 acre. The dominant group of this village, the backward Hindus, cluster in a range of 1 to 5 acres. Very different from Ghaghsi, inequality seems comparatively lower between marginalized groups in Boyar where 20 to 30 per cent households of Dalits, backward Hindus, Azlafs, and Ashrafs cluster between 0.1 and 2 acres. Over two-third households of upper-caste Hindus are clustered in this range as landlessness is very low among them.

The picture is a bit complicated in Digaliati where if backward Hindus are clustered between 0.1 and 1 acre range and three-fourth upper-caste Hindus households own land between 1 and 5 acres, Ashraf households are scattered all over the landownership spectrum because this category is inclusive of two communities—Bengali Muslims and Assamese Muslims—with wide inequalities between them. Qualitative observations reveal that if the Bengali Muslims are concentrated towards the lower end of the spectrum, the Assamese Muslims are generally clustered around the middle segment.

In Salehpur, inequality appears very high as masses are submerged in landlessness, but a section of Dalits and Ashrafs cluster between 1 and 5 acres. But similarities between these two groups end here as sources of their ownership and their social location differ completely. While most of the land owned by the Muslims is inherited, the Dalits have got ceiling surplus and government land pattas. It is no hidden fact that in many cases infertile, unirrigated village common land is allotted as pattas and whereas land is cultivable, it is likely to remain under possession of somebody else belonging to a powerful social class. This reality reflects in data on income when most of the Dalit households report to have no income from agriculture.

Average landownership of each social group also reveals persisting inequalities between them (see Figure 14.1). Average land owned by Azlaf households in Ghaghsi is a little higher than half of the corresponding figure for backward Hindus. Altogether, on account of average landownership, both groups of Muslims are placed at the bottom except in Boyar. A similar story is repeated in Digaliati with wide gaps between upper-caste Hindus and Ashrafs. Surprisingly though, average landownership of the Ashrafs is lower than that of the Dalits in Salehpur. A second look at the landownership structure confirms that the enormous disparity within the Muslim community of this village is partly responsible for this. Taking all the villages into account, upper-caste Hindus emerge as the biggest landowners, followed by backward Hindus, Ashrafs, Dalits, and Azlafs.

Although Azlafs are the most deprived social group in terms of landownership, in some instances they are buying land both for agricultural and homestead purposes. Out of a total 132 cases of land transactions studied, Azlafs bought in 38 cases and sold in 24 cases.

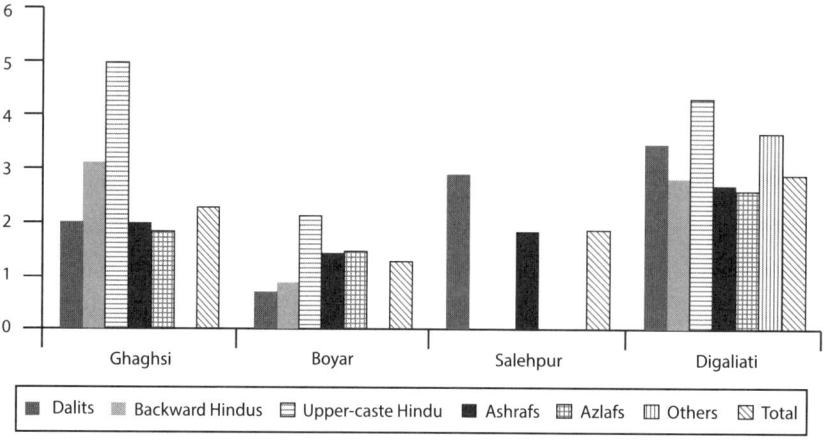

Figure 14.1   Average Landownership of Different Social Groups (in acres)
Source: 'Socio-Economic Household Survey of Different Social and Religious Groups in Four States', CSD, 2012.

Although this data does not capture the quantum and quality of land transferred, on the basis of the number of transactions, backward Hindus emerge as the central figure in the rural land market, making the highest number of transactions. The Azlafs from Ghaghsi and Boyar prefer buying agricultural land whereas in Digaliati and Salehpur, demand among the Ashrafs for homestead land is high, reflecting their homelessness.

OCCUPATIONAL PATTERN

In rural India, land continues to be such an important economic and political asset that an individual's location in the agrarian structure could have an impact on his occupational opportunities.

In Ghaghsi, peppermint cultivation mainly benefits rich peasantry, but because it requires a huge labour supply during the peak season, it also provides wage employment to poor Muslims and Dalits for a few days in a year. Earnings from cash crop cultivation have given a boost to construction activities in the area in which Muslim workers too find wage employment. Some of these Azlaf households cultivate vegetables on their tiny plots and others trade in these perishable commodities, keeping them at risk of indebtedness in case of price fluctuations. At least one-third of them also work as wage labour which is comparable to that of the Dalits. But one thing distinguishes a Dalit labour from an Azlaf labour. Dalits generally avoid going to the local labour market,[1] finding it demeaning and exploitative to work for an unknown employer and prefer to work in the vicinity of their village. Azlafs cannot afford to avoid any opportunity that they come across. Most of the male members of this community shift across agriculture, wage employment, and self-employment during different seasons of the year. It consequently reduces migration. Backward Hindus are mainly involved in self-cultivation on their own land, with some of them going for salaried jobs, self-employment, and wage labour.

The difference between Dalit and Muslim labour is seen in Uttar Pradesh because a larger part of the Dalit labour force is still involved in agriculture whereas a majority of Muslim workers earn their livelihood from the construction industry. Probably hailing from artisan communities, Muslim workers could easily get absorbed in the construction industry whereas the Dalits are traditionally involved in agriculture. In the case of Ghaghsi, Muslim construction workers generally work in neighbouring villages. From Boyar, they migrate to big cities starting mostly as headload workers graduating to the mason level. Most of the males from upper-caste Hindus,

a majority of the backward Hindus, and one-third of Ashrafs of this village cultivate their own land.

The proportion of individuals in salaried jobs are almost negligible in all three villages (mentioned above) but in Digaliati. Connectivity through the highway facilitates them in this, but again, a distinction needs to be made between jobs taken up by upper-caste Hindus and Ashrafs, and between two groups within the Ashraf category. While the Bengali Muslims and a few Assamese Muslims of this village are mainly employed as drivers, white-collar jobs seem to be mostly going the upper-caste Hindu way. Almost half of the Ashraf males reported as having been 'self-employed'. These are mostly vendors selling eatables on trains running between the Guwahati and Chaparmukh rail section on the Dibrugarh line.

Salehpur differs from Ghaghsi on account of the absence of opportunities for self-employment and scale of migration. Banana cultivation does not require as much labour as peppermint. Very high landlessness in Salehpur almost ensures that over three-fourths of the male population derives their livelihood as wage labour—both as agricultural labour in their own village and in agriculturally developed states as well as construction workers in other metropolitan cities (Table 14.2). The proportion of these workers is the lowest among the Ashrafs, some among whom form a tiny landed class drawing income from agriculture while others work as salaried employees.

If patterns of male occupation vary vastly across states and social groups, there are similarities as well as differences in the patterns of female occupation. A vast majority of females in the working age group are reported as taking care of household chores as well as collection of firewood, cattle feed, vegetables and sewing, weaving, among others. Moreover, a sizeable proportion of females, especially among Dalits and Azlafs, work as daily wage labour, while a significant number of them are involved in agriculture and self-employment. Although this information is not necessarily provided by women themselves, it can be easily deciphered by observing in these communities that women contribute substantially to the economy of their households. The female input is mostly unacknowledged because the nature of their contribution remains non-monetary or they are absent at the time of monetary transactions. They are not just discriminated against in resource allocation within the family, but the labour market also exploits them in terms of involvement in tedious activities and lower wages as compared to their male counterparts.

Table 14.2 Social Group-wise and Gender-wise Pattern of Main Occupations

Village	Social Group	Salaried Job	Agriculture	Self-Employed	Daily Wage Worker	Search for Employment	Others	Household Chores and Non-monetary Economic Activities	Student	Total
Ghaghsi (Uttar Pradesh)										
					Female					
	Dalit	0.0	13.6	4.5	6.8	0.0	0.0	61.4	13.6	100.0
	Backward Hindu	1.8	2.7	0.0	0.0	0.0	2.7	84.7	8.1	100.0
	Upper-caste Hindu	0.0	0.0	0.0	0.0	0.0	0.0	100.0	0.0	100.0
	Asharf	0.0	0.0	0.0	0.0	0.0	0.0	100.0	0.0	100.0
	Ajlaf	0.0	3.7	0.9	4.6	0.0	7.3	73.4	10.1	100.0
	Total	0.5	4.5	1.1	3.4	0.0	5.0	75.7	9.8	100.0
					Male					
	Dalit	2.5	55.0	2.5	32.5	5.0	0.0	0.0	2.5	100.0
	Backward Hindu	3.6	61.3	8.0	11.7	2.9	2.2	1.5	8.8	100.0
	Upper-caste Hindu	50.0	25.0	0.0	0.0	0.0	25.0	0.0	0.0	100.0
	Asharf	0.0	0.0	0.0	100.0	0.0	0.0	0.0	0.0	100.0
	Ajlaf	1.6	27.9	14.3	35.9	3.2	2.4	4.8	10.0	100.0
	Total	2.8	40.9	11.1	27.7	3.2	2.3	3.2	8.8	100.0
Boyar (West Bengal)										
					Female					
	Dalit	0.0	3.7	1.2	28.4	3.7	14.8	44.4	3.7	100.0
	Backward Hindu	0.0	6.5	3.2	0.0	6.5	16.1	64.5	3.2	100.0
	Upper-caste Hindu	3.7	7.4	7.4	0.0	0.0	22.2	51.9	7.4	100.0
	Asharf	0.0	0.0	2.9	0.0	0.0	19.1	64.7	13.2	100.0
	Ajlaf	0.7	0.0	0.0	2.0	2.0	5.9	80.9	8.6	100.0
	Total	0.6	1.9	1.7	7.2	2.2	12.5	66.0	7.8	100.0
					Male					
	Dalit	1.2	3.5	5.8	69.8	5.8	9.3	0.0	4.7	100.0
	Backward Hindu	0.0	53.8	11.5	23.1	0.0	11.5	0.0	0.0	100.0
	Upper-caste Hindu	5.6	83.3	5.6	0.0	0.0	5.6	0.0	0.0	100.0
	Asharf	0.0	31.7	9.5	33.3	1.6	12.7	0.0	11.1	100.0
	Ajlaf	3.8	18.9	3.1	61.0	0.6	5.7	1.9	5.0	100.0
	Total	2.3	23.3	5.7	52.3	2.0	8.2	0.9	5.4	100.0

Salehpur (Bihar)

Female

Group									
Dalit	0.0	3.1	3.1	12.5	0.0	0.0	81.3	0.0	100.0
Backward Hindu	0.0	0.0	0.0	0.0	0.0	0.0	100.0	0.0	100.0
Asharf	0.9	2.6	1.3	14.8	0.0	5.7	69.9	4.8	100.0
Ajlaf	0.0	0.0	0.0	15.4	0.0	0.0	84.6	0.0	100.0
Others	0.0	0.0	0.0	0.0	0.0	0.0	100.0	0.0	100.0
Total	0.7	2.5	1.4	14.4	0.0	4.7	72.2	4.0	100.0

Male

Group									
Dalit	0.0	3.2	0.0	93.5	0.0	0.0	3.2	0.0	100.0
Backward Hindu	0.0	0.0	0.0	100.0	0.0	0.0	0.0	0.0	100.0
Asharf	1.8	10.1	4.3	73.3	0.4	2.2	0.4	7.6	100.0
Ajlaf	0.0	6.3	0.0	81.3	0.0	12.5	0.0	0.0	100.0
Others	0.0	0.0	0.0	100.0	0.0	0.0	0.0	0.0	100.0
Total	1.5	9.1	3.7	75.9	0.3	2.4	0.6	6.4	100.0

Digaliati (Assam)

Female

Group									
Dalit	50.0	0.0	0.0	50.0	0.0	0.0	0.0	0.0	100.0
Backward Hindu	3.0	0.0	6.1	6.1	0.0	0.0	69.7	15.2	100.0
Upper-caste Hindu	10.2	2.0	10.2	4.1	6.1	0.0	59.2	8.2	100.0
Asharf	2.4	1.3	3.7	3.7	1.3	2.4	79.5	5.7	100.0
Ajlaf	0.0	0.0	0.0	0.0	0.0	12.5	75.0	12.5	100.0
Others	0.0	0.0	0.0	0.0	0.0	0.0	100.0	0.0	100.0
Total	3.5	1.3	4.6	4.1	1.8	2.0	75.9	6.8	100.0

Male

Group									
Dalit	0.0	0.0	33.3	33.3	0.0	0.0	0.0	33.3	100.0
Backward Hindu	8.0	8.0	40.0	8.0	4.0	16.0	8.0	8.0	100.0
Upper-caste Hindu	23.1	23.1	25.6	10.3	2.6	7.7	2.6	5.1	100.0
Asharf	6.4	11.3	44.8	20.2	6.7	3.1	3.1	4.3	100.0
Ajlaf	9.1	0.0	63.6	0.0	0.0	0.0	0.0	27.3	100.0
Others	11.1	33.3	33.3	11.1	11.1	0.0	0.0	0.0	100.0
Total	8.2	12.3	42.9	17.9	6.1	4.1	3.1	5.3	100.0

Source: 'Socio-Economic Household Survey of Different Social and Religious Groups in Four States', CSD, 2012.

EDUCATION

The dominant view among educationists is that education up to Class X is a basic requirement to make educational achievement operational in terms of better employment opportunities. From this point of view, wide gaps are visible among social groups (see Table 14.3). In Ghaghsi, the proportion of Azlafs having completed matriculation or higher education is comparable to that of the Dalits and lower than that of the backward Hindus. At the same time in Boyar, their educational achievements are closer to that of the backward Hindus. The gap between the upper-caste Hindus and the Ashrafs is the widest in Digaliati. In this Assam village, very few Muslims go beyond Class VIII. These are mainly the Assamese Muslims. In fact, a sizeable number of children who reach Class VIII are from this community itself. Most of the Bengali Muslims are concentrated in the primary-level segment. Though the Muslims have managed to narrow gaps vis-à-vis other social groups as far as literacy is concerned, when it comes to crossing the threshold of secondary education, wide inequality still persists.

In Ghaghsi, the proportion of Azlafs finishing college education is less than that of the Dalits and way below the backward Hindus. Similarly, the Ashrafs of Boyar are comparable to the Dalits, but the Azlafs are still behind them. The upper-caste Hindus are way ahead of all other social groups in all the villages.

It is widely perceived that the Muslims prefer to send their children to madrasas instead of modern schools. This study reveals a very strong urge among Muslims for

Table 14.3   Educational Achievement Pattern

Village	Social Group	Illiterate	Up to Primary	Junior High School (Class VIII)	High School (Class X)	Inter-mediate (Class XII)	Technical and Others	Graduate and Above	Total
Ghaghsi	Dalit	45.3	29.9	16.2	4.3	2.6	0.0	1.7	100.0
(Uttar Pradesh)	Backward Hindu	21.5	28.9	23.6	11.2	7.7	1.5	5.6	100.0
	Upper-caste Hindu	14.3	0.0	0.0	14.3	28.6	0.0	42.9	100.0
	Ashraf	50.0	50.0	0.0	0.0	0.0	0.0	0.0	100.0
	Azlaf	42.0	42.3	7.6	2.9	1.4	3.3	0.6	100.0
	Total	36.2	36.9	13.0	5.5	3.5	2.4	2.4	100.0
Boyar	Dalit	55.3	28.9	10.2	2.5	2.0	0.5	0.5	100.0
(West Bengal)	Backward Hindu	23.8	55.0	11.3	5.0	2.5	0.0	2.5	100.0
	Upper-caste Hindu	5.6	18.5	22.2	29.6	5.6	0.0	18.5	100.0
	Ashraf	20.4	42.6	20.4	8.0	5.6	0.0	3.1	100.0
	Azlaf	26.0	49.2	15.9	5.3	1.3	1.3	0.9	100.0
	Total	29.8	42.6	15.4	6.6	2.5	0.7	2.3	100.0
Salehpur	Dalit	61.9	27.4	9.5	1.2	0.0	0.0	0.0	100.0
(Bihar)	Backward Hindu	44.4	33.3	11.1	0.0	11.1	0.0	0.0	100.0
	Ashraf	49.2	36.9	7.4	4.2	0.8	0.9	0.5	100.0
	Azlaf	50.0	33.3	14.6	0.0	0.0	2.1	0.0	100.0
	Others	66.7	16.7	16.7	0.0	0.0	0.0	0.0	100.0
	Total	50.5	35.7	8.1	3.6	0.8	0.9	0.4	100.0
Digaliati	Dalit	0.0	42.9	14.3	14.3	14.3	0.0	14.3	100.0
(Assam)	Backward Hindu	2.7	44.6	23.0	18.9	5.4	0.0	5.4	100.0
	Upper-caste Hindu	2.0	15.2	26.3	25.3	9.1	0.0	22.2	100.0
	Ashraf	7.9	47.6	32.5	6.5	3.8	0.5	1.2	100.0
	Azlaf	9.5	14.3	42.9	33.3	0.0	0.0	0.0	100.0
	Others	0.0	36.8	47.4	10.5	5.3	0.0	0.0	100.0
	Total	6.8	43.4	31.6	9.8	4.4	0.4	3.6	100.0

Source: 'Socio-Economic Household Survey of Different Social and Religious Groups in Four States', CSD, 2012.

modern education albeit a section of them would like a combination of both. That is why in Salehpur and Digaliati both institutions—madrasa and modern school—exist. Muslim children go to the madrasa in the morning and then attend the school in daytime. This arrangement of children spending only two hours in the madrasa for learning Arabic, Urdu, and religious instructions while spending six hours in school clearly reveals an inclination towards modern instruction. In Boyar, all children go to the government school.

The scenario in the Uttar Pradesh village is very different. Till a few years back, a majority of the Muslim children were attending only the government school here in spite of a government-recognized madrasa in the village. But slowly, most of the Muslim students have shifted to the madrasa due to the hostile and discriminatory environment in the school. These students were made to sit in separate rows behind Kurmi students who often sat in the front row. Muslim students were also subjected to a more severe form of corporal punishment than students from the dominant-caste background. Although the headmistress and the only permanent teacher of the school happen to be Muslims, all the four *para* teachers are from the dominant Kurmi community. Influential people in the village keep intervening in the school affairs and use pressure tactics to keep the teachers under check. One incident reveals the vulnerability of the Muslim teachers in this school. When a Muslim male teacher joined the school a couple of years back, the Kurmis of the village got alerted as he was the second Muslim teacher after the headmistress to have joined the school. The very next day, this teacher was accused of attempting to molest one Dalit girl who lives close to the school. The widely held belief in the village is that he was innocent. Coming from a well-to-do family of the area and a lawyer himself, this teacher managed to escape police action against him, but the incident has left him permanently scarred and he is anxious never to go against the interests of the dominant group. Under these circumstances, Muslim parents preferred to withdraw their children from the school and started sending them to the madrasa.

HEALTH-RELATED ISSUES

Data from this survey shows that wherever any Accredited Social Health Activist (ASHA) is appointed from among the marginalized communities, the proportion of institutional deliveries have gone up. In Boyar, a majority of the deliveries in recent years took place at the government hospital where a Muslim woman is working as an ASHA. She thus assists the government in encouraging people to access health services and also remains approachable to the community. It is not clear whether it is the availability of a government facility or the fact that private facilities are unaffordable that ensures that almost nobody goes to private hospitals for deliveries. But even here, the Azlafs are still lagging behind the others and the community has a higher infant mortality rate (IMR) than the others. The situation is even better in Digaliati where a Bengali Muslim woman has also been working as an ASHA. In total contrast, institutional deliveries are below one-third of the total deliveries in Ghaghsi where the poor state of the government hospital is compounded by the appointment of a woman from the Kurmi background as an ASHA who would not prefer to visit the Dalit and poor Muslim homes. Around 50 per cent households of every social group reported to have never received a visit of an ASHA for the care of their newborn babies. A sizeable section of the backwards prefer private health care and do not encourage ASHAs' visits, but the absence of such visits to homes of marginalized communities gives a sense of discrimination. The situation is the worst in Bihar where neither private nor government systems work for the underclass. Consequently, three-fourths of the births take place at home with the help of a *dai* (Table 14.4).

Same is the case of drinking water in which well-to-do sections prefer private sources, but the poor are compelled to spend money on private supply in the absence of public services. In Boyar, most of the poor households draw drinking water from government hand pumps while the upper-caste Hindus choose not to do so. A higher proportion of the Dalits of Ghaghsi get public water supply as compared to the Muslims because of a special provision regarding installation of hand pumps in Dalit localities. Absence of such services in Salehpur leaves all communities to their fate and they have to make their own arrangements about procuring drinking water. The only difference is that some Dalit and Muslim households, who cannot afford to have hand pumps of their own, opt for sharing hand pumps (Table 14.5).

HOUSING AND ELECTRICITY

There is remarkable consistency in the pattern of space available for agriculture and dwelling, which is a reflection of not only intergroup inequality, but also geographical variations. The Dalits and Azlafs of Ghaghsi are again found comparable with each other, concentrated in the 200–1,000 square feet range while some of the backwards of the same village also going beyond 2,000 square feet. Similarly, the underclass of Boyar shows very little difference among themselves, mostly having smaller

Table 14.4 Facility Where the Delivery Took Place

Village	Social Group	Home Delivery (Trained Mid-wife)	Home Delivery (Dai)	Government Hospital	Private Hospital	Total
Ghaghsi	Dalit	12.5	68.8	12.5	6.3	100.0
(Uttar Pradesh)	Backward Hindu	4.7	53.5	18.6	23.3	100.0
	Ashraf	0.0	100.0	0.0	0.0	100.0
	Azlaf	2.4	72.2	20.6	4.8	100.0
	Total	3.8	67.7	19.4	9.1	100.0
Boyar	Dalit	32.1	3.6	60.7	3.6	100.0
(West Bengal)	Backward Hindu	41.7	8.3	50.0	0.0	100.0
	Ashraf	0.0	12.5	87.5	0.0	100.0
	Azlaf	20.8	33.3	44.4	1.4	100.0
	Total	22.7	21.9	53.9	1.6	100.0
Salehpur	Dalit	4.2	91.7	4.2	0.0	100.0
(Bihar)	Backward Hindu	0.0	100.0	0.0	0.0	100.0
	Ashraf	8.0	58.9	29.5	3.6	100.0
	Azlaf	28.6	57.1	14.3	0.0	100.0
	Others	0.0	75.0	25.0	0.0	100.0
	Total	8.9	65.2	23.4	2.5	100.0
Digaliati	Dalit	33.3	33.3	33.3	0.0	100.0
(Assam)	Backward Hindu	0.0	0.0	87.5	12.5	100.0
	Upper-caste Hindu	10.0	10.0	40.0	40.0	100.0
	Ashraf	4.5	19.1	71.8	4.5	100.0
	Azlaf	0.0	0.0	100.0	0.0	100.0
	Others	0.0	0.0	100.0	0.0	100.0
	Total	5.2	17.0	70.4	7.4	100.0

Source: 'Socio-Economic Household Survey of Different Social and Religious Groups in Four States', CSD, 2012.

houses of less than 200 square feet. In Digaliati, houses are generally bigger, but intergroup inequalities are also sharper than other states. These differences in size are also magnified by the fact that the caste Hindus and Assamese Muslims own their homestead plots whereas the Bengali Muslims generally reside on government land between the highway and railway line. Two-fifths of the Ashrafs and a tiny section of the Dalits in Salehpur live in bigger houses than most of the others (Table 14.6).

The pattern that is emerging is indicative of the orientation towards using easily available material for construction of dwellings. Availability is enhanced by the presence of the material within that agro-climatic zone. At the same time, people of the higher class use tougher material to increase durability of the house as the usage of asbestos or metal sheets in Boyar as against the usage of bamboo, straw, wood, leaves, and others by Dalits, Azlafs, Ashrafs. Distinction between the social categories is not

so much in Digaliati and Salehpur. In Digaliati, asbestos or metal sheets are used and in Salehpur, bamboo and straw are used (Table 14.7).

Access to electricity largely seems to have a function of spatial location. Like many other aspect of everyday life, intergroup inequalities do exist in this as well. The village in Bihar did not have electricity supply although there have been some signs of supply lines being set up for the last two years. Proximity to the highway seems to have benefited the residents of Digaliati as almost all of them have access to electricity (Figure 14.2).

* * *

On the basis of evidence gathered from these villages, one is inclined to suggest that experiences of marginalization of Muslims in rural India vary in different contexts. Ghaghsi appears to be a communally divided village. It is this communal character that induces discrimination

Table 14.5   Source of Drinking Water

Village	Social Group	Government Hand Pump	Private Hand Pump	Well with Brick Walls	Well without Brick Walls	Pond	Sharing Hand Pump	Others	Total
Ghaghsi	Dalit	30.0	30.0	0.0	0.0	0.0	0.0	40.0	100.0
(Uttar Pradesh)	Backward Hindu	5.2	50.6	0.0	0.0	0.0	0.0	44.2	100.0
	Upper-caste Hindu	0.0	100.0	0.0	0.0	0.0	0.0	0.0	100.0
	Muslim Ashraf	0.0	100.0	0.0	0.0	0.0	0.0	0.0	100.0
	Muslim Ajlaf	4.6	60.3	0.0	0.0	0.0	4.6	30.5	100.0
	Total	7.9	53.8	0.0	0.0	0.0	2.5	35.8	100.0
Boyar	Dalit	89.7	6.9	0.0	0.0	0.0	0.0	3.4	100.0
(West Bengal)	Backward Hindu	75.0	25.0	0.0	0.0	0.0	0.0	0.0	100.0
	Upper-caste Hindu	17.6	76.5	0.0	0.0	0.0	0.0	5.9	100.0
	Muslim Ashraf	97.7	2.3	0.0	0.0	0.0	0.0	0.0	100.0
	Muslim Ajlaf	93.1	2.6	0.0	0.9	1.7	0.0	1.7	100.0
	Total	86.4	10.5	0.0	0.4	0.8	0.0	1.9	100.0
Salehpur	Dalit	6.3	56.3	0.0	0.0	0.0	34.4	3.1	100.0
(Bihar)	Backward Hindu	0.0	100.0	0.0	0.0	0.0	0.0	0.0	100.0
	Muslim Ashraf	16.4	64.6	0.0	0.0	0.0	12.7	6.3	100.0
	Muslim Ajlaf	18.2	72.7	0.0	0.0	0.0	9.1	0.0	100.0
	Others	25.0	50.0	0.0	0.0	0.0	25.0	0.0	100.0
	Total	15.1	64.0	0.0	0.0	0.0	15.5	5.4	100.0
Digaliati	Dalit	0.0	50.0	0.0	0.0	0.0	50.0	0.0	100.0
(Assam)	Backward Hindu	4.3	60.9	4.3	0.0	0.0	17.4	13.0	100.0
	Upper-caste Hindu	7.4	77.8	0.0	0.0	0.0	11.1	3.7	100.0
	Muslim Ashraf	8.1	86.7	0.0	0.5	0.0	2.4	2.4	100.0
	Muslim Ajlaf	0.0	80.0	0.0	0.0	0.0	20.0	0.0	100.0
	Others	0.0	100.0	0.0	0.0	0.0	0.0	0.0	100.0
	Total	7.4	83.4	0.4	0.4	0.0	5.2	3.3	100.0

Source: 'Socio-Economic Household Survey of Different Social and Religious Groups in Four States', CSD, 2012.

in the form of social welfare schemes not reaching the Muslims. The Hindus have a slightly higher number of votes than the Muslims in Ghaghsi panchayat as it includes a neighbouring village also. In panchayat elections, for a Hindu candidate, polarization between the two communities has always been considered a winning tactic for elections. Just before one such election, the route of the Holi procession was diverted towards the mosque, which has never been the case before. Seemingly, it was a deliberate attempt on part of a Kurmi candidate to spite the Muslim community. Similarly, in another election, the Dalits were incited by caste Hindus to detour their Ambedkar birth anniversary procession through the same road which passes in front of the mosque. It is well known in the village that the cacophony in these processions would irk the Muslims. On both the occasions,

the Muslims had raised objections to the passage of these processions near the mosque which stoked communal tension. Votes were thus polarized between the Hindus and Muslims making the Hindu candidate victorious in both the elections. When the panchayat president got elected on the basis of communal polarization, it was almost natural for him to make sure that all development schemes routed through the panchayat did not reach the Muslims. Our survey clearly shows that most of the Muslims are poor and homeless, but in 2002, when the Below Poverty Line (BPL) survey was conducted, very few Muslims could find place in the BPL list and consequently were blocked out from Indira Awaas Yojana (IAY) list also. The Mahatma Gandhi National Rural Employment Guarantee Act (MNREGA) card scenario too is no different.

Table 14.6 Plinth Area of the House (in square feet)

Villages	Social Group	0 to 100	101 to 200	201 to 500	501 to 1,000	1,001 to 2,000	2001 to Highest	Total
Ghaghsi	Dalit	0.0	6.7	43.3	40.0	10.0	0.0	100.0
(Uttar Pradesh)	Backward Hindu	0.0	1.3	31.2	42.9	16.9	7.8	100.0
	Upper-caste Hindu	0.0	0.0	0.0	100.0	0.0	0.0	100.0
	Muslim Ashraf	0.0	0.0	0.0	100.0	0.0	0.0	100.0
	Muslim Ajlaf	1.5	5.3	34.4	45.8	13.0	0.0	100.0
	Total	0.8	4.2	34.2	44.6	13.8	2.5	100.0
Boyar	Dalit	46.6	48.3	5.2	0.0	0.0	0.0	100.0
(West Bengal)	Backward Hindu	41.7	41.7	12.5	4.2	0.0	0.0	100.0
	Upper-caste Hindu	29.4	23.5	41.2	5.9	0.0	0.0	100.0
	Muslim Ashraf	34.9	48.8	16.3	0.0	0.0	0.0	100.0
	Muslim Ajlaf	25.0	55.2	19.0	0.0	0.9	0.0	100.0
	Total	33.3	49.2	16.3	0.8	0.4	0.0	100.0
Salehpur	Dalit	31.3	43.8	3.1	0.0	21.9	0.0	100.0
(Bihar)	Backward Hindu	33.3	33.3	0.0	33.3	.0	0.0	100.0
	Muslim Ashraf	7.9	33.3	17.5	1.1	22.8	17.5	100.0
	Muslim Ajlaf	36.4	54.5	9.1	0.0	0.0	0.0	100.0
	Others	0.0	25.0	0.0	0.0	50.0	25.0	100.0
	Total	12.6	35.6	14.6	1.3	21.8	14.2	100.0
Digaliati	Dalit	0.0	0.0	50.0	50.0	0.0	0.0	100.0
(Assam)	Backward Hindu	0.0	0.0	17.4	17.4	43.5	21.7	100.0
	Upper-caste Hindu	0.0	0.0	33.3	11.1	25.9	29.6	100.0
	Muslim Ashraf	0.9	6.2	30.3	21.3	24.6	16.6	100.0
	Muslim Ajlaf	0.0	0.0	0.0	60.0	40.0	0.0	100.0
	Others	0.0	0.0	33.0	33.3	0.0	33.3	100.0
	Total	0.7	4.8	29.2	21.0	26.2	18.1	100.0

Source: 'Socio-Economic Household Survey of Different Social and Religious Groups in Four States', CSD, 2012.

Similarly, the general economic backwardness in Murshidabad has a compound effect on a larger section of the Muslims who are already placed at the lower rungs of class hierarchy. Since most of the people in Boyar either earn their livelihood as wage labour in the construction industry or as unsecured tenants on land owned by absentee landowners, they mostly suffer from economic exploitation rather than social discrimination that is prevalent in Ghaghsi. One thing that strikes is that labour wages are higher in Boyar as compared to Ghaghsi in spite of backward agriculture. It seems that labour wages are not just economic function, but also political function.

Again, unlike Ghaghsi, caste and religious identities seem to play comparatively less significant roles in public life and also in shaping social perceptions in Boyar. If the landed upper-caste Hindus settled outside the village visit the village to celebrate Durga Puja, the Muslim construction workers also make it a point to be there. A deeper probe unearths evidence of upper-caste households practising untouchability vis-à-vis the Muslims and Dalits, but as these Hindus are settled outside the village and their estates are managed by resident managers who deal with tenants and labours, village public spaces are freely accessible for the marginalized communities. The class composition of this village also differs from that of Ghaghsi with little differentiation among marginalized communities, while in the latter village, graded inequalities are prominently reflected. Residents of this village have far better formal access to government schemes. Most of them possess BPL cards and a majority of them have also got MNREGA job cards, but they are unable

Table 14.7 Material Used for Construction of Roof

Villages	Social Group	Clay/Bamboo/ Grass/Wood/ Straw/Leaves/Reeds, etc.	Tin/Asbestos/ Metal Sheet	Burnt Brick	Others	Total
Ghaghsi	Dalit	60.0	0.0	40.0	0.0	100.0
(Uttar Pradesh)	Backward Hindu	31.2	7.8	59.7	1.3	100.0
	Upper-caste Hindu	0.0	0.0	100.0	0.0	100.0
	Ashraf	100.0	0.0	0.0	0.0	100.0
	Azlaf	65.6	1.5	32.8	0.0	100.0
	Total	53.8	3.3	42.5	0.4	100.0
Boyar	Dalit	82.8	17.2	0.0	0.0	100.0
(West Bengal)	Backward Hindu	62.5	37.5	0.0	0.0	100.0
	Upper-caste Hindu	41.2	58.8	0.0	0.0	100.0
	Ashraf	48.8	44.2	7.0	0.0	100.0
	Azlaf	75.0	23.3	1.7	0.0	100.0
	Total	69.0	29.1	1.9	0.0	100.0
Salehpur	Dalit	93.8	3.1	3.1	0.0	100.0
(Bihar)	Backward Hindu	100.0	0.0	0.0	0.0	100.0
	Ashraf	82.5	9.0	7.9	0.5	100.0
	Azlaf	81.8	0.0	18.2	0.0	100.0
	Others	75.0	0.0	25.0	0.0	100.0
	Total	84.1	7.5	7.9	0.4	100.0
Digaliati	Dalit	0.0	100.0	0.0	0.0	100.0
(Assam)	Backward Hindu	0.0	100.0	0.0	0.0	100.0
	Upper-caste Hindu	0.0	96.3	3.7	0.0	100.0
	Ashraf	7.6	91.5	0.9	0.0	100.0
	Azlaf	0.0	100.0	0.0	0.0	100.0
	Others	33.3	66.7	0.0	0.0	100.0
	Total	6.3	92.6	1.1	0.0	100.0

Source: 'Socio-Economic Household Survey of Different Social and Religious Groups in Four States', CSD, 2012.

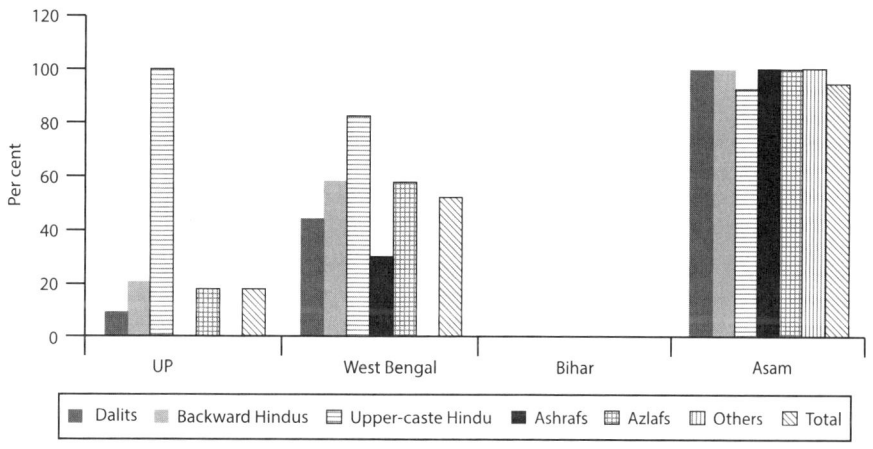

Figure 14.2 Access to Electricity

Source: 'Socio-Economic Household Survey of Different Social and Religious Groups in Four States', CSD, 2012.

to derive tangible benefits in the absence of MNREGA work and supply of limited items at the Public Distribution System (PDS) shop. Still, the fact that Muslim-populated areas are generally backward raises questions about whether this 'general backwardness' can be attributed to a certain kind of a bias at the macro-level or that it is owing to historical reasons, including 'political economy of community formation' (Ahmad 2007).

Salehpur confirms our argument that continuation of zamindari, dominated by a person of any caste, would not have helped any section of the society. In a village where a Muslim sheikh possesses unaccounted quantum of land, a significant number of households from the same community remains landless. It is true that with the abolition of intermediaries, the interest of the Muslim community as a whole in land came down drastically, but at the same time it is also true that internal differentiation in the community has been more skewed than other communities, which is reflected from the data presented in this study. The Muslim elite has always projected their own interests as the interest of the whole community. Besides, this village also reveals limitations of the land reforms as they were conceived and implemented. At one level, enough loopholes were left that could be utilized to evade confiscation of land and at another level, the Muslims, in spite of appalling landlessness, could not get land.

Digaliati brings forth complexities compounded by an intermeshing of religious and nationality questions with power and class structure. If the Bengali Muslims try to forge a common identity with the Assamese Muslims, the latter emphasize on differences between them and choose to associate with the Assamese Hindus, foregrounding linguistic identity. In both these efforts, a quest for getting closer to the power structure is reflected. Although the Assamese Muslims join the Bengali Muslims during religious gatherings, they avoid conjugal relations with them even if the latter seem ready or even eager for these alliances. Similarly, even the poor among the Assamese Muslims consider it demeaning to work for the Bengali Muslims although the reverse of it is quite common. The Assamese Muslims share the perception of the Hindus that migration has altered the demographic and political landscape of the state and if the Bengali Muslims are allowed to access resources, especially land, nothing would be left for the future generations of the 'local' population. Under the circumstances, it is near impossible for the Bengali Muslims to buy land from the market, and getting land through government land distribution programmes is unthinkable. Village panchayat data show that only 19 households from all the communities have benefited from land reforms programmes. Even if they are able to buy land in some cases, it is generally either a very small piece for homestead purposes or infertile, potholed land which, too, comes for a disproportionally higher price.

The Bengali Muslims are discriminated against not just in the land distribution programmes. Their representation in the IAY waitlist also reflects the same bias. Schemes such as the BPL and MGNREGA also do not present a hopeful picture for this community. On these counts, this village bears a close resemblance to Ghaghsi. The two villages may be very different in terms of economy, politics, and sociology, but both witness a marked failure of the state in overcoming hurdles put up by dominant classes in providing legitimate rights to the marginalized communities in general and the poor Muslims in particular. Alienation from the state, resourcelessness and insecurity arising out of being labelled as a 'foreigner' render the Bengali Muslims in Digaliati vulnerable to economic exploitation and political domination. Multiple dependencies on landed classes for access to land, occasional advances, and wage labour weakens their bargaining power in the labour market and compels them to accept inferior terms in the lease market. Wages in this area can cross Rs 100 per day at times, but mostly after a day's work, these people may be paid as low as a quarter of this sum. Inability to resist also fetches menial, inferior quality work. If in order to escape humiliation they try to flee to towns leaving their families behind, they can be coerced into coming back.

Search for protection from the police in the background of criminalization of the community reinforces their patron–client relationship with the local political leaders invariably hailing from the dominant groups. This leaves very little space for them to fight against injustice or pursue their own political agenda during the elections. The previous panchayat polls are a reflection of the marginal electoral influence of the Bengali Muslims despite their significant numerical presence in the village. They supported the local candidate put up by the All India United Democratic Front (AIUDF), but he lost. In the case of this village also, the time-tested technique of reserving seats for Scheduled Castes (SCs)/Scheduled Tribes (STs), in Muslim-majority constituencies was applied. Reservation in this village had two interrelated consequences. Firstly, because of the thin presence of his own community, the elected ST president remained dependent on the caste Hindus. Secondly, the claim of the Muslims to the elected post was easily sidelined in this process.

The voting pattern was also influenced by the above-mentioned dependencies leading to some of the AIUDF supporters too voting for the Congress candidate and polarization of all other communities against the AIUDF candidate. The AIUDF is generally seen as a party of the Bengali Muslim community, but beyond elections this party has failed to enthuse the masses to agitate on issues of everyday life. This is analogous to that of the Bahujan Samaj Party (BSP) in Uttar Pradesh which is also rarely seen at the forefront of protests on issues such as atrocities against the Dalits in Uttar Pradesh. The behaviour is consistent with identity-based parties who appear to believe in bringing change through state power rather than by way of mobilization.

Suggestions for the Way Forward

There is an intersectionality of class and other relationships which characterizes the axis of deprivation in all the four cases. In most of the cases, social discrimination plays a role in their marginalization with varying intensity. It appears most intense in Ghaghsi and Digaliati. The nationality question worsens the situation for a section of Muslims in the latter village.

Exclusion of Muslims from government schemes reflects faulty design and consequent erroneous implementation of the government's initiatives that, in turn, gives room to the local power elite for manipulation. For instance, the Planning Commission provides all-India and state-wise estimates of the BPL population whereas identification of BPL households is done by the BPL census. Often, the BPL census comes out with a higher number of BPL households than the Planning Commission estimates. Difference between these figures leads to problems of exclusion as well as inclusion. If there are more households which are poor as per the BPL criterion, then it is obvious that a number of poor families have been excluded from what the Planning Commission finally recognizes as BPL. This discrepancy certainly leads to an unhealthy competition among the poor to get BPL cards. It also leaves room for manoeuvring the entire process by the locally dominant groups and bureaucracy as is the case in Ghaghsi, Uttar Pradesh.

It is rightly suggested that universalization of PDS would justifiably deal with the problem of exclusion and inclusion. But this may not suffice as throughout this study it has come out very clearly that the interests of the privileged class lie in keeping the downtrodden in a continuous state of deprivation and poverty. To maintain their influence, they try to subvert initiatives for economic empowerment of the excluded. For the marginalized, the

situation is aggravated in the continuing failure of the state to remove impediments created by the influential. The strategy should be such that the programme is immune to the influence of the dominant groups to ensure participation of all the intended beneficiaries.

The dark irony of the situation on the ground is that whereas madrasas are often used to politically isolate the Muslims, almost all the Muslims in the present study showed a preference for modern education and schools for their children. It was clear that they feel that even the government-supported madrasas do not offer quality education. Hence, in the name of supporting madrasas, the government cannot abdicate its responsibility of providing modern school education to Muslim children. The issue is not just setting-up high-quality schools in Muslim majority areas, it is also about creating a discrimination-free environment in the schools. Absence of infrastructure impacts everyone in a village, but its severity varies along one's social location. For provisioning infrastructural facilities, such as electricity, *pucca* roads, health care, drinking water, PDS shops, and others, Muslim-populated localities should be prioritized.

In rural India, a majority of the Muslims belong to either of these categories—landless-marginal peasant, wage labour, and self-employed. These three categories appear different from each other, but separation between them is only conceptual. Empirically, clear-cut distinctions between them is questionable. This is the same class of people who represent these categories in a different time and space. Deprived of ownership of land and capital, crucial means of production, they share a similar social situation wherein they opt for a range of similar occupations in different seasons and places for subsistence. Some of them may stick only to one of these occupations, but that happens in the absence of other options. In fact, the informal sector is seen as a 'dumping ground' for all those who could not get employment in the organized sector.

The issues relating to this class will have to be dealt with both in the long and short term. The state's social welfare strategies do not focus on specificities of this class. For instance, the phenomenon of 'floating population' does not reflect adequately in social security schemes of the government. It has long been deduced by the scholars that in a bid to avoid providing social security to those engaged in wage labour, frequently changing employers has been falsely cited as a cause. They advocate a comprehensive strategy to facilitate transfer of labour from unorganized labour into organized employment. And simultaneously, investment is needed to be diverted to the informal sector to sustain its growth and to enhance labour productivity (Ghose 2010).

Until the highly skewed structure of resource ownership is modified, significant transformation in society and in the lives of poor Muslims would remain only a rhetorical goal. In the name of 'inclusive growth', a few steps can be taken to ameliorate the conditions of a tiny section without disturbing the existing structures. But when resources are to be redistributed in favour of a large mass of exploited class, this cannot be done without giving a serious blow to the interests of the propertied class. This kind of a change is necessary not just for the empowerment of the poor, but also for the disempowerment of the influential. Weakening of the elite stronghold over the rural power structure is also necessary for facilitating state initiatives to reach their intended beneficiaries. Extensive land reforms are considered a prerequisite for bringing in substantive democracy in rural areas.

It is difficult to conceive of such a change in the absence of transformative politics that connects with the other exploited sections of the society to form a broader resistance against the status quo. Some have advocated a strong Muslim party with an all-India reach to pursue the interests of the Muslims. This view has never found resonance among the Muslims masses, who always support secular parties. This is not to say that Muslim-specific issues should not be raised, but identity politics merely emphasizes on 'recognition' at the cost of 'redistribution'. It is true that different social groups such as Dalits, Muslims, Adivasis, and women suffer from different types of social oppression, but at the same time, they are also exploited by the capital. In this situation, non-recognition of this commonness prevents these exploited groups from coming together to pose a challenge to the rule of the capital. This focus on 'experiences' and 'difference' misses an important point that even if oppression based on caste, ethnic identity, and gender is taken care of, the exploitation of the same group will continue as long as capitalist order remains untouched.

Equity on the lines of religion will not be overemphasized if a comprehensive, multifaceted approach for the progress of the Muslim community is developed. This will not happen with minor modifications in the existing development paradigm, but will entail an alternative path of development.

Note

1. In this cash crop growing area labour markets have emerged where labourers and their potential employer would collect in the morning and negotiate the daily wages before getting into a contract. In these markets daily wages fluctuate with agricultural seasons and in keeping with the demand and supply of labour. These markets generally offer higher wages to the labourers than prevailing wages in the villages.

References

Ahmad, Imtiaz. 2007. 'Exploring the Status of Muslims in the Economy', *Economic and Political Weekly*, 42(35, 15 September): 3703–4.

Alam, Arshad. 2003. 'Understanding Madrasas', *Economic and Political Weekly*, 38(22, 31 May): 2123–6.

———. 2009. 'Contextualising Muslim Identity: Ansaris, Deobandis, Barelwis', *Economic and Political Weekly*, 44(24, 13 June): 86–92.

Alam, Mohd. Sanjeer and Saraswati Raju. 2007. 'Contextualising Inter-, Intra-religious and Gendered Literacy and Educational Disparities in Rural Bihar', *Economic and Political Weekly*, 42(8, 5 May): 1613–22.

Aleaz, Bonita. 2005. 'Madrasa Education, State and Community Consciousness: Muslims in West Bengal', *Economic and Political Weekly*, 40(6, 5 February): 555–65.

Ara, Arjumand. 2006. 'Reinterpreting Madrasas', *Economic and Political Weekly*, 41(25, 24 June): 2544–7.

Bandyopadhyay, D. 2002. 'Madrasa Education and the Condition of Indian Muslims', *Economic and Political Weekly*, 37(16, 20 April): 1481–4.

Bhagat, R.B. and Purujit Praharaj. 2005. 'Hindu–Muslim Fertility Differentials', *Economic and Political Weekly*, 40(5, 29 January): 411–18.

Brass, Paul R. 2004. 'Development of an Institutionalised Riot System in Meerut City, 1961 to 1982', *Economic and Political Weekly*, 39(44, 30 October): 4839–48.

Dharmalingam, A., K. Navaneetham, and S. Philip Morgan. 2005. 'Muslim–Hindu Fertility Differences: Evidence from National Family Health Survey-II', *Economic and Political Weekly*. 40(5, 29 January): 429–36.

Engineer, Asghar Ali. 2001. 'Muslims and Education', *Economic and Political Weekly*, 36(34, 25 August): 3221–2.

———. 2004. 'A Handy Tool for Anti-Minorityism', *Economic and Political Weekly*, 39(39, 25 September): 4304–5.

Godbole, Madhav. 2001. 'Madarsas: Need for a Fresh Look', *Economic and Political Weekly*, 36(41, 13 October): 3889–90.

Ghose, Ajit K. 2010. 'Informal Employment in India', in Manoranjan Mohanty (ed.), *India: Social Development Report 2010—The Land Question and the Marginalized*. New Delhi: Oxford University Press and the Council for Social Development, pp. 116–20.

Gupta, Charu. 2004. 'Censuses, Communalism, Gender and Identity: A Historical Perspective', *Economic and Political Weekly*, 39(39, 25 September: 4302–4.

Hartung, Jan-Peter and Helmut Reifeld (eds). 2006. *Islamic Education, Diversity and National Identity: Dīnī Madrasas in India Post 9/11*. New Delhi: Sage Publications.

James, K.S. and Sajini B. Nair. 2005. 'Accelerated Decline in Fertility in India since the 1980s: Trends among Hindus and Muslims', *Economic and Political Weekly*, 40(5, 29 January): 375–84.

Jhingran, Saral. 2005. 'Madrasa Modernisation Programme—An Assessment', *Economic and Political Weekly*, 40(53, 31 December): 5540–2.

Krishnan, P.S. 'Understanding the Backward Classes of Muslim Society', *Economic and Political Weekly*, 45(34, 21 August): 46–56.

Kulkarni, P.M. and Manoj Alagrajan. 2005. 'Population Growth, Fertility, and Religion in India', *Economic and Political Weekly*, 40(5, 29 January): 403–10.

Premi, Mahendra. 2004. 'Religion in India: A Demographic Perspective', *Economic and Political Weekly*, 39(39, 25 September): 4297–4302.

Rajan, S. Irudaya. 2005. 'District Level Fertility Estimates for Hindus and Muslims', *Economic and Political Weekly*, 40(5, 29 January): 437–46.

Reddy, P.H. 2003. 'Religion, Population Growth, Fertility and Family Planning Practice in India', *Economic and Political Weekly*, 38(33, 16 August): 3500–9.

Sikand, Yoginder. 2003. 'Madrasa Reform and the Indian State', *Economic and Political Weekly*, 38(43, 25 October): 4503–6.

Trivedi, Prashant K. 2010. 'Changing Agrarian Scene: Sociology of Land, Wages, and Indebtedness in UP', in Manoranjan Mohanty (ed.), *India: Social Development Report 2010—The Land Question and the Marginalized*. New Delhi: Oxford University Press, pp. 243–56.

Zavier, A.J. Francis and P.N. Mari Bhat. 2005. 'Role of Religion in Fertility Decline: The Case of Indian Muslims', *Economic and Political Weekly*, 40(5, 29 January): 385–402.

15

Assessing UPA Government's Response to Muslim Deprivation

Zoya Hasan and Mushirul Hasan

In March 2005, within six months of the United Progressive Alliance (UPA) government coming to power, the Sachar Committee was set up to analyse the conditions of Muslims and to identify areas of intervention by the government to improve their socio-economic and educational conditions.[1] The Sachar Committee Report (SCR) highlighted the deep deficiencies and deprivation of the Muslim communities. The cabinet approved its recommendations with the Ministry of Minority Affairs (MoMA) designated as the nodal ministry to monitor implementation. The report sparked a lively debate among political parties, academics, and civil society.

The Committee revealed that the Muslims lagged behind in every aspect of socio-economic development, thus exposing the hollowness of the propaganda that they are being appeased. Most Muslims are much worse-off because they benefit from no affirmative action. Their status in contemporary India was not very different from that of the Dalits in the mid-twentieth century, which led to constitutionally mandated affirmative action in their favour. If we take 1947 as the baseline, Muslims have suffered downward mobility. This is not a new assessment for those who have investigated the socio-economic status of Muslims in India.[2] However, the significance of the report lies in the fact that it carries with it an official stamp, and, more importantly, the report used data from state institutions, which are important sources of social statistics all around the world. It confirms that the Muslims face economic deprivation, social exclusion, and political under-representation.

The SCR provides extensive data to bolster the case for government intervention for the development of Muslims, though not for treating them as an undifferentiated community. It saw a way out of the deprivation trap for Muslims through 'inclusive development and mainstreaming of the community, while respecting diversity'. This, it felt, could be attained by following a two-pronged approach of adopting general policy initiatives buttressed by specific policy measures, dealing with particular deprivations of minorities.

The Sachar report and its recommendations has been the subject of a major debate in the Muslim community as well. One of the biggest gains of the Sachar Committee was its reconstruction of the Muslim community as 'developmental subjects' of the state rather than primarily as a cultural and religious community. The report marks a decisive shift from the politics of identity to the politics of development because it was amply clear that the problems of the Muslims necessitated going beyond identity politics and the customary allegiance to secularism and pluralism. It led to a major shift in the focus of the government's social policies as it introduced the language of equality, of opportunity, and anti-discrimination evident in its recommendations for an equal opportunity commission and diversity index in public institutions. This is noticeable in the overall policy approach, principles, and the criterion for recognizing beneficiary groups as well as schemes for minorities. A new set of public programmes and schemes now exist to promote their development. These include improving infrastructure, creating assets in minority concentration districts, and making provision of merit-cum-means scholarships. While some of these initiatives have been more successful than others, many other have been ineffective in conception and implementation. Sixty-five years after Independence and six years after the submission of the SCR, a number of anomalies continue to trouble scholars and policymakers. They are principally concerned with the concept of minorities and the scope of state intervention in regard to their social and economic development. Public debates in the run-up to the Twelfth Five Year Plan focus on two aspects—whether the government should target Muslims qua Muslims or all the five officially recognized religious minorities or disadvantaged groups. This issue has been framed in terms of whether or not it is constitutionally appropriate to plan schemes along community lines or areas or sectoral lines. We seek to discuss this aspect, as also the response of the UPA government to the SCR. Moreover, we shed light on the implementation of programmes and schemes working on the ground and the extent to which they benefit those most in need of assistance.

The Prime Minister's 15-Point Programme

The Prime Minister's 15-Point Programme was recast to focus on the social, educational, and economic uplift of minorities. Although not new in conception or thrust, it seeks to ensure that the benefits of the government's welfare schemes must reach the minorities. Five ministries come under the ambit of the programme—Ministries of Human Resources and Development, Rural Development, Housing and Urban Poverty Alleviation, Women and Child Development, and Finance. The schemes under this programme include Sarva Shiksha Abhiyan (SSA), Integrated Child Development Services (ICDS), Kasturba Gandhi Balika Vidyalaya (KGBV), Swarnajayanti Gram Swarojgar Yojana (SGSY), Swarna Jayanti Shahari Rozgar Yojana (SJSRY), upgradation of existing industrial training institutes (ITIs), bank credit under priority lending, and Indira Awas Yojana (IAY). The government can allocate 15 per cent from the budget of these programmes for minorities.

There are several weaknesses of the 15-Point Programme however. To start with, it is obvious that very few schemes are included in the 15-Point Programme and those included the utilization of funds is tardy. Apart from narrow coverage, the programme focuses on basic services. It simply allocates funds to ongoing schemes without regard to specific needs of deprived

groups (CES 2011). Many of the schemes have to be administered by the states and there is no special assistance for states or districts with large minority populations to implement them. Moreover, in the beneficiary schemes, especially employment and livelihood, the 15 per cent fund allocation formula cannot be applied because they are demand-driven in nature, and hence no targets can be fixed (ibid.). Only individual beneficiary-oriented schemes such as IAY are amenable to the 15 per cent targeting for minorities; most of the others such as ICDS or SSA do not lend themselves to separate allocation for minorities as these are area development programmes. Besides a major chunk of the 15-Point Programme allocation in 2009–10 (62 per cent) went to the three Jawaharlal Nehru National Urban Renewal Mission (JNNURM) projects for urban development, which does not specifically benefit minorities.

The main constraint is the absence of institutional mechanisms and implementing staff at the district and block levels (ibid.). As to monitoring, no independent assessments, including a two-year in-depth evaluation mentioned in the guidelines or social audit reports have been done so far. No social audit reports or assessments have been placed in the public domain.

EDUCATION-RELATED SCHEMES

Access to education is an important equalizing force in an unequal society. For the Muslims, underachievement in education is a major reason for their deprivation. Government policy seeks to alleviate the educational gaps principally through two approaches. For school education, emphasis has been given to madrasas by funding posts and supporting their modernization to enable them to provide a small amount of modern education along with religious instruction for which they have been primarily established. While the modernization of madrasas is desirable, given their limited reach it cannot be a substitute for access to regular schools. As for higher education, there has been a growing reliance on minority educational institutions and private minority institutions established under Article 30 of the Constitution, which have been allowed by the Supreme Court the right to reserve seats for minorities. These minority institutions are expected to take up the responsibility of educating the Muslims. The single most important initiative of the UPA government in this regard was the establishment of the National Commission for Minority Educational Institutions (NCMEI) in 2004. The NCEMI supports direct affiliation of minority professional institutions with central universities to upgrade the standard and quality of education offered in the minority institutions, provided the relevant laws under which such universities are created allow such affiliation.

While there is no systematic attempt to evaluate the outcomes of these policies, there is no denying that this approach has not plugged the gap in educational disparities. In fact, the limited participation of Muslims in school and higher education calls into question the efficacy of existing policy as also the commitment to implement policies that would bridge the gap. The SCR makes it clear that there is no substitute for regular schools and colleges and the state's role in removal of supply-side constraints for the minorities is absolutely critical.

The UPA government has introduced four educational scholarship schemes to be implemented by the MoMA. These schemes are pre-matric, post-matric, merit-cum-means, and free coaching.[3] Apart from pre- and post-matric scholarship and fee reimbursement schemes, which are meant for both the sexes, the specific initiatives of the minorities welfare department include pre- and post-matric hostels and residential schools for girls. All scholarship schemes, including the fellowship scheme, have 30 per cent earmarking for girls. In fact, the MoMA states that 49 per cent of the total scholarships awarded by the Ministry went to women.[4] In the pre-matric, post-matric, and merit-cum-means schemes, 48.50, 52.95, and 34.44 per cent, respectively, went to girl students.[5] In addition, the Maulana Azad Education Foundation (MAEF) has awarded 59,303 scholarships to girl students with a total disbursement of Rs 69 crores since 2003.[6] Overall, the government has sanctioned Rs 1,094.94 crores as scholarships to 62.72 lakh students in 2011–12. Even with improvement in enrolment it still means only 1 out of each 4.55 enrolled Muslim children in Classes I–VII receives a scholarship (CES 2011: 23). Of the 20,000-odd post-matric scholarships to pursue professional and technical education, 14,585 have gone to Muslims. The allocation for scholarships for minorities in 2010–11 was Rs 256 crores, which is a rather small intervention to deal with the huge backlog of educational backwardness (ibid.). In higher education, the share of Muslims has improved the least compared with all socio-religious categories between 2004–5 and 2009–10. This is despite the much lower base level for them compared with other communities.[7]

A study by the Institute for Human Development (IHD) of the scholarship schemes in 2012 reveals the immense demand for such support as evident from the large numbers of minority students applying for the scholarships, especially at the pre- and post-matric levels (GoI 2012). It points out that the number of scholarships is few and the amount is small in comparison to the demand. The major difficulties reported are regarding opening a bank account and getting information about the scholarships.[8] If the scholarships are made universal and demand-driven then it would be possible to fund all the deserving minority students (ibid.).

MULTI-SECTORAL DEVELOPMENT PROGRAMME

A special scheme called the Multi-sectoral Development Programme (MsDP) was initiated in 90 minority concentration districts in 2008–9 for addressing the 'development deficits' of these districts and bringing them at par with the national average. The MsDP is the largest ever programme for the development of minorities since Independence directed at improving the overall parameters of minority concentration districts. Under this programme, funds are given to ongoing government schemes and public provisioning in minority concentration areas rather than target specific deprivations of minorities or Muslims. This was a follow-up to the SCR's finding that Muslims are concentrated in locations with poor infrastructural facilities and, therefore, the emphasis of government intervention should be infrastructure related.[9] The idea behind this scheme was to address the development deficit in minority concentration districts on the pattern of the Backward Regions Grant Fund (BRGF), Rashtriya Sam Vikas Yojana (RSYV), and Border Area Development Programme (BADP).

The selected districts are relatively backward and below the national average in terms of socio-economic and basic amenities indicators, and have a minority population of at least 25 per cent of all five minority communities and not Muslims alone. This means the MsDP does not focus only on the minority population as districts also cover several blocks/villages which have a substantially high non-minority population. Being a special area development programme, it envisages inclusive growth with benefits flowing to everyone in the district, and not the minorities alone and certainly not targeting of individual beneficiaries. In fact, the MoMA has repeatedly stated that no benefits can be given selectively to families of the minority communities. Hence, the focus has gone to the construction of health sub-centres (such as primary health centres or PHCs), school buildings, and anganwadi centres (AWCs). which are meant to benefit everyone and not just minorities. In fact, activities which could benefit minority groups, such as skill development, technical education, and income generation, which are essential for improving the socio-economic condition of minorities, are eschewed by the district administration and the government.

The MsDP is intended to replenish and top-up the existing centrally sponsored schemes (CSS), particularly those in the New 15-Point Programme for the development of social, economic, educational, and civic infrastructure. District plans of only 60 out of 90 districts had been approved by October 2011. The main reason for the slow pace of progress is delay in conceptualization of plans and transfer of funds to district authorities/implementing agencies by states/union territories (Shariff 2010). This in turn delays the actual execution of works by the districts/implementing agencies. The total allocation was Rs 3,780 crores, but the reported expenditure undertaken by the states until mid-2011 was a mere Rs 940 crores (ibid.). During 2007–12, state governments did not use even half of the allocated funds (Ali 2012). Of the 20 states, only 12 were able to utilize less than 50 per cent of the funds, and some states only 20 per cent. States which were unable to spend even 50 per cent of the funds include Uttarakhand, Sikkim, Arunachal Pradesh, Mizoram, Karnataka, Bihar, Uttar Pradesh, Assam, Meghalaya, Kerala, Maharashtra, and Jammu and Kashmir. Both Bihar and Uttar Pradesh with a high concentration of Muslims utilized less than 50 per cent of funds allocated to them (ibid.). Bihar was allocated Rs 523.20 crores, but it used only Rs 167.50 crores or 45.58 per cent of the funds, whereas Uttar Pradesh utilized Rs 347.61 crores or 48.08 per cent of the Rs 722.94 provided to it.[10]

The Parliamentary Standing Committee of the Ministry of Social Justice and Empowerment (2011–12) report noted that even the general works were not done. For example, 295,162 houses were supposed to be built under the IAY, but only 175,008 had been built (Tripathi 2012). As against 689 schools and 2,498 primary health care centres to be built under the MsDP, only 334 schools and 1,623 primary health care centres were ready by June 2012 (ibid.).

For the most part, the MsDP has been quite ineffective in alleviating the socio-economic deprivation of Muslims. There is a dissonance between the identified development deficits of minorities and the interventions rolled out for them. Poor access to basic services remains a major problem in Muslim-dominated areas. The provision of electricity and drinking water, a major problem in these areas for instance, is not earmarked for special attention. It does not find reflection in the priority list of needs identified for the districts. Efforts were made

initially by districts and states to propose projects aimed at the development of Muslims, but these were either turned down or were later reworked by districts to fit MoMA preferences, encouraging area-based projects rather than those targeted at the community (ibid.). The 'area development' as opposed to 'targeting' approach' prevents a focus on the particular needs of Muslims, and moreover the area approach is marked by its inability to take-up projects in Muslim concentration pockets up to the village level, limiting this to districts or blocks (ibid.).

There were strong protests against making district the unit of intervention because there are considerable problems in making it the lowest unit of disaggregation. With district as the unit, funds could be spent anywhere and a project could be set up anywhere where Muslims are not present in substantial numbers, and yet it will meet the criteria regardless of its benefits going to the intended beneficiaries. A better way would have been to make blocks, even villages and hamlets, rather than districts, the unit for planning projects. Government personnel admitted that there was a need to bring down the unit of planning from the district to the block level, but were constrained by the non-availability of block-level data to cover more and more population of the minorities.[11] The Planning Commission's Eleventh Plan Working Group on Empowering the Minorities recommended the same, but this was not accepted. This point has been gone over innumerable times by various committees. Although these programmes are specially designed to address Muslim backwardness, preference is given to the area approach arguing that benefits will also flow to the Muslims and minorities in them. Further, most interventions target 'minorities' rather than Muslims, but hardly any other religious minority suffers the development deficits that the Muslims do. Only a handful of interventions, such as those that deal with Waqf property and institutions, aim specifically at Muslims (CES 2011).

As to the 'trickle down' assumptions of the area approach—develop the district and 'backward' sections in it will also develop equitably—the logic has not quite worked.[12] The institutional weaknesses of the programme—absence of participatory planning and implementation, and exclusion of Panchayati Raj institutions and beneficiary groups from the process—means even the little promise of area development are belied. Nonetheless, but the area logic is taken further, by ensuring that where individual beneficiary schemes are taken up, benefits of that flow to all in the project area, and not only to minorities. Above all, the MsDP has been reduced to augmenting resources for existing flagship programmes.[13]

This underlines the flawed logic of the programme—that locating a project in an area of minority concentration solves the 'access' problem. Expecting that a project will benefit a disadvantaged community through a process of trickle down is disregarding the barriers that prevent the group from equitably accessing those benefits to begin with (CES 2011).

Targeting area or community

A critical issue that arises from this discussion is whether government programmes should directly benefit individuals, households, and settlements of minorities, and provide education, skills, livelihood, water, and sanitation to them or should they focus on the development of the area. The government is reluctant to go beyond the area development approach because of the fear that any minority-specific scheme runs the risk of challenge in courts, whereas the area development programme does not attract any legal challenge. However, the Bombay, Gujarat, and Delhi high courts rejected four petitions that questioned the constitutionality of the merit-cum-means scholarship scheme for students of minority communities. The courts ruled that these schemes do not violate the constitutional principles of equality or affect any of the fundamental rights guaranteed to the members of the other communities. Since only a minuscule of total tax revenue or education cess was utilized for providing some facilities to any religious denomination, especially the underprivileged and disadvantaged among them, the students of the majority community were not discriminated against. What emerges is that if it can be established that a group of persons are socially and educationally backward minority communities included, they would be entitled to affirmative action under Article 15(4). Only schemes directed at the entire community run the risk of falling foul of the Constitution. Nonetheless, the proposal for a Minority Sub-plan on the lines of the tribal sub-plan or the Scheduled Castes Component Plan did not find favour with the Planning Commission during the discussions on the Eleventh Plan for fear that it would be charged with commnalizing the planning process. This objection was driven by the argument that the Constitution makes special mention of Scheduled Castes (SCs) and Scheduled Tribes (STs) for affirmative intervention, not of Muslims (Hasan 2009: Chapter 6). The scepticism had more to do with fears of a political fallout than conceptual or constitutional doubts with regard to the efficacy of a sub-plan.

Hence, the MsDP, steers clear of targeting minorities. The contention is that minorities have to be un-derstood as a collective group and all interventions have to be for the disadvantaged and underprivileged among them in consonance with Articles 15 and 16 of the Constitution.[14] The Ministry of Law and Justice has repeatedly raised objections to a minority-specific proposal whenever it is mooted stating that the Constitution does not permit to be treated favourably except with regard to rights relating to religion, cultural, and education rights. Discrimination in their favour would be contrary to guarantees under Articles 14, 15, and 16.[15] For instance, it also objected to proposals of increasing the authorized share capital of National Finance and Development Corporation (NFDC), again on the same ground. In short, the schemes should have universal coverage and not target minorities.

The area approach also follows from the Sachar Committee's finding of Muslims being concentrated in locations with poor infrastructure facilities. It uses the same logic as 15-Point Programme—augment social and economic infrastructure in the identified districts so as to bring the district at par with the national level assuming again that benefits will flow equitably to all, including minorities, in them. It is theoretically possible to raise the district's overall development indicators, while making little impact on that of Muslims or even other minorities. By creating facilities such as a PHC in a village with a high concentration of Muslims, or an ITI in the district, it was hoped that the Muslims would be able to make use of those facilities. But the experience so far shows that the benefits are not reaching the minorities as funds are flowing to blocks which have their negligible presence.

A civil society based assessment of minority welfare schemes carried out by the Centre for Equity Studies (CES) entitled 'Promises To Keep: Investigating the Government's Response to the Sachar Committee Recommendations' submitted to the National Advisory Council (NAC) in May 2011 concluded that 'the UPA government's minority welfare agenda was floundering due to lack of will, outreach and funds' (CES 2011). It criticized government schemes for being too small in scale and not sufficiently targeted, for instance, at Muslims in particular, to have an impact. Government programmes have been reduced to area schemes that mostly miss the minorities. It notes that right from the MoMA to the district level and below, the officers lack conviction, clout, and even a mandate to directly tackle the socio-economic structural discrimination faced by the Muslims (ibid.). Diffidence at the policy level to clearly focus on Muslim deprivation translates into active reluctance by the implementing agencies on the ground to target the

Muslims even in districts with high Muslim concentration. The report stated that district plans should target Muslim-dominated villages, hamlets, or urban settlements so that the benefits reach the right people rather than reaching everybody else. The NAC also asked the government to direct minority welfare schemes not to districts as a whole, but to individual hamlets and settlements. The NAC members felt that targeting the government's 15-Point plan at minority-dominated districts was flawed as the benefits are not reaching the intended targets. For the Twelfth Plan, the MoMA has taken a decision to make blocks (instead of districts) the criteria of its implementation for MsDP and also to extend it to towns and cities.

NOT ENOUGH HAS BEEN DONE

Although it is too early to offer a comprehensive assessment of government interventions as many of the measures have been introduced quite recently and, therefore, are yet to demonstrate their effectiveness. However, six years after the submission of the Sachar report not enough has been done on the ground. Internal assessments indicate that minority schemes are underperforming and need a boost to inject a fresh sense of purpose in programmes seen as politically significant. There are serious concerns with regard to institutional capacity, poor monitoring and coordination, and delays in fund releases, among others. However, Prime Minister Manmohan Singh in 2011 claimed that his government's initiatives have begun to impact the status of minorities.[16] Referring to the persisting impression that the government had set up the Sachar Committee, but was lackadaisical in implementing its recommendations, he said the reality was the opposite. 'I have often heard people comment that we have not implemented the Sachar recommendations. I want to tell you today that this is not true at all. We have not only drawn up schemes and plans based on Sachar recommendations, these initiatives have begun to impact the status of minorities,' he said (ibid.).[17]

Rejecting the government's claims that it was according high priority to the execution of decisions taken on Sachar Committee's recommendations, the Standing Committee of the Ministry of Social Justice and Empowerment found fault with its implementation, and said that the MoMA was not addressing the root of the problems highlighted in the report (Ghosh 2011). The Committee came out with a damning report card on the performance of the UPA government with regard to minority-related initiatives. It suggested that the government should bring a law to ensure time-bound implementation.

For over five decades after Independence, the development of minorities was constrained by the absence of a substantive conception of minority rights to promote equal opportunity. Until the Eleventh Plan, there were no developmental plans attending to minorities. Now the issue is not the absence of policies for minority development, but the failure to enlarge the scope of state intervention and budgetary allocations to reverse their deprivation. Recognition of religious minorities for policy attention is constitutionally acceptable, yet it is still not politically acceptable because it can lead to a majoritarian backlash or communalization of the polity. Even so, these are choices that governments are called upon to make in relation to their social priorities. The basic issue, therefore, is not with regard to policy but political processes, because of which the minority category remains contentious and is seen as perpetrating vote-bank politics.[18]

The Congress, which has always claimed that it is the party most concerned about Muslim interests and in keeping with this concern it had appointed the Sachar Committee to look into the problems of the community, has not shown the requisite political will to implement its major recommendations. An Expert Group on Diversity Index had in 2008 recommended the setting up of Diversity Commission and Diversity Implementation Boards as institutional mechanisms for affirmative action and policy targeting (GoI 2008). Another Expert Group Report that year suggested the creation of an Equal Opportunity Commission (EOC), aimed at promoting diversity in education and employment by exercising the powers of a civil court to give shape to the equality jurisprudence of the Constitution and ensure inclusive development (Menon 2008).[19] Visualized as a body to tackle all kinds of discrimination, the EOC faced hostility from the established social constituencies and national commissions amid fears that it would make several existing commissions redundant. The larger mandate of working for all disadvantaged sections was seen to be an encroachment on their turf and, therefore, they want it to be confined to minorities. A Group of Ministers (GoM) headed by Defence Minister A.K. Antony in August 2010 duly concluded that the EOC should confine only to minorities. This failed to resolve the jurisdiction issue. This decision faced opposition from the National Commission for Minorities (NCM), which tackles cases of violation of minority rights, over possible overlap in functions.

A major problem in regard to minority development is too little funding of government programmes for their welfare. The proposed allocation for the Eleventh Plan was Rs 17,224 crores against which the final allocation was fixed at Rs 7,000 crores. The per capita allocation for minorities in 2010–11 was much lower than for the other disadvantaged groups (CES 2011: 39). The minority share in the total fund allocation in 2010–11 was 5.33 per cent which was insufficient. The funding for the Scheduled Caste Plan was higher at 7.19 per cent with a population share of 16 per cent and 14.13 per cent for the Scheduled Tribe Plan with a population of 8.2 per cent. The bulk of the 15-Point Programme allocations in 2010–11 went to the JNUURM projects for urban development, urban infrastructure, and governance.

Apart from under-funding, the matter of even greater concern was under-utilization of these meagre funds, especially schemes implemented by the MoMA. The Twelfth Plan Steering Committee Report on 'Empowerment of Minorities' noted the under-spending in areas relating to education and the MsDP because of non-submission of proposals (GoI 2012b).

The central government can devise programmes and increase outlays for centrally sponsored schemes, but it has to depend upon the states to implement them. Most issues such as education, security, and employment fall under the purview of state governments rather than the central government and states require institutional capacity for implementing these schemes. The institutional strength and absorptive capacities in the state and district levels are still very weak in many states even today (ibid.). Most of them do not even have separate and well-endowed Department of Minorities Welfare (ibid.).

Overall, it is fair to say that the UPA government's response has been cautious and minimalist to do what is absolutely necessary to bolster its support among the Muslims at a time when the Congress has seen erosion in its social support, particularly among the Muslims. But it has been reluctant to unveil serious and sustained measures to plug the gaps in intergroup inequalities. The cautious response in regard to the Muslims has much to do with the politics of polarization practised by the BJP, which has targeted minority groups, especially the Muslims and Christians, charging them with extra-territorial loyalties with the intention of diluting their national credentials and thereby questioning their claim to special measures and benefits given by the state. As in the past, the BJP objects to the incorporation of any special measures or budgetary allocations for minorities, and disparaged the latter as 'communal budgeting'. But the weak-kneed response also has to do with the politics of tokenism the Congress resorts to which has been

accentuated after the BJP's rise to power at the centre. Before the 2009 elections, the Congress had identified the implementation of the SCR as one of the major challenges facing it. Muslim support played a significant part in its re-election in the 2009 Lok Sabha polls and hence the expectation that the UPA government would give priority to SCR implementation. But this did not happen. Members of Parliament (MPs) belonging to different parties expressed dissatisfaction regarding government inaction during the Rajya Sabha debate on the SCR.

The Sachar Report recommendations, if implemented and monitored well, have the capacity to alter the social and political position of the Muslim minority. Yet, the UPA has failed to live up to the expectations it has created because its implementation has not been a priority. Hence, the objectives of the inclusive agenda relating to the Muslim minority remains work in progress. The Planning Commission's Approach Paper to the Twelfth Plan says that 'the acceleration of growth in recent years has been accompanied by efforts at greater inclusiveness which has had resonance in many of the slower growing states. However, within this framework of acceleration, despite efforts to be inclusive, there are concerns whether historically disadvantaged groups have benefited adequately…. The Twelfth Plan needs to proactively address these concerns.'

In 2006, the decision to carve out a separate ministry for minority affairs seemed like a bold decision. Since then, all that it seems to be doing is vetting minority-related initiatives of other ministries. The Ministry has not been able to translate its mandate into a broader agenda of affirmative action. On the one hand, its programmes are too small or not sufficiently targeted (Manoj 2012). On the other hand, having made the MoMA the pivot for the implementation of minority development, it did not introduce minority-specific initiatives beyond the MsDP and scholarships. The minority-specific schemes were generally uncoordinated and, therefore, unlikely to have a significant impact on their welfare. Basically, these schemes are not based on a proper assessment of minority needs and requirements. In addition to specific minority-targeted schemes, there is a need for durable structural changes, a recognition that deprivation amongst Muslims exists due to systemic causes which can be set right by mainstreaming and greater inclusion in existing government programmes and by helping them to access their share within the mainstream line of ministries, departments, and programmes.

NOTES

1. The Prime Minister constituted a 'High Level Committee on the Social, Economic and Educational Status of the Muslim Community of India', charged with investigating the socio-economic status of Muslims in 2005 (GoI 2006). The Committee chaired by Rajinder Sachar, Former Chief Justice of the Delhi High Court, submitted the report to the Prime Minister in November 2006.

2. For example, the study of the socio-economic status of Muslim women based on the national-level survey of 10,000 Muslim and Hindu women covering a range of issues from education, work, access to welfare, etc., found that Muslims are generally poor and disadvantaged and that they are only slightly better-off than the SCs. See Hasan and Menon (2004), especially Chapter 2 on 'Socioeconomic Status of Households'.

3. The MoMA started in 2006 with five schemes and a budget allocation of Rs 130.89 crores. By 2009 it was running 12 schemes on a budget of Rs 2,600 crores. The MoMA's allocation was Rs 7,000 crores which is 0.32 per cent of the Eleventh Plan outlay. The bulk of this funding went to the states which are expected to implement these programmes.

4. See 'Follow Up on Sachar Committee Report', status as on 31 March 2012. Available at minorityaffairs.gov.in/sites/upload_files/moma/.../sachar%20updated_0.pdf (accessed 4 August 2012).

5. Ibid.

6. Ibid.

7. Note by Abusaleh Shariff submitted to the Planning Commission, reported in Ghosh (2011).

8. Ibid.

9. For more details of the MSDP, see http://www.minorityaffairs.gov.in/MSDP.

10. The 27th Report, Standing Committee on Social Justice and Empowerment (2011–2012), Ministry of Minority Affairs, presented to the Lok Sabha on 9.5.2012, Lok Sabha Secretariat, New Delhi, 2012.

11. Ibid.

12. Empowered Committee (EC) meeting minutes: 'the scheme, while giving priority to villages/areas having a substantial minority population, (is) intended to benefit the district as a whole, as it is a special area development programme.' This point is reiterated in every EC meeting. See Minutes of the 16th Meeting of EC, 28 July 2009, p. 1 in CES (2011).

13. This point was made very clearly in EC meetings: 'The programme envisages providing additional resources to various existing Centrally Sponsored Schemes (CSS)....' Minutes of the 16th Meeting of EC, 28 July 2009.

14. Response of the MoMA submitted to the NAC, p. 7.

15. Ibid, p. 8.

16. 'Minorities have benefited after Sachar Committee report, says Manmohan'. Prime Minister Manmohan Singh's speech reported in The Hindu, 30 December 2011.

17. Ibid.

18. On this, see Hasan (2009: Chapter 3).

19. The expert group constituted by the MoMA recommended that the EOC will cover all deprived and discriminated groups. However, in August 2010, the GoM decided to limit the mandate of the EOC to minorities. This recommendation was made after most minorities shot down the proposal for an EOC with a mandate to cover multiple groups across religious barriers.

REFERENCES

Ali, Mohammed. 2012. 'Minority Funds Go a-begging', The Hindu, 27 July.

CES (Centre of Equity Studies). 2011. 'Promises to Keep: Investigating Government's Response to the Sachar Committee Recommendations', Study report submitted to the NAC. New Delhi: CES.

Ghosh, Abantika. 2011. 'PM Urged to Review Sachar Panel's Recommendations', The Times of India, 6 September.

GoI (Government of India). 2006. Social, Economic and Educational Status of the Muslim Community of India, November. New Delhi: Prime Minister's High Level Committee, Cabinet Secretariat, GoI.

———. 2008. 'Report of the Expert Group on Diversity Index', submitted to the MoMA. Available at www.minorityaffairs.gov.in/sites/upload_files/moma/files/.../di_expgrp.pdf (accessed 7 August 2011).

———. 2012a. 'Evaluation and Impact Assessment Study of the Educational Scholarship Programmes of Ministry of Minority Affairs'. New Delhi: Government of India, coordinated by Indian Council of Social Science Research (ICSSR).

———. 2012b. 'Report of the Steering Committee on "Empowerment of Minorities"'. New Delhi: Planning Commission, GoI.

Hasan, Zoya. 2009. Politics of Inclusion: Caste, Minority, and Affirmative Action. New Delhi: Oxford University Press.

Hasan, Zoya and Ritu Menon. 2004. Unequal Citizens: Socioeconomic Status of Muslim Women in India. New Delhi: Oxford University Press.

Manoj, C.G. 2012. 'Ministry of Minor Achievements', The Indian Express, 10 October.

Menon, Madhava. 2008. 'Equal Opportunity Commission: What, Why and How?' Report submitted to the MoMA, GoI. Available at www.minorityaffairs.gov.in/sites/upload_files/moma/files/.../eoc_wwh.pdf (accessed 7 August 2011).

Menon, Meena. 2012. 'Muslims Bear the Brunt of Faulty Scholarship Schemes', The Hindu, 2 September.

Shariff, Abusaleh. 2010. 'Muslims: The Lamb's Share', Outlook, 23 August.

Tripathi, Purnima. 2012. 'Hollow Promise', Frontline, 29(12, 16–29 June). Available at http://www.frontlineonnet.com/fl2912/stories/20120629291209900.htm.

16

Government's Commitment towards Development of Muslims

A Post-Sachar Assessment of Uttar Pradesh and Haryana[*]

Jawed Alam Khan and Pooja Parvati

Sixty-three years before, the Constitution of India put down as fundamental guarantees to all its citizens—social justice, liberty of faith and worship, equality of status and opportunity, and dignity of the individual. Given the vast diversity of the country's population, the underlying philosophy of governance for the country could not have been more apt. However, when we review the status of the minority community, more specifically the Muslims in the country, we find that this promise to secure for all citizens equality, liberty, and justice has not been honoured in full measure.

'Minority' as a term is mentioned in the Constitution in Articles 29 to 30 and 350A to 350 B, but no definitions are given. Article 29 refers to 'minorities' and speaks of 'any sections of citizens … having a distinct language, script or culture'. Article 30 speaks specifically of two categories of minorities—religious and linguistic. The remaining two Articles—350A and 350B—relate only to linguistic minorities. The Oxford Dictionary defines 'Minority' as a 'smaller number or part; a number or part representing less than half of the whole; a relatively small group of people, differing from others in race, religion, language or political persuasion'. A special Sub-Committee on the Protection of Minority Rights appointed by the United Nations Human Rights Commission (UNHRC) in 1946 defined 'minority' as those 'non-dominant groups in a population which possess a wish to preserve stable ethnic, religious and linguistic traditions or characteristics markedly different from those of the rest of population' (Mishra 2007: 3).

The Indian Constitution distinguishes 212 listed ethnic communities, which collectively form around 7.5 per cent of India's population. As regards religious minorities at the national level in India, all those who profess a religion other than Hinduism are considered minorities, since over 80 per cent population of the country professes Hinduism. At the national level, the Muslims are the largest minority (13.4 per cent). Next to them are the Christians (2.34 per cent) and Sikhs (1.9 per cent), while all other religious groups are still smaller.

With the growing realization among policymakers that the minorities are confronted by diverse and unique challenges, it led to the expectation that the needs of minority communities would have to be recognized separately and provisions made for their welfare in the national Five Year Plans. However, it was not until the Sixth Plan that the minorities were acknowledged as a separate socio-economic group and provisions were made for them through the Minimum Needs Programme.

---

[*] This is a substantially revised version of the chapter available at http://www.cbgaindia.org/files/recent_publications/Policy%20priorities%20for%20Development%20of%20Muslims%20in%20the%2011th%20Plan-An%20assessment.pdf.

In light of the acknowledgment of the dearth of authentic information about the social, economic, and educational condition of the Muslims in India, a Prime Minister's High Level Committee (PMHLC) was formed to assess the social, economic, and educational status of the Muslim community in India in 2005. Also known as the Sachar Committee Report (SCR), the detailed report out in the end of 2006 highlighted the socio-economic plight of the Indian Muslims as compared to the general population. The Report attempted to understand the exclusion of the Muslims in the policy space by moving away from the 'identity' and 'security' question to concerns pertaining to 'development' and 'participation'.

Looking at the development indicators, poverty among the Muslims is higher than that in rural areas. The percentage share of poverty among the Muslims in urban areas was 44 per cent, while the comparable estimate for other minority groups was found to be 16 per cent of poor people. Around 35 per cent of Muslim women had body mass index less than 18.5, and 54.7 per cent women were anaemic as of 2005–6. The indicators with respect to children are also dismal with the infant mortality rate (IMR) found to be around 52.4 per cent and under 5 mortality rate (U5MR) as high as 82.7 per cent in 2005–6.

According to data available from SCR (GoI 2006), the literacy rate among the Muslims (59.1 per cent) in 2001 was far below the national average (65.1 per cent) and other socio-religious communities (SRCs) (70.8 per cent). State-level estimates suggested that the literacy gap between the Muslims and the general average was greater in urban areas and particularly for women. The gap between the Muslims and other SRCs increased with the increase in the level of education. Besides, around 29 per cent of children (aged 6 to 17 years) reported to be out-of-school were from the Muslim community, which is much higher than the figures for other religious groups in the country.

Related to employment, there is an incidence of low aggregate work participation ratios for the Muslims and particularly Muslim women. The participation of the Muslims in salaried jobs, both in the public and private sectors is quite low compared to the Scheduled Castes (SCs) and Scheduled Tribes (STs). Most of the Muslims are involved in self-employment. The presence of the Muslims was found to be low in government-sector employment. It is only 3 per cent in the Indian Administrative Services, 1.8 per cent in the Indian Foreign Services, and 4 per cent in the Indian Police Services including other police and security services. The share of Muslims in employment in various departments and public sector undertakings (PSUs) was abysmally low at all levels.

The situation pertaining to the share of Muslims in availing institutional credit in 'unpaid/outstanding amount' was only 4.7 per cent as compared to 6.5 per cent of other minorities. The Reserve Bank of India's (RBI) efforts to extend banking and credit facilities under the Prime Minister's 15-Point Programme have mainly benefited other minorities and the Muslims have remained marginalized. Another important finding was that as compared to the Muslim majority areas, the areas inhabiting fewer Muslims had better roads, sewage and drainage, and water supply facilities. In 2008–9, only 67.5 per cent of Muslim households had access to electricity for domestic use compared too much higher rates for other groups (UNDP 2011).

Following from the report findings, the union government stepped up its commitment to address the problems of inequality, deprivation, and exclusion among the Muslims in the Eleventh Plan period, which included educational and economic empowerment, access to public services, strengthening of minority institutions, and area development programmes.

OVERVIEW OF POLICY COMMITMENTS FOR MUSLIMS IN INDIA

In 2006, the union government revamped the Prime Minister's 15-Point Programme and brought to focus the vital concerns of education, employment and skill development, living conditions, and security among the Muslims by bringing within its ambit select flagship schemes and interventions.[1] In 2007–8, the Ministry of Minority Affairs (MoMA) launched the Multi-sectoral Development Programme (MsDP) that adopted an area development approach with a bouquet of schemes to address deficits related to housing, drinking water, electricity, female and total literacy, institutional delivery and vaccination, and female and total work participation.

The MsDP was introduced in 90 Minority Concentration Districts (MCDs) of 29 states/union territories. Under MCDs, the districts were selected where there is at least 25 per cent minority population or more than 5 lakh minority population and also those districts where the minority population falls between 20 and 25 per cent of the total population. In the six states/union territories, where a minority community is in majority, 15 per cent of the minority population criteria has been used for selecting the MCDs in those states. These relatively backward states/union territories had also lagged behind the national average in terms of eight socio-economic and basic amenities indicators were identified for the overall development of minorities as per the 2001 Census.

Out of the 90 districts, 53 districts were classified under Category A as those lagging behind in terms of socio-economic indicators and provision of basic amenities. The remaining 37 districts fell under Category B of which 20 districts lagged behind in terms of socio-economic parameters and 17 districts with regard to basic amenities parameters. Among the 90 MCDs, around 66 districts belonged to Muslim-concentrated districts. In terms of institutional strengthening, the government resolved to strengthen the National Minorities Development and Finance Corporation (NMDFC) and the Maulana Azad Education Foundation (MAEF).

To promote access to credit among the backward sections within the minorities, the NMDFC[3] was established in 1994. It focuses on providing microfinance to the poorest of poor among minorities through non-governmental organizations (NGOs), educational loans to persons belonging to the minority community, facilitating vocational training programmes among the minority community, and financing tailor-made market assistance options to artisans and crafts persons. The RBI focuses on opening more branches in areas that have a concentration of minority population and distributing 15 per cent of total credit to minorities under PSL as per the RBI Master Circular, 2006.

The MoMA implements five scholarship schemes apart from the MAEF[4] that aim at addressing education deficit among the minority community. These schemes include (a) pre-matric for up to Class X; (b) post-matric for Class XI to PhD; (c) merit-cum-means for technical and professional courses at undergraduate and postgraduate levels; (d) free coaching and allied scheme for competitive examinations; and (e) Maulana Azad National Fellowship for minority students pursuing MPhil and PhD.[5]

A commonly held critique of most of these interventions has been that they have targeted the minority community at large and not really addressed the specific disadvantages confronting the Muslim community. The MsDP was seen as a gap-filling measure to address the development deficits in MCDs that would be implemented on the lines of schemes like the Backward Regions Grant Fund (BRGF). This notwithstanding, the MsDP was found wanting in terms of institutional mechanisms (clarity of planning, implementation channels, and coordination among various agencies involved in many states and districts).

Evaluating the progress made in terms of integrating concerns of the Muslims, we find that even after six years of supposed policy initiatives in this direction, there remain gaps in policy provisions and concomitant budgets, utilization of funds, and fine-tuning the design of government programmes specific to the development of minorities. This chapter reviews the adequacy of the government's policy initiatives and budgetary provisions in the backdrop of the Sachar Committee recommendations.

The chapter is based on primary as well as secondary data sources. Two districts were selected for primary data collection: Barabanki in Uttar Pradesh and Mewat in Haryana. At the district level, perceptions were gathered from government officials, panchayat functionaries, and the intended beneficiaries, that is, the Muslim community. Household surveys were conducted in four gram panchayats in each district and 40 questionnaires were administered in each gram panchayat. The gram panchayats include the following: in Barabanki, Mohsand, and Bahrauli in Nindura block, and Badagaon and Bansa in Masauli block; and in Mewat, Pinagua, and Singar in Punahna block, and Goila and Mohammedpur Ahir in Tauru block.

ALLOCATION AND FUND UTILIZATION

According to the 2001 Census, minorities constitute approximately 19 per cent of the total population in the country. In the Eleventh Plan period, total allocations for minorities accounted for about 6 per cent of the total plan outlay that includes central sector plan and central assistance to state plan. The share of MoMA in total allocations being 0.79 per cent of the total central sector plan is insignificant to address development of minorities. Akin to the allocations made under the Scheduled Caste Sub-Plan (SCSP) and the Tribal Sub-Plan (TSP), where budgetary outlays are made in proportion to the share of SC and ST population in the country, the time is right to initiate a discussion on whether such budgetary strategies (that is, of allocating budgets in proportion to the share of minority population) can be thought of for the minorities as well (Table 16.1).

The total resource availability for minorities includes allocations made towards the MoMA, the Prime Minister's New 15-Point Programme, and some programmes like madrasa modernization, promotion of Urdu language, and Haj subsidies. Disaggregating this, we find that major allocations were made through four of the Jawaharlal

Table 16.1   Share of Resource Allocation by Union
Government for Minorities during the
Eleventh Plan (in Rs crores)

A. Total plan allocation earmarked for minorities	105,807.2
B. Total plan allocation of union govt. (including central assistance to state plan)	1,588,273
A as % of B	6.66

Source: MoMA, Government of India (GoI) and *Expenditure Budget*, vols I and II, Union Budget documents, GoI, available at www.india.budget.nic.in.

Nehru National Urban Renewal Mission (JNNURM) projects [Basic Services to Urban Poor (BSUP), Integrated Housing and Slum Development Programme (IHSDP), Urban Infrastructure Development Scheme for Small and Medium Towns (UIDSSMT), and Urban Infrastructure and Governance (UIG)] for urban infrastructure constituting 70 per cent of the total allocation meant for minorities. However, the operationalization and accounting system appears unclear about the inclusion of minorities in JNNURM at the state and district levels in Bihar, Haryana, Uttar Pradesh, and West Bengal. From this, it can be safely inferred that details of most of the allocations given on the MoMA website under JNNURM are *notional* as most of the schemes do not report beneficiary data on minorities (Table 16.2).

Further, funds for scholarship schemes, given the level of educational backwardness among the Muslims, is woefully inadequate. As per the annual target, the union government has provided 24 lakh pre-matric scholarships annually for minorities. According to District Information System for Education (DISE) data on enrolment, there are around 2.45 crore students from the Muslim community enrolled up to the upper primary level in 2009–10, which shows that per-student availability of pre-matric scholarships is highly uneven. Moreover, there is a very low unit cost reimbursed for pre-matric scholarships which is just Rs 1,000 per annum. In case of the MsDP, Rs 8 crore per district annually has been allocated in 90 MCDs during the plan period. With regard to the MAEF, the allocation has been insignificant to cater to the educational requirements of the Muslims.

With regard to fund utilization, the average utilization of funds accounted for 78 per cent of the total outlay for MoMA in the Eleventh Plan period (total tentative plan outlay for MoMA was Rs 8,690 crores). The MoMA shared that poor utilization is also owing to a late start (in 2008–9) in the implementation of major schemes such as pre-matric scholarship and the MsDP for select MCDs.

Table 16.2   Resource Allocation for Minorities during the
Eleventh Plan Period

Schemes	Amount (in Rs crores)	Share (in %)
BSUP	31,431.08	29.73
IHSDP	8,147.59	7.71
UIG	26,495.95	25.06
UIDSSMT	7,825.81	7.40
Indira Awas Yojana (IAY)	8,216.426	7.77
National Rural Drinking Water Programme (NRDWP)	14,045.31	13.28
Industrial Training Institutes (ITIs)	163	0.15
Swarna Jayanti Shahari Rozgar Yojana (SJSRY)	192	0.18
Madrasa modernization programme	450	0.43
Other schemes**	150	0.14
MoMA	8,690	8.22
Total	105,807.2	100.00

Source: MoMA, GoI and *Expenditure Budget*, vols I and II, Union Budget documents, GoI, available at www.india.budget.nic.in.
Notes: ** Other schemes include promotion of Urdu language and Haj subsidies; Prime Minister's New 15-Point Programme does not provide fund allocation data for Sarva Shiksha Abhiyan (SSA), Swarnajayanti Gram Swarojgar Yojana (SGSY), and Integrated Child Development Services (ICDS).

Moving on to review the status of fund utilization for specific programmes, we find that utilization trends for Prime Minister's New 15-Point programme are not captured at all. In the programme, no scheme other than IAY and SGSY reports expenditure data disaggregated on the basis of minorities.

Related factors for delays include non-submission of complete proposals by the state governments for MsDP and delays in the submission of utilization certificates. These bottlenecks are evidenced more in the scholarship schemes and the MsDP where lack of institutional arrangements, inadequate planning capacity, shortage of staff and infrastructure and insufficient funds to monitor the programmes have crippled effective working of these schemes (Table 16.3).

Fund utilization under all the four schemes[6] has improved in the Eleventh Plan period although the three schemes, that is, pre-matric, post-matric, and merit-cum-means, report inadequate utilization[7] (Table 16.4). The low rate of utilization in scholarship schemes is mostly reflective of the government's inability to make these schemes popular among the beneficiaries although actual

Table 16.3   Status of Fund Utilization under the MoMA
(in Rs crore)

Year	Allocation (BE)	Expenditure	Utilization (in %)
2007–8	500	196.65	39.33
2008–9	1000	619.09	61.86
2009–10	1740	1,709.42	98.24
2010–11	2600	2,080.86	77.26
2011–12	2850	2,292.27	80.43
Total	8690	6,826.22	78.55

Source: MoMA, GoI.
Note: BE = Budget Estimate.

performance would depend on how far the physical targets are met.

Table 16.4   Fund Utilization in Education-related
Schemes for Minorities during the
Eleventh Plan

Schemes	Allocation	Expenditure	Utilization (in %)
Pre-matric	1,400	1,327.33	94.81
Post-matric	1,150	820.85	71.38
Merit-cum-means	600	427.35	71.23
Free coaching	45	54.61	121.36

Source: Budget allocation and expenditure for the Eleventh Five Year Plan, MoMA, GoI.

In this regard, all five schemes (Table 16.5) show improvement in meeting targets. Pre-matric, post-matric, and merit-cum-means scholarships fare better in terms of the physical targets, but not well enough to achieve the financial targets set in the Eleventh Plan (Table 16.5). There is a significant increase in the number of scholarships which could be due to the inclusion of renewal of existing scholarship grantees along with fresh allotments. However, the mismatch between financial and physical

achievements could be due to scholarships getting concentrated within courses (non-vocational, non-technical, day scholars) or income groups that require lower fees.[8]

Table 16.5   Physical Performance in Select Schemes
during the Eleventh Plan (in Rs lakhs)

Scheme	Target	Achievement
Pre-matric	72	121.91
Post-matric	14.25	17.87
Merit-cum-means	2.07	1.62
Free coaching	0.25	0.28
Maulana Azad National Fellowship	0.02	0.02
Total	88.59	141.7

Source: MoMA, GoI.

The initial Eleventh Plan outlays for the MsDP of Rs 2,750 crores (total plan outlay for MoMA being Rs 7,000 crores) was raised to Rs 3,747crores. Moving on to look at expenditures, only 47 per cent of the total Plan outlay was spent by the 89 approved projects. At the district level, Mewat (Haryana) reported 25 per cent utilization while Barabanki (Uttar Pradesh) spent 60 per cent of the allocated funds. Under-utilization of funds also impacted completion of activities. Based on perceptions shared by the district-level officials, the slow pace and poor utilization has been due to delays in fund releases from the centre to states and further down to districts/implementing agencies.

In terms of the priority and nature of projects approved, the focus has been mainly on IAY (28 per cent), Anganwadi Centre or AWC (26 per cent), education (21 per cent), skill upgradation (11 per cent), health facilities (9 per cent), and drinking water supply (5 per cent). Table 16.7 reveals that the targets for provisioning of major services are not even near the halfway mark even though it has been more than five years of implementation of the programme; ideally, all these activities should have been completed by 2010.

Table 16.6   Financial Performance of MsDP in Uttar Pradesh and Haryana* (in Rs crore)

State	No. of MCDs	No. of MCDs with Approved Plans	Approved Cost of Projects in MCDs	Expenditure	% of Utilization
Uttar Pradesh	21	21	1,003.9	505	50.31
Haryana	2	2	49	30	61
Total	90	90	3,734	1769	47

Source: MoMA, GoI.
Note: *As per the Eleventh Five Year Plan.

Table 16.7 Physical Progress in MsDP in Uttar Pradesh and Haryana*

		IAY	Total of Health	AWC	Hand Pumps/DWS	Additional Classroom	School Building	ITI Building	Polytechnic	Hostels
Uttar Pradesh	T	84,730	960	9,581	11,984	626	59	32	19	9
	A	54,045	429	3,798	5,203	78	0	0	0	0
	% completion	64	45	40	43	12	0	0	0	0
Haryana	T	2000	6	142		183	8	1		
	A	1911	0	71		63	6			
	% completion	95.95	0	50		34	75	0		
Total	T	301,556	2,624	27,797	34,553	13,825	696	71	31	332
	A	126,128	953	9,956	15,761	4,416	103			2
	% completion	42	36	36	46	32	15	0	0	1

Source: MoMA, GoI.
Notes: * As per the Eleventh Five Year Plan; T = Target; A = Achievement; ITI = Industrial Training Institutes.

To cite some instances, construction of primary health centres (PHCs), community health centres (CHCs), and other education-related infrastructure have been delayed in Mewat while in Pinagua and Singar gram panchayats, although the foundation of the CHC was laid in 2010, there has been no progress since. In Barabanki, more than 50 per cent of works under different components have been completed. While there has been substantial progress in the construction of IAY houses and AWCs, the pace of work on upgradation and construction of senior secondary schools is sluggish.[9]

The delays in meeting the physical targets have occurred mainly due to lack of requisite institutional arrangements. Examples abound, Bihar and Haryana suffer from the absence of a minority welfare department at the district level. It is worth noting that the MsDP is being implemented by the District Planning Office in Bihar, while in Haryana, it is the Mewat Development Agency. Poor planning capacity, delay in identifying executing agencies, and indifference of the line departments busy implementing their own projects with little time to spare, are some of the related factors.

POLICY DESIGN AND IMPLEMENTATION CHALLENGES

Having looked at the concerns relating to budgetary allocations and concomitant utilization, it is useful to also scrutinize the design of these planned interventions and examine whether the design addresses specific disadvantages confronting the community. This section would focus on three specific programmes—the Prime Minister's New 15-Point Programme, the MsDP, and scholarship schemes.

PRIME MINISTER'S NEW 15-POINT PROGRAMME

This programme was aimed at channelling resources equitably to minorities and more specifically to the Muslims, but the guidelines do not actually mention 15 per cent as the targeted share for earmarking benefits for beneficiaries; it says ,'a certain percentage of the physical and financial targets will be earmarked for poor beneficiaries from minority communities'. This does not specify clearly the numbers/share of beneficiaries and leads to confusion at the time of operationalization of the scheme. The objectives and design of Prime Minister's New 15-Point Programme reveal the union government's intent to provide policy-driven benefits for minorities are akin to the adoption of budgetary strategies such as the SCSP for the SCs and TSP for STs. The 15-Point Programme has borrowed certain features of the SCSP and TSP in terms of allocating a share of fund flows to minorities but does not base this on the share of minority population.

It is worth noting that the SCSP and TSP promises plan allocations to the SCs and STs in terms of their proportion within total population that would be channelled through central ministries or departments and state government departments, along with additional funds in the form of Central Plan Assistance. However, in terms of expenditure reporting and accounting at the union, state, and district levels, the SCSP and TSP are better placed than the Prime Minister's New 15-Point Programme. The allocation for the SCs and STs are reported through budget (minor) heads 789 and 796 in the Detailed Demand for Grants in the union and state budget documents.

The existing policy guidelines of centrally sponsored schemes (CSSs) covered under the 15-Point Programme do not allow for tailor-made interventions for minorities/Muslims within the general sector programme. Due to rigidity in scheme guidelines, these CSSs are not able to address the gaps in terms of development deficits of the Muslims and also fail to fulfil the regional aspirations of the community. In the reporting format, there is scant scope to monitor and track the benefits accruing to the Muslims as most of the schemes have minority-focused development interventions, for instance, the JNNURM projects. Further, most of the CSS guidelines (except in the case of IAY, SGSY, and SJSRY) do not clarify the proportion of earmarked benefits accruing to the minorities.

Given the deeply entrenched deprivation among the majority of the Muslim community, it is necessary to initiate specific policy measures and adequate coverage of schemes along with requisite budgetary allocations in the 15-Point Programme. These schemes should have enough scope for tailor-made interventions that suit specific needs of the community. However, very few departments or ministries are allocating the requisite funds and reporting physical targets disaggregated in terms of the minority population and it is not in keeping with the proportional share of the minority population in the country which is pegged at 19 per cent of the total population.[10] A large number of schemes under the 15-Point Programme focus on essential services and employment generation while critical sectors—such as information and technology, commerce and industry, and micro, small, and medium enterprises—that would address long-term development of minorities remaining out of the programme's ambit.

Most of the CSSs that are part of the 15-Point Programme have not been altered in any way (by way of bringing about changes in the scheme guidelines) to cater to the specific disadvantages and needs of the community. The state- and district-level implementing agencies do not have adequate clarity on the share of allocations available towards the programme given the lack of disaggregated data in most schemes. Weak implementing mechanisms with state-level functionaries and panchayati raj institution (PRI) representatives remaining unclear about their role in the district-level planning process and subsequent implementation of the programme contribute to the design concerns. Therefore, the design of this programme could be made more appropriate to ensure comprehensive coverage of the minority population and addressing their developmental needs by integrating more

interventions that cater exclusively to the specific disadvantages confronting minorities in the country.

MULTI-SECTORAL DEVELOPMENT PROGRAMME

Although the MsDP is implemented in 90 MCDs with a substantial minority population, the criteria for identification tend to be more exclusionary, leaving a significant proportion of the Muslims out of the programme. Data reveal that only 30 per cent of the Muslim population in 90 MCDs are covered through the programme. The MsDP was designed as an umbrella programme in order to prioritize the developmental needs of the minorities, specifically the Muslims, in critical sectors; however, by adopting an area development approach, the programme ended up benefiting the general populace in MCDs with scant focus on the Muslims. A summary scan of the projects approved by the Empowered Committee (Minority Welfare) revealed that the MsDP caters to sectors like housing (IAY), child development and education (construction of AWCs, primary/secondary schools, more specifically construction of additional classrooms), provision of health and basic services (primary health centres or PHCs, drinking water supply, electricity, sanitation), and employment (skill-development and income-generating activities).

However, when it comes to selection of activities by the districts, the bulk of spending is directed towards the construction of IAY houses, AWCs, school buildings and health sub-centres, provisions that would cater to the common populace and are not exclusive to the minorities. Based on perceptions gathered at the district level in implementing IAY, there seem to be several grey areas in the implementation of the MsDP. The District Magistrate of Barabanki in Uttar Pradesh had been allotting 15 per cent of the houses to minorities following IAY guidelines for both MsDP and the 15-Point Programme. Adhering to these guidelines, houses were allotted to people falling within the below the poverty line (BPL) category; an assessment of the 6,000 IAY beneficiaries under MsDP in Barabanki district reveals more than half of the total benefits going to non-minority communities owing to non-inclusion of the Muslims in the BPL list with only 1–2 per cent Muslims being covered in the BPL list in Uttar Pradesh. Thus, the design flaw pertaining to making the BPL category a prerequisite leads to the exclusion of the targeted community from benefiting from the programme, as a majority of the BPL Muslims are not counted in the first place.

Strict adherence to scheme guidelines has also led to gaps in programme implementation. Activities related to ensuring girls' education, skill development, technical education, and income-generating activities (as proposed by the district administration in many MCDs) that are essential to advance the educational and economic conditions of the community have been neglected by the MoMA. For instance, Darbhanga district in Bihar proposed building additional classrooms in recognized madrasas that got shot down by the MoMA on the grounds that SSA guidelines do not sanction additional classrooms to madrasas. The baseline survey conducted for MsDP in Mewat district in Haryana suggested more focus be given to programmes promoting female literacy in rural areas, but the district administration built additional classrooms, staff quarters, and a hostel in Mewat Model School that already has adequate and quality infrastructure. Thus, it becomes clear that the MoMA has not accepted any of the innovative projects prescribed by the Empowered Committee (Minority Welfare) like handloom projects for the weaver community in Barabanki (Uttar Pradesh) or additional classrooms for recognized madrasas in Darbhanga (Bihar).

Another concern relates to the diversion of benefits of MsDP to non-minority areas as evidenced in the infrastructure projects in Bihar, Uttar Pradesh, and Haryana. The MoMA directive to the officials to follow an area approach, wherein benefits may go to non-minority areas to avoid social disruption, is a clear instance of the design of the programme curtailing its ability to achieve the desired impact on Muslims.

Recommendations pertaining to channelling MsDP outlays to building neighbourhood schools for Muslim girls with female teachers in MCDs could be considered given the stated focus of the programme on girl's education, health, skill development, and livelihood support in Muslim-dominated bastis. Another vital objective pertaining to promoting gainful employment among the Muslims could be furthered by apportioning adequate outlays for creation of artisan clusters in MCDs across the country. Needless to add, the success of these interventions would largely depend on the extent and scope of community participation in planning and implementing the services.

SCHOLARSHIP SCHEMES

The scholarship schemes are ridden with many basic, design-related problems, particularly the application procedures that are cumbersome and time-consuming. Most of the scholarship schemes entail opening bank accounts and providing supporting documents such as income and religion certificates. Related concerns of the absence of clear-cut institutional mechanisms for submission of application forms, unrealistic unit costs in terms of amounts provided as admission, tuition fees, and maintenance costs, and prevalent eligibility norms of supporting not more than two students from a family for the scholarship constrain effective implementation and comprehensive coverage of beneficiaries.

In comparison, the unit costs of scholarships, eligibility criteria, and coverage of courses for the SCs and STs are more realistic despite the Sachar Panel equating the Muslims as being confronted by the same level of disadvantages as the SCs and STs in terms of educational attainments, even though the latest outcome assessments point to the Muslims continuing to be at the periphery while other social groups (SCs and STs) fare better than them. Had the intent of the government been to promote educational opportunities among students of the minority community, particularly Muslim students, it would be setting the scholarship amounts at a higher level to act as significant 'pull' factors. However, the inverse of this is true.

Not only is the income eligibility criterion kept favourable for the SCs and STs (to avail pre-matric scholarships, the income level of family is limited to Rs 2 lakhs, while for minorities it is Rs 1 lakh), but also the varying amounts that are given as scholarship (SC/ST students are provided Rs 150 per month while those of the minority community are given Rs 100 per month). Not only are the existing amounts provided to SC/ST students woefully inadequate, lowering these further for those of the minority groups is clearly an unresponsive measure and does not in any way present itself as a positive step. This discriminatory approach within social groups is compounded by a lack of awareness among the community about various schemes. Finally, as in the case of most other government programmes, budgeting inadequate administrative costs leads to ineffective implementation of these schemes as most of the offices do not even have resources to hire contractual managerial staff.

In this context, some critical implementation challenges also merit attention. Based on the scrutiny of available data and perceptions of officials at the state and district levels, it is found that the MoMA continues to be confronted by critical implementation challenges. The coordination with other line departments at the union government level needs significant strengthening given that umbrella programmes (such as the Prime Minister's New 15-Point Programme and the MsDP) are implemented in tandem with other agencies or ministries. At the state level, the Minority Welfare Department is starved of financial resources and implements schemes without a clear policy mandate or conducting regular needs assessment of the community. Poor coordination mars scheme implementation even at the sub-state level as the nodal department is provided with information by other line departments with regard to Prime Minister's New 15-Point Programme only at the behest of the District Magistrate.

In order to effectively monitor the 15-Point Programme and other schemes, guidelines[11] made provision for setting up central (committee of secretaries), state, and district level committees to report progress on a quarterly basis for various schemes under the Prime Minister's New 15-Point Programme since 2007. A scrutiny of the notifications by the governments of Bihar and Haryana reveal that state level committees (SLCs) were formed only on 10 August 2010 and 3 June 2010 for Bihar and Haryana, respectively, which was at a delay of more than three years.

Apart from the delays in constituting the SLCs, the norm of holding quarterly meetings have also not been adhered to in most MCD states.[12] At the district level too, although the district level committees (DLCs) are constituted, they lack representation from the minority community. Lack of clarity and proper awareness among government officials is also believed to inhibit effective implementation of schemes exclusively for the welfare of minorities. Further, the prevailing perception among government functionaries that interventions focusing only on the Muslims might lead to social disruption also compounds the problem.

Summary of Field Observations from Uttar Pradesh and Haryana

Primary surveys and perceptions of relevant stakeholders also formed part of the research methodology for this chapter to understand the extent of marginalization faced by the Muslims and the percolation of government programmes within the community. The districts of Barabanki in Uttar Pradesh and Mewat in Haryana were selected.

Uttar Pradesh has about 19 per cent of the total Muslim population in the state and is largest in terms of absolute numbers of Muslims in the country. The state with a per capita income of Rs 23,132[13] is among the lowest in the country. In 2007–8, the union government identified 21 MCDs for the overall development of Muslims and Barabanki with 22 per cent of total Muslim population was one of the MCDs.

While Haryana has just about 6 per cent of the total Muslim population of the country, Mewat district has 74 per cent of Muslim population and is the lone Muslim majority district in north India (excluding Jammu and Kashmir). This makes the district a unique case study. Key indicators substantiate this further: Mewat's literacy rate is 44 per cent as against the state average of 68 per cent. The region has remained backward despite other parts of the state experiencing agricultural prosperity owing to Green Revolution. The district is one of the most agriculturally and industrially backward districts and is marked by poor infrastructure in terms of education, health, and basic amenities.

FIELD OBSERVATIONS FROM BARABANKI

Government officials

Perceptions of officials from departments like rural development, district rural development agency, education, women and child development, and minority welfare were gathered in order to understand the functioning of minority-related development programmes. On the question of priority to the Muslims, it was shared that as most of the schemes focused on universalization, it was not necessary to have any special focus on the welfare of Muslims in the Prime Minister's New 15-Point Programme.[14] While most of the programmes were implemented (construction of additional classrooms, AWCs, and payment of scholarships), the officers were not aware about the provisions and guidelines of the MsDP.

With regard to the inclusion of Muslims in rural development programmes, although the reporting format of IAY and SGSY allows for furnishing details of minority beneficiaries as per the 15-Point Programme guidelines,[15] reviewing the reporting format of IAY and SGSY for 2009–10, 2010–11, and 2011–12 reveals that the percentage share of physical targeting is not proportionate to minority population.

Another concern relating to ineffective coordination was also found as the Minority Welfare Department felt it did not play a significant role in coordinating with and monitoring other departments (with regard to the 15-Point Programme) as the other departments did not take instructions from Minority Welfare being stronger in terms of financial and human resources and having their own priorities; it was only when the District Magistrate issued any directives that these agencies were compelled to take action. Other constraints relating to insufficient office space, poor infrastructure, inadequate staff, and low budgets for monitoring and supervision of the programme also compounded the situation.

A key concern echoed by many officials was that most of the so-called minority-related programmes catered to the general population as well[16] and problems such as getting disaggregated village-wise population data, data on BPL Muslims, and support in preparation of the Detailed Project Report apart from those mentioned earlier led to ineffective implementation. It was also shared that the districts did not get to select the activities to be carried out as part of the MsDP. A case in point was a livelihood proposal on handlooms submitted by the Minority Welfare Department to MoMA that was rejected. Most Muslims in the district were engaged by local traders in low-wage-earning small enterprises (such as handloom, zardozi, and poultry farming). Projects that rid them of their indebtedness (through provision of soft loans for handloom trade) would have been a practical solution.

With regard to functioning of the NMDFC, it was seen as a total failure in the state and in Barabanki due to inadequate administrative support and staff. Issues such as poor outreach, low involvement of the bank in providing credit, unrealistic and antiquated loan support, and eligibility criteria have all contributed to this failure.

The coverage of pre-matric, post-matric, and merit-cum-means scholarships has also been limited among its intended beneficiaries; the pre-matric scholarship was provided to a mere 37 per cent of the total students enrolled up to upper primary level in 2011–12. Lack of awareness of these interventions among the district officials could be a significant factor.

Gram panchayats

All the four gram panchayats surveyed[17] are characterized by the absence of awareness among the Muslims of any policy initiatives exclusively for the Muslims such as the MsDP or 15-Point Programme. The community is mainly confronted with low levels of girls' education and inadequate health facilities (nutrition and health check-ups for children up to six years). These and the distance to schools have encouraged the trend of sending girls to madrasas. With regard to livelihood-related problems, lack of access to credit was cited as a key factor by all respondents through NMDFC and priority sector lending (PSL). The landless weavers with no collateral found it hard to get loans. The discriminatory mindset of officials against the Muslims is also a constraint in terms of accessing the loan.

Households

Survey findings from the four gram panchayats[18] reveal similar patterns: 80 per cent of the surveyed households were illiterate with average monthly incomes not exceeding Rs 3,000. The main occupations were weaving and farming (mostly as casual labour). With regard to access to key government programmes such as ICDS, 50 per cent of the eligible children were availing these facilities, but did not seem satisfied. While the enrolment at government upper-primary level was 80 per cent, parents showed preference to sending their wards to madrasas or private schools owing to their perception of the poor quality of education imparted in government schools.

When quizzed about other facilities such as scholarships, uniforms, books and Midday Meals (MDMs), respondents shared that these were not provided on time. Overall, the access to school-related services and entitlements by the community was weak. Further, the enrolment of children in secondary (60 per cent) and senior secondary (40 per cent) schools shows a gradual decline. Low income of parents and the distance from school were identified as main factors and, expectedly, the dropout rate was higher among girls.

With regard to accessing social security schemes like widow pension and old age pension, less than 50 per cent of eligible beneficiaries availed of these benefits primarily due to non-inclusion of names of beneficiaries in the BPL list. While there were about 50 per cent Muslim ration card holders, there were just 10 per cent of Muslim BPL card holders among the total respondents. In this regard, most of the BPL respondents received housing facilities either through the MsDP or the 15-Point Programme in all the surveyed villages but there were large deserving people without access as their names were not included in the BPL list.

Sanitation-related services were almost non-existent and the reasons for poor access were cited to be the ridiculously low unit cost of toilets set as per the guidelines. Access to credit support was also non-existent as none of the 160 respondents (from all four gram panchayats) had been provided credit through PSL for minorities or the 15-Point Programme. Lack of awareness among the community was seen to be the single-most important factor.

FIELD OBSERVATIONS FROM MEWAT (HARYANA)

Government officials

In Mewat officials concurred on the grim educational status of this district and linked it with systemic weaknesses such as inadequate staff and existing staff focusing on non-educational work assignments. While most of the villages (78 per cent) had primary schools, population covered by upper primary (9 per cent), secondary (7 per cent), and senior secondary (4 per cent) schools in the district is abysmal. Not only does it lead to a high dropout rate among girls, it also acts as a 'push' factor to send them to madrasas. Another basic sector that remains neglected in Mewat is health and child development. The officials opined that the community's general lack of awareness and unwillingness to participate in carrying out the schemes coupled with inadequacy of funds for various schemes was responsible for poor outcomes.

Views were also shared that the government should run fewer schemes to ensure the focus is on improving the outcomes rather than the supply-based interventions. While the officials blamed the community for their backwardness, statistics present a different picture. Out of 1,100 posts of Anganwadi workers, only 300 are filled by Muslims. Among 3,184 junior basic teachers, only 545 are from the Muslim community. At the district level, little representation from the community was found in the government departments.

Gram panchayats

Four gram panchayats were surveyed[19] to assess the functioning of policies designed for minorities. Most of the Muslim population is engaged in driving, casual labour, and producing handmade fans and mats, and lack of funds stops them from stocking the finished product for long, making them under-price it to sell. The community felt that the main reason for ineffective implementation was lack of information and awareness among the community on the programmes. Thus, backwardness in Mewat was owing to illiteracy, poor economic situation, government apathy, and officials' biases towards the community.

During discussions, two aspects were pointed out to prove discrimination: (*a*) lack of water facilities—both for irrigation and drinking, and (*b*) lack of hospitals. In all other neighbouring districts of Haryana, water through canals was provided, but Muslim-inhabited areas were deprived of canal facilities for irrigation. Drinking water facility has been directed to non-Muslim-dominated border villages within Mewat district. The government had announced a 100-bedded hospital in the area, but this was divided and 50 beds along with all the equipment meant for the hospital were taken away. Police apathy and discrimination is another sore point with the community feeling that the police discriminate against them and frame them on wrongful charges.

At Goila, in response to the reasons for backwardness, lack of education, poverty, and lack of information about the policies were highlighted. Surprisingly, bias as a factor was not mentioned even though no child had ever received a pre-matric scholarship, which could be due to their ignorance about such schemes. Similar to community perceptions in Barabanki, the community believed that private school teachers were motivated to teach unlike government school teachers. A similar refrain (as in Barabanki) noticed in Mewat was the problems related to BPL lists. Many well-off households were included in the BPL list, while the deserving were left out. At Mohammedpur Ahir, villagers and the sarpanch expressed dissatisfaction at the quality of government services. Of the five AWCs, not a single one had its own building and scholarships were an unknown entity in the village.

Households

Similar to the results from the household surveys in Barabanki, responses in Mewat too pointed to problems of infrastructure and provision of entitlements. Only 60 per cent children had access to Anganwadi facilities and complained about facilities like supplementary nutrition programme (SNP) health check-ups and informal education. Although 70–80 per cent children in the school-going age attended primary and upper primary schools, there was a massive drop in enrolment at secondary and senior secondary levels, particularly among girls. Akin to Barabanki and owing to high out-of-pocket expenses,[20] there is a strong preference among parents to send their children to private schools or madrasas. During discussions, respondents shared that having higher degrees would not help in getting government jobs as there was deep-rooted discrimination against the Muslims in Haryana. Therefore, children start working at an early age to support their families. With regard to availing MDMs, scholarships, books, and uniforms, most of the respondents complained about irregularity. Similarly, huge numbers of eligible beneficiaries for widow pension (50 per cent) and old age pension (30–40 per cent) were left out. As in the case of Barabanki, while over 50 per cent Muslims had ration cards, only 7 per cent Muslims had BPL/Antodaya cards.

With regard to employment, people were unwilling to work through the Mahatma Gandhi National Rural Employment Guarantee Scheme (MGNREGS) due to low wages and subsequent delays. Over 50 per cent respondents from Singar and Pinagua were engaged in self-help group (SHG) activities, while in Goila and Mohammedpur Ahir, SHG activities were not the mainstay. SHG-related work was undertaken by Mewat Development Agency supported by NMDFC through a separate unit called the SHG Federation for Community Mobilisation and Networking. With regard to availing credit from PSL, only four to five people had availed it from the four surveyed grampanchayats. Concerns of discriminatory mindsets of officials to extend credit to Muslims and inadequate awareness among the community resonated views coming from the other districts.

* * *

A thorough scrutiny of the government programmes meant for minorities reveals major constraints in terms of policy design, programme implementation, and access by the community. Firstly, budgets are inadequate when compared to the size of minority/Muslim population. Secondly, policy design, norms, and guidelines (Prime Minister's New 15-Point Programme and MsDP) do not adequately address the needs and aspirations of minorities, particularly the Muslims. The design of the 15-Point Programme and MsDP are inappropriate in terms of comprehensive coverage and addressing the specific disadvantages confronting the Muslims. These umbrella interventions focus on the existing CSSs without proposing any changes in their guidelines. Further, the assumptions related to fund allocation and setting physical targets for the Muslims remains unclear. Thirdly, poor planning, absence of proper institutional mechanisms, and related systemic weaknesses (of staff shortage and infrastructure) at the district and block levels have led to delays in implementation and overall poor outcomes. Fourthly, lack of awareness about the interventions cuts across beneficiaries and service providers. Finally, exclusion of the panchayats and the Muslim community from the implementation and planning processes of critical interventions has proved disastrous. Further, minuscule proportions of benefits of the intended initiatives have gone to the Muslims owing to a variety of factors ranging from continued discrimination, inadequate targeting, electoral considerations, and weak implementing apparatus. A major share of benefits is diverted to non-Muslims and non-minority areas due to ambiguity in policy provisions and unclear guidelines.

There are several policy challenges in the Twelfth Plan that require sustained policy interventions in terms of ensuring that the programme policy design is appropriate, and that there are adequate funds, proper institu-

tions, and staff to ensure effective implementation by the states to bring Muslims at par with other communities in terms of socio-economic development. In order to address these challenges, it is proposed that the Twelfth Plan take some forward-looking steps. Firstly, strengthening the 15-Point Programme on the lines of the SCSP and TSP along with reforms in the budgetary processes and institutions is recommended. At least 19 per cent of the funds should be allocated for minorities, out of which 73 per cent should go to the Muslims. Secondly, a separate budget statement on the 15-Point Programme along with earmarked budget (minor) heads in the detailed demands for grants like the SCSP and TSP could be considered. Thirdly, annual reports of all departments/ministries must provide disaggregated religious group-wise data on Muslim beneficiaries in schemes, public employment, and access to credit. Fourthly, creating effective institutional mechanisms (Minority Welfare Department at district and state levels) and providing adequate staff for effective implementation at the state level is suggested. Fifthly, extending the coverage of the MsDP beyond the 90 MCDs is critical to ensuring that the benefits percolate deeper into the community. In this regard, the benefits must be located in Muslim hamlets/bastis rather than at the village/gram panchayat level (as is implemented in Prime Minister's Adarsh Gram Yojana or PMAGY for the SCs and STs). Finally, priority to girls' education, skill development, and financial assistance for livelihood support in the umbrella programmes for minorities is recommended. There is need for revision in the prevalent unit cost of scholarships and doing away the norms and eligibility criteria (marks, domicile, income and caste certificates, and two child norms) making them uniform to schemes catering to the SC/ST students.

NOTES

1. Seven union government ministries/departments are involved in implementing the programme. These include: Ministries of Rural Development (IAY, SGSY, and NRDWP), Urban Development (UIDSSMT), Housing and Urban Poverty Alleviation (IHSDP, BSUP, and SJSRY), Labour and Employment (ITIs), School Education and Literacy (SSA, KGBVs and madrasa modernization programme), Women and Child Development (ICDS), and Finance (PSL to minorities).

2. Region specific socio-economic indicators at the district level include: literacy rate, female literacy rate, work participation, and female work participation rate. Basic amenities indicators at the district level include: percentage of household with *pucca* walls, percentage of household with safe drinking water, percentage of household with electricity, and percentage of household with water closets/latrines.

3. The NMDFC is a GoI undertaking run by the MoMA. NMDFC finances income-generating activities among minorities at concessional rates of interest through the state channelizing agencies. Families having annual income less than Rs 40,000 in rural areas and Rs 55,000 in urban areas are categorized as below double the poverty line and they can access credit through the NMDFC. It receives contributions from the Union government (65 per cent), state governments (26 per cent) and individuals/organizations (9 per cent) towards its share capital.

4. The MAEF is a non-profit-making social service organization established to promote education amongst educationally backward minorities through providing scholarships to girls and grant-in-aid to NGOs for infrastructure.

5. Some of the common features of all these scholarship schemes introduced in the Eleventh Plan for minorities are: (*a*) 30 per cent of scholarships are earmarked for girl students; (*b*) students should have secured not less than 50 per cent marks in the previous final examination; (*c*) not more than two students from the family; (*d*) scholarship allocation to states/union territories on the basis of population of minorities; (*e*) scholarship can be allowed from not more than one source; (*f*) eligibility criteria vary across schemes—the parent's annual income must not exceed Rs 1 lakh in the case of pre-matric, while it is Rs 2 lakhs for post-matric. The limit is Rs 2.5 lakhs for merit-cum-means, while the same is Rs 4.5 lakhs for Maulana Azad National Fellowship.

6. The schemes include pre-matric, post-matric, merit-cum-means, and free coaching.

7. See *Mid-term Appraisal of the Eleventh Plan*, Planning Commission, 2010, available at http://planningcommission.nic.in/.

8. Report of the Steering Committee on Empowerment of Minorities in the Twelfth Plan.

9. See 'Baseline Survey of MCDs of Barabanki & Mewat', 2008, available at http://www.icssr.org/.

10. See Department/Ministry-wise status of implementation on the follow-up action on the major recommendations of the Sachar Committee, available from the MoMA, GoI website, http://www.minorityaffairs.gov.in/.

11. Guidelines for implementation of Prime Minister's New 15-Point Programme are accessible at http://www.*minorityaffairs*.gov.in/sites/upload_files/moma/files/pdfs/pm15points_eguide.pdf.

12. Two meetings of the SLCs have been held in Assam, two in Bihar, three in Haryana, six in West Bengal, and nine in Uttar Pradesh since early 2007.

13. Data as on 2009–10 from RBI, *Handbook of Statistics on Indian Economy 2010–11*.

14. Project Officer from ICDS and Basic Shiksha Adhikari.

15. Project Director (IAY, SGSY), Rural Development Department.

16. As per instructions issued by the MoMA to the department.

17. The four gram panchayats in Barabanki were Badagoan, Bansa, Mohsand and Bahrauli.

18. The survey compiles the information on profiles of the respondents, access to ICDS and schools facilities by their children, out-of-pocket expenses on education of children, social security schemes, access to PDS system, employment programmes, PSL and knowledge about ongoing development programmes. Forty household questionnaires were administered in each gram panchayat.

19. The gram panchayats surveyed were Pinagua, Singar, Goila, and Mohammedpur Ahir.

20. Parents spend anywhere between Rs 500 and Rs 1,500 on education-related expenses.

References

GoI (Government of India). 2006. *Social, Economic and Educational Status of the Muslim Community of India*, November. New Delhi: PMHLC, Cabinet Secretariat, GoI.

Mishra, Ranganath. 2007. *Report of the National Commission for Linguistic and Religious Minorities (NCRLM)*, July. New Delhi: MoMA, GoI.

UNDP (United Nations Development Programme). 2011. *Human Development Report 2011, Sustainability and Equity: A Better Future for All*. New York: UNDP.

17

Social Development of the Christian Community in India

SAVIO ABREU AND ROWENA ROBINSON

In the context of expanding concerns about inclusive development and equal opportunities, the development of minorities, whether religious, ethnic, gender, sexual, or linguistic, assumes importance. In this chapter, we look at the issue of development with respect to the Christian community in India. Obviously, the analysis of the socio-economic development of a society from the perspective of a religious community raises certain pertinent questions. For instance, will comparing social development at the level of religious communities as a whole provide a realistic picture of development/underdevelopment within these various minority groups? This issue of the usefulness and the limitations of pitching the discussion of development at the level of intercommunity comparisons has been discussed previously (see, for instance, Robinson 2010).

For a more in-depth picture of social development of religious minorities, it may be necessary to combine all-India community-level comparisons of development with intra-community differences and regional variations in social development. While the Christian community numerically is a small minority in India, going back perhaps to AD 52, when St. Thomas, one of the disciples of Jesus, is said to have brought Christianity to India, the idea of 'minority consciousness' is certainly a product of more recent historical and political realities. The idea of the 'minority' in India has been inherited from the Independence struggle and Partition history, and sanctioned by provisions in favour of minorities in the Constitution. The pre-eminent minority during the colonial period was, of course, the Muslim community. However, other groups were recognized for purposes of positive discrimination by the Government of India (GoI) Acts of 1919 and 1935, thus allowing these groups to develop some understanding of themselves as 'minorities' with the capacity to make claims on the state.

Another significant issue that needs to be discussed in relation to the theme of this chapter is whether an analysis of specific development indicators such as education, poverty, gender, and employment provides a representative picture of the social development of a religious community. Any conclusions and simulations based on empirical analysis of data collected through survey methods may give an impression of precision, but they rely on many assumptions about data quality and measurement, and may be affected by systematic bias and sampling errors, inferences of causality between variables, and potential errors of the reliability and practicality of the measuring instruments. In a report on the Millennium Development Goals (MDGs) in India, Deolalikar (2005: 1) mentions right at the outset that while the results and simulations presented in the report may appear precise, they are only indicative of possible broad trends and require to be complemented with other analyses using different methodological approaches.

This chapter bases itself on the understanding that along with a descriptive analysis of the available survey data on the above-mentioned development indicators, there is a need to elucidate using participatory and qualitative research methods. In particular, attention needs to be paid to the various struggles of, attacks on, and forms of discrimination against the Christian minority, especially the Dalit Christians, that lead Christians sometimes to look at themselves as new islands of underdevelopment (Dayal 2008: 7).

HISTORY OF CHRISTIANITY IN INDIA

Historians disagree on the exact beginning of Christianity in India. As mentioned earlier, some argue that Christianity was brought in India by St. Thomas in AD 52. Others argue that it was within a few hundred years of the birth of Christ. But it has been well established by various historians that during the period of St. Thomas, Christianity in India formed part of the mainstream of Kerala society, enjoying civil autonomy and social privileges under the local kings (see the works of historians such as David 1985 or Mundadan 1984).

Western Christianity in India began with the arrival of the Portuguese in 1498 CE. Their colonial ventures were in the form of a mercantile expansion couched in a military and ecclesiastical mould. The religious mission of conversion was combined with mercantilism and furthering trade and commerce. Due to the enterprise of Portuguese and other European chaplains and missionaries, several Catholic communities emerged along the west coast with Goa as the centre. The Latin Church was closely connected to the colonial power and received state patronage. In the Portuguese enclaves, the Christians lived a privileged life compared to the Hindus and Muslims. Due to the strenuous efforts of the Portuguese in the spread of Christianity, by 1851 Goa was a Christian colony with 63.8 per cent of the population being Christians (Fonseca 1878).

Protestant Christianity began in India from the beginning of the eighteenth century with the Tranquebar mission on the southeast coast of India in 1706, started by the Lutherans, and followed by other Protestant missions such as the Serampore mission and the Mission Movement in Calcutta (Mundadan 1984: 160). The passing of the Charter Act in 1813 by the British Parliament opened the way for many Protestant denominations from Britain, Europe, and the USA to preach the gospel in India. This proliferation of Protestant missionary work was in conjunction with the expansion of the British Empire in India. While there was growth and expansion of Christianity in India in the eighteenth century, it was the period following the first war of independence of 1857 that witnessed tremendous growth in the Indian Church. The failure of the missionaries to convert the Brahmins necessitated a shift of emphasis to working among the depressed classes and tribals. Almost every organization—both Catholic and Protestant—reported phenomenal growth, so much so that the majority of the Christians in India today are from the Scheduled Castes (SCs) and Scheduled Tribes (STs), as the demographic profile of the Christian community will show.

The above description of the history of the Christians raises the question that given the diversity among them, can they be sociologically classified as a distinct category? The Syrian Christians of Kerala and the Christians of the Konkan coast (Mangalore and Goa) mainly belong to the upper castes and are educationally advanced and economically and politically powerful (Fernandes 1988: 22). On the other hand, the majority of the sixteenth-century Latin Christians of the Kerala–Tamil Nadu coast and the seventeenth–eighteenth century Christian converts are from the backward classes. Almost all the late nineteenth and early twentieth century Christians are from the Dalit community (the so-called ex-untouchables). Finally, the converts from the northeast and Chota Nagpur area are tribals. Besides, the Indian Christian community comprises of Catholics, Syrian Orthodox Christians, various Protestant denominations, Pentecostals, and different born-again Christian sects. These are all significant divisions, based on theological and doctrinal issues. Thus, we find Indian Christians are placed at opposite ends of the power and social status graph and belong to different denominations and groupings.

The Christians, on the eve of India's Independence, were not integrated as a community, but were categorized as a 'minority' community both by the colonial state and independent India's Constitution. In more recent decades, various events have contributed to the anxieties of many groups in India, particularly the minorities. The increasing communalization of politics and the rise of hard-line Hindutva ideology in the context of the controversy over the Babri Masjid in Ayodhya are crucial. National-level political parties such as the Bharatiya Janata Party (BJP) and some of its allies have publicly questioned the value of the constitutional commitment to secularism. This has created a great deal of unease among minorities such as the Sikhs, Muslims, and Christians, who have also increasingly been targets of violence. Such upheaval has contributed to religion increasingly competing with caste as the main unit of identification in Indian society. The emphasis on religion as a marker of identity and its link with altering social and political realities is the reason why this chapter compares social development at the level of religious communities and not at the linguistic, regional, or caste levels.

Social Development and Demographic Profile

Since the 2011 Census data on distribution of population by religious groups[1] is still not available, the chapter describes only the main features of the demographic profile of the Christian community from Census 2001,[2] which has been described extensively in Robinson (2010). The percentage of the Indian Christians in terms of the total population in 2001 is 2.3 per cent, while the population changes from 1961 to 2001 show that this percentage has remained relatively unchanged over this period. During this period, the proportion of Christians in the national population has tended to range between 2.3 and 2.6. The relatively stable percentage of Christians assumes significance in the light of the arguments by Hindutva forces and other Right-wing fundamentalist forces that the Church is involved in widespread conversion to Christianity leading to a large-scale increase in the Christian population. Also, in terms of the growth of different religious communities, the growth rate of the Christians has only marginally increased from 21.5 per cent during 1981–91 to 22.6 per cent during 1991–2001, which is below the national growth rate of 22.7 per cent during 1991–2001. If we compare this with other religious communities, only the Hindus (20.3 per cent) and the Sikhs (18.2 per cent) have lower growth rates than the Christians during the period 1991–2001.

With regard to other social indicators such as the sex ratio and literacy rates, the Christians compare reasonably favourably with other religious communities. The Christians are the only community to show up a positive adult sex ratio (1,009 females), which is much higher than 931 for the Hindus, 936 for the Muslims, and only 893 for the Sikhs. At the same time, the child sex ratio for the Christians dips to 964. While it still compares favourably with 950 for the Muslims, 925 for the Hindus, and 786 for the Sikhs, it nevertheless offers some evidence that the Christians are engaging in sex-selective abortions. In fact, in the northern Indian states such as Jammu and Kashmir, Himachal Pradesh, and Punjab, the 0–6 sex ratios among Christians plummet to 834, 898, and 870, respectively. The literacy rate for Christians (80.3 per cent) is higher than all other religious communities, except the Jains who have a literacy rate of 94.1 per cent. It is much higher than the 64.8 per cent literacy rate for the entire country. Also the gap of male–female literacy rates for the Christians is as low as 8.2 per cent points, with only the Jains (6.8 per cent points) being lower than them, as against the national gender literacy gap of 21.6 per cent points.

In terms of their population in the 0–6 age group, the Christians show a lower proportion (13.5 per cent) than the national average (15.9 per cent). This indicates a decline in fertility rates. Only the Jains (10.6 per cent) and Sikhs (12.8 per cent) exhibit lower proportions than the Christians. The work participation rate, that is, the percentage of workers to the total population, for Christians is 39.7 per cent, slightly above the national work participation rate of 39.1 per cent, but slightly below the Buddhists (40.6 per cent) and Hindus (40.4 per cent). But the female work participation rate among the Christians (28.7 per cent) is significantly higher than the national level of 25.6 per cent and most of the religious communities, except the Buddhists (31.7 per cent). The gender gap in the work participation rate of Christians (22 per cent points) is favourable when compared to the Jains (46 per cent points), Muslims (33.4 per cent points), and Sikhs (33.1 per cent points), and even the national level of 26.1 per cent points, with only the Buddhists (17.5 per cent points) having a lower gender work participation rate gap. Among the Christians, 29.2 per cent of the total population is engaged in cultivation, while 15.3 per cent are agricultural labourers, as opposed to 31.7 per cent and 26.5 per cent, respectively, at the national level. Also, only 2.7 per cent Christians are engaged in the household industry as opposed to 8.2 per cent Muslims and a national average of 4.2 per cent. It is no wonder then that the majority of Christians, 52.8 per cent, are engaged in other work, that is, in the non-agricultural sector, which includes the services, manufacturing, trade and commerce, and allied activities. Only the Jains with 81.7 per cent have a higher percentage of such 'other workers' compared to the Christians.

Regional Variations in Social Development

While the above analysis of the demographic and developmental profile of the Indian Christian community gives a pan-India picture, it ignores the regional variations between the mainly upper-caste and middle-upper-class Syrian Christians of Kerala and the Christians of the Konkan coast, and the predominantly backward-class sixteenth-century Latin Christians of the Kerala–Tamil Nadu coast and the later Christian converts, mainly from the Dalit community, spread in different states of India and the predominantly tribal Christians from the northeast and Chota Nagpur area. The concentration of Christians is not uniform in India as the state-wise break-up of their population in India, as per the 2001 Census, in Table 17.1 shows. The majority of the Christians (12 million or 50.6 per cent of the total Christian

Table 17.1 Demographic Profile of Christians, State-wise, 2001

Code	State/Union Territory	Total Population	Christian Population	Proportion of Christian Population	Sex Ratio	Sex Ratio (0–6)	Proportion of Child Population in the Age Group 0–6 Years	Literacy Rate	Female Literacy Rate	Work Participation Rate
	India*	1,028,610,328	24,080,016	2.3	1,009	964	13.5	80.3	76.2	39.7
01	Jammu and Kashmir	10,143,700	20,299	0.2	594	834	11.6	74.8	60.9	50.6
02	Himachal Pradesh	6,077,900	7,687	0.1	822	898	12.8	82.8	79.5	47.6
03	Punjab	24,358,999	292,800	1.2	893	870	16.1	54.6	47.0	35.7
04	Chandigarh	900,635	7,627	0.8	932	939	12.1	88.5	85.1	41.7
05	Uttaranchal	8,489,349	27,116	0.3	960	989	11.7	87.9	85.3	37.0
06	Haryana	21,144,564	27,185	0.1	918	921	12.4	85.3	81.8	39.0
07	Delhi	13,850,507	130,319	0.9	1,076	965	11.4	94.0	91.7	44.9
08	Rajasthan	56,507,188	72,660	0.1	986	956	14.6	83.0	77.7	42.9
09	Uttar Pradesh	166,197,921	212,578	0.1	961	936	14.6	72.8	67.4	33.9
10	Bihar	82,998,509	53,137	0.1	974	918	14.8	71.1	66.4	39.2
11	Sikkim	540,851	36,115	6.7	960	929	14.6	72.4	65.2	47.4
12	Arunachal Pradesh	1,097,968	205,548	18.7	1,003	960	20.5	47.0	37.8	43.5
13	Nagaland	1,990,036	1,790,349	90.0	941	968	14.6	66.2	61.6	42.2
14	Manipur*	2,166,788	737,578	34.0	977	959	14.0	65.9	58.5	44.2
15	Mizoram	888,573	772,809	87.0	986	969	16.1	93.1	91.4	51.7
16	Tripura	3,199,203	102,489	3.2	941	975	15.7	67.9	57.3	38.7
17	Meghalaya	2,318,822	1,628,986	70.3	1,004	973	21.1	65.3	63.3	41.9
18	Assam	26,655,528	986,589	3.7	962	964	17.6	56.4	48.0	41.7
19	West Bengal	80,176,197	515,150	0.6	1,002	973	13.4	69.7	62.3	38.9
20	Jharkhand	26,945,829	1,093,382	4.1	1,018	975	16.2	67.9	59.8	45.6
21	Odisha	36,804,660	897,861	2.4	1,026	981	17.8	54.9	44.1	44.6
22	Chhattisgarh	20,833,803	401,035	1.9	1,021	972	15.3	75.3	68.2	46.1
23	Madhya Pradesh	60,348,023	170,381	0.3	996	976	13.3	85.8	81.4	40.5
24	Gujarat	50,671,017	284,092	0.6	988	927	12.8	77.7	71.2	45.9
25	Daman and Diu	158,204	3,362	2.1	944	918	9.8	88.2	82.7	43.2
26	Dadra and Nagar Haveli	220,490	6,058	2.7	902	1009	19.3	64.6	50.8	47.4
27	Maharashtra	96,878,627	1,058,313	1.1	993	958	10.3	91.0	87.4	38.9
28	Andhra Pradesh	76,210,007	1,181,917	1.6	1,037	977	12.3	75.3	69.8	42.8
29	Karnataka	52,850,562	1,009,164	1.9	1,030	961	11.1	87.4	84.0	39.5
30	Goa	1,347,668	359,568	26.7	1,107	945	9.6	83.8	78.8	32.4
31	Lakshadweep	60,650	509	1	206	333	3	97	96	82
32	Kerala	31,841,374	6,057,427	19.0	1,031	960	11.2	94.8	93.5	33.9
33	Tamil Nadu	62,405,679	3,785,060	6.1	1,031	968	11.2	85.8	81.6	39.0
34	Puducherry	974,345	67,688	6.9	1,101	962	11.0	87.3	82.9	34.9
35	Andaman and Nicobar Islands	356,152	77,178	21.7	904	990	12.7	77.0	71.6	40.3

Source: The First Report on Religion, Census of India, 2001.
Note: * Excludes Mao-Maram, Paomata, and Paurul subdivisions of Senapati district of Manipur.

population) is found in south India (the four southern states of Kerala, Tamil Nadu, Karnataka, Andhra Pradesh, and the union territories of Lakshadweep, Puducherry, and Andaman and Nicobar Islands), as Table 17.2 shows. Table 17.3 illustrates that the next major concentration of Christians is found in northeast India (the eight states of Assam, Arunachal Pradesh, Meghalaya, Manipur, Mizoram, Nagaland, Sikkim, and Tripura), which has more than 6 million Christians or 26 per cent of the total Christian population. Thus, more than three-fourths of the Christian community is found in south and northeast India as indicated by Figure 17.1.

Table 17.2   Christian Population in South India

State / Union Territory	Christian Population	Proportion of State Christian Population
India	24,080,016	
Andhra Pradesh	1,181,917	4.9
Karnataka	1,009,164	4.2
Lakshadweep	509	
Kerala	6,057,427	25.2
Tamil Nadu	3,785,060	15.7
Puducherry	67,688	0.3
Andaman and Nicobar Islands	77,178	0.3
South India	12,178,943	50.6

Source: Adapted from 'The First Report on Religion', Census of India, 2001.

Table 17.3   Christian Population in Northeast India

State / Union Territory	Christian Population	Proportion of State Christian Population
India*	24,080,016	
Sikkim	36,115	0.1
Arunachal Pradesh	205,548	0.8
Nagaland	1,790,349	7.4
Manipur*	737,578	3.1
Mizoram	772,809	3.2
Tripura	102,489	0.4
Meghalaya	1,628,986	6.8
Assam	986,589	4.1
Northeast India	6,260,463	26.0

Source: Adapted from 'The First Report on Religion', Census of India, 2001.
Note: * Excludes Mao-Maram, Paomata, and Purul subdivisions of Senapati district of Manipur.

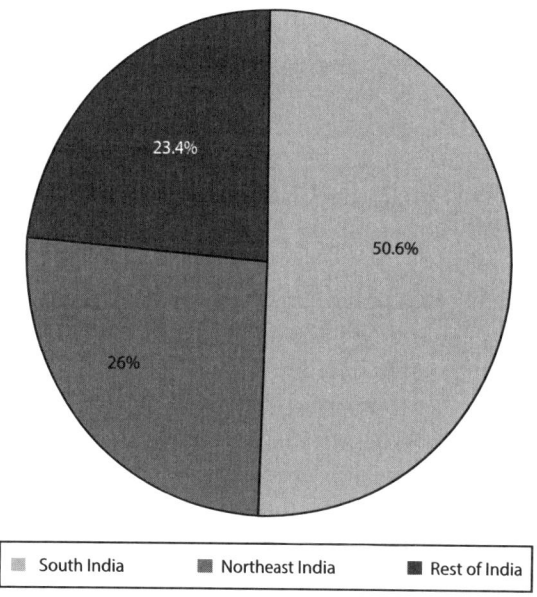

Figure 17.1   Regional Distribution of Christian Population in India

Source: Prepared on the basis of 'The First Report on Religion', Census of India, 2001.

DISCRIMINATION AGAINST DALIT AND TRIBAL CHRISTIANS

DALIT CHRISTIANS

Whenever issues affecting the Christian community as a whole occupy centre-stage in the national minority discourse, the Christian identity gets strengthened, but when the minority discourse dwells on the socially backward classes in India, especially the Dalits and the STs, religious identity weakens or breaks down completely in the face of SC or ST unity. Such changes are perceived particularly when one looks at discussions and debates surrounding the issue of reservations for Dalit Christians. During the colonial period, the Christian depressed classes of south India had presented a memorandum to the Simon Commission, stating that while the Hindu depressed classes have found favour with the government of Madras with various schemes and benefits, the Christian depressed classes have been pathetically neglected, ignored, and forgotten for no fault of theirs (Arokiaraj 2010a: 17).

After Indian Independence, the Presidential Order of 1950 allotted the benefits of reservation only to SC Hindus, though exemption was given to the Sikhs through an amendment in 1956, and this was upheld by the Supreme Court in a judgement in the *Soosai Case*, delivered on

1 October 1985 (Manickam 1988: 154–77). In 1990, this Order was amended to include the Buddhists. Thus, as it stands, the Order deprives Dalit Christians and Dalit Muslims of the benefits of positive discrimination and the right to seek protection and safeguards provided to all Dalits under the SC/ST Prevention of Atrocities Act 1989. Instead of social, economic, and educational backwardness being the criteria for affirmative action, the 1950 Order created a linkage between caste and religion, and thus could be said to have divided the entire Dalit community on the basis of religion.

This has led the Dalit Christians, supported by the Church, to fight for the same reservation and welfare benefits that are granted to the SCs professing Hindu, Sikh, and neo-Buddhist religions through different organizations such as the Christian Dalit Liberation Movement, formed in the 1980s and the All India Christian People's Forum comprising various Christian denominations and non-governmental organizations (NGOs) (Stanislaus 2004: 271–91). This denial of the benefits of reservation to Dalit Christians by the state is countered by innovative strategies employed by the Dalit Lutheran Christians of coastal Andhra Pradesh. They employ Hindu names in order to gain access to benefits reserved under the law for the SCs. Kumar and Robinson in their chapter 'Legally Hindu: Dalit Lutheran Christians of Coastal Andhra Pradesh' argue that the economically deprived Lutherans adopt the Hindu SC identity primarily, for the protection offered from upper-caste oppression and violence by the legal provisions of the Scheduled Castes and Scheduled Tribes (Prevention of Atrocities) Act 1989, and not merely for the benefits of reservation in education and employment (see Kumar and Robinson 2010). This maintaining of a dual identity is not unique to the Lutheran Dalit Christians of coastal Andhra Pradesh, but is also found among the rural Christian Vankars in Gujarat (Lobo 2001: 246). Since the government has denied the Christians the benefits granted to Hindu SCs, the Christian Vankars use their Hindu identity in order to get economic benefits and revert to their Christian identity in order to retain their social status.

While there are no clear figures available regarding the exact number of Dalit Christians, most authors would agree that much more than half of all Christians (65–70 per cent) are from the former 'untouchable' castes (Lobo 2001; Robinson and Kujur 2010: 5). The Christian SCs include the Pulayans in Kerala, Pariahs in Tamil Nadu, Tigalas in Karnataka, Malas and Madigas in Andhra Pradesh, Chamars (Ravidasis) in Madhya Pradesh, Uttar Pradesh, and Bihar, Vankars from Gujarat, and Mahars

from Maharashtra (Lobo 2001: 242). The case of the Dalit Christians is special since they face discrimination at three levels. The first level of discrimination which all Dalits, including Dalit Christians, face is from caste Hindus. Several examples of such discrimination can be cited. For instance, caste Hindus in the countryside in Andhra Pradesh do not differentiate between a converted Dalit Christian and a Dalit (Kumar and Robinson 2010). All Dalits are meted out the same treatment by those considered high in the caste hierarchy. In Zafferwal village, Gurdaspur district, Punjab, both Dalit Sikhs, known as Majhoabli Sikh and Dalit Christians, known as Issai, stay side by side in the *thathis* (place of mockery), which is outside the village (Massey 2007: 71).

The second level of discrimination, which the Dalit Christians face is by the state, which has already been mentioned earlier. The third level of discrimination that they face is at the hands of fellow Christians who continue to claim their upper-caste status even after conversion. S.M. Michael points out how, in some places, there are separate seating arrangements for the Dalits in churches, while in others liturgical services are performed separately for those presumed 'high' or 'low' in caste (2010: 51–74). Sometimes, Dalits are asked to sit on the floor, even where raised seating is available and there are, in some places, two cemeteries and two hearses for dead bodies. In some places, separate queues are formed for receiving Holy Communion. Archbishop George Zur, Apostolic Pro-Nuncio to India, in his address to the Catholic Bishops' Conference of India (CBCI) in December 1991 said that 'Casteism is rampant among the clergy and the religious. Though Dalit Christians make 65 per cent of the 10 million Christians in the South, less than 4 per cent of the parishes are entrusted to Dalit priests' (Massey 2007: 74). The second and third levels of discrimination by the state and at the hands of the upper-caste Christians make the case of Dalit Christians even more complex as compared to the other SCs.

Many backward class commissions have acknowledged the social and economic backwardness of Christians of SC origin and have recommended SC status for them. The National Commission for Religious and Linguistic Minorities (NCRLM), or the Ranganath Misra Commission, which was asked by the GoI to study the issue of assigning SC status to Dalit Christians and Muslims, visited 26 states and two union territories conducting seminars, workshops, and public hearings, and collecting the views and opinions of individuals, NGOs, church organizations, and social organizations. It submitted its report to the Prime Minister in May 2007, and this was tabled in Parliament on 18 December 2009. The NCRLM report recommended to the Union of India that

Para 3 of the Constitution (Scheduled Castes) Order 1950—which originally restricted the Scheduled Caste net to the Hindus and later opened it to Sikhs and Buddhists, thus still excluding from its purview the Muslims, Christians, Jains and Parsis, etc.—should be wholly deleted by appropriate action so as to completely de-link the Scheduled Caste status from religion and make the Scheduled Castes net fully religion-neutral like that of the Scheduled Tribes. (Arokiaraj 2010a: 19)

Despite the unequivocal findings of the Ranganath Misra Commission, the idea of caste as Hindu underlies the continued exclusion of Christian and Muslim converts from the Indian state's statutory concessions and protections for the SCs (Mosse 2012: 58).

The National Commission for Scheduled Castes, a constitutional body, while endorsing the recommendations of the NCRLM report concerning Dalit Christians and Dalit Muslims has recommended that reservation should be extended to Dalit Christians and Dalit Muslims. From the viewpoint of the institutional response to this issue of denial of SC status to Dalit Christians and Dalit Muslims, it is seen that the state governments of Tamil Nadu, West Bengal, Uttar Pradesh, Bihar, Madhya Pradesh, Punjab, Andhra Pradesh, and Puducherry have asked the Indian government to extend SC status to Dalit Christians. However, the response of the union government to the Writ Petition 180/2004 filed by the Centre for Public Interest Litigation in 2004, praying for the deletion of Para 3 of the Constitution (Scheduled Castes Order) 1950, and other petitions concerning Dalit Christians and Muslims appears to be one of delaying the case (Arokiaraj 2010b). The union government has been regularly postponing giving a reply to the Supreme Court on the issues raised in the Writ Petitions. When a sizeable proportion of the Christian population, belonging to the SCs, are excluded from the process of development this must reflect poorly on the institutional response and the governmental measures apparently aimed at ensuring the equitable socio-economic development of all sections of society.

While Dalit Christians and church organizations involved in the struggle for Dalit rights have joined forces with other SCs on common issues, the main concern of the Christians about acquiring reservation benefits from the government have differed from the concerns of the rest of the Dalits. This is highlighted in 'A Dalit Vision for a New India', the document of the National Dalit policy drafted by Dalit academicians and activists, and

civil society organizations, released in November 2006. The efforts and steps to obtain reservation and other SC benefits for the Dalit Christians can be classified under three periods: (a) the period of meeting with political leaders and submitting memoranda (1950s–80s); (b) the period of public rallies, strikes, lobbying with political leaders, litigation, private member bills (1990s–2000); and (c) the period of an intense legal battle, lobbying with national and international bodies and leaders, gathering information under the Right to Information (RTI) Act, demonstrations, collaboration with Dalit Muslims and other human rights groups (2000 onwards) (Arokiaraj 2010a: 20). In December 2006, the National Council of Dalit Christians, a lay movement of various Dalit Christian movements, conducted a relay hunger strike at the national level to demand SC status for Dalit Christians and Muslims. During the sessions of Parliament in 2007, 2008, 2009, and 2010, this movement, in collaboration with the National Coordination Committee for Dalit Christians, organized rallies and dharnas in New Delhi and were involved in intense lobbying.

The Church in India has overtly supported the Dalit and tribal struggles and in the process has expanded the identity of the Church in India to include these and other marginalized groups

The Dalits and Tribals are politically exploited, educationally most backward and socially discriminated against. The Church should be in solidarity with the poor and make a preferential option for them.... To realize this objective, the Church should join other people of good will and work towards the dismantling of structures like caste and class that cause and perpetuate poverty and oppression.[3]

The CBCI, at its general body meetings at Jamshedpur in February 2008 and at Guwahati in March 2010, sent signed memoranda to the Prime Minister urging the union government to include Dalit Christians in the SC list. On the other hand, the Dalit Christians continue to accuse the Church hierarchy of being ambivalent about their problems and raise issues such as marginalization in admissions and appointments to Christian institutions, discrimination in vocations to priesthood and religious life, and the lack of sharing of power and authority in the Church.

TRIBAL CHRISTIANS

Tribal Christians are found mainly in two regional enclaves—northeast India and the Chota Nagpur region of central India. In both places, Christianity entered the area in the second half of the nineteenth century.

Many authors on Christianity in India agree that around 15 to 20 per cent of the Christians in India are tribals (Robinson and Kujur 2010: 5). In fact, the states of Meghalaya (70.3 per cent Christians, 85.9 per cent tribals), Mizoram (87.0 per cent Christians, 94.5 per cent tribals), and Nagaland (90.0 per cent Christians, 89.1 per cent tribals) in northeast India—all having more than two-thirds Christian population, also have more than two-thirds tribal population (refer to Table 17.4 and Figure 17.2). The tribals of the Chota Nagpur area are mainly found in the states of Jharkhand, Chhattisgarh, Madhya Pradesh, Odisha, and West Bengal. The tribal Christians are mainly from the Oraon, Munda, Kharia, Santhal, and Ho tribes. Jharkhand with over a million Christians, comprising 4.1 per cent of the total population, had the largest tribal Christian concentration in the Chota Nagpur area. Today the tribal Christians of Chota Nagpur are spread all over the country, including the Andaman Islands, Assam, West Champaran in north Bihar, and north Bengal, besides in many urban centres of north India, especially New Delhi.

Tribals all over India who converted to Christianity have benefited and developed through the activities of the missionaries in the areas of education, health, and welfare, but this has also led to conflicts with the dominant non-Adivasi interests. For tribals, land and

Table 17.4 Percentages of Tribal and Christian Populations in Northeast India

State/Union Territory	Proportion of Christian Population	Proportion of Tribal Population
Sikkim	6.7	20.6
Arunachal Pradesh	18.7	64.2
Nagaland	90.0	88.9
Manipur	34.0	34.4
Mizoram	87.0	94.5
Tripura	3.2	31.1
Meghalaya	70.3	85.9
Assam	3.7	12.4

Source: Prepared on the basis of *The First Report on Religion*, and *Population Profiles*, Census of India, 2001.

other natural resources such as forests or water are not merely commodities, but the centre of their culture, identity, and world view. According to Lobo (2010), in the tribal belt of the state of Gujarat, the work of education, health care, and developmental projects by the Christians among the Bhils has led to the empowerment of the deprived Adivasis and has also partly resulted in giving voice to Adivasi independence and indigenous revival movements. Such movements certainly do not

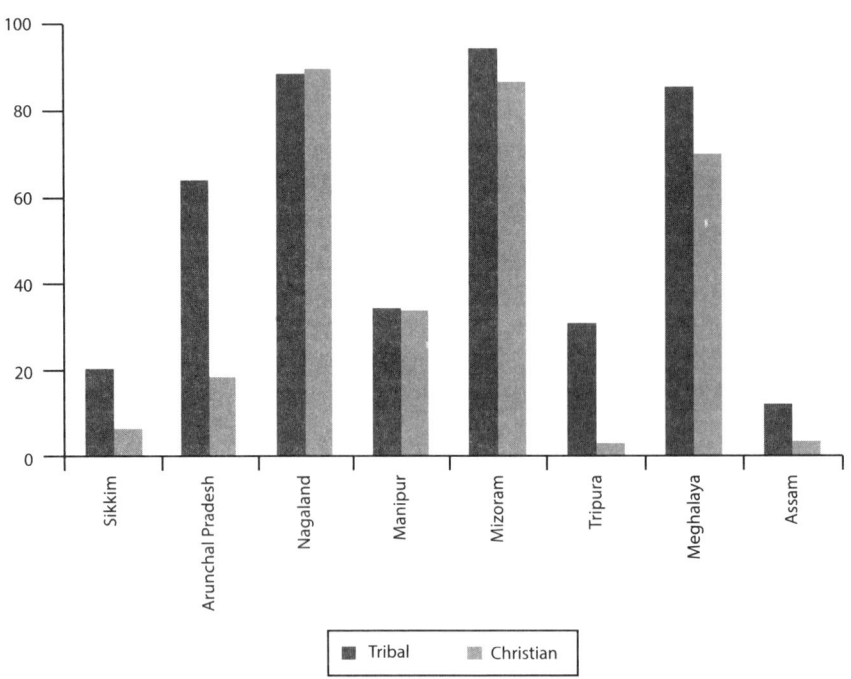

Figure 17.2 Percentages of Tribal and Christian Populations in Northeast India

Source: Prepared on the basis of 'The First Report on Religion', and 'Population Profiles', Census of India, 2001.

have the backing either of the elite Adivasis or of those who espouse the Hindutva ideology. Also, Adivasis empowered by the work of the missionaries might no longer submit to the exploitation of the non-Adivasi vested interests such as shopkeepers, moneylenders, and landlords. Lakshmi Bhatia (2010) links the growth of Christianity in Mizoram with the progress of education since education was delegated to the missions right from the start. The Church in Mizoram, which is predominantly tribal, has been instrumental in the creation and maintenance of an educated and aware middle class and this class has provided the leadership for Mizoram's political movement. Christianity has created a radically altered Mizo society, a highly literate, westernized, and politically aware people. The middle class in Mizoram is constituted of the Church leaders, the educated members of the government machinery, the political elite, school teachers, and medical professionals. Many of them occupy important positions both in the sacred and secular realms. This explains why Christianity, as a way of life, overshadows and dominates the public and private spheres of Mizo life.

While Dalit Christians face discrimination at three levels, as seen in the previous section, the tribal Church in the Chota Nagpur area faces a double marginalization (Kujur 2010: 30). First, the tribal Church has always been in the periphery, defending itself from the attacks at the local level by those who accuse it of distorting the traditional culture and dividing the tribal community. In the case of the Oraons of Chota Nagpur, there is tension between Christians, non-Christian Sarnas, and those seeking to 'Hinduize' the tribals. Conversion to Christianity among the Oraons led to those adhering to the traditional tribal religion, that is, the Sarna Oraons viewing the Christian Oraons with suspicion because of their betrayal of the parental community. Also under missionary influence, the converts had to cut themselves off from all aspects of the old religion and culture. Fundamentalist Hindu forces such as the Hindu Dharm Sansad, the Rashtriya Swayamsevak Sangh (RSS), and others are attempting to Hinduize the tribals, on the one hand, by organizing 'homecoming' events for conversion to Hinduism, and, on the other, to de-recognize the tribal identity of Christians and Sarnas who refuse the 'Hindu' label. These Hindutva organizations consider the work of education and health provision, among the tribals of Gujarat by the Christians as insidious ways, whereby the Christians gain the loyalty of the 'innocent' and 'backward' tribes (Lobo 2010: 230–1). Second, the local tribal Church faces criticism and censorship from the orthodox Church

hierarchy for its innovations and experimentations in tribal liturgy, tribal theology, and tribal ecclesiology.

India has one of the most extensive and comprehensive programmes of affirmative action both for the SCs and STs written into statutory law and government policies. Unlike the Dalit Christians, who are discriminated against by the state on the basis of religion, the tribal Christians are constitutionally entitled to get reservations as STs. Yet, due to the big gap between intent and implementation, the geographically isolated and marginalized tribals are pushed into violence. Thus, in northeast India, the sense of alienation from the Indian mainstream led to various nationalist and ethnic conflicts (Fernandes 2012). The Naga National Council, the Mizo National Front, and other organizations led the struggle for autonomy and sovereignty. Quite often the government treats these disturbances as a law and order problem and the action on the ground is not only inadequate, but often counterproductive. Whether in its repressive policing or in a non-participative top-down approach towards the STs, the state response is at best patronizing and at worst leading to a creation of dependencies that stymie tribal autonomy. The cultural hegemony of the institutional response imposes compromises or violates the dignity of the tribals and treats them as inferior (Heredia 2012).

ATTACKS AGAINST CHRISTIANS AND THE INSTITUTIONAL RESPONSE

'The Indian government's insistence at the international level that existing laws and judicial decisions are sufficient to deal with egregious violations such as torture and attacks on religious minorities is very disappointing,' read the draft report of the Working Group on India's Universal Periodic Review (UPR), a mechanism of the United Nations to review the human rights record of all its member states (Malhotra 2012). UN member countries that participated in India's UPR on 24 May 2012 in Geneva expressed concerns over India's right to freedom of religion and belief, anti-conversion laws, and the targeting of religious minorities. The GoI's oral response during the UPR session was marked by a 'general lack of acceptance of human rights challenges in the country and a mere reiteration of domestic laws, policies and Constitutional provisions' and even on the Communal Violence Bill, the Human Rights Council took note of the government's 'uncertainty' regarding such a law that aims to protect minorities (ibid.).

Though most of the attacks on Christian missionaries and institutions in Independent India had been isolated and sporadic, the last two decades have seen a spurt and a pattern of sustained attacks on the Christian community. The violence in Gujarat, Madhya Pradesh, Uttar Pradesh, Odisha, and the attacks on churches in Karnataka have shaken the Christian community and led their leaders to re-emphasize the need for a pan-Indian Christian unity, leaving aside all other differences of caste, class, region, rites, and denominations. 'Mr. Prime Minister, long ago we left our fathers and our homes. We have worked without fear in distant forests and villages. Now, for the first time, we are feeling afraid,' Sister Dolores, the National Secretary of the Catholic Religious in India, the association of priests and nuns in India, told Atal Bihari Vajpayee at a meeting with him in 2000 (Dayal 2000). Due to the constant targeting of Christians, a sense of fear has entered because of which many in the Church leadership are afraid to speak out, lest their patriotism be questioned or their institutions singled out. Fear and a sense of uncertainty and vulnerability have now begun to creep into the self-consciousness of the Christian community as it increasingly sees itself as an insecure and embattled minority community. Sajan George, President of the Global Council of Indian Christians, while documenting cases of attacks against Christians all over India mentions that out of 405 cases of Christians being persecuted from January 2006 till May 2007, over 325 were from the Dalit background. So while the Christian community as a whole is feeling vulnerable and insecure, the Christians belonging to the lower socio-economic strata are affected the most by these anti-Christians attacks and forms of persecution. At the same time, the increased attacks on Christians are seen by extremist and fundamentalist Christian groups as a divine sign to go on the offensive and intensify their proselytizing activities. Persecution and attacks embolden them to fulfil their desire of bringing into being a 'Christian India' in the near future.

The increasing number of attacks on Christians are quite definitely part of a hate campaign by the Sangh Parivar and other right-wing Hindutva forces targeting Muslims and Christians throughout India. This hate campaign questions the roots of Christianity branding it as a foreign religion, questions the patriotism and loyalty of the Christians, and targets priests, nuns, and Christian institutions. This discourse brands the minorities as being well-off at the cost of the majority Hindu community who are suffering and, therefore, the Muslims and Christians are the enemies of the Hindus. In particular, the Christians are targeted for engaging in conversion by force or inducement, thus manipulating innocent tribals and Dalits, and threatening the demographic strength of the Hindus. A sample of the type of writing that constructs this type of discourse on the minorities is given below:

The minorities are safe only under the BJP. One country, one people is its core ideology.... But the definition of minorities in India is strangely distorted. Here the minorities are better off than Hindus and were the ruling class for centuries.... The vote-bank politics has deprived the Hindu his status. This is at the root of the tension in places where conversion is tearing apart the social fabric. In states where the minorities are in majority their tyranny has totally subjugated the Hindu. (Balashankar 2008)

The impact of the minority discourse of the Sangh Parivar was seen vividly in December 2007 in the anti-Christian attacks in Kandhamal district of Odisha that, according to the All-India Christian Council's (AICC) reports and corroborated by the National Commission for Minorities' (NCM) report, resulted in 95 churches and 730 houses being destroyed in the clashes and six people seriously wounded, multiple reports of women molested or raped, and four people confirmed dead (Bauman 2010: 267). But the ferocity of these riots paled in comparison to the events of the last week of August 2008, when the Dalit Pana Christians experienced the fury of the worst-ever communal rage in Odisha—churches were set on fire; Christian institutions, orphanages, and hamlets were destroyed; pastors were attacked; one nun was burnt alive and another was gangraped. At the height of the violence there were over 20,000 refugees, mostly Christians, in relief camps, while according to the AICC, there were over a hundred deaths by November. An opposition party report put the total much higher, though government officials reported in May 2009 that only 42 persons were confirmed dead. Militant Hinduization had deeply divided the Adivasis (Kandhas have become increasingly Hinduized) and the Dalits (around 70 per cent of the Panas are Christians) on communal lines in Kandhamal district and the Kandha–Pana ethnic divide was ingeniously be converted by the Sangh Parivar into a Hindu–Christian communal confrontation (Kanungo 2008). Chad Bauman argues that the Odisha violence was exacerbated by the involvement of those who intentionally politicized and communalized local tensions, in part by portraying communal identities at both the local and national levels as if they were singular, rigid, and mutually exclusive (2010: 263–90). The Odisha violence brought to the fore the lack of bargaining power of the Christian minority with the government authorities in a country ruled by vote-bank politics.

At the same time these attacks worked as a catalyst in uniting the Christians and making them realize their Christian communitarian identity. When the Sangh Parivar activists attacked churches in Mangalore on 14 September 2008, church bells were rung and on hearing them big crowds of Christians, especially the youth, gathered at the churches and thwarted the plans of the aggressors. The tolling of the church bells is a powerful symbol for the Christians, reminding them that they need to come together as a community in the face of crisis.[4] If the attacks against the Dalit Christians in Odisha in August 2008 weakened the Christian community's trust in the state authorities, the subsequent attacks on various Christian places of worship in BJP-ruled Karnataka made the Christians sceptical of the intent and capability of the state machinery and law enforcement agencies to protect the interests of the minorities.

The report of the Justice B.K. Somasekhara Commission of Inquiry,[5] constituted by the Karnataka government, was submitted on 28 January 2011 and it found that attacks had taken place at various places of worship across Karnataka, particularly in the towns of Mangalore and Davanagere. Some of the attacks were deliberate and well-planned. Clearly, forms of communal antagonism and fundamentalism had been brewing for several years. The Commission indicted the district administration functionaries including the corporation, municipality, electricity board, and village panchayat authorities for failing to protect the rights of the religious minorities guaranteed under the Constitution, but found no evidence to show that the politicians, the BJP, the Sangh Parivar or the state government were, directly or indirectly, involved in the attacks. On the other hand, an independent inquiry by Justice (Retired) Michael F.J. Saldanha found that each and every attack was state-sponsored in that it was not only supported by the state, but also covered up by the state. Justice Saldanha, Transparency International India (TII) Chairman and former judge of the Bombay and Karnataka high courts, held the then Chief Minister B.S. Yediyurappa and the then Home Minister B.V. Acharya fully responsible for the unfortunate incidents. To write this 304-page report, which was released on 24 February 2011 in Mangalore, Justice Saldanha visited 413 places, examined 673 witnesses, and collected evidence and testimonies from 2,114 victims after visiting hospitals, courts, police stations, jails, and government offices. The attacks against Christians in Odisha and Karnataka in 2008 evoked protests not just from within the country, but also from several Christian nations, highlighting the global dimension of the Indian Christian community. This was noticed again in India's UPR at Geneva on 24 May 2012, when UN member countries expressed concerns over India's right to freedom of religion and belief, the anti-conversion laws of different states, and the targeting of religious minorities.

* * *

In conclusion, the issue of attacks against Christians or Christian places of worship speaks of the violence increasingly visible at all levels of contemporary Indian society—domestic violence, violence in public places, as well as varied forms of political violence. Violence by the state has also increased, and the role of media in its reportage of the use of egregious force against different categories of citizens—women, workers, Dalits, or tribals—is worthy of further investigation. But for the Christian community, certainly, the issues of persecution and harassment of the Christian clergy and laity, anti-conversion laws, the lack of a strong institutional response to attacks against religious minorities, the denial of constitutional rights for Dalit Christians, and the violation of the dignity of Christian tribals continue to erode their confidence in the intention or ability of the state to promote and safeguard the social development of minorities. Thus, though the economic and social indicators of the Christians, such as with regard to education, poverty, gender, employment, may appear to place them in a relatively better position in comparison to some of the other religious communities, the increasingly precarious position they find themselves in, in the highly polarized and communalized situation of present-day India, raises troubling questions about their overall social security and development.

Notes

1. See 'Distribution of Population by Religions', Census of India 2011, Drop-in-Article. Available at http://www.censusindia.gov.in/CensusWebResults.aspx?cx=012918 038926302546381%3Ajjz7p38u6ma&cof=FORID%3 A9&q=Distribution%20of%20Population%20by%20 Religions&sa=Search#156.

2. See 'Population Profiles, RGI', Census of India 2001. Available at http://delhiplanning.nic.in/Economic%20Survey/ ES2007-08/T18.pdf.

3. CBCI statement on 'The Church in Dialogue', 25th General Body Meeting, Jalandhar, 1–8 March 2002.

4. 'An Open Letter to the Catholics of Mangalore', email sent by Cedric Prakash on 25 September 2008.

5. 'Final Report of Justice B.K. Somsekhara Commission of Inquiry', prepared by B.K. Somasekhara, Bangalore, 28 January 2011.

REFERENCES

Abreu, Savio. 2009. 'The Making of a Christian Minority', *Seminar*, 602(October): 64–9.

Arokiaraj, Cosmon G. 2010a. 'Dalit Christian Struggles for Equal Rights and the Way Forward', *Jeevadhara*, XLI(241): 14–25.

———. 2010b. 'The NCRLM Report—Additional Term of Reference, A Ray of Hope for the Socially Excluded Dalit Christians and Dalit Muslims', *Catholic India*, 22(2): 32–9.

Balashankar, R. 2008. 'Are Minorities Safe in BJP-Ruled States?' *Economic Times*, 22 September.

Bauman, Chad. 2010. 'Identity, Conversion, and Violence: Dalits, Adivasis, and the 2007–08 Riots in Orissa', in Rowena Robinson and Joseph Marianus Kujur (eds), *Margins of Faith: Dalit and Tribal Christianity in India*. Thousand Oaks, CA: Sage Publications, pp. 263–90.

Bhatia, Lakshmi. 2010. 'Contradiction and Change in the Mizo Church', in Rowena Robinson and Joseph M. Kujur (eds), *Margins of Faith: Dalit and Tribal Christianity in India*. New Delhi: Sage Publications, pp. 169–84.

David, M.D. (ed.). 1985. 'History of the Church in India', in *Asia and Christianity*. Bombay: Himalaya Publishing House.

Dayal, John. 2000. 'India's Plural Culture, Secular Democracy Challenge and Opportunity', unpublished paper presented at the hearings of the US Commission on International Religious Freedom, Washington, 18 September.

———. 2008. 'New Islands of Underdevelopment', *Communalism Combat*, 132(14 June): 7–13.

Deolalikar, Anil K. 2005. *Attaining the Millennium Development Goals in India*. New Delhi: Oxford University Press.

Fernandes, Walter. 1988. *The Role of Christians in National Integration*. New Delhi: Indian Social Institute.

———. 2012. 'Challenges to Theology from the Social Reality of Northeast India', Unpublished paper presented at the Seminar on Tribal Theology in Northeast India, Guwahati, organized by NESRC, Guwahati & Tribal Study Centre, ETC, Jorhat, 17–19 April.

Fonseca, J.N. 1878. *An Historical and Archaeological Sketch of the City of Goa*. Bombay: Thacker & Co. Limited.

Heredia, R.C. 2012. 'Tribals at the Margins: Inferiorised Identity, Violated Dignity', Unpublished paper presented at the Seminar on Tribal Theology in Northeast India, Guwahati, organized by NESRC, Guwahati and Tribal Study Centre, ETC, Jorhat, 17–19 April.

Kanungo, Pralay. 2008. 'Hindutva's Fury against Christians in Orissa', *Economic and Political Weekly*, 43(37, 13 September): 16–9.

Kujur, Joseph Marianus. 2010. 'Tribal Church in the Margins: Oraons of Central India', in Rowena Robinson and Joseph Marianus Kujur (eds), *Margins of Faith: Dalit and Tribal Christianity in India*. New Delhi and Thousand Oaks: Sage Publications, pp. 22–50.

Kumar, Ashok and Rowena Robinson. 2010. 'Legally Hindu: Dalit Lutheran Christians of Coastal Andhra Pradesh', in Rowena Robinson and Joseph Marianus Kujur (eds), *Margins of Faith: Dalit and Tribal Christianity in India*. New Delhi and Thousand Oaks: Sage Publications, pp. 149–68.

Lobo, Lancy. 2001. 'Visions, Illusions and Dilemmas of Dalit Christians in India', in Ghanshyam Shah (ed.), *Dalit Identity and Politics*. New Delhi: Sage Publications, pp. 242–57.

———. 2010. 'Christianization, Hinduization and Indigenous Revivalism among the Tribals of Gujarat', in Rowena Robinson and Joseph M. Kujur (eds), *Margins of Faith: Dalit and Tribal Christianity in India*. New Delhi: Sage Publications, pp. 211–34.

Malhotra, John. 2012. 'Tough Questions on Religious Freedom at UN Human Rights Periodic Review', *Christian Today India*, 4 June. Available at http://in.christiantoday.com/articles/tough-questions-on-religious-freedom-at-un-human-rights-periodic-review/7353.htm (accessed 7 July 2012).

Manickam, S. 1988. *Studies in Missionary History: Reflections on a Culture-Contact*. Madras: The Christian Literature Society.

Massey, James. 2007. 'An Analysis of the Dalit Situation with Special Reference to Dalit Christians and Dalit Theology', *Religion and Society*, 52(3 and 4, September–December): 56–86.

Michael, S.M. 2010. 'Dalit Encounter with Christianity', in Rowena Robinson and Joseph Marianus Kujur (eds), *Margins of Faith: Dalit and Tribal Christianity in India*. New Delhi and Thousand Oaks: Sage Publications, pp. 51–74.

Mosse, David. 2012. 'Caste and Christianity', *Seminar*, 633(May): 58–62.

Mundadan, A.M. 1984. *Indian Christians: Search for Identity and Struggle for Autonomy*. Bangalore: Dharmaram Publications.

Robinson, Rowena. 2010. 'Indian Christians: Trajectories of Development', in Gurpreet Mahajan and Surinder S. Jodhka (eds), *Religion, Communities and Development: Changing Contours of Politics and Policy in India*. New Delhi: Routledge, pp. 151–72.

Robinson, Rowena and Joseph M. Kujur (eds). 2010. *Margins of Faith: Dalit and Tribal Christianity in India*. New Delhi: Sage Publications.

Stanislaus, L. 2004. 'Empowering the Oppressed in Society', in S. Ponnumuthan, Chacko Aerath, and George Menachery (eds), *Christian Contribution to Nation Building: A Third Millennium Enquiry*. Cochin: Documentary Committee of CBCI-KCBC, pp. 271–91.

18

Social Development Index 2012

Surajit Deb

The aggregate indicators of development spanning several dimensions of human well-being are increasingly becoming more relevant measures of social progress. The conventional economic measures such as per capita income or Gross Domestic Product (GDP) are increasingly being recognized as inadequate measures of progress. The Commission on the Measurement of Economic Performance and Social Progress (CMEPSP) was constituted in the recent past, with the aim to identify the limits of GDP as an indicator of economic performance and social sustainability, and consider additional indicators relevant to capture the social progress so as to improve upon the metrics of societal well-being (Stiglitz *et al.* 2010). The Human Development Index (HDI) and Social Development Index (SDI) are multidimensional indicators as compared to the measures of economic performance or poverty, which are one-dimensional. However, much of the quality and reliability of such comprehensive indices depend on the choice of components included and the method of aggregation. In HDI, the deprivation with regard to other aspects of well-being, namely, health and education, are added to the indicator of economic deprivation. The HDI methodology also employs the assumption of equal weighting of the three components. The methodology of combining indicators by making the HDI a simple average of the values of a number of separate indicators, however, remained open to criticism in the literature (Decanq and Lugo 2009; Noorbakhsh 1998; Ranis *et al.* 2005; Srinivasan 1994). In recent years, there is a growing concern that composite indices spanning different development dimensions like the HDI should be supported by theoretical perspectives as

well as a statistical system and not just remain a *mash-up index* that is based on averages (Ravallion 2012).

The primary focus of human development remained on health, education, and income attainments, whereas the social dimension of development would require the aspects of social discrimination that exclude the marginalized groups from equal access to basic needs. The aspects of livelihood insecurity, unemployment, and social inequalities have to be added in the analysis. The notion of SDI can, therefore, be conceived as a broader conception than the HDI, in the sense that elements such as social exclusion, gender discrimination, unemployment, people's living standards, access to basic amenities, social issues such as female foeticide, which generally act as possible barriers to social integration, are incorporated in the aggregate index. In the present case, SDI is a composite index, taking into account six important dimensions of social development: (*a*) demographic parameters; (*b*) health indicators; (*c*) educational attainment; (*d*) basic amenities; (*e*) economic deprivation; and (*f*) social deprivation parameters.

The SDI-2008 was developed using a simplistic methodology based on equal weights in aggregating components into a composite indicator. The SDI-2010 revised the methodology and used the principal component analysis (PCA) to estimate the composite indices of SDI for the Indian states, but applied it on a restricted data set. The SDI-2012, developed in this chapter, follows the same methodology used earlier in the construction of the SDI-2010, and uses the PCA to determine the set of weights that are to be employed for deriving the composite index on the basis of their statistical importance. This is necessary, since the use of equal weights among indicators—as is done in the case of HDI—can encounter potential methodological problems in case two or more indicators in our analysis are interlinked and correlated. The PCA basically aggregates individual dimensions of social development that are correlated to form a composite indicator that captures to the maximum extent possible the information common to individual indicators. Thus, the PCA is not only useful when there is a severe high degree of correlation present in the multiple attributes, but has also been argued to be better suited in establishing the optimal weights of variables in comparison to the method of equal weights.

While the essential methodology of the present SDI has remained the same as in the SDI-2010, the SDI-2012 has used recent data information as much as possible. We have made use of data from Census 2011 for literacy and child sex ratio (CSR), the NSS 55th Round (2009–10) for employment and per capita consumption, the District Level Health and Facility Survey (DLHFS-3) 2007–8 data for basic amenities indicators and the Planning Commission's data on poverty for 2009–10. The SDI-2012 can also be seen as an improvement over the earlier series in terms of the states' coverage in the analysis. Thus, states like Delhi and Goa—which have recently registered significant progress in various socio-economic indicators—have also been included in the present version.

The social inequality and exclusion can take different forms, but in India they mainly operate along the lines of caste, tribe, gender, or religious bias. It is also argued that the contemporary development policies have generated inequality between the rural and urban areas of living. Therefore, in addition to the aggregate index for a particular state, we have also provided separate SDIs for rural and urban areas of each state. Further, we also construct separate SDIs, which are disaggregated over social groups, namely, Scheduled Caste (SC), Scheduled Tribe (ST), and non-SC/ST groups of population, as well as gender classes for each state. Thus, SDI-Rural, SDI-Urban, SDI-SC, SDI-ST, SDI-Male, and SDI-Female have been provided to examine the disparity across states.

The rest of the chapter is structured as follows. The following section elaborates the methodology on how uncorrelated principal components are extracted through linear transformations of the original variables by retaining most of the variations in the original dataset. In the third section, we discuss in detail the definition and

data source of each of the indicators that are used in the analysis. The analyses of our results are included in the section that follows. Finally, the last section is devoted to a discussion of the findings and conclusions.

METHODOLOGY

A major methodological issue with regard to most composite indices relates to the selection of appropriate weights that are used in the aggregation. A number of methods can be used to determine the weights, for example, the use of equal weights among indicators or employing statistical procedures such as PCA or determination of weights through regression analysis. The HDI, for instance, has restricted itself in using equal weights among the three basic dimensions, namely, health, knowledge, and income. It may be noted that although the original HDI methodology was revised in 2010, the new HDI continues to assign equal weight to all three dimension indices on the assumption that that all three dimensions are equally important. Under the previous HDI formula, health was measured by life expectancy at birth; education or knowledge by a combination of the adult literacy rate, primary school enrolment, secondary school enrolment, and university enrolment; and income or standard of living by GDP per capita adjusted for purchasing power parity (PPP US$). While health is still measured by life expectancy at birth, the HDI-2010 differed in measuring achievements in knowledge by combining the expected years of schooling for a school-age child in a country entering school today with the mean years of prior schooling for adults aged 25 years and older. Similarly, the income measurement was changed from purchasing-power-adjusted per-capita GDP to purchasing-power-adjusted per-capita Gross National Income (GNI). In the previous HDI, each of the dimensions carried equal weight, that is, one-third in producing the final HDI score, while indicators within the dimension of education accounted for one-twelfth. The new HDI continues to assign equal weight to all three dimension indices, with the two education sub-indices that are also weighted equally. A range of statistical procedures have also been used by researchers to determine the suitable weighting scheme in specific cases, for example, the World Bank's *Doing Business Indicators* (see World Bank 2012), which uses PCA to assign weights on the basis of factor loadings or the *Quality of Life Index* produced by the Economist Intelligence Unit (2011), which determines weights through regression analysis.

In the present case, the derivation of a single composite index of social development out of numerous indicators bears a key concern that some of the development (or deprivation) indicators may be interlinked, and thereby display a high statistical correlation. For instance, studies on malnutrition in India reiterated that the children of illiterate mothers are also more malnourished, which would point towards a correlation between the education and health indicators. In case two or more indicators are correlated, the use of equal weights among indicators could encounter potential problems for the robustness of the composite index. The PCA involves a multivariate statistical technique that helps transform a number of possibly correlated variables into a smaller number of uncorrelated ones, which we call principal components. In this study, PCA is used to derive the composite index by aggregating over indicators on the basis of their statistical importance. The PCA-determined weights of the indicators are designed in such a way that the resultant composite index accounts for a maximum variance in the data set. The method of principal component has been argued to be better suited in establishing the optimal weights of variables in relation to the method of equal weights.

As our first step, we convert some of the negative indicators in the list of 21 indicators positive. That is, since the SDI is linked to development, the negative (or deprivation) indicators such as total fertility rate, infant mortality rate, percentage of under-nourished children, pupil–teacher ratio, school dropout rate, percentage of population below poverty line, unemployment rate, and ratio of female to total unemployment rates are made positive by taking the inverse of the respective values. Second, it is important that before we perform the PCA each of the individual indicators must have been normalized and made scale-free. The normalization of data is important given that the indicators are measured in different units and also display widely different means as well as relatively large standard deviations. It is therefore necessary to convert them in some standard comparable units such that the initial scale chosen for measuring them do not bias the results. Thus, each of these raw indicators is mapped onto a unit-free scale by subtracting the lowest value of the particular indicator among states from each of the states value under that indicator, and then dividing by the indicator-range among states, namely, $(x_{np} - x_{npmin}) \div (x_{npmax} - x_{npmin})$. In the present exercise, we have employed a method of normal or single-stage PCA, which requires that all the respective indicators under each development dimensions have to be combined. Therefore, for our second step, we add the scale-free values of the indicators within each dimension

to arrive at the representative development dimensions for each state. These normalized values are finally subjected to PCA for the determination of statistical weights, as discussed below.

Our data set can now be considered as a $(n \times p)$ data matrix $(X_{n,p})$, where n is the number of Indian states $(n = 22)$ and p is the number of social development dimensions $(p = 6)$. The elements of this matrix are $x_{i,j}$, where $x_{i,j}$ is the value of the j-th indicator for the i-th state. The application of PCA needs a significant correlation among individual dimensions because the weights are set in accordance to the correlation among dimensions. The correlation matrices involving relevant dimensions used for working out each of the eight SDIs are provided in Appendix Tables 18A.1 through 18A.8. We can identify some clear relationships among various dimensions of social development in these tables. For instance, a high and positive correlation can be observed in the case of the aggregate SDI between demographic and health indicators $(r = 0.89)$ and between demographic and educational indicators $(r = 0.79)$, or between health and education indicators $(r = 0.74)$ and between health and basic amenities indicators $(r = 0.75)$, and so on (Appendix Table 18A.3).

The principle of PCA lies in finding weights to be given to each of the concerned dimensions, where weights maximize the sum of the squares of correlation of the dimension with the composite index. Suppose that y_1 is a principal component of $x_1, x_2, x_3, ..., x_p$, such that $y_1 = a_{11}x_1 + a_{12}x_2 + ... + a_{1p}x_p$. Then the variance of y_1 is maximized given the constraint that the sum of the squared weights of $x_1, x_2, x_3, ... x_p$ is equal to 1. The PCA determines the weight vector $(a_{11}, a_{12}, ... a_{1p})$ by selecting higher weights for those series that vary a lot so that they influence the composite index relatively more. Once the weights are chosen, the first principle component would indicate the dominant pattern of variance in the indicators. The second principal component (y_2) similarly finds out a second weight vector $(a_{21}, a_{22}, ... a_{2p})$ such that the variance is maximized subject to the constraints that it is uncorrelated with the first principal component. This signifies that y_2 has the next largest sum of squared correlations with the original variables, and the variances of the subsequent principal components would be smaller. The analysis also produces an estimate of how much variance in the x's is explained by each principal component.

One problem of using PCA in indexing is to decide on how many components to retain. It can be noticed in the applied literature that using the first principal component has remained the standard practice. To capture the total system variability of the original variables, we could use all the components, but if the first component accounts for a large proportion of the variability (around 70–80 per cent), it implies that there is one dominant component in the underlying variables. In the present analysis we use the first principal component since it explains about 76 per cent of the variance in the data in most cases. In PCA, each of the principal components are described by the pair of eigen-value and eigen-vector, where each eigen-value describes the amount of variance explained by each principal component and the factor-loadings are the coordinates of the eigen-vector. The factor-loadings measure the importance of each dimension in accounting for the variability in the particular principal component. The eigen-vectors provide the weights to compute the uncorrelated principal components, and the principal component scores are then worked out as linear combinations of normalized original variables with the factor-loadings as weights.

In order to construct our composite indices of aggregate SDI, SDI-Rural, SDI-Urban, SDI-Social, and SDI-Gender for the Indian states, we have consistently used the PCA scores based on the first principal component. The aggregate SDI, SDI-Rural, and SDI-Urban are determined by the first principal component of the combination of six development dimensions covering 21 indicators. The SDI-Social is constructed for different social classes using the first principal component of the four development dimensions involving nine indicators. Finally, the SDI-Gender is computed for male and females by the first principal component of three development dimensions comprising six indicators. The method of using the first principal component, which is the linear combination of the initial indicators and has the largest variance, appears to be a better estimate than the simple average of original variables that have high degrees of correlation present.

DATA SOURCE

The description of the indicators used in the construction of each SDI along with the account of their database is discussed below. See also Table 18.1.

SDI: RURAL, URBAN, AND AGGREGATE

In these indices, six dimensions, namely, demographic, health, educational, basic amenities, economic deprivation, and social deprivation have been used, separately for the rural, urban, and total areas of each state.

Demographic indicators

1. Contraceptive Prevalence Rate (CPR): It refers to the proportion of currently married women using any form of contraceptive. The data has been collected from the state-wise fact sheets of the National Family Health Survey (NFHS-III), 2005–6, International Institute of Population Science (IIPS) and Ministry of Health and Family Welfare (MoHFW).
2. Total Fertility Rate (TFR): This is defined as the number of children that would be born to each woman if she were to live to the end of her child-bearing years (15–49 years) and if the likelihood of her giving birth to children at each age was the currently prevailing age-specific fertility rates. This data is compiled from the Sample Registration System, 2011, Registrar General of India.
3. Infant Mortality Rate (IMR): This refers to the number of infants dying under one year of age in a year per 1,000 live births of the same year. This data is made available from the Sample Registration System, 2011, Registrar General of India.

Health indicators

1. Percentage of institutional delivery: It represents the percentage of delivery that took place in an institution in both public and private sectors in the state. The data have been compiled from the state-wise fact sheets of NFHS-III, 2005–6, IIPS and MoHFW.
2. Percentage of undernourished children: The nutritional status of children is calculated according to anthropometric measure (weight-for-age) from NFHS-III, 2005–6.

Educational attainment indicators

1. Literacy rate: This data have been compiled from the Census 2011 information provided by the Registrar General and Census Commissioner, Ministry of Home Affairs, Government of India (GoI).
2. Pupil–teacher ratio: This is the ratio of the number of students to a teacher in primary schools in different states of India and the data have been compiled from the 'Seventh All India School Education Survey, 2002', MoHRD, GoI.
3. School attendance rate: It captures percentage of the population currently attending school. The data for all the states are gathered from NSS 64th Round the Survey, 2007–8 (Report No. 532), which represents

the current attendance rate in educational institutions per 1,000 persons for the 5–14 age group population.

Basic amenities indicators

We have considered four variables to measure access to basic amenities, namely, percentage of households which live in *pucca* houses, have access to safe drinking water, have access to toilet facilities, and have electricity connection. The data for all the states have been taken from the DLHFS-III, 2007–8, IIPS and MoHFW.

Economic deprivation indicators

We have used three indicators in this dimension, namely, head count ratio (HCR) of poverty, unemployment rate (according to current daily status), and the monthly per capita expenditure (rural + urban) for different states. The data on the per cent of population living below poverty line (Tendulkar Methodology) in 2009–10 has been taken from Planning Commission, GoI. The unemployment rate as defined by the number of persons unemployed per 1,000 persons in the labour force has been compiled from the NSS 66th Round Survey, 2009–10, Key Indicators. Finally, the data on monthly per capita expenditure (Modified Mixed Reference Period) are compiled from the NSS 66th Round Survey, 2009–10, Key Indicators.

Social deprivation indicators

We have used six indicators in this dimension, which are the disparity ratio between the SCs and general population in literacy rate, disparity ratio between the STs, and general population in literacy rate, disparity ratio between female and male literacy rates, ratio between female unemployment rate to total unemployment rate, disparity ratio of per capita expenditure of Muslims to the total population, and the child (or juvenile) sex ratio. While the first three indicators are intended to capture the educational deprivation of the SCs, STs, and women, the remaining three would assess the female deprivation of employment, economic deprivation of Muslims, and the survival of girl child. The data on SC, ST, and general literacy rates are taken from the NSS 61st Round Survey, 2004–5 (Report No. 516). The female and male literacy data have been compiled from the Census 2011 information provided by the Registrar General and Census Commissioner, Ministry of Home Affairs, GoI. The female and male unemployment rates are gathered from the NSS 66th Round Survey, 2009–10, Key Indicators. The data on monthly per capita expenditure of Muslims

and general population are taken from the SCR (GoI 2006). Finally, the CSR referring between 0 and 6 years were taken from the recent Census 2011 data.

The 22 states covered for this part of our analysis are Andhra Pradesh, Assam, Bihar, Chhattisgarh, Delhi, Goa, Gujarat, Haryana, Himachal Pradesh, Jammu and Kashmir, Jharkhand, Karnataka, Kerala, Madhya Pradesh, Maharashtra, Odisha, Punjab, Rajasthan, Tamil Nadu, Uttar Pradesh, Uttarakhand, and West Bengal. Box 18.1 lists all the 21 indicators under six dimensions along with their years of reference for each data indicator series.

SDI-SOCIAL

We have used four dimensions, namely, demographic, health, educational, and economic deprivation in these indices separately for the SC, ST, and non-SC/ST groups of population for each state.

Demographic indicators

We have used three indicators in this dimension as before, namely, CPR, TFR, and IMR on each social group. The data for all the three series have been collected from the state-wise fact sheets of NFHS-III, 2005–6, IIPS and MoHFW.

Health indicators

We have utilized two indicators under the health dimension, namely percentage of institutional deliveries and percentage of undernourished children, and the data have been compiled from the state-wise fact sheets of NFHS-III, 2005–6.

Educational attainment indicators

The literacy rate and dropout rates have been as two indicators in this dimension. For literacy rates, we have used the data on SC, ST, and general literacy rate from the NSS 61st Round Survey, 2004–5 (Report No. 516). The data on dropout rates are gathered from 'Selected Educational Statistics, 2005-06', Department of Higher Education, MoHRD, GoI.

Economic deprivation indicators

As before, we have used the per cent of population living below poverty line, the head count ratio (HCR) and unemployment rate (current daily status) in this dimension. The unemployment rate as defined by the number of person unemployed per thousand persons in the labour force of that particular social group has been compiled

Box 18.1 Dimensions/Indicators and the Database for SDI-2012

Dimension/Indicator	Database
Dimension 1: Demographic	
1.1 CPR	NFHS-III, 2005–6
1.2 TFR	SRS, 2009
1.3 IMR	SRS, 2009
Dimension 2: Health	
2.1% of institutional delivery	NFHS-III, 2005–6
2.2% of undernourished children	NFHS-III, 2005–6
Dimension 3: Education	
3.1 Literacy rate	Census 2011
3.2 Pupil–teacher ratio	Ministry of Human Resource Development (MoHRD) 2002
3.3 School attendance rate	NSS, 64th Round, 2007–8
Dimension 4: Basic amenities	
4.1 % of households living in pucca houses	DLHFS-3, 2007–8
4.2 % of households having access to drinking water	DLHFS-3, 2007–8
4.3 % of households having access to toilet facility	DLHFS-3, 2007–8
4.4 % of households having electricity connection	DLHFS-3, 2007–8
Dimension 5: Economic deprivation	
5.1 Percentage of population living below poverty line	Planning Commission, 2009–10
5.2 Unemployment rate (current daily status)	NSS, 66th Round, 2009–10
5.3 Monthly per capita expenditure	NSS, 66th Round, 2009–10
Dimension 6: Social	
6.1 Disparity between SC and general population in literacy rate	NSS, 61st Round, 2004–5
6.2 Disparity between ST and general population in literacy rate	NSS, 61st Round, 2004–5
6.3 Disparity between female and male population in literacy rate	Census 2011
6.4 Disparity between female and total unemployment rate	NSS, 66th Round, 2009–10
6.5 Disparity between per capita expenditure of Muslims and total population	Sachar Committee Report (SCR), 2002
6.6 CSR	Census 2011

from the NSS 61st Round Survey, 2004–5, Report No. 516. The head count poverty ratio data for the SC, ST, and non-SC/ST has been sourced from data provided by the Planning Commission, as reported in the Ministry of Tribal Affairs, and Ministry of Social Justice and Empowerment, GoI.

The 20 states covered for this analysis are Andhra Pradesh, Assam, Bihar, Chhattisgarh, Gujarat, Haryana, Himachal Pradesh, Jammu and Kashmir, Jharkhand, Karnataka, Kerala, Madhya Pradesh, Maharashtra, Odisha, Punjab, Rajasthan, Tamil Nadu, Uttar Pradesh, Uttarakhand, and West Bengal. Box 18.2 lists all the nine indicators under four dimensions along with their years of reference for each data indicator series.

SDI-gender

Three dimensions, namely, health, educational, and economic deprivation have been used in these indices,

separately for the male and female class of population for each state.

Health indicators

The two indicators used in this dimension are the IMR and percentage of undernourished children on each gender class. The data for both the series are taken from the state-wise fact sheets of NFHS-III, 2005–6, IIPS and MoHFW.

Education indicators

Two indicators have been under this dimension, which are literacy rate and higher secondary completion rate. The male and female literacy rates have been taken from the recent Census (2011) data provided by the Registrar General and Census Commissioner, Ministry of Home Affairs, GoI. The higher secondary completion rates of boy and girl students are compiled from 'Selected

Box 18.2   Dimensions/Indicators and the Database for SDI-Social

Dimension/Indicator	Database
Dimension 1: Demographic	
1.1 CPR	NFHS-III, 2005–6
1.2 TFR	NFHS-III, 2005–6
1.3 IMR	NFHS-III, 2005–6
Dimension 2: Health	
2.1 % of institutional delivery	NFHS-III, 2005–6
2.2 % of undernourished children	NFHS-III, 2005–6
Dimension 3: Education	
3.1 Literacy rate	NSS, 61st Round, 2004–5
3.2 Dropout rate (High school)	MoHRD, 2005–6
Dimension 4: Economic deprivation	
4.1 Percentage of population living below poverty line	Ministry of Tribal Affairs, 2004–5
4.2 Unemployment rate (current daily status)	NSS, 61st Round, 2004–5

Educational Statistics, 2005–6', Department of Higher Education, MoHRD, GoI.

Economic deprivation indicators

We have considered the unemployment rate and wage rate, classified by males and females, under this dimension. The data on male and female unemployment rates has been compiled from the NSS 66th Round Survey, 2009–10, Key Indicators.

For the wage data, we have used the data series on average daily wage rate by directly employed workers in states during 2003–4, Labour Bureau's, Ministry of Labour and Employment.

The 21 states covered for the analysis are Andhra Pradesh, Assam, Bihar, Chhattisgarh, Gujarat, Haryana, Himachal Pradesh, Jharkhand, Karnataka, Kerala, Madhya Pradesh, Maharashtra, Odisha, Punjab, Rajasthan, Tamil Nadu, Uttar Pradesh, Uttarakhand, West Bengal, Delhi,

and Goa. Box 18.3 lists all the six indicators under three dimensions along with their years of reference for each data indicator series.

RESULTS

SDI: RURAL, URBAN, AND AGGREGATE

The individual states are ranked in Figure 18.1 on the basis of their aggregate SDI scores build over six dimensions covering 21 indicators. The states of Delhi, Goa, Kerala, Himachal Pradesh, and Punjab belonged to the top five ranks, while Odisha, Madhya Pradesh, Uttar Pradesh, Jharkhand, and Bihar occupied the bottom five ranks. It can be seen that more number of states have done better than the all-India SDI position, which remained at the 16th position out of 22 states in our sample. However, with 15 states remaining above the all-India level and yet a low score of all-India SDI would signify that social

Box 18.3   Dimensions/Indicators and the Database for SDI-Gender

Dimension/Indicator	Database
Dimension 1: Health	
1.1 IMR	NFHS-III, 2005–6
1.2 % of undernourished children	NFHS-III, 2005–6
Dimension 2: Education	
2.1 Literacy rate	Census 2011
2.2 High school completion rate	MoHRD 2005–6
Dimension 3: Economic Deprivation	
3.1 Unemployment rate (current daily status)	NSS, 66th Round, 2009–10
3.2 Wage rate	Ministry of Labour and Employment, 2003–4

development remained remote for a large section of the Indian population, which is concentrated in the seven highly populated states of Chhattisgarh, Rajasthan, Odisha, Madhya Pradesh, Uttar Pradesh, Jharkhand, and Bihar.

The top two positions in SDI scores are occupied by Delhi and Goa, respectively, while Kerala's ranking remained at third. To understand the mechanism of the aggregate SDI score, we looked into individual state's rankings in all the six constituent dimensions (Table 18.1). It is apparent that Delhi did extremely well in the SDI ranking due to the basic amenities, economic, and social factors, despite scoring low in demographic, health, and educational progress. On the contrary, Kerala ranked first among the major Indian states in many indicators of social development, namely, demographic, health, educational, and social aspects, but its overall SDI rank lagged behind due to poor performances in economic as well as basic amenities indicators. Similarly, the other two top states in aggregate SDI, namely, Goa and Himachal Pradesh revealed significant progress in the majority of social development indicators, yet lagged due to one or two remaining indicators.

It is sometimes argued that the reason for widening the economic divide between the rich and poor in the country is due to the biased growth strategy in favour of urban India in comparison to rural India. In the background of recent evidence of the growing income inequality between the rural and urban Indian, it would be interesting to study how social development has moved across rural and urban areas. The individual state's SDI scores bifurcated over the rural and urban areas are provided in Figures 18.2 and 18.3, respectively. It can be seen that the same states of Delhi, Goa, Kerala, Himachal Pradesh, and Punjab—which belonged to the top five ranks in the aggregate SDI—also occupy the top ranks as per the SDI-Rural ranking (Figure 18.2). When the SDI-Urban classification is used, the ranking changes slightly so that Jammu and Kashmir replaces Punjab in the list of top five ranks (Figure 18.3). Correspondingly, the same states that belonged to the lower down rankings in the aggregate SDI—Odisha, Madhya Pradesh, Uttar Pradesh, Jharkhand, and Bihar—perform worst in the SDI ranking, either in rural or urban classification.

Interestingly, while Delhi topped the SDI ranking in the rural and total categories, its ranking in the urban category remained at number four. With the rural classification being somewhat artificial for the state of Delhi, the lower-down position of SDI-Urban is due to the lower levels of social development in the slums of urban Delhi. Appendix Table 18A.9 provides a comparison of the PCA scores and ranks of SDI-Rural, SDI-Urban, and aggregate SDI of individual states. We find uniformity between the rankings of SDI-Rural and SDI-Urban for a large number of state and also all India. However, there are indications that the SDI rankings for a particular state differed widely when viewed from the rural–urban perspective. Thus, the SDI-Urban recorded progress ahead of the SDI-Rural in Andhra Pradesh, Maharashtra, and West Bengal, whereas the SDI-Rural moved ahead of the

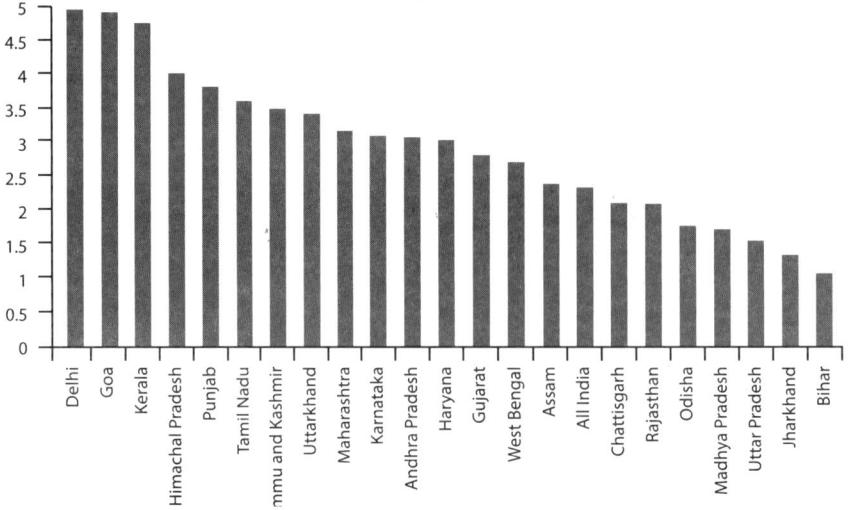

Figure 18.1 Aggregate SDI Scores
Source: Table 18A.9.

Table 18.1 State Rankings in Individual Indicators of Aggregate SDI, Rural, Urban, and Total

States	Demographic			Health			Education		
	Rural	Urban	Total	Rural	Urban	Total	Rural	Urban	Total
Andhra Pradesh	6	3	6	7	5	7	19	19	18
Assam	20	21	20	16	17	18	10	5	10
Bihar	22	22	23	20	23	22	23	22	23
Chhattisgarh	18	15	18	22	19	21	14	18	15
Delhi	9	10	7	5	16	6	4	10	5
Goa	2	4	2	3	2	2	1	6	3
Gujarat	13	13	13	14	13	12	11	9	11
Haryana	11	17	11	12	18	14	13	12	12
Himachal Pradesh	4	1	4	8	10	10	2	3	2
Jammu and Kashmir	14	7	14	6	3	5	5	2	4
Jharkhand	21	19	21	23	20	23	22	17	22
Karnataka	8	9	8	9	8	9	9	4	8
Kerala	1	2	1	1	1	1	3	1	1
Madhya Pradesh	15	18	19	21	21	20	15	11	14
Maharashtra	5	5	5	10	9	8	6	7	7
Odisha	16	16	16	13	12	16	17	13	19
Punjab	7	12	9	4	6	4	12	21	13
Rajasthan	19	20	17	18	15	17	21	20	20
Tamil Nadu	3	8	3	2	4	3	8	8	6
Uttar Pradesh	23	23	22	19	22	19	20	23	21
Uttarakhand	12	11	12	11	11	11	7	15	9
West Bengal	10	6	10	15	7	13	16	16	16
All India	17	14	15	17	14	15	18	14	17

(contd.)

Table 18.1 (contd.)

States	Basic Amenities			Economic Deprivation			Social		
	Rural	Urban	Total	Rural	Urban	Total	Rural	Urban	Total
Andhra Pradesh	9	6	10	12	7	14	17	6	17
Assam	17	18	18	19	17	21	2	2	1
Bihar	21	23	22	21	23	22	21	23	21
Chhattisgarh	19	21	20	11	15	13	7	9	13
Delhi	1	1	1	1	2	1	1	5	2
Goa	6	11	4	2	1	2	12	3	5
Gujarat	11	7	11	13	4	11	11	18	16
Haryana	5	9	3	9	5	8	22	14	19
Himachal Pradesh	3	5	5	3	3	3	4	12	8
Jammu and Kashmir	8	2	8	4	14	4	8	17	11
Jharkhand	23	20	23	22	22	19	18	20	9
Karnataka	12	16	14	10	8	10	10	11	14
Kerala	4	13	6	8	9	9	3	1	3
Madhya Pradesh	18	17	17	20	18	20	19	19	22
Maharashtra	13	12	13	14	6	12	14	10	15
Odisha	22	22	21	23	21	23	15	13	10
Punjab	2	3	2	6	12	7	6	16	12
Rajasthan	16	10	16	7	10	6	23	22	23
Tamil Nadu	10	15	9	16	11	15	13	8	7
Urtar Pradesh	20	19	19	17	19	18	20	21	20
Utrarakhand	7	4	7	5	20	5	9	7	4
West Bengal	15	8	15	18	16	17	5	4	6
All India	14	14	12	15	13	16	16	15	18

Source: Author's calculations.

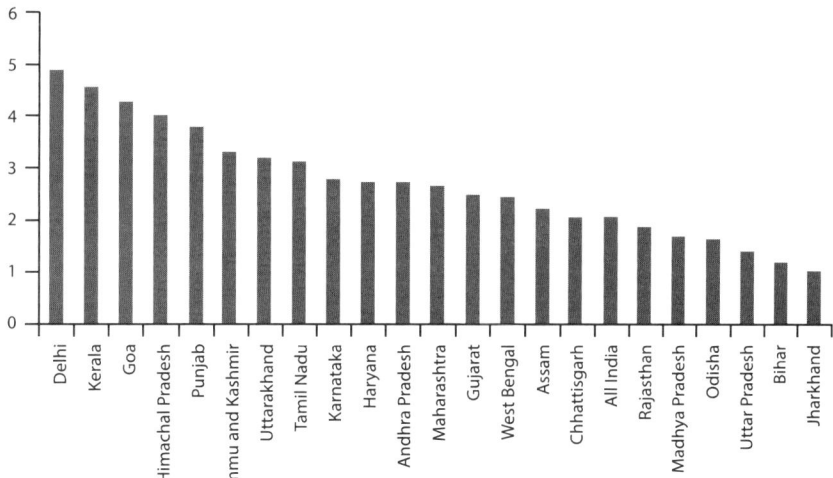

Figure 18.2   Aggregate SDI Scores, Rural
Source: Table 18A.9.

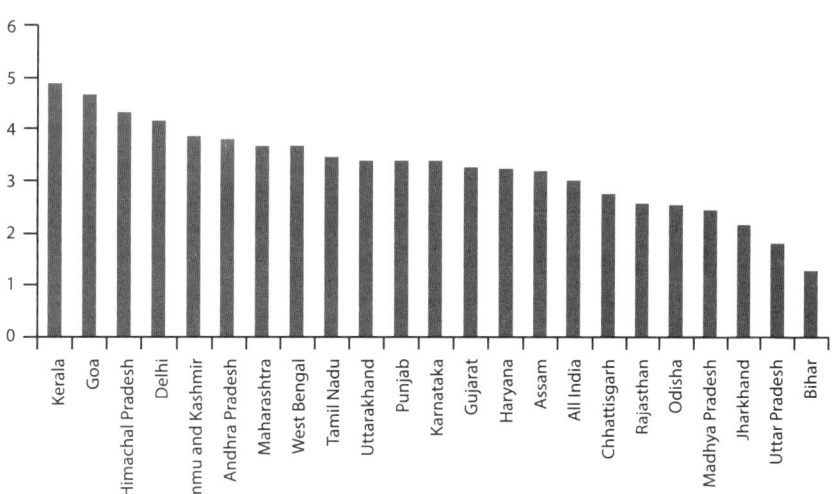

Figure 18.3   Aggregate SDI Scores, Urban
Source: Table 18A.9.

SDI-Urban in Delhi, Haryana, Karnataka, Punjab, and Uttarakhand.

SDI-SOCIAL: SC, ST, AND NON-SC/ST

The backward classes, namely, SCs, STs, and Other Backward Classes (OBCs) continue to suffer social and economic exclusion in India and thereby get in the way of the country's inclusive development (GoI 2011c, 2012). Thus, we have also worked out the SDI for social groups, namely, SC, ST, and non-SC/ST to assess the progress made by these marginalized sections of the society vis-à-vis the general population. The progress in social

development across social classes are examined considering the four development dimensions of demography, health, education, and economic deprivation, and considering nine indicators, as given in Box 18.2. The rankings of SDI-Social are provided individually in Figures 18.4 to 18.6 for SC, ST, and non-SC/ST, respectively.

While the states of Kerala, Tamil Nadu, Maharashtra, West Bengal, and Andhra Pradesh captured the top five ranks in the SDI-SC, the top five ranks in SDI-ST belonged to Kerala, Himachal Pradesh, Tamil Nadu, Punjab, and Haryana. It is apparent that both Kerala and Tamil Nadu have done well in the upliftment of SCs, STs

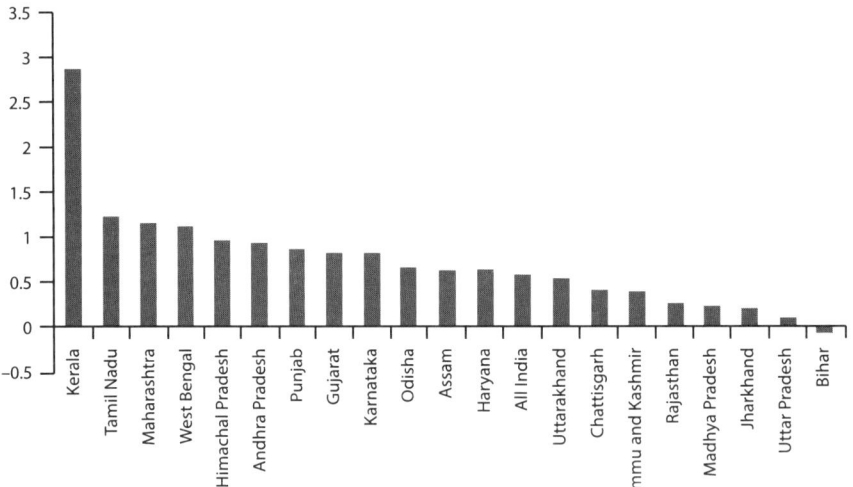

Figure 18.4 SDI Social Scores, SC
Source: Table 18A.10.

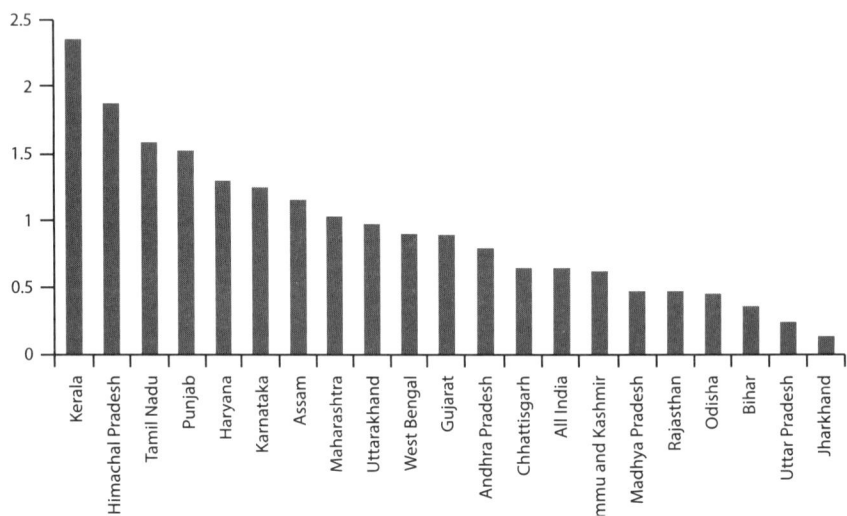

Figure 18.5 SDI Social Scores, ST
Source: Table 18A.10.

as well as non-SC/STs. On the contrary, states like Bihar, Jharkhand, Madhya Pradesh, Uttar Pradesh, Odisha, and Rajasthan continue to record social deprivation for the SCs and STs, and, therefore, remained at the bottom of the rankings. Table 18.2 includes the state's rankings in all the four individual dimensions, namely demographic, health, educational, and economic deprivation. It is apparent once again that Kerala (and also Maharashtra) ranked high among states in the dimensions of demographic, health, and educational but lagged behind in the economic indicator. Some other states such as Tamil Nadu, Andhra Pradesh, and Himachal Pradesh

have also successfully attained progress for the backward classes in the areas of demography, health, or education.

The comparison of PCA scores and rankings of SDI-SC, SDI-ST, and SDI-non-SC/ST of individual states are provided in Appendix Table 18A.10, and it can be seen that the all-India scores recorded a position of around 13 among 20 states in all the three indices. The equivalence among rankings of SDI-SC, SDI-ST, and SDI-non-SC/ST can similarly be noted for a majority of states. A wide variation between the rankings of SDI-SC or SDI-ST vis-à-vis SDI-non-SC/ST would indicate minorities lagging behind (or drawing level) with the

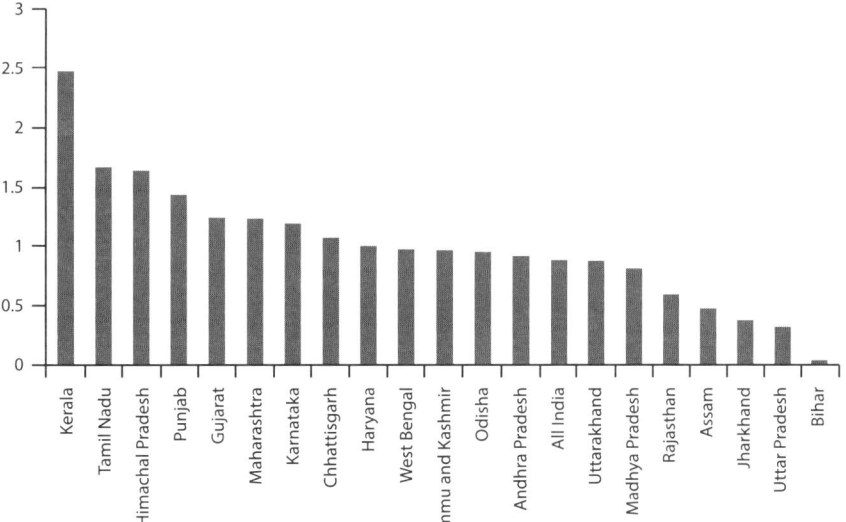

Figure 18.6   SDI Social Scores, Non-SC/ST
Source: Table 18A.10.

general population. It appears that states like Andhra Pradesh and Assam have done well in the upliftment of the marginalized groups, but Gujarat and Jammu and Kashmir lagged behind in the social development specific to the backward classes of SC and ST. Further, within the backward classes, the rankings of SDI-SC moved ahead of SDI-ST in the states of Andhra Pradesh, Gujarat, Maharashtra, Odisha, and West Bengal whereas the SDI-ST progressed more than SDI-ST in Assam, Haryana, Himachal Pradesh, Karnataka, Punjab, and Uttarakhand.

SDI-GENDER: MALE AND FEMALE

Gender discrimination is another form of socio-economic inequality which bears an adverse impact on the social development goals. While there has been a marginal increase in the country's sex ratio from 933 in 2001 to 940 in 2011, significant variations exist between the states such as Kerala recording a sex ratio in favour of women and Delhi, Chandigarh, or Haryana having an adverse ratio. Some of the states display gender inequality in health and education, so that it is common to find girls recording higher IMR or school dropout rates. In other states, high female unemployment rates are common along with the concentration of women in casual, unskilled, and low-paid work. To capture the male–female disparity in social development, the SDI across gender is built on the basis of three dimensions of health, education, and economic deprivation and covering six indicators as given in Box 18.3. The rankings of SDI-Gender are provided individually in Figure 18.7 and Figure 18.8 for males

and females, respectively. It can be seen that Kerala, Goa, Tamil Nadu, Punjab, and Delhi represented the top five ranks in both the SDI-Male as well as SDI-Female. On the other hand, states like Jharkhand, Madhya Pradesh, Chhattisgarh, Uttarakhand, Uttar Pradesh, Bihar, Odisha, and Gujarat remained at the bottom of the rankings of both in SDI-Male and SDI-Female. Interestingly, 13 states have performed better than the all-India level in SDI-Female as compared to 12 states achieving better than the all-India in SDI-Male.

The individual state's rankings in all the three constituent dimensions across gender reveal that Kerala, once again ranked high among the states in the health and educational indicators but lagged behind in economic provisions (Table 18.3). It may be noted that states such as Uttar Pradesh, Jharkhand, Chhattisgarh, Uttarakhand, Rajasthan, or Haryana may have been progressive enough in providing economic opportunities to females, but are also the worst performers in the areas of female health and education. Delhi remains the only exception, which has confined the female's economic deprivation as well as demonstrated progress in the remaining dimensions. Correspondingly, there are states such as Goa, Punjab, Tamil Nadu, and Karnataka that have progressed well in the areas of girl's education or health. The comparison of the PCA scores and rankings of SDI-Male and SDI-Female of individual states are provided in Appendix Table 18A.11. While gender parity is observed in the SDI rankings for the all-India and a number of states, wide divergences between the rankings of SDI-Male

Table 18.2 State Rankings in Individual Indicators of SDI-Social, SC, ST, and Non-SC/ST

States	Demographic			Health		
	SC	ST	Non-SC/ST	SC	ST	Non-SC/ST
Andhra Pradesh	5	12	15	3	9	5
Assam	11	10	18	12	4	21
Bihar	21	19	21	21	12	20
Chhattisgarh	16	14	8	17	18	9
Gujarat	9	9	5	8	14	10
Haryana	10	11	10	16	8	13
Himachal Pradesh	6	2	1	9	5	11
Jammu and Kashmir	13	15	12	11	7	4
Jharkhand	19	21	19	20	19	19
Karnataka	8	6	6	6	6	6
Kerala	1	1	2	1	1	2
Madhya Pradesh	17	16	16	19	20	16
Maharashtra	4	5	7	4	11	8
Odisha	12	17	11	10	16	7
Punjab	7	4	4	5	3	3
Rajasthan	18	18	17	15	10	15
Tamil Nadu	3	3	3	2	2	1
Uttar Pradesh	20	20	20	18	21	18
Uttarakhand	15	7	14	14	17	14
West Bengal	2	8	9	7	15	17
All India	14	13	13	13	13	12

States	Education			Economic Deprivation		
	SC	ST	Non-SC/ST	SC	ST	Non-SC/ST
Andhra Pradesh	17	20	16	5	5	1
Assam	6	4	15	7	15	20
Bihar	21	21	21	10	20	13
Chhattisgarh	7	6	12	4	6	19
Gujarat	4	8	8	9	7	2
Haryana	13	10	7	14	1	10
Himachal Pradesh	3	1	2	13	9	11
Jammu and Kashmir	9	15	19	1	11	5
Jharkhand	20	19	20	19	14	18
Karnataka	16	7	10	12	2	7
Kerala	1	2	1	18	21	16
Madhya Pradesh	11	16	13	2	8	4
Maharashtra	2	5	3	20	17	9
Odisha	14	18	14	21	16	21
Punjab	12	11	6	11	3	3
Rajasthan	18	13	17	6	12	8
Tamil Nadu	5	14	4	15	4	12
Uttar Pradesh	19	12	18	3	19	6
Uttarakhand	10	3	5	8	10	15
West Bengal	8	17	9	16	18	17
All India	15	9	11	17	13	14

Source: Author's calculations.

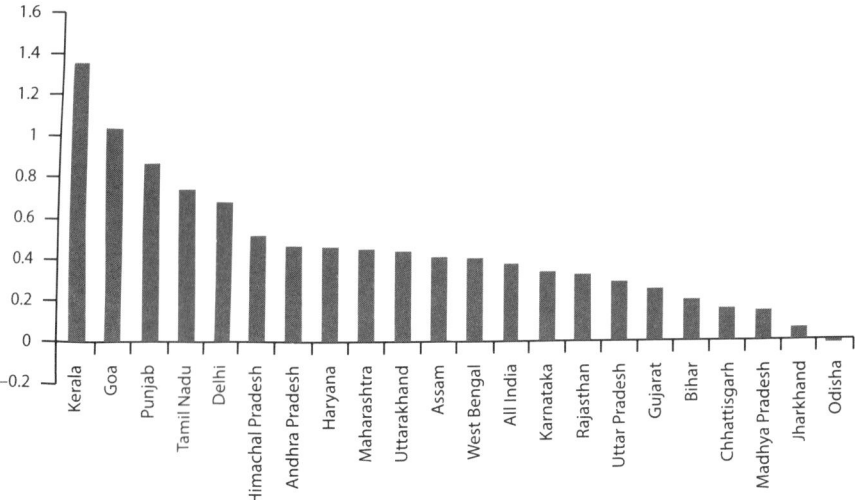

Figure 18.7   SDI-Gender Scores, Male
Source: Table 18A.11.

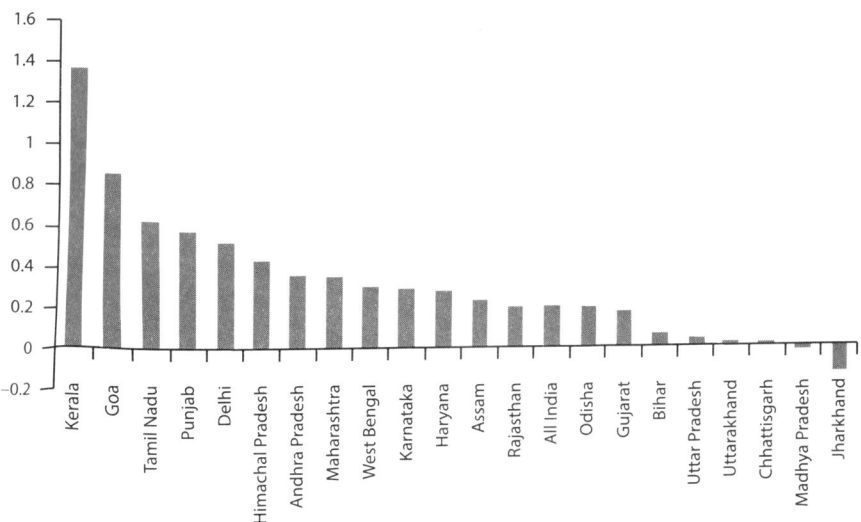

Figure 18.8   SDI-Gender Scores, Female
Source: Table 18A.11.

and SDI-Female is evident for specific states. Thus, a higher ranking of SDI-Female in comparison to SDI-Male is noticed for Karnataka, Odisha, and West Bengal whereas a lower ranking of SDI-Female is revealed for Haryana, Uttar Pradesh, and quite strikingly, in the case of Uttarakhand.

* * *

While India's robust economic growth over the past few years has helped to reduce its average per capita income gap with developed countries, the country still lags far behind in terms of its ranking in human development,

upliftment of the socially marginalized groups, and removal of gender disparity (Deolalikar 2005; Desai *et al.* 2010; GoI 2009, 2011b; UNDP 2011). As part of the planning strategy, the Approach Paper to the Twelfth Five Year Plan (2012–17) has committed itself to achieving inclusive development through the economic and social empowerment of the disadvantaged groups and marginalized sections of society (GoI 2011c). The *Economic Survey* (GoI 2012) has further emphasized that much is needed to be done to reduce disparities between men and women in economic and social outcomes. The various SDIs constructed in this report can be seen as useful tools

Table 18.3   State Rankings in Individual Indicators of SDI-Gender, Male and Female

States	Health		Education		Economic Deprivation	
	Male	Female	Male	Female	Male	Female
Andhra Pradesh	9	8	18	10	19	20
Assam	12	14	4	20	20	19
Bihar	20	21	21	21	12	21
Chhattisgarh	19	20	14	17	4	3
Delhi	4	3	2	2	2	4
Goa	2	2	3	5	3	14
Gujarat	17	18	13	18	9	15
Haryana	8	10	10	14	10	7
Himachal Pradesh	6	6	7	8	15	8
Jharkhand	21	22	9	9	1	2
Karnataka	13	9	5	4	6	13
Kerala	1	1	1	1	22	23
Madhya Pradesh	22	23	23	22	17	16
Maharashtra	7	7	8	7	7	17
Odisha	23	15	19	19	14	9
Punjab	3	4	16	6	21	12
Rajasthan	16	16	22	23	5	6
Tamil Nadu	5	5	6	3	23	22
Uttar Pradesh	18	13	20	15	8	1
Uttarakhand	10	19	17	12	16	5
West Bengal	14	12	12	16	18	10
All India	15	17	15	13	13	18

Source: Author's calculations.

that can be used to determine the progress made by the states of India in the directions of *inclusive growth*. It may be noted that the scope of the present SDI remains much broader than HDI, since six development dimensions covering 21 indicators have been used as opposed to the Indian HDI, which uses three dimensions encompassing four indicators.[1] Further, to properly understand the unequal progress made by Indian states in the overall social development, we have also worked out disaggregated SDIs from different perspectives of inequality, namely, areas of residence, social groups, and gender. Thus, SDI-Rural, SDI-Urban, SDI-SC, SDI-ST, SDI-Male, and SDI-Female have been constructed to examine the disparity across states.

The states that have performed well in overall SDI include Delhi, Goa, Kerala, Himachal Pradesh, and Punjab, while states like Bihar, Jharkhand, Uttar Pradesh, Madhya Pradesh, Odisha, Rajasthan, and Chhattisgarh continue to rank low in many indicators of social development.

The overall social development in the states of Haryana, Karnataka, Punjab, and Uttarakhand appears to be driven more by the rural sector, while there is an obvious urban orientation of social developments in Andhra Pradesh, Maharashtra, and West Bengal. The states of Andhra Pradesh and Assam have done well in supporting the marginalized groups (SCs and STs), whereas Gujarat and Jammu and Kashmir failed in the social empowerment of the disadvantaged groups. Finally, there are states that lagged quite noticeably in female-specific social development, namely, Haryana, Uttar Pradesh, and Uttarakhand while Karnataka, Odisha, and West Bengal appear to have done well in women's upliftment by reducing the gender discrimination in social development. Kerala has remained as an outlier in various scales of human and social development indicators, even though its economic base remained at an average level. Besides Kerala, a small state like Goa has presented an all-round performance in social development and projected figures above m...

states as well as the national average in all respects. Interestingly, states that are economically quite progressive based on the real per capita net state domestic product, namely, Haryana, Punjab, and Uttarakhand are not the top-ranking states in aggregate SDI, SDI-Social, or SDI-Gender.

We have provided a comparison among SDI-2012, SDI-2010, and HDI-2007–8. It is important to note that these three series may not be strictly comparable for differences in definition, coverage, and data-point of reference. The HDI and SDI are different in nature due to the obvious definitional variation and coverage. Thus, the states that performed well in the domains of health, education, and income attainments need not be expected to experience similar achievements in the social dimensions of development. On the other hand, there are some differences between SDI-2012 and SDI-2010, although they are similar by definition. In fact, the SDI-2012 differs from SDI-2010 in two major respects, namely, states' coverage and use of recent data. The HDI has covered more number of states than the SDI-2010, but failed to use recent data for some of the variables. The SDI-2012 has made use of the recent data that includes Census 2011 for literacy and CSR, NSS 55th Round data (2009–10) for employment and per capita consumption, DLHFS, 2007–8 data for basic amenities indicators and the Planning Commission's data on poverty for 2009–10. In spite of the differences, one can notice a broad similarity in the ranking orders (Table 18.4). The states of Bihar, Jharkhand, Uttar Pradesh, Madhya Pradesh, Odisha, Rajasthan, and Chhattisgarh are ranked low in both the social and human development indicators. It, therefore, appears that development in India may not remain inclusive and broad-based unless significant progresses are attained in the human

and social development of the states that are consistently placed lower down in the ranking order.

Table 18.4 Comparison of State Rankings in SDI 2012, SDI 2010, and HDI 2007–8

States	SDI-2012	SDI-2010	HDI-2007–8
Delhi	1		2
Goa	2		4
Kerala	3	1	1
Himachal Pradesh	4		3
Punjab	5	2	5
Tamil Nadu	6	3	8
Jammu and Kashmir	7		10
Uttarakhand	8		14
Maharashtra	9	4	7
Karnataka	10	6	12
Andhra Pradesh	11	5	15
Haryana	12	8	9
Gujarat	13	7	11
West Bengal	14	10	13
Assam	15	9	16
Chhattisgarh	16	13	23
Rajasthan	17	12	17
Odisha	18	11	22
Madhya Pradesh	19	14	20
Uttar Pradesh	20	15	18
Jharkhand	21	16	19
Bihar	22	17	21

Sources: Author's calculation, CSD (2011), and GoI (2011a).
Note: The 6th rank in HDI belongs to north eastern states (excluding Assam), which is not included here.

APPENDIX

Table 18A.1 Correlation among Indicators in Aggregate SDI-Rural

	Demographic	Health	Education	Basic Amenities	Economic Deprivation	Social
Demographic	1					
Health	0.83	1				
Education	0.78	0.75	1			
Basic amenities	0.71	0.79	0.71	1		
Economic deprivation	0.50	0.60	0.69	0.81	1	
Social	0.37	0.50	0.59	0.50	0.44	1

Source: Author's calculations.

Table 18A.2 Correlation among Indicators in Aggregate SDI-Urban

	Demographic	Health	Education	Basic Amenities	Economic Deprivation	Social
Demographic	1					
Health	0.81	1				
Education	0.77	0.63	1			
Basic amenities	0.54	0.50	0.37	1		
Economic deprivation	0.55	0.51	0.46	0.59	1	
Social	0.61	0.61	0.59	0.22	0.44	1

Source: Author's calculations.

Table 18A.3 Correlation among Indicators in Aggregate SDI

	Demographic	Health	Education	Basic Amenities	Economic Deprivation	Social
Demographic	1					
Health	0.89	1				
Education	0.79	0.74	1			
Basic amenities	0.72	0.75	0.67	1		
Economic deprivation	0.60	0.62	0.67	0.79	1	
Social	0.34	0.42	0.56	0.35	0.35	1

Source: Author's calculations.

Table 18A.4 Correlation among Indicators in SDI-Social, SC

	Demographic	Health	Education	Economic Deprivation
Demographic	1			
Health	0.93	1		
Education	0.89	0.75	1	
Economic deprivation	−0.31	−0.33	−0.14	1

Source: Author's calculations.

Table 18A.5 Correlation among Indicators in SDI-Social, ST

	Demographic	Health	Education	Economic Deprivation
Demographic	1			
Health	0.81	1		
Education	0.65	0.43	1	
Economic deprivation	0.26	0.28	−0.11	1

Source: Author's calculations.

Table 18A.6 Correlation among Indicators in SDI-Social, Non-SC/ST

	Demographic	Health	Education	Economic Deprivation
Demographic	1			
Health	0.68	1		
Education	0.71	0.52	1	
Economic deprivation	0.04	0.25	-0.16	1

Source: Author's calculations.

Table 18A.7　Correlation among Indicators in SDI-Gender, Male

	Health	Education	Economic Deprivation
Health	1		
Education	0.70	1	
Economic deprivation	−0.19	0.04	1

Source: Author's calculations.

Table 18A.8　Correlation among Indicators in SDI-Gender, Female

	Health	Education	Economic Deprivation
Health	1		
Education	0.80	1	
Economic deprivation	−0.25	−0.08	1

Source: Author's calculations.

Table 18A.9　Aggregate SDI Scores and Ranks of Individual States, Rural, Urban, and Total

States	SDI-Rural		SDI-Urban		SDI-Total	
	Scores	Ranks	Scores	Ranks	Scores	Ranks
Andhra Pradesh	2.73	11	3.79	6	3.08	11
Assam	2.21	15	3.21	15	2.40	15
Bihar	1.19	22	1.29	23	1.11	23
Chhattisgarh	2.07	16	2.76	17	2.12	17
Delhi	4.91	1	4.17	4	4.93	1
Goa	4.31	3	4.68	2	4.86	2
Gujarat	2.51	13	3.29	13	2.81	13
Haryana	2.77	10	3.25	14	3.05	12
Himachal Pradesh	4.04	4	4.32	3	3.99	4
Jammu and Kashmir	3.32	6	3.88	5	3.48	7
Jharkhand	0.97	23	2.18	21	1.40	22
Karnataka	2.78	9	3.39	12	3.11	10
Kerala	4.58	2	4.86	1	4.72	3
Madhya Pradesh	1.69	19	2.46	20	1.77	20
Maharashtra	2.67	12	3.71	7	3.17	9
Odisha	1.66	20	2.55	19	1.79	19
Punjab	3.81	5	3.39	11	3.78	5
Rajasthan	1.88	18	2.60	18	2.11	18
Tamil Nadu	3.13	8	3.48	9	3.59	6
Uttar Pradesh	1.40	21	1.79	22	1.59	21
Uttarakhand	3.21	7	3.42	10	3.40	8
West Bengal	2.47	14	3.68	8	2.71	14
All India	2.06	17	3.02	16	2.36	16

Source: Author's calculations.

Table 18A.10 SDI-Social Scores and Ranks of Individual States, SC, ST, and Non-SC/ST

States	SDI-SC		SDI-ST		SDI-Non-SC/ST	
	Scores	Ranks	Scores	Ranks	Scores	Ranks
Andhra Pradesh	0.94	6	0.80	12	0.92	13
Assam	0.65	11	1.16	7	0.47	18
Bihar	−0.06	21	0.35	19	0.03	21
Chhattisgarh	0.42	15	0.64	13	1.07	8
Gujarat	0.84	8	0.90	11	1.24	5
Haryana	0.64	12	1.30	5	1.01	9
Himachal Pradesh	0.97	5	1.88	2	1.64	3
Jammu and Kashmir	0.40	16	0.62	15	0.96	11
Jharkhand	0.21	19	0.14	21	0.38	19
Karnataka	0.81	9	1.24	6	1.19	7
Kerala	2.89	1	2.35	1	2.47	1
Madhya Pradesh	0.24	18	0.48	16	0.81	16
Maharashtra	1.16	3	1.03	8	1.23	6
Odisha	0.67	10	0.44	18	0.95	12
Punjab	0.87	7	1.52	4	1.43	4
Rajasthan	0.27	17	0.47	17	0.60	17
Tamil Nadu	1.23	2	1.58	3	1.67	2
Uttar Pradesh	0.12	20	0.25	20	0.31	20
Uttarakhand	0.55	14	0.98	9	0.87	15
West Bengal	1.14	4	0.90	10	0.98	10
All India	0.57	13	0.64	14	0.87	14

Source: Author's calculations.

Table 18A.11   SDI-Gender Scores and Ranks of Individual States, Male and Female

States	SDI-Male		SDI-Female	
	Scores	Ranks	Scores	Ranks
Andhra Pradesh	0.47	7	0.36	7
Assam	0.41	11	0.24	12
Bihar	0.20	18	0.07	17
Chhattisgarh	0.16	19	0.01	20
Delhi	0.68	5	0.52	5
Goa	1.04	2	0.85	2
Gujarat	0.26	17	0.18	16
Haryana	0.46	8	0.28	11
Himachal Pradesh	0.52	6	0.43	6
Jharkhand	0.06	21	−0.12	22
Karnataka	0.34	14	0.29	10
Kerala	1.36	1	1.37	1
Madhya Pradesh	0.15	20	−0.01	21
Maharashtra	0.45	9	0.35	8
Odisha	−0.01	22	0.20	15
Punjab	0.87	3	0.57	4
Rajasthan	0.33	15	0.21	13
Tamil Nadu	0.74	4	0.62	3
Uttar Pradesh	0.29	16	0.05	18
Uttarakhand	0.44	10	0.03	19
West Bengal	0.41	12	0.30	9
All India	0.37	13	0.20	14

Source: Author's calculations.

NOTE

1. The Indian HDI is constructed as a simple average of three indices in the dimensions of health, education, and income, considering life expectancy at birth, literacy rate, adjusted mean years of schooling, and inequality adjusted per capita real consumption expenditure as the four indicators (refer to GOI 2011a).

REFERENCES

CSD (Council for Social Development). (2011). *India: Social Development Report, 2010*. New Delhi: Oxford University Press.

Decanq, K. and M.A. Lugo. 2009. 'Setting Weights in Multidimensional Indices of Well-Being and Deprivation', *Oxford Poverty and Human Development Initiative (OPHI)*, Working Paper No. 18, University of Oxford. Available at www.ophi.org.uk (accessed 28 April 2013).

Deolalikar, A.B. 2005. *Attaining the Millennium Development Goals in India*. New Delhi: Oxford University in collaboration with The World Bank, Human Development Unit, South Asia Region.

Desai, S., A. Dubey, B.L. Joshi, M. Sen, A. Sharif, and R. Vanneman. 2010. *Human Development in India: Challenges for a Society in Transition*. New Delhi: Oxford University Press.

Economist Intelligence Unit. 2011. *Quality of Life Index*. London: The Economist Group.

GoI (Government of India). 2006. *Social, Economic and Educational Status of the Muslim Community in India: A Report* (Sachar Committee Report). New Delhi: Prime Minister's High Level Committee, Cabinet Secretariat, GoI.

———. 2009. *Gendering Human Development Indices: Recasting the Gender Development Index and Gender Empowerment Measure for India*. New Delhi: Ministry of Women and Child Development, GoI in collaboration with Indian Institute of Public Administration and UNDP.

———. 2011a. *India, Human Development Report, 2011*. New Delhi: Oxford University Press, Institute of Applied Manpower Research, Planning Commission.

GoI (Government of India). 2011b. *Millennium Development Goals, India Country Report, 2011*. New Delhi: Central Statistical Organisation (CSO), Ministry of Statistics and Programme Implementation, GoI.

———. 2011c. *Faster, Sustainable and More Inclusive Growth: An Approach to the 12th Five Year Plan, 2012–17*, October. New Delhi: Planning Commission, GoI.

———. 2012. *Economic Survey, 2011–12*. New Delhi: Ministry of Finance.

Noorbakhsh, F. 1998 'The Human Development Index: Some Technical Issues and Alternative Indices', *Journal of International Development*, 10: 589–605.

Ranis, G., F. Stewart, and E. Samman. 2005. 'Human Development: Beyond the HDI', Economic Growth Center Paper No. 916. New Haven: Yale University.

Ravallion, Martin. 2012. 'Mash-up Indices of Development', *World Bank Research Observer*, 27(1): 1–32.

Srinivasan, T.N. 1994. 'Human Development: A New Paradigm or Reinvention of the Wheel?' *American Economic Review*, 84(2): 238–43.

Stiglitz, J.E., Amartya Sen, and Jean-Paul Fitoussi. 2010. 'Mis-Measuring Our Lives: Why GDP Doesn't Add Up', Report by the Commission on the Measurement of Economic Performance and Social Progress. New York: The New Press.

UNDP (United Nations Development Programme). 2011. *Human Development Report, 2011, Sustainability and Equity: A Better Future for All*. New York: Palgrave Macmillan for UNDP.

World Bank. 2012. *Doing Business Indicators: Doing Business in a More Transparent World*. Washington, DC: Co-publication of World Bank and International Finance Corporation.

Editors and Contributors

Savio Abreu is Director, Xavier Centre of Historical Research, Alto Porvorim, Goa.

Nilachala Acharya is Senior Research Officer, Centre for Budget and Governance Accountability, New Delhi.

Indu Agnihotri is Director, Centre for Women's Development Studies, New Delhi.

Arshad Alam is Assistant Professor, Centre for the Study of Social Systems, School of Social Sciences, Jawaharlal Nehru University, New Delhi.

Mohammad Sanjeer Alam is Associate Fellow, Centre for the Study of Developing Societies, New Delhi.

Surajit Deb is Associate Professor, Department of Economics, Ram Lal Anand College (Evening), University of Delhi, New Delhi.

Muchkund Dubey is President, Council for Social Development, New Delhi.

Tanweer Fazal is Associate Professor, Nelson Mandela Centre for Peace and Conflict Resolution, Jamia Millia Islamia, New Delhi.

Jayati Ghosh is Professor, Centre for Economic Studies and Planning, School of Social Sciences, Jawaharlal Nehru University, New Delhi.

Prabir Kumar Ghosh is Senior Research Fellow and Head—Field Operation, National Council of Applied Economic Research–Centre for Macro Consumer Research, New Delhi.

Tajamul Haque is Director, Council for Social Development, New Delhi.

Mushirul Hasan is Professor, Department of History, Jamia Millia Islamia, New Delhi.

Zoya Hasan is Professor, Centre for Political Studies, School of Social Sciences, Jawaharlal Nehru University, New Delhi.

Himanshu is Assistant Professor, Centre for Informal Sector and Labour Studies, School of Social Sciences, Jawaharlal Nehru University, New Delhi.

Praveen Jha is Professor, Centre for Economic Studies and Planning, School of Social Sciences, Jawaharlal Nehru University, New Delhi.

Jawed Alam Khan is Senior Research Officer, Centre for Budget and Governance Accountability, New Delhi.

P.M. Kulkarni is Professor, Centre for the Study of Regional Development, School of Social Sciences, Jawaharlal Nehru University, New Delhi.

Rajeev Kumar is Senior Researcher, Collaborative Research and Dissemination, New Delhi.

Oommen C. Kurian is Senior Research Officer, Centre for Enquiry into Health and Allied Themes, Mumbai.

Pooja Parvati is an independent consultant based in New Delhi.

R. Ramakumar is Associate Professor, Centre for Study of Developing Economies, Research Facilities: Nutrition Research Facility, School of Development Studies, Tata Institute of Social Sciences, Mumbai.

Mohan Rao is Professor, Centre of Social Medicine and Community Health, School of Social Sciences, Jawaharlal Nehru University, New Delhi.

Rowena Robinson is Visiting Professor, Department of Humanities and Social Sciences, Indian Institute of Technology Guwahati, Assam, and Professor, Department of Humanities and Social Sciences, Indian Institute of Technology Bombay, Mumbai.

Abusaleh Shariff is Chairperson, Centre for Research and Debates in Development Policy, New Delhi, and Executive Director, US-India Policy Institute, Washington, DC.

Amit Sharma is Research Analyst, National Council of Applied Economic Research, New Delhi.

Khursheed Anwar Siddiqui is Consultant, ACNielsen ORG-MARG Pvt. Ltd. New Delhi.

Avanindra Nath Thakur is Research Scholar, Centre for Economic Studies and Planning, School of Social Sciences, Jawaharlal Nehru University, New Delhi.

Prashant K. Trivedi is Assistant Professor, Giri Institute of Development Studies, Lucknow.